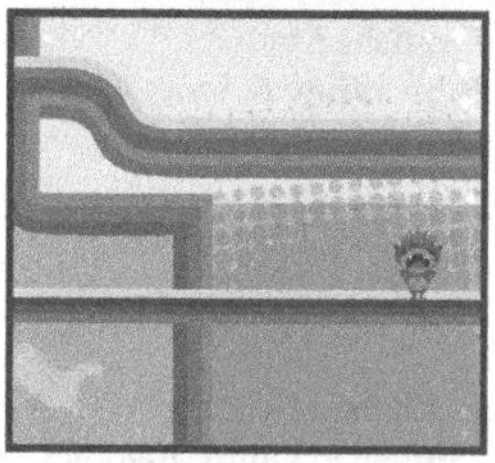

Threat Modeling

Designing for Security

Adam Shostack

WILEY

Threat Modeling: Designing for Security

Published by
John Wiley & Sons, Inc.
10475 Crosspoint
BoulevardIndianapolis, IN 46256
www.wiley.com

Published by John Wiley & Sons, Inc., Indianapolis, Indiana
Published simultaneously in Canada

ISBN: 978-1-118-80999-0
ISBN: 978-1-118-82269-2 (ebk)
ISBN: 978-1-118-81005-7 (ebk)

Manufactured in the United States of America

SKY10068029_022224

Library of Congress Control Number: 2013954095

For all those striving to deliver more secure systems

Credits

Executive Editor
Carol Long

Project Editors
Victoria Swider
Tom Dinse

Technical Editor
Chris Wysopal

Production Editor
Christine Mugnolo

Copy Editor
Luann Rouff

Editorial Manager
Mary Beth Wakefield

Freelancer Editorial Manager
Rosemarie Graham

Associate Director of Marketing
David Mayhew

Marketing Manager
Ashley Zurcher

Business Manager
Amy Knies

Vice President and Executive Group Publisher
Richard Swadley

Associate Publisher
Jim Minatel

Project Coordinator, Cover
Todd Klemme

Technical Proofreader
Russ McRee

Proofreader
Nancy Carrasco

Indexer
Robert Swanson

Cover Image
Courtesy of Microsoft

Cover Designer
Wiley

About the Author

Adam Shostack is currently a program manager at Microsoft. His security roles there have included security development processes, usable security, and attack modeling. His attack-modeling work led to security updates for Autorun being delivered to hundreds of millions of computers. He shipped the SDL Threat Modeling Tool and the *Elevation of Privilege* threat modeling game. While doing security development process work, he delivered threat modeling training across Microsoft and its partners and customers.

Prior to Microsoft, he has been an executive at a number of successful information security and privacy startups. He helped found the CVE, the Privacy Enhancing Technologies Symposium and the International Financial Cryptography Association. He has been a consultant to banks, hospitals and startups and established software companies. For the first several years of his career, he was a systems manager for a medical research lab. Shostack is a prolific author, blogger, and public speaker. With Andrew Stewart, he co-authored *The New School of Information Security* (Addison-Wesley, 2008).

About the Technical Editor

Chris Wysopal, Veracode's CTO and Co-Founder, is responsible for the company's software security analysis capabilities. In 2008 he was named one of InfoWorld's Top 25 CTO's and one of the 100 most influential people in IT by eWeek. One of the original vulnerability researchers and a member of L0pht Heavy Industries, he has testified on Capitol Hill in the US on the subjects of government computer security and how vulnerabilities are discovered in software. He is an author of L0phtCrack and netcat for Windows. He is the lead author of *The Art of Software Security Testing* (Addison-Wesley, 2006).

Acknowledgments

First and foremost, I'd like to thank countless engineers at Microsoft and elsewhere who have given me feedback about their experiences threat modeling. I wouldn't have had the opportunity to have so many open and direct conversations without the support of Eric Bidstrup and Steve Lipner, who on my first day at Microsoft told me to go "wallow in the problem for a while." I don't think either expected "a while" to be quite so long. Nearly eight years later with countless deliverables along the way, this book is my most complete answer to the question they asked me: "How can we get better threat models?"

Ellen Cram Kowalczyk helped me make the book a reality in the Microsoft context, gave great feedback on both details and aspects that were missing, and also provided a lot of the history of threat modeling from the first security pushes through the formation of the SDL, and she was a great manager and mentor. Ellen and Steve Lipner were also invaluable in helping me obtain permission to use Microsoft documents.

The *Elevation of Privilege* game that opens this book owes much to Jacqueline Beauchere, who saw promise in an ugly prototype called "Threat Spades," and invested in making it beautiful and widely available.

The SDL Threat Modeling Tool might not exist if Chris Peterson hadn't given me a chance to build a threat modeling tool for the Windows team to use. Ivan Medvedev, Patrick McCuller, Meng Li, and Larry Osterman built the first version of that tool. I'd like to thank the many engineers in Windows, and later across Microsoft, who provided bug reports and suggestions for improvements in the beta days, and acknowledge all those who just flamed at us, reminding us of the importance of getting threat modeling right. Without that tool, my experience and breadth in threat modeling would be far poorer.

Larry Osterman, Douglas MacIver, Eric Douglas, Michael Howard, and Bob Fruth gave me hours of their time and experience in understanding threat modeling at Microsoft. Window Snyder's perspective as I started the Microsoft job has been invaluable over the years. Knowing when you're done . . . well, this book is nearly done.

Rob Reeder was a great guide to the field of usable security, and Chapter 15 would look very different if not for our years of collaboration. I can't discuss usable security without thanking Lorrie Cranor for her help on that topic; but also for the chance to keynote the *Symposium on Usable Privacy and Security*, which led me to think about usable engineering advice, a perspective that is now suffused throughout this book.

Andy Steingrubl, Don Ankney, and Russ McRee all taught me important lessons related to operational threat modeling, and how the trade-offs change as you change context. Guys, thank you for beating on me—those lessons now permeate many chapters. Alec Yasinac, Harold Pardue, and Jeff Landry were generous with their time discussing their attack tree experience, and Chapters 4 and 17 are better for those conversations. Joseph Lorenzo Hall was also a gem in helping with attack trees. Wendy Nather argued strongly that assets and attackers are great ways to make threats real, and thus help overcome resistance to fixing them. Rob Sama checked the Acme financials example from a CPA's perspective, correcting many of my errors. Dave Awksmith graciously allowed me to include his threat personas as a complete appendix. Jason Nehrboss gave me some of the best feedback I've ever received on very early chapters.

I'd also like to acknowledge Jacob Appelbaum, Crispin Cowan, Dana Epp (for years of help, on both the book and tools), Jeremi Gosney, Yoshi Kohno, David LeBlanc, Marsh Ray, Nick Mathewson, Tamara McBride, Russ McRee, Talhah Mir, David Mortman, Alec Muffet, Ben Rothke, Andrew Stewart, and Bryan Sullivan for helpful feedback on drafts and/or ideas that made it into the book in a wide variety of ways.

Of course, none of those acknowledged in this section are responsible for the errors which doubtless crept in or remain.

Writing this book "by myself" (an odd phrase given everyone I'm acknowledging) makes me miss working with Andrew Stewart, my partner in writing on *The New School of Information Security*. Especially since people sometimes attribute that book to me, I want to be public about how much I missed his collaboration in this project.

This book wouldn't be in the form it is were it not for Bruce Schneier's willingness to make an introduction to Carol Long, and Carol's willingness to pick up the book. It wasn't always easy to read the feedback and suggested changes from my excellent project editor, Victoria Swider, but this thing is better where I did. Tom Dinse stepped in as the project ended and masterfully took control of a very large number of open tasks, bringing them to resolution on a tight schedule.

Lastly, and most importantly, thank you to Terri, for all your help, support, and love, and for putting up with "it's almost done" for a very, very long time.

—Adam Shostack

Contents

Introduction

All models are wrong, some models are useful.

— George Box

This book describes the useful models you can employ to address or mitigate these potential threats. People who build software, systems, or things with software need to address the many predictable threats their systems can face.

Threat modeling is a fancy name for something we all do instinctively. If I asked you to threat model your house, you might start by thinking about the precious things within it: your family, heirlooms, photos, or perhaps your collection of signed movie posters. You might start thinking about the ways someone might break in, such as unlocked doors or open windows. And you might start thinking about the sorts of people who might break in, including neighborhood kids, professional burglars, drug addicts, perhaps a stalker, or someone trying to steal your Picasso original.

Each of these examples has an analog in the software world, but for now, the important thing is not how you guard against each threat, but that you're able to relate to this way of thinking. If you were asked to help assess a friend's house, you could probably help, but you might lack confidence in how complete your analysis is. If you were asked to secure an office complex, you might have a still harder time, and securing a military base or a prison seems even more difficult. In those cases, your instincts are insufficient, and you'd need tools to help tackle the questions. This book will give you the tools to think about threat modeling technology in structured and effective ways.

In this introduction, you'll learn about what threat modeling is and why individuals, teams, and organizations threat model. Those reasons include finding security issues early, improving your understanding of security requirements, and being able to engineer and deliver better products. This introduction has five main sections describing what the book is about, including a definition of threat modeling and reasons it's important; who should read this book; how to use it, and what you can expect to gain from the various parts, and new lessons in threat modeling.

What Is Threat Modeling?

Everyone threat models. Many people do it out of frustration in line at the airport, sneaking out of the house or into a bar. At the airport, you might idly consider how to sneak something through security, even if you have no intent to do so. Sneaking in or out of someplace, you worry about who might catch you. When you speed down the highway, you work with an implicit threat model where the main threat is the police, who you probably think are lurking behind a billboard or overpass. Threats of road obstructions, deer, or rain might play into your model as well.

When you threat model, you usually use two types of models. There's a model of what you're building, and there's a model of the threats (what can go wrong). What you're building with software might be a website, a downloadable program or app, or it might be delivered in a hardware package. It might be a distributed system, or some of the "things" that will be part of the "Internet of things." You model so that you can look at the forest, not the trees. A good model helps you address classes or groups of attacks, and deliver a more secure product.

The English word *threat* has many meanings. It can be used to describe a person, such as "Osama bin Laden was a threat to America," or people, such as "the insider threat." It can be used to describe an event, such as "There is a threat of a hurricane coming through this weekend," and it can be used to describe a weakness or possibility of attack, such as "What are you doing about confidentiality threats?" It is also used to describe viruses and malware such as "This threat incorporates three different methods for spreading." It can be used to describe behavior such as "There's a threat of operator error."

Similarly, the term *threat modeling* has many meanings, and the term *threat model* is used in many distinct and perhaps incompatible ways, including:

- As a verb—for example, "Have you threat modeled?" That is, have you gone through an analysis process to figure out what might go wrong with the thing you're building?
- As a noun, to ask what threat model is being used. For example, "Our threat model is someone in possession of the machine," or "Our threat model is a skilled and determined remote attacker."
- It can mean building up a set of idealized attackers.
- It can mean abstracting threats into classes such as tampering.

There are doubtless other definitions. All of these are useful in various scenarios and thus correct, and there are few less fruitful ways to spend your time than debating them. Arguing over definitions is a strange game, and the only way to win is not to play. This book takes a big tent approach to threat modeling and includes a wide range of techniques you can apply early to make what you're designing or building more secure. It will also address the reality that some techniques are more effective than others, and that some techniques are more likely to work for people with particular skills or experience.

Threat modeling is the key to a focused defense. Without threat models, you can never stop playing whack-a-mole.

In short, threat modeling is the use of abstractions to aid in thinking about risks.

Reasons to Threat Model

In today's fast-paced world, there is a tendency to streamline development activity, and there are important reasons to threat model, which are covered in this section. Those include finding security bugs early, understanding your security requirements, and engineering and delivering better products.

Find Security Bugs Early

If you think about building a house, decisions you make early will have dramatic effects on security. Wooden walls and lots of ground-level windows expose you to more risks than brick construction and few windows. Either may be a reasonable choice, depending on where you're building and other factors. Once you've chosen, changes will be expensive. Sure, you can put bars over your windows, but wouldn't it be better to use a more appropriate design from the start? The same sorts of tradeoffs can apply in technology. Threat modeling will help you find design issues even before you've written a line of code, and that's the best time to find those issues.

Understand Your Security Requirements

Good threat models can help you ask "Is that really a requirement?" For example, does the system need to be secure against someone in physical possession of the device? Apple has said yes for the iPhone, which is different from the traditional world of the PC. As you find threats and triage what you're going to do with them, you clarify your requirements. With more clear requirements, you can devote your energy to a consistent set of security features and properties.

There is an important interplay between requirements, threats, and mitigations. As you model threats, you'll find that some threats don't line up with your business requirements, and as such may not be worth addressing. Alternately, your requirements may not be complete. With other threats, you'll find that addressing them is too complex or expensive. You'll need to make a call between addressing them partially in the current version or accepting (and communicating) that you can't address those threats.

Engineer and Deliver Better Products

By considering your requirements and design early in the process, you can dramatically lower the odds that you'll be re-designing, re-factoring, or facing a constant stream of security bugs. That will let you deliver a better product on a more predictable schedule. All the effort that would go to those can be put into building a better, faster, cheaper or more secure product. You can focus on whatever properties your customers want.

Address Issues Other Techniques Won't

The last reason to threat model is that threat modeling will lead you to categories of issues that other tools won't find. Some of these issues will be errors of omission, such as a failure to authenticate a connection. That's not something that a code analysis tool will find. Other issues will be unique to your design. To the extent that you have a set of smart developers building something new, you might have new ways threats can manifest. Models of what goes wrong, by abstracting away details, will help you see analogies and similarities to problems that have been discovered in other systems.

A corollary of this is that threat modeling should not focus on issues that your other safety and security engineering is likely to find (except insofar as finding them early lets you avoid re-engineering). So if, for example, you're building a product with a database, threat modeling might touch quickly on SQL injection attacks, and the variety of trust boundaries that might be injectable. However, you may know that you'll encounter those. Your threat modeling should focus on issues that other techniques can't find.

Who Should Read This book?

This book is written for those who create or operate complex technology. That's primarily software engineers and systems administrators, but it also includes a variety of related roles, including analysts or architects. There's also a lot of information in here for security professionals, so this book should be useful to them and those who work with them. Different parts of the book are designed for different people—in general, the early chapters are for generalists (or specialists in something other than security), while the end of the book speaks more to security specialists.

You don't need to be a security expert, professional, or even enthusiast to get substantial benefit from this book. I assume that you understand that there are people out there whose interests and desires don't line up with yours. For example, maybe they'd like to take money from you, or they may have other goals, like puffing themselves up at your expense or using your computer to attack other people.

This book is written in plain language for anyone who can write or spec a program, but sometimes a little jargon helps in precision, conciseness, or clarity, so there's a glossary.

What You Will Gain from This Book

When you read this book cover to cover, you will gain a rich knowledge of threat modeling techniques. You'll learn to apply those techniques to your projects so you can build software that's more secure from the get-go, and deploy it more securely. You'll learn to how to make security tradeoffs in ways that are considered, measured, and appropriate. You will learn a set of tools and when to bring them to bear. You will discover a set of glamorous distractions. Those distractions might seem like wonderful, sexy ideas, but they hide an ugly interior. You'll learn why they prevent you from effectively threat modeling, and how to avoid them.

You'll also learn to focus on the actionable outputs of threat modeling, and I'll generally call those "bugs." There are arguments that it's helpful to consider code issues as bugs, and design issues as flaws. In my book, those arguments are a distraction; you should threat model to find issues that you can address, and arguing about labels probably doesn't help you address them.

Lessons for Different Readers

This book is designed to be useful to a wide variety of people working in technology. That includes a continuum from those who develop software to those who combine it into systems that meet operational or business goals to those who focus on making it more secure.

For convenience, this book pretends there is a bright dividing line between development and operations. The distinction is used as a way of understanding who has what capabilities, choices, and responsibilities. For example, it is "easy" for a developer to change what is logged, or to implement a different authentication system. Both of these may be hard for operations. Similarly, it's "easy" for operations to ensure that logs are maintained, or to ensure that a computer is in a locked cage. As this book was written, there's also an important model of "devops" emerging. The lessons for developers and operations can likely be applied with minor adjustments. This book also pretends that security expertise is separate from either development or operations expertise, again, simply as a convenience.

Naturally, this means that the same parts of the book will bring different lessons for different people. The breakdown below gives a focused value proposition for each audience.

Software Developers and Testers

Software developers—those whose day jobs are focused on creating software—include software engineers, quality assurance, and a variety of program or project managers. If you're in that group, you will learn to find and address design issues early in the software process. This book will enable you to deliver more secure software that better meets customer requirements and expectations. You'll learn a simple, effective and fun approach to threat modeling, as well as different ways to model your software or find threats. You'll learn how to track threats with bugs that fit into your development process. You'll learn to use threats to help make your requirements more crisp, and vice versa. You'll learn about areas such as authentication, cryptography, and usability where the interplay of mitigations and attacks has a long history, so you can understand how the recommended approaches have developed to their current state. You'll learn about how to bring threat modeling into your development process. And a whole lot more!

Systems Architecture, Operations, and Management

For those whose day jobs involve bringing together software components, weaving them together into systems to deliver value, you'll learn to find and address threats as you design your systems, select your components, and get them ready for deployment. This book will enable you to deliver more secure systems that better meet business, customer, and compliance requirements. You'll learn a simple, effective, and fun approach to threat modeling, as well as different ways to model the systems you're building or have built. You'll learn how to find security and privacy threats against those systems. You'll learn about the building blocks which are available for you to operationally address those threats. You'll learn how to make tradeoffs between the threats you face, and how to ensure that those threats are addressed. You'll learn about specific threats to categories of technology, such as web and cloud systems, and about threats to accounts, both of which are deeply important to those in operations. It will cover issues of usability, and perhaps even change your perspective on how to influence the security behavior of people within your organization and/ or your customers. You will learn about cryptographic building blocks, which you may be using to protect systems. And a whole lot more!

Security Professionals

If you work in security, you will learn two major things from this book: First, you'll learn structured approaches to threat modeling that will enhance your productivity, and as you do, you'll learn why many of the "obvious" parts of threat modeling are not as obvious, or as right, as you may have believed. Second, you'll learn about bringing security into the development, operational and release processes that your organization uses.

Even if you are an expert, this book can help you threat model better. Here, I speak from experience. As I was writing the case study appendix, I found myself turning to both the tree in Appendix B and the requirements chapter, and finding threats that didn't spring to mind from just considering the models of software.

TO MY COLLEAGUES IN INFORMATION SECURITY

I want to be frank. This book is not about how to design abstractly perfect software. It is a practical, grounded book that acknowledges that most software is built in some business or organizational reality that requires tradeoffs. To the dismay of purists, software where tradeoffs were made runs the world these days, and I'd like to make such software more secure by making those tradeoffs better. That involves a great many elements, two of which are making security more consistent and more accessible to our colleagues in other specialties.

This perspective is grounded in my time as a systems administrator, deploying security technologies, and observing the issues people encountered. It is grounded in my time as a startup executive, learning to see security as a property of a system which serves a business goal. It is grounded in my responsibility for threat modeling as part of Microsoft's Security Development Lifecycle. In that last role, I spoke with thousands of people at Microsoft, its partners, and its customers about our approaches. These individuals ranged from newly hired developers to those with decades of experience in security, and included chief security officers and Microsoft's Trustworthy Computing Academic Advisory Board. I learned that there are an awful lot of opinions about what works, and far fewer about what does not. This book aims to convince my fellow security professionals that pragmatism in what we ask of development and operations helps us deliver more secure software over time. This perspective may be a challenge for some security professionals. They should focus on Parts II, IV, and V, and perhaps give consideration to the question of the best as the enemy of the good.

How To Use This Book

You should start at the very beginning. It's a very good place to start, even if you already know how to threat model, because it lays out a framework that will help you understand the rest of the book.

The Four-Step Framework

This book introduces the idea that you should see threat modeling as composed of steps which accomplish subgoals, rather than as a single activity. The essential questions which you ask to accomplish those subgoals are:

1. What are you building?
2. What can go wrong with it once it's built?
3. What should you do about those things that can go wrong?
4. Did you do a decent job of analysis?

The methods you use in each step of the framework can be thought of like Lego blocks. When working with Legos, you can snap in other Lego blocks. In Chapter 1, you'll use a data flow diagram to model what you're building, STRIDE to help you think about what can go wrong and what you should do about it, and a checklist to see if you did a decent job of analysis. In Chapter 2, you'll see how diagrams are the most helpful way to think about what you're building. Different diagram types are like different building blocks to help you model what you're building. In Chapter 3, you'll go deep into STRIDE (a model of threats), while in Chapter 4, you'll learn to use attack trees instead of STRIDE, while leaving everything else the same. STRIDE and attack trees are different building blocks for considering what can go wrong once you've built your new technology.

Not every approach can snap with every other approach. It takes crazy glue to make an Erector set and Lincoln logs stick together. Attempts to glue threat modeling approaches together has made for some confusing advice. For example, trying to consider how terrorists would attack your assets doesn't really lead to a lot of actionable issues. And even with building blocks that snap together, you can make something elegant, or something confusing or bizarre.

So to consider this as a framework, what are the building blocks? The four-step framework is shown graphically in Figure I-1.

The steps are:

1. Model the system you're building, deploying, or changing.
2. Find threats using that model and the approaches in Part II.

3. Address threats using the approaches in Part III.
4. Validate your work for completeness and effectiveness (also Part III).

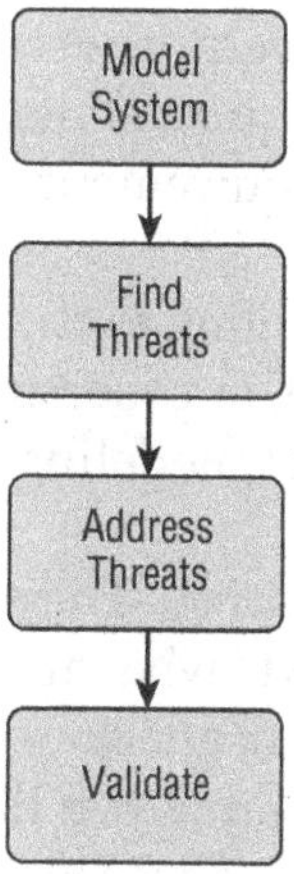

Figure I-1: The Four-Step Framework

This framework was designed to align with software development and operational deployment. It has proven itself as a way to structure threat modeling. It also makes it easier to experiment without replacing the entire framework. From here until you reach Part V, almost everything you encounter is selected because it plugs into this four-step framework.

This book is roughly organized according to the framework:

Part I "Getting Started" is about getting started. The opening part of the book (especially Chapter 1) is designed for those without much security expertise. The later parts of the book build on the security knowledge you'll gain from this material (or combined with your own experience). You'll gain an understanding of threat modeling, and a recommended approach for those who are new to the discipline. You'll also learn various ways to model your software, along with why that's a better place to start than other options, such as attackers or assets.

Part II "Finding Threats" is about finding threats. It presents a collection of techniques and tools you can use to find threats. It surveys and analyzes the different ways people approach information technology threat modeling, enabling you to examine the pros and cons of the various techniques that people bring to bear. They're grouped in a way that enables you to either read them from start to finish or jump in at a particular point where you need help.

Part III "Managing and Addressing Threats" is about managing and addressing threats. It includes processing threats and how to manage them, the tactics and technologies you can use to address them, and how to make risk tradeoffs you might need to make. It also covers validating that your threats are addressed, and tools you can use to help you threat model.

Part IV "Threat Modeling in Technologies and Tricky Areas" is about threat modeling in specific technologies and tricky areas where a great deal of threat modeling and analysis work has already been done. It includes chapters on web and cloud, accounts and identity, and cryptography, as well as a requirements "cookbook" that you can use to jump-start your own security requirements analysis.

Part V "Taking it to the Next Level" is about taking threat modeling to the next level. It targets the experienced threat modeler, security expert, or process designer who is thinking about how to build and customize threat modeling processes for a given organization.

Appendices include information to help you apply what you've learned. They include sets of common answers to "what's your threat model," and "what are our assets"; as well as threat trees that can help you find threats, lists of attackers and attacker personas; and details about the *Elevation of Privilege* game you'll use in Chapter 1; and lastly, a set of detailed example threat models. These are followed by a glossary, bibliography, and index.

Website: This book's website, `www.threatmodelingbook.com` will contain a PDF of some of the figures in the book, and likely an errata list to mitigate the errors that inevitably threaten to creep in.

What This Book Is Not

Many security books today promise to teach you to hack. Their intent is to teach you what sort of attacks need to be defended against. The idea is that if you have an empirically grounded set of attacks, you can start with that to create your defense. This is *not* one of those books, because despite millions of such books being sold, vulnerable systems are still being built and deployed. Besides, there are solid, carefully considered defenses against many sorts of attacks. It may be useful to know how to execute an attack, but it's more important to know where each attack might be executed, and how to effectively defend against it. This book will teach you that.

This book is not focused on a particular technology, platform, or API set. Platforms and APIs influence may offer security features you can use, or mitigate some threats for you. The threats and mitigations associated with a platform change from release to release, and this book aims to be a useful reference volume on your shelf for longer than the release of any particular technology.

This book is not a magic pill that will make you a master of threat modeling. It is a resource to help you understand what you need to know. Practice will help you get better, and deliberative practice with feedback and hard problems will make you a master.

New Lessons on Threat Modeling

Most experienced security professionals have developed an approach to threat modeling that works for them. If you've been threat modeling for years, this book will give you an understanding of other approaches you can apply. This book also give you a structured understanding of a set of methods and how they inter-relate. Lastly, there are some deeper lessons which are worth bringing to your attention, rather than leaving them for you to extract.

There's More Than One Way to Threat Model

If you ask a programmer "What's the right programming language for my new project?" you can expect a lot of clarifying questions. There is no one ideal programming language. There are certainly languages that are better or worse at certain types of tasks. For example, it's easier to write text manipulation code in Perl than assembler. Python is easier to read and maintain than assembler, but when you need to write ultra-fast code for a device driver, C or assembler might be a better choice. In the same way, there are better and worse ways to threat model, which depend greatly on your situation: who will be involved, what skills they have, and so on.

So you can think of threat modeling like programming. Within programming there are languages, paradigms (such as waterfall or agile), and practices (pair programming or frequent deployment). The same is true of threat modeling. Most past writing on threat modeling has presented "the" way to do it. This book will help you see how "there's more than one way to do it" is not just the Perl motto, but also applies to threat modeling.

The Right Way Is the Way That Finds Good Threats

The right way to threat model is the way that empowers a project team to find more good threats against a system than other techniques that could be employed with the resources available. (A "good threat" is a threat that illuminates work that needs to be done.) That's as true for a project team of one as it is for a project team of thousands. That's also true across all levels of resources, such as time, expertise, and tooling. The right techniques empower a team to really find and address threats (and gain assurance that they have done so).

There are lots of people who will tell you that they know the one true way. (That's true in fields far removed from threat modeling.) Avoid a religious war and find a way that works for you.

Threat Modeling Is Like Version Control

Threat modeling is sometimes seen as a specialist skill that only a few people can do well. That perspective holds us back, because threat modeling is more like version control than a specialist skill. This is not intended to denigrate or minimize threat modeling; rather, no professional developer would think of building software of any complexity without a version control system of some form. Threat modeling should aspire to be that fundamental.

You expect every professional software developer to know the basics of a version control system or two, and similarly, many systems administrators will use version control to manage configuration files. Many organizations get by with a simple version control approach, and never need an expert. If you work at a large organization, you might have someone who manages the build tree full time. Threat modeling is similar. With the lessons in this book, it will become reasonable to expect professionals in software and operations to have basic experience threat modeling.

Threat Modeling Is Also Like Playing a Violin

When you learn to play the violin, you don't start with the most beautiful violin music ever written. You learn to play scales, a few easy pieces, and then progress to trickier and trickier music.

Similarly, when you start threat modeling, you need to practice to learn the skills, and it may involve challenges or frustration as you learn. You need to understand threat modeling as a set of skills, which you can apply in a variety of ways, and which take time to develop. You'll get better if you practice. If you expect to compete with an expert overnight, you might be disappointed. Similarly, if you threat model only every few years, you should expect to be rusty, and it will take you time to rebuild the muscles you need.

Technique versus Repertoire

Continuing with the metaphor, the most talented violinist doesn't learn to play a single piece, but they develop a repertoire, a set of knowledge that's relevant to their field.

As you get started threat modeling, you'll need to develop both techniques and a repertoire—a set of threat examples that you can build from to imagine how new systems might be attacked. Attack lists or libraries can act as a partial substitute for the mental repertoire of known threats an expert knows about. Reading about security issues in similar products can also help you develop a repertoire of threats. Over time, this can feed into how you think about new and different threats. Learning to think about threats is easier with training wheels.

"Think Like an Attacker" Considered Harmful

A great deal of writing on threat modeling exhorts people to "think like an attacker." For many people, that's as hard as thinking like a professional chef. Even if you're a great home cook, a restaurant-managing chef has to wrestle with problems that a home cook does not. For example, how many chickens should you buy to meet the needs of a restaurant with 78 seats, each of which will turn twice an evening? The advice to think like an attacker doesn't help most people threat model.

Worse, you may end up with implicit or incorrect assumptions about how an attacker will think and what they will choose to do. Such models of an attacker's mindset may lead you to focus on the wrong threats. You don't need to focus on the attacker to find threats, but personification may help you find resources to address them.

The Interplay of Attacks, Mitigations, & Requirements

Threat modeling is all about making more secure software. As you use models of software and threats to find potential problems, you'll discover that some threats are hard or impossible to address, and you'll adjust requirements to match. This interplay is a rarely discussed key to useful threat modeling.

Sometimes it's a matter of wanting to defend against administrators, other times it's a matter of what your customers will bear. In the wake of the 9/11 hijackings, the US government reputedly gave serious consideration to banning laptops from airplanes. (A battery and a mass of explosives reportedly look the same on the x-ray machines.) Business customers, who buy last minute expensive tickets and keep the airlines aloft, threatened to revolt. So the government implemented other measures, whose effectiveness might be judged with some of the tools in this book.

This interplay leads to the conclusion that there are threats that cannot be effectively mitigated. That's a painful thought for many security professionals. (But as the Man in Black said, "Life is pain, Highness! Anyone who says differently is selling something.") When you find threats that violate your requirements and cannot be mitigated, it generally makes sense to adjust your requirements. Sometimes it's possible to either mitigate the threat operationally, or defer a decision to the person using the system.

With that, it's time to dive in and threat model!

Part I

Getting Started

This part of the book is for those who are new to threat modeling, and it assumes no prior knowledge of threat modeling or security. It focuses on the key new skills that you'll need to threat model and lays out a methodology that's designed for people who are new to threat modeling.

Part I also introduces the various ways to approach threat modeling using a set of toy analogies. Much like there are many children's toys for modeling, there are many ways to threat model. There are model kits with precisely molded parts to create airplanes or ships. These kits have a high degree of fidelity and a low level of flexibility. There are also numerous building block systems such as Lincoln Logs, Erector Sets, and Lego blocks. Each of these allows for more flexibility, at the price of perhaps not having a propeller that's quite right for the plane you want to model.

In threat modeling, there are techniques that center on attackers, assets, or software, and these are like Lincoln Logs, Erector Sets, and Lego blocks, in that each is powerful and flexible, each has advantages and disadvantages, and it can be tricky to combine them into something beautiful.

Part I contains the following chapters:

- **Chapter 1: Dive In and Threat Model!** contains everything you need to get started threat modeling, and does so by focusing on four questions:
  - What are you building?
  - What can go wrong?
  - What should you do about those things that can go wrong?
  - Did you do a decent job of analysis?

  These questions aren't just what you need to get started, but are at the heart of the four-step framework, which is the core of this book.
- **Chapter 2: Strategies for Threat Modeling** covers a great many ways to approach threat modeling. Many of them are "obvious" approaches, such as thinking about attackers or the assets you want to protect. Each is explained, along with why it works less well than you hope. These and others are contrasted with a focus on software. Software is what you can most reasonably expect a software professional to understand, and so models of software are the most important lesson of Chapter 2. Models of software are one of the two models that you should focus on when threat modeling.

CHAPTER

1

Dive In and Threat Model!

Anyone can learn to threat model, and what's more, everyone should. Threat modeling is about using models to find security problems. Using a model means abstracting away a lot of details to provide a look at a bigger picture, rather than the code itself. You model because it enables you to find issues in things you haven't built yet, and because it enables you to catch a problem before it starts. Lastly, you threat model as a way to anticipate the threats that could affect you.

Threat modeling is first and foremost a practical discipline, and this chapter is structured to reflect that practicality. Even though this book will provide you with many valuable definitions, theories, philosophies, effective approaches, and well-tested techniques, you'll want those to be grounded in experience. Therefore, this chapter avoids focusing on theory and ignores variations for now and instead gives you a chance to learn by experience.

To use an analogy, when you start playing an instrument, you need to develop muscles and awareness by playing the instrument. It won't sound great at the start, and it will be frustrating at times, but as you do it, you'll find it gets easier. You'll start to hit the notes and the timing. Similarly, if you use the simple four-step breakdown of how to threat model that's exercised in Parts I-III of this book, you'll start to develop your muscles. You probably know the old joke about the person who stops a musician on the streets of New York and asks "How do I get to Carnegie Hall?" The answer, of course, is "practice, practice, practice." Some of that includes following along, doing the exercises, and developing an understanding of the steps involved. As you do so, you'll start to understand how the various tasks and techniques that make up threat modeling come together.

In this chapter you're going to find security flaws that might exist in a design, so you can address them. You'll learn how to do this by examining a simple web application with a database back end. This will give you an idea of what can go wrong, how to address it, and how to check your work. Along the way, you'll learn to play *Elevation of Privilege*, a serious game designed to help you start threat modeling. Finally you'll get some hands-on experience building your own threat model, and the chapter closes with a set of checklists that help you get started threat modeling.

Learning to Threat Model

You begin threat modeling by focusing on four key questions:

1. What are you building?
2. What can go wrong?
3. What should you do about those things that can go wrong?
4. Did you do a decent job of analysis?

In addressing these questions, you start and end with tasks that all technologists should be familiar with: drawing on a whiteboard and managing bugs. In between, this chapter will introduce a variety of new techniques you can use to think about threats. If you get confused, just come back to these four questions.

Everything in this chapter is designed to help you answer one of these questions. You're going to first walk through these questions using a three-tier web app as an example, and after you've read that, you should walk through the steps again with something of your own to threat model. It could be software you're building or deploying, or software you're considering acquiring. If you're feeling uncertain about what to model, you can use one of the sample systems in this chapter or an exercise found in Appendix E, "Case Studies."

The second time you work through this chapter, you'll need a copy of the *Elevation of Privilege* threat-modeling game. The game uses a deck of cards that you can download free from `threatmodelingbook.com/resources`. You should get two–four friends or colleagues together for the game part.

You start with building a diagram, which is the first of four major activities involved in threat modeling and is explained in the next section. The other three include finding threats, addressing them, and then checking your work.

What Are You Building?

Diagrams are a good way to communicate what you are building. There are lots of ways to diagram software, and you can start with a whiteboard diagram of how data flows through the system. In this example, you're working with a simple web app with a web browser, web server, some business logic and a database (see Figure 1-1).

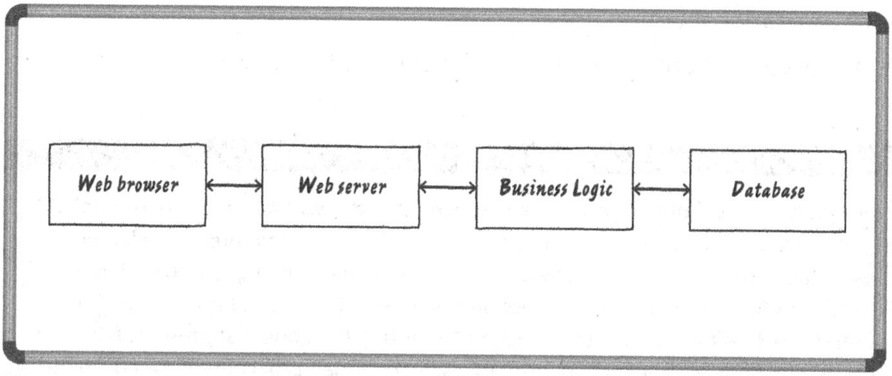

Figure 1-1: A whiteboard diagram

Some people will actually start thinking about what goes wrong right here. For example, how do you know that the web browser is being used by the person you expect? What happens if someone modifies data in the database? Is it OK for information to move from one box to the next without being encrypted? You might want to take a minute to think about some things that could go wrong here because these sorts of questions may lead you to ask "is that allowed?" You can create an even better model of what you're building if you think about "who controls what" a little. Is this a website for the whole Internet, or is it an intranet site? Is the database on site, or at a web provider?

For this example, let's say that you're building an Internet site, and you're using the fictitious Acme storage-system. (I'd put a specific product here, but then I'd get some little detail wrong and someone, certainly not you, would get all wrapped around the axle about it and miss the threat modeling lesson. Therefore, let's just call it Acme, and pretend it just works the way I'm saying. Thanks! I knew you'd understand.)

Adding boundaries to show who controls what is a simple way to improve the diagram. You can pretty easily see that the threats that cross those boundaries are likely important ones, and may be a good place to start identifying threats. These boundaries are called *trust boundaries*, and you should draw them wherever different people control different things. Good examples of this include the following:

- Accounts (UIDs on unix systems, or SIDS on Windows)
- Network interfaces
- Different physical computers
- Virtual machines
- Organizational boundaries
- Almost anywhere you can argue for different privileges

TRUST BOUNDARY VERSUS ATTACK SURFACE

A closely related concept that you may have encountered is *attack surface*. For example, the hull of a ship is an attack surface for a torpedo. The side of a ship presents a larger attack surface to a submarine than the bow of the same ship. The ship may have internal "trust" boundaries, such as waterproof bulkheads or a Captain's safe. A system that exposes lots of interfaces presents a larger attack surface than one that presents few APIs or other interfaces. Network firewalls are useful boundaries because they reduce the attack surface relative to an external attacker. However, much like the Captain's safe, there are still trust boundaries inside the firewall. A trust boundary and an attack surface are very similar views of the same thing. An attack surface is a trust boundary and a direction from which an attacker could launch an attack. Many people will treat the terms are interchangeable. In this book, you'll generally see "trust boundary" used.

In your diagram, draw the trust boundaries as boxes (see Figure 1-2), showing what's inside each with a label (such as "corporate data center") near the edge of the box.

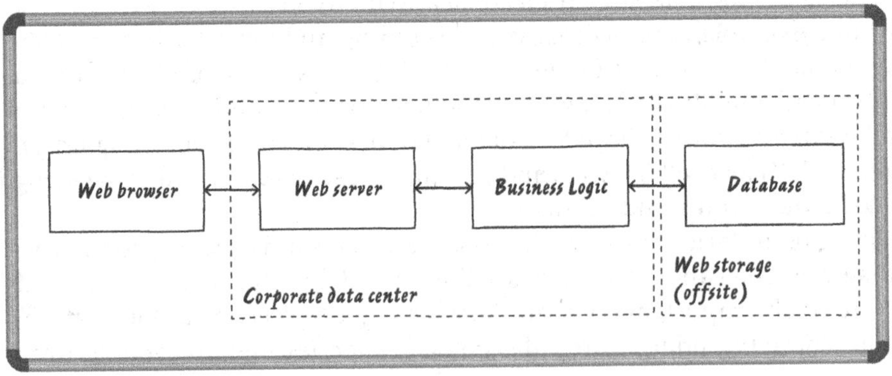

Figure 1-2: Trust boundaries added to a whiteboard diagram

As your diagram gets larger and more complex, it becomes easy to miss a part of it, or to become confused by labels on the data flows. Therefore, it can be very helpful to number each process, data flow, and data store in the diagram, as shown in Figure 1-3. (Because each trust boundary should have a unique name, representing the unique trust inside of it, there's limited value to numbering those.)

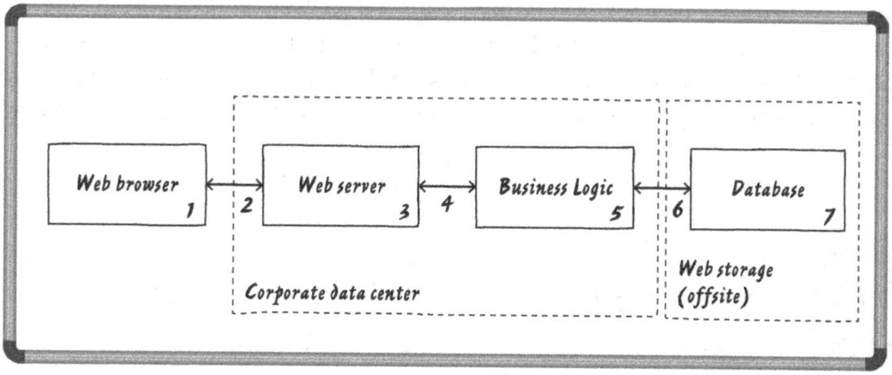

Figure 1-3: Numbers and trust boundaries added to a whiteboard diagram

Regarding the physical form of the diagram: Use whatever works for you. If that's a whiteboard diagram and a camera phone picture, great. If it's Visio, or OmniGraffle, or some other drawing program, great. You should think of threat model diagrams as part of the development process, so try to keep it in source control with everything else.

Now that you have a diagram, it's natural to ask, is it the right diagram? For now, there's a simple answer: Let's assume it is. Later in this chapter there are some tips and checklists as well as a section on updating the diagram, but at this stage you have a good enough diagram to get started on identifying threats, which is really why you bought this book. So let's identify.

What Can Go Wrong?

Now that you have a diagram, you can really start looking for what can go wrong with its security. This is so much fun that I turned it into a game called, *Elevation of Privilege*. There's more on the game in Appendix D, "Elevation of Privilege: The Cards," which discusses each card, and in Chapter 11, "Threat Modeling Tools," which covers the history and philosophy of the game, but you can get started playing now with a few simple instructions. If you haven't already done so, download a deck of cards from `http://www.microsoft.com/security/sdl/adopt/eop.aspx`. Print the pages in color, and cut them into individual cards. Then shuffle the deck and deal it out to those friends you've invited to play.

NOTE Some people aren't used to playing games at work. Others approach new games with trepidation, especially when those games involve long, complicated instructions. *Elevation of Privilege* takes just a few lines to explain. You should give it a try.

How To Play Elevation of Privilege

Elevation of Privilege is a serious game designed to help you threat model. A sample card is shown in Figure 1-4. You'll notice that like playing cards, it has a number and suit in the upper left, and an example of a threat as the main text on the card. To play the game, simply follow the instructions in the upcoming list.

3
Tampering
An attacker can take advantage of your custom key exchange or integrity control which you built instead of using standard crypto.
3

Figure 1-4: An Elevation of Privilege card

1. Deal the deck. (Shuffling is optional.)
2. The person with the 3 of Tampering leads the first round. (In card games like this, rounds are also called "tricks" or "hands.")

3. Each round works like so:
   A. Each player plays one card, starting with the person leading the round, and then moving clockwise.
   B. To play a card, read it aloud, and try to determine if it affects the system you have diagrammed. If you can link it, write it down, and score yourself a point. Play continues clockwise with the next player.
   C. When each player has played a card, the player who has played the highest card wins the round. That player leads the next round.
4. When all the cards have been played, the game ends and the person with the most points wins.
5. If you're threat modeling a system you're building, then you go file any bugs you find.

There are some folks who threat model like this in their sleep, or even have trouble switching it off. Not everyone is like that. That's OK. Threat modeling is not rocket science. It's stuff that anyone who participates in software development can learn. Not everyone wants to dedicate the time to learn to do it in their sleep.

Identifying threats can seem intimidating to a lot of people. If you're one of them, don't worry. This section is designed to gently walk you through threat identification. Remember to have fun as you do this. As one reviewer said: "Playing *Elevation of Privilege* should be *fun*. Don't downplay that. We play it every Friday. It's enjoyable, relaxing, and still has business value."

Outside of the context of the game, you can take the next step in threat modeling by thinking of things that might go wrong. For instance, how do you know that the web browser is being used by the person you expect? What happens if someone modifies data in the database? Is it OK for information to move from one box to the next without being encrypted? You don't need to come up with these questions by just staring at the diagram and scratching your chin. (I didn't!) You can identify threats like these using the simple mnemonic STRIDE, described in detail in the next section.

Using the STRIDE Mnemonic to Find Threats

STRIDE is a mnemonic for things that go wrong in security. It stands for Spoofing, Tampering, Repudiation, Information Disclosure, Denial of Service, and Elevation of Privilege:

- **Spoofing** is pretending to be something or someone you're not.

- **Tampering** is modifying something you're not supposed to modify. It can include packets on the wire (or wireless), bits on disk, or the bits in memory.
- **Repudiation** means claiming you didn't do something (regardless of whether you did or not).
- **Information Disclosure** is about exposing information to people who are not authorized to see it.
- **Denial of Service** are attacks designed to prevent a system from providing service, including by crashing it, making it unusably slow, or filling all its storage.
- **Elevation of Privilege** is when a program or user is technically able to do things that they're not supposed to do.

NOTE This is where *Elevation of Privilege*, the game, gets its name. This book uses *Elevation of Privilege*, italicized, or abbreviated to EoP, for the game—to avoid confusion with the threat.

Recall the three example threats mentioned in the preceding section:

- How do you know that the web browser is being used by the person you expect?
- What happens if someone modifies data in the database?
- Is it ok for information to go from one box to the next without being encrypted?

These are examples of spoofing, tampering, and information disclosure. Using STRIDE as a mnemonic can help you walk through a diagram and select example threats. Pair that with a little knowledge of security and the right techniques, and you'll find the important threats faster and more reliably. If you have a process in place for ensuring that you develop a threat model, document it, and you can increase confidence in your software.

Now that you have STRIDE in your tool belt, walk through your diagram again and look for more threats, this time using the mnemonic. Make a list as you go with the threat and what element of the diagram it affects. (Generally, the software, data flow, or storage is affected, rather than the trust boundary.) The following list provides some examples of each threat.

- **Spoofing:** Someone might pretend to be another customer, so you'll need a way to authenticate users. Someone might also pretend to be your website, so you should ensure that you have an SSL certificate and that you use a single domain for all your pages (to help that subset of customers who read URLs to see if they're in the right place). Someone might also place a deep link to one of your pages, such as `logout.html` or `placeorder.aspx`. You should be checking the Referrer field before taking action. That's not a complete solution to what are called CSRF (Cross Site Request Forgery) attacks, but it's a start.

- **Tampering:** Someone might tamper with the data in your back end at Acme. Someone might tamper with the data as it flows back and forth between their data center and yours. A programmer might replace the operational code on the web front end without testing it, thinking they're uploading it to staging. An angry programmer might add a coupon code "PayBobMore" that offers a 20 percent discount on all goods sold.
- **Repudiation:** Any of the preceding actions might require digging into what happened. Are there system logs? Is the right information being logged effectively? Are the logs protected against tampering?
- **Information Disclosure:** What happens if Acme reads your database? Can anyone connect to the database and read or write information?
- **Denial of Service:** What happens if a thousand customers show up at once at the website? What if Acme goes down?
- **Elevation of Privilege:** Perhaps the web front end is the only place customers should access, but what enforces that? What prevents them from connecting directly to the business logic server, or uploading new code? If there's a firewall in place, is it correctly configured? What controls access to your database at Acme, or what happens if an employee at Acme makes a mistake, or even wants to edit your files?

The preceding possibilities aren't intended to be a complete list of how each threat might manifest against every model. You can find a more complete list in Chapter 3, "STRIDE." This shorter version will get you started though, and it is focused on what you might need to investigate based on the very simple diagram shown in Figure 1-2. Remember the musical instrument analogy. If you try to start playing the piano with Ravel's Gaspard (regarded as one of the most complex piano pieces ever written), you're going to be frustrated.

Tips for Identifying Threats

Whether you are identifying threats using *Elevation of Privilege,* STRIDE, or both, here are a few tips to keep in mind that can help you stay on the right track to determine what could go wrong:

- **Start with external entities:** If you're not sure where to start, start with the external entities or events which drive activity. There are many other valid approaches though: You might start with the web browser, looking for spoofing, then tampering, and so on. You could also start with the business logic if perhaps your lead developer for that component is in the room. Wherever you choose to begin, you want to aspire to some level of organization. You could also go in "STRIDE order" through the diagram. Without some organization, it's hard to tell when you're done, but be careful not to add so much structure that you stifle creativity.

- **Never ignore a threat because it's not what you're looking for right now.** You might come up with some threats while looking at other categories. Write them down and come back to them. For example, you might have thought about "can anyone connect to our database," which is listed under information disclosure, while you were looking for spoofing threats. If so, that's awesome! Good job! Redundancy in what you find can be tedious, but it helps you avoid missing things. If you find yourself asking whether "someone not authorized to connect to the database who reads information" constitutes spoofing or information disclosure, the answer is, who cares? Record the issue and move along to the next one. STRIDE is a tool to guide you to threats, not to ask you to categorize what you've found; it makes a lousy taxonomy, anyway. (That is to say, there are plenty of security issues for which you can make an argument for various different categorizations. Compare and contrast it with a good taxonomy, such as the taxonomy of life. Does it have a backbone? If so, it's a vertebrate.)
- **Focus on feasible threats:** Along the way, you might come up with threats like "someone might insert a back door at the chip factory," or "someone might hire our janitorial staff to plug in a hardware key logger and steal all our passwords." These are real possibilities but not very likely compared to using an exploit to attack a vulnerability for which you haven't applied the patch, or tricking someone into installing software. There's also the question of what you can do about either, which brings us to the next section.

Addressing Each Threat

You should now have a decent-sized list or lists of threats. The next step in the threat modeling process is to go through the lists and address each threat. There are four types of action you can take against each threat: Mitigate it, eliminate it, transfer it, or accept it. The following list looks briefly at each of these ways to address threats, and then in the subsequent sections you will learn how to address each specific threat identified with the STRIDE list in the "What Can Go Wrong" section. For more details about each of the strategies and techniques to address these threats, see Chapters 8 and 9, "Defensive Building Blocks" and "Tradeoffs When Addressing Threats."

- **Mitigating threats** is about doing things to make it harder to take advantage of a threat. Requiring passwords to control who can log in mitigates the threat of spoofing. Adding password controls that enforce complexity or expiration makes it less likely that a password will be guessed or usable if stolen.
- **Eliminating threats** is almost always achieved by eliminating features. If you have a threat that someone will access the administrative function of

a website by visiting the /admin/URL, you can mitigate it with passwords or other authentication techniques, but the threat is still present. You can make it less likely to be found by using a URL like /j8e8vg21euwq/, but the threat is still present. You can eliminate it by removing the interface, handling administration through the command line. (There are still threats associated with how people log in on a command line. Moving away from HTTP makes the threat easier to mitigate by controlling the attack surface. Both threats would be found in a complete threat model.) Incidentally, there are other ways to eliminate threats if you're a mob boss or you run a police state, but I don't advocate their use.

- **Transferring threats** is about letting someone or something else handle the risk. For example, you could pass authentication threats to the operating system, or trust boundary enforcement to a firewall product. You can also transfer risk to customers, for example, by asking them to click through lots of hard-to-understand dialogs before they can do the work they need to do. That's obviously not a great solution, but sometimes people have knowledge that they can contribute to making a security tradeoff. For example, they might know that they just connected to a coffee shop wireless network. If you believe the person has essential knowledge to contribute, you should work to help her bring it to the decision. There's more on doing that in Chapter 15, "Human Factors and Usability."
- **Accepting the risk** is the final approach to addressing threats. For most organizations most of the time, searching everyone on the way in and out of the building is not worth the expense or the cost to the dignity and job satisfaction of those workers. (However, diamond mines and sometimes government agencies take a different approach.) Similarly, the cost of preventing someone from inserting a back door in the motherboard is expensive, so for each of these examples you might choose to accept the risk. And once you've accepted the risk, you shouldn't worry over it. Sometimes worry is a sign that the risk hasn't been fully accepted, or that the risk acceptance was inappropriate.

The strategies listed in the following tables are intended to serve as examples to illustrate ways to address threats. Your "go-to" approach should be to mitigate threats. Mitigation is generally the easiest and the best for your customers. (It might look like accepting risk is easier, but over time, mitigation is easier.) Mitigating threats can be hard work, and you shouldn't take these examples as complete. There are often other valid ways to address each of these threats, and sometimes trade-offs must be made in the way the threats are addressed.

Addressing Spoofing

Table 1-1 and the list that follows show targets of spoofing, mitigation strategies that address spoofing, and techniques to implement those mitigations.

Table 1-1: Addressing Spoofing Threats

THREAT TARGET	MITIGATION STRATEGY	MITIGATION TECHNIQUE
Spoofing a person	Identification and authentication (usernames and something you know/have/are)	Usernames, real names, or other identifiers: ❖ Passwords ❖ Tokens ❖ Biometrics Enrollment/maintenance/expiry
Spoofing a "file" on disk	Leverage the OS	❖ Full paths ❖ Checking ACLs ❖ Ensuring that pipes are created properly
	Cryptographic authenticators	Digital signatures or authenticators
Spoofing a network address	Cryptographic	❖ DNSSEC ❖ HTTPS/SSL ❖ IPsec
Spoofing a program in memory	Leverage the OS	Many modern operating systems have some form of application identifier that the OS will enforce.

- When you're concerned about a person being spoofed, ensure that each person has a unique username and some way of authenticating. The traditional way to do this is with passwords, which have all sorts of problems as well as all sorts of advantages that are hard to replicate. See Chapter 14, "Accounts and Identity" for more on passwords.
- When accessing a file on disk, don't ask for the file with `open(file)`. Use `open(/path/to/file)`. If the file is sensitive, after opening, check various security elements of the file descriptor (such as fully resolved name, permissions, and owner). You want to check with the file descriptor to avoid *race conditions*. This applies doubly when the file is an executable, although checking after opening can be tricky. Therefore, it may help to ensure that the permissions on the executable can't be changed by an attacker. In any case, you almost never want to call `exec()` with `./file`.
- When you're concerned about a system or computer being spoofed when it connects over a network, you'll want to use DNSSEC, SSL, IPsec, or a combination of those to ensure you're connecting to the right place.

Addressing Tampering

Table 1-2 and the list that follows show targets of tampering, mitigation strategies that address tampering, and techniques to implement those mitigations.

Table 1-2: Addressing Tampering Threats

THREAT TARGET	MITIGATION STRATEGY	MITIGATION TECHNIQUE
Tampering with a file	Operating system	ACLs
	Cryptographic	❖ Digital Signatures ❖ Keyed MAC
Racing to create a file (tampering with the file system)	Using a directory that's protected from arbitrary user tampering	ACLs Using private directory structures (Randomizing your file names just makes it annoying to execute the attack.)
Tampering with a network packet	Cryptographic	❖ HTTPS/SSL ❖ IPsec
	Anti-pattern	Network isolation (See note on network isolation anti-pattern.)

- **Tampering with a file:** Tampering with files can be easy if the attacker has an account on the same machine, or by tampering with the network when the files are obtained from a server.
- **Tampering with memory:** The threats you want to worry about are those that can occur when a process with less privileges than you, or that you don't trust, can alter memory. For example, if you're getting data from a shared memory segment, is it ACLed so only the other process can see it? For a web app that has data coming in via AJAX, make sure you validate that the data is what you expect after you pull in the right amount.
- **Tampering with network data:** Preventing tampering with network data requires dealing with both spoofing and tampering. Otherwise, someone who wants to tamper can simply pretend to be the other end, using what's called a *man-in-the-middle attack*. The most common solution to these problems is SSL, with IP Security (IPsec) emerging as another possibility. SSL and IPsec both address confidentiality and tampering, and can help address spoofing.

- **Tampering with networks anti-pattern:** It's somewhat common for people to hope that they can isolate their network, and so not worry about tampering threats. It's also very hard to maintain isolation over time. Isolation doesn't work as well as you would hope. For example, the isolated United States SIPRNet was thoroughly infested with malware, and the operation to clean it up took 14 months (Shachtman, 2010).

NOTE A program can't check whether it's authentic after it loads. It may be possible for something to rely on "trusted bootloaders" to provide a chain of signatures, but the security decisions are being made external to that code. (If you're not familiar with the technology, don't worry, the key lesson is that a program cannot check its own authenticity.)

Addressing Repudiation

Addressing repudiation is generally a matter of ensuring that your system is designed to log and ensuring that those logs are preserved and protected. Some of that can be handled with simple steps such as using a reliable transport for logs. In this sense, syslog over UDP was almost always silly from a security perspective; syslog over TCP/SSL is now available and is vastly better.

Table 1-3 and the list that follows show targets of repudiation, mitigation strategies that address repudiation, and techniques to implement those mitigations.

Table 1-3: Addressing Repudiation Threats

THREAT TARGET	MITIGATION STRATEGY	MITIGATION TECHNIQUE
No logs means you can't prove anything.	Log	Be sure to log all the security-relevant information.
Logs come under attack	Protect your logs.	❖ Send over the network. ❖ ACL
Logs as a channel for attack	Tightly specified logs	Documenting log design early in the development process

- **No logs means you can't prove anything:** This is self-explanatory. For example, when a customer calls to complain that they never got their order, how will this be resolved? Maintain logs so that you can investigate what happens when someone attempts to repudiate something.

- **Logs come under attack:** Attackers will do things to prevent your logs from being useful, including filling up the log to make it hard to find the attack or forcing logs to "roll over." They may also do things to set off so many alarms that the real attack is lost in a sea of troubles. Perhaps obviously, sending logs over a network exposes them to other threats that you'll need to handle.
- **Logs as a channel for attack:** By design, you're collecting data from sources outside your control, and delivering that data to people and systems with security privileges. An example of such an attack might be sending mail addressed to "</html> haha@example.com", causing trouble for web-based tools that don't expect inline HTML.

You can make it easier to write secure code to process your logs by clearly communicating what your logs can't contain, such as "Our logs are all plaintext, and attackers can insert all sorts of things," or "Fields 1–5 of our logs are tightly controlled by our software, fields 6–9 are easy to inject data into. Field 1 is time in GMT. Fields 2 and 3 are IP addresses (v4 or 6)..." Unless you have incredibly strict control, documenting what your logs can contain will likely miss things. (For example, can your logs contain Unicode double-wide characters?)

Addressing Information Disclosure

Table 1-4 and the list which follows show targets of information disclosure, mitigation strategies that address information disclosure, and techniques to implement those mitigations.

Table 1-4: Addressing Information Disclosure Threats

THREAT TARGET	MITIGATION STRATEGY	MITIGATION TECHNIQUE
Network monitoring	Encryption	❖ HTTPS/SSL ❖ IPsec
Directory or filename (for example layoff-letters/adamshostack.docx)	Leverage the OS.	ACLs
File contents	Leverage the OS.	ACLS
	Cryptography	File encryption such as PGP, disk encryption (FileVault, BitLocker)
API information disclosure	Design	Careful design control Consider pass by reference or value.

- **Network monitoring:** Network monitoring takes advantage of the architecture of most networks to monitor traffic. (In particular, most networks now broadcast packets, and each listener is expected to decide if the packet matters to them.) When networks are architected differently, there are a variety of techniques to draw traffic to or through the monitoring station.

  If you don't address spoofing, much like tampering, an attacker can just sit in the middle and spoof each end. Mitigating network information disclosure threats requires handling both spoofing and tampering threats. If you don't address tampering, then there are all sorts of clever ways to get information out. Here again, SSL and IP Security options are your simplest choices.

- **Names reveal information:** When the name of a directory or a filename itself will reveal information, then the best way to protect it is to create a parent directory with an innocuous name and use operating system ACLs or permissions.
- **File content is sensitive:** When the contents of the file need protection, use ACLs or cryptography. If you want to protect all the data should the machine fall into unauthorized hands, you'll need to use cryptography. The forms of cryptography that require the person to manually enter a key or passphrase are more secure and less convenient. There's file, filesystem, and database cryptography, depending on what you need to protect.
- **APIs reveal information:** When designing an API, or otherwise passing information over a trust boundary, select carefully what information you disclose. You should assume that the information you provide will be passed on to others, so be selective about what you provide. For example, website errors that reveal the username and password to a database are a common form of this flaw, others are discussed in Chapter 3.

Addressing Denial of Service

Table 1-5 and the list that follows show targets of denial of service, mitigation strategies that address denial of service, and techniques to implement those mitigations.

Table 1-5: Addressing Denial of Service Threats

THREAT TARGET	MITIGATION STRATEGY	MITIGATION TECHNIQUE
Network flooding	Look for exhaustible resources.	❖ Elastic resources ❖ Work to ensure attacker resource consumption is as high as or higher than yours.
		Network ACLS
Program resources	Careful design	Elastic resource management, proof of work
	Avoid multipliers.	Look for places where attackers can multiply CPU consumption on your end with minimal effort on their end: Do something to require work or enable distinguishing attackers, such as client does crypto first or login before large work factors (of course, that can't mean that logins are unencrypted).
System resources	Leverage the OS.	Use OS settings.

- **Network flooding:** If you have static structures for the number of connections, what happens if those fill up? Similarly, to the extent that it's under your control, don't accept a small amount of network data from a possibly spoofed address and return a lot of data. Lastly, firewalls can provide a layer of network ACLs to control where you'll accept (or send) traffic, and can be useful in mitigating network denial-of-service attacks.
- **Look for exhaustible resources:** The first set of exhaustible resources are network related, the second set are those your code manages, and the third are those the OS manages. In each case, elastic resourcing is a valuable technique. For example, in the 1990s some TCP stacks had a hardcoded limit of five half-open TCP connections. (A half-open connection is one in the process of being opened. Don't worry if that doesn't make sense, but rather ask yourself why the code would be limited to five of them.) Today, you can often obtain elastic resourcing of various types from cloud providers.

- **System resources:** Operating systems tend to have limits or quotas to control the resource consumption of user-level code. Consider those resources that the operating system manages, such as memory or disk usage. If your code runs on dedicated servers, it may be sensible to allow it to chew up the entire machine. Be careful if you unlimit your code, and be sure to document what you're doing.
- **Program resources:** Consider resources that your program manages itself. Also, consider whether the attacker can make you do more work than they're doing. For example, if he sends you a packet full of random data and you do expensive cryptographic operations on it, then your vulnerability to denial of service will be higher than if you make him do the cryptography first. Of course, in an age of botnets, there are limits to how well one can reassign this work. There's an excellent paper by Ben Laurie and Richard Clayton, "Proof of work proves not to work," which argues against proof of work schemes (Laurie, 2004).

Addressing Elevation of Privilege

Table 1-6 and the list that follows show targets of elevation of privilege, mitigation strategies that address elevation of privilege, and techniques to implement those mitigations.

Table 1-6: Addressing Elevation of Privilege Threats

THREAT TARGET	MITIGATION STRATEGY	MITIGATION TECHNIQUE
Data/code confusion	Use tools and architectures that separate data and code.	❖ Prepared statements or stored procedures in SQL ❖ Clear separators with canonical forms ❖ Late validation that data is what the next function expects
Control flow/ memory corruption attacks	Use a type-safe language.	Writing code in a type-safe language protects against entire classes of attack.
	Leverage the OS for memory protection.	Most modern operating systems have memory-protection facilities.

THREAT TARGET	MITIGATION STRATEGY	MITIGATION TECHNIQUE
	Use the sandbox.	❖ Modern operating systems support sandboxing in various ways (AppArmor on Linux, AppContainer or the MOICE pattern on Windows, Sandboxlib on Mac OS). ❖ Don't run as the "nobody" account, create a new one for each app. Postfix and QMail are examples of the good pattern of one account per function.
Command injection attacks	Be careful.	❖ Validate that your input is the size and form you expect. ❖ Don't sanitize. Log and then throw it away if it's weird.

- **Data/code confusion:** Problems where data is treated as code are common. As information crosses layers, what's tainted and what's pure can be lost. Attacks such as XSS take advantage of HTML's freely interweaving code and data. (That is, an .html file contains both code, such as Javascript, and data, such as text, to be displayed and sometimes formatting instructions for that text.) There are a few strategies for dealing with this. The first is to look for ways in which frameworks help you keep code and data separate. For example, prepared statements in SQL tell the database what statements to expect, and where the data will be.

  You can also look at the data you're passing right before you pass it, so you know what validation you might be expected to perform for the function you're calling. For example, if you're sending data to a web page, you might ensure that it contains no <, >, #, or & characters, or whatever.

  In fact, the value of "whatever" is highly dependent on exactly what exists between "you" and the rendition of the web page, and what security checks it may be performing. If "you" means a web server, it may be very important to have a few < and > symbols in what you produce. If "you" is something taking data from a database and sending it to, say PHP, then the story is quite different. Ideally, the nature of "you" and the additional steps are clear in your diagrams.

- **Control flow/memory corruption attacks:** This set of attacks generally takes advantage of weak typing and static structures in C-like languages to enable an attacker to provide code and then jump to that code. If you use a type-safe language, such as Java or C#, many of these attacks are harder to execute.

Modern operating systems tend to contain memory protection and randomization features, such as Address Space Layout Randomization (ASLR). Sometimes the features are optional, and require a compiler or linker switch. In many cases, such features are almost free to use, and you should at least try all such features your OS supports. (It's not completely effortless, you may need to recompile, test, or make other such small investments.)

The last set of controls to address memory corruption are sandboxes. Sandboxes are OS features that are designed to protect the OS or the rest of the programs running as the user from a corrupted program.

NOTE Details about each of these features are outside the scope of this book, but searching on terms such as type safety, ASLR, and sandbox should provide a plethora of details.

- **Command injection attacks:** Command injection attacks are a form of code/data confusion where an attacker supplies a control character, followed by commands. For example, in SQL injection, a single quote will often close a dynamic SQL statement; and when dealing with unix shell scripts, the shell can interpret a semicolon as the end of input, taking anything after that as a command.

In addition to working through each STRIDE threat you encounter, a few other recurring themes will come up as you address your threats; these are covered in the following two sections.

Validate, Don't Sanitize

Know what you expect to see, how much you expect to see, and validate that that's what you're receiving. If you get something else, throw it away and return an error message. Unless your code is perfect, errors in sanitization will hurt a lot, because after you write that sanitize input function you're going to rely on it. There have been fascinating attacks that rely on a sanitize function to get their code into shape to execute.

Trust the Operating System

One of the themes that recurs in the preceding tables is "trust the operating system." Of course, you may want to discount that because I did much of this work while working for Microsoft, a purveyor of a variety of fine operating system software, so there might be some bias here. It's a valid point, and good for you for being skeptical. See, you're threat modeling already!

More seriously, trusting the operating system is a good idea for a number of reasons:

- The operating system provides you with security features so you can focus on your unique value proposition.
- The operating system runs with privileges that are probably not available to your program or your attacker.
- If your attacker controls the operating system, you're likely in a world of hurt regardless of what your code tries to do.

With all of that "trust the operating system" advice, you might be tempted to ask why you need this book. Why not just rely on the operating system?

Well, many of the building blocks just discussed are discretionary. You can use them well or you can use them poorly. It's up to you to ensure that you don't set the permissions on a file to 777, or the ACLs to allow Guest accounts to write. It's up to you to write code that runs well as a normal or even sandboxed user, and it's certainly up to you in these early days of client/server, web, distributed systems, web 2.0, cloud, or whatever comes next to ensure that you're building the right security mechanisms that these newfangled widgets don't yet offer.

File Bugs

Now that you have a list of threats and ways you would like to mitigate them, you're through the complex, security-centered parts of the process. There are just a few more things to do, the first of which is to treat each line of the preceding tables as a bug. You want to treat these as bugs because if you ship software, you've learned to handle bugs in some way. You presumably have a way to track them, prioritize them, and ensure that you're closing them with an appropriate degree of consistency. This will mean something very different to a three-person start-up versus a medical device manufacturer, but both organizations will have a way to handle bugs. You want to tap into that procedure to ensure that threat modeling isn't just a paper exercise.

You can write the text of the bugs in a variety of ways, based on what your organization does. Examples of filing a bug might include the following:

- Someone might use the `/admin/` interface without proper authorization.
- The admin interface lacks proper authorization controls,
- There's no automated security testing for the `/admin/` interface.

Whichever way you go, it's great if you can include the entire threat in the bug, and mark it as a security bug if your bug-tracking tool supports that. (If you're a super-agile scrum shop, use a uniquely colored Post-it for security bugs.)

You'll also have to prioritize the bugs. Elevation-of-privilege bugs are almost always going to fall into the highest priority category, because when they're exploited they lead to so much damage. Denial of service often falls toward the bottom of the stack, but you'll have to consider each bug to determine how to rank it.

Checking Your Work

Validation of your threat model is the last thing you do as part of threat modeling. There are a few tasks to be done here, and it is best to keep them aligned with the order in which you did the previous work. Therefore, the validation tasks include checking the model, checking that you've looked for each threat, and checking your tests. You probably also want to validate the model a second time as you get close to shipping or deploying.

Checking the model

You should ensure that the final model matched what you built. If it doesn't, how can you know that you found the right, relevant threats? To do so, try to arrange a meeting during which everyone looks at the diagram, and answer the following questions:

- Is this complete?
- Is it accurate?
- Does it cover all the security decisions we made?
- Can I start the next version with this diagram without any changes?

If everyone says yes, your diagram is sufficiently up to date for the next step. If not, you'll need to update it.

Updating the Diagram

As you went through the diagram, you might have noticed that it's missing key data. If it were a real system, there might be extra interfaces that were not drawn in, or there might be additional databases. There might be details that you jumped to the whiteboard to draw in. If so, you need to update the diagram with those details. A few rules of thumb are useful as you create or update diagrams:

- Focus on data flow, not control flow.
- Anytime you need to qualify your answer with "sometimes" or "also," you should consider adding more detail to break out the various cases. For example, if you say, "Sometimes we connect to this web service via SSL,

and sometimes we fall back to HTTP," you should draw both of those data flows (and consider whether an attacker can make you fall back like that).

- Anytime you find yourself needing more detail to explain security-relevant behavior, draw it in.
- Any place you argued over the design or construction of the system, draw in the agreed-on facts. This is an important way to ensure that everyone ended that discussion on the same page. It's especially important for larger teams when not everyone is in the room for the threat model discussions. If they see a diagram that contradicts their thinking, they can either accept it or challenge the assumptions; but either way, a good clear diagram can help get everyone on the same page.
- Don't have data sinks: You write the data for a reason. Show who uses it.
- Data can't move itself from one data store to another: Show the process that moves it.
- The diagram should tell a story, and support you telling stories while pointing at it.
- Don't draw an eye chart (a diagram with so much detail that you need to squint to read the tiny print).

Diagram Details

If you're wondering how to reconcile that last rule of thumb, don't draw an eye chart, with all the details that a real software project can entail, one technique is to use a sub diagram that shows the details of one particular area. You should look for ways to break things out that make sense for your project. For example, if you have one hyper-complex process, maybe everything in that process should be covered in one diagram, and everything outside it in another. If you have a dispatcher or queuing system, that's a good place to break things up. Your databases or the fail-over system is also a good split. Maybe there's a set of a few elements that really need more detail. All of these are good ways to break things out.

The key thing to remember is that the diagram is intended to help ensure that you understand and can discuss the system. Recall the quote that opens this book: "All models are wrong. Some models are useful." Therefore, when you're adding additional diagrams, don't ask, "Is this the right way to do it?" Instead, ask, "Does this help me think about what might go wrong?"

Checking Each Threat

There are two main types of validation activities you should do. The first is checking that you did the right thing with each threat you found. The other is asking if you found all the threats you should find.

In terms of checking that you did the right thing with each threat you did find, the first and foremost question here is "Did I do something with each unique threat I found?" You really don't want to drop stuff on the floor. This is "turning the crank" sort of work. It's rarely glamorous or exciting until you find the thing you overlooked. You can save a lot of time by taking meeting minutes and writing a bug number next to each one, checking that you've addressed each when you do your bug triage.

The next question is "Did I do the right something with each threat?" If you've filed bugs with some sort of security tag, run a query for all the security bugs, and give each one a going-over. This can be as lightweight as reading each bug and asking yourself, "Did I do the right thing?" or you could use a short checklist, an example of which ("Validating threats") is included at the end of this chapter in the "Checklists for Diving in and Threat Modeling" section.

Checking Your Tests

For each threat that you address, ensure you've built a good test to detect the problem. Your test can be a manual testing process or an automated test. Some of these tests will be easy, and others very tricky. For example, if you want to ensure that no static web page under `/beta` can be accessed without the beta cookie, you can build a quick script that retrieves all the pages from your source repository, constructs a URL for it, and tries to collect the page. You could extend the script to send a cookie with each request, and then re-request with an admin cookie. Ideally, that's easy to do in your existing web testing framework. It gets a little more complex with dynamic pages, and a lot more complex when the security risk is something such as SQL injection or secure parsing of user input. There are entire books written on those subjects, not to mention entire books on the subject of testing. The key question you should ask is something like "Are my security tests in line with the other software tests and the sorts of risks that failures expose?"

Threat Modeling on Your Own

You have now walked through your first threat model. Congratulations! Remember though: You're not going to get to Carnegie Hall if you don't practice, practice, practice. That means it is time to do it again, this time on your own, because doing it again is the only way to get better. Pick a system you're working on and threat model it. Follow this simplified, five-step process as you go:

1. Draw a diagram.
2. Use the EoP game to find threats.

3. Address each threat in some way.
4. Check your work with the checklists at the end of this chapter.
5. Celebrate and share your work.

Right now, if you're new to threat modeling, your best bet is to do it often, applying it to the software and systems that matters to you. After threat modeling a few systems, you'll find yourself getting more comfortable with the tools and techniques. For now, the thing to do is practice. Build your first muscles to threat model with.

This brings up the question, what should you threat model next?

What you're working on now is the first place to look for the next system to threat model. If it has a trust boundary of some sort, it may be a good candidate. If it's too simple to have trust boundaries, threat modeling it probably won't be very satisfying. If it has too many boundaries, it may be too big a project to chew on all at once. If you're collaborating closely on it with a few other people who you trust, that may be a good opportunity to play *EoP* with them. If you're working on a large team, or across organizational boundaries, or things are tense, then those people may not be good first collaborators on threat modeling. Start with what you're working on now, unless there are tangible reasons to wait.

Checklists for Diving In and Threat Modeling

There's a lot in this chapter. As you sit down to really do the work yourself, it can be tricky to assess how you're doing. Here are some checklists that are designed to help you avoid the most common problems. Each question is designed to be read aloud and to have an affirmative answer from everyone present. After reading each question out loud, encourage questions or clarification from everyone else involved.

Diagramming

1. Can we tell a story without changing the diagram?
2. Can we tell that story without using words such as "sometimes" or "also"?
3. Can we look at the diagram and see exactly where the software will make a security decision?
4. Does the diagram show all the trust boundaries, such as where different accounts interact? Do you cover all UIDs, all application roles, and all network interfaces?
5. Does the diagram reflect the current or planned reality of the software?

6. Can we see where all the data goes and who uses it?
7. Do we see the processes that move data from one data store to another?

Threats

1. Have we looked for each of the STRIDE threats?
2. Have we looked at each element of the diagram?
3. Have we looked at each data flow in the diagram?

NOTE Data flows are a type of element, but they are sometimes overlooked as people get started, so question 3 is a belt-and-suspenders question to add redundancy. (A belt-and-suspenders approach ensures that a gentleman's pants stay up.)

Validating Threats

1. Have we written down or filed a bug for each threat?
2. Is there a proposed/planned/implemented way to address each threat?
3. Do we have a test case per threat?
4. Has the software passed the test?

Summary

Any technical professional can learn to threat model. Threat modeling involves the intersection of two models: a model of what can go wrong (threats), applied to a model of the software you're building or deploying, which is encoded in a diagram. One model of threats is STRIDE: spoofing, tampering, repudiation, information disclosure, denial of service, and elevation of privilege. This model of threats has been made into the *Elevation of Privilege* game, which adds structure and hints to the model.

With a whiteboard diagram and a copy of *Elevation of Privilege,* developers can threat model software that they're building, systems administrators can threat model software they're deploying or a system they're constructing, and security professionals can introduce threat modeling to those with skillsets outside of security.

It's important to address threats, and the STRIDE threats are the inverse of properties you want. There are mitigation strategies and techniques for developers and for systems administrators.

Once you've created a threat model, it's important to check your work by making sure you have a good model of the software in an up-to-date diagram, and that you've checked each threat you've found.

CHAPTER 2

Strategies for Threat Modeling

The earlier you find problems, the easier it is to fix them. Threat modeling is all about finding problems, and therefore it should be done early in your development or design process, or in preparing to roll out an operational system. There are many ways to threat model. Some ways are very specific, like a model airplane kit that can only be used to build an F-14 fighter jet. Other methods are more versatile, like Lego building blocks that can be used to make a variety of things. Some threat modeling methods don't combine easily, in the same way that Erector set pieces and Lego set blocks don't fit together. This chapter covers the various strategies and methods that have been brought to bear on threat modeling, presents each one in depth, and sets the stage for effectively finding threats.

You'll start with very simple methods such as asking "what's your threat model?" and brainstorming about threats. Those can work for a security expert, and they may work for you. From there, you'll learn about three strategies for threat modeling: focusing on assets, focusing on attackers, and focusing on software. These strategies are more structured, and can work for people with different skillsets. A focus on software is usually the most appropriate strategy. The desire to focus on assets or attackers is natural, and often presented as an unavoidable or essential aspect of threat modeling. It would be wrong not to present each in its best light before discussing issues with those strategies. From there, you'll learn about different types of diagrams you can use to model your system or software.

NOTE This chapter doesn't include the specific threat building blocks that discover threats, which are the subject of the next few chapters.

"What's Your Threat Model?"

The question "what's your threat model?" is a great one because in just four words, it can slice through many conundrums to determine what you are worried about. Answers are often of the form "an attacker with the laptop" or " insiders," or (unfortunately, often) "huh?" The "huh?" answer is useful because it reveals how much work would be needed to find a consistent and structured approach to defense. Consistency and structure are important because they help you invest in defenses that will stymie attackers. There's a compendium of standard answers to "what's your threat model?" in Appendix A, "Helpful Tools," but a few examples are listed here as well:

- A thief who could steal your money
- The company stakeholders (employees, consultants, shareholders, etc.) who access sensitive documents and are not trusted
- An untrusted network
- An attacker who could steal your cookie (web or otherwise)

NOTE Throughout this book, you'll visit and revisit the same example for each of these approaches. Your main targets are the fictitious Acme Corporation's "Acme/SQL," which is a commercial database server, and Acme's operational network. Using Acme examples, you can see how the different approaches play out against the same systems.

Applying the question "what's your threat model?" to the Acme Corporation example, you might get the following answers:

- For the Acme SQL database, the threat model would be an attacker who wants to read or change data in the database. A more subtle model might also include people who want to read the data without showing up in the logs.
- For Acme's financial system, the answers might include someone getting a check they didn't deserve, customers who don't make a payment they owe, and/or someone reading or altering financial results before reporting.

If you don't have a clear answer to the question, "what's your threat model?" it can lead to inconsistency and wasted effort. For example, start-up Zero-Knowledge

Systems didn't have a clear answer to the question "what's your threat model?" Because there was no clear answer, there wasn't consistency in what security features were built. A great deal of energy went into building defenses against the most complex attacks, and these choices to defend against such attackers had performance impacts on the whole system. While preventing governments from spying on customers was a fun technical challenge and an emotionally resonant goal, both the challenge and the emotional impact made it hard to make technical decisions that could have made the business more successful. Eventually, a clearer answer to "what's your threat model?" let Zero-Knowledge Systems invest in mitigations that all addressed the same subset of possible threats.

So how do you ensure you have a clear answer to this question? Often, the answers are not obvious, even to those who think regularly about security, and the question itself offers little structure for figuring out the answers. One approach, often recommended is to brainstorm. In the next section, you'll learn about a variety of approaches to brainstorming and the tradeoffs associated with those approaches.

Brainstorming Your Threats

Brainstorming is the most traditional way to enumerate threats. You get a set of experienced experts in a room, give them a way to take notes (whiteboards or cocktail napkins are traditional) and let them go. The quality of the brainstorm is bounded by the experience of the brainstormers and the amount of time spent brainstorming.

Brainstorming involves a period of idea-generation, followed by a period of analyzing and selecting the ideas. Brainstorming for threat modeling involves coming up with possible attacks of all sorts. During the idea generation phase, you should forbid criticism. You want to explore the space of possible threats, and an atmosphere of criticism will inhibit such idea generation. A moderator can help keep brainstorming moving.

During brainstorming, it is key to have an expert on the technology being modeled in the room. Otherwise, it's easy to make bad assumptions about how it works. However, when you have an expert who's proud of their technology, you need to ensure that you don't end up with a "proud parent" offended that their software baby is being called ugly. A helpful rule is that it's the software being attacked, not the software architects. That doesn't always suffice, but it's a good start. There's also a benefit to bringing together a diverse grouping of experts with a broader set of experience.

Brainstorming can also devolve into out-of-scope attacks. For example, if you're designing a chat program, attacks by the memory management unit against the CPU are probably out of scope, but if you're designing a motherboard, these attacks may be the focus of your threat modeling. One way to handle this issue is to list a set of attacks that are out of scope, such as "the administrator is malicious" or "an attacker edits the hard drive on another system," as well as a set of attack equivalencies, like, "an attacker can smash the stack and execute code," so that those issues can be acknowledged and handled in a consistent way. A variant of brainstorming is the exhortation to "think like an attacker," which is discussed in more detail in Chapter 18, "Experimental Approaches."

Some attacks you might brainstorm in threat modeling the Acme's financial statements include breaking in over the Internet, getting the CFO drunk, bribing a janitor, or predicting the URL where the financials will be published. These can be a bit of a grab bag, so the next section provides somewhat more focused approaches.

Brainstorming Variants

Free-form or "normal" brainstorming, as discussed in the preceding section, can be used as a method for threat modeling, but there are more specific methods you can use to help focus your brainstorming. The following sections describe variations on classic brainstorming: scenario analyses, pre-mortems, and movie-plotting.

Scenario Analysis

It may help to focus your brainstorming with scenarios. If you're using written scenarios in your overall engineering, you might start from those and ask what might go wrong, or you could use a variant of Chandler's law ("When in doubt, have a man come through a door with a gun in his hand.") You don't need to restrict yourself to a man with a gun, of course; you can use any of the attackers listed in Appendix C, "Attacker Lists."

For an example of scenario-specific brainstorming, try to threat model for handing your phone to a cute person in a bar. It's an interesting exercise. The recipient could perhaps text donations to the Red Cross, text an important person to "stop bothering me," or post to Facebook that "I don't take hints well" or "I'm skeevy," not to mention possibilities of running away with the phone or dropping it in a beer.

Less frivolously, your sample scenarios might be based on the product scenarios or use cases for the current development cycle, and therefore cover failover and replication, and how those services could be exploited when not properly authenticated and authorized.

Pre-Mortem

Decision-sciences expert Gary Klein has suggested another brainstorming technique he calls the *pre-mortem* (Klein, 1999). The idea is to gather those involved in a decision and ask them to assume that it's shortly after a project deadline, or after a key milestone, and that things have gone totally off the rails. With an "assumption of failure" in mind, the idea is to explore why the participants believe it will go off the rails. The value to calling this a pre-mortem is the framing it brings. The natural optimism that accompanies a project is replaced with an explicit assumption that it has failed, giving you and other participants a chance to express doubts. In threat modeling, the assumption is that the product is being successfully attacked, and you now have permission to express doubts or concerns.

Movie Plotting

Another variant of brainstorming is movie plotting. The key difference between "normal brainstorming" and "movie plotting" is that the attack ideas are intended to be outrageous and provocative to encourage the free flow of ideas. Defending against these threats likely involves science-fiction-type devices that impinge on human dignity, liberty, and privacy without actually defending anyone. Examples of great movies for movie plot threats include *Ocean's Eleven, The Italian Job,* and every Bond movie that doesn't stink. If you'd like to engage in more structured movie plotting, create three lists: flawed protagonists, brilliant antagonists, and whiz-bang gadgetry. You can then combine them as you see fit.

Examples of movie plot threats include a foreign spy writing code for Acme SQL so that a fourth connection attempt lets someone in as admin, a scheming CFO stealing from the firm, and someone rappelling from the ceiling to avoid the pressure mats in the floor while hacking into the database from the console. Note that these movie plots are equally applicable to Acme and its customers.

The term movie plotting was coined by Bruce Schneier, a respected security expert. Announcing his contest to elicit movie plot threats, he said: "The purpose of this contest is absurd humor, but I hope it also makes a point. Terrorism is a real threat, but we're not any safer through security measures that require us to correctly guess what the terrorists are going to do next" (Schneier, 2006). The point doesn't apply only to terrorism; convoluted but vividly described threats can be a threat to your threat modeling methodology.

Literature Review

As a precursor to brainstorming (or any other approach to finding threats), reviewing threats to systems similar to yours is a helpful starting point in threat modeling. You can do this using search engines, or by checking the academic literature and following citations. It can be incredibly helpful to search on competitors or related products. To start, search on a competitor, appending terms such as "security," "security bug," "penetration test," "pwning," or "Black Hat," and use your creativity. You can also review common threats in this book, especially Part III, "Managing and Addressing Threats" and the appendixes. Additionally, Ross Anderson's *Security Engineering* is a great collection of real world attacks and engineering lessons you can draw on, especially if what you're building is similar to what he covers (Wiley, 2008).

A *literature review* of threats against databases might lead to an understanding of SQL injection attacks, backup failures, and insider attacks, suggesting the need for logs. Doing a review is especially helpful for those developing their skills in threat modeling. Be aware that a lot of the threats that may come up can be super-specific. Treat them as examples of more general cases, and look for variations and related problems as you brainstorm.

Perspective on Brainstorming

Brainstorming and its variants suffer from a variety of problems. Brainstorming often produces threats that are hard or impossible to address. Brainstorming intentionally requires the removal of scoping or boundaries, and the threats are very dependent on the participants and how the session happens to progress. When experts get together, unstructured discussion often ensues. This can be fun for the experts and it usually produces interesting results, but oftentimes, experts are in short supply. Other times, engineers get frustrated with the inconsistency of "ask two experts, get three answers."

There's one other issue to consider, and that relates to exit criteria. It's difficult to know when you're done brainstorming, and whether you're done because you have done a good job or if everyone is just tired. Engineering management may demand a time estimate that they can insert into their schedule, and these are difficult to predict. The best approach to avoid this timing issue is simply to set a meeting of defined length. Unfortunately, this option doesn't provide a high degree of confidence that all interesting threats have been found.

Because of the difficulty of addressing threats illuminated with a limitless brainstorming technique and the poorly defined exit criteria to a brainstorming session, it is important to consider other approaches to threat modeling that are more prescriptive, formal, repeatable, or less dependent on the aptitudes and knowledge of the participants. Such approaches are the subject of the rest of this chapter and also discussed in the rest of Part II, "Finding Threats."

Structured Approaches to Threat Modeling

When it's hard to answer "What's your threat model?" people often use an approach centered on models of their assets, models of attackers, or models of their software. Centering on one of those is preferable to using approaches that attempt to combine them because these combinations tend to be confusing.

Assets are the valuable things you have. The people who might go after your assets are attackers, and the most common way for them to attack is via the software you're building or deploying.

Each of these is a natural place to start thinking about threats, and each has advantages and disadvantages, which are covered in this section. There are people with very strong opinions that one of these is right (or wrong). Don't worry about "right" or "wrong," but rather "usefulness." That is, does your approach help you find problems? If it doesn't, it's wrong for you, however forcefully someone might argue its merits.

These three approaches can be thought of as analogous to Lincoln Log sets, Erector sets, and Lego sets. Each has a variety of pieces, and each enables you to build things, but they may not combine in ways as arbitrary as you'd like. That is, you can't snap Lego blocks to an Erector set model. Similarly, you can't always snap attackers onto a software model and have something that works as a coherent whole.

To understand these three approaches, it can be useful to apply them to something concrete. Figure 2-1 shows a data flow diagram of the Acme/SQL system.

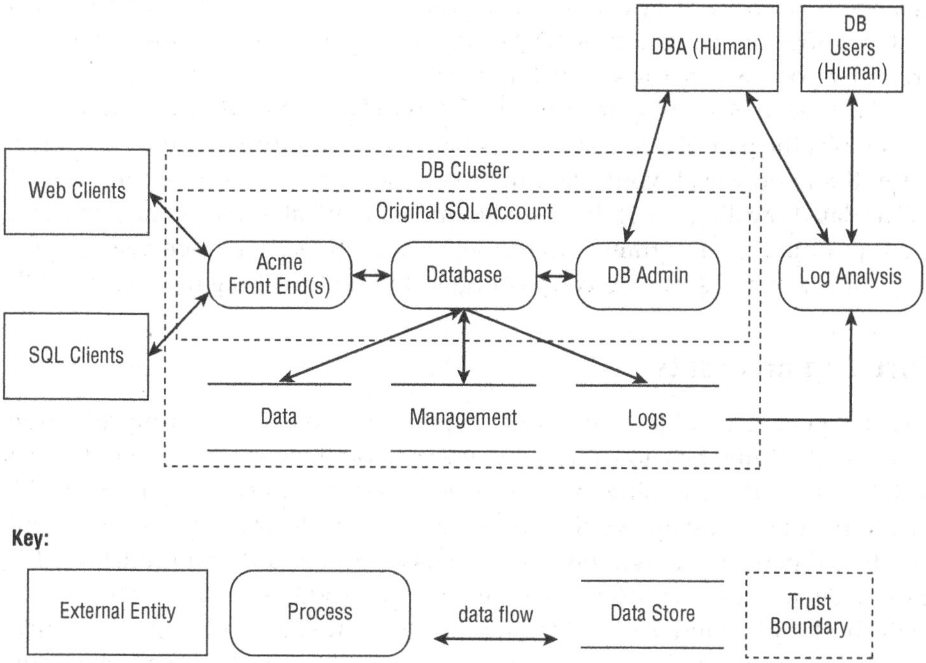

Figure 2-1: Data flow diagram of the Acme/SQL database

Looking at the diagram, and reading from left to right, you can see two types of clients accessing the front ends and the core database, which manages transactions, access control, atomicity, and so on. Here, assume that the Acme/SQL system comes with an integrated web server, and that authorized clients are given nearly raw access to the data. There could simultaneously be web servers offering deeper business logic, access to multiple back ends, integration with payment systems, and so on. Those web servers would access Acme/SQL via the SQL protocol over a network connection.

Back to the diagram, Figure 2-1 also shows there is also a set of DB Admin tools that the DBA (the human database administrator) uses to manage the system. As shown in the diagram, there are three conceptual data stores: Data, Management (including metadata such as locks, policies, and indices), and Logs. These might be implemented in memory, as files, as custom stores on raw disk, or delegated to network storage. As you dig in, the details matter greatly, but you usually start modeling from the conceptual level, as shown.

Finally, there's a log analysis package. Note that only the database core has direct access to the data and management information in this design. You should also note that most of the arrows are two-way, except Database ⇨ Logs and Logs ⇨ Log Analysis. Of course, the Log Analysis process will be querying the logs, but because it's intended as a read-only interface, it is represented as a one-way arrow. Very occasionally, you might have strictly one-way flows, such as those implemented by SNMP traps or syslog. Some threat modelers prefer two one-way arrows, which can help you see threats in each direction, but also lead to busy diagrams that are hard to label or read. If your diagrams are simple, the pair of one way arrows helps you find threats, and is therefore better than two-way. If your diagram is complex, either approach can be used.

The data flow diagram is discussed in more detail later in this chapter, in the section "Data Flow Diagrams." In the next few sections, you'll see how to apply asset, attacker, and software-centric models to find threats against Acme/SQL.

Focusing on Assets

It seems very natural to center your approach on assets, or things of value. After all, if a thing has no value, why worry about how someone might attack it? It turns out that focusing on assets is less useful than you may hope, and is therefore not the best approach to threat modeling. However, there are a small number of people who will benefit from asset-centered threat modeling. The most likely to benefit are a team of security experts with experience structuring their thinking around assets. (Having found a way that works for them, there may be no reason to change.) Less technical people may be able to contribute to threat modeling by saying "focus on this asset." If you are in either of these groups, or work with them, congratulations! This section is for you. If you aren't one of those people, however, don't be too quick to skip ahead. It is still important to have a good understanding of the role assets can play in threat modeling, even if they're not in a starring role). It can also help for you to understand why the approach is not as useful as it may appear, so you can have an informed discussion with those advocating it.

The term asset usually refers to something of value. When people bring up assets as part of a threat modeling activity, they often mean something an attacker wants to access, control, or destroy. If everyone who touches the threat modeling process doesn't have a working agreement about what an asset is, your process will either get bogged down, or participants will just talk past each other.

There are three ways the term asset is commonly used in threat modeling:

- Things attackers want
- Things you want to protect
- Stepping stones to either of these

You should think of these three types of assets as families rather than categories because just as people can belong to more than one family at a time, assets can take on more than one meaning at a time. In other words, the tags that apply to assets can overlap, as shown in Figure 2-2. The most common usage of asset in discussing threat models seems to be a marriage of "things attackers want" and "things you want to protect."

Figure 2-2: The overlapping definitions of assets

NOTE **There are a few other ways in which the term asset is used by those who are threat modeling—such as a synonym for computer, or a type of computer (for example, "Targeted assets: mail server, database"). For the sake of clarity, this book only uses asset with explicit reference to one or more of the three families previously defined, and you should try to do the same.**

Things Attackers Want

Usually assets that attackers want are relatively tangible things such as "this database of customer medical data." Good examples of things attackers want include the following:

- User passwords or keys
- Social security numbers or other identifiers
- Credit card numbers
- Your confidential business data

Things You Want to Protect

There's also a family of assets you want to protect. Unlike the tangible things attackers want, many of these assets are intangibles. For example, your company's reputation or goodwill is something you want to protect. Competitors or activists may well attack your reputation by engaging in smear tactics. From a threat modeling perspective, your reputation is usually too diffuse to be able to technologically mitigate threats against it. Therefore, you want to protect it by protecting the things that matter to your customers.

As an example of something you want to protect, if you had an empty safe, you intuitively don't want someone to come along and stick their stethoscope to it. But there's nothing in it, so what's the damage? Changing the combination and letting the right folks (but only the right folks) know the new combination requires work. Therefore you want to protect this empty safe, but it would be an unlikely target for a thief. If that same safe has one million dollars in it, it would be much more likely to pique a thief's interest. The million dollars is part of the family of things you want that attackers want, too.

Stepping Stones

The final family of assets is stepping stones to other assets. For example, everything drawn in a threat model diagram is something you want to protect because it may be a stepping stone to the targets that attackers want. In some ways, the set of stepping stone assets is an attractive nuisance. For example, every computer has CPU and storage that an attacker can use. Most also have Internet connectivity, and if you're in systems management or operational security, many of the computers you worry most about will have special access to your organization's network. They're behind a firewall or have VPN access. These are stepping stones. If they are uniquely valuable stepping stones in some way, note that. In practice, it's rarely helpful to include "all our PCs" in an asset list.

NOTE Referring back to the safe example in the previous section, the safe combination is a member of the stepping stone family. It may well be that stepping-stones and things you protect are, in practice, very similar. The list of technical elements you protect that are not members of the stepping-stone family appears fairly short.

Implementing Asset-Centric Modeling

If you were to threat model with an asset-focused approach, you would make a list of your assets and then consider how an attacker could threaten each. From there, you'd consider how to address each threat.

After an asset list is created, you should connect each item on the list to particular computer systems or sets of systems. (If an asset includes something like "Amazon Web Services" or "Microsoft Azure," then you don't need to be able to point to the computer systems in question, you just need to understand where they are—eventually you'll need to identify the threats to those systems and determine how to mitigate them.)

The next step is to draw the systems in question, showing the assets and other components as well as interconnections, until you can tell a story about them. You can use this model to apply either an attack set like STRIDE or an attacker-centered brainstorm to understand how those assets could be attacked.

Perspective on Asset-Centric Threat Modeling

Focusing on assets appears to be a common-sense approach to threat modeling, to the point where it seems hard to argue with. Unfortunately, much of the time, a discussion of assets does *not* improve threat modeling. However, the misconception is so common that it's important to examine why it doesn't help.

There's no direct line from assets to threats, and no prescriptive set of steps. Essentially, effort put into enumerating assets is effort you're not spending finding or fixing threats. Sometimes, that involves a discussion of what's an asset, or which type of asset you're discussing. That discussion, at best, results in a list of things to look for in your software or operational model, so why not start by creating such a model? Once you have a list of assets, that list is not (ahem) a stepping stone to finding threats; you still need to apply some methodology or approach. Finally, assets may help you prioritize threats, but if that's your goal, it doesn't mean you should start with or focus on assets. Generally, such information comes out naturally when discussing impacts as you prioritize and address threats. Those topics are covered in Part III, "Managing and Addressing Threats."

How you answer the question "what are our assets?" should help focus your threat modeling. If it doesn't help, there is no point to asking the question or spending time answering it.

Focusing on Attackers

Focusing on attackers seems like a natural way to threat model. After all, if no one is going to attack your system, why would you bother defending it? And if you're worried because people will attack your systems, shouldn't you understand them? Unfortunately, like asset-centered threat modeling, attacker-centered threat modeling is less useful than you might anticipate. But there are also a small number of scenarios in which focusing on attackers can come in handy, and they're the same scenarios as assets: experts, less-technical input to your process, and prioritization. And similar to the "Focusing on Assets" section, you can also learn for yourself why this approach isn't optimal, so you can discuss the possibility with those advocating this approach.

Implementing Attacker-Centric Modeling

Security experts may be able to use various types of attacker lists to find threats against a system. When doing so, it's easy to find yourself arguing about the resources or capabilities of such an archetype, and needing to flesh them out. For example, what if your terrorist is state-sponsored, and has access to government labs? These questions make the attacker-centric approach start to resemble "*personas*," which are often used to help think about human interface issues. There's a spectrum of detail in attacker models, from simple lists to data-derived personas, and examples of each are given in Appendix C, "Attacker Lists" That appendix may help security experts and will help anyone who wants to try attacker-centric modeling and learn faster than if they have to start by creating a list.

Given a list of attackers, it's possible to use the list to provide some structure to a brainstorming approach. Some security experts use attacker lists as a way to help elicit the knowledge they've accumulated as they've become experts. Attacker-driven approaches are also likely to bring up possibilities that are human-centered. For example, when thinking about what a spy would do, it may be more natural (and fun) to think about them seducing your sysadmin or corrupting a janitor, rather than think about technical attacks. Worse, it will probably be challenging to think about what those human attacks mean for your system's security.

Where Attackers Can Help You

Talking about human threat agents can help make the threats real. That is, it's sometimes tough to understand how someone could tamper with a configuration file, or replace client software to get around security checks. Especially when dealing with management or product teams who "just want to ship," it's helpful to be able to explain who might attack them and why. There's real value in this, but it's not a sufficient argument for centering your approach on those threat agents; you can add that information at a later stage. (The risk associated with talking about attackers is the claim that "no one would ever do that." Attempting to humanize a risk by adding an actor can exacerbate this, especially if you add a type of actor who someone thinks "wouldn't be interested in us.").

You were promised an example, and the spies stole it. More seriously, carefully walking through the attacker lists and personas in Appendix C likely doesn't help you (or the author) figure out what they might want to do to Acme/SQL, and so the example is left empty to avoid false hope.

Perspective on Attacker-Centric Modeling

Helping security experts structure and recall information is nice, but doesn't lead to reproducible results. More importantly, attacker lists or even personas are not enough structure for most people to figure out what those people will do. Engineers may subconsciously project their own biases or approaches into what an attacker might do. Given that the attacker has his own motivations, skills, background, and perspective (and possibly organizational priorities), avoiding such projection is tricky.

In my experience, this combination of issues makes attacker-centric approaches less effective than other approaches. Therefore, I recommend against using attackers as the center of your threat modeling process.

Focusing on Software

Good news! You've officially reached the "best" structured threat modeling approach. Congrats! Read on to learn about software-centered threat modeling, why it's the most helpful and effective approach, and how to do it.

Software-centric models are models that focus on the software being built or a system being deployed. Some software projects have documented models of various sorts, such as architecture, UML diagrams, or APIs. Other projects don't bother with such documentation and instead rely on implicit models.

Having large project teams draw on a whiteboard to explain how the software fits together can be a surprisingly useful and contentious activity. Understandings differ, especially on large projects that have been running for a while, but finding where those understandings differ can be helpful in and of itself because it offers a focal point where threats are unlikely to be blocked. ("I thought *you* were validating that for a SQL call!")

The same complexity applies to any project that is larger than a few people or has been running longer than a few years. Projects accumulate complexity, which makes many aspects of development harder, including security. Software-centric threat modeling can have a useful side effect of exposing this accumulated complexity.

The security value of this common understanding can also be substantial, even before you get to looking for threats. In one project it turned out that a library on a trust boundary had a really good threat model, but unrealistic assumptions had been made about what the components behind it were doing. The work to create a comprehensive model led to an explicit list of common assumptions that could and could not be made. The comprehensive model and resultant understanding led to a substantial improvement in the security of those components.

NOTE As complexity grows, so will the assumptions that are made, and such lists are never complete. They grow as experience requires and feedback loops allow.

Threat Modeling Different Types of Software

The threat discovery approaches covered in Part II, can be applied to models of all sorts of software. They can be applied to software you're building for others to download and install, as well as to software you're building into a larger operational system. The software they can be applied to is nearly endless, and is not dependent on the business model or deployment model associated with the software.

Even though software no longer comes in boxes sold on store shelves, the term *boxed software* is a convenient label for a category. That category is all the software whose architecture is definable, because there's a clear edge to what is the software: It's everything in the box (installer, application download, or open source repository). This edge can be contrasted with the deployed systems that organizations develop and change over time.

NOTE You may be concerned that the techniques in this book focus on either boxed software or deployed systems, and that the one you're concerned about isn't covered. In the interests of space, the examples and discussion only cover both when there's a clear difference and reason. That's because the recommended ways to model software will work for both with only a few exceptions.

The boundary between boxed software models and network models gets blurrier every year. One important difference is that the network models tend to include more of the infrastructural components such as routers, switches, and data circuits. Trust boundaries are often operationalized by these components, or by whatever group operates the network, the platforms, or the applications.

Data flow models (which you met in Chapter 1, "Dive In and Threat Model!" and which you'll learn more about in the next section) are usually a good choice for both boxed software and operational models. Some large data center operators have provided threat models to teams, showing how the data center is laid out. The product group can then overlay its models "on top" of that to align with the appropriate security controls that they'll get from operations. When you're using someone else's data center, you may have discussions about their infrastructure choices that make it easy to derive a model, or you might have to assume the worst.

Perspective on Software-Centric Modeling

I am fond of software-centric approaches because you should expect software developers to understand the software they're developing. Indeed, there is nothing else you should expect them to understand better. That makes software an ideal place to start the threat-modeling tasks in which you ask developers to participate. Almost all software development is done with software models that are good enough for the team's purposes. Sometimes they require work to make them good enough for effective threat modeling.

In contrast, you can merely hope that developers understand the business or its assets. You may aspire to them understanding the people who will attack their product or system. But these are hopes and aspirations, rather than reasonable expectations. To the extent that your threat modeling strategy depends on these hopes and aspirations, you're adding places where it can fail. The remainder of this chapter is about modeling your software in ways that help you find threats, and as such enabling software centric-modeling. (The methods for finding these threats are covered in the rest of Part II.)

Models of Software

Making an explicit model of your software helps you look for threats without getting bogged down in the many details that are required to make the software function properly. Diagrams are a natural way to model software.

As you learned in Chapter 1, whiteboard diagrams are an extremely effective way to start threat modeling, and they may be sufficient for you. However, as a system hits a certain level of complexity, drawing and redrawing on whiteboards becomes infeasible. At that point, you need to either simplify the system or bring in a computerized approach.

In this section, you'll learn about the various types of diagrams, how they can be adapted for use in threat modeling, and how to handle the complexities of larger systems. You'll also learn more detail about trust boundaries, effective labeling, and how to validate your diagrams.

Types of Diagrams

There are many ways to diagram, and different diagrams will help in different circumstances. The types of diagrams you'll encounter most frequently are probably data flow diagrams (DFDs). However, you may also see UML, swim lane diagrams, and state diagrams. You can think of these diagrams as Lego blocks, looking them over to see which best fits whatever you're building. Each diagram type here can be used with the models of threats in Part II.

The goal of all these diagrams is to communicate how the system works, so that everyone involved in threat modeling has the same understanding. If you can't agree on how to draw how the software works, then in the process of getting to agreement, you're highly likely to discover misunderstandings about the security of the system. Therefore, use the diagram type that helps you have a good conversation and develop a shared understanding.

Data Flow Diagrams

Data flow models are often ideal for threat modeling; problems tend to follow the data flow, not the control flow. Data flow models more commonly exist for network or architected systems than software products, but they can be created for either.

Data flow diagrams are used so frequently they are sometimes called "threat model diagrams." As laid out by Larry Constantine in 1967, DFDs consist of numbered elements (data stores and processes) connected by data flows, interacting with external entities (those outside the developer's or the organization's control).

The data flows that give DFDs their name almost always flow two ways, with exceptions such as radio broadcasts or UDP data sent off into the Ethernet. Despite that, flows are usually represented using one-way arrows, as the threats and their impact are generally not symmetric. That is, if data flowing to a web server is read, it might reveal passwords or other data, whereas a data flow from the web server might reveal your bank balance. This diagramming convention doesn't help clarify channel security versus message security. (The channel might be something like SMTP, with messages being e-mail messages.) Swim lane diagrams may be more appropriate as a model if this channel/message distinction is important. (Swim lane diagrams are described in the eponymous subsection later in this chapter.)

The main elements of a data flow diagram are shown in Table 2-1.

Table 2-1: Elements of a Data Flow Diagram

ELEMENT	APPEARANCE	MEANING	EXAMPLES
Process	Rounded rectangle, circle, or concentric circles	Any running code	Code written in C, C#, Python, or PHP
Data flow	Arrow	Communication between processes, or between processes and data stores	Network connections, HTTP, RPC, LPC
Data store	Two parallel lines with a label between them	Things that store data	Files, databases, the Windows Registry, shared memory segments
External entity	Rectangle with sharp corners	People, or code outside your control	Your customer, Microsoft.com

Figure 2-3 shows a classic DFD based on the elements from Table 2-1; however, it's possible to make these models more usable. Figure 2-4 shows this same model with a few changes, which you can use as an example for improving your own models.

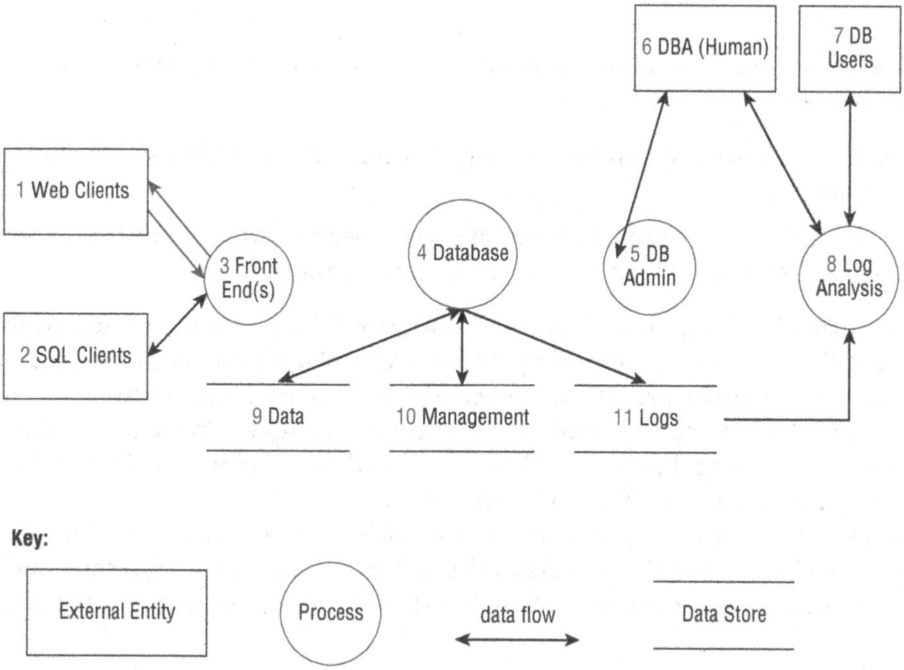

Figure 2-3: A classic DFD model

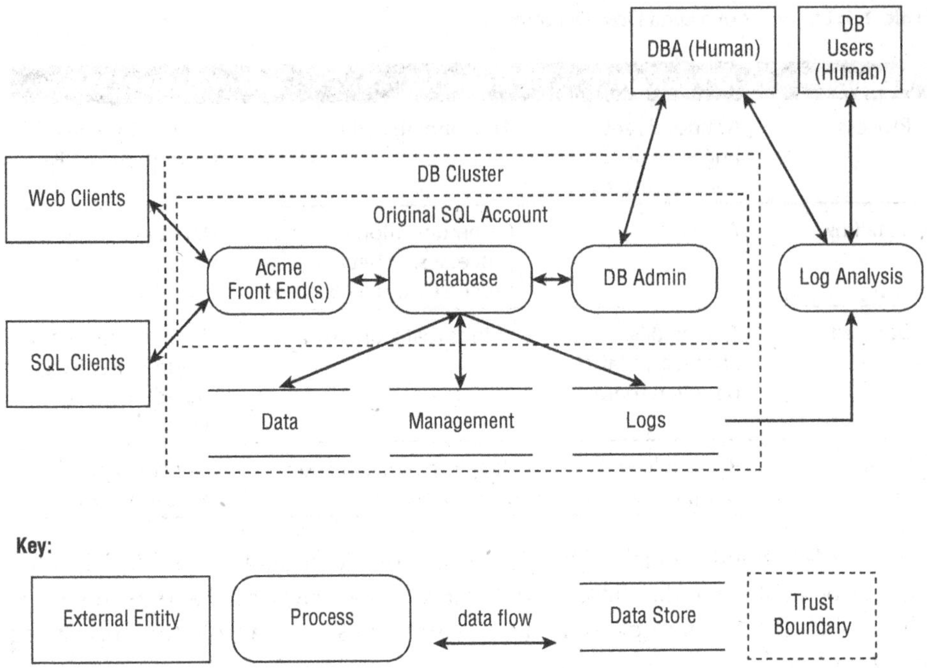

Figure 2-4: A modern DFD model (previously shown as Figure 2-1)

The following list explains the changes made from classic DFDs to more modern ones:

- The processes are rounded rectangles, which contain text more efficiently than circles.
- Straight lines are used, rather than curved, because straight lines are easier to follow, and you can fit more in larger diagrams.

Historically, many descriptions of data flow diagrams contained both "process" elements and "complex process" elements. A process was depicted as a circle, a complex process as two concentric circles. It isn't entirely clear, however, when to use a normal process versus a complex one. One possible rule is that anything that has a subdiagram should be a complex process. That seems like a decent rule, if (ahem) a bit circular.

DFDs can be used for things other than software products. For example, Figure 2-5 shows a sample operational network in a DFD. This is a typical model for a small to mid-sized corporate network, with a representative sampling of systems and departments shown. It is discussed in depth in Appendix E, "Case Studies."

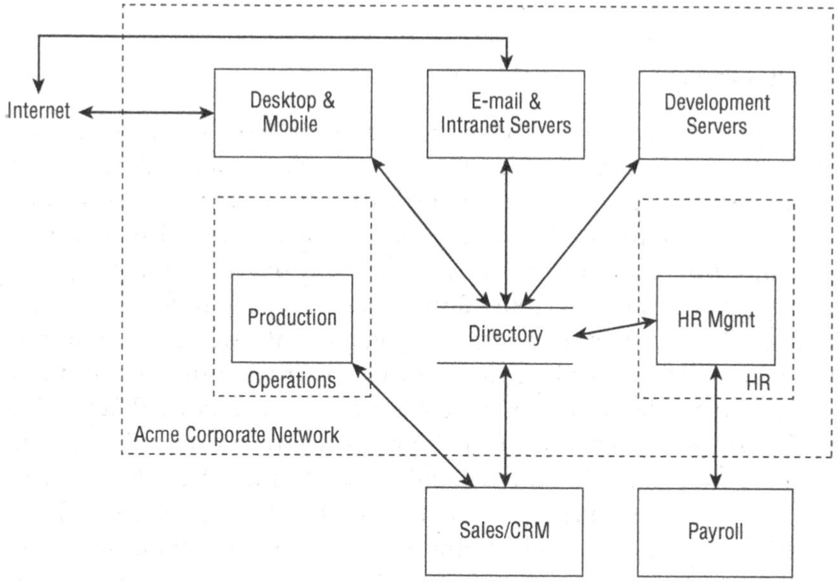

Figure 2-5: An operational network model

UML

UML is an abbreviation for Unified Modeling Language. If you use UML in your software development process, it's likely that you can adapt UML diagrams for threat modeling, rather than redrawing them. The most important way to adapt UML for threat modeling diagrams is the addition of trust boundaries.

UML is fairly complex. For example, the Visio stencils for UML offer roughly 80 symbols, compared to six for DFDs. This complexity brings a good deal of nuance and expressiveness as people draw structure diagrams, behavior diagrams, and interaction diagrams. If anyone involved in the threat modeling isn't up on all the UML symbols, or if there's misunderstanding about what those symbols mean, then the diagram's effectiveness as a tool is greatly diminished. In theory, anyone who's confused can just ask, but that requires them to know they're confused (they might assume that the symbol for fish excludes sharks). It also requires a willingness to expose one's ignorance by asking a "simple" question. It's probably easier for a team that's invested in UML to add trust boundaries to those diagrams than to create new diagrams just for threat modeling.

Swim Lane Diagrams

Swim lane diagrams are a common way to represent flows between various participants. They're drawn using long lines, each representing participants in a protocol, with each participant getting a line. Each lane edge is labeled to identify the participant; each message is represented by a line between participants; and time is represented by flow down the diagram lanes. The diagrams end up looking a bit like swim lanes, thus the name. Messages should be labeled with their contents; or if the contents are complex, it may make more sense to have a diagram key that abstracts out some details. Computation done by the parties or state should be noted along that participant's line. Generally, participants in such protocols are entities like computers; and as such, swim lane diagrams usually have implicit trust boundaries between each participant. Cryptographer and protocol designer Carl Ellison has extended swim lanes to include the human participants as a way to structure discussion of what people are expected to know and do. He calls this extension *ceremonies*, which is discussed in more detail in Chapter 15, "Human Factors and Usability."

A sample swim lane diagram is shown in Figure 2-6.

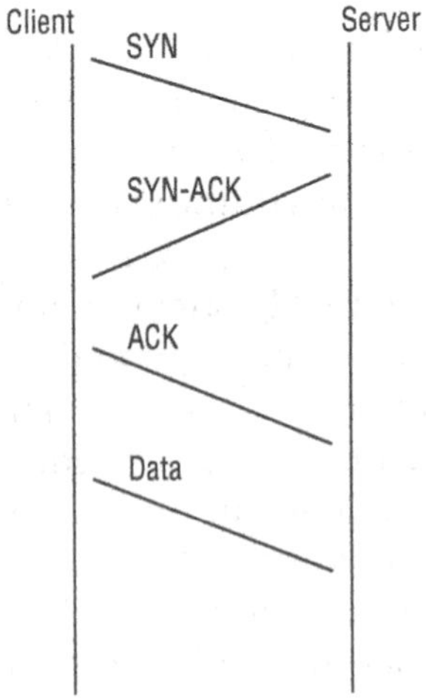

Figure 2-6: Swim lane diagram (showing the start of a TCP connection)

State Diagrams

State diagrams represent the various states a system can be in, and the transitions between those states. A computer system is modeled as a machine with state, memory, and rules for moving from one state to another, based on the valid messages it receives, and the data in its memory. (The computer should course test the messages it receives for validity according to some rules.) Each box is labeled with a state, and the lines between them are labeled with the conditions that cause the state transition. You can use state diagrams in threat modeling by checking whether each transition is managed in accordance with the appropriate security validations.

A very simple state machine for a door is shown in Figure 2-7 (derived from Wikipedia). The door has three states: opened, closed, and locked. Each state is entered by a transition. The "deadbolt" system is much easier to draw than locks on the knob, which can be locked from either state, creating a more complex diagram and user experience. Obviously, state diagrams can become complex quickly. You could imagine a more complex state diagram that includes "ajar," a state that can result from either open or closed. (I started drawing that but had trouble deciding on labels. Obviously, doors that can be ajar are poorly specified and should not be deployed.) You don't want to make architectural decisions just to make modeling easier, but often simple models are easier to work with, and reflect better engineering.

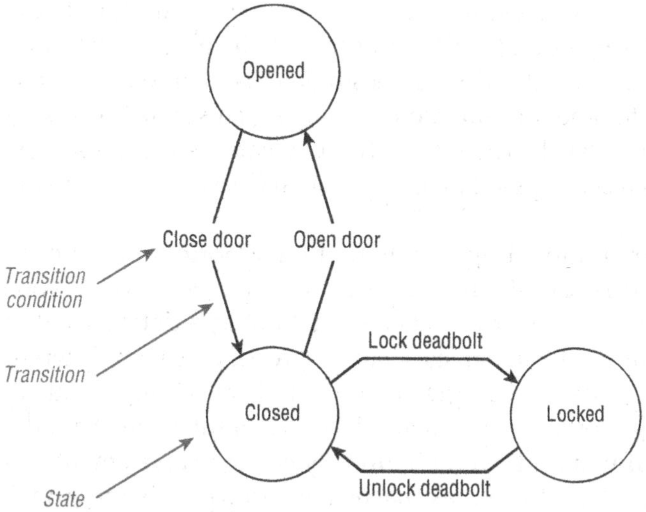

Figure 2-7: A state machine diagram

Trust Boundaries

As you saw in Chapter 1, a trust boundary is anyplace where various principals come together—that is, where entities with different privileges interact.

Drawing Boundaries

After a software model has been drawn, there are two ways to add boundaries: You can add the boundaries you know and look for more, or you can enumerate principals and look for boundaries. To start from boundaries, add any sorts of enforced trust boundary you can. Boundaries between unix UIDs, Windows sessions, machines, network segments, and so on should be drawn in as boxes, and the principal inside each box should be shown with a label.

To start from principals, begin from one end or the other of the privilege spectrum (often that's root/admin or anonymous Internet users), and then add boundaries each time they talk to "someone else."

You can always add at least one boundary, as all computation takes place in some context. (So you might criticize Figure 2-1 for showing Web Clients and SQL Clients without an identified context.)

If you don't see where to draw trust boundaries of any sort, your diagram may be detailed as everything is inside a single trust boundary, or you may be missing boundaries. Ask yourself two questions. First, does everything in the system have the same level of privilege and access to everything else on the system? Second, is everything your software communicates with inside that same boundary? If either of these answers are a no, then you should now have clarified either a missing boundary or a missing element in the diagram, or both. If both are yes, then you should draw a single trust boundary around everything, and move on to other development activities. (This state is unlikely except when every part of a development team has to create a software model. That "bottom up" approach is discussed in more detail in Chapter 7, "Processing and Managing Threats.")

A lot of writing on threat modeling claims that trust boundaries should only cross data flows. This is useful advice for the most detailed level of your model. If a trust boundary crosses over a data store (that is, a database), that might indicate that there are different tables or stored procedures with different trust levels. If a boundary crosses over a given host, it may reflect that members of, for example, the group "software installers," have different rights from the "web content updaters." If you find a trust boundary crossing an element of a diagram other than a data flow, either break that element into two (in the model, in reality, or both), or draw a subdiagram to show them separated into multiple entities. What enables good threat models is clarity about what boundaries exist and how those boundaries are to be protected. Contrariwise, a lack of clarity will inhibit the creation of good models.

Using Boundaries

Threats tend to cluster around trust boundaries. This may seem obvious: The trust boundaries delineate the attack surface between principals. This leads some to expect that threats appear *only* between the principals on the boundary, or only matter on the trust boundaries. That expectation is sometimes incorrect. To see why, consider a web server performing some complex order processing. For example, imagine assembling a computer at Dell's online store where thousands of parts might be added, but only a subset of those have been tested and are on offer. A model of that website might be constructed as shown in Figure 2-8.

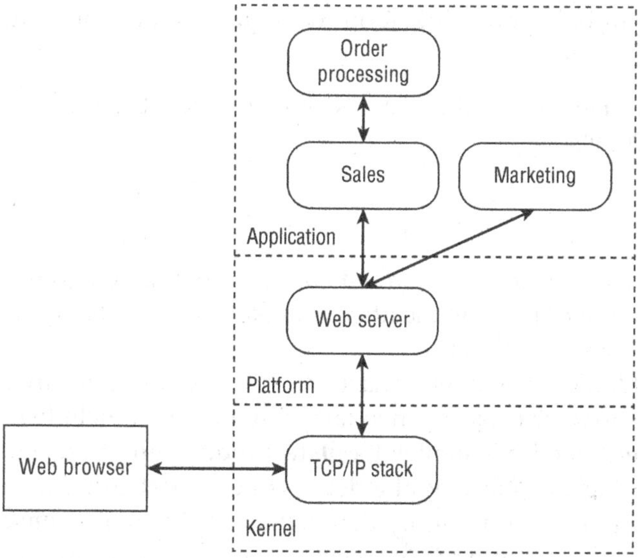

Figure 2-8: Trust boundaries in a web server

The web server in Figure 2-8 is clearly at risk of attack from the web browser, even though it talks through a TCP/IP stack that it presumably trusts. Similarly, the sales module is at risk; plus an attacker might be able to insert random part numbers into the HTML post in which the data is checked in an order processing module. Even though there's no trust boundary between the sales module and the order processing module, and even though data might be checked at three boundaries, the threats still follow the data flows. The client is shown simply as a web browser because the client is an external entity. Of course, there are many other components around that web browser, but you can't do anything about threats to them, so why model them?

Therefore, it is more accurate to say that threats tend to cluster around trust boundaries and complex parsing, but may appear anywhere that information is under the control of an attacker.

What to Include in a Diagram

So what should be in your diagram? Some rules of thumb include the following:

- Show the events that drive the system.
- Show the processes that are driven.
- Determine what responses each process will generate and send.
- Identify data sources for each request and response.
- Identify the recipient of each response.
- Ignore the inner workings, focus on scope.
- Ask if something will help you think about what goes wrong, or what will help you find threats.

This list is derived from Howard and LeBlanc's *Writing Secure Code, Second Edition* (Microsoft Press, 2009).

Complex Diagrams

When you're building complex systems, you may end up with complex diagrams. Systems do become complex, and that complexity can make using the diagrams (or understanding the full system) difficult.

One rule of thumb is "don't draw an eye chart." It is important to balance all the details that a real software project can entail with what you include in your actual model. As mentioned in Chapter 1, one technique you can use to help you do this is a subdiagram showing the details of one particular area. You should look for ways to break out highly-detailed areas that make sense for your project. For example, if you have one very complex process, maybe everything inside it is one diagram, and everything outside it is another. If you have a dispatcher or queuing system, that might be a good place to break things up. Maybe your databases or the fail over system is a good place to split. Maybe there are a few elements that really need more detail. All of these are good ways to break things out.

One helpful approach to subdiagrams is to ensure that there are not more subdiagrams than there are processes. Another approach is to use different diagrams to show different scenarios.

Sometimes it's also useful to simplify diagrams. When two elements of the diagram are equivalent from a security perspective, you can combine them. Equivalent means inside the same trust boundary, relying on the same technology, and handling the same sort of data.

The key thing to remember is that the diagram is intended to help ensure that you understand and can discuss the system. Remember the quote that opens this book: "All models are wrong, some models are useful." Therefore, when you're adding additional diagrams, don't ask "is this the right way to do it?" Instead, ask "does this help us think about what might go wrong?"

Labels in Diagrams

Labels in diagrams should be short, descriptive, and meaningful. Because you want to use these names to tell stories, start with the outsiders who are driving the system; those are nouns, such as "customer" or "vibration sensor." They communicate information via data flows, which are nouns or noun phrases, such as "books to buy" or "vibration frequency." Data flows should almost never be labeled using verbs. Even though it can be hard, you should work to find more descriptive labels than "read" or "write," which are implied by the direction of the arrows. In other words, data flows communicate their information (nouns) to processes, which are active: verbs, verb phrases, or verb/noun chains.

Many people find it helpful to label data flows with sequence numbers to help keep track of what happens in what order. It can also be helpful to number elements within a diagram to help with completeness or communication. You can number each thing (data flow 1, a process 1, et cetera) or you can have a single count across the diagram, with external entity 1 talking over data flows 2 and 3 to process 4. Generally, using a single counter for everything is less confusing. You can say "number 1" rather than "data flow 1, not process 1."

Color in Diagrams

Color can add substantial amounts of information without appearing overwhelming. For example, Microsoft's Peter Torr uses green for trusted, red for untrusted and blue for what's being modeled (Torr, 2005). Relying on color alone can be problematic. Roughly one in twelve people suffer from color blindness, the most common being red/green confusion (Heitgerd, 2008). The result is that even with a color printer, a substantial number of people are unable to easily access this critical information. Box boundaries with text labels address both problems. With box trust boundaries, there is no reason not to use color.

Entry Points

One early approach to threat modeling was the "asset/entry point" approach, which can be effective at modeling operational systems. This approach can be partially broken down into the following steps:

1. Draw a DFD.
2. Find the points where data flows cross trust boundaries.
3. Label those intersections as "entry points."

NOTE **There were other steps and variations in the approaches, but we as a community have learned a lot since then, and a full explanation would be tedious and distracting.**

In the Acme/SQL example (as shown in Figure 2-1) the entry points are the "front end(s)" and the "database admin" console process. "Database" would also be an entry point, because nominally, other software could alter data in the databases and use failures in the parsers to gain control of the system. For the financials, the entry points shown are "external reporting," "financial planning and analysis," "core finance software," "sales" and "accounts receivable."

Validating Diagrams

Validating that a diagram is a good model of your software has two main goals: ensuring accuracy and aspiring to goodness. The first is easier, as you can ask whether it reflects reality. If important components are missing, or the diagram shows things that are not being built, then you can see that it doesn't reflect reality. If important data flows are missing, or nonexistent flows are shown, then it doesn't reflect reality. If you can't tell a story about the software without editing the diagram, then it's not accurate.

Of course, there's that word "important" in there, which leads to the second criterion: aspiring to goodness. What's important is what helps you find issues. Finding issues is a matter of asking questions like "does this element have any security impact?" and "are there things that happen sometimes or in special circumstances?" Knowing the answers to these questions is a matter of experience, just like many aspects of building software. A good and experienced architect can quickly assess requirements and address them, and a good threat modeler can quickly see which elements will be important. A big part of gaining that experience is practice. The structured approaches to finding threats in Part II, are designed to help you identify which elements are important.

How To Validate Diagrams

To best validate your diagrams, bring together the people who understand the system best. Someone should stand in front of the diagram and walk through the important use cases, ensuring the following:

- They can talk through stories about the diagram.
- They don't need to make changes to the diagram in its current form.
- They don't need to refer to things not present in the diagram.

The following rules of thumb will be useful as you update your diagram and gain experience:

- Anytime you find someone saying "sometimes" or "also" you should consider adding more detail to break out the various cases. For example, if you say, "Sometimes we connect to this web service via SSL, and sometimes we fall back to HTTP," you should draw both of those data flows (and consider whether an attacker can make you fall back like that).
- Anytime you need more detail to explain security-relevant behavior, draw it in.
- Each trust boundary box should have a label inside it.
- Anywhere you disagreed over the design or construction of the system, draw in those details. This is an important step toward ensuring that everyone ended that discussion on the same page. It's especially important for larger teams where not everyone is in the room for the threat model discussions. If anyone sees a diagram that contradicts their thinking, they can either accept it or challenge the assumptions; but either way, a good clear diagram can help get everyone on the same page.
- Don't have data sinks: You write the data for a reason. Show who uses it.
- Data can't move itself from one data store to another: Show the process that moves it.
- All ways data can arrive should be shown.
- If there are mechanisms for controlling data flows (such as firewalls or permissions) they should be shown.
- All processes must have at least one entry data flow and one exit data flow.
- As discussed earlier in the chapter, don't draw an eye chart.
- Diagrams should be visible on a printable page.

NOTE ***Writing Secure Code*** **author David LeBlanc notes that "A process without input is a miracle, while one without output is a black hole. Either you're missing something, or have mistaken a process for people, who are allowed to be black holes or miracles."**

When to Validate Diagrams

For software products, there are two main times to validate diagrams: when you create them and when you're getting ready to ship a beta. There's also a third triggering event (which is less frequent), which is if you add a security boundary.

For operational software diagrams, you also validate when you create them, and then again using a sensible balance between effort and up-to-dateness. That sensible balance will vary according to the maturity of a system, its scale, how tightly the components are coupled, the cadence of rollouts, and the nature of new rollouts. Here are a few guidelines:

- Newer systems will experience more diagram changes than mature ones.
- Larger systems will experience more diagram changes than smaller ones.
- Tightly coupled systems will experience more diagram changes than loosely coupled systems.
- Systems that roll out changes quickly will likely experience fewer diagram changes per rollout.
- Rollouts or sprints focused on refactoring or paying down technical debt will likely see more diagram changes. In either case, create an appropriate tracking item to ensure that you recheck your diagrams at a good time. The appropriate tracking item is whatever you use to gate releases or rollouts, such as bugs, task management software, or checklists. If you have no formal way to gate releases, then you might focus on a clearly defined release process before worrying about rechecking threat models. Describing such a process is beyond the scope of this book.

Summary

There's more than one way to threat model, and some of the strategies you can employ include modeling assets, modeling attackers, or modeling software. "What's your threat model" and brainstorming are good for security experts, but they lack structure that less experienced threat modelers need. There are more structured approaches to brainstorming, including scenario analysis, pre-mortems, movie plotting, and literature reviews, which can help bring a little structure, but they're still not great.

If your threat modeling starts from assets, the multiple overlapping definitions of the term, including things attackers want, things you're protecting, and stepping stones, can trip you up. An asset-centered approach offers no route to figure out what will go wrong with the assets.

Attacker modeling is also attractive, but trying to predict how another person will attack is hard, and the approach can invite arguments that "no one would do that." Additionally, human-centered approaches may lead you to human-centered threats that can be hard to address.

Software models are focused on that what software people understand. The best models are diagrams that help participants understand the software and find threats against it. There are a variety of ways you can diagram your software, and DFDs are the most frequently useful.

Once you have a model of the software, you'll need a way to find threats against it, and that is the subject of Part II.

Part

II

Finding Threats

At the heart of threat modeling are the threats.

There are many approaches to finding threats, and they are the subject of Part II. Each has advantages and disadvantages, and different approaches may work in different circumstances. Each of the approaches in this part is like a Lego block. You can substitute one for another in the midst of this second step in the four-step framework and expect to get good results.

Knowing what aspects of security can go wrong is the unique element that makes threat modeling threat modeling, rather than some other form of modeling. The models in this part are abstractions of threats, designed to help you think about these security problems. The more specific models (such as attack libraries) will be more useful to those new to threat modeling, and are less freewheeling. As you become more experienced, the less structured approaches such as STRIDE become more useful.

In this part, you'll learn about the following approaches to finding threats:

- **Chapter 3: STRIDE** covers the STRIDE mnemonic you met in chapter 1, and its many variants.
- **Chapter 4: Attack Trees** are either a way for you to think through threats against your system, or a way to help others structure their thinking about those threats. Both uses of attack trees are covered in this chapter.

- **Chapter 5: Attack Libraries** are libraries constructed to track and organize threats. They can be very useful to those new to security or threat modeling.
- **Chapter 6: Privacy Tools** covers a collection of tools for finding privacy threats.

Part II focuses on the second question in the four-step framework: What can go wrong? As you'll recall from Part I, before you start finding threats with any of the techniques in this part, you should first have an idea of scope: where are you looking for threats? A diagram, such as a data flow diagram discussed in Part I, can help scope the threat modeling session, and thus is an excellent input condition. As you discuss threats, however, you'll likely find imperfections in the diagram, so it isn't necessary to "perfect" your diagram before you start finding threats.

CHAPTER 3

STRIDE

As you learned in Chapter 1, "Dive in and Threat Model!," STRIDE is an acronym that stands for Spoofing, Tampering, Repudiation, Information Disclosure, Denial of Service, and Elevation of Privilege. The STRIDE approach to threat modeling was invented by Loren Kohnfelder and Praerit Garg (Kohnfelder, 1999). This framework and mnemonic was designed to help people developing software identify the types of attacks that software tends to experience.

The method or methods you use to think through threats have many different labels: finding threats, threat enumeration, threat analysis, threat elicitation, threat discovery. Each connotes a slightly different flavor of approach. Do the threats exist in the software or the diagram? Then you're finding them. Do they exist in the minds of the people doing the analysis? Then you're doing analysis or elicitation. No single description stands out as always or clearly preferable, but this book generally talks about finding threats as a superset of all these ideas. Using STRIDE is more like an elicitation technique, with an expectation that you or your team understand the framework and know how to use it. If you're not familiar with STRIDE, the extensive tables and examples are designed to teach you how to use it to discover threats.

This chapter explains what STRIDE is and why it's useful, including sections covering each component of the STRIDE mnemonic. Each threat-specific section provides a deeper explanation of the threat, a detailed table of examples for that threat, and then a discussion of the examples. The tables and examples are designed to teach you how to use STRIDE to discover threats. You'll also learn about approaches built on STRIDE: STRIDE-per-element, STRIDE-per-interaction, and DESIST. The other approach built on STRIDE, the *Elevation of Privilege* game, is covered in Chapters 1, "Dive In and Threat Model!" and 12, "Requirements Cookbook," and Appendix C, "Attacker Lists."

Understanding STRIDE and Why It's Useful

The STRIDE threats are the opposite of some of the properties you would like your system to have: authenticity, integrity, non-repudiation, confidentiality, availability, and authorization. Table 3-1 shows the STRIDE threats, the corresponding property that you'd like to maintain, a definition, the most typical victims, and examples.

Table 3-1: The STRIDE Threats

THREAT	PROPERTY VIOLATED	THREAT DEFINITION	TYPICAL VICTIMS	EXAMPLES
Spoofing	Authentication	Pretending to be something or someone other than yourself	Processes, external entities, people	Falsely claiming to be Acme.com, winsock .dll, Barack Obama, a police officer, or the Nigerian Anti-Fraud Group
Tampering	Integrity	Modifying something on disk, on a network, or in memory	Data stores, data flows, processes	Changing a spreadsheet, the binary of an important program, or the contents of a database on disk; modifying, adding, or removing packets over a network, either local or far across the Internet, wired or wireless; changing either the data a program is using or the running program itself

THREAT	PROPERTY VIOLATED	THREAT DEFINITION	TYPICAL VICTIMS	EXAMPLES
Repudiation	Non-Repudiation	Claiming that you didn't do something, or were not responsible. Repudiation can be honest or false, and the key question for system designers is, what evidence do you have?	Process	Process or system: "I didn't hit the big red button" or "I didn't order that Ferrari." Note that repudiation is somewhat the odd-threat-out here; it transcends the technical nature of the other threats to the business layer.
Information Disclosure	Confidentiality	Providing information to someone not authorized to see it	Processes, data stores, data flows	The most obvious example is allowing access to files, e-mail, or databases, but information disclosure can also involve filenames ("Termination for John Doe.docx"), packets on a network, or the contents of program memory.
Denial of Service	Availability	Absorbing resources needed to provide service	Processes, data stores, data flows	A program that can be tricked into using up all its memory, a file that fills up the disk, or so many network connections that real traffic can't get through
Elevation of Privilege	Authorization	Allowing someone to do something they're not authorized to do	Process	Allowing a normal user to execute code as admin; allowing a remote person without any privileges to run code

In Table 3-1, "typical victims" are those most likely to be victimized: For example, you can spoof a program by starting a program of the same name, or by putting a program with that name on disk. You can spoof an endpoint on the same machine by squatting or splicing. You can spoof users by capturing their authentication info by spoofing a site, by assuming they reuse credentials across sites, by brute forcing (online or off) or by elevating privilege on their machine. You can also tamper with the authentication database and then spoof with falsified credentials.

Note that as you're using STRIDE to look for threats, you're simply enumerating the things that might go wrong. The exact mechanisms for how it can go wrong are something you can develop later. (In practice, this can be easy or it can be very challenging. There might be defenses in place, and if you say, for example, "Someone could modify the management tables," someone else can say, "No, they can't because...") It can be useful to record those possible attacks, because even if there is a mitigation in place, that mitigation is a testable feature, and you should ensure that you have a test case.

You'll sometimes hear STRIDE referred to as "STRIDE categories" or "the STRIDE taxonomy." This framing is not helpful because STRIDE was not intended as, nor is it generally useful for, categorization. It is easy to find things that are hard to categorize with STRIDE. For example, earlier you learned about tampering with the authentication database and then spoofing. Should you record that as a tampering threat or a spoofing threat? The simple answer is that it doesn't matter. If you've already come up with the attack, why bother putting it in a category? The goal of STRIDE is to help you find attacks. Categorizing them might help you figure out the right defenses, or it may be a waste of effort. Trying to use STRIDE to categorize threats can be frustrating, and those efforts cause some people to dismiss STRIDE, but this is a bit like throwing out the baby with the bathwater.

Spoofing Threats

Spoofing is pretending to be something or someone other than yourself. Table 3-1 includes the examples of claiming to be Acme.com, winsock.dll, Barack Obama, or the Nigerian Anti-Fraud Office. Each of these is an example of a different subcategory of spoofing. The first example, pretending to be Acme.com (or Google.com, etc.) entails spoofing the identity of an entity across a network. There is no mediating authority that takes responsibility for telling you that Acme.com is the site I mean when I write these words. This differs from the second example, as Windows includes a `winsock.dll`. You should be able to ask the operating system to act as a mediating authority and get you to `winsock`. If you have your own DLLs, then you need to ensure that you're opening them with the appropriate path (`%installdir%\dll`); otherwise, someone might substitute one in a working directory, and get your code to do what they want. (Similar issues exist with unix and `LD_PATH`.) The third example, spoofing Barack Obama, is an instance of pretending to be a specific person. Contrast that with the fourth example, pretending to be the President of the United States or the Nigerian Anti-Fraud Office. In those cases, the attacker is pretending to be in a role. These spoofing threats are laid out in Table 3-2.

Table 3-2: Spoofing Threats

THREAT EXAMPLES	WHAT THE ATTACKER DOES	NOTES
Spoofing a process on the same machine	Creates a file before the real process	
	Renaming/linking	Creating a Trojan "su" and altering the path
	Renaming	Naming your process "sshd"
Spoofing a file	Creates a file in the local directory	This can be a library, executable, or config file.
	Creates a link and changes it	From the attacker's perspective, the change should happen between the link being checked and the link being accessed.
	Creates many files in the expected directory	Automation makes it easy to create 10,000 files in `/tmp`, to fill the space of files called `/tmp/"pid.NNNN`, or similar.
Spoofing a machine	ARP spoofing	
	IP spoofing	
	DNS spoofing	Forward or reverse
	DNS Compromise	Compromise TLD, registrar or DNS operator
	IP redirection	At the switch or router level
Spoofing a person	Sets e-mail display name	
	Takes over a real account	
Spoofing a role	Declares themselves to be that role	Sometimes opening a special account with a relevant name

Spoofing a Process or File on the Same Machine

If an attacker creates a file before the real process, then if your code is not careful to create a new file, the attacker may supply data that your code interprets, thinking that your code (or a previous instantiation or thread) wrote that data, and it can be trusted. Similarly, if file permissions on a pipe, local procedure call, and so on, are not managed well, then an attacker can create that endpoint, confusing everything that attempts to use it later.

Spoofing a process or file on a remote machine can work either by creating spoofed files or processes on the expected machine (possibly having taken admin rights) or by pretending to be the expected machine, covered next.

Spoofing a Machine

Attackers can spoof remote machines at a variety of levels of the network stack. These spoofing attacks can influence your code's view of the world as a client, server, or peer. They can spoof ARP requests if they're local, they can spoof IP packets to make it appear that they're coming from somewhere they are not, and they can spoof DNS packets. DNS spoofing can happen when you do a forward or reverse lookup. An attacker can spoof a DNS reply to a forward query they expect you to make. They can also adjust DNS records for machines they control such that when your code does a reverse lookup (translating IP to FQDN) their DNS server returns a name in a domain that they do not control—for example, claiming that 10.1.2.3 is `update.microsoft.com`. Of course, once attackers have spoofed a machine, they can either spoof or act as a man-in-the-middle for the processes on that machine. Second-order variants of this threat involve stealing machine authenticators such as cryptographic keys and abusing them as part of a spoofing attack.

Attackers can also spoof at higher layers. For example, *phishing attacks* involve many acts of spoofing. There's usually spoofing of e-mail from "your" bank, and spoofing of that bank's website. When someone falls for that e-mail, clicks the link and visits the bank, they then enter their credentials, sending them to that spoofed website. The attacker then engages in one last act of spoofing: They log into your bank account and transfer your money to themselves or an accomplice. (It may be one attacker, or it may be a set of attackers, contracting with one another for services rendered.)

Spoofing a Person

Major categories of spoofing people include access to the person's account and pretending to be them through an alternate account. Phishing is a common way to get access to someone else's account. However, there's often little to prevent anyone from setting up an account and pretending to be you. For example, an attacker could set up accounts on sites like LinkedIn, Twitter, or Facebook and pretend to be you, the Adam Shostack who wrote this book, or a rich and deposed prince trying to get their money out of the country.

Tampering Threats

Tampering is modifying something, typically on disk, on a network, or in memory. This can include changing data in a spreadsheet (using either a program such as Excel or another editor), changing a binary or configuration file on disk, or modifying a more complex data structure, such as a database on disk. On a network, packets can be added, modified, or removed. It's sometimes easier to add packets than to edit them as they fly by, and programs are remarkably bad about handling extra copies of data securely. More examples of tampering are in Table 3-3.

Table 3-3: Tampering Threats

THREAT EXAMPLES	WHAT THE ATTACKER DOES	NOTES
Tampering with a file	Modifies a file they own and on which you rely	
	Modifies a file you own	
	Modifies a file on a file server that you own	
	Modifies a file on their file server	Loads of fun when you include files from remote domains
	Modifies a file on their file server	Ever notice how much XML includes remote schemas?
	Modifies links or redirects	
Tampering with memory	Modifies your code	Hard to defend against once the attacker is running code as the same user
	Modifies data they've supplied to your API	Pass by value, not by reference when crossing a trust boundary
Tampering with a network	Redirects the flow of data to their machine	Often stage 1 of tampering
	Modifies data flowing over the network	Even easier and more fun when the network is wireless (WiFi, 3G, et cetera)
	Enhances spoofing attacks	

Tampering with a File

Attackers can modify files wherever they have write permission. When your code has to rely on files others can write, there's a possibility that the file was written maliciously. While the most obvious form of tampering is on a local disk, there are also plenty of ways to do this when the file is remotely included, like most of the JavaScript on the Internet. The attacker can breach your security by breaching someone else's site. They can also (because of poor privileges, spoofing, or elevation of privilege) modify files you own. Lastly, they can modify links or redirects of various sorts. Links are often left out of integrity checks. There's a somewhat subtle variant of this when there are caches between things you control (such as a server) and things you don't (such as a web browser on the other side of the Internet). For example, *cache poisoning attacks* insert data into web caches through poor security controls at caches (OWASP, 2009).

Tampering with Memory

Attackers can modify your code if they're running at the same privilege level. At that point, defense is tricky. If your API handles data by reference (a pattern often chosen for speed), then an attacker can modify it after you perform security checks.

Tampering with a Network

Network tampering often involves a variety of tricks to bring the data to the attacker's machine, where he forwards some data intact and some data modified. However, tricks to bring you the data are not always needed; with radio interfaces like WiFi and Bluetooth, more and more data flow through the air. Many network protocols were designed with the assumption you needed special hardware to create or read arbitrary packets. The requirement for special hardware was the defense against tampering (and often spoofing). The rise of software-defined radio (SDR) has silently invalidated the need for special hardware. It is now easy to buy an inexpensive SDR unit that can be programmed to tamper with wireless protocols.

Repudiation Threats

Repudiation is claiming you didn't do something, or were not responsible for what happened. People can repudiate honestly or deceptively. Given the increasing knowledge often needed to understand the complex world, those honestly repudiating may really be exposing issues in your user experiences or service architectures. Repudiation threats are a bit different from other security threats, as they often appear at the business layer. (That is, above the network layer such as TCP/IP, above the application layer such as HTTP/HTML, and where the business logic of buying products would be implemented.)

Repudiation threats are also associated with your logging system and process. If you don't have logs, don't retain logs, or can't analyze logs, repudiation threats are hard to dispute. There is also a class of attacks in which attackers will drop data in the logs to make log analysis tricky. For example, if you display your logs in HTML and the attacker sends `</tr>` or `</html>`, your log display needs to treat those as data, not code. More repudiation threats are shown in Table 3-4.

Table 3-4: Repudiation Threats

THREAT EXAMPLES	WHAT THE ATTACKER DOES	NOTES
Repudiating an action	Claims to have not clicked	Maybe they really did
	Claims to have not received	Receipt can be strange; does mail being downloaded by your phone mean you've read it? Did a network proxy pre-fetch images? Did someone leave a package on the porch?
	Claims to have been a fraud victim	
	Uses someone else's account	
	Uses someone else's payment instrument without authorization	
Attacking the logs	Notices you have no logs	
	Puts attacks in the logs to confuse logs, log-reading code, or a person reading the logs	

Attacking the Logs

Again, if you don't have logs, don't retain logs, or can't analyze logs, repudiation actions are hard to dispute. So if you aren't logging, you probably need to start. If you have no log centralization or analysis capability, you probably need that as well. If you don't properly define what you will be logging, an attacker may be able to break your log analysis system. It can be challenging to work through the layers of log production and analysis to ensure reliability, but if you don't, it's easy to have attacks slip through the cracks or inconsistencies.

Repudiating an Action

When you're discussing repudiation, it's helpful to discuss "someone" rather than "an attacker." You want to do this because those who repudiate are often not actually attackers, but people who have been failed by technology or process. Maybe they really didn't click (or didn't perceive that they clicked). Maybe the spam filter really did eat that message. Maybe UPS didn't deliver, or maybe UPS delivered by leaving the package on a porch. Maybe someone claims to have been a victim of fraud when they really were not (or maybe someone else in a household used their credit card, with or without their knowledge). Good technological systems that both authenticate and log well can make it easier to handle repudiation issues.

Information Disclosure Threats

Information disclosure is about allowing people to see information they are not authorized to see. Some information disclosure threats are shown in Table 3-5.

Table 3-5: Information Disclosure Threats

THREAT EXAMPLES	WHAT THE ATTACKER DOES	NOTES
Information disclosure against a process	Extracts secrets from error messages	
	Reads the error messages from username/passwords to entire database tables	
	Extracts machine secrets from error cases	Can make defense against memory corruption such as ASLR far less useful
	Extracts business/personal secrets from error cases	
Information disclosure against data stores	Takes advantage of inappropriate or missing ACLs	
	Takes advantage of bad database permissions	
	Finds files protected by obscurity	
	Finds crypto keys on disk (or in memory)	
	Sees interesting information in filenames	
	Reads files as they traverse the network	
	Gets data from logs or temp files	
	Gets data from swap or other temp storage	
	Extracts data by obtaining device, changing OS	

THREAT EXAMPLES	WHAT THE ATTACKER DOES	NOTES
Information disclosure against a data flow	Reads data on the network	
	Redirects traffic to enable reading data on the network	
	Learns secrets by analyzing traffic	
	Learns who's talking to whom by watching the DNS	
	Learns who's talking to whom by social network info disclosure	

Information Disclosure from a Process

Many instances in which a process will disclose information are those that inform further attacks. A process can do this by leaking memory addresses, extracting secrets from error messages, or extracting design details from error messages. Leaking memory addresses can help bypass ASLR and similar defenses. Leaking secrets might include database connection strings or passwords. Leaking design details might mean exposing anti-fraud rules like "your account is too new to order a diamond ring."

Information Disclosure from a Data Store

As data stores, well, store data, there's a profusion of ways they can leak it. The first set of causes are failures to properly use security mechanisms. Not setting permissions appropriately or hoping that no one will find an obscure file are common ways in which people fail to use security mechanisms. Cryptographic keys are a special case whereby information disclosure allows additional attacks. Files read from a data store over the network are often readable as they traverse the network.

An additional attack, often overlooked, is data in filenames. If you have a directory named "May 2013 layoffs," the filename itself, "Termination Letter for Alice.docx," reveals important information.

There's also a group of attacks whereby a program emits information into the operating environment. Logs, temp files, swap, or other places can contain data. Usually, the OS will protect data in swap, but for things like crypto keys, you should use OS facilities for preventing those from being swapped out.

Lastly, there is the class of attacks whereby data is extracted from the device using an operating system under the attacker's control. Most commonly (in 2013), these attacks affect USB keys, but they also apply to CDs, backup tapes, hard drives, or stolen laptops or servers. Hard drives are often decommissioned without full data deletion. (You can address the need to delete data from hard drives by buying a hard drive chipper or smashing machine, and since such machines are awesome, why on earth wouldn't you?)

Information Disclosure from a Data Flow

Data flows are particularly susceptible to information disclosure attacks when information is flowing over a network. However, data flows on a single machine can still be attacked, particularly when the machine is shared by cloud co-tenants or many mutually distrustful users of a compute server. Beyond the simple reading of data on the network, attackers might redirect traffic to themselves (often by spoofing some network control protocol) so they can see it when they're not on the normal path. It's also possible to obtain information even when the network traffic itself is encrypted. There are a variety of ways to learn secrets about who's talking to whom, including watching DNS, friend activity on a site such as LinkedIn, or other forms of social network analysis.

NOTE Security mavens may be wondering if side channel attacks and covert channels are going to be mentioned. These attacks can be fun to work on (and side channels are covered a bit in Chapter 16, "Threats to Cryptosystems"), but they are not relevant until you've mitigated the issues covered here.

Denial-of-Service Threats

Denial-of-service attacks absorb a resource that is needed to provide service. Examples are described in Table 3-6.

Table 3-6: Denial-of-Service Threats

THREAT EXAMPLES	WHAT THE ATTACKER DOES	NOTES
Denial of service against a process	Absorbs memory (RAM or disk)	
	Absorbs CPU	
	Uses process as an amplifier	
Denial of service against a data store	Fills data store up	
	Makes enough requests to slow down the system	
Denial of service against a data flow	Consumes network resources	

Denial-of-service attacks can be split into those that work while the attacker is attacking (say, filling up bandwidth) and those that persist. Persistent attacks can remain in effect until a reboot (for example, `while(1){fork();}`), or even past a reboot (for example, filling up a disk). Denial-of-service attacks can also be divided into amplified and unamplified. Amplified attacks are those whereby small attacker effort results in a large impact. An example would take advantage of the old unix chargen service, whose purpose was to generate a semi-random character scheme for testing. An attacker could spoof a single packet from the chargen port on machine A to the chargen port on machine B. The hilarity continues until someone pulls a network cable.

Elevation of Privilege Threats

Elevation of privilege is allowing someone to do something they're not authorized to do—for example, allowing a normal user to execute code as admin, or allowing a remote person without any privileges to run code. Two important ways to elevate privileges involve corrupting a process and getting past authorization checks. Examples are shown in Table 3-7.

Table 3-7: Elevation of Privilege Threats

THREAT EXAMPLES	WHAT THE ATTACKER DOES	NOTES
Elevation of privilege against a process by corrupting the process	Send inputs that the code doesn't handle properly	These errors are very common, and are usually high impact.
	Gains access to read or write memory inappropriately	Writing memory is (hopefully obviously) bad, but reading memory can enable further attacks.
Elevation through missed authorization checks		
Elevation through buggy authorization checks		Centralizing such checks makes bugs easier to manage
Elevation through data tampering	Modifies bits on disk to do things other than what the authorized user intends	

Elevate Privileges by Corrupting a Process

Corrupting a process involves things like smashing the stack, exploiting data on the heap, and a whole variety of exploitation techniques. The impact of these techniques is that the attacker gains influence or control over a program's control flow. It's important to understand that these exploits are not limited to the attack surface. The first code that attacker data can reach is, of course, an important target. Generally, that code can only validate data against a limited subset of purposes. It's important to trace the data flows further to see where else elevation of privilege can take place. There's a somewhat unusual case whereby a program relies on and executes things from shared memory, which is a trivial path for elevation if everything with permissions to that shared memory is not running at the same privilege level.

Elevate Privileges through Authorization Failures

There is also a set of ways to elevate privileges through authorization failures. The simplest failure is to not check authorization on every path. More complex for an attacker is taking advantage of buggy authorization checks. Lastly, if a program relies on other programs, configuration files, or datasets being trustworthy, it's important to ensure that permissions are set so that each of those dependencies is properly secured.

Extended Example: STRIDE Threats against Acme-DB

This extended example discusses how STRIDE threats could manifest against the Acme/SQL database described in Chapter 1, "Dive In and Threat Model!" and 2, "Strategies for Threat Modeling," and shown in Figure 2-1. You'll first look at these threats by STRIDE category, and then examine the same set according to who can address them.

Spoofing

- A web client could attempt to log in with random credentials or stolen credentials, as could a SQL client.
- If you assume that the SQL client is the one you wrote and allow it to make security decisions, then a spoofed (or tampered with) client could bypass security checks.
- The web client could connect to a false (spoofed) front end, and end up disclosing credentials.
- A program could pretend to be the database or log analysis program, and try to read data from the various data stores.

Tampering

- Someone could also tamper with the data they're sending, or with any of the programs or data files.
- Someone could tamper with the web or SQL clients. (This is nominally out of scope, as you shouldn't be trusting external entities anyway.)

NOTE These threats, once you consider them, can easily be addressed with operating system permissions. More challenging is what can alter what data within the database. Operating system permissions will only help a little there; the database will need to implement an access control system of some sort.

Repudiation

- The customers using either SQL or web clients could claim not to have done things. These threats may already be mitigated by the presence of logs and log analysis. So why bother with these threats? They remind you that you need to configure logging to be on, and that you need to log the "right things," which probably include successes and failures of authentication attempts, access attempts, and in particular, the server needs to track attempts by clients to access or change logs.

Information Disclosure

- The most obvious information disclosure issues occur when confidential information in the database is exposed to the wrong client. This information may be either data (the contents of the salaries table) or metadata (the existence of the termination plans table). The information disclosure may be accidental (failure to set an ACL) or malicious (eavesdropping on the network). Information disclosure may also occur by the front end(s)—for example, an error message like "Can't connect to database foo with password bar!"
- The database files (partitions, SAN attached storage) need to be protected by the operating system and by ACLs for data within the files.
- Logs often store confidential information, and therefore need to be protected.

Denial of Service

- The front ends could be overwhelmed by random or crafted requests, especially if there are anonymous (or free) web accounts that can craft requests designed to be slow to execute.
- The network connections could be overwhelmed with data.
- The database or logs could be filled up.

- If the network between the main processes, or the processes and databases, is shared, it may become congested.

Elevation of Privilege

- Clients, either web or SQL, could attempt to run queries they're not authorized to run.
- If the client is enforcing security, then anyone who tampers with their client or its network stream will be able to run queries of their choice.
- If the database is capable of running arbitrary commands, then that capability is available to the clients.
- The log analysis program (or something pretending to be the log analysis program) may be able to run arbitrary commands or queries.

NOTE The log analysis program may be thought of as trusted, but it's drawn outside the trust boundaries. So either the thinking or the diagram (in Figure 2-1) is incorrect.

- If the DB cluster is connected to a corporate directory service and no action is taken to restrict who can log in to the database servers (or file servers), then anyone in the corporate directory, including perhaps employees, contractors, build labs, and partners can make changes on those systems.

NOTE The preceding lists in this extended example are intended to be illustrative; other threats may exist.

It is also possible to consider these threats according to the person or team that must address them, divided between Acme and its customers. As shown in Table 3-8, this illustrates the natural overlap of threat and mitigation, foreshadowing the Part III, "Managing and Addressing Threats" on how to mitigate threats. It also starts to enumerate things that are not requirements for Acme/SQL. These non-requirements should be documented and provided to customers, as covered in Chapter 12. In this table, you're seeing more and more actionable threats. As a developer or a systems administrator, you can start to see how to handle these sorts of issues. It's tempting to start to address threats in the table itself, and a natural extension to the table would be a set of ways for each actor to address the threats that apply.

Table 3-8: Addressing Threats According to Who Handles Them

THREAT	INSTANCES THAT ACME MUST HANDLE	INSTANCES THAT IT DEPARTMENTS MUST HANDLE
Spoofing	Web/SQL/other client brute forcing logins DBA (human) DB users	Web client SQL client DBA (human) DB users
Tampering	Data Management Logs	Front end(s) Database DB admin
Repudiation	Logs (Log analysis must be protected.) Certain actions from web and SQL clients will need careful logging. Certain actions from DBAs will need careful logging.	Logs (Log analysis must be protected.) If DBAs are not fully trusted, a system in another privilege domain to log all commands might be required.
Information disclosure	Data, management, and logs must be protected. Front ends must implement access control. Only the front ends should be able to access the data.	ACLs and security groups must be managed. Backups must be protected.
Denial of service	Front ends must be designed to minimize DoS risks.	The system must be deployed with sufficient resources.

Continues

Table 3-8 ***(continued)***

THREAT	INSTANCES THAT ACME MUST HANDLE	INSTANCES THAT IT DEPARTMENTS MUST HANDLE
Elevation of privilege	Trusting client The DB should support prepared statements to make injection harder. No "run this command" tools should be in the default install. No default way to run commands on the server, and calls like `exec()` and `system()` must be permissioned and configurable if they exist.	Inappropriately trusting clients that are written locally Configure the DB appropriately.

STRIDE Variants

STRIDE can be a very useful mnemonic when looking for threats, but it's not perfect. In this section, you'll learn about variants of STRIDE that may help address some of its weaknesses.

STRIDE-per-Element

STRIDE-per-element makes STRIDE more prescriptive by observing that certain threats are more prevalent with certain elements of a diagram. For example, a data store is unlikely to spoof another data store (although running code can be confused as to which data store it's accessing.) By focusing on a set of threats against each element, this approach makes it easier to find threats. For example, Microsoft uses Table 3-9 as a core part of its Security Development Lifecycle threat modeling training.

Table 3-9: STRIDE-per-Element

	S	T	R	I	D	E
External Entity	x		x			
Process	x	x	x	x	x	x
Data Flow		x		x	x	
Data Store		x	?	x	x	

Applying this chart, you can focus threat analysis on how an attacker might tamper with, read data from, or prevent access to a data flow. For example, if data is flowing over a network such as Ethernet, it's trivial for someone attached to that same Ethernet to read all the content, modify it, or send a flood of packets to cause a TCP timeout. You might argue that you have some form of network segmentation, and that may mitigate the threats sufficiently for you. The question mark under repudiation indicates that logging data stores are involved in addressing repudiation, and sometimes logs will come under special attack to allow repudiation attacks.

The threat is to the element listed in Table 3-9. Each element is the victim, not the perpetrator. Therefore, if you're tampering with a data store, the threat is to the data store and the data within. If you're spoofing in a way that affects a process, then the process is the victim. So, spoofing by tampering with the network is really a spoof of the endpoint, regardless of the technical details. In other words, the other endpoint (or endpoints) are confused about what's at the other end of the connection. The chart focuses on spoofing of a process, not spoofing of the data flow. Of course, if you happen to find spoofing when looking at the data flow, obviously you should record the threat so you can address it, not worry about what sort of threat it is. STRIDE-per-element has the advantage of being prescriptive, helping you identify what to look for where without being a checklist of the form "web component: XSS, XSRF..." In skilled hands, it can be used to find new types of weaknesses in components. In less skilled hands, it can still find many common issues.

STRIDE-per-element does have two weaknesses. First, similar issues tend to crop up repeatedly in a given threat model; second, the chart may not represent your issues. In fact, Table 3-9 is somewhat specific to Microsoft. The easiest place to see this is "information disclosure by external entity," which is a good description of some privacy issues. (It is by no means a complete description of privacy.) However, the table doesn't indicate that this could be a problem. That's because Microsoft has a separate set of processes for analyzing privacy problems. Those privacy processes are outside the security threat modeling space. Therefore, if you're going to adopt this approach, it's worth analyzing whether the table covers the set of issues you care about, and if it doesn't, create a version that suits your scenario. Another place you might see the specificity is that many people want to discuss spoofing of data flows. Should that be part of STRIDE-per-element? The spoofing action is a spoofing of the endpoint, but that description may help some people to look for those threats. Also note that the more "x" marks you add, the closer you come to "consider STRIDE for each element of the diagram." The editors ask if that's a good or bad thing, and it's a fine question. If you want to be comprehensive, this is helpful; if you want to focus on the most likely issues, however, it will likely be a distraction.

So what are the exit criteria for STRIDE-per-element? When you have a threat per checkbox in the STRIDE-per-element table, you are doing reasonably well.

If you circle around and consider threats against your mitigations (or ways to bypass them) you'll be doing pretty well.

STRIDE-per-Interaction

STRIDE-per-element is a simplified approach to identifying threats, designed to be easily understood by the beginner. However, in reality, threats don't show up in a vacuum. They show up in the interactions of the system. STRIDE-per-interaction is an approach to threat enumeration that considers tuples of (*origin, destination, interaction*) and enumerates threats against them. Initially, another goal of this approach was to reduce the number of things that a modeler would have to consider, but that didn't work out as planned. STRIDE-per-interaction leads to the same number of threats as STRIDE-per-element, but the threats may be easier to understand with this approach. This approach was developed by Larry Osterman and Douglas MacIver, both of Microsoft. The STRIDE-per-interaction approach is shown in Tables 3-10 and 3-11. Both reference two processes, Contoso.exe and Fabrikam.dll. Table 3-10 shows which threats apply to each interaction, and Table 3-11 shows an example of STRIDE per interaction applied to Figure 3-1. The relationships and trust boundaries used for the named elements in both tables are shown in Figure 3-1.

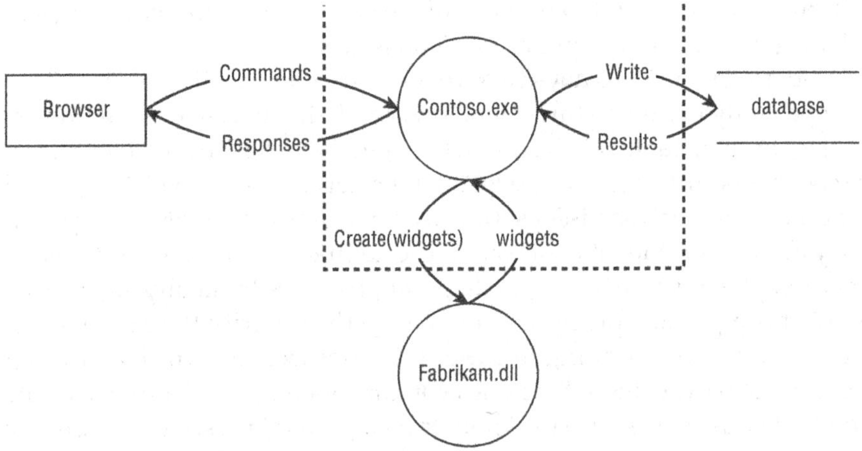

Figure 3-1: The system referenced in Table 3-10

In Table 3-10, the table columns are as follows:

- A number for referencing a line (For example, "Looking at line 2, let's look for spoofing and information disclosure threats.")

- The main element you're looking at
- The interactions that element has
- The STRIDE threats applicable to the interaction

Table 3-10: STRIDE-per-Interaction: Threat Applicability

#	ELEMENT	INTERACTION	S	T	R	I	D	E
1	Process (Contoso)	Process has outbound data flow to data store.	x			x		
2		Process sends output to another process.	x		x	x	x	x
3		Process sends output to external interactor (code).	x		x	x	x	
4		Process sends output to external interactor (human).			x			
5		Process has inbound data flow from data store.	x	x			x	x
6		Process has inbound data flow from a process.	x		x		x	x
7		Process has inbound data flow from external interactor.	x				x	x
8	Data Flow (commands/ responses)	Crosses machine boundary		x		x	x	
9	Data Store (database)	Process has outbound data flow to data store.		x	x	x	x	
10		Process has inbound data flow from data store.			x	x	x	
11	External Interactor (browser)	External interactor passes input to process.	x		x	x		
12		External interactor gets input from process.	x					

Table 3-11: STRIDE-per-Interaction (Example)

	ELEMENT	INTERACTION	S	T	R	I	D	E
1	Process (Contoso)	Process has outbound data flow to data store.	"Database" is spoofed, and Contoso writes to the wrong place.			P2: Contoso writes information in "database which should not be in database" (e.g., passwords).		
2		Process sends output to other process.	Fabrikam is spoofed, and Contoso writes to the wrong place.		Fabrikam claims not to have been called by Contoso.	P2: Fabrikam is not authorized to receive data.	None unless calls are synchronous	Fabrikam can impersonate Contoso and use its privileges.
3		Process sends output to external interactor (with the interactor being code).	Contoso is confused about the identity of the browser.		Browser disclaims and doesn't acknowledge the output.	P2: Browser gets data it's not authorized to get.	None unless calls are synchronous	
4		Process sends output to external interactor (for a human interactor).			Human disclaims seeing the output.			

Table 3-11 (continued)

ELEMENT	INTERACTION	S	T	R	I	D	E
5	Process has inbound data flow from data store.	"Database" is spoofed, and Contoso reads the wrong data.	Contoso state is corrupted by data read from the data store.			Process state is corrupted by the data retrieved from the data store.	Process internal state is corrupted based on data read from the file, leading to code execution .
6	Process has inbound data flow from a process.	Contoso believes it's getting data from Fabrikam.		Contoso denies getting data from Fabrikam.		Contoso crashes/ stops due to Fabrikam interaction.	Fabrikam passes data or args that allow it to change flow of execution of Contoso.
7	Process has inbound data flow from external interactor.	Contoso believes it's getting data from the browser, when in fact it's a random attacker.				Contoso crashes/ stops due to browser interaction.	Browser passes data or args that allow it to change flow of execution of Contoso.

Continues

Table 3-11 ***(continued)***

	ELEMENT	INTERACTION	S	T	R	I	D	E
8	Data Flow (commands/ responses)	Crosses machine boundary		Data flow is modified by MITM attack.		The contents of the data flow are sniffed on the wire.	The data flow is interrupted by an external entity (e.g., messing with TCP sequence numbers.)	
9	Data Store (database)	Process has outbound data flow to data store.		Database is corrupted.	Contoso claims not to have written to database.	Database reveals information.	Database cannot be written to.	
10		Process has inbound data flow from data store.			Contoso claims not to have read from database.	Database discloses information.	Database cannot be read from.	
11	External Interactor (browser)	External interactor passes input to process.	Contoso is confused about the identity of the browser.		Contoso claims not to have received the data.	~~P2: process not authorized to receive the data~~ (We can't stop it.)		
12		External interactor gets input from process.	Browser is confused about the identity of Contoso.		~~Contoso claims not to have sent the data~~ (Not our problem.)			

When you have a threat per checkbox in the STRIDE-per-interaction table, you are doing reasonably well. If you circle through and consider threats against your mitigations (or ways to bypass them) you'll be doing pretty well.

STRIDE-per-interaction is too complex to use without a reference chart handy. (In contrast, STRIDE is an easy mnemonic, and STRIDE-per-element is simple enough that the chart can be memorized or printed on a wallet card.)

DESIST

DESIST is a variant of STRIDE created by Gunnar Peterson. DESIST stands for Dispute, Elevation of privilege, Spoofing, Information disclosure, Service denial, and Tampering. (Dispute replaces repudiation with a less fancy word, and Service denial replaces Denial of Service to make the acronym work.) Starting from scratch, it might make sense to use DESIST over STRIDE, but after more than a decade of STRIDE, it would be expensive to displace at Microsoft. (CEO of Scorpion Software, Dana Epp, has pointed out that acronyms with repeated letters can be challenging, a point in STRIDE's favor.) Therefore, STRIDE-per-element, rather than DESIST-per-element, exists as the norm. Either way, it's always useful to have mnemonics for helping people look for threats.

Exit Criteria

There are three ways to judge whether you're done finding threats with STRIDE. The easiest way is to see if you have a threat of each type in STRIDE. Slightly harder is ensuring you have one threat per element of the diagram. However, both of these criterion will be reached before you've found all threats. For more comprehensiveness, use STRIDE-per-element, and ensure you have one threat per check.

Not having met these criteria will tell you that you're not done, but having met them is not a guarantee of completeness.

Summary

STRIDE is a useful mnemonic for finding threats against all sorts of technological systems. STRIDE is more useful with a repertoire of more detailed threats to draw on. The tables of threats can provide that for those who are new to security, or act as reference material for security experts (a function also served by Appendix B, "Threat Trees"). There are variants of STRIDE that attempt to add focus and attention. STRIDE-per-element is very useful for this purpose, and can be customized to your needs. STRIDE-per-interaction provides more focus, but requires a crib sheet (or perhaps software) to use. If threat modeling experts were to start over, perhaps DESIST would help us make better ... progress in finding threats.

CHAPTER

4

Attack Trees

As Bruce Schneier wrote in his introduction to the subject, "Attack trees provide a formal, methodical way of describing the security of systems, based on varying attacks. Basically, you represent attacks against a system in a tree structure, with the goal as the root node and different ways of achieving that goal as leaf nodes" (Schneier, 1999).

In this chapter you'll learn about the attack tree building block as an alternative to STRIDE. You can use attack trees as a way to find threats, as a way to organize threats found with other building blocks, or both. You'll start with how to use an attack tree that's provided to you, and from there learn various ways you can create trees. You'll also examine several example and real attack trees and see how they fit into finding threats. The chapter closes with some additional perspective on attack trees.

Working with Attack Trees

Attack trees work well as a building block for threat enumeration in the four-step framework. They have been presented as a full approach to threat modeling (Salter, 1998), but the threat modeling community has learned a lot since then.

There are three ways you can use attack trees to enumerate threats: You can use an attack tree someone else created to help you find threats. You can create a tree to help you think through threats for a project you're working on. Or you can create trees with the intent that others will use them. Creating new trees for general use is challenging, even for security experts.

Using Attack Trees to Find Threats

If you have an attack tree that is relevant to the system you're building, you can use it to find threats. Once you've modeled your system with a DFD or other diagram, you use an attack tree to analyze it. The attack elicitation task is to iterate over each node in the tree and consider if that issue (or a variant of that issue) impacts your system. You might choose to track either the threats that apply or each interaction. If your system or trees are complex, or if process documentation is important, each interaction may be helpful, but otherwise that tracking may be distracting or tedious. You can use the attack trees in this chapter or in Appendix B "Threat Trees" for this purpose.

If there's no tree that applies to your system, you can either create one, or use a different threat enumeration building block.

Creating New Attack Trees

If there are no attack trees that you can use for your system, you can create a project-specific tree. A project-specific tree is a way to organize your thinking about threats. You may end up with one or more trees, but this section assumes you're putting everything in one tree. The same approach enables you to create trees for a single project or trees for general use.

The basic steps to create an attack tree are as follows:

1. Decide on a representation.
2. Create a root node.
3. Create subnodes.
4. Consider completeness.
5. Prune the tree.
6. Check the presentation.

Decide on a Representation

There are AND trees, where the state of a node depends on all of the nodes below it being true, and OR trees, where a node is true if any of its subnodes are true. You need to decide, will your tree be an AND or an OR tree? (Most will be OR trees.) Your tree can be created or presented graphically or as an outline. See the section "Representing a Tree" later in this chapter for more on the various forms of representation.

Create a Root Node

To create an attack tree, start with a root node. The root node can be the component that prompts the analysis, or an adversary's goal. Some attack trees use the problematic state (rather than the goal) as the root. Which you should use is a matter of preference. If the root node is a component, the subnodes should be labeled with what can go wrong for the node. If the root node is an attacker goal, consider ways to achieve that goal. Each alternative way to achieve the goal should be drawn in as a subnode.

The guidance in "Toward a Secure System Engineering Methodology" (Salter, 1999) is helpful to security experts; however, it doesn't shed much light on how to actually generate the trees, comparative advice about what a root node should be (in other words, whether it's a goal or a system component and, most important, when one is better than the other), or how to evaluate trees in a structured fashion that would be suitable for those who are not security experts. To be prescriptive:

- Create a root node with an attacker goal or high-impact action.
- Use OR trees.
- Draw them into a grid that the eye can track linearly.

Create Subnodes

You can create subnodes by brainstorming, or you can look for a structured way to find more nodes. The relation between your nodes can be AND or OR, and you'll have to make a choice and communicate it to those who are using your tree. Some possible structures for first-level subnodes include:

- Attacking a system:
  - physical access
  - subvert software
  - subvert a person
- Attacking a system via:
  - People
  - Process
  - Technology
- Attacking a product during:
  - Design
  - Production
  - Distribution
  - Usage
  - Discard

You can use these as a starting point, and make them more specific to your system. Iterate on the trees, adding subnodes as appropriate.

NOTE Here the term subnode is used to include leaf (end) nodes and nodes with children, because as you create something you may not always know whether it is a leaf or whether it has more branches.

Consider Completeness

For this step, you want to determine whether your set of attack trees is complete enough. For example, if you are using components, you might need to add additional trees for additional components. You can also look at each node and ask "is there another way that could happen?" If you're using attacker motivations, consider additional attackers or motivations. The lists of attackers in Appendix C "Attacker Lists" can be used as a basis.

An attack tree can be checked for quality by iterating over the nodes, looking for additional ways to reach the goal. It may be helpful to use STRIDE, one of the attack libraries in the next chapter, or a literature review to help you check the quality.

Prune the Tree

In this step, go through each node in the tree and consider whether the action in each subnode is prevented or duplicative. (An attack that's worth putting in a tree will generally only be prevented in the context of a project.) If an attack is prevented, by some mitigation you can mark those nodes to indicate that they don't need to be analyzed. (For example, you can use the test case ID, an "I" for impossible, put a slash through the node, or shade it gray.) Marking the nodes (rather than deleting them) helps people see that the attacks were considered. You might choose to test the assumption that a given node is impossible. See the "Test Process Integration" section in Chapter 10 "Validating That Threats Are Addressed" for more details.

Check the Presentation

Regardless of graphical form, you should aim to present each tree or subtree in no more than a page. If your tree is hard to see on a page, it may be helpful to break it into smaller trees. Each top level subnode can be the root of a new tree, with a "context" tree that shows the overall relations. You may also be able to adjust presentation details such as font size, within the constraints of usability.

The node labels should be of the same form, focusing on active terms. Finally, draw the tree on a grid to make it easy to track. Ideally, the equivalent level subnodes will show on a single line. That becomes more challenging as you go deeper into a tree.

Representing a Tree

Trees can be represented in two ways: as a free-form (human-viewable) model without any technical structure, or as a structured representation with variable types and/or metadata to facilitate programmatic analysis.

Human-Viewable Representations

Attack trees can be drawn graphically or shown in outline form. Graphical representations are a bit more work to create but have more potential to focus attention. In either case, if your nodes are not all related by the same logic (AND/OR), you'll need to decide on a way to represent the relationship and communicate that decision. If your tree is being shown graphically, you'll also want to decide if you use a distinct shape for a terminal node: The labels in a node should be carefully chosen to be rich in information, especially if you're using a graphical tree. Words such as "attack" or "via" can distract from the key information. Choose "modify file" over "attack via modifying file." Words such as "weak" are more helpful when other nodes say "no." So "weak cryptography" is a good contrast to "no cryptography."

As always, care should be taken to ensure that the graphics are actually information-rich and communicative. For instance, consider the three representations of a tree shown in Figure 4–1.

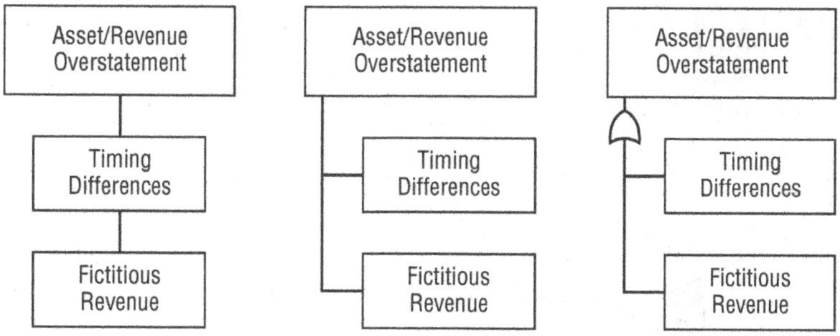

Figure 4–1: Three representations of a tree

The left tree shows an example of a real tree that simply uses boxes. This representation does not clearly distinguish hierarchy, making it hard to tell which nodes are at the same level of the tree. Compare that to the center tree, which uses a tree to show the equivalence of the leaf nodes. The rightmost tree adds the "OR gate" symbol from circuit design to show that any of the leaf nodes lead to the parent condition.

Additionally, tree layout should make considered use of space. In the very small tree in Figure 4–2, note the pleasant grid that helps your eye follow the layout. In contrast, consider the layout of Figure 4–3, which feels jumbled. To focus your attention on the layout, both are shown too small to read.

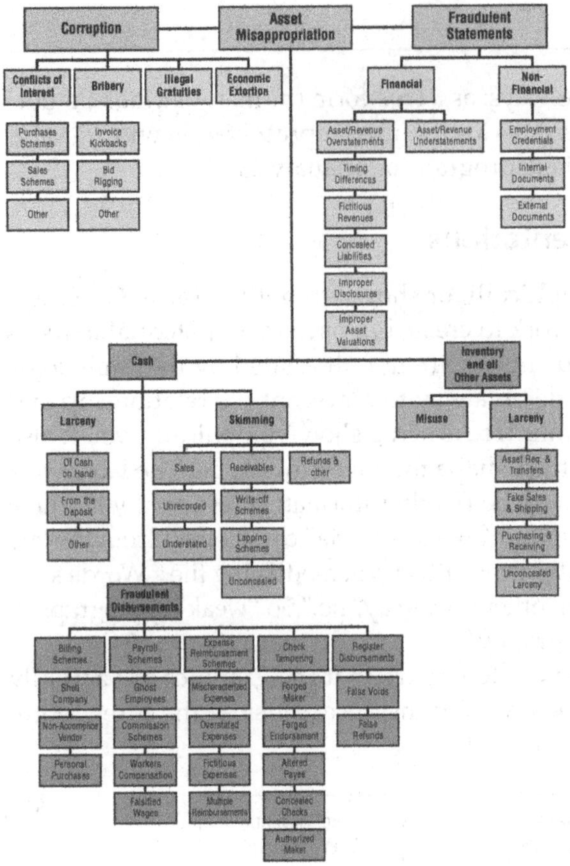

Figure 4-2: A tree drawn on a grid

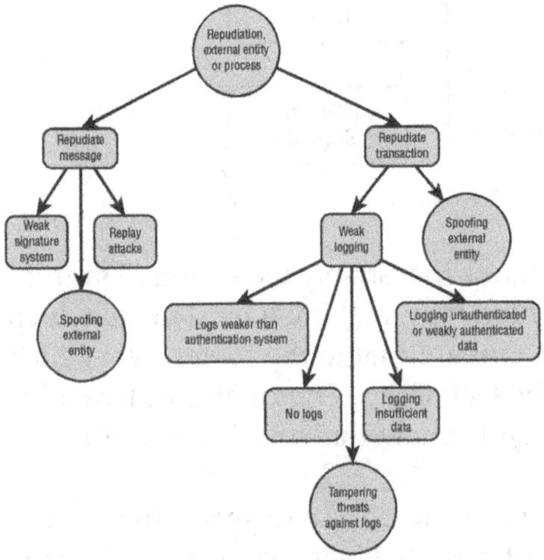

Figure 4-3: A tree drawn without a grid

NOTE In *Writing Secure Code 2* (Microsoft Press, 2003), Michael Howard and David LeBlanc suggest the use of dotted lines for unlikely threats, solid lines for likely threats, and circles to show mitigations, although including mitigations may make the trees too complex.

Outline representations are easier to create than graphical representations, but they tend to be less attention-grabbing. Ideally, an outline tree is shown on a single page, not crossing pages. The question of how to effectively represent AND/OR is not simple. Some representations leave them out, others include an indicator either before or after a line. The next three samples are modeled after the trees in "Election Operations Assessment Threat Trees" later in this chapter. As you look at them, ask yourself precisely what is needed to achieve the goal in node 1, "Attack voting equipment."

1. Attack voting equipment
   - 1.1 Gather knowledge
     - 1.1.1 From insider
     - 1.1.2 From components
   - 1.2 Gain insider access
     - 1.2.1 At voting system vendor
     - 1.2.2 By illegal insider entry

The preceding excerpt isn't clear. Should the outline be read as a need to do each of these steps, or one or the other to achieve the goal of attacking voting equipment? Contrast that with the next tree, which is somewhat better:

1. Attack voting equipment
   - 1.1 Gather knowledge (and)
     - 1.1.1 From insider (or)
     - 1.1.2 From components
   - 1.2 Gain insider access (and)
     - 1.2.1 At voting system vendor (or)
     - 1.2.2 By illegal insider entry

This representation is useful at the end nodes: It is clearly 1.1.1 or 1.1.2. But what does the "and" on line 1.1 refer to? 1.1.1 or 1.1.2? The representation is not clear. Another possible form is shown next:

1. Attack voting equipment
   O 1.1 Gather knowledge
      T 1.1.1 From insider
      O 1.1.2 From components
   O 1.2 Gain insider access
      T 1.2.1 At voting system vendor
      T 1.2.2 By illegal insider entry

This is intended to be read as "AND Node: 1: Attack voting equipment, involves 1.1, gather knowledge either from insider or from components AND 1.2, gain insider access . . ." This can be confusing if read as the children of that node are to be ORed, rather than being ORed with its sibling nodes. This is much clearer in the graphical presentation. Also note that the steps are intended to be sequential. You must gather knowledge, then gain insider access, then attack the components to pull off the attack.

As you can see from the preceding examples, the question of how to use an outline representation of a tree is less simple than you might expect. If you are using someone else's tree, be sure you understand their intent. If you are creating a tree, be sure you are clear on your intent, and clear in your communication of your intent.

Structured Representations

Graphical and outline presentation of trees are useful for humans, but a tree is also a data structure, and a structured representation of a tree makes it possible to apply logic to the tree and in turn, the system you're modeling. Several software packages enable you to create and manage complex trees. One such package allows the modeler to add costs to each node, and then assess what attacks an attacker with a given budget can execute. As your trees become more complex, such software is more likely to be worthwhile. See Chapter 11 "Threat Modeling Tools" for a list of tree management software.

Example Attack Tree

The following simple example of an attack tree (and a useful component for other attack tree activity) models how an attacker might get into a building. The entire tree is an OR tree; any of the methods listed will achieve the goal. (This tree is derived from "An Attack Tree for the Border Gateway Protocol" [Convery, 2004].)

Goal: Access to the building

1. Go through a door
   a. When it's unlocked:
      i. Get lucky.
      ii. Obstruct the latch plate (the "Watergate Classic").
      iii. Distract the person who locks the door at night.
   b. Drill the lock.
   c. Pick the lock.
   d. Use the key.
      i. Find a key.
      ii. Steal a key.
      iii. Photograph and reproduce the key.
      iv. Social engineer a key from someone.
         1. Borrow the key.
         2. Convince someone to post a photo of their key ring.
   e. Social engineer your way in.
      i. Act like you're authorized and follow someone in.
      ii. Make friends with an authorized person.
      iii. Carry a box, a cup of coffee in each hand, etc.
2. Go through a window.
   a. Break a window.
   b. Lift the window.
3. Go through a wall.
   a. Use a sledgehammer or axe.
   b. Use a truck to go through the wall.
4. Gain access via other means.
   a. Use a fire escape.
   b. Use roof access from a helicopter (preferably black) or adjacent building.
   c. Enter another part of the building, using another tenant's access.

Real Attack Trees

A variety of real attack trees have been published. These trees may be helpful to you either directly, because they model systems like the one you're modeling, or as examples of how to build an attack tree. The three attack trees in this section show how insiders commit financial fraud, how to attack elections, and threats against SSL.

Each of these trees has the nice property of being available now, either as an extended example, as a model for you to build from, or (if you're working around fraud, elections, or SSL), to use directly in analyzing a system which matters to you.

The fraud tree is designed for you to use. In contrast, the election trees were developed to help the team think through their threats and organize the possibilities.

Fraud Attack Tree

An attack tree from the Association of Certified Fraud Examiners is shown with their gracious permission in Figure 4-4, and it has a number of good qualities. First, it's derived from actual experience in finding and exposing fraud. Second, it has a structure put together by subject matter experts, so it's not a random collection of threats. Finally, it has an associated set of mitigations, which are discussed at great length in Joseph Wells' *Corporate Fraud Handbook* (Wiley, 2011).

Election Operations Assessment Threat Trees

The largest publicly accessible set of threat trees was created for the Elections Assistance Commission by a team centered at the University of Southern Alabama. There are six high-level trees. They are useful both as an example and for you to use directly, and there are some process lessons you can learn.

NOTE **This model covers a wider scope of attacks than typical for software threat models, but is scoped like many operational threat models.**

1. Attack voting equipment.
2. Perform an insider attack.
3. Subvert the voting process.
4. Experience technical failure.
5. Attack audit.
6. Disrupt operations.

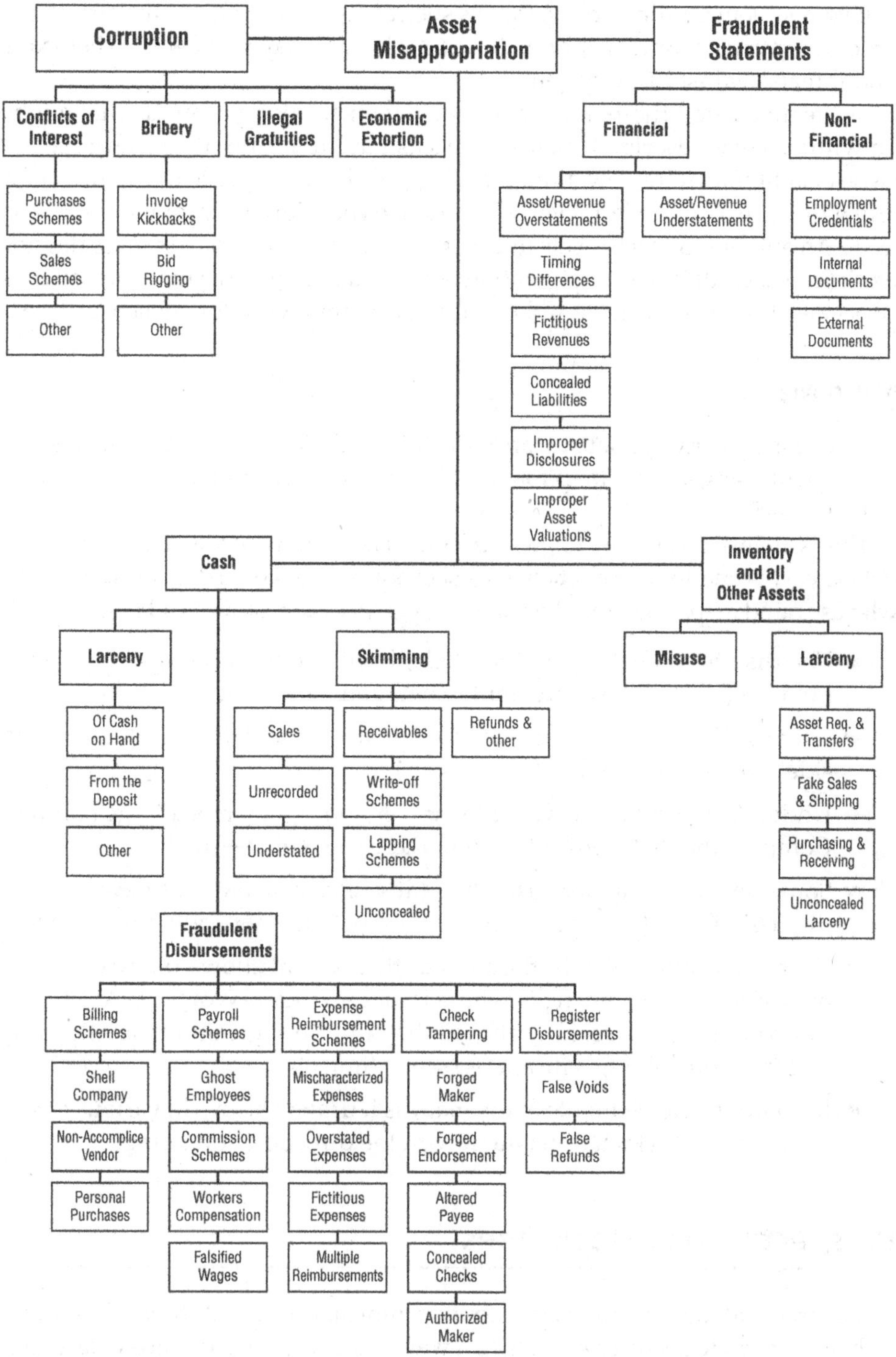

Figure 4-4: The ACFE fraud tree

If your system is vulnerable to threats such as equipment attack, insider attack, process subversion or disruption, these attack trees may work well to help you find threats against those systems.

The team created these trees to organize their thinking around what might go wrong. They described their process as having found a very large set of issues via literature review, brainstorming, and original research. They then broke the threats into high-level sets, and had individuals organize them into trees. An attempt to sort the sets into a tree in a facilitated group process did not work (Yanisac, 2012). The organization of trees may require a single person or a very close-knit team; you should be cautious about trying for consensus trees.

Mind Maps

Application security specialist Ivan Ristic (Ristić, 2009) conducted an interesting experiment using a mind map for what he calls an SSL threat model, as shown in Figure 4–5.

This is an interesting way to present a tree. There are very few mind-map trees out there. This tree, like the election trees, shows a set of editorial decisions and those who use mind maps may find the following perspective on this mind map helpful:

- The distinction between "Protocols/Implementation bugs" and "End points/Client side/secure implementation" is unclear.
- There's "End points/Client side/secure implementation" but no "server side" counterpart to that.
- Under "End points/server side/server config" there's a large subtree. Compare that to Client side where there's no subtree at all.
- Some items have an asterisk (*) but it's unclear what that means. After discussion with Ivan, it turns out that those "may not apply to everyone."
- There's an entire set of traffic analytic threats that allow you to see where on a secure site someone is. These issues are made worse by AJAX, but more important here, how should they fit into this mind map? Perhaps under "Protocols/specifications/scope limits"?
- It's hard to find elements of the map, as it draws the eye in various directions, some of which don't align with the direction of reading.

Perspective on Attack Trees

Attack trees can be a useful way to convey information about threats. They can be helpful even to security experts as a way to quickly consider possible attack types. However, despite their surface appeal, it is very hard to create attack trees.

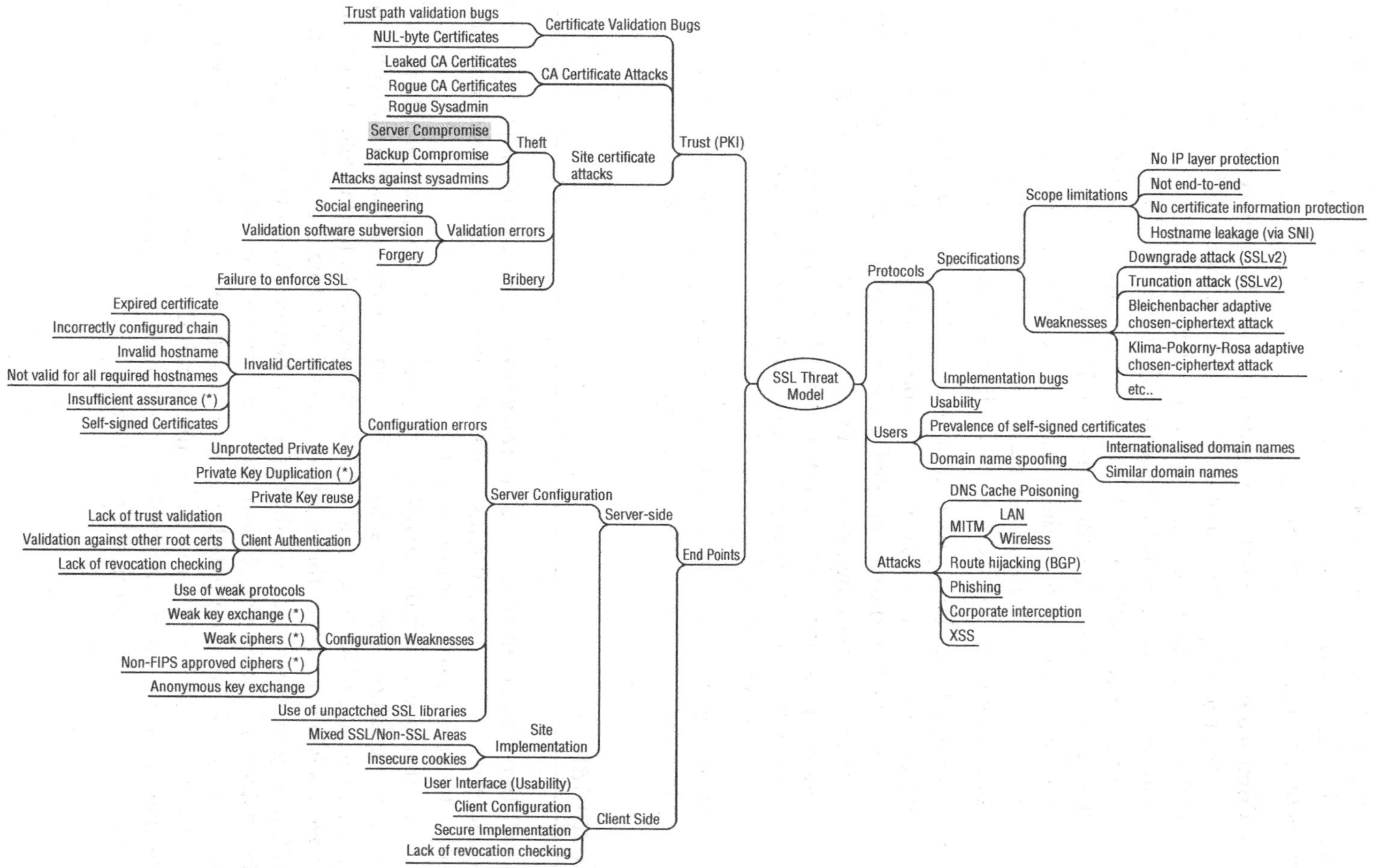

Figure 4-5: Ristic's SSL mind map

I hope that we'll see experimentation and perhaps progress in the quality of advice. There are also a set of issues that can make trees hard to use, including completeness, scoping, and meaning:

- **Completeness:** Without the right set of root nodes, you could miss entire attack groupings. For example, if your threat model for a safe doesn't include "pour liquid nitrogen on the metal, then hit with a hammer," then your safe is unlikely to resist this attack. Drawing a tree encourages specific questions, such as "how could I open the safe without the combination?" It may or may not bring you to the specific threat. Because there's no way of knowing how many nodes a branch should have, you may never reach that point. A close variant of the this is how do you know that you're done? (Schneier's attack tree article alludes to these problems.)
- **Scoping:** It may be unreasonable to consider what happens when the computer's main memory is rapidly cooled and removed from the motherboard. If you write commercial software for word processing, this may seem like an operating system issue. If you create commercial operating systems, it may seem like a hardware issue. The nature of attack trees means many of the issues discovered will fall under the category of "there's no way for us to fix that."
- **Meaning:** There is no consistency around AND/OR, or around sequence, which means that understanding a new tree takes longer.

Summary

Attack trees fit well into the four-step framework for threat modeling. They can be a useful tool for finding threats, or a way to organize thinking about threats (either for your project or more broadly).

To create a new attack tree to help you organize thinking, you need to decide on a representation, and then select a root node. With that root node, you can brainstorm, use STRIDE, or use a literature review to find threats to add to nodes. As you iterate over the nodes, consider if the tree is complete or overly-full, aiming to ensure the right threats are in the tree. When you're happy with the content of the tree, you should check the presentation so others can use it. Attack trees can be represented as graphical trees, as outlines, or in software.

You saw a sample tree for breaking into a building, and real trees for fraud, elections, and SSL. Each can be used as presented, or as an example for you to consider how to construct trees of your own.

CHAPTER

5

Attack Libraries

Some practitioners have suggested that STRIDE is too high level, and should be replaced with a more detailed list of what can go wrong. Insofar as STRIDE being abstract, they're right. It could well be useful to have a more detailed list of common problems.

A library of attacks can be a useful tool for finding threats against the system you're building. There are a number of ways to construct such a library. You could collect sets of attack tools; either proof-of-concept code or fully developed ("weaponized") exploit code can help you understand the attacks. Such a collection, where no modeling or abstraction has taken place, means that each time you pick up the library, each participant needs to spend time and energy creating a model from the attacks. Therefore, a library that provides that abstraction (and at a more detailed level than STRIDE) could well be useful. In this chapter, you'll learn about several higher-level libraries, including how they compare to checklists and literature reviews, and a bit about the costs and benefits of creating a new one.

Properties of Attack Libraries

As stated earlier, there are a number of ways to construct an attack library, so you probably won't be surprised to learn that selecting one involves trade-offs, and that different libraries address different goals. The major decisions to be made, either implicitly or explicitly, are as follows:

- Audience
- Detail versus abstraction
- Scope

Audience refers to whom the library targets. Decisions about audience dramatically influence the content and even structure of a library. For example, the "Library of Malware Traffic Patterns" is designed for authors of intrusion detection tools and network operators. Such a library doesn't need to spend much, if any, time explaining how malware works.

The question of detail versus abstraction is about how many details are included in each entry of the library. Detail versus abstraction is, in theory, simple. You pick the level of detail at which your library should deliver, and then make sure it lands there. Closely related is structure, both within entries and between them. Some libraries have very little structure, others have a great deal. Structure between entries helps organize new entries, while structure within an entry helps promote consistency between entities. However, all that structure comes at a cost. Elements that are hard to categorize are inevitable, even when the things being categorized have some form of natural order, such as they all descend from the same biological origin. Just ask that egg-laying mammal, the duck-billed platypus. When there is less natural order (so to speak), categorization is even harder. You can conceptualize this as shown in Figure 5-1.

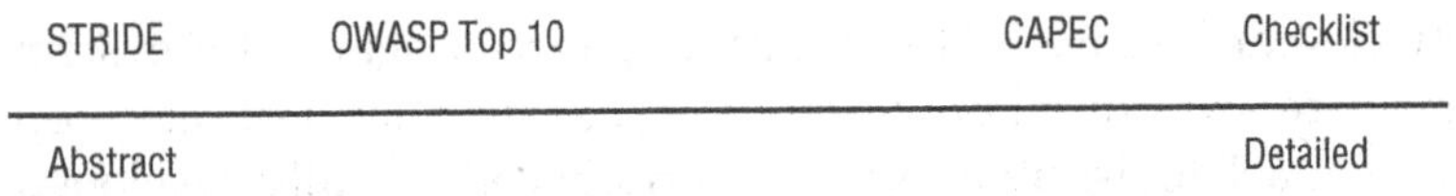

Figure 5-1: Abstraction versus detail

Scope is also an important characteristic of an attack library. If it isn't shown by a network trace, it probably doesn't fit the malware traffic attack library. If it doesn't impact the web, it doesn't make sense to include it in the OWASP attack libraries.

There's probably more than one sweet spot for libraries. They are a balance of listing detailed threats while still being thought provoking. The thought-provoking nature of a library is important for good threat modeling. A thought-provoking list means that some of the engineers using it will find interesting and different threats. When the list of threats reaches a certain level of granularity, it stops prompting thinking, risks being tedious to apply, and becomes more and more of a checklist.

The library should contain something to help remind people using it that it is not a complete enumeration of what could go wrong. The precise form of that reminder will depend on the form of the library. For example, in *Elevation of Privilege*, it is the ace card(s), giving an extra point for a threat not in the game.

Closely related to attack libraries are checklists and literature reviews, so before examining the available libraries, the following section looks at checklists and literature reviews.

Libraries and Checklists

Checklists are tremendously useful tools for preventing certain classes of problems. If a short list of problems is routinely missed for some reason, then a checklist can help you ensure they don't recur. Checklists must be concise and actionable.

Many security professionals are skeptical, however, of "checklist security" as a substitute for careful consideration of threats. If you hate the very idea of checklists, you should read *The Checklist Manifesto* by Atul Gawande. You might be surprised by how enjoyable a read it is. But even if you take a big-tent approach to threat modeling, that doesn't mean checklists can replace the work of trained people using their judgment.

A checklist helps people avoid common problems, but the modeling of threats has already been done when the checklist is created. Therefore, a checklist can help you avoid whatever set of problems the checklist creators included, but it is unlikely to help you think about security. In other words, using a checklist won't help you find any threats not on the list. It is thus narrower than threat modeling.

Because checklists can still be useful as part of a larger threat modeling process, you can find a collection of them at the end of Chapter 1, "Dive In and Threat Model!" and throughout this book as appropriate. The *Elevation of Privilege* game, by the way, is somewhat similar to a checklist. Two things distinguish it. The first is the use of aces to elicit new threats. The second is that by making threat modeling into a game, players are given social permission to playfully analyze a system, to step beyond the checklist, and to engage with the security questions in play. The game implicitly abandons the "stop and check in" value that a checklist provides.

Libraries and Literature Reviews

A literature review is roughly consulting the library to learn what has happened in the past. As you saw in Chapter 2, "Strategies for Threat Modeling," reviewing threats to systems similar to yours is a helpful starting point in threat modeling. If you write up the input and output of such a review, you may have the start of an attack library that you can reuse later. It will be more like an attack library if you abstract the attacks in some way, but you may defer that to the second or third time you review the attack list.

Developing a new library requires a very large time investment, which is probably part of why there are so few of them. However, another reason might be the lack of prescriptive advice about how to do so. If you want to develop a literature review into a library, you need to consider how the various attacks are similar and how they differ. One model you can use for this is a zoo. A *zoo* is a grouping—whether of animals, malware, attacks, or other things—that taxonomists can use to test their ideas for categorization. To track your zoo of attacks, you can use whatever form suits you. Common choices include a wiki, or a Word or Excel document. The main criteria are ease of use and a space for each entry to contain enough concrete detail to allow an analyst to dig in.

As you add items to such a zoo, consider which are similar, and how to group them. Be aware that all such categorizations have tricky cases, which sometimes require reorganization to reflect new ways of thinking about them. If your categorization technique is intended to be used by multiple independent people, and you want what's called "inter-rater consistency," then you need to work on a technique to achieve that. One such technique is to create a flowchart, with specific questions from stage to stage. Such a flowchart can help produce consistency.

The work of grouping and regrouping can be a considerable and ongoing investment. If you're going to create a new library, consider spending some time first researching the history and philosophy of taxonomies. Books like *Sorting Things Out: Classification and Its Consequences* (Bowker, 2000) can help.

CAPEC

The CAPEC is MITRE's Common Attack Pattern Enumeration and Classification. As of this writing, it is a highly structured set of 476 attack patterns, organized into 15 groups:

- Data Leakage
- Attacks Resource Depletion
- Injection (Injecting Control Plane content through the Data Plane)
- Spoofing
- Time and State Attacks
- Abuse of Functionality

- Probabilistic Techniques
- Exploitation of Authentication
- Exploitation of Privilege/Trust
- Data Structure Attacks
- Resource Manipulation
- Network Reconnaissance
- Social Engineering Attacks
- Physical Security Attacks
- Supply Chain Attacks

Each of these groups contains a sub-enumeration, which is available via MITRE (2013b). Each pattern includes a description of its completeness, with values ranging from "hook" to "complete." A complete entry includes the following:

- Typical severity
- A description, including:
  - Summary
  - Attack execution flow
- Prerequisites
- Method(s) of attack
- Examples
- Attacker skills or knowledge required
- Resources required
- Probing techniques
- Indicators/warnings of attack
- Solutions and mitigations
- Attack motivation/consequences
- Vector
- Payload
- Relevant security requirements, principles and guidance
- Technical context
- A variety of bookkeeping fields (identifier, related attack patterns and vulnerabilities, change history, etc.)

An example CAPEC is shown in Figure 5-2.

You can use this very structured set of information for threat modeling in a few ways. For instance, you could review a system being built against either each CAPEC entry or the 15 CAPEC categories. Reviewing against the individual entries is a large task, however; if a reviewer averages five minutes for each of the 475 entries, that's a full 40 hours of work. Another way to use this information is to train people about the breadth of threats. Using this approach, it would be possible to create a training class, probably taking a day or more.

Exit Criteria

The appropriate exit criteria for using CAPEC depend on the mode in which you're using it. If you are performing a category review, then you should have at least one issue per categories 1–11 (Data Leakage, Resource Depletion, Injection, Spoofing, Time and State, Abuse of Functionality, Probabilistic Techniques, Exploitation of Authentication, Exploitation of Privilege/Trust, Data Structure Attacks, and Resource Manipulation) and possibly one for categories 12–15 (Network Reconnaissance, Social Engineering, Physical Security, Supply Chain).

Perspective on CAPEC

Each CAPEC entry includes an assessment of its completion, which is a nice touch. CAPECs include a variety of sections, and its scope differs from STRIDE in ways that can be challenging to unravel. (This is neither a criticism of CAPEC, which existed before this book, nor a suggestion that CAPEC change.)

The impressive size and scope of CAPEC may make it intimidating for people to jump in. At the same time, that specificity may make it easier to use for someone who's just getting started in security, where specificity helps to identify attacks. For those who are more experienced, the specificity and apparent completeness of CAPEC may result in less creative thinking. I personally find that CAPEC's impressive size and scope make it hard for me to wrap my head around it.

CAPEC is a classification of common attacks, whereas STRIDE is a set of security properties. This leads to an interesting contrast. CAPEC, as a set of attacks, is a richer elicitation technique. However, when it comes to addressing the CAPEC attacks, the resultant techniques are far more complex. The STRIDE defenses are simply those approaches that preserve the property. However, looking up defenses is simpler than finding the attacks. As such, CAPEC may have more promise than STRIDE for many populations of threat modelers. It would be fascinating to see efforts made to improve CAPEC's usability, perhaps with cheat sheets, mnemonics, or software tools.

Pharming

Attack Pattern ID: 89 **Typical Severity:** Very High **Status:** Draft
*(**Standard** Attack Pattern Completeness: **Complete**)*

Description

Summary

A pharming attack occurs when the victim is fooled into entering sensitive data into supposedly trusted locations, such as an online bank site or a trading platform. An attacker can impersonate these supposedly trusted sites and have the victim be directed to his site rather than the originally intended one.

Pharming does not require script injection or clicking on malicious links for the attack to succeed.

Attack Execution Flow

1. Attacker sets up a system mocking the one trusted by the users. This is usually a website that requires or handles sensitive information.
2. The attacker then poisons the resolver for the targeted site. This is achieved by poisoning the DNS server, or the local hosts file, that directs the user to the original website
3. When the victim requests the URL for the site, the poisoned records direct the victim to the attacker's system rather than the original one.
4. Because of the identical nature of the original site and the attacker controlled one, and the fact that the URL is still the original one, the victim trusts the website reached and the attacker can now "farm" sensitive information such as credentials or account numbers.

Attack Prerequisites

Vulnerable DNS software or improperly protected hosts file or router that can be poisoned

A website that handles sensitive information but does not use a secure connection and a certificate that is valid is also prone to pharming

Typical Likelihood of Exploit

Figure 5-2: A sample CAPEC entry

OWASP Top Ten

OWASP, The Open Web Application Security Project, offers a Top Ten Risks list each year. In 2013, the list was as follows:

- Injection
- Broken Authentication and Session Management
- Cross-Site Scripting
- Insecure Direct Object References
- Security Misconfiguration
- Sensitive Data Exposure
- Missing Function Level Access Control
- Cross Site Request Forgery
- Components with Known Vulnerabilities
- Invalidated Requests and Forwards [sic]

This is an interesting list from the perspective of the threat modeler. The list is a good length, and many of these attacks seem like they are well-balanced in terms of attack detail and its power to provoke thought. A few (cross-site scripting and cross-site request forgery) seem overly specific with respect to threat modeling. They may be better as input into test planning.

Each has backing information, including threat agents, attack vectors, security weaknesses, technical and business impacts, as well as details covering whether you are vulnerable to the attack and how you prevent it.

To the extent that what you're building is a web project, the OWASP Top Ten list is probably a good adjunct to STRIDE. OWASP updates the Top Ten list each year based on the input of its volunteer membership. Over time, the list may be more or less valuable as a threat modeling attack library.

The OWASP Top Ten are incorporated into a number of OWASP-suggested methodologies for web security. Turning the Top Ten into a threat modeling methodology would likely involve creating something like a STRIDE-per-element approach (Top Ten per Element?) or looking for risks in the list at each point where a data flow has crossed a trust boundary.

Summary

By providing mode specifics, attack libraries may be useful to those who are not deeply familiar with the ways attackers work. It is challenging to find generally useful sweet spots between providing lots of details and becoming tedious. It is also challenging to balance details with the threat of fooling a reader into thinking a checklist is comprehensive. Performing a literature review and capturing the details in an attack library is a good way for someone to increase their knowledge of security.

There are a number of attack libraries available, including CAPEC and the OWASP Top Ten. Other libraries may also provide value depending on the technology or system on which you're working.

CHAPTER

6

Privacy Tools

Threat modeling for privacy issues is an emergent and important area. Much like security threats violate a required security property, privacy threats are where a required privacy property is violated. Defining privacy requirements is a delicate balancing act, however, for a few reasons: First, the organization offering a service may want or even need a lot of information that the people using the service don't want to provide. Second, people have very different perceptions of what privacy is, and what data is private, and those perceptions can change with time. (For example, someone leaving an abusive relationship should be newly sensitive to the value of location privacy, and perhaps consider their address private for the first time.) Lastly, most people are "privacy pragmatists" and will make value tradeoffs for personal information.

Some people take all of this ambiguity to mean that engineering for privacy is a waste. They're wrong. Others assert that concern over privacy is a waste, as consumers don't behave in ways that expose privacy concerns. That's also wrong. People often pay for privacy when they understand the threat and the mitigation. That's why advertisements for curtains, mailboxes, and other privacy-enhancing technologies often lead with the word "privacy."

Unlike the previous three chapters, each of which focused on a single type of tool, this chapter is an assemblage of tools for finding privacy threats. The approaches described in this chapter are more developed than "worry about privacy," yet they are somewhat less developed than security attack libraries such as CAPEC (discussed in Chapter 5, "Attack Libraries"). In either event, they are important enough to include. Because this is an emergent area, appropriate exit criteria are less clear, so there are no exit criteria sections here.

In this chapter, you'll learn about the ways to threat model for privacy, including Solove's taxonomy of privacy harms, the IETF's "Privacy Considerations for Internet Protocols," privacy impact assessments (PIAs), the nymity slider, contextual integrity, and the LINDDUN approach, a mirror of STRIDE created to find privacy threats. It may be reasonable to treat one or more of contextual integrity, Solove's taxonomy or (a subset of) LINDDUN as a building block that can snap into the four-stage model, either replacing or complementing the security threat discovery.

NOTE **Many of these techniques are easier to execute when threat modeling operational systems, rather than boxed software. (Will your database be used to contain medical records? Hard to say!) The IETF process is more applicable than other processes to "boxed software" designs.**

Solove's Taxonomy of Privacy

In his book, *Understanding Privacy* (Harvard University Press, 2008), George Washington University law professor Daniel Solove puts forth a taxonomy of privacy *harms*. These harms are analogous to threats in many ways, but also include impact. Despite Solove's clear writing, the descriptions might be most helpful to those with some background in privacy, and challenging for technologists to apply to their systems. It may be possible to use the taxonomy as a tool, applying it to a system under development, considering whether each of the harms presented is enabled. The following list presents a version of this taxonomy derived from Solove, but with two changes. First, I have added "identifier creation," in parentheses. I believe that the creation of an identifier is a discrete harm because it enables so many of the other harms in the taxonomy. (Professor Solove and I have agreed to disagree on this issue.) Second, exposure is in brackets, because those using the other threat modeling techniques in this Part should already be handling such threats.

- (Identifier creation)
- Information collection: surveillance, interrogation
- Information processing: aggregation, identification, insecurity, secondary use, exclusion
- Information dissemination: breach of confidentiality, disclosure, increased accessibility, blackmail, appropriation, distortion, [exposure]
- Invasion: intrusion, decisional interference

Many of the elements of this list are self-explanatory, and all are explained in depth in Solove's book. A few may benefit from a brief discussion. The harm of surveillance is twofold: First is the uncomfortable feeling of being watched and second are the behavioral changes it may cause. *Identification* means the association of information with a flesh-and-blood person. *Insecurity* refers to the psychological state of a person made to feel insecure, rather than a technical state. The harm of secondary use of information relates to societal trust. Exclusion is the use of information provided to exclude the provider (or others) from some benefit.

Solove's taxonomy is most usable by privacy experts, in the same way that STRIDE as a mnemonic is most useful for security experts. To make use of it in threat modeling, the steps include creating a model of the data flows, paying particular attention to personal data.

Finding these harms may be possible in parallel to or replacing security threat modeling. Below is advice on where and how to focus looking for these.

- Identifier creation should be reasonably easy for a developer to identify.
- Surveillance is where data is collected about a broad swath of people or where that data is gathered in a way that's hard for a person to notice.
- Interrogation risks tend to correlate around data collection points, for example, the many "* required" fields on web forms. The tendency to lie on such forms may be seen as a response to the interrogation harm.
- Aggregation is most frequently associated with inbound data flows from external entities.
- Identification is likely to be found in conjunction with aggregation or where your system has in-person interaction.
- Insecurity may associate with where data is brought together for decision purposes.
- Secondary use may cross trust boundaries, possibly including boundaries that your customers expect to exist.
- Exclusion happens at decision points, and often fraud management decisions.
- Information dissemination threats (all of them) are likely to be associated with outbound data flows; you should look for them where data crosses trust boundaries.
- Intrusion is an in-person intrusion; if your system has no such features, you may not need to look at these.
- Decisional interference is largely focused on ways in which information collection and processing may influence decisions, and as such it most likely plays into a requirements discussion.

Privacy Considerations for Internet Protocols

The Internet Engineering Task Force (IETF) requires consideration of security threats, and has a process to threat model focused on their organizational needs, as discussed in Chapter 17, "Bringing Threat Modeling to Your Organization." As of 2013, they sometimes require consideration of privacy threats. An informational RFC "Privacy Considerations for Internet Protocols," outlines a set of security-privacy threats, a set of pure privacy threats, and offers a set of mitigations and some general guidelines for protocol designers (Cooper, 2013). The combined security-privacy threats are as follows:

- Surveillance
- Stored data compromise
- Mis-attribution or intrusion (in the sense of unsolicited messages and denial-of-service attacks, rather than break-ins)

The privacy-specific threats are as follows:

- Correlation
- Identification
- Secondary use
- Disclosure
- Exclusion (users are unaware of the data that others may be collecting)

Each is considered in detail in the RFC. The set of mitigations includes data minimization, anonymity, pseudonymity, identity confidentiality, user participation and security. While somewhat specific to the design of network protocols, the document is clear, free, and likely a useful tool for those attempting to threat model privacy. The model, in terms of the abstracted threats and methods to address them, is an interesting step forward, and is designed to be helpful to protocol engineers.

Privacy Impact Assessments (PIA)

As outlined by Australian privacy expert Roger Clarke in his "An Evaluation of Privacy Impact Assessment Guidance Documents," a PIA "is a systematic process that identifies and evaluates, from the perspectives of all stakeholders, the potential effects on privacy of a project, initiative, or proposed system or scheme, and includes a search for ways to avoid or mitigate negative privacy impacts." Thus, a PIA is, in several important respects, a privacy analog to security threat modeling. Those respects include the systematic tools for identification and evaluation of privacy issues, and the goal of not simply identifying issues, but also mitigating them. However, as usually presented, PIAs have too much integration between their steps to snap into the four-stage framework used in this book.

There are also important differences between PIAs and threat modeling. PIAs are often focused on a system as situated in a social context, and the evaluation is often of a less technical nature than security threat modeling. Clarke's evaluation criteria include things such as the status, discoverability, and applicability of the PIA guidance document; the identification of a responsible person; and the role of an oversight agency; all of which would often be considered out of scope for threat modeling. (This is not a critique, but simply a contrast.) One sample PIA guideline from the Office of the Victorian Privacy Commissioner states the following:

"Your PIA Report might have a Table of Contents that looks something like this:

1. Description of the project
2. Description of the data flows
3. Analysis against 'the' Information Privacy Principles
4. Analysis against the other dimensions to privacy
5. Analysis of the privacy control environment
6. Findings and recommendations"

Note that step 2, "description of the data flows," is highly reminiscent of "data flow diagrams," while steps 3 and 4 are very similar to the "threat finding" building blocks. Therefore, this approach might be highly complementary to the four-step model of threat modeling.

The appropriate privacy principles or other dimensions to consider are somewhat dependent on jurisdiction, but they can also focus on classes of intrusion, such as those offered by Solove, or a list of concerns such as informational, bodily, territorial, communications, and locational privacy. Some of these documents, such as those from the Office of the Victorian Privacy Commissioner (2009a), have extensive lists of common privacy threats that can be used to support a guided brainstorming approach, even if the documents are not legally required. Privacy impact assessments that are performed to comply with a law will often have a formal structure for assessing sufficiency.

The Nymity Slider and the Privacy Ratchet

University of Waterloo professor Ian Goldberg has defined a measurement he calls *nymity*, the "amount of information about the identity of the participants that is revealed [in a transaction]." Nymity is from the Latin for name, from which *anonymous* ("without a name") and *pseudonym* ("like a name") are derived.

Goldberg has pointed out that you can graph nymity on a continuum (Goldberg, 2000). Figure 6-1 shows the nymity slider. On the left-hand side, there is less privacy than on the right-hand side. As Goldberg points out, it is easy to move towards more nymity, and extremely difficult to move away from it. For example, there are protocols for electronic cash that have most of the privacy-preserving properties of physical cash, but if you deliver it over a TCP connection you lose many of those properties. As such, the nymity slider can be used to examine how privacy-threatening a protocol is, and to compare the amount of nymity a system uses. To the extent that it can be designed to use less identifying information, other privacy features will be easier to achieve.

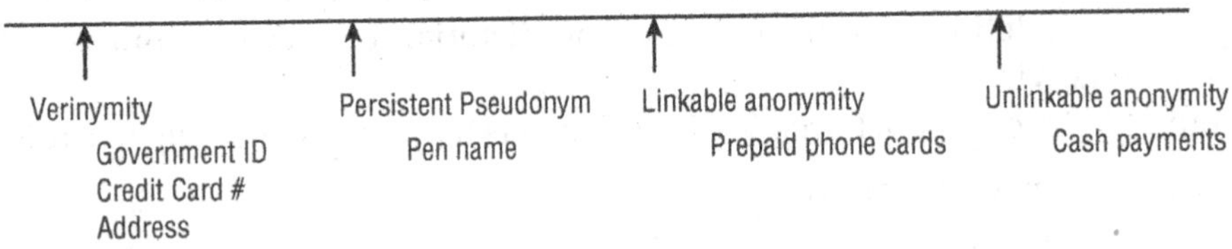

Figure 6-1: The nymity slider

When using nymity privacy in threat modeling, the goal is to measure how much information a protocol, system, or design exposes or gathers. This enables you to compare it to other possible protocols, systems, or designs. The nymity slider is thus an adjunct to other threat-finding building blocks, not a replacement for them.

Closely related to nymity is the idea of *linkability*. Linkability is the ability to bring two records together, combining the data in each into a single record or virtual record. Consider several databases, one containing movie preferences, another containing book purchases, and a third containing telephone records. If each contains an e-mail address, you can learn that `joe@example.org` likes religious movies, that he's bought books on poison, and that several of the people he talks with are known religious extremists. Such intersections might be of interest to the FBI, and it's a good thing you can link them all together! (Unfortunately, no one bothered to include the professional database showing he's a doctor, but that's beside the point!) The key is that you've engaged in linking several datasets based on an identifier. There is a set of identifiers, including e-mail addresses, phone numbers, and government-issued ID numbers, that are often used to link data, which can be considered strong evidence that multiple records refer to the same person. The presence of these strongly linkable data points increases linkability threats.

Linkability as a concept relates closely to Solove's concept of *identification* and *aggregation*. Linkability can be seen as a spectrum from strongly linkable with multiple validated identifiers to weakly linkable based on similarities in the data.

("John Doe and John E. Doe is probably the same person.") As data becomes richer, the threat of linkage increases, even if the strongly linkable data points are removed. For example, Harvard professor Latanya Sweeney has shown how data with only date of birth, gender, and zip code uniquely identifies 87 percent of the U.S. population (Sweeney, 2002). There is an emergent scientific research stream into "re-identification" or "de-anonymization," which discloses more such results on a regular basis. The release of anonymous datasets carries a real threat of re-identification, as AOL, Netflix, and others have discovered. (McCullagh, 2006; Narayanan, 2008; Buley, 2010).

Contextual Integrity

Contextual integrity is a framework put forward by New York University professor Helen Nissenbaum. It is based on the insight that many privacy issues occur when information is taken from one context and brought into another. A *context* is a term of art with a deep grounding in discussions of the spheres, or arenas, of our lives. A context has associated roles, activities, norms, and values. Nissenbaum's approach focuses on understanding contexts and changes to those contexts. This section draws very heavily from Chapter 7 of her book *Privacy in Context*, (Stanford Univ. Press, 2009) to explain how you might apply the framework to product development.

Start by considering what a context is. If you look at a hospital as a context, then the roles might include doctors, patients, and nurses, but also family members, administrators, and a host of other roles. Each has a reason for being in a hospital, and associated with that reason are activities that they tend to perform there, norms of behavior, and values associated with those norms and activities.

Contexts are places or social areas such as restaurants, hospitals, work, the Boy Scouts, and schools (or a type of school, or even a specific school). An event can be "in a work context" even if it takes place somewhere other than your normal office. Any instance in which there is a defined or expected set of "normal" behaviors can be treated as a context. Contexts nest and overlap. For example, normal behavior in a church in the United States is influenced by the norms within the United States, as well as the narrower context of the parishioners. Thus, what is normal at a Catholic Church in Boston or a Baptist Revival in Mississippi may be inappropriate at a Unitarian Congregation in San Francisco (or vice versa). Similarly, there are shared roles across all schools, those of student or teacher, and more specific roles as you specify an elementary school versus a university. There are specific contexts within a university or even the particular departments of a university.

Contextual integrity is violated when the informational norms of a context are breached. Norms, in Nissenbaum's sense, are "characterized by four key parameters: context, actors, attributes, and transmission principles." Context is roughly as just described. Actors are senders, recipients, and information subjects. Attributes refer to the nature of the information—for example, the nature or particulars of a disease from which someone is suffering. A transmission principle is "a constraint on the flow (distribution, dissemination, transmission) of information from party to party." Nussbaum first provides two presentations of contextual integrity, followed by an augmented contextual integrity heuristic. As the technique is new, and the "augmented" approach is not a strict superset of the initial presentation, it may help you to see both.

Contextual Integrity Decision Heuristic

Nissenbaum first presents contextual integrity as a post-incident analytic tool. The essence of this is to document the context as follows:

1. Establish the prevailing context.
2. Establish key actors.
3. Ascertain what attributes are affected.
4. Establish changes in principles of transmission.
5. Red flag

Step 5 means "if the new practice generates changes in actors, attributes, or transmission principles, the practice is flagged as violating entrenched informational norms and constitutes a prima facie violation of contextual integrity." You might have noticed a set of interesting potential overlaps with software development and threat modeling methodologies. In particular, actors overlap fairly strongly with personas, in Cooper's sense of personas (discussed in Appendix B, "Threat Trees"). A contextual integrity analysis probably does not require a set of personas for bad actors, as any data flow outside the intended participants (and perhaps some between them) is a violation. The information transmissions, and the associated attributes are likely visible in data flow or swim lane diagrams developed for normal security threat modeling.

Thus, to the extent that threat models are being enhanced from version to version, a set of change types could be used to trigger contextual integrity analysis. The extant diagram is the "prevailing context." The important change types would include the addition of new human entities or new data flows.

Nissenbaum takes pains to explore the question of whether a violation of contextual integrity is a worthwhile reason to avoid the change. From the perspective of threat elicitation, such discussions are out of scope. Of course, they are in scope as you decide what to do with the identified privacy threats.

Augmented Contextual Integrity Heuristic

Nissenbaum also presents a longer, 'augmented' heuristic, which is more prescriptive about steps, and may work better to predict privacy issues.

1. Describe the new practice in terms of information flows.
2. Identify the prevailing context.
3. Identify information subjects, senders, and recipients.
4. Identify transmission principles.
5. Locate applicable norms, identify significant changes.
6. Prima facie assessment
7. Evaluation
    a. Consider moral and political factors.
    b. Identify threats to autonomy and freedom.
    c. Identify effects on power structures.
    d. Identify implications for justice, fairness, equality, social hierarchy, democracy and so on.
8. Evaluation 2
    a. Ask how the system directly impinges on the values, goals, and ends of the context.
    b. Consider moral and ethical factors in light of the context.
9. Decide.

This is, perhaps obviously, not an afternoon's work. However, in considering how to tie this to a software engineering process, you should note that steps 1, 3, and 4 look very much like creating data flow diagrams. The context of most organizations is unlikely to change substantially, and thus descriptions of the context may be reusable, as may be the work products to support the evaluations of steps 7 and 8.

Perspective on Contextual Integrity

I very much like contextual integrity. It strikes me as providing deep insight into and explanations for a great number of privacy problems. That is, it may be possible to use it to predict privacy problems for products under design. However, that's an untested hypothesis. One area of concern is that the effort to spell out all the aspects of a context may be quite time consuming, but without spelling out all the aspects, the privacy threats many be missed. This sort of work is challenging when you're trying to ship software and Nissenbaum goes so far as to describe it as "tedious" (*Privacy In Context*, page 142). Additionally, the act of fixing a context in software or structured definitions may present risks that the fixed representation will deviate as social norms evolve.

This presents a somewhat complex challenge to the idea of using contextual integrity as a threat modeling methodology within a software engineering process. The process of creating taxonomies or categories is an essential step in structuring data in a database. Software engineers do it as a matter of course as they develop software, and even those who are deeply cognizant of taxonomies often treat it as an implicit step. These taxonomies can thus restrict the evolution of a context—or worse; generate dissonance between the software-engineered version of the context or the evolving social context. I encourage security and privacy experts to grapple with these issues.

LINDDUN

LUNDDUN is a mnemonic developed by Mina Deng for her PhD at the Katholieke Universiteit in Leuven, Belgium (Deng, 2010). LINDDUN is an explicit mirroring of STRIDE-per-element threat modeling. It stands for the following violations of privacy properties:

- Linkability
- Identifiability
- Non-Repudiation
- Detectability
- Disclosure of information
- Content Unawareness
- Policy and consent Noncompliance

LINDDUN is presented as a complete approach to threat modeling with a process, threats, and requirements discovery method. It may be reasonable to use the LINDDUN threats or a derivative as a tool for privacy threat enumeration in the four-stage framework, snapping it either in place of or next to STRIDE security threat enumeration. However, the threats in LINDDUN are somewhat unusual terminology; therefore, the training requirements may be higher, or the learning curve steeper than other privacy approaches.

NOTE LINDDUN leaves your author deeply conflicted. The privacy terminology it relies on will be challenging for many readers. However, it is, in many ways, one of the most serious and thought-provoking approaches to privacy threat modeling, and those seriously interested in privacy threat modeling should take a look. As an aside, the tension between non-repudiation as a privacy threat and repudiation as a security threat is delicious.

Summary

Privacy is no less important to society than security. People will usually act to protect their privacy given an understanding of the threats and how they can address them. As such, it may help you to look for privacy threats in addition to security threats. The ways to do so are less prescriptive than ways to look for security threats.

There are many tools you can use to find privacy issues, including Solove's taxonomy of privacy harms. (A harm is a threat with its impact.) Solove's taxonomy helps you understand the harm associated with a privacy violation, and thus, perhaps, how best to prioritize it. The IETF has an approach to privacy threats for new Internet protocols. That approach may complement or substitute Privacy Impact Assessments. PIAs and the IETF's processes are appropriate when a regulatory or protocol design context calls for their use. Both are more prescriptive than the nymity slider, a tool for assessing the amount of personal information in a system and measuring privacy invasion for comparative purposes. They are also more prescriptive than contextual integrity, an approach which attempts to tease out the social norms of privacy. If your goal is to identify when a design is likely to raise privacy concerns, however, then contextual integrity may be the most helpful. Far more closely related to STRIDE-style threat identification is LINDDUN, which considers privacy violations in the manner that STRIDE considers security violations.

Part III

Managing and Addressing Threats

Part III is all about managing threats and the activities involved in threat modeling. While threats themselves are at the heart of threat modeling, the reason you threat model is so that you can deliver more secure products, services, or technologies. This part of the book focuses on the third step in the four-step framework, what to do after you've found threats and need to do something about them; but it also covers the final step: validation.

Chapters in this part include the following:

- **Chapter 7: Processing and Managing Threats** describes how to start a threat modeling project, how to iterate across threats, the tables and lists you may want to use, and some scenario-specific process elements.
- **Chapter 8: Defensive Tactics and Technologies** are tools you can use to address threats, ranging from simple to complex. This chapter focuses on a STRIDE breakdown of security threats and a variety of ways to address privacy.
- **Chapter 9: Trade-Offs When Addressing Threats** includes risk management strategies, how to use those strategies to select mitigations, and threat-modeling specific prioritization approaches.

- **Chapter 10: Validating That Threats Are Addressed** includes how to test your threat mitigations, QA'ing threat modeling, and process aspects of addressing threats. This is the last step of the four-step approach.
- **Chapter 11: Threat Modeling Tools** covers the various tools that you can use to help you threat model, ranging from the generic to the specific.

CHAPTER

7

Processing and Managing Threats

Finding threats against arbitrary things is fun, but when you're building something with many moving parts, you need to know where to start, and how to approach it. While Part II is about the tasks you perform and the methodologies you can use to perform them, this chapter is about the processes in which those tasks are performed. Questions of "what to do when" naturally come up as you move from the specifics of looking at a particular element of a system to looking at a complete system. To the extent that these are questions of what an individual or small team does, they are addressed in this chapter; questions about what an organization does are covered in Chapter 17, "Bringing Threat Modeling to Your Organization."

Each of the approaches covered here should work with any of the "Lego blocks" covered in Part II. In this chapter, you'll learn how to get started looking for threats, including when and where to start and how to iterate through a diagram. The chapter continues with a set of tables and lists that you might use as you threat model, and ends with a set of scenario-specific guidelines, including the importance of the vendor-customer trust boundary, threat modeling new technologies, and how to threat model an API.

Starting the Threat Modeling Project

The basic approach of "draw a diagram and use the *Elevation of Privilege* game to find threats" is functional, but people prefer different amounts of prescriptiveness, so this section provides some additional structure that may help you get started.

When to Threat Model

You can threat model at various times during a process, with each choice having a different value. Most important, you should threat model as you get started on a project. The act of drawing trust boundaries early on can greatly help you improve your architecture. You can also threat model as you work through features. This allows you to have smaller, more focused threat modeling projects, keeping your skills sharp and reducing the chance that you'll find big problems at the end. It is also a good idea to revisit the threat model as you get ready to deliver, to ensure that you haven't made decisions which accidentally altered the reality underlying the model.

Starting at the Beginning

Threat modeling as you get started involves modeling the system you're planning or building, finding threats against the model, and filing bugs that you'll track and manage, such as other issues discovered throughout the development process. Some of those bugs may be test cases, some might be feature work, and some may be deployment decisions. It depends on what you're threat modeling.

Working through Features

As you develop each feature, there may be a small amount of threat modeling work to do. That work involves looking deeply at the threats to that feature (and possibly refreshing or validating your understanding of the context by checking the software model). As you start work on a feature or component, it can also be a good time to work through second- or third-order threats. These are the threats in which an attacker will try to bypass the features or design elements that you put in place to block the most immediate threats. For example, if the primary threat is a car thief breaking a window, a secondary threat is them jumping the ignition. You can mitigate that with a steering-wheel lock, which is thus a second-order mitigation. There's more on this concept of ordered threats in the "Digging Deeper into Mitigations" section later in this chapter, as well as more on considering planned mitigations, and how an attacker might work around them.

Threat modeling as you work through a feature has several important value propositions. One is that if you do a small threat model as you start a component or feature, the design is probably closer to mind. In other words, you'll have a more detailed model with which to look for threats. Another is that if you find threats, they are closer to mind as you're working on that feature. Threat modeling as you work through features can also help you maintain your awareness of threats and your skills at threat modeling. (This is especially true if your project is a long one.)

Close to Delivery

Lastly, you should threat model as you get ready to ship by reexamining the model and checking your bugs. (Shipping here is inclusive of delivering, deploying, or going live.) Reexamining the model means ensuring that everyone still agrees it's a decent model of what you're building, and that it includes all the trust boundaries and data flows that cross them. Checking your bugs involves checking each bug that's tagged threat modeling (or however else you're tracking them), and ensuring it didn't slip through the cracks.

Time Management

So how long should all this take? The answer to that varies according to system size and complexity, the familiarity of the participants with the system, their skill in threat modeling, and even the culture of meetings in an organization. Some very rough rules of thumb are that you should be able to diagram and find threats against a "component" and decide if you need to do more enumeration in a one-hour session with an experienced threat modeler to moderate or help. For the sort of system that a small start-up might build, the end-to-end threat modeling could take a few hours to a week, or possibly longer if the data the system holds is particularly sensitive. At the larger end of the spectrum, a project to diagram the data flows of a large online service has been known to require four people working for several months. That level of effort was required to help find threat variations and alternate routes through a system that had grown to serve millions of people.

Whatever you're modeling, familiarity with threat modeling helps. If you need to refer back to this book every few minutes, your progress will be slower. One of the reasons to threat model regularly is to build skill and familiarity with the tasks and techniques. Organizational culture also plays a part. Organizations that run meetings with nowhere to sit will likely create a list of threats faster than a consensus-oriented organization that encourages exploring ideas. (Which list will be better is a separate and fascinating question.)

What to Start and (Plan to) End With

When you start looking for threats, a diagram is something between useful and essential input. Experienced modelers may be able to start without it, but will likely iterate through creating a diagram as they find threats. The diagram is likely to change as you use it to find threats; you'll discover things you missed or don't need. That's normal, and unless you run a strict waterfall approach to engineering, it's a process that evolves much like the way requirements evolve as you discover what's easy or hard to build.

Use the following two testable states to help assess when you're done:

- You have filed bugs.
- You have a diagram or diagrams that everyone agrees represents the system.

To be more specific, you should probably have a number of bugs that's roughly scaled to the number of things in your diagram. If you're using a data flow diagram and STRIDE, expect to have about five threats per diagram element.

NOTE **Originally, this text suggested that you should have: (# of processes * 6) + (# of data flows * 3) + (# of data stores * 3.5) + (# of distinct external entities *2) threats, but that requires keeping four separate counts, and is thus more work to get approximately the same answer.**

You might notice that says "STRIDE" rather than "STRIDE-per-element" or "STRIDE-per-interaction," and five turns out to match the number you get if you tally up the checkmarks in those charts. That's because those charts are derived from where the threats usually show up.

Where to Start

When you are staring at a blank whiteboard and wondering where to start, there are several commonly recommended places. Many people have recommended assets or attackers, but as you learned in Chapter 2, "Strategies for Threat Modeling," the best starting place is a diagram that covers the system as a whole, and from there start looking at the trust boundaries. For advice on how to create diagrams, see Chapter 2.

When you assemble a group of people in a room to look for threats, you should include people who know about the software, the data flows and (if possible) threat modeling. Begin the process with the component(s) on which the participants in the room are working. You'll want to start top-down, and then work across the system, going "breadth first," rather than delving deep into any component ("depth first").

Finding Threats Top Down

Almost any system should be modeled from the highest-level view you can build of the entire system, for some appropriate value of "the entire system". What constitutes an entire system is, of course, up for debate, just like what constitutes the entire Internet, the entirety of (say) Amazon's website, and so on, isn't a simple question. In such cases more scoping is needed. The ideal is probably what is within an organization's control and, to the extent possible, cross-reviews with those responsible for other components.

In contrast, bottom-up threat modeling starts from features, and then attempts to derive a coherent model from those feature-level models. This doesn't work well, but advice that implies you should do this is common, so a bit of discussion may be helpful. The reason this doesn't work is because it turns out to be very challenging to bring threat models together when they are not derived from a system-level view. As such, you should start from the highest-level view you can build of the entire system.

MICROSOFT'S BOTTOM-UP EXPERIENCE

It may help to understand the sorts of issues that can lead to a bottom-up approach. At Microsoft in the mid-2000s, there was an explosion of bottom-up threat modeling. There were three drivers for this: specific words in the Security Development Lifecycle (SDL) threat model requirement, aspects of Microsoft's approach to function teams, and the work involved in creating top-level models. The SDL required "all new features" be threat modeled. This intersected with an approach to features whereby a particular team of developer, tester, and program manager owns a feature and collaborates to ship it. Because the team owned its feature, it was natural to ask it to add threat models to the specifications involved in producing it. As Microsoft's approach to security evolved, product security teams had diverse sets of important tasks to undertake. Creating all-up threat models was usually not near the top of the list. (Many large product diagrams have now done that work and found it worthwhile. Some of these diagrams require more than one poster-size sheet of paper.)

Finding Threats "Across"

Even with a top-down approach, you want to go breadth first, and there are three different lists you can iterate "across": A list of the trust boundaries, a list of diagram elements, or a list of threats. A structure can help you look for threats, either because you and your team like structure, or because the task feels intimidating and you want to break it down, Table 7-1 shows three approaches.

Table 7-1: Lists to Iterate Across

METHOD	SAMPLE STATEMENT	COMMENTS
Start from what goes across trust boundaries.	"What can go wrong as foo comes across this trust boundary?	This is likely to identify the highest-value threats.
Iterate across diagram elements.	"What can go wrong with this database file?" "What can go wrong with the logs?"	Focusing on diagram elements may work well when a lot of teams are collaborating.
Iterate across the threats.	"Where are the spoofing threats in this diagram?" "Where are the tampering threats?"	Making threats the focus of discussion may help you find related threats.

Each of these approaches can be a fine way to start, as long as you don't let them become straightjackets. If you don't have a preference, try starting from what crosses trust boundaries, as threats tend to cluster there. However you iterate, ensure that you capture each threat as it comes up, regardless of the planned approach.

Digging Deeper into Mitigations

Many times threats will be mitigated by the addition of features, which can be designed, developed, tested and delivered much like other features. (Other times, mitigation might be a configuration change, or at the other end of the effort scale, require re-design.) However, mitigations are not quite like other features. An attacker will rarely try to work around the bold button and find an unintended, unsupported way to bold their text.

Finding threats is great, and to the extent that you plan to be attacked only by people who are exactly lazy enough to find a threat but not enthusiastic enough to try to bypass your mitigation, you don't need to worry about going deeper into the mitigations. (You may have to worry about a new job, but that, as they say, is beyond the scope of this book. I recommend Mike Murray's *Forget the Parachute: Let Me Fly the Plane.*) In this section, you'll learn about how to go deeper into the interplay of how attackers can attempt to bypass the design choices and features you put in place to make their lives harder.

The Order of Mitigation

Going back to the example of threat modeling a home from the introduction, it's easy and fun for security experts to focus on how attackers could defeat the security system by cutting the alarm wire. If you consider the window to be the attack surface, then threats include someone smashing through it and someone opening it. The smashing is addressed by re-enforced glass, which is thus "first-order" mitigation. The smashing threat is also addressed by an alarm, which is a second-order defense. But, oh no! Alarms can be defeated by cutting power. To address that third-level threat, the system designer can add more defenses. For example, alarm systems can include an alert if the line is ever dropped. Therefore, the defender can add a battery, or perhaps a cell phone or some other radio. (See how much fun this is?) These multiple layers, or orders, of attack and defense are shown in Table 7-2.

NOTE If you become obsessed with the window-smashing threat and forget to put a lock on the window, or you never discover that there's a door key under the mat, you have unaddressed problems, and are likely mis-investing your resources.

Table 7-2: Threat and Mitigation "Orders" or "Layers"

ORDER	THREAT	MITIGATION
1st	Window smashing	Reinforced glass
2nd	Window smashing	Alarm
3rd	Cut alarm wire	Heartbeat
4th	Fake heartbeat	Cryptographic signal integrity

Threat modeling should usually proceed from attack surfaces, and ensure that all first-order threats are mitigated before attention is paid to the second-order threats. Even if a methodology is in place to ensure that the full range of first-order threats is addressed, a team may run out of time to follow the methodology. Therefore, you should find threats breadth-first.

Playing Chess

It's also important to think about what an attacker will do next, given your mitigations. Maybe that means following the path to faking a heartbeat on the alarm wire, but maybe the attacker will find that door key, or maybe they'll move on to another victim. Don't think of attacks and mitigations as static. There's a dynamic interplay between them, usually driven by attackers. You might think of threats and mitigations like the black and white pieces on a chess board. The attacker can move, and when they move, their relationship to other pieces can change. As you design mitigation, ask what an attacker could do once you deliver that mitigation. How could they work around it? (This is subtly different from asking what they *will* do. As Nobel-prize winning physicist Niels Bohr said, "Prediction is very difficult, especially about the future.")

Generally, attackers look for the weakest link they can easily find. As you consider your threats and where to go into depth, start with the weakest links. This is an area where experience, including a repertoire of real scenarios, can be very helpful. If you don't have that repertoire, a literature review can help, as you saw in Chapter 2. This interplay is a place where artful threat modeling and clever redesign can make a huge difference.

Believing that an attacker will stop because you put a mitigation in place is optimistic, or perhaps naive would be a better word. What happens several moves ahead can be important. (Attackers are tricky like that.) This differs from thinking through threat ordering in that your attacker will likely move to the "next easiest" attack available. That is, an attacker doesn't need to stick to the attack you're planning for or coding against at the moment, but rather can go anywhere in your system. The attacker gets to choose where to go, so you need to defend everywhere. This isn't really fair, but no one promised you fair.

Prioritizing

You might feel that the advice in this section about the layers of mitigations and the suggestion to find threats across first is somewhat contradictory. Which should you do first? Consider the chess game or cover everything? Covering breadth first is probably wise. As you manage the bugs and select ways to mitigate threats, you can consider the chess game and deeper threat variants. However, it's important to cover both.

The unfortunate reality is that attackers with enough interest in your technology will try to find places where you didn't have enough time to investigate or build defenses. Good requirements, along with their interplay with threats and mitigations, can help you create a target that is consistently hard to attack.

Running from the Bear

There's an old joke about Alice and Bob hiking in the woods when they come across an angry bear. Alice takes off running, while Bob pauses to put on some running shoes. Alice stops and says, "What the heck are you doing?"

Bob looks at her and replies, "I don't need to outrun the bear, I just need to outrun you."

OK, it's not a very good joke. But it is a good metaphor for bad threat modeling. You shouldn't assume that there's exactly one bear out there in the woods. There are a lot of people out there actively researching new vulnerabilities, and they publish information about not only the vulnerabilities they find, but also about their tools and techniques. Thus, more vulnerabilities are being found more efficiently than in past years. Therefore, not only are there multiple bears, but they have conferences in which they discuss techniques for eating both Alice and Bob for lunch.

Worse, many of today's attacks are largely automated, and can be scaled up nearly infinitely. It's as if the bears have machine guns. Lastly, it will get far worse as the rise of social networking empowers automated social engineering attacks (just consider the possibilities when attackers start applying modern behavior-based advertising to the malware distribution business).

If your iteration ends with "we just have to run faster than the next target," you may well be ending your analysis early.

Tracking with Tables and Lists

Threat modeling can lead you to generate a lot of information, and good tracking mechanisms can make a big difference. Discovering what works best for you may require a bit of experimentation. This section lays out some sample lists and sample entries in such lists. These are all intended as advice, not straightjackets. If you regularly find something that you're writing on the side, give yourself a way to track it.

Tracking Threats

The first type of table to consider is one that tracks threats. There are (at least) three major ways to organize such a table, including by diagram element (see Table 7-3), by threat type (see Table 7-4), or by order of discovery (see Table 7-5). Each of these tables uses these methods to examine threats against the super-simple diagram from Chapter 1, "Dive In and Threat Model!" reprised here in Figure 7-1.

If you organize by diagram element, the column headers are Diagram Element, Threat Type, Threat, and Bug ID/Title. You can check your work by validating that the expected threats are all present in the table. For example, if you're using STRIDE-per-element, then you should have at least one tampering, information disclosure, and denial-of-service threat for each data flow. An example table for use in iterating over diagram elements is shown in Table 7-3.

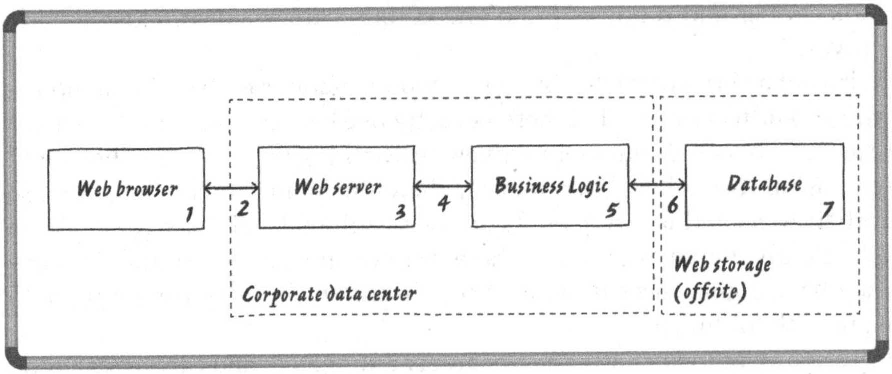

Figure 7-1: The diagram considered in threat tables

Table 7-3: A Table of Threats, Indexed by Diagram Element (excerpt)

DIAGRAM ELEMENT	THREAT TYPE	THREAT	BUG ID AND TITLE
Data flow (4) web server to Biz Logic	Tampering	Add orders without payment checks.	4553 "need integrity controls on channel"
	Information disclosure	Payment instruments in the clear	4554 "need crypto" #PCI #p0
	Denial of service	Can we just accept all these inside the data center?	4555 "Check with Alice in IT if these are acceptable".

To check the completeness of Table 7-3, confirm that each element has at least one threat. If you're using STRIDE-per-element, each process should have six threats, each data flow three, each external entity two, and each data store three or four if the data store is a log.

You can also organize a table by threats, and use threats as what's being iterated "across." If you do that, you end up with a table like the one shown in Table 7-4.

Table 7-4: A Table of Threats, Organized by Threat (excerpt)

THREAT	DIAGRAM ELEMENT	THREAT	BUG ID AND TITLE
Tampering	Web browser (1)	Attacker modifies our JavaScript order checker.	4556 "Add order-checking logic to the server".
	Data flow (2) from browser to server	Failure to use HTTPS*	4557 "Build unit tests to ensure that there are no HTTP listeners for endpoints to these data flows."

THREAT	DIAGRAM ELEMENT	THREAT	BUG ID AND TITLE
	Web server	Someone who tampers with the web server can attack our customers.	4558 "Ensure all changes to server code are pulled from source control so changes are accountable".
	Web server	Web server can add items to orders.	4559 "Investigate moving controls to Biz Logic, which is less accessible to attackers".

* The entry for "failure to use HTTPS" is an example that illustrates how knowledge of the scenario and mitigating techniques can lead you to jump to a fix, rather than perhaps tediously working through the threats. Be careful that when you (literally) jump to a conclusion like this, you're not missing other threats.

NOTE You may have noticed that Table 7-4 has two entries for web server—this is totally fine. You shouldn't let having something in a space prevent you from finding more threats against that thing, or recording additional threats that you discover.

The last way to formulate a table is by order of discovery, as shown in Table 7-5. This is the easiest to fill out, as the next threat is simply added to the next line. It is, however, the hardest to validate, because the threats will be "jumbled together."

Table 7-5: Threats by Order of Discovery (excerpt)

THREAT	DIAGRAM ELEMENT	THREAT	BUG ID
Tampering	Web browser (1)	Attacker modifies the JavaScript order checker.	4556 "Add order-checking logic to the server".

With three variations, the obvious question is which one should you use? If you're new to threat modeling and need structure, then either of the first two forms help you organize your approach. The third is more natural, but requires checking at the end; so as you become more comfortable threat modeling, jumping around will become natural, and therefore the third type of table will become more useful.

Making Assumptions

The key reason to track assumptions as you discover them is so that you can follow up and ensure that you're not assuming your way into a problem. To do that, you should track the following:

- The assumption
- The impact if it's wrong

- Who can tell you if it's wrong
- Who's going to follow-up
- When they need to do so
- A bug for tracking

Table 7-6 shows an example entry for such a table of assumptions.

Table 7-6: A Table for Recording Assumptions

ASSUMPTION	IMPACT IF WRONG (IF NOT OBVIOUS)	WHO TO TALK TO (IF KNOWN)	WHO'S FOLLOWING UP	FOLLOW-UP BY DATE	BUG #
It's OK to ignore denial of service within the data center.	Unhandled vulnerabilities	Alice	Bob	April 15	4555

External Security Notes

Many of the documented Microsoft threat-modeling approaches have a section for "external security notes." That name frames these notes with respect to the threat model. That is, they're notes for those outside the threat discovery process in some way, and they'll probably emerge or crystalize as you look for threats. Therefore, like tracking threats and assumptions, you want to track external security notes. You can be clearer by framing the notes in terms of two sets of audiences: your customers and those calling your APIs. One of the most illustrative forms of these notes appears in the IETF "RFC Security Considerations" section, so you'll get a brief tour of those here.

Notes for Customers

Security notes that are designed for your customers or the people using your system are generally of the form "we can't fix problem X." Not being able to fix problem X may be acceptable, and it's more likely to be acceptable if it's not a surprise—for example, "This product is not designed to defend against the system administrator." This sort of note is better framed as "non-requirements," and they are discussed at length in Chapter 12, "Requirements Cookbook."

Notes for API Callers

The right design for an API involves many trade-offs, including utility, usability, and security. Threat modeling that leads to security notes for your callers can serve two functions. First, those notes can help you understand the security implications of your design decisions before you finalize those decisions. Second, they can help your customers understand those implications.

These notes address the question "What does someone calling your API need to do to use it in a secure way?" The notes help those callers know what threats you address (what security checks you perform), and thus you can tell them about a subset of the checks they'll need to perform. (If your security depends on not telling them about threats then you have a problem; see the section on Kerckhoffs's Principles in Chapter 16, "Threats to Cryptosystems.") Notes to API callers are generally one of the following types:

- **Our threat model is [description]**—That is, the things you worry about are... This should hopefully be obvious to readers of this book.
- **Our code will only accept input that looks like [some description]**—What you'll accept is simply that—a description of what validation you'll perform, and thus what inputs you would reject. This is, at a surface level, at odds with the Internet robustness principle of "be conservative in what you send, and liberal in what you accept"; but being liberal does not require foolishness. Ideally, this description is also matched by a set of unit tests.
- **Common mistakes in using our code include [description]**—This is a set of things you know callers should or should not do, and are two sides of the same coin:
  - **We do not validate this property that callers might expect us to validate**—In other words, what should callers check for themselves in their context, especially when they might expect you to have done something?
  - **Common mistakes that our code doesn't or can't address**—In other words, if you regularly see bug reports (or security issues) because your callers are not doing something, consider treating that as a design flaw and fixing it.

For an example of callers having trouble with an API, consider the `strcpy` function. According to the manual pages included with various flavors of unix, "`strcpy` does not validate that s2 will fit buffer s1," or "`strcpy` requires that s1 be of at least length (s2) + 1." These examples are carefully chosen, because as the fine manual continues, "Avoid using `strcat`." (You should now use `SafeStr*` on Windows, `strL*` on unix.) The manual says this because, although notes about safer use were eventually added, the function was simply too hard to use correctly, and no amount of notes to callers was going to overcome that. If your notes to those calling your API boil down to "it is impossible to use this API without jumping through error-prone hoops," then your API is going to need to change (or deliver some outstanding business value).

Sometimes, however, it's appropriate to use these sorts of notes to API callers—for example, "This API validates that the SignedDataBlob you pass in is signed by a valid root CA. You will still need to ensure that the OrganizationName field matches the name in the URL, as you do not pass us the URL." That's a reasonable note, because the blob might not be associated with a URL. It might also be reasonable to have a `ValidateSignatureURL()` API call.

RFC Security Considerations

IETF RFCs are a form of external security notes, so it's worth looking at them as an evolved example of what such notes might contain (Rescorla, 2003). If you need a more structured form of note, this framework is a good place to start. The security considerations of a modern RFC include discussion of the following:

- What is in scope
- What is out of scope—and why
- Foreseeable threats that the protocol is susceptible to
- Residual risk to users or operators
- Threats the protocol protects against
- Assumptions which underlie security

Scope is reasonably obvious, and the RFC contains interesting discussion about not arbitrarily defining either foreseeable threats or residual risk as out of scope. The point about residual risk is similar to non-requirements, as covered in Chapter 12. It discusses those things that the protocol designers can't address at their level.

Scenario-Specific Elements of Threat Modeling

There are a few scenarios where the same issues with threat modeling show up again and again. These scenarios include issues with customer/vendor boundaries, threat modeling new technologies, and threat modeling an API (which is broader than just writing up external security notes). The customer/vendor trust boundary is dropped with unfortunate regularity, and how to approach an API or new technology often appears intimidating. The following sections address each scenario separately.

Customer/Vendor Trust Boundary

It is easy to assume that because someone is running your code, they trust you, and/or you can trust them. This can lead to things like Acme engineers saying, "Acme.com isn't really an external entity... " While this may be true, it may also be wrong. Your customers may have carefully audited the code they received from you. They may believe that your organization is generally trustworthy without wanting to expose their secrets to you. You holding those secrets is a different security posture. For example, if you hold backups of their cryptographic keys, they may be subject to an information disclosure threat via a subpoena or other legal demand that you can't reveal to them. Good security design involves minimizing risk by appropriate design and enforcement of the customer/vendor trust boundary.

This applies to traditional programs such as installed software packages, and it also applies to the web. Believing that a web browser is faithfully executing the code you sent it is optimistic. The other end of an HTTPS connection might not even be a browser. If it is a browser, an attacker may have modified your JavaScript, or be altering the data sent back to you via a proxy. It is important to pay attention to the trust boundary once your code has left your trust context.

New Technologies

From mobile to cloud to industrial control systems to the emergent "Internet of Things," technologists are constantly creating new and exciting technologies. Sometimes these technologies genuinely involve new threat categories. More often, the same threats manifest themselves. Models of threats that are intended to elicit or organize thinking about skilled threat modelers (such as STRIDE in its mnemonic form) can help in threat modeling these new technologies. Such models of threats enable skilled practitioners to find many of the threats that can occur even as the new technologies are being imagined.

As your threat elicitation technique moves from the abstract to the detailed, changes in the details of both the technologies and the threats may inhibit your ability to apply the technique.

From a threat-modeling perspective, the most important thing that designers of new technologies can do is clearly define and communicate the trust relationships by drawing their trust boundaries. What's essential is not just identification, but also communication. For example, in the early web, the trust model was roughly as shown in Figure 7-2.

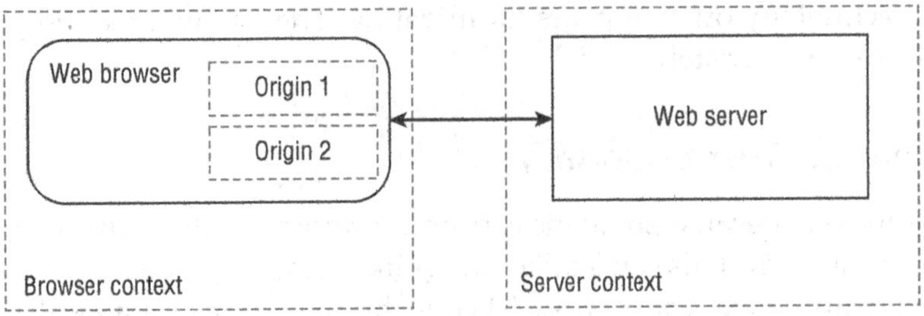

Figure 7-2: The early web threat model

In that model, servers and clients both ran code, and what passed between them via HTTP was purely data in the form of HTML and images. (As a model, this is simplified; early web browsers supported more than HTTP, including gopher and FTP.) However, the boundaries were clearly drawable. As the web evolved and web developers pushed the boundary of what was possible with the browser's built-in functionality, a variety of ways for the server to run code on the client were added, including JavaScript, Java, ActiveX, and Flash. This was an active transformation of the security model, which now looks more like Figure 7-3.

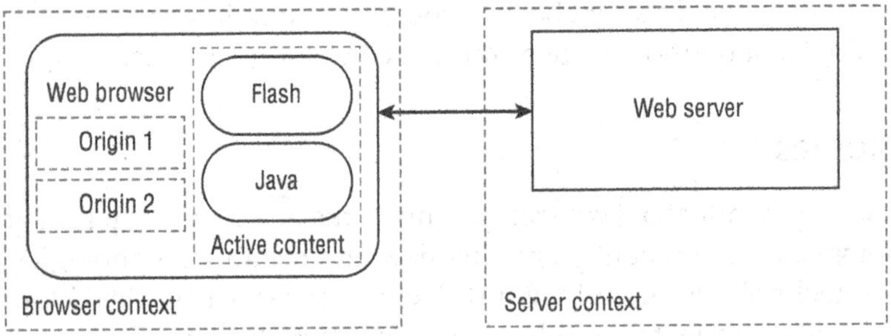

Figure 7-3: The evolved web threat model

In this model, content from the server has dramatically more access to the browser, leading to two new categories of threats. One is *intra-page threats*, whereby code from different servers can attack other information in the browser. The other is *escape threats*, whereby code from the server can find a way to influence what's happening on the client computer. In and of themselves, these changes are neither good nor bad. The new technologies created a dramatic transformation of what's possible on the web for both web developers and web attackers. The transformation of the web would probably have been accomplished with more security if boundaries had been clearly identified. Thus, those using new technology will get substantial security benefits from its designers by defining, communicating, and maintaining clear trust boundaries.

Threat Modeling an API

API threat models are generally very similar. Each API has a low trust side, regardless of whether it is called from a program running on the local machine or called by anonymous parties on the far side of the Internet. On a local machine, the low trust side is more often clear: The program running as a normal user is running at a low trust level compared to the kernel. (It may also be running at the same trust level as other code running with the same user ID, but with the introduction of things like AppContainer on Windows and Mac OS sandbox, two programs running with the same UID may not be fully equivalent. Each should treat the other as being untrusted.) In situations where there's a clear "lower trust" side, that unprivileged code has little to do, except ensure that data is validated for the context in which that data will be used. If it really is at a lower trust level, then it will have a hard time defending itself from a malicious kernel, and should generally not try. This applies only to relationships like that of a program to a kernel, where there's a defined hierarchy of privilege. Across the Internet, each side must treat the other as untrusted. The "high trust" side of the API needs to do the following seven things for security:

- **Perform all security checks inside the trust boundary.** A system has a trust boundary because the other side is untrusted or less trusted. To allow the less trusted side to perform security checks for you is missing the point of having a boundary. It is often useful to test input before sending it (for example, a user might fill out a long web form, miss something, and then get back an error message). However, that's a usability feature, not a security feature. You must test inside the trust boundary. Additionally, for networked APIs/restful APIs/protocol endpoints, it is important to consider authentication, authorization, and revocation.
- **When reading, ensure that all data is copied in before validation for purpose (see next bullet).** The low, or untrusted side, can't be trusted to validate data. Nor can it be trusted to not change data under its control after you've checked it. There is an entire genus of security flaws called *TOCTOU* ("time of check, time of use") in which this pattern is violated. The data that you take from the low side needs to be copied into secured memory, validated for some purpose, and then used without further reference to the data on the low side.
- **Know what purpose the data will be put to, and validate that it matches what the rest of your system expects from it.** Knowing what the data will be used for enables you to check it for that purpose—for example, ensure an IPv4 address is four octets, or that an e-mail address matches some regular expression (an e-mail regular expression is an easily grasped example, but sending e-mail to the address is better [Celis, 2006]). If the

API is a pass-through (for example, listening on a socket), then you may be restricted to validating length, length to a C-style string, or perhaps nothing at all. In that case, your documentation should be very clear that you are doing minimal or no validation, and callers should be cautious.

- **Ensure that your messages enable troubleshooting without giving away secrets.** Trusted code will often know things that untrusted code should not. You need to balance the capability to debug problems with returning too much data. For example, if you have a database connection, you might want to return an error like "can't connect to server instance with username `dba` password `dfug90845b4j`," but anyone who connected then now knows the DBA's password. Oops! Messages of the form "An error of type *X* occurred. This is instance *Y* in the error log *Z*" are helpful enough to a systems administrator, who can search for *Y* in *Z* while only disclosing the existence of the logs to the attacker. Even better are errors that include information about who to contact. Messages that merely say "Contact your system administrator" are deeply frustrating.
- **Document what security checks you perform, and the checks you expect callers to perform for themselves.** Very few APIs take unconstrained input. The HTTP interface is a web interface: It expects a verb (`GET`, `POST`, `HEAD`) and data. For a `GET` or `HEAD`, the data is a URL, an HTTP version, and a set of HTTP headers. Old-fashioned CGI programs knew that the web server would pass them a set of headers as environment variables and then a set of name-value pairs. The environment variables were not always unique, leading to a number of bugs. What a CGI could rely on could be documented, but the diverse set of attacks and assumptions that people could read into it was not documentable.
- **Ensure that any cryptographic function runs in a constant time.** All your crypto functions should run in constant time from the perspective of the low trust side. It should be obvious that cryptographic keys (except the public portion of asymmetric systems) are a critical subset of the things you should not expose to low. Crypto keys are usually both a stepping stone asset and a thing you want to protect asset. See also Chapter 16 on threats to cryptosystems.
- **Handle the unique security demands of your API.** While the preceding issues show up with great consistency, you're hopefully building a new API to deliver new value, and that API may also bring new risks that you should consider. Sometimes it's useful to use the "rogue insider" model to help ask "what could we do wrong with this?"

In addition to the preceding checklist, it may be helpful to look to similar or competitive APIs and see what security changes they've executed, although the security changes may not be documented as such.

Summary

There are a set of tools and techniques that you can use to help threat modeling fit with other development, architecture, or technology deployments. Threat modeling tasks that use these tools happen at the start of a project, as you're working through features, and as you're close to delivery.

Threat modeling should start with the creation of a software diagram (or updating the diagram from the previous release). It should end with a set of security bugs being filed, so that the normal development process picks up and manages those bugs.

When you're creating the diagram, start with the broadest description you can, and add details as appropriate. Work top down, and as you do, at each level of the diagram(s), work across something: trust boundaries, software elements or your threat discovery technique.

As you look to create mitigations, be aware that attackers may try to bypass those mitigations. You want to mitigate the most accessible (aka "first order") threats first, and then mitigate attacks against your mitigations. You have to consider your threats and mitigations not as a static environment, but as a game where the attacker can move pieces, and possibly cheat.

As you go through these analyses, you'll want to track discoveries, including threats, assumptions, and things your customers need to know. Customers here include your customers, who need to understand what your goals and non-goals are, and API callers, who need to understand what security checks you perform, and what checks they need to perform.

There are some scenario-specific call outs: It is important to respect the customer/vendor security boundary; new technologies can and should be threat modeled, especially with respect to all the trust boundaries, not just the customer/vendor one; all APIs have very similar threat models, although there may be new and interesting security properties of your new and interesting API.

CHAPTER

8

Defensive Tactics and Technologies

So far you've learned to model your software using diagrams and learned to find threats using STRIDE, attack trees, and attack libraries. The next step in the threat modeling process is to address every threat you've found.

When it works, the fastest and easiest way to address threats is through technology-level implementations of defensive patterns or features. This chapter covers the standard tactics and technologies that you will use to mitigate threats. These are often operating system or program features that you can configure, activate, apply or otherwise rapidly engage to defend against one or more threats. Sometimes, they involve additional code that is widely available and designed to quickly plug in. (For example, tunneling connections over SSH to add security is widely supported, and some unix packages even have options to make that easier.)

Because you likely found your threats via STRIDE, the bulk of this chapter is organized according to STRIDE. The main part of the chapter addresses STRIDE and privacy threats, because most pattern collections already include information about how to address the threats.

Tactics and Technologies for Mitigating Threats

The mitigation tactics and technologies in this chapter are organized by STRIDE because that's most likely how you found them. This section is therefore organized by ways to mitigate each of the STRIDE threats, each of which includes a brief recap of the threat, tactics that can be brought to bear against it, and the techniques for accomplishing that by people with various skills and responsibilities. For example, if you're a developer who wants to add cryptographic authentication to address spoofing, the techniques you use are different from those used by a systems administrator. Each subsection ends with a list of specific technologies.

Authentication: Mitigating Spoofing

Spoofing threats against code come in a number of forms: faking the program on disk, squatting a port (IP, RPC, etc.), splicing a port, spoofing a remote machine, or faking the program in memory (related problems with libraries and dependencies are covered under tampering); but in general, only programs running at the same or a lower level of trust are spoofable, and you should endeavor to trust only code running at a higher level of trust, such as in the OS.

There is also spoofing of people, of course, a big, complex subject covered in Chapter 14, "Accounts and Identity." Mitigating spoofing threats often requires unusually tight integration between layers of systems. For example, a maintenance engineer from Acme, Inc. might want remote (or even local) access to your database. Is it enough to know that the person is an employee of Acme? Is it enough to know that he or she can initiate a connection from Acme's domain? You might reasonably want to create an account on your database to allow Joe Engineer to log in to it, but how do you bind that to Acme's employee database? When Joe leaves Acme and gets a job at Evil Geniuses for a Better Tomorrow, what causes his access to Acme's database to go away?

NOTE **Authentication and authorization are related concepts, and sometimes confused. Knowing that someone really is Adam Shostack should not authorize a bank to take money from my account (there are several people of that name in the U.S.). Addressing authorization is covered in the Authorization: Mitigating Elevation of Privilege**

From here, let's dig into the specific ways in which you can ensure authentication is done well.

Tactics for Authentication

You can authenticate a remote machine either with or without cryptographic trust mechanisms. Without crypto involves verifying via IP or "classic" DNS entries. All the noncryptographic methods are unreliable. Before they existed, there were attempts to make hostnames reliable, such as the double-reverse DNS lookup. At the time, this was sometimes the best tactic for authentication.

Today, you can do better, and there's rarely an excuse for doing worse. (SNMP may be an excuse, and very small devices may be another). As mentioned earlier, authenticating a person is a complex subject, covered in Chapter 14. Authenticating on-system entities is somewhat operating system dependent.

Whatever the underlying technical mechanisms are, at some point cryptographic keys are being managed to ensure that there's a correspondence between technical names and names people use. That validation cannot be delegated entirely to machines. You can choose to delegate it to one of the many companies that assert they validate these things. These companies often do business as "PKI" or "public key infrastructure" companies, and are often referred to as "certification authorities" or "CAs". You should be careful about relying on that delegation for any transaction valued at more than what the company will accept for liability. (In most cases, certificate authorities limit their liability to nothing). Why you should assign it a higher value is a question their marketing departments hope will not be asked, but the answer roughly boils down to convenience, limited alternatives, and accepted business practice.

Developer Ways to Address Spoofing

Within an operating system, you should aim to use full and canonical path names for libraries, pipes, and so on to help mitigate spoofing. If you are relying on something being protected by the operating system, ensure that the permissions do what you expect. (In particular, unix files in `/tmp` are generally unreliable, and Windows historically has had similarly shared directories.) For networked systems in a single trust domain, using operating system mechanisms such as Active Directory or LDAP makes sense. If the system spans multiple trust domains, you might use persistence or a PKI. If the domains change only rarely, it may be appropriate to manually cross-validate keys, or to use a contract to specify who owns what risks.

You can also use cryptographic ways to address spoofing, and these are covered in Chapter 16, "Threats to Cryptosystems." Essentially, you tie a key to a person, and then work to authenticate that the key is correctly associated with the person who's connecting or authenticating.

Operational Ways to Address Spoofing

Once a system is built, a systems administrator has limited options for improving spoofing defenses. To the extent that the system is internal, pressure can be brought to bear on system developers to improve authentication. It may also be possible to use DNSSEC, SSH, or SSL tunneling to add or improve authentication. Some network providers will filter outbound traffic to make spoofing harder. That's helpful, but you cannot rely on it.

Authentication Technologies

Technologies for authenticating computers (or computer accounts) include the following:

- IPSec
- DNSSEC
- SSH host keys
- Kerberos authentication
- HTTP Digest or Basic authentication
- "Windows authentication" (NTLM)
- PKI systems, such as SSL or TLS with certificates

Technologies for authenticating bits (files, messages, etc.) include the following:

- Digital signatures
- Hashes

Methods for authenticating people can involve any of the following:

- Something you know, such as a password
- Something you have, such as an access card
- Something you are, such as a biometric, including photographs
- Someone you know who can authenticate you

Technologies for maintaining authentication across connections include the following:

- Cookies

Maintaining authentication across connections is a common issue as you integrate systems. The cookie pattern has flaws, but generally, it has fewer flaws than re-authenticating with passwords.

Integrity: Mitigating Tampering

Tampering threats come in several flavors, including tampering with bits on disk, bits on a network, and bits in memory. Of course, no one is limited to tampering with a single bit at a time.

Tactics for Integrity

There are three main ways to address tampering threats: relying on system defenses such as permissions, use of cryptographic mechanisms, and use of logging technology and audit activities as a deterrent.

Permission mechanisms can protect things that are within their scope of control, such as files on disk, data in a database, or paths within a web server. Examples of such permissions include ACLs on Windows, unix file permissions, or `.htaccess` files on a web server.

There are two main cryptographic primitives for integrity: hashes and signatures. A *hash* takes an input of some arbitrary length, and produces a fixed-length digest or hash of the input. Ideally, any change to the input completely transforms the output. If you store a protected hash of a digital object, you can later detect tampering. Actually, anyone with that hash can detect tampering, so, for example, many software projects list a hash of the software on their website. Anyone who gets the bits from any source can rely on them being the bits described on the project website, to a level of security based on the security of the hash and the operation of the web site. A signature is a cryptographic operation with a private key and a hash that does much the same thing. It has the advantage that once someone has obtained the right public key, they can validate a lot of hashes. Hashes can also be used in binary trees of various forms, where large sets of hashes are collected together and signed. This can enable, for example, inserting data into a tree and noting the time in a way that's hard to alter. There are also systems for using hashes and signatures to detect changes to a file system. The first was co-invented by Gene Kim, and later commercialized by Tripwire, Inc. (Kim, 1994).

Logging technology is a weak third in this list. If you log how files change, you may be able to recover from integrity failures.

Implementing Integrity

If you're implementing a permission system, you should ensure that there's a single permissions kernel, also called a *reference monitor*. That reference monitor should be the one place that checks all permissions for everything. This has two main advantages. First, you have a single monitor, so there are no bugs, synchronization failures, or other issues based on which code path called. Second, you only have to fix bugs in one place.

Creating a good reference monitor is a fairly intricate bit of work. It's hard to get right, and easy to get wrong. For example, it's easy to run checks on references (such as symlinks) that can change when the code finally opens the file. If you need to implement a reference monitor, perform a literature review first.

If you're implementing a cryptographic defense, see Chapter 16. If you're implementing an auditing system, you need to ensure it is sufficiently performant that people will leave it on, that security successes and failures are both logged, and that there's a usable way to access the logs. You also need to ensure that the data is protected from attackers. Ideally, this involves moving it off the generating system to an isolated logging system.

Operational Assurance of Integrity

The most important element of assuring integrity is about process, not technology. Mechanisms for ensuring integrity only work to the extent that integrity failures generate operational exceptions or interruptions that are addressed by a person. All the cryptographic signatures in the world only help if someone investigates the failure, or if the user cannot or does not override the message about a failure. You can devote all your disk access operations to running checksums, but if no one investigates the alarms, they won't do any good. Some systems use "whitelists" of applications so only code on the whitelist runs. That reduces risk, but carries an operational cost.

It may be possible to use SSH or SSL tunneling or IPSec to address network tampering issues. Systems like Tripwire, OSSEC, or L5 can help with system integrity.

Integrity Technologies

Technologies for protecting files include:

- ACLs or permissions
- Digital signatures
- Hashes
- Windows Mandatory Integrity Control (MIC) feature
- Unix immutable bits

Technologies for protecting network traffic:

- SSL
- SSH
- IPSec
- Digital signatures

Non-Repudiation: Mitigating Repudiation

Repudiation is a somewhat different threat because it bridges the business realm, in which there are four elements to addressing it: preventing fraudulent transactions, taking note of contested issues, investigating them, and responding to them. In an age when anyone can instantly be a publisher, assuming that you can ignore the possibility of a customer (or noncustomer) complaint or contested charge is foolish. Ensuring you can accept customer complaints and investigate them is outside the scope of this book, but the output from such a system provides a key validation that you have the right logs.

Note that repudiation is sometimes a feature. As Professor Ian Goldberg pointed out when introducing his *Off-the-Record* messaging protocol, signed conversations can be embarrassing, incriminating, or otherwise undesirable (Goldberg, 2008). Two features of the *Off-the-Record* (OTR) messaging system are that it's secure (encrypted and authenticated) and deniable. This duality of feature or threat also comes up in the LINDDUN approach to privacy threat modeling.

Tactics for Non-Repudiation

The technical elements of addressing repudiation are fraud prevention, logs, and cryptography. Fraud prevention is sometimes considered outside the scope of repudiation. It's included here because managing repudiation is easier if you have fewer contested transactions. Fraud prevention can be divided into fraud by internal actors (embezzlement and the like) and external fraud. Internal fraud prevention is a complex matter; for a full treatment see *The Corporate Fraud Handbook* (Wells, 2011). You should have good account management practices, including ensuring that your tools work well enough that people are not tempted or forced to share passwords as part of getting their jobs done. Be sure you log and audit the data in those logs.

Logs are the traditional technical core of addressing repudiation issues. What is logged depends on the transaction, but generally includes signatures or an IP address and all related information. There are also cryptographic ways to address repudiation, which are currently mostly used between larger businesses.

Tactics for Preventing Fraud by External Parties

External fraud prevention can be seen as a matter of payment fraud prevention, and ensuring that your customers remain in control of their account. In both cases, details about the state of the art changes quickly, so talk to your peers. Even the most tight-lipped companies have been willing to have very frank discussions with peers under NDA.

In essence, stability is good. For example, someone who has been buying two romance novels a month from you for a decade and is still living at the same address is likely the person who just ordered another one. If that person suddenly moves to the other side of the world, and orders technical books in Slovakian with a new credit card with a billing address in the Philippines, you might have a problem. (Then again, they might have finally found true love, and you don't want to upset your loyal customers.)

Tools for Preventing Fraud by External Parties

In their annual report on online fraud, CyberSource includes a survey of popular fraud detection tools and their perceived effectiveness (CyberSource, 2013). Their 2013 survey includes a set of automated tools:

- Validation services
- Proprietary data/customer history
- Multi-merchant data
- Purchase device tracing

Validation services include tracking verification numbers (aka CVN/CVV), address verification services, postal address verification, Verified by Visa/MasterCard SecureCode, telephone number verification/reverse lookups, public records services, credit checks, and "out-of-wallet/in-wallet" verification services.

Proprietary data and customer history includes customer order history, in house "negative lists" of problematic customers, "positive lists" of VIP or reliable customers, order velocity monitoring, company-specific fraud models (these are usually built with manual, statistical, or machine learning analyses of past fraudulent orders), and customer website behavioral analysis.

Multi-merchant data focuses on shared negative lists or multi-merchant purchase velocity analyzed by the merchant. (This analysis is nominally also performed by the card processors and clearing houses, so the additional value may be transient.)

Finally, purchase device tracking includes device "fingerprinting" and IP address geolocation. The CyberSource report also discusses the importance of tools to help manual review, and how a varied list is both very helpful and time consuming. Because manual review is one of the most expensive components of an anti-fraud approach to repudiation threats, it may be worth investing in tools to gather all the data into one (or at least fewer) places to improve analyst productivity.

Implementing Non-Repudiation

The two key tools for non-repudiation are logging and digital signatures. Digital signatures are probably most useful for business-to-business systems.

Log as much as you can keep for as long as you need to keep it. As the price of storage continues to fall, this advice becomes easier and easier to follow. For example, with a web transaction, you might log IP address, current geolocation of that address, and browser details. You might also consider services that either provide information on fraud or allow you to request decision advice. To the extent that these companies specialize, and may have broader visibility into fraud, this may be a good area of security to outsource. Some of the information you log or transfer may interact with your privacy policies, and it's important to check.

There are also cryptographic digital signatures. Digital signature should be distinguished from electronic signature, which is a term of art under U.S. law referring to a variety of mechanisms with which to produce a signature, some as minimalistic as "press 1 to agree to these terms and conditions." In contrast, a digital signature is a mathematical transformation that demonstrates irrefutably that someone in possession of a mathematical key took an action to cause a signature to be made. The strength of "irrefutable" here depends on the strength of the math, and the tricky bits are possession of the key and what human intent (if any) may have lain behind the signature.

Operational Assurance of Non-Repudiation

When a customer or partner attempts to repudiate a transaction, someone needs to investigate it. If repudiation attempts are frequent, you may need dedicated people, and those people might require specialized tools.

Non-Repudiation Technologies

Technologies you can use to address repudiation include:

- Logging
- Log analysis tools
- Secured log storage
- Digital signatures
- Secure time stamps
- Trusted third parties
- Hash trees
- As mentioned in "tools for preventing fraud" above

Confidentiality: Mitigating Information Disclosure

Information disclosure can happen with information at rest (in storage) or in motion (over a network). The information disclosed can range from the content of communication to the existence of an entity with which someone is communicating.

Tactics for Confidentiality

Much like with integrity, there are two main ways to prevent information disclosure: Within the confines of a system, you can use ACLs, and outside of it you must use cryptography.

If what must be protected is the content of the communication, then traditional cryptography will be sufficient. If you need to hide who is communicating with whom and how often, you'll need a system that protects that data, such as a cryptographic mix or onion network. If you must hide the fact that communication is taking place at all, steganography will be required.

Implementing Confidentiality

If your system can act as a reference monitor and control all access to the data, you can use a permissions system. Otherwise, you'll need to encrypt either the data or its "container." The data might be a file on disk, a record in a database, or an e-mail message as it transits over the network. The container might be a file system, database, or network channel, such as all e-mail between two systems, or all packets between a web client and a web server.

In each cryptographic case, you have to consider who needs access to the keys for encrypting and decrypting data. For file encryption, that might be as simple as asking the operating system to securely store the key for the user so that the user can get to it later. Also, note that encrypted data is not integrity controlled. The details can be complex and tricky, but consider a database of salaries, where the cells are encrypted. You don't need to know the CEO's salary to know that replacing your salary with it is likely a good thing (for you); and if there's no integrity control, replacing the encrypted value of your salary with the CEO's salary will do just fine.

An important subset of information disclosure cases related to the storage of passwords or backup authentication mechanisms is considered in depth in Chapter 14.

Operational Assurance of Confidentiality

It may be possible to add ACLs to an already developed system, or to use chroot or similar sandboxes to restrict what it can access. On Windows, the addition of a SID to a program and an inherited deny ACL for that SID may help (or it may break things). It is usually possible to add a disk or file encryption layer to protect information at rest from disclosure. Disk crypto will work "by default" with all the usual caveats about how keys are managed. It works for adversarial custody of the machine, but not if the password is written down or otherwise stored with the machine. With regard to a network, it may be possible to use SSH or SSL tunneling or IPSec to address network confidentiality issues.

Confidentiality Technologies

Technologies for confidentiality include:

- Protecting files:
  - ACLs/permissions
  - Encryption
  - Appropriate key management
- Protecting network data:
  - Encryption
  - Appropriate key management
- Protecting communication headers or the fact of communication:
  - Mix networks
  - Onion routing
  - Steganography

NOTE In the preceding lists, "appropriate key management" is not quite a technology, but is so important that it's included.

Availability: Mitigating Denial of Service

Denial-of-service attacks work by exhausting some resource. Traditionally, those resources are CPU, memory (both RAM and hard drive space can be exhausted), and bandwidth. Denial-of-service attacks can also exhaust human availability. Consider trying to call the reservations line of a very exclusive restaurant—the French Laundry in Napa Valley books all its tables within 5 minutes of the phone being open every day (for a day 30 days in the future). The resource under contention is the phone lines, and in particular the people answering them.

Tactics for Availability

There are two forms of denial of service attacks: brute force and clever. Using the restaurant example, brute force involves bringing 100 people to a restaurant that can seat only 25. Clever attacks bring 20 people, each of whom makes an ever-escalating list of requests and changes, and runs the staff ragged. In the online world, brute force attacks on networks are somewhat common under the name DDoS (Distributed Denial of Service). They can also be carried out against CPU (for example, `while(1) fork()`) or disk. It's simple to construct a small zip file that will expand to whatever limit might be in place: the maximum size of a file or space on the file system. Recall that a zip file is structured to describe the contents of the real file as simply as possible, such as 65,535 0s. That three-byte description will expand to 64K, for a magnification effect of over 21,000—which is awfully cool if you're an attacker.

Clever denial-of-service attacks involve a small amount of work by an attacker that causes you to do a lot of work. For example, connecting to an SSL v2 server, the client sends a client master key challenge, which is a random key encrypted such that the server does (relatively) expensive public key operations to decrypt it. The client does very little work compared to the server. This can be partially addressed in a variety of ways, most notably the Photuris key management protocol. The core of such protocols is proof that the client has done more work than the server, and the body of approaches is called *proof of work*. However, in a world of abundant bots and volunteers to run DDoS software for political causes, Ben Laurie and Richard Clayton have shown reasonably conclusively that "Proof-of-Work Proves Not to Work" (in a paper of that name [Laurie]).

A second important strategy for defending against denial-of-service attacks is to ensure your attacker can receive data from you. For example, defenses against SYN flooding attacks now take this form. In a SYN flood attack, a host receives a lot of connection attempts (TCP SYNchronize) and it needs to keep track of each one to set up new connections. By sending a slew of those, operating systems in the 1990s could be run out of memory in the fixed-size buffers allocated to track SYNs, and no new connections could be established. Modern TCP stacks calculate certain parts of their response to a SYN packet using some cryptography. They maintain no state for incoming packets, and use the cryptographic tools to validate that new connections are real (Rescorla, 2003).

Implementing Availability

If you're implementing a system, consider what resources an attacker might consume, and look for ways to limit those resources on a per-user basis. Understand that there are limits to what you can achieve when dealing with systems on the other side of a trust boundary, and some of the response needs to be operational. Ensure that the operators have such mechanisms.

Operational Assurance of Availability

Addressing brute force denial-of-service attacks is simple: Acquire more resources such that they don't run out, or apply limits so that one bad apple can't spoil things for others. For example, multi-user operating systems implement quota systems, and business ISPs may be able to filter traffic coming from certain sources.

Addressing clever attacks is generally in the realm of implementation, not operations.

Availability Technologies

Technologies for protecting files include:

- ACLs
- Filters
- Quotas (rate limiting, thresholding, throttling)
- High-availability design
- Extra bandwidth (rate limiting, throttling)
- Cloud services

Authorization: Mitigating Elevation of Privilege

Elevation of privilege threats are one category of unauthorized use, and the only one addressed in this section. The overall question of designing authorization systems fills other books.

Tactics for Authorization

As discussed in the section "Implementing Integrity," having a reference monitor that can control access between objects is a precursor to avoiding several forms of a problem, including elevation of privilege. Limiting the attack surface makes the problem more tractable. For example, limiting the number of `setuid` programs limits the opportunity for a local user to become root. (Technically, programs can be `setuid` to something other than root, but generally those other accounts are also privileged.) Each program should do a small number of things, and carefully manage their input, including user input, environment, and so on. Each should be sandboxed to the extent that the system supports it. Ensure that you have layers of defense, such that an anonymous Internet user can't elevate to administrator with a single bug. You can do this by having the code that listens on the network run as a limited user. An attacker who exploits a bug will not have complete run of the system. (If they're a normal user, they may well have easy access to many elevation paths, so lock down the account.)

The permission system needs to be comprehensible, both to administrators trying to check things and to people trying to set things. A permission system that's hard to use often results in people incorrectly setting permissions, (technically) enabling actions that policy and intent mean to forbid.

Implementing Authorization

Having limited the attack surface, you'll need to very carefully manage the input you accept at each point on the attack surface. Ensure that you know what you want to accept and how you're going to use that input. Reject anything that doesn't match, rather than trying to make a complete list of bad characters. Also, if you get a non-match, reject it, rather than try to clean it up.

Operational Assurance of Authorization

Operational details, such as "we need to expose this to the Internet" can often lead to those deploying technology wanting to improve their defensive stance. This usually involves adding what can be referred to as *defense in depth* or *layered defense*. There are several ways to do this.

First, run as a normal or limited user, not as administrator/root. While technically that's not a mitigation against an elevation-of-privilege threat, but a harbinger of such, it's inline with the "principle of least privilege." Each program should run as its own limited user. When unix made "nobody" the default account for services, the nobody account ended up with tremendous levels of authorization. Second, apply all the sandboxing you can.

Authorization Technologies

Technologies for improving authorization include:

- ACLs
- Group or role membership
- Role based access control
- Claims-based access control
- Windows privileges (runas)
- Unix sudo
- Chroot, AppArmor or other unix sandboxes
- The "MOICE" Windows sandbox pattern
- Input validation for a defined purpose

NOTE **MOICE is the "Microsoft Office Isolated Conversion Environment." The name comes from the problem that led to the pattern being invented, but the approach can now be considered a pattern for sandboxing on Windows. For more on MOICE, see (LeBlanc, 2007).**

NOTE Many Windows privileges are functionally equivalent to administrator, and may not be as helpful as you desire. See (Margosis, 2006) for more details.

Tactic and Technology Traps

There are two places where it's easy to get pulled into wasting time when working through these technologies and tactics. The first distraction is risk management. The tactics and technologies in this chapter aren't the only ways to address threats, but they are the best place to start. When you can use them, they will be easier to implement and work better than more complex or nuanced risk management approaches. For example, if you can address a threat by changing a network endpoint to a local endpoint, there's no point to engaging in the more time consuming risk management approaches covered in the next chapter. The second distraction is trying to categorize threats. If you found a threat via brainstorming or just the free flow of ideas, don't let the organization of this chapter fool you into thinking you should try to categorize that threat. Instead, focus on finding the best way to address it. (Teams can spend longer in debate around categorization than it would take to implement the fix they identified—changing permissions on a file.)

Addressing Threats with Patterns

In his book, *A Pattern Language*, architect Christopher Alexander and his colleagues introduced the concept of architectural patterns (Alexander, 1977). A *pattern* is a way of expressing how experts capture ways of solving recurring problems. Patterns have since been adapted to software. There are well-understood development patterns, such as the three-tier enterprise app.

Security patterns seem like a natural way to group and communicate about tactics and technologies to address security problems into something larger. You can create and distribute patterns in a variety of ways, and this section discusses some of them. However, in practice, these patterns have not been popular. The reasons for this are not clear, and those investing in using patterns to address security problems would likely benefit from studying the factors that have limited their popularity.

Some of those factors might include engineers not knowing when to reach for such a text, or the presentation of security patterns as a distinct subset, apart from other patterns. At least one web patterns book (Van Duyne, 2007) includes a chapter on security patterns. Embedding security patterns where non-specialists are likely to find them seems like a good pattern.

Standard Deployments

In many larger organizations, an operations group will have a standard way to deploy systems, or possibly several standard ways, depending on the data's sensitivity. In these cases, the operations group can document what sorts of threats their standard deployment mitigates, and provide that document as part of their "on-boarding" process. For example, a standard data center at an organization might include defenses against DDoS, or state that "network information disclosure is an accepted risk for risk categories 1–3."

Addressing CAPEC Threats

CAPEC (MITRE's Common Attack Pattern Enumeration and Classification) is primarily a collection of attack patterns, but most CAPEC threat patterns include defenses. This chapter has primarily organized threats according to STRIDE. If you are using CAPEC, each CAPEC pattern includes advice about how to address it in its "Solutions and Mitigations" section. The CAPEC website is the authoritative source for such data.

Mitigating Privacy Threats

There are essentially three ways to address privacy threats: Avoid collecting information (minimization), use crypto in various clever ways, and control how data is used (compliance and policy). Cryptography is a technology, while minimization and compliance are more tactics you can apply. Each requires effort to integrate into your design or implementation.

Minimization

Perhaps obviously, it is impossible to use information you don't have in a way that impacts someone's privacy. Therefore, minimizing your collection and retention of information reduces risk. Minimizing what you collect is by far more reliable than attempting to use policy controls on the data. Of course, it also eliminates any utility that you can get from that data. As such, minimization is generally a business call regarding risk and reward. Over the past decade, with breach disclosure laws, the balance of factors related to decisions about the collection and retention of information have changed dramatically. Some legal scholars have gone so far as to compare personal data to toxic waste. Holly

Towle, an attorney specializing in electronic commerce, offers 10 principles for handling toxic waste, or personally identifying information (PII). Each of these is addressed in depth in her article (Towle, 2009):

- Do not touch it unless you have to.
- If you have to touch it, learn how or whether to do so—mistakes can be fatal or at least seriously damaging.
- Do not use normal methods to transport (transfer) it.
- Attempt to crack the whip over contractor handling it.
- Do not store some of it at all.
- Store what you need but in a manner avoiding spills, and limit access.
- Be alert for suspicious odors and other red flags.
- Report spills to the relevant people and agencies.
- Dispose of it only by special means.
- Get ready to be sued or incur often unreasonable expenses no matter how much care you take.

Minimization is a conceptually simple way to address privacy. In practice, however, it can become complex and contentious. The value of collecting data is easy to see, and it's hard to know what you'll be unable to do if you don't collect it.

Cryptography

There are a variety of ways to use cryptographic techniques to address privacy concerns. The applicability of each is dependent on the threat model, in the sense of who you're worried about. Each of these techniques is the subject of a great deal of research, so rather than try to provide a full description of each technique and risk leaving out key details, the following sections explain where each is useful as a response to a threat.

Hashing or Encrypting Data

If your privacy concern is someone accidentally viewing data, or running simple database queries, it may help to encrypt the data. If you want a record that can only be accessed once someone has a specific string (such as an e-mail address or SSN), you can use a cryptographic hash of that data. For example, if you store `hash(adam.shostack@example.com)`, then only someone who knows that e-mail address can look it up.

WARNING **Simple hashing doesn't protect your data if the attacker is willing to build a "dictionary" and hash each term in the dictionary. For SSNs, that's only a billion hashes to run, which is cheap on modern hardware. Hashing is therefore not the right defense if your data is low entropy, either because the data is short strings, or because it's highly structured. In those cases, you'll likely want to encrypt, and use a unique key and initialization vector per plaintext.**

Split-Key Systems

Splitting keys is useful when you're concerned about the threat of someone decrypting the data without authorization. It's possible to encrypt data with multiple keys, such that all or some fraction of the keys is needed to decrypt it. For example, if you store `m = ` e_{k1}`(`e_{k2}`(plaintext))`, then to decrypt `m`, you need the party that holds `k1` to decrypt the `m`, then send that to whomever holds `k2`.

If you're worried about availability threats, there are split-key cryptographic systems for which the keys are mathematically related, and you only need `k-of-n` keys to get the plaintext out of the system. Such systems encrypt the data with `n` keys. Those `n` keys are mathematically related in ways which allow any `k` of the `n` keys to decrypt the data. These are useful, for example, for backing up the master key to a system where that master key may be needed a decade later. Such a system is used to backup the root keys for DNSSEC.

Private Information Retrieval

If the threat is a database owner watching a client's queries and learning from them, then a set of techniques called *private information retrieval* may be useful. Private information retrieval techniques are generally fairly bandwidth intensive, as they often retrieve far more information than is desired to get at the data without revealing anything to the database owner.

Differential Privacy

When the threat is a database client running multiple queries to violate the database owner's privacy policies, *differential privacy* provides the database owner with a way to first measure how much information has been given out, and then stop answering queries that provide additional information. This does not mean that the database needs to stop answering queries. Many queries will not change, or differentiate, the amount of information that can be inferred, even after the database has reached a specified privacy limit.

NOTE Differential privacy offers very strong protection for a very specific definition of privacy.

Mixes and Mix-Like Systems

A *mix* is a system for preventing traffic analysis and providing untracability to message senders or recipients. That is, an observer should not be able to trace a message back to a person after it has been through a mix. Mixes work by maintaining a pool of messages, and now and then sending messages out. To avoid trusting a single mix, there may be a network of mixes operated by different parties.

There are two major modes in which mixes operate: interactive-time and batch. Interactive-time mixes can be used for scenarios like web browsing, but are less secure against traffic analysis. There are also interactive systems that do not mix traffic but aim to conceal its source and destination. Such interactive systems include Tor.

Blinding

Blinding helps defend against surveillance threats that use cryptographic keys as identifiers. For example, if Alice is worried that a certificate authority might track her vote, then she might want a voting registration system that can do deep checking to ensure that she is authorized to vote, providing her with an anonymous voting chit that can be used to prove her right to vote. Online, this can be done through the use of blinding.

Blinding is a cool math trick that can solve real problems. The math may look a little intimidating, but you can understand it with high school algebra. Think of signing as doing exponentiation modulo p. (Modulo is a remainder—1 mod 12 is 1, 14 mod 12 is 2, where 14 mod 10 is 4. The modulo math is needed for certain security properties.) Therefore if s is the signature, a is Alice's key, and c is the CA's key, then a signature is $s = a^c \mod p$. Normally, the CA calculates the signature, and sends s back to Alice. Now the CA knows s, and can use that knowledge. So how can the CA calculate s without knowing it? Because multiplication is commutative, the CA can calculate something related to s. Blinding works by Alice multiplying her key by some blinding factor (b) before sending the product of that multiplication (ab) to the CA. The CA then calculates $s = (ab)c \mod p$, and sends s to Alice. Alice then divides s by b, and $s/b = ac$. So Alice now knows s/b, which appears for all the world like a signature on a, but the CA doesn't know that a is associated with Alice. The math shown here is a subset of what's needed to do this securely, with the goal of giving you an idea of how it works. Proper blinding requires that you deal with a plethora of mathematical threats, which are covered in a book such as (Ferguson, 2012).

Compliance and Policy

To the extent that a business decision has been made to gather and store sensitive information about people, the organization needs to put controls around it. Those controls can either be policy or technical, and they can meet either your business need or regulatory needs, or both. These approaches are not as crisp as the tools and tactics you can apply to security problems, and to the extent that you can apply minimization or cryptography to privacy problems, it will be easier and more effective.

Policies

The first class of controls are organizational policies that specify who can do what with the information. From the technologist's perspective, these can be frustratingly vague statements, such as "only authorized people will be allowed access." However, they are an important first step in setting requirements. From a statement like that you can derive a technical approach, such as "only a security group can access the data." Then you'll need to ensure that that policy is enforced across a variety of information systems, and then you're at the level of tactics and technologies.

Regulatory Requirements

Personal data is subject to a long and complex list of privacy rules that differ from jurisdiction to jurisdiction. As with everything else covered in this book, this section on mitigating privacy threats is not intended to replace proper legal advice.

There's one other thing to be said about mitigating privacy threats to your organization. In many cases, organizations are required by law to collect and protect a set of information that they must treat as toxic waste, at great expense. It makes a great deal of privacy sense for organizations and their industry groups to argue against requirements to gather such data. That includes rolling back existing mandates and holding firm against new mandates to collect data that you'd prefer not to hold.

Summary

The best way to address threats is to use standard, well-tested features or products that add security against the threats you've identified. These tactics and technologies are available to address each of the STRIDE threats. There are tactics and technologies available to both developers and operations.

Authentication technologies mitigate spoofing threats. You can authenticate computers, bits, or people. Integrity technologies mitigate tampering threats. Generally, you want integrity protection for files and network connections. Non-repudiation technologies mitigate repudiation, which can include fraud and other repudiations. Anti-fraud technologies include validation services, or use of customer history that's either local or shared by others. There are also a variety of cryptographic and operational measures you can take to increase assurance around your logs. Information disclosure threats are addressed by confidentiality technologies. Those can be most easily applied to files or network connections; however, it can also be important to protect container data, such as filenames or the fact of communication. Preventing denial of service involves ensuring that code doesn't have arbitrary limits that prevent it from taking advantage of all the available resources. Preventing elevation of privilege generally works by first ensuring that the code is constrained by mechanisms such as ACLs, and then by more complex sandboxes.

Patterns are collections of tactics and technologies. They seem like a natural approach. For reasons which are unclear, they haven't really taken off, and those who are considering using them would be advised to understand why.

Mitigating privacy threats is best done by minimizing what you collect, and then applying cryptography; however, there are limits to the tactics and technologies available, and sometimes you must fall back to compliance tools or policy.

The issue of standard tactics and technologies not being applicable everywhere is not limited to privacy. In the next chapter, you'll learn about making structured tradeoffs between ways to address threats.

CHAPTER

9

Trade-Offs When Addressing Threats

After you create a list of threats, you should consider whether standard approaches will work. It is often faster to do so than to assess the risk trade-offs and the variety of ways you might deal with the problem. Of course, it's helpful to understand that there are ways to manage risks other than the tactics and technologies you learned about in Chapter 8, "Defensive Tactics and Technologies," and those more complex approaches are the subject of this chapter.

For each threat in your list, you need to make one or more decisions. The first decision is your strategy: Should you accept the risk, address it, avoid it, or transfer it? If you're going to address it, you must next decide when, and then how? There are a variety of ways to think about when to address the threat. Table 9-1 provides an example to make these choices appear more concrete and to help separate them:

Table 9-1: Sample Risk Approach Tracking Table

ITEM #	THREAT	WHY NOT USE STANDARD MITIGATION?	STRATEGY	APPROACH
1	Physical tampering	We don't own the hardware.	Accept	Document on website

This may seem like a lot of things to do for every threat, but the first approach to fixing most issues is to try to apply standard mitigations, and only look for an alternative when that fails.

This chapter first teaches you about risk management, in the sense of avoiding, addressing, accepting, or transferring risks. You'll learn how to apply risk management to software design. From there, you'll learn about a variety of threat-specific prioritization approaches, ranging from the simple to the complex. The chapter also covers risk acceptance, and closes with a brief discussion of arms races in mitigation strategies.

Classic Strategies for Risk Management

As you consider each threat, you should make three decisions. Logically, these can be ordered as follows:

1. What's the level of risk?
2. What do you want to do to address that risk?
3. How are you going to achieve that?

Strategizing in this manner can be expensive. Therefore, when there is an easy way to address a problem, you should skip strategizing and just address it. Not only is it easier, it avoids the possibility that your risk management approach will lead you astray.

When you do find it necessary to strategize, a few classic strategies exist for addressing risks: You can avoid them, address them, accept them, or transfer them. You can also ignore risks, but that option is not ignored in this section.

Avoiding Risks

Avoiding risks is a great approach to the extent that you can do so. A good risk assessment can help you determine whether a risk is greater than the potential reward. If it is, then the risk may be worth avoiding. As the saying goes, "a ship in the harbor is safe, but that is not what ships are for." So how do you avoid a risk? You don't build the feature, or you change the design sufficiently that the risk disappears.

Addressing Risks

Addressing risks is also a perfectly valid approach. The main ways you do so are via design changes (such as adding cryptography) or operational processes. Design and operational changes were covered in Chapter 8.

Accepting Risks

You can choose to accept a risk by deciding to accept all the costs of things going wrong. This is easier when you're operating a service than when you're building a product. You can't accept risk on behalf of your users or customers—if there's risk that affects them, that risk is transferred.

Sometimes a threat is real but the probability is very low, or the impact is minor. In these situations, it's probably reasonable to accept the risk. Before doing so, it may be helpful to reassess both the probability and the impact, asking whether there are any factors that would change either (e.g., "do not use Panexa while pregnant or when you might become pregnant"). It can also be illuminating to ask whether you would accept the risk for yourself, if you couldn't hand it to customers or others. Note that the word "illuminating" is used, rather than "useful."

Risk acceptance differs from "ignore it" or "wait and see" (see the sections on each later in this chapter) insofar as it entails accepting that certain things are real risks. For example, Microsoft treats threats that involve unconstrained access to hardware as non-threats (Culp, 2013), and is explicit about the risk acceptance and the rationale behind that decision.

Transferring Risks

Risks that fall on your customers or end users are transferred risks. Many products bundle some level of risk with them, and use some combination of terms of service, licensing agreements, or user interface to transfer the risk. You should clearly disclose such risks.

Ignoring Risks

A traditional approach to risk in information security is to ignore it. Approaches to measuring risk have been hampered by an orientation towards secrecy and obscurity. Historically, both the occurrence of each breach and impact information has been generally kept secret. As a result, calculating frequency and making predictions have been hard, and a de facto strategy of ignoring risks emerged. From an executive standpoint, this strategy was highly effective, if frustrating for security staff.

This approach is becoming less effective as a combination of contracts, lawsuits, and laws increase the risk of ignoring risks. In particular, a variety of new American laws make ignoring information security risks more risky. They include breach disclosure laws, general information security laws, sectorial information security laws, and Federal law for public companies. Breach disclosure laws usually do not (directly) regulate information security, but require disclosure when it fails. Some states now have general security laws that apply to any storage of certain types of personal information. Outside of the U.S., there may also be requirements to disclose security breaches, especially those that involve a loss of control of personal information, or in certain sectors (such as telecommunications in Europe). The overall regulatory situation around security risks is also rapidly evolving, and disclosures are helping security professionals learn from each other's mistakes, and focus attention on important issues.

Finally, if you are threat modeling and create a list of security problems that you decide not to address, please send a copy of the list to the author, care of the publisher. There will be quarterly auctions to sell them to plaintiff's attorneys (or other interested parties). Even if you don't send them to me, they may be revealed by whistleblowers, accidentally shared or disclosed, or discovered as part of a legal action. All in all, it seems that "ignore it" is a riskier proposition than it has been before.

Selecting Mitigations for Risk Management

There are many ways to select mitigations. The following sections describe how to integrate risk management into your decisions about how to mitigate threats. The ways to mitigate cover a spectrum, with risk increasing as you move from changing the design through standard tactics and technologies to designing your own.

Changing the Design

The first way to address risks in a design is to eliminate the features to eliminate the risks. For example, if you have payroll software that is accessible to the entire Internet without authentication, then changing the design so that it's only available on your corporate intranet will reduce the risk. This aligns with the risk-avoidance approach. Unfortunately, carried to its logical conclusion, this leaves you with software that doesn't do anything at all. While that has a Zen simplicity to it, Zen simplicity is usually not a requirement; features are.

This brings you to the second way to address risks: Change the design by adding features that reduce risks. For example, you can redesign the software to add authentication and authorization features.

There are two ways to think about changing designs: *iterative* and *comparative*. Iterative means altering a small number of components, with each change intended to reduce the number of components or trust boundaries or otherwise eliminate some threats. The comparative method means coming up with two or more designs, and then comparing them. This would appear to be more expensive, and in the short term it is. However, it is common for iterative design to involve many iterations, so often it is more cost-effective (especially in the early days) to consider several designs and choose between them.

For an example of how one might change a design, consider Figure 9-1, which depicts a threat model for sending single-use login tokens to phones. (These tokens are often called *one time tokens*, abbreviated OTT.) There are many advantages to this type of authentication, including the capability to deploy to all sorts of phones, including voice-only phones, "dumb" mobile phones, and smartphones. The downside is a plethora of places where that token is subject to information disclosure.

Those places include the varied systems responsible for mobile phone roaming and the "femtocell" base stations that telephone companies distribute. They also include things such as Google Voice or iMessage, which put text messages onto the Internet in various ways. (These products are mentioned only as examples, rather than a comment on their security.)

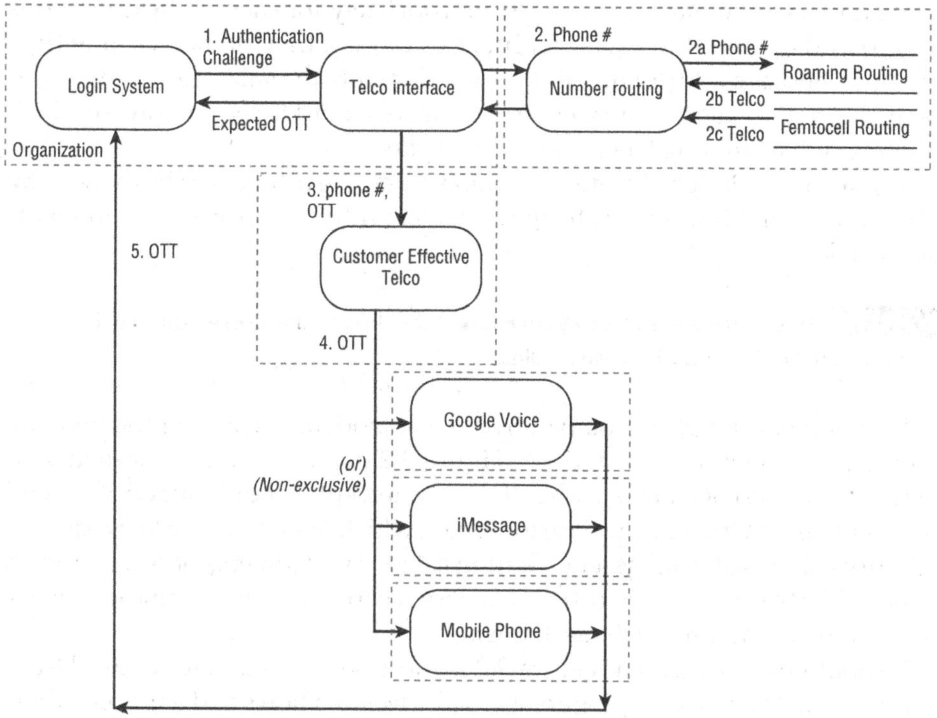

Figure 9-1: An OTT threat model

There's a variety of ways to change the design and address the information disclosure threats that apply to Figure 9-1. Simplified versions of ways to address these threats follow. In each, m_1 is a message from the server to the client, while m_2 is a response.

- Send a nonce, encrypted to a key held on a smartphone, and then send the decrypted nonce to the authentication server. The server checks that the $nonce_n$ is the one that it encrypted for the phone, and if it is, approves the transaction. ($m_1 = e_{phone}(nonce_n)$, $m_2 = nonce_n$).
- Send a nonce to the smartphone, and then send a signed version of the nonce to the server. The server validates that the signature on the $nonce_{phone}$ is from the expected phone, and that it is a good signature on the expected nonce. If both checks pass, then the server approves the transaction. ($m_1 = nonce_{phone}$, $m_2 = sign_{phone}(nonce_{phone})$).
- Send a nonce to the smartphone. The smartphone hashes the nonce with a secret value it shares with the server, and then sends that hash back. $m_1 = nonce_{phone}$, $m_2 = hash_{phone}(nonce_{phone})$).

It's important to manage the keys appropriately for each of these methods and to understand these are simplified examples; they do not include time stamps, message addressing, and other elements to make the system fully secure. Including those in this discussion makes it hard to see the ways in which cryptographic building blocks could be applied.

The key in all design changes is to understand the differences introduced by the changes, and how those changes interact with the software requirements as a whole.

NOTE This model and some ways to address the threats, are worked through in more detail in Appendix E, "Case Studies."

For another example of comparative threat modeling, consider the two systems shown in Figures 9-2 and 9-3. Figure 9-2 depicts an e-mail system, and Figure 9-3 is a version of 9-2 with a "lawful intercept" module added. ("Lawful intercept" is an Orwellian phrase for "thing which allows people to bypass the security features of your system." Setting aside any arguments of "should we as a society have such a mechanism?" it's possible to assess the technical security implications of adding such mechanisms.)

It should be obvious that Figure 9-2 is more secure than Figure 9-3. Using software-centric modeling, Figure 9-3 adds two data flows and a process; thus, by STRIDE-per-element, it has an additional 12 threats (tampering, information disclosure, DoS with each flow, for 6; and the six S,T,R, I, D, and E threats against the process for a total of 12). Additionally, Figure 9-3 has two apparent groupings of elevation-of-privilege threats: those posed by outsiders and those posed by software-allowed, but human-policy-violating, use. Thus, if Figure 9-2 has a list of threats (1...*n*), then Figure 9-3 has a list of threats (1...*n*+14).

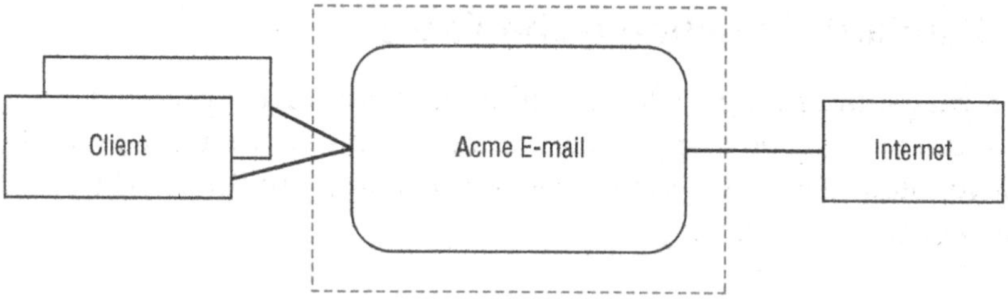

Figure 9-2: An e-mail system

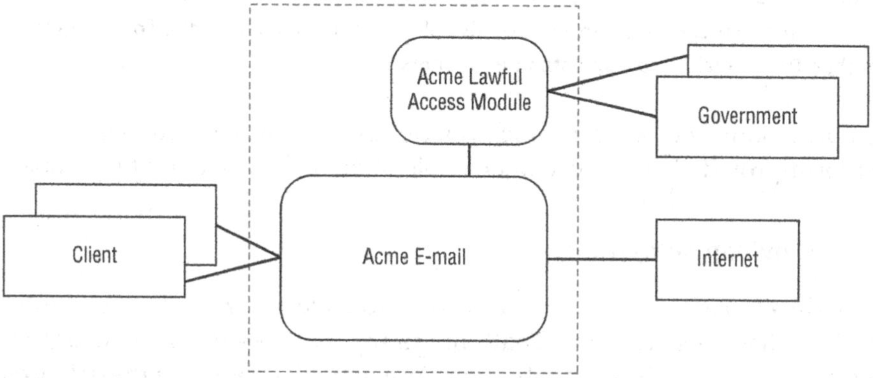

Figure 9-3: The same e-mail system with a lawful access module

If instead of software-centric modeling you use attacker-centered modeling on the systems shown in Figures 9-2 and 9-3, you find two sets of threats: First, each law enforcement agency that is authorized to connect adds its employees and IT systems as possible threats, and possible threat vectors. Second, attackers are likely to attack these features of the system to abuse them. The 2010 "Aurora" attacks on Google and others allegedly did exactly this (McMillan, 2010, and Adida, 2013). Thus, by comparing them you can see that the addition of these features creates additional risk. You might also wonder where those risks fall, but that's outside the scope of this example.

More subtly, the addition of the code in Figure 9-3 is an obvious source of security vulnerabilities. As such, it may draw attention and possibly effort away from the rest of the system. Thus, the components that comprise Figure 9-2 are likely to be less secure, even ignoring the threats to the additional components. In the same vein, the requests and implementations for such back-doors may be confidential or classified. If that's the case, the features may not go through normal tracking for implementation, testing, or review, again reducing the odds that they are secure. Of course, because such a system is designed to bypass other security controls, any weaknesses are likely to have outsized impact.

Applying Standard Mitigation Technologies

To the extent that standard approaches will effectively solve a problem, they should be used. Devising new approaches to defense is very simple and lots of fun. Unfortunately, devising *effective* new approaches, building, and testing them can be very time consuming.

NOTE To be fair, testing newly devised mitigation approaches can actually be super-quick sometimes, as the new defense will fall with just a few minutes of expert scrutiny. PGP creator Phil Zimmermann tells the story of bringing the cipher he created for the first version of his popular encryption software to a large gathering of cryptographers, where he saw months of his painstaking work demolished over lunch. After that, PGP switched to using standard ciphers.

There are a number of ways in which you can use standard mitigations, including platform-provided ones, developer-implemented ones, or operational ones.

Platform-Provided Mitigations

Software developers have a number of ways to code mitigations to common threats. Each has pros and cons. That's not to say that they're all equal, or that any one has advantages in every situation. As a general rule, using the defenses in whatever platform you're building on is a good idea for several reasons: First, they often run at a higher trust level than defenses you can build. Second, they're generally well designed and subjected to a high level of scrutiny before you get to them. Related to that, they're often more intensively tested than what you can justify. Finally, they're usually either free or included in the price of the platform.

Developer-Implemented Mitigations

There is an entire set of mitigations that are not platform provided, and must be implemented by developers. Almost all of these can be seen as feature development work: Implement a cryptographic scheme to address a spoofing threat; implement a better logging system to address a repudiation threat, and so on.

An interesting and growing set of software is built and operated by the same organization. This creates an additional class of defensive opportunities that you can design. This class focuses on attack detection, whereby attempts to execute injection or overflow attacks can be found and repaired. With the right investment in detection and response capabilities, this allows some deferment of security costs to find and fix those bugs. Doing so requires developing the features to detect such attacks. It also increases the importance of information disclosure attacks, which disclose your source (or binary) to an attacker, possibly enabling them to develop a reliable exploit without triggering your attack detection.

Operational Mitigations

Systems administrators should consider a number of trade-offs in terms of policy, procedural, and software defenses. To the extent that software defenses are available, they will scale better and be more reliable than process-oriented controls. Operationally, process-oriented controls provide defense against a broader swath of issues. In particular, effective change control helps manage a wide variety of issues. A firewall to control issues at the network or edge is easier to manage and maintain. However, at the machine level, there is less doubt about what a packet means (Ptacek, 1998). Highly targeted defensive programs are often technically superior to more general ones, but they are less well-integrated into operations, which may mean that they are less effective overall. Many classes of mitigations that have become commercial standards are "arms race" technology.

For example, a signature-based anti-virus program is only as good as its last update. In contrast, a firewall will block packets according to its rules. Some firewalls were implemented as packet filters, and can be fooled, but others implemented connection proxying (meaning the connection terminates at the firewall, and code on the firewall makes an additional connection to the target system). Those firewalls don't engage in a meaningful arms race, although some of them include signature-driven intrusion detection or prevention code, and that code requires regular updating. (Arms races are so much "fun" that they get their own section, towards the end of this chapter.)

It is valuable for developers to understand the system administrator's perspective on defenses, and vice versa. This is especially true of standard mitigations, where you can rely on a body of knowledge, analogies, and other facets of the mitigation being a standard approach to make it easier to operate. Developing a defensive system that no one can operate is about as bad as developing one that doesn't work. The ultimate goal of deploying operational technology that meets business needs requires developers and system administrators to understand the limits of available defenses. The example defenses shown in Table 9-2 are for the Acme SQL Database introduced previously in the book.

Table 9-2: Defenses by Who Can Implement Them

THREAT	INSTANCES THAT DEVELOPERS MUST IMPLEMENT	INSTANCES THAT IT DEPARTMENTS MUST IMPLEMENT
Spoofing	Web/SQL/other client brute-forcing logins Authentication for DBA (human), DB users	Authentication infrastructure for: web client, SQL client DBA (human), DB users
Tampering	Integrity protection for Data, Management, Logs	Integrity protection for front end(s), Database admin
Repudiation	Logs (log analysis must be protected) Certain actions from web and SQL clients will need careful logging. Certain actions from DBAs will need careful logging.	Logs (log analysis must be protected) If DBAs are not fully trusted, a system in another privilege domain to log all commands might be required.
Information Disclosure	Data, management, and logs must be protected. Front ends must implement access control. Only the front ends should be able to access the data.	ACLs and security groups must be managed. Backups must be protected.
Denial of Service	Front ends must be designed to minimize DoS risks	The system must be deployed with sufficient resources.
Elevation of Privilege	Trusting client DB should support prepared statements to make injection harder. There should be no default way to run commands on the server, and calls like `exec()` or `system()` must be permissioned and configurable if they exist.	Avoiding improperly trusting clients which were written locally. Configure DB appropriately.

Designing a Custom Mitigation

As explained earlier, custom approaches are risky and expensive to verify, but sometimes you have no choice. Aspects of your design or implementation could prevent all the standard approaches. For example, if you're implementing a low-cost device with an eight-bit processor, it's probably not going to be able to use 2,048-bit RSA keys at acceptable speeds. At that point, you need to consider what you can do.

Because the defense will be custom, there are fewer specifics to talk about. However, some general guidelines apply. Ensure that you have a clearly written definition of the goal of the custom system, along with the constraints you're operating under. Consider what will happen when it breaks, and in particular what you'll do to update it.

Custom mitigations differ from non-security code in a very important way: It's hard to see that they're ineffective. The mistakes made by inexperienced database designers are easy to see; problems like performance will crop up relatively quickly and obviously. With security mitigations, it's easier to be fooled.

When you're designing a custom approach to mitigation, it's worthwhile to take a couple of unusual steps early in the process. The first is to share your motivation and design. You may well get useful feedback on it. You'll get more useful feedback if you make the design public (rather than requiring an NDA), and/or if you pay for feedback, perhaps by hiring experts to break it or by offering a prize to anyone who can break it.

WARNING **Be careful to explain what you did separately from why you think those defenses make it hard to break; the interleaving can inhibit the free flow of ideas in the same way that criticism can shut down a brainstorming session.**

Fuzzing Is Not a Mitigation

Oftentimes, to address a variety of threats, people will say "we'll fuzz that!" *Fuzzing* is the technique of generating random input for a program, and it is stunningly effective at finding bugs in code that's never been fuzzed. This is especially true of parsers. However, fuzzing is not a way of mitigating threats; it's a way of testing mitigations. Fuzzing will not make your code secure, it will help you find bugs, and as those bugs are fixed, the average time to find the next bug using random input goes up. However, the time for a clever human to find that next bug does not change. Therefore, over time, fuzzing becomes less effective. When you are tempted to fuzz, you should ensure it's in your test plan, but at design time you need to take other actions.

You can do several things to make parsers more secure at design/code time. The first is to design your file format or network protocol for safe parsing (Sassaman, 2013). If the format is not Turing complete, parsing it is easier. If it doesn't contain macros, loops, multiple ways to encode things, or the capability to encapsulate layers of encoding, your parser can be a lot simpler, and thus safer. The next thing you can do to make parsers safer is to use a safer language than the C family. C's lack of type safety and primitive, unsafe string handling functions make safe coding of parsers hard. If the thing being parsed is already defined and you can't redefine it (say, HTML), it may help to create a state machine for your parser. You may, quite appropriately, be laughing at the idea of creating a state machine for HTML. Well, if you can't describe it, good luck with making a safe parser for it. Finally, if there's a canonicalization step, canonicalize early, and run the input through it until the output matches the input.

Threat-Specific Prioritization Approaches

This section is all about risks you're going to address (rather than avoid, accept, or transfer). For the problems you decide to address, you have choices to make about how to approach those risks. Those choices include simply waiting and seeing whether the risks materialize or fixing the easy stuff first, using threat-ranking techniques of various sorts, or using some approach to estimate the cost of the problem.

Simple Approaches

The very simplest approaches to threat prioritization don't involve any math or calculation. They are "wait and see" and "do the easy fixes first."

Wait and See

The wait and see approach to security issues sometimes works pretty well, and often fails catastrophically. It can differ from "ignore it" when the system in question is either an internal network or a service offering that can be monitored for problems. Wait and see is a worse technique for, say, a gas tank, than it is for a website. It can also be an example of what 451 Group analyst Wendy Nather calls "the cheeseburger case": "Doc, I'm gonna keep eating cheeseburgers until I have a heart attack. Then we'll deal with it" (Nather, 2013). The cheeseburger case is less about accepting risks, but more about ignoring those risks—and doing nothing to mitigate them until a catastrophe forces you to pay attention. Most businesses have long used monitoring as a part of their risk management strategy. For example, if a bank notices that one of its employees suddenly has a flashy car, someone is likely to question where the money came from. Monitoring, the "see" part of "wait and see," needs to be planned effectively. There are four main types of monitoring: change detection, signature attack detection, anomaly attack detection, and impact detection.

NOTE Related to the cheeseburger approach in risk management is the ostrich approach of sticking ones head in the sand. Of course, your colleagues don't really stick their heads in the sand, they say "no one would ever do that!" The best response to this is to say "if I can give you an example where someone did that, will you agree to fix it?" (This is another place where the repertoire that people develop en route to becoming an expert can come in very handy.)

Change Detection

Change detection focuses on the operational discipline of ensuring that change is managed. To the extent that changes are managed, anything outside the change management process must be treated as a problem. (Kim, 2006)

Signature Attack Detection

Signature attack detection is based on the idea that an interesting subset of attacks has certain definable signatures, either sequences of bytes or messages that will appear only in an attack. With the rise of production-quality exploit software, this signature-oriented approach appeared promising. However, as the products to detect signatures proliferated, the attack tools added polymorphism, and simple signature detection is less effective than its proponents had hoped.

Anomaly Attack Detection

Anomaly attack detection is based on the idea that there's a normal and unchanging set of network traffic. This is a pipe dream. As business changes, the normal traffic changes; and when it does, the anomaly detector needs to be retrained about what's normal. As business accelerates and change accelerates, it becomes increasingly difficult to continue training the system so that it knows what's normal. There are also normal abnormalities (for example, every Friday evening, there's an audit run, and every close of quarter there's another one). It may be possible to use people to investigate every anomaly, although the cost of doing so rises very quickly.

Impact Detection

The final major form of detection is impact detection. If suddenly the shipped product count for the quarter is out of whack with your accounts receivable, there's a problem. (A friend once did a penetration test in which he ordered minus three copies of a book. The system credited his credit card the cost of the three books, minus shipping, and a week later he got the three books in the mail. When the merchant was told what happened, it turned out that the shipping clerk had seen the negative three copies, figured it was a bug, and sent the three copies.)

Generally, mature operations use some combination of all the techniques—change detection, signature attack detection, anomaly attack detection, and impact detection. The precise combination that will work for a given organization's threat profile, risk acceptance, culture, regulatory environment, and so on, are specific to that organization. Wait and see is less valid in (at least) three cases. First, when there's a risk of injury or death. Duh. Enough said. Second, when you're shipping a product to your customer, especially physical products. Regardless of whether the product is a baby's crib, a car, or a piece of software, wait and see what goes wrong cannot be the primary risk management approach. Third, when you don't have a response planned. For example, if you operate banking software, you probably have an adjustable dollar level at which you manually check transactions for fraud. You might adjust it based on current capacity in the fraud management department or on the cost effectiveness of the activity.

Easy Fixes First

Some organizations just starting to threat model may begin by fixing those things that are easy to fix before going on to harder fixes. For many experienced security practitioners, this seems like an odd choice, but it's worth discussing the pros and cons of the approach. On the pro side, fixing security issues is a good thing, and demonstrating that threat modeling is producing actionable bugs may help ensure that threat modeling continues. The downside is that the issues you're fixing may be the wrong things, or things that don't seem relevant to other parts of an organization, and thus appear to be a waste of time.

If you need to start from an easy fix first approach, ensure that you do so in consultation with the people who are performing the fixes, and ensure they don't perceive it as busywork. In addition, plan to move from easy fixes to a more mature approach, as described in the remainder of this section.

Threat-Ranking with a Bug Bar

There are a few techniques that enable you to rank your threats with a little more precision than "easy" and "everything else." These ranking techniques are designed to provide you with a consistent approach to addressing threats.

DREAD

One of the first of these was DREAD. This awesome acronym stands for discoverability, reproducibility, exploitability, affected users, and damage. Unfortunately, DREAD is fairly subjective and leads to odd results in many circumstances. Therefore, as of 2010, DREAD is no longer recommended for use by the Microsoft SDL team.

The most effective simple prioritization technique is a bug bar. In a bug bar, bugs are given a severity based on a shared understanding of their impact. That shared understanding comes from a "bug bar" table that lists the criteria used to classify bugs, and might include examples. Over the product lifecycle, the bar defining what bugs must be fixed is adjusted. Thus, six months before shipping, a medium-impact bug would be fixed, whereas a bug discovered on the day of shipping would be fixed in a hotfix. The bar will likely be refined, and what must be fixed may change as your security processes mature. Microsoft makes fairly heavy use of the bug bar concept.

A version of the complete Microsoft SDL bug bar is available online. The bug bar is made available under a Creative Commons license that allows you to use it within your organization (Microsoft, 2012).

Cost Estimation Approaches

Sometimes there are business reasons to use a threat prioritization approach that produces cost estimates. This section covers two such approaches: probability/impact assessments and FAIR.

Probability/Impact Assessments

Assessing probability and impact is an obvious approach, but effective implementations are rare. There are a few sticking points, including that, unlike hurricanes or tornados, information security events are often caused by malice. However, insurance companies still write theft insurance, and don't go out of business too often. Over time, the industry will likely learn more about both probabilities and impacts from incidents disclosure because of breach disclosure laws, and probability/impact assessments will become a more useful part of threat modeling. If you're going to use a probability/impact assessment of any form, you'll need to figure out the cost of mitigation, and few approaches help you do that (Gordon, 2006).

Probability assessments in information security are notoriously hard to get right. Well-engineered systems can often be broken with very inexpensive equipment. Kryptonite bike locks were found vulnerable to a Bic pen (Kahney, 2004). Facial recognition systems have been found to recognize photographs of an authorized person (Nguyen, 2009). Fingerprint readers have been beaten by gummy candy and laser printers (Matsumoto, 2002). Expensive equipment may be easier to get than you anticipate, for example, graduate students often have access to million-dollar lab equipment. At the other end of the spectrum, most people would consider an attack that allows someone to steal a few dollars as not worth a lot of time. However, a billion people worldwide live on less than one dollar a day, and their lives would be improved by stealing just a few dollars.

(This isn't to say that everyone living at that level of poverty would become a criminal given the opportunity, only that typical Western assessments of cost/benefit trade-offs are challenged by global networking.)

FAIR

FAIR is the acronym for Factor Analysis of Information Risk, developed by Jack Jones while he was Chief Security Officer for a large bank. FAIR focuses on defining business risk associated with technology systems. FAIR defines a threat as "anything (e.g., object, substance, human) that is capable of acting against an asset in a manner that can result in harm."

The primary use of FAIR is for systems that a business is deploying, regardless of the source of the components (off the shelf or local). It defines risk as a function of loss event frequency and probable loss magnitude. Each of these is decomposed further, as shown in Figure 9-4.

FAIR has 10 defined steps in four stages:

Stage 1: Identify scenario components

1. Identify the asset at risk.
2. Identify the threat community under consideration.

Stage 2: Evaluate loss event frequency

3. Estimate the probable threat event frequency.
4. Estimate the threat capability.
5. Estimate control strength.
6. Derive vulnerability.
7. Derive loss event frequency.

Stage 3: Estimate probable loss magnitude

8. Estimate worst-case loss.
9. Estimate probable loss.

Stage 4: Derive and articulate risk

10. Derive and articulate risk.

The document "An Introduction to FAIR" (Jones, 2006) presents FAIR as an approach to risk management in business. The FAIR white paper starts out at what you might see as a very philosophical level. If you find that frustrating, consider jumping to page 64 of that introductory paper, where FAIR is presented in a more concrete and compact fashion.

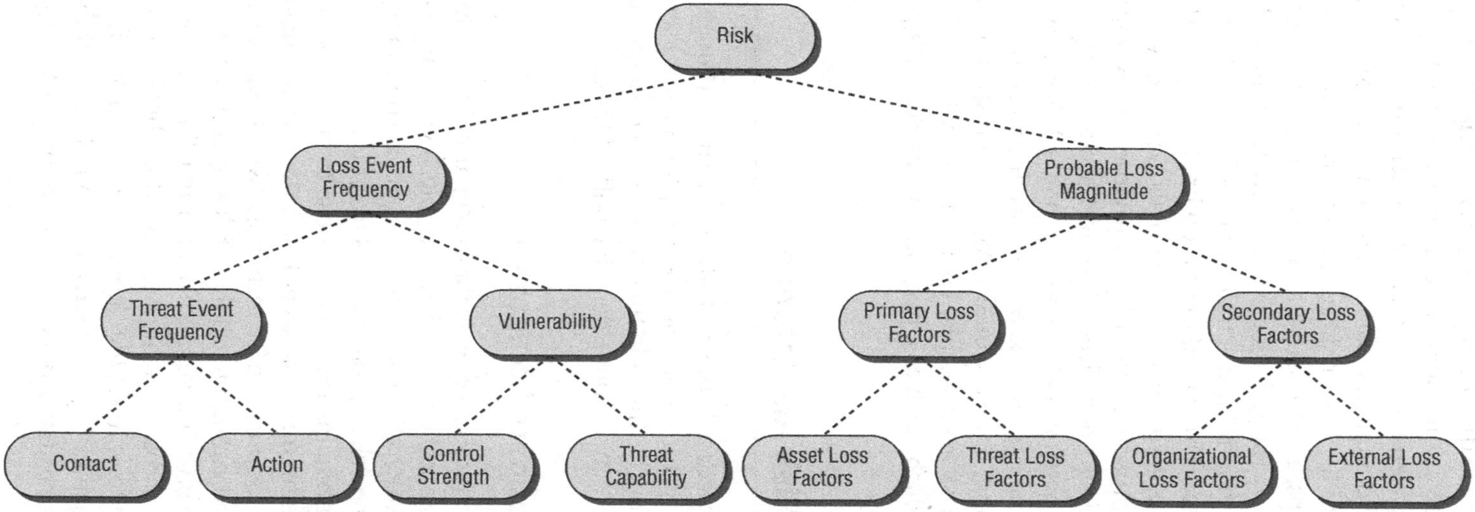

Figure 9-4: FAIR's risk decomposition

There are two issues to discuss regarding FAIR. The first is the way in which it assigns numbers to various elements of risk. The white paper acknowledges these in a remarkably frank discussion in the conclusions. It's worth reiterating that without incident data, FAIR is a repeatable way to get to the same results, but the results are hard to compare to results for other systems. The second issue is FAIR's opening steps, and the asset- and attacker-centricity of the system. An asset is defined as "any data, device, or other component of the environment that supports information-related activities, and which can be affected in a manner that results in loss." This broad definition implies a remarkable amount of work, as FAIR analysis is run on each asset. This is probably ameliorated by an intuitive ranking approach. FAIR at least provides an "example" set of threat communities, but it does not address the effort needed to analyze their behaviors, nor the risks in getting that analysis wrong. FAIR is probably the best of the approaches for quantifying risk. My lovely editor would like to know if that means it's worth using, and so would I. More seriously, if your organization relies on quantified risk assessments, FAIR has many things to recommend it, but if a simpler approach, such as a bug bar will work, that's probably a better return on investment.

Mitigation via Risk Acceptance

As discussed in the section "Classic Strategies for Risk Management," it is perfectly reasonable to address risk via risk acceptance, and there are two ways that is commonly done: either via business risk acceptance or via user risk acceptance. The following sections describe both of these.

Mitigation via Business Acceptance

If an organization is building software for its own use, it is free to make whatever risk acceptance decisions it chooses. For example, if your inventory site exposes your product inventory to the world, that's a choice you can reasonably make, by applying whatever risk approach works for you.

In a number of cases, a business may choose to take into account other perspectives beyond its own in risk acceptance decisions. Those cases include privacy and "fitness for purpose," a term borrowed from the lawyers to mean something that's good enough to do the job it's intended to serve.

If the software involves personal, private information, then the risk acceptance must take into account the myriad laws that apply to such things. Many of those laws require something like "appropriate security." This constrains the decisions that the business can make regarding risk. Even if those laws do not apply, losing all your customer data may enable competitors to use that data to market to your customers, or it may upset your customers. Lastly, it may have an impact on your reputation.

Fitness for purpose is the other element that may influence a business's willingness to accept risk. If your system is being sold with the expectation that it can connect to the Internet, then there may be a reasonable expectation that it's sufficiently secure for that purpose. If it's being sold for medical use, "critical infrastructure," or similar areas, there may be substantial additional expectations. In these types of cases, the business cannot silently accept the risk; at the very least the risk acceptance decisions must be communicated to customers. (I'm not a lawyer, but if you decide not to communicate such risks, I suspect you'll get to know some very unfriendly lawyers.)

Mitigation via User Acceptance

There are times when a software developer or systems administrator can't make a decision for the user. For example, there may be a business reason to visit Playboy.com. (For instance, consider an investment bank. No reason to allow adult content, right? Except when Playboy's CEO visits to pitch her stock to the bank's analysts, she'll want to demo their new digital media line of business.) There may be a reason to have viruses on a system. Or maybe there's something that is "obviously" a security error, but the user wants to accept the risk involved.

If you need to warn someone about a potential risk, ensure that such warnings are NEAT: necessary, explanatory, actionable, and tested. These four relatively simple steps work well for designing warnings (or improving existing ones), and NEAT is covered in more detail in Chapter 15, "Human Factors and Usability."

When authenticating, ensure that the authentication is two-way. If any details have changed since the last authentication, inform the user about what's different. This requires persisting some information, explaining it to the user, and walking them through evaluating it.

Arms Races in Mitigation Strategies

An *arms race* describes the predictable set of steps that both attackers and defenders engage in that leave both sides approximately where they were at the start of the arms race, only poorer. A classic example is signature-driven anti-virus software. Such software is only as good as its latest update. There will almost always be viruses that the signature authors have not yet discovered, or for which the signatures have not been tested, shipped, or applied.

It should perhaps go without saying that such arms races are to be avoided, but because they are frequent it's worth a few words on why arms races happen, and what you can do should you find it hard to avoid one.

Arms races happen because some factor makes a perfect defense hard. For example, it turns out that bolting on security defenses that block only what viruses do is nearly impossible. Commercial operating systems support a wide variety of behavior, and legitimate programs make use of those defined behaviors, sometimes in ways that are hard to distinguish from malicious use. Therefore, heuristic modules in anti-virus programs have a high rate of false positives. Similarly, whitelisting of programs in advance is an excellent defensive technique, but one that turns out to be very inhibitory to the normal use of computers.

When you find yourself in an arms race, you are playing an economic game, and your goal should be to both minimize your cost while maximizing your profit, while simultaneously maximizing your opponent's cost and minimizing their profit. Your costs go up when you must scramble, and your profits will be maximized the longer your opponent spends time reacting to your latest moves. This leads to two related strategies: Aim for the last-mover advantage and have a bag of tricks.

Last-mover advantage is a term credited to cryptographer extraordinaire Paul Kocher (Kocher, 2006). It refers to the idea that the last side to take action has an advantage. Further, your moves should be designed, in part, to flummox the other side, and make it tricky for them to respond. Therefore, here, the use of obfuscation or anti-debugging techniques can pay dividends. Having a system that's designed to roll forward to a new configuration can also help, and here's where a bag of tricks comes in. A *bag of tricks* is a set of moves in the arms race that are already coded and tested. When you detect that your opponent has taken a new move, you deploy something from your bag of tricks. For example, if you have a DRM scheme to prevent people from using your music files as they choose, you might have a set of additional restrictions coded up and ready to ship as attackers break your current scheme. This enables you to maximize how long you have the last-mover advantage.

Summary

There are many strategies you can apply to risk management. The classic risk management strategies of avoid, address, accept, or transfer are applicable to how you address threats.

More specific to threats and security are the approaches of changing the design, applying standard mitigations, and designing custom mitigations. It's expensive and time consuming to test your custom mitigation, and easy to get the design wrong, so custom mitigations should be a fallback. The department of "easy to get wrong" also includes fuzzing, which is more appropriately seen as a test technique. (It's a great technique, but you can't fuzz your way to a secure design or implementation.)

Sometimes you need to prioritize your mitigation approaches, and there's a variety of ways to do so, ranging from simple ones like wait and see (and the associated actions to ensure you do see) to bug bars and quantified risk management approaches such as FAIR.

Now and then you need to accept risks, or ask others to do so. When you need to accept risk, you should ensure that you're doing so with some structure and not using "accepted risk" as a synonym for ignoring it. When you need to ask others to accept risk, you should do so clearly, and the NEAT approach can help you do so.

Sometimes arms races are hard to avoid. If you do find yourself there, there are some strategies to drive your opponent's costs up while keeping yours low. You want to aim for a last-mover advantage that forces your opponent to scramble while you relax. That's what good risk management can get you.

CHAPTER 10

Validating That Threats Are Addressed

You've been hard at work to address your threats, first by simply fixing them, and then by assessing risks around them. But are your efforts working? It is important that you test the fixes, and have confidence that anything previously identified has been addressed.

Good testers have a lot in common with good threat modelers: Both focus on how stuff is going to break, and work on preventing it. Working closely with your testers can have surprisingly positive payoff for threat modeling proponents, a synergy explored in more detail in Chapter 17, "Bringing Threat Modeling to Your Organization."

A brief note on terminology: In this chapter, the term *testing* is used to refer to a key functional task that "quality assurance" performs: the creation and management of tests. This chapter focuses only on the subset of testing that intersects with threat modeling. As shown in Figure 10-1, threat-model-driven testing can overlap heavily with security testing, but the degree of overlap will vary across organizations. Some organizations have reliability testing specialists. They need to understand the issues you find when looking for denial-of-service threats. Others might manage repudiation as part of customer readiness. Your security testers might also use fuzzing, look for SQL injection, or create and manage tests that are not driven by threat modeling.

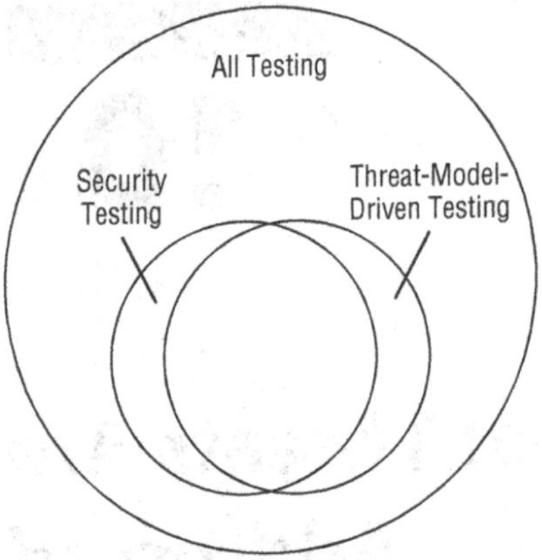

Figure 10-1: Different types of testing

This chapter will teach you about testing threat mitigations, how to examine software you acquire from elsewhere to check that threats are addressed to your satisfaction, explain how to perform quality assurance on your threat modeling activity, and discuss some of the mechanical and process elements of threat modeling validation. It closes with a set of tables designed to help you track your threat modeling testing activity.

Testing Threat Mitigations

You'll need both process and skills to test the mitigations you're developing. This section explains both, and also discusses penetration testing, which is often mistaken for a complete approach to testing security.

Test Process Integration

Anything you do to address a threat is subject to being tested. However you manage test cases, you should include testing the threats you've found and chosen to address. If you're an agile team that uses test-driven development, develop at least two tests per threat: one that exploits the easy (no mitigation) case, and at least one that attempts to bypass the mitigation. It can be easy, fun, and even helpful for your testers to go nuts with this. It may be worth the effort to ensure they start with the highest-risk threats, or the ones that developers don't want to fix. If you use bugs to track test development, you might want to file two test-creation bugs per threat. One will track the threat, and the other the test code for the threat. Then again, you might find this overkill. Giving threat model bugs unique tags can help you when you search for threat model test bugs. (For example, you can use "threatmodel" to find all bugs that come from threat enumeration, and "tmtest" for the test bugs.)

If you have some form of test planning, then you should ensure that the list of threats feeds into the test planning. A good list of threats delivered to a tester can produce an avalanche of new tests.

How to Test a Mitigation

If you think of threats as bugs, then testing threats is much like doing heavy testing on those bugs. You'll want to set up a way to reproduce the conditions that cause the bug to trigger, and create a test that demonstrates whether a fix is working. That test can be manual or automated. Sometimes the level of effort needed to code an automated test can be high, and you'll be tempted to test manually. At the same time, these are bugs you'd really prefer do not regress, which is an argument for automation.

Of course, unlike normal bugs, attackers will vary conditions to help them trigger your bugs, so good testing will include variations of the attack. The exact variation you'll want depends heavily on the threat. You should vary whatever the mitigation code depends on. For a simple example, consider an XSS bug in a website. Such bugs are often demonstrated by use of the JavaScript `alert` function. Therefore, perhaps someone has coded a test that looks for the string "alert." Try replacing that with "`%61%6C%65%72%74%0A`." Robert "RSnake" Hansen has a site dedicated to creating such variants—his "XSS (Cross Site Scripting) Cheat Sheet Calculator" (OWASP, 2013b). You can use such a site to develop the skills to create your own variations.

As you develop tests for a threat, you can also consider how the mitigations you're developing can be attacked. This is very similar to attack variations, but goes back to the idea of second-and third-order threats discussed in Chapter 7, "Processing and Managing Threats."

The skills required to perform testing of threat mitigations vary according to the type of threat and mitigation. There are test engineers at large companies who are experts at *shell coding*, that is, the specialized attack code used to take over control flow. There are others who are expert cryptographers, spending their days looking for mathematical attacks on the cryptography their employers develop.

Penetration Testing

Some organizations choose to use penetration testing to validate their threat models and/or add a level of confidence in their software. Penetration testing (aka pen testing) can supplement threat modeling. But there's a saying that "you can't test quality in." That means all the testing you might possibly do will never make a product great. It will just help you fix the defects you happen to find. To make a quality product, you need to start with good design, good raw materials and good production processes, and then check that your output matches your expectation. In the same way, you can't test your product to secure. So, pen testing can't replace threat modeling.

Pen testing can be either black box or glass box. Black box pen testing provides only the software to the testers, who will then explicitly test assumptions you have about how much effort it takes to gain an understanding of the software. This is an expensive undertaking, especially compared to glass box pen testing, whereby testers are given access to code, designs, and threat models, and they are able to use those to better understand the goals of the software and the intentions of the developers.

If you choose to use pen testing as an adjunct to threat modeling, the most important thing is to ensure that you're aligned with the penetration testers regarding what's in scope. If they come back with a list of SQL injections and cross-site scripting attacks, will you be happy? (Either a yes or a no is fine as long as you're clear with the pen testers. An "I don't know" is likely to leave you unhappy.)

Checking Code You Acquire

Most of this book is focused on what you're building. But the reality is that much of the code in today's products comes from elsewhere, in either binary or source form. And not all of it comes with well-formed security operations guidance and non-requirements. Less of it comes with explicit threat models telling you what the creators worried about. This section shows you how to threat model code you've acquired, so you can validate if threats are addressed. The steps here are aligned with the four-stage framework expressed in the Introduction and in Chapter 1, "Dive In and Threat Model!". You'll use a variety of tools to learn about the software you're looking at, create a model of the software from what you've learned, and then analyze that model. From there, standard operational approaches to addressing threats can come into play. You can apply these techniques to code you acquire from outside, or if you're an operations team, to code which is handed to you for deployment. This section is inspired by work by consultant Ollie Whitehouse (Whitehouse, 2013).

NOTE **The approaches here assume you do not have the time or the skills to decompile or reverse engineer the binaries. Of course, if you do, you have more options and the capability to dig deeper. If you have source, you can of course compile it, and so the binary approaches will work, and may be easier (for example, find listening ports or account information by running the installer). Of course, that dynamic analysis has limitations; if on the third Wednesday of the month, the software opens a backdoor, bad luck if you start the next day and trust runtime analysis. This section also assumes you're looking at software which you have reason to believe you can trust. (For example, unexpected binaries on your USB drives may well be malware.)**

Constructing a Software Model

Even if the product comes with an architecture diagram, it may not suffice for threat modeling. For example, it probably doesn't show trust boundaries. So you'll need to construct a model that's useful for threat analysis. To do that you need to dig into a set of questions, and then synthesize. In theory, you'll want to move from the outside in, enumerating architectural aspects of the software, including the following:

- Accounts and processes:
  - New accounts created
  - Running processes
  - Start-up processes
  - Invoked or spawned processes
- Listening ports:
  - Sockets
  - RPC
  - Web
  - Local inter-process communication
- Administrative interfaces:
  - Documented
  - Account recovery
  - Service personnel accounts
- Web and database implementation
- Technical dependencies and platform information:
  - Changes to OS (for appliances/virtual machines)
  - Firewall rule changes
  - Permission changes
  - Auto-updater status
  - Unpatched vulnerabilities

If the software is delivered in binary form, you can use unix tools like `ps`, `netstat`, find (with the –newer option), or their equivalents on your platform to find listeners and processes. Similarly, the operating system can show you new accounts and start-up processes. Tools like Sysinternals' Autoruns on Windows can walk through the many possible ways to start a program on boot. Administrative interfaces are probably documented, although it's unfortunately common to have backdoors for service or recovery, so you can look into how you'd get in "if you forget your password."

With this information, you can start to construct a software model. The components are the trust boundaries, and the processes are the processes within each. The listening ports get drawn as one end of data flows. If present, you'll need to dig deeper into web and databases, in technology-appropriate ways, to better understand what's happening in those complex subsystems. The administrative interfaces can add additional trust boundaries and possibly data flows. Technical dependencies (such as a web server or framework) may also introduce new processes or data flows, and the approach here can be applied recursively to those dependencies. There's one other aspect to check for dependencies: Are the dependencies up to date with security fixes? Searching a database like the US National Vulnerability Database for the dependency can give you an idea of what's been discovered in the version you have, or you can use free tools such as nmap or Metasploit to test it.

All of the preceding can be performed by any systems administrator who's willing to learn a bit about new tools. If you also have source code, it may be possible to, and even worth, digging in. You may learn about additional accounts where Windows impersonates, or unix sets `uid`. System calls such as `fork` and `exec` will show you where processes are spawned. `Open`, `read`, and especially `socket` and `listen` calls can reveal trust boundaries. (There are a near-infinite number of higher-level variants which implicitly create a `socket` and `listen`.) Finding extra login interfaces is easier with the code, but will likely require more than just grepping.

Using the Software Model

When you have a model of the software you acquired, you can apply the techniques in Part II of this book to bear to find threats. You can look to see if they are appropriately mitigated. If you're looking for threats during a software evaluation or acquisition phase, you have a number of choices about the threats you find that are not mitigated to your satisfaction. Those choices include:

- Bring them to the attention of the software producer.
- Look for an alternate package.
- Mitigate them yourself.

If you are bringing them to the software producer, be prepared for a discussion of the correct requirements, the tradeoffs involved in a fix, or other disagreements about the threats you've found. (For example, many proposed "improvements" to Windows permissions fail to consider what may break if those changes are made.)

Some backwards looking vendors may even threaten you, asserting that you've violated the license, although fortunately this is becoming less common.

If the producer is open source, don't be surprised if the answer is "we're accepting patches."

If you're looking at threats after the software has been acquired, selected or deployed, your ability to select an alternative is dramatically lower. (Once again, threat modeling early gives you more flexibility.) Bringing them to the vendor or mitigating them yourself are your main choices.

Mitigating issues yourself means applying the "operational" mitigations found in Chapter 8, "Defensive Tactics and Technologies." The most common forms of this are "slap a firewall in front of it," and tunnel the network traffic over SSL or SSH.

You can make all this work a lot easier by looking for operational security guides and threat model documents as you select components. Components that come with such documentation are likely to require a lot less work on your part.

QA'ing Threat Modeling

While it is common for security enthusiasts to claim that you're never done threat modeling, at some point you need to ship, deploy, or otherwise deliver the software, and you may or may not be planning to do another version. As you get close to finishing (say, feature complete), you'll want to be able to close out the threat modeling work. If you use checklists or some other means of tracking what needs to be done to pass through the gate and call it feature complete, you should add threat model verification to the checklist. Verifying the threat model consists of ensuring the following:

- The model actually matches reality closely enough.
- Everything in the threat list is addressed and the threat model portion of the test plan is complete.
- Threat model bugs are closed.

Model/Reality Conformance

As you finish addressing threats, you need to ensure that the threats you're addressing were found using a model that relates to what you built. In other words, if you did three major architecture revamps between the last time you did an architectural diagram of the system and now, the list of threats you found might not be relevant to what you've built. Therefore, you need to check whether your model is close enough to reality to be useful. Ideally, you do this along the way, by including threat modeling in your list of activities to do during an architectural redesign or major refactoring work. This also applies to deploying complex systems. The complexities of deployment often lead to on-the-fly changes. If those are substantial (say, turning off a firewall), then the threat model probably needs a revamp.

If your threat model leads to substantial redesign or architecture changes to address threats, "closing that loop" is tremendously important. If that's the goal, make sure you re-check the software model against the code around the time the code is getting checked in, or when the new systems are being deployed. Ideally, bring the people who made the changes into a room, and have them explain the changes that were made and the new security features.

NOTE **A meeting like this can sometimes devolve into security finding new threats against the new system. That may be acceptable, or it may seem like moving the goalposts. Upfront agreement on the meeting goals will reduce contention.**

Task and Process Completion

Have you gone through each threat, and decided on a strategy and a tactic for addressing it? That might be to accept the risk and monitor, or it might be to use an operating system feature to manage it. You need to track these and ensure that you do an appropriate amount of work to avoid any falling through the cracks. (You might say that anything of severity less than some bar isn't worth the effort to track.) Good threat modeling tools make it easy to file a bug per threat. If you're using something without that feature, you need to file bugs manually.

There are two reasons why threats should lead to bugs that are like your other bugs, rather than a separate document. First, anyone shipping software has a way to manage bugs; and if you want your security issues managed, making them bugs puts them into the same machinery your organization is already using to assure quality. Second, bugs act as an exit point from threat modeling, allowing the normal machinery to take over, and enabling you to say, "We're done threat modeling that."

Bug Checking

As you get closer to shipping, review the mitigation test bugs, ensuring that you've closed each one. This is where a tag such as `tmtest` is really helpful. Bugs that haven't been closed should be triaged like other bugs (with appropriate attention to the gravity of the bug), and fixed or, if appropriate, moved to the next revision.

Process Aspects of Addressing Threats

There are a few final aspects of how testing and threat modeling complement each other, and a few red flags that testers can use to quickly find issues, including a belief that data is "validated" where people are making assumptions.

Threat Modeling Empowers Testing; Testing Empowers Threat Modeling

Writing code is hard; thinking through all the things needed to make the code work leaves little space in the brain for thinking about anything else, including what might go wrong. This level of focus and concentration on the problem at hand is part of why engineers can get so upset at interruptions: The problem at hand is complex enough to require full attention, and there's no room for minor issues like eating properly. There's "no room" in two senses: rational and emotional. In the rational sense, developers usually want to focus on developing great code. Thinking about all the ways to make the code better, faster, more capable, more elegant, and so on, requires less of a mental shift than thinking about what will go wrong. Many great developers have learned that they need to think about writing testable code and collaborating with testers, but that doesn't mean they're great at finding what will go wrong. The emotional sense of lacking room to think about what might go wrong means that after a lot of effort to make the code work, thinking about making it break is challenging.

Threat modeling has a natural ally in testers, especially when testing is seen as an "inferior" function to developing. If testing "owns" threat modeling, then test has a reason to be in architecture meetings. They need to be there to talk about how to threat model, and to start conducting tests early. If threat modeling is the reason testers are brought in early, then testers have a reason to drive effective threat modeling processes.

Validation/Transformation

It's common to see threat models that assert, incorrectly, that this input or that has been "validated." This claim should be a red flag for testers, because it is never completely true. The data may well have been validated for some purpose or purposes. For example, is the following data valid? `http://www.example.org/this/url/will/pwn/you`.

It's a valid URL, in accordance with RFC 1738. It uses a domain that is nominally reserved for example use. Were it a real URL, a path `this/url/will/pwn/you` is probably unsafe to visit. It's easy to construct similar examples.

For example, the e-mail address `adam+threat@example.org` is valid (see RFC 822), but just try convincing many web forms of that. Many filter out the plus sign to make SQL injection attacks harder to carry out, along with the single quote character ('), which annoys a great many Irish people with names like O'Malley or O'Leary. Therefore, data can only be validated for a particular purpose or, better, to comply with certain rules.

The other approach to data is to filter and transform it. For example, if you have a system that is taking input that will be displayed on a website, you can do so more safely by ensuring it is ASCII, eliminating everything but a known good set and transforming bracketed strings into approved HTML strings. Your known good set could be A–Z, 0–9 and some set of punctuation. The advantage to a filter and transform approach is safety by design. By filtering out everything but known good, and then transforming them into something that includes "dangerous" input, attack code will need to pass through multiple bugs to succeed.

Document Assumptions as You Go

As you threat model, you'll find yourself saying, "I assume that ..." You should write those things down, and testers should test the assumptions. How to do that will vary according to the assumption. Generally, you can test the assumptions by asking, "Could it ever not be true?" and "What can I break if this is false, incomplete, or an overgeneralization?"

This differs in a subtle but important way from the common prescription to "document all assumptions." That advice leads people to try to document all assumptions as they start threat modeling, but what assumptions? When do you stop? Do you assume that no one will find a new solution to the factoring problem that underlies many public key cryptography schemes? It's usually a reasonable assumption, but documenting that in advance often feels like an exercise in pedantry. In contrast, documenting as you go is easier, constrained, and helps those who review the threat models.

Tables and Lists

Now that you know about the defensive tactics and technologies and the various strategies you can apply to manage risks, it's time to learn about the blocking and tackling elements. If you think back to Chapter 7, many of the tables there have a bug ID as their last column. The tables here, therefore, start with a bug ID. A simple table might look something like Table 10-1.

Table 10-1: Tracking Bugs for Fixing

BUG ID	THREAT	RISK MANAGEMENT TECHNIQUE	PRIORITIZATION APPROACH	TACTIC	TESTER	DONE?
4556	Orders not checked at server	Design change	Fix now to address, avoid dependencies.	Code changes	Alice	
4558	Ensure all changes to server code are pulled from source control so changes are accountable.	Operational change	Wait and see.	Deploy ment tooling change	Bob	No
4559	Investigate moving controls to business logic, which is less accessible to attackers.	Design change	Wait and see.	Include in user stories for next refactoring.	Bob	no

However, you'll notice that these threats are all being addressed, or have a strategy for addressing them. As you'll recall, this isn't always possible, so you might have additional tables for accepted risks (see Table 10-3) and transferred risks (see Table 10-4). That leaves out avoided risks, which are rarely worth tracking as bugs. If you maintain architecture documentation, you might include the insecure designs that were avoided. You can use a table like Table 10-2 to track how you're handling various risks, which can help you get an overview of where you stand overall. (With the right fields, you can also extract such a table from your bug tracking system.) In this list and the lists that follow, italics are used for fields that you might choose to include if you're a more process-intensive shop.

Table 10-2 shows the following:

- Bug ID
- Threat
- Risk management approach
- Risk management technique or building blocks
- Is it done?
- Test IDs if you have test code (optional).

Table 10-2: Overall Threat Modeling Bug Tracking (Example)

BUG ID	THREAT	RISK MANAGEMENT APPROACH	TECHNIQUE/ BUILDING BLOCKS	DONE?
1234	Criminals sending money orders	Avoid	Don't accept checks/ACH/ money orders.	Yes!
4556	Orders not checked at server	Address	Fix now.	Check with Alice.
1235	People will mistype URL, visit phishing site.	Accept	Document in security advice page, advising bookmark, since we can't fix the browsers.	Yes
1236	People will order things they don't want.	Transfer	Terms of service state that all orders are final.	Yes

In tracking accepted risks, the key deliverable is an understanding of the risks you're accepting, so that executives can have a single view. You might choose to sort such a table by bug ID, cost, or the business owner who has accepted the risk. Of course, as you've learned, putting a dollar value on threats can be challenging. If you do put a cost on threats, then unlike most of the other tables, the accepted risks table can actually be summarized or totaled.

As shown in Table 10-3, you should track at least the following:

- Bug ID
- Threat
- Cost or impact estimate
- Who made the estimate and how (optional)
- Why the risk is accepted
- Who accepted it
- The sign off procedure that was followed (optional)

Table 10-3: Accepted Risks (Example)

BUG ID	THREAT	COST/IMPACT ESTIMATE	REASON TO ACCEPT	BUSINESS SIGN-OFF FROM
1237	A janitor will plug a keylogger into the CEO's desktop.	High	The CEO still has a desktop.	IT director
1238				
...	...	...		...
Total	(above)	$1,000,000		Charlene, Dave

The "transferred to" column may or may not be needed. You may find that all risks are transferred to the customer, but you might find that some risks are transferred to other parties. For example, if your product has a file-sharing feature, risk may be transferred to copyright owners; or if your product has a messaging feature, you may create a new channel for spam. Of course, in practice, those risks may fall on your customers.

If you want to track to whom it's transferred, you can do so as shown in Table 10-4, which includes the following:

- Bug ID
- Threat
- Why you can't fix it
- To whom it's transferred (optional)
- The way it's being transferred
- Whether the transfer mechanism is completed

Table 10-4: Transferred Risks (Example)

BUG ID	THREAT	REASON WE CAN'T FIX	FORM OF TRANSFER	DONE?
1238	Insiders	Need an admin role	Non-requirements, presented in security operations guide	Yes
1239	Buffer overflow in our custom document format	After careful redesign and fuzzing, residual risks exist.	Warning on opening document	No—requires user testing.

Summary

Like everything else in the development of software or the deployment of systems, threat models can be subjected to a quality assurance process. It's important to "close the loop" and ensure that threats have been appropriately handled. Those tasks may fall outside what's normally thought of as threat modeling. How you handle them will vary according to your organization.

Thus, there's a need to integrate threat model testing into your test process, and to test that each threat is addressed. You'll also want to look for variants and second- or third-order attacks as you test for threats.

When you perform quality assurance, you'll want to confirm that the software model conforms to what you ended up building, deploying or acquiring. Modeling the architecture of software you acquire involves a different process than software you create in-house. In addition, you should verify that each task and process associated with threat modeling was completed, and check the threat model bugs to ensure that each was handled appropriately.

There's an interesting overlap between "the security mindset" and the way many testers approach their work. This may lead to an interesting career opportunity for testers. Also, at larger organizations, this offers an opportunity for security and testers to create a virtuous circle of mutual reinforcement.

The term "validated" is, by itself, a red flag for security analysis and testing. Without a clear statement of what the validation is for, it is impossible to test whether it's correct, and whether the assumption (or group of assumptions) is accurate or shared by everyone touching the supposedly validated data. "The exact purpose data is being validated" is often left as an assumption, rather than being made explicit. There are many others, and all of them should be validated as you threat model, and tested at an appropriate time.

CHAPTER

11

Threat Modeling Tools

This chapter covers tools to help you threat model. Tooling can help threat modeling in a number of ways. It can help you create better models, or create models more fluidly. Tools can help you remember to engage in various steps, or provide assistance performing those steps. Tools can help create a more legible or even beautiful threat model document. Tools can help you check your threat model for completeness. Finally, tools can help you create actionable output from a threat model.

Tools can also act as a constraint. You may find yourself stymied by usability issues, such as fields you're unsure how to fill out. Or you might find that a tool cramps your style. Some trade-offs are unavoidable as tools are created, so the chapter starts with general tools that are useful in threat modeling, and then progresses to more specialized tools.

A few disclosures: I do not have personal experience with each tool described here, and some of the tools I created myself. (Those are treated at greater length, because there's less risk of me insulting the authors.)

This chapter starts by describing some generally useful tools and how to apply them to threat modeling. You'll then learn about the open-source tools that are available, followed by commercial tools. The chapter closes with a few words about tools that don't yet exist.

Generally Useful Tools

This section discusses tools that are not specialized for threat modeling but can be tremendously useful. It covers a few of the more useful tools to encourage you to think about the tools you already use and with which you are familiar.

Whiteboards

I can hardly imagine threat modeling without a whiteboard. No technology I've used has the immediacy, flexibility, and visibility to a group than a whiteboard when iteratively drawing system architecture. Whiteboards also have the advantage of transience—drawing on paper just isn't the same. On a whiteboard, no one tries to correct details such as a line not being connected properly, so the discussion can be focused on how the system actually works.

For distributed teams, a webcam focused on a whiteboard may work, or you may have "virtual whiteboarding" technologies that work for you.

Office Suites

Microsoft Office contains a number of tools that are very useful in threat modeling. Word is a great tool for recording threats in free-form. What to record is dependent on the approach you've chosen. Excel can be used for issue tracking and status. Visio is great for turning whiteboards into more precise documents. Of course, Office is one of several suites with word processing, spreadsheet, and drawing functionality. The only caveats would be the limitations of the tools. The document tool should be more than text—a feature such as embedded images is extremely useful. Similarly, use a vector drawing tool that enables you to move symbols as symbols. Automatic connector management is also super-useful, and of course this feature is not unique to Visio.

To state the obvious, Microsoft Word, Excel, and Visio are commercially licensed tools.

Bug-Tracking Systems

Whatever bug-tracking system you use should also be used to track threats. A good bug from threat modeling can take many forms. The form you use will influence how you title and discuss bugs, and there is no universally right way to approach it. (The right way is the way that works best for you and your organization.) The title could express any of the following:

- **The threat itself**: Here the bug title is of a form such as "an attacker can threaten the component" or "the component is vulnerable to threat."

For example, "the front end is vulnerable to spoofing because we use reusable passwords."

- **The mitigation:** Here, the bug title is of a form such as "the component needs mitigation." For example, "the front end needs to run only over SSH." In the text of the bug, you should also explain the threat.
- **The need to test a mitigation:** This is what you can title a bug if someone says, "Oh, the front end isn't vulnerable to that." Rather than absorb time in the meeting to discuss or check the threat, file a bug, "Test front end vulnerability to *threat*" and ensure that there are good tests for the bug.
- **The need to validate an assumption:** These bugs are filed to ensure that someone follows up on an assumption you discover while threat modeling, and on which you depend for a security property. The bug should have a title such as "security depends on assumption A" or "security property X of component Y depends on assumption Z." For example, "Security depends on the assumption that no one would ever find the key in the fake rock that looks exactly like the rocks at our last house."
- **Other tracking items:** You should treat the preceding items as suggestions, not a form into which all bugs need to fit. If you find something worth tracking, file a bug.

When tracking security bugs from threat modeling, there are a few fields that can make running queries and analysis more reliable. These include whether the bug is a security bug, whether it's "stop ship," and how the bug was found (for example, threat modeling, fuzzing, code review, customer report). You can also check the tables in Chapter 7, "Processing and Managing Threats," and Chapter 9, "Trade-Offs When Addressing Threats," for useful fields. For example, you might want a risk management approach field whose values could be avoid, address, accept, or transfer.

The right fields to use will depend in large part on the queries you want to run, which of course depend on the questions you want to ask. Some questions you might want to ask include the following:

- Do we have any open security bugs?
- Do we have any open threat modeling bugs?
- Do we have any high-severity threat modeling bugs left to fix?
- How much risk are we transferring to end-users in the security operations guide or via warning dialogs?
- What department head has signed off on the largest business risk? Which department head has signed off on the most risks?

Open-Source Tools

A variety of open-source tools for threat modeling are available. The open source tools illustrate some of the challenges in creating a high-quality threat modeling tool.

TRIKE

There are two tools named TRIKE. The first was a standalone desktop tool, written in Smalltalk. That tool is no longer being maintained, and TRIKE is now implemented in a spreadsheet. According to documentation, it works best in Excel 2011 for the Macintosh (Trike, 2013). TRIKE is sometimes referred to as "OctoTrike."

TRIKE does not fit cleanly into the four-stage framework defined in this book. The TRIKE spreadsheet contains 19 pages, which are grouped as follows: one overview, seven main threat pages (actors, data model, intended actions, connections, protocols, threats, and security objectives), four record-keeping pages (use case index, use case details, document index, and development team) and seven reference sheets (actor types, data types, action, network layers, meaningful threats, intended response, and guide words). As of this writing, the help spreadsheet appears to be a reference document, not an introduction of the system.

SeaMonster

SeaMonster is an Eclipse-based attack tree and misuse case tool that was developed by students at the Norwegian University of Science and Technology. It appears to be abandoned since 2010 (SeaMonster, 2013). The code is still available.

Elevation of Privilege

Elevation of Privilege (the game) is designed to be the easy way to get started threat modeling. It works by inviting individuals to participate in a game. The game consists of 74 physical playing cards in six suits, named for the STRIDE threats, with most suits having cards 2 through Ace. Two suits have fewer cards in order to avoid redundant threats, and it was challenging to find broadly applicable threat instances that were easily explained on a card. Each card has a specific instance of a STRIDE threat. For example, the 6 of Tampering reads "An attacker can write to a data store your code relies on." Another example card is shown in Figure 11-1.

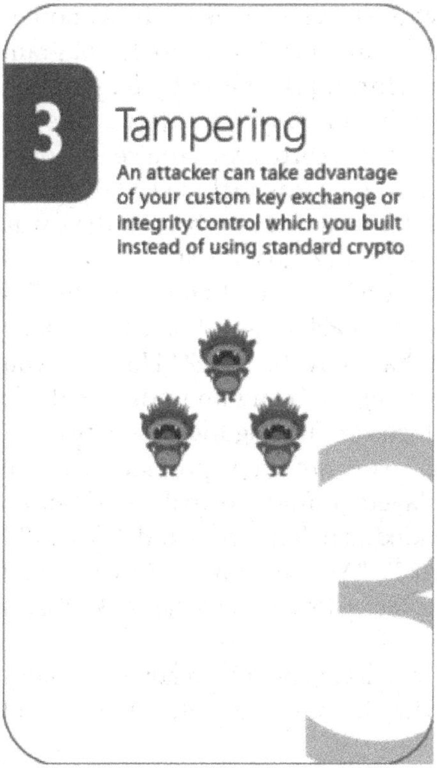
3
Tampering
An attacker can take advantage of your custom key exchange or integrity control which you built instead of using standard crypto

Figure 11-1: An *Elevation of Privilege* card

The *Elevation of Privilege* files can be downloaded from `http://www.microsoft.com/sdl/adopt/eop.aspx`. Before starting *Elevation of Privilege,* participants or the game organizer create a diagram of a system being modeled. People then come together for a game. The organizer explains the rules, and may ask people to "put their skepticism on hold." The game starts by dealing out the deck, and is then structured into turns. The first card played is always the 3 of Tampering. Play proceeds around the table in hands.

Each hand starts with a player selecting a suit to lead and playing in that suit. Each player plays by selecting a card and connecting it to the diagram. The player must play in the suit that was led if they have a card in that suit. If they don't, they may play any card. When play has gone once around the table, the hand ends. The player who played the highest card wins the hand. The highest card is either in the suit that was led, or, if a card in the Elevation of Privilege suit card was played, the highest card played from the EoP played wins the hand. (All Elevation of Privilege threat cards are higher ranked than the suit that was led, and only Elevation of Privilege cards can win when someone leads in another suit.) Players get a point for connecting the threat on their card to the diagram with a "buggable threat," and a point for winning the hand by playing the highest card either in the suit that was led or in EoP. Any EoP card trumps the suit that was led. To encourage creativity, each ace card says "You've invented a new threat," and the threats are enumerated on cards included in the pack. The game ends either when time allocated has elapsed or when all the cards have been played. The winner is the player with the most points.

A buggable threat is one a team identifies and is willing to file a bug for. It's a simple and implicit element of most software development. Some teams may find it more helpful to ask "would we add that to the backlog?" However you want to approach it (in the context of the game), you want an understandable and shared bar to test threats, so that you focus on finding the good ones.

Games are less threatening than "serious" work, and they provide structure and hints to the beginner, enabling new players to find a threat based on the cards in their hands. The game is also intended to help players find a *flow state*, a concept that is covered in depth in Chapter 19, "Architecting for Success." EoP is covered in greater depth in my paper *Elevation of Privilege: Drawing Developers into Threat Modeling* [Shostack, 2012].

Microsoft makes the files (source and PDF) available under a Creative Commons BY-3.0 license, allowing you to take it, modify it, make derivative works, and even sell them.

Commercial Tools

Here are a few commercially licensed threat modeling tools. I mention a few commercial tools as examples, but *caveat emptor.*

ThreatModeler

ThreatModeler from MyAppSecurity.com is a defense-oriented tool based on data elements, roles, and components. It uses a set of attack libraries, including the MITRE CAPEC (see Chapter 4, "Attack Trees"), the WASC threat classification, and others. The tool generates attack trees with the component as the root, requirements that can be violated as a first level of subnode, and then threats and attacks as the next layers. According to the documentation, ThreatModeler is intended to be used by architects, developers, security professionals, QA professionals, or senior executives. ThreatModeler requires Windows.

Corporate Threat Modeller

Corporate Threat Modeller from SensePost is a tool built to support a methodology designed after an analysis of the strengths and weaknesses of a number of threat modeling approaches. Those approaches included threat trees and OCTAVE, a US-CERT-originated system for threat modeling a business (White, 2010). The analysis also looked at Microsoft's SDL Threat Modeling Tool v3, and the Microsoft "IT Infrastructure Threat Modeling Guide," (McRee, 2009) which shows how to use STRIDE-per-element to threat model IT infrastructure.

The Corporate Threat Modeler was explicitly designed for consultants. Insofar as it was developed with an explicitly stated target user (not "everyone"), it is one of the most interesting tools on the market. The approach starts with an architectural overview, and then applies a somewhat complex risk equation. The tool is free to download.

Secur*I*Tree

Secur*I*Tree is threat risk software from Amenaza Technologies, which launched in 2007 to positive reviews (SC Magazine, 2007). The product seems like a well thought through tool for constructing, managing and interpreting threat trees. It contains not only the ability to manage trees, but a set of ways to filter those trees. Each node in the tree has behavioral/capability indicators: a cost to execute, noticability, and a technical ability. It also has impact/attacker benefit indicators of attacker gain and victim loss, along with stored notes for a node or subtree. You can filter the tree based on a given attacker ability. Secur*I*Tree comes with a library of threat trees, which is likely to help its customers get to the interesting part of the threat modeling work faster. Secur*I*Tree also includes some excellent screencast-delivered training (Ingoldsby, 2009). Secur*I*Tree runs on Windows, Mac, and Linux.

Little-JIL

If you're making use of threat trees at a research institution, the Little-JIL software may be helpful. "Little-JIL is a graphical language for defining processes that coordinate the activities of autonomous agents and their use of resources during the performance of a task." It has been used for creating an elections process model and a set of fault trees for that model (Simidchieva, 2010). The full fault trees are available as a graphML model. The software used to create and process the models may be freely used at research institutions (Laser, undated).

Microsoft's SDL Threat Modeling Tool

Microsoft has shipped at least four families of threat modeling tools. They are the *Elevation of Privilege* card game, the SDL Threat Modeling Tool v3, the Threat Analysis and Modeling Tool, and the Threat Modeling Tool v1 and 2. I was the project lead for *Elevation of Privilege* and the SDL Threat Modeling Tool v3 and 3.1. The currently available SDL Threat Modeling Tool is (or has been) available free from Microsoft.

The SDL Threat Modeling Tool v3 was designed in reaction to the complexities and usability issues encountered when engineers who were not threat modeling experts tried to use the older tools. It was the first tool designed around the four-stage framework. The tool has four major screens, designed around the tasks that naturally fit together: Draw Diagrams, Analyze Model, Describe Environment, and Generate Reports. The Draw Diagrams screen, shown in Figure 11-2, includes both the capability to draw diagrams with a constrained Visio stencil set and a diagram validation section with heuristics. The Analyze Model screen, shown in Figure 11-3, is automatically filled out with threats according to STRIDE-per-element.

Each threat instance contains a set of guiding questions to help engineers think through the threat, and an area to record the threat, mitigation, to track whether work on the threat is complete, and to file a bug. The Describe Environment screen is something of a catch-all to track assumptions, external notes and the context of the threat model. The Reports screen includes an all-up report, an open issues report, a list of bugs, and a diagrams-only report intended to facilitate printing. The tool also contains a manual, a sample threat model (for the tool itself), and a getting started guide, all accessible via the Help menu.

As shown in Figure 11-2, the main Draw Diagrams screen contains the following, clockwise from upper left (excluding the menu):

- The diagrams control, enabling you to create sub-diagrams
- The Visio shapes you can use as diagram elements
- The "default" diagram (discussed in the next paragraph)
- The numbered Screens control
- Diagram validation (feedback)
- A help pane

The default diagram is present because human factor testing has shown that less experienced threat modelers are sometimes stymied by a blank screen. Providing them with a starting diagram serves two purposes. One, it demonstrates what is expected in that space. Two, rather than needing to create a diagram, a novice can modify what's there, which is an easier task.

One other feature worth mentioning from Figure 11-2 is the help field. Generally, help is a menu option that software engineers ignore, because they believe they're too smart to need to read what they expect will be a badly written help file. Therefore, the tool has basic help onscreen.

The Analyze Model screen shown in Figure 11-3 has two panes. The left pane is a list of diagram elements and the threats associated with them, presented as a tree with a single level of branches. The right pane is titled with the element name ("Results") and a description of the element. Under that is a reminder of the STRIDE-per-element threats to which it is subject, and an option to not generate threat placeholders, with a reason box. A large portion of the screen is devoted to onscreen guidance: "Some questions to ask about this threat type." The guidance is specific to threat and element category (process, data store, data flow, or external entity).

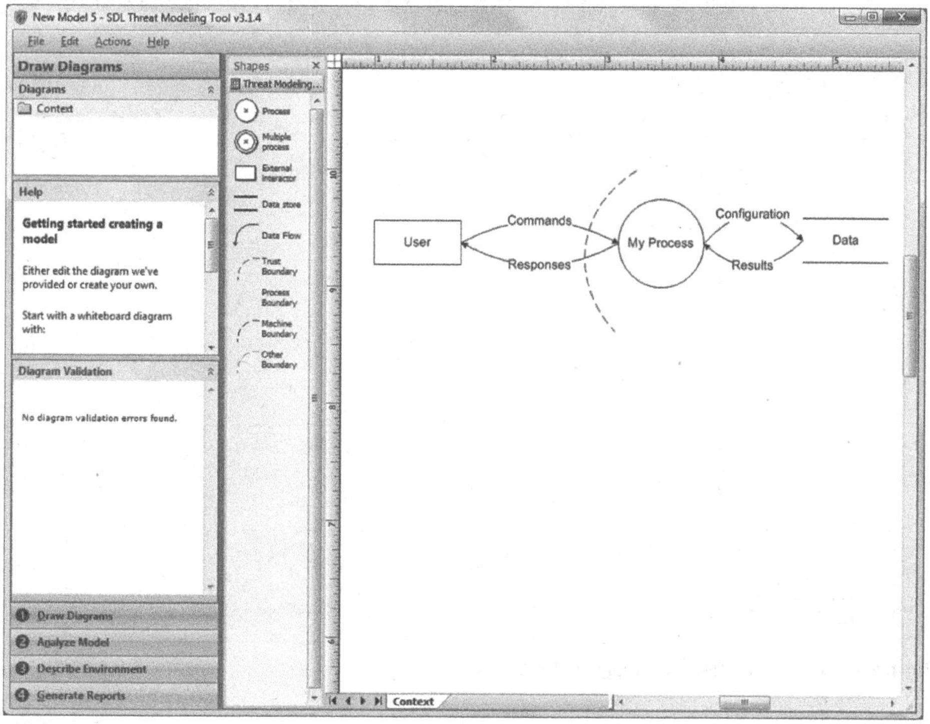

Figure 11-2: The SDL Threat Modeling Tool "Draw Diagrams" screen

There's also a command link to "Certify that there are no threats of this type." The word *certify* was carefully chosen to convey gravity. The last element on the screen is where the threat modeler describes the threat impact, and how it will be mitigated. Most of that is done in two large text entry boxes, but there is also a Finished check box, a "file bug" command link, and a completion bar. The completion bar (shown empty, under the word *completion*) fills out in four segments to encourage text entry in the Impact and Solution fields, as well as checking "finished" and filing a bug. There is also an Add Threat command link in case someone discovers an additional tampering threat against the results data flow.

The bug filing is intentionally abstracted into an API, and the tool ships with sample code to connect to a variety of bug tracking systems, or allow you to connect to whatever you use. When developing the tool, we intentionally spent time to create an API and to ship it under the Microsoft Public License (an Open

Source Initiative Approved License), because bugs are a critical part of ensuring that the threat model leads to something actionable.

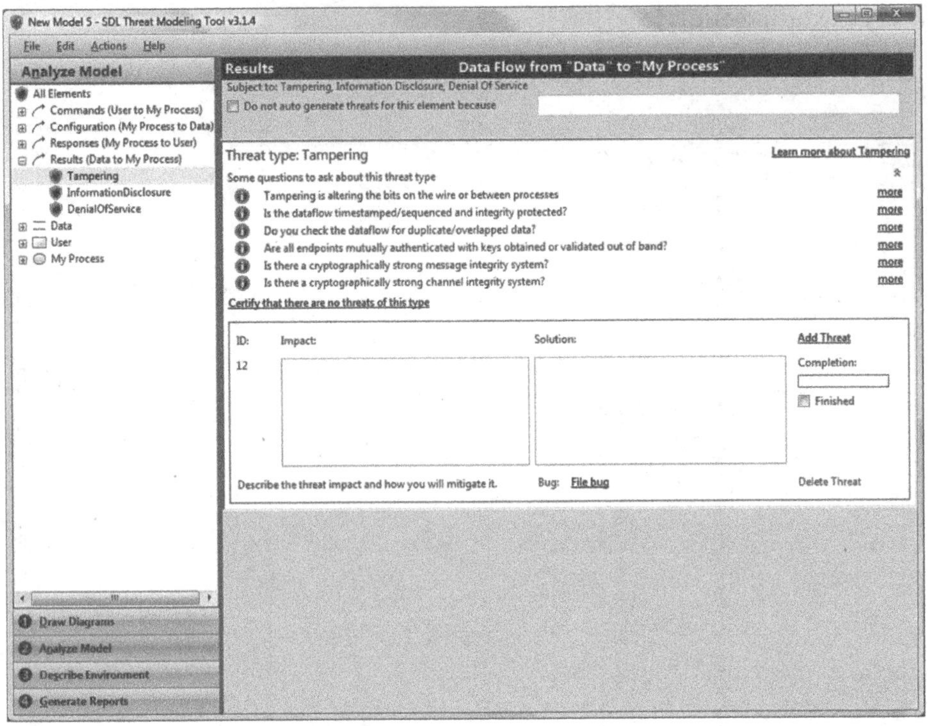

Figure 11-3: The SDL TM Tool Analyze Model screen

NOTE **Within the Draw Diagrams screen, the term "validation" causes consternation when diagrams don't conform. For example, one heuristic is to show where all data comes from. That can be addressed by including three extra elements: an installer external entity, a data flow, and a trust boundary. Doing so is not obvious, and requires roughly 10 steps. In a future version, it would be great to see diagram feedback that includes advice on how to address each. Also, boxed trust boundaries would be one of several improvements that could be made to the shapes in the default set. Others include rounded rectangles for processes, less curvy lines, and better positioning of text.**

The SDL TM Tool v3.1 series is a no-cost download from Microsoft (`www.microsoft.com/security/sdl/adopt/threatmodeling.aspx`) and it requires Visio 2007 or 2010 to use. The tool is compatible with the Visio 2010 evaluation version. Newer versions of the tool may become available (after this book goes to press) with different dependencies.

Tools That Don't Exist Yet

There are two categories of features that people often ask for that are worth a brief discussion: automated model creation and automated threat identification. A great many people want tools that can take a piece of software that's already been written and extract a data flow or other architectural diagram. This is an attractive goal, and one that might be feasible for programs written in strongly typed languages. Marwan Abi-Antoun has done some work showing how to extract data flow diagrams for Java (Abi-Antoun, 2009). (The system with open code and published DFDs he found to use for testing was only 3,000 lines of code.) If technology to do this is further developed, it will present great value to threat modeling, but also create a temptation to not perform any threat modeling or analysis until late in a project. Threat modeling after the code has been completed limits options for addressing issues. This is discussed further in Chapter 7, "Processing and Managing Threats" and Chapter 17, "Bringing Threat Modeling to Your Organization."

Similarly, tools that can take a diagram or other model and produce lists of threats would be lovely. A Spanish graduate student, Guifré Ruiz, and colleagues have created a first version of such a tool (Ruiz, 2012). However, these tools carry a risk that security analysis will focus only on known threats from an attack library. Such tools cannot (currently) analogize from closely related threats the way an experienced person can. Threat analysis that could reliably extend that knowledge to prevent new systems from making mistakes others have made would be a useful step forward. As more such tools are developed, it will be important to consider the balance between human and automated security design analysis. After all, to the extent that you need software engineers to create new functionality, that new functionality and the new combinations that result may expose new threats. It's not impossible to imagine a tool that would find threats against code not yet written, but it's hard to imagine one that would do so as comprehensively as an expert threat modeler.

Summary

A wide variety of tools are available for threat modeling. General-purpose tools such as whiteboards and bug-tracking systems can be very helpful, and tools such as word processors, spreadsheets, and diagramming tools can be used to help you threat model. Also available are a variety of specialized threat modeling tools. Microsoft has shipped several of these free, including *Elevation of Privilege* and the SDL Threat Modeling Tool, and you can find other commercial and open-source tools that may aid your efforts. There is also demand for tools that can automate model creation or threat identification, although such tools may come at a high price if they appear to find threats while missing new threats or are used too late in the development process.

Part

IV

Threat Modeling in Technologies and Tricky Areas

Part IV is where this book moves away from threat modeling as a generic approach, and focuses on threat modeling of specific technologies and tricky areas. In other words, this part moves from a focus on technique to a focus on the repertoire you'll need to address these tricky areas.

All of these technologies and areas (except requirements) share three properties that make it worth discussing them in depth:

- Systems will have similar threats.
- Those threats and the approaches to mitigating them have been extensively worked through, so there's no need to start from scratch.
- Naïve mitigations fall victim to worked-through attacks. Therefore, you can abstract what's been done in these areas into models, and you can learn the current practical state of the art in handling each.

The following chapters are included in this part:

- **Chapter 12: Requirements Cookbook** lays out a set of security requirements so that you don't have to start your requirements from a blank slate, but can borrow and adapt. Much like the other chapters in this part, requirements are a tricky area where specific advice can help you.
- **Chapter 13: Web and Cloud Threats** are the most like other threat modeling, but with a few recurring threats to consider. (That is, while an awful

lot of words have been written on the security properties of web and cloud, they're actually only a little more complex to threat model than other operational environments.)

- **Chapter 14: Accounts and Identity** are far more nuanced than web or cloud, and begin to intrude on the human world, where poor choices in design can cause people to avoid your service or work around your security measures.
- **Chapter 15: Human Factors and Usability** issues are at the overlap of the human and technological worlds, and both the modeling of threats and how to address them are less developed. That makes them no less critical, only more of a challenge and opportunity for innovation.
- **Chapter 16: Threats to Cryptosystems** is a chapter with more modest goals, not because cryptography is any harder than the other subjects, but because it's easier to get wrong in ways that look fine under casual inspection. As such, this chapter aims to familiarize you with the world of cryptography and the threat terminology that is unique to the field, relating it to the rest of the threats in the book.

CHAPTER

12

Requirements Cookbook

Important threats violate important security requirements. Ideally, those requirements are explicit, crisp, agreed-on within the development organization, and understood by customers and the people impacted by the system. Unfortunately, this is rarely the case. In part, that's because requirements are very difficult to do well. That makes requirements a tedious way to start a project, and as the agile folks will tell you, YAGNI ("you ain't gonna need it")—so we should skip straight to user stories, right? Maybe, but maybe not.

As you discover threats, you'll be forced to decide whether the threat matters. Some of that decision will be based on a risk calculation, and some will be based on a requirements calculation. If your system is not designed to maintain security in the face of hostile administrators, then all effort spent on mitigating hostile administrators will be wasted.

That said, this chapter starts with an explanation of the cookbook approach and a discussion of the interplay of requirements, threats, and mitigations. You'll then learn about ways to think about business requirements, and look at how to use common security frames to help with your requirements. (A *frame* here is a way of structuring how you look at a problem, while a *framework* is a breakdown which includes specific process steps.) The frames are "prevent/detect/respond" and "people, process, technology," with requirements in development contrasted with requirements in acquisition. Next you'll learn how to use compliance frameworks and privacy to drive your requirements. You can use these sections to decide what sort of requirements you might need.

Each of these sections may be more useful to product management than to developers. The chapter then delves deep into the more technology-centered STRIDE requirements. The STRIDE requirements are the most deeply technical and "actionable" of the requirements. You should not succumb to the temptation to make those the only requirements you consider. The chapter closes with a discussion of non-requirements.

Why a "Cookbook"?

A great many systems are available for requirements elicitation. Most of them (at best) skim over security. This chapter does not intend to replace your requirements approach, but to supplement it with a set of straw-man requirements, designed to be easily adapted to the specific needs of your system. The intent is, much like a cookbook, to give you ideas that you can easily turn into real "food." Also like a cookbook, you can't simply take what's here (the raw ingredients) and serve it to your dinner guests; but you can use what's here to prepare a scrumptious set of requirements. As you consider what you want to build, you can refer to this section for requirements that crystalize what you're thinking about.

Of course, you'll need more detail than the sample requirements can provide. For example, "Anonymous people can create/read/update/delete item" is a good starting point, but what sort of items can they create, read, update, or delete? Wikipedia has a nuanced set of answers for create, update, and delete, and another set of nuanced answers for what can be read. There's a very different set of answers on Google.com or Whitehouse.gov. The requirements examples shown cannot include the local or specific knowledge needed to make them concrete.

Most of these starting points are grouped with several related starting points. To take some examples from the section on STRIDE authentication requirements, after the requirement "Anonymous people can create/read/update/delete items," the next requirement is "All authenticated users can create/read/update/delete item," followed by "An enumerated subset of users can create/read/update/delete items." In this case, you might well need all three requirements expanded into your project's authentication requirements. In contrast, the section on authentication strength includes "We will control the authentication database" and "We will allow an outside organization (such as Facebook) to control our authentication database." These are both reasonable choices that organizations make, but you can't make both of them. The next requirement splits the difference with "We will allow an outside organization (such as Facebook) to control part of our authentication database, such as 'signed in users,' but not administrators."

The Interplay of Requirements, Threats, and Mitigations

The same sort of task interplay as discussed in the previous section takes place on a broader scale between threats, requirements, and mitigations. As threats are discovered, some of them will violate explicit requirements. Others will violate implicit requirements, offering an opportunity to improve the requirements list. Other threats may lead to discussion of whether they violate a requirement or not, again leading to possible clarification. Thus, finding threats helps you identify requirements. Discussion of threats may also lead to a discussion about the difficulty of addressing a given threat. Such discussion can also feed back into requirements when a threat can't be mitigated. Mitigations drive requirements far more often than requirements drive mitigations. (In fact, I can't think of a case where a requirement drives a mitigation without a threat, except perhaps it's a fine definition of compliance, and that may be why so many security professionals resent compliance work.) This interplay is shown visually in Figure 12-1.

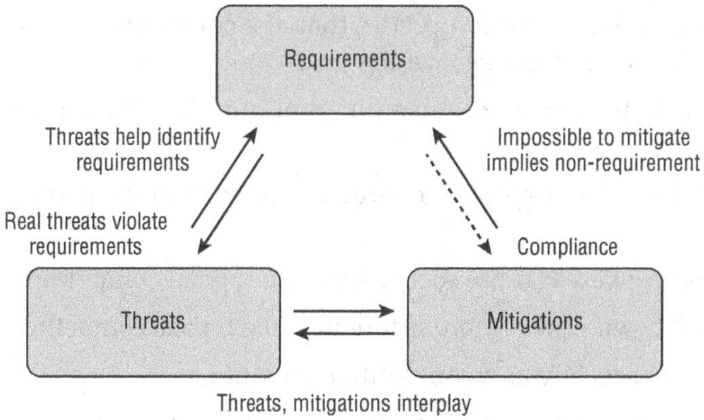

Figure 12-1: The interplay of threats, requirements, and mitigations

You might have noticed a *reductio ad absurdum* attack on this perspective. That is, taken to an extreme, it quickly becomes ridiculous. For example, if a product were to declare that the network is trusted, and all network threats are irrelevant, that would be a pretty silly decision to make, and hard to justify in front of customers if the product handles any sensitive data. However, the extreme position isn't what you should take. If you are new to threat modeling, be extremely cautious about removing requirements because you're unsure how to mitigate the threats. To check your assumption that mitigation is impossible, you should plan to spend days to weeks investigating what others have done in similar circumstances. As you develop more experience in security, that investigation will go faster, as your toolbox will be more varied.

Business Requirements

In this section you learn about the business requirements for security. These are the requirements that will make the most sense to business people. Some organizations may call these "goals," or "mission," or "vision."

Outshining the Competition

Your organization may be in a situation in which security properties or features are either a customer requirement or a competitive differentiator. In those scenarios, you can start with a requirement or requirements selected from the following list:

1. The product is no less secure than the typical competitor.
2. The product is no less secure as measured by *X* than the typical competitor.
3. The product is no less secure as measured by *X* than market leader *Y*.
4. The product will ship fewer security updates than the competition. (This can incentivize hiding vulnerabilities, which you shouldn't do.)
5. The product will have fewer exploitable vulnerabilities than the typical competitor.
6. The product will have fewer exploitable vulnerabilities than the market leader *Y*.
7. The product will be viewed as more secure than the typical competitor.
8. The product line will be viewed as more secure than the typical competitor.
9. We will be able to use security as a competitive advantage.
10. We will be able to use this security feature/property as a competitive advantage.

Industry Requirements

If your product is sold for a particular industry or use, there may be industry-specific requirements which apply. For example, if you're building payment processing software, you'll need to comply with industry rules. If you sell medical devices, you'll want to ensure that your devices have substantial defense in depth, as your ability to get them recertified quickly may be controlled by law. If you're building tools for emergency responders, they may come under particular attack. You should consider how your particular circumstances will drive your requirements.

Scenario-Driven Requirements

The use of stories, scenarios, or use cases can be a strong general approach to requirements elicitation, so it is natural to hope that security requirements might also be derived from them. That is a reasonable hope, but I am not aware of any structured approach for doing so for security requirements.

The primary challenge is that security is rarely a goal of a feature. When explaining what Alice will do as she goes about her day, few product managers say "and then we'll force her to log in again, since her session timed out over lunch" or "and then Mallory will try to break into the product by. . ." Even for security features, such as access control, it's rare to have a product manager define a scenario like "Alice adds a group to allow write access to this file, and then tests to see whether the explicit deny rule for Bob still holds."

Prevent/Detect/Respond as a Frame for Requirements

Prevent/detect/respond is a common way for organizations to think about operational security. I'm aware of a large bank that, having adopted this way of seeing the world, focuses most of its energy on response, assuming that its systems will be compromised, and focusing on reducing mean time to repair. Prevent/detect/respond can be used as a frame for thinking about requirements in development, to ensure that your technology addresses each area. It can also be used in technology acquisition or operations.

Prevention

STRIDE threat modeling is very focused on ensuring that you prevent threats. One element not well covered by STRIDE is vulnerabilities, and their management. Another is operational security approaches to prevention.

Operational Security Preventive Requirements

Operational isolation requirements focus on reducing attack surface by isolating systems from each other.

1. All production systems will be isolated from the public Internet by firewalls.
2. All production systems will be isolated from internal development and operational systems (such as HR).
3. All traversals of isolation boundaries will be authenticated by something beyond IP and port numbers.

4. All production systems will be deployed on VMs that are distinct from other production systems (that is, one application, one VM).
5. All cloud systems will be isolated from competitors. (This is easy to write, and hard to achieve.)

Least privilege requirements are focused on making it more difficult for an attacker to take advantage of an intrusion. Least privilege is easy to say and practically challenging to achieve. In the list that follows, "with privileges" means emphatically "as root/administrator," but also those points in between a "normal" user and the most privileged.

1. No production application will run with privileges.
2. No production application will run with privileges without undergoing a threat model analysis and penetration test.
3. Any production application we create that requires privileges will have those privileges isolated into a small component.
4. Application acquisition will include a discussion of threat models and operational security guidance.

Account management for prevention includes account lifecycle (as discussed in Chapter 14, "Accounts and Identity"), when it's made operational. Managing accounts across a small organization was challenging even before the days of cloud services, which make it even harder.

1. Account creation will be managed and tracked, and all service accounts will have a responsible person.
2. Accounts for people will be terminated when a person leaves.
3. Accounts will be periodically audited or reviewed to ensure that there is someone responsible for each.

Vulnerability Management

Vulnerability is a term of art that refers those accidental flaws which can be exploited by an attacker. This is in contrast to features that can be abused. In other words, a vulnerability is something that everyone agrees ought to be fixed. The exploitation of vulnerabilities can often be automated, so in order to prevent exploitation it's important to consider the vulnerability lifecycle from discovery through coding a fix, testing that fix, and delivering it. If you develop software, some of the vulnerabilities discovered will be in your code, while others will be in code on which you depend. You'll need to be able to handle both sorts. In each case, you'll need to take the fix, test it, and deliver it onwards to people in operations. Sometimes those operations people will be in the same organization, but oftentimes they'll be external. If you're in operations, you'll need to be able to discover vulnerability reports from your suppliers, and manage them. You may also get vulnerability reports about the systems you operate, and you'll need to manage those as well.

Once you have a way to learn about the updates, you'll need a way to flow those updates through to your software and/or deployed systems. If you develop complex software, good unit tests of the functionality you use in outside components will help you rapidly test security updates and identify issues that might come with them. Maybe that's part of a continuous deployment strategy for your site, or perhaps it's something like running a security response process the way Microsoft does (Rains, 2013) so your customers can learn about, receive, and deploy your updates in their environment.

Vulnerability Reports about Your Products or Systems

Properly managing inbound vulnerability reports is an important task, and you should consider how you'll encourage people to report vulnerabilities to you. There is an alternative approach, which is "we will sue security researchers to inhibit discovery and reporting of security flaws." This backfires. For example, after Cisco sued researcher Mike Lynn for exposing flaws in its products, Cisco CSO John Stewart said "we did some silly things" and "we created a firestorm" (McMillan, 2008).

Product vulnerability management requirements might include:

1. We will have a public policy encouraging the reporting of security flaws.
2. We will have a public policy encouraging the reporting of security flaws and make it easy to do so.
3. We will have a public policy encouraging the reporting of security flaws by paying for them.
4. We will have a public policy encouraging the reporting of security flaws in our online services.
5. We will have a public policy encouraging the reporting of security flaws in our online services, and explain what testing is acceptable or unacceptable.
6. We will have automatic update functionality built into our product.
7. We will have automatic update functionality built into our product, and it will be on by default.
8. We will support only the latest version of this product, and security fixes will require an update.
9. We will support only the latest version of this product, and security fixes will require an update and those updates may include feature changes.

10. We will have a public policy on support lifetime, and produce security fixes for all currently supported products.
11. We will have a public channel for vulnerability announcements that is designed to satisfy those looking to sign up to lots of channels to track all the software they operate. As such, it will be nothing but vulnerability announcements.

Managing Vulnerabilities in External Code

It is important to track the components on which you depend and their security updates. This applies to both development and operations, and to both commercial and open-source components. Your acquisition process should include understanding how an organization notifies customers of security updates. If there's no mail list, RSS feed, or other mechanism established for security update notifications, that's probably a problem. Some possible requirements include:

1. We will only discover security issues when they're important enough for the media to talk about.
2. Each group will maintain its own list of dependencies.
3. We will maintain a single list of dependencies to track for software updates.
4. We will ensure that we track dependencies, and have a person assigned to reading the updates and generating action as appropriate.
5. Our dependency-tracking SLA will be no more than four hours from announcement to bug filed, 24 × 365.
    a. The response will be a risk assessment and possibly an action plan.
    b. The response will be to test and roll all patches of severity *X* without bothering with risk assessment.
    c. The response will be to deploy all patches and believe in our rollback practices.
6. We will maintain a testbed to roll out new patches before putting them into production.
7. We will use virtual machines taken from production to test new patches before rolling them into production.
8. We will have patch management software that can deploy to all operational services.

Operationally managing vulnerabilities is more broad than managing patches. Sometimes a vendor will release an advisory about a problem before there's a patch, and you'll have to decide if and how you want to manage such reports. An advisory may involve work in addition to or in place of patching.

Detection

Detecting security problems is a challenge in the chaos of modern operations. Even in regulated industries, most intrusions are detected by a third party. The right way to perform security logging and analysis seems to be elusive. Nevertheless, if you want to use prevent/detect/respond as a frame for thinking about requirements, useful requirements can be found in this section. There are two major goals to think about: incident detection and incident analysis. From a requirements perspective, incident detection involves logging and ensuring that the logs are analyzed. There are four main types of monitoring: change detection, signature attack detection, anomaly attack detection, and impact detection. These are discussed further in Chapter 9 "Tradeoffs When Addressing Threats" under "Wait and See." Incident analysis involves recording enough state transitions that an analyst can reconstruct what happened.

Operational requirements:

1. We will detect attacks of type *X* within time *Y*.
2. We will detect 75 percent of attacks of type *X* within time *Y*, and 50 percent of the remainder within *Z*.

Product requirements:

1. Our product will use the word "security" in all log messages that we expect are security related.
2. Our product will log in a way to help detect attacks.
3. Our product will log login attempts in a way to help detect attacks.
4. Our product will track repeated attempts to perform any action, and flag such in the logs.

There is a fuzzy line between detection and response requirements. Rigidly categorizing them probably isn't useful.

Response

Incident response teams often use an approach that mirrors the one suggested by Ripley in the movie *Aliens*, "I say we take off and nuke the entire site from orbit. It's the only way to be sure." Planning for that in product threat modeling involves a good separation between your product and its configuration and data. That separation enables the response team to nuke the product install (which may be compromised) while preserving the configuration and data (which may also be compromised, but can perhaps be cleaned up). In the same vein, publishing a set of signatures or hashes for the code you ship will help a response team check the integrity of your product after a compromise.

In operational threat modeling for response, there is a much longer set of requirements from which you can build:

1. We will have an incident response plan.
2. We will have an incident response plan in a binder on a shelf somewhere.
3. We will have an incident response plan and run annual/quarterly/monthly drills to ensure we know how to operate.
4. Our intrusion-detection SLA will be no more than four hours from detection to incident response execution, 24 × 365.
5. Our intrusion-detection SLA will be no more than eight business hours from detection to incident response execution during normal business hours.
6. Our incident response plan will [not] be designed to preserve court-quality evidence.
7. The senior administrators will be trained in our incident response plan.
8. All administrators will be trained in our incident response plan.
9. All administrators will have a wallet card with first response steps and contact information.
10. All incidents will have a lessons learned document produced.
11. All incidents will have a lessons learned document produced, appropriate to the scale of the incident.
12. Lessons learned documents will be shared with the appropriate people.
13. Lessons learned documents will be shared with all employees.
14. Lessons learned documents will be shared with all employees and partners.
15. Lessons learned documents will be published when we are required to report a breach so others can learn from our mistakes.
16. Lessons learned documents will be published so others can learn from our mistakes.

The act of publishing lessons learned documents may seem unusual, but it is increasingly common practice, and the transparency has been beneficial to business. For example, after a major outage at Amazon, they published a root cause analysis, and Netflix announced that they had used the information to improve their own service (Netflix, 2011).

CROSS-REFERENCE See also the earlier section "Vulnerability Management."

People/Process/Technology as a Frame for Requirements

It's also common for people to use people/process/technology as a frame for thinking about security, so it may help you to use it as a way to find requirements.

People

There are two major categories of security requirements for people: trustworthiness and skills. Trustworthiness is a matter of how much authority and discretion the people in the system are expected to have. Organizations do various levels of background checking at hiring time or as an ongoing matter. Such checks can be expensive and intrusive, and may be constrained or required by local law. If your product is intended for use by highly trusted people, you should be explicit about that. Requirements for trustworthiness can be somewhat managed by audit and retributive measures, which impose development requirements regarding logging and operational requirements around the audit process. Skill requirements should also be clearly documented. It is sometimes helpful (and usually tricky) to have a certification of some sort that attempts to assess the skills of an individual.

Security requirements focused on people might include:

1. Employees with cash management responsibility will undergo background checks for financial crimes.
2. Employees with cash management responsibility will undergo credit checks.
3. Employees with cash management responsibility will undergo regular credit checks.
4. Employees dealing with children will be required to certify that they do not have a criminal conviction.
5. Employees dealing with children will be required to certify that they do not have a criminal conviction in the last seven years.
6. Employees dealing with children will undergo a criminal background check.
7. Prospective employees will have an opportunity to contest information that is returned, as we are aware that background checks are often inaccurate.

If you are not familiar with the issues of accuracy in background checks, there are fascinating reports available, including ones from the National Consumer Law Center (Yu, 2012) or the National Employment Law Project (Neighly, 2013).

Process

Understanding how the product's technology is to be operated can also drive security requirements. Drafting a security operations guide can be a good way to elicit product security requirements.

Technology

It is very tempting to say that this entire book is about the technology, so "this section intentionally left blank." But that's not really the case. This book shows that models of your technology are the best place to start threat modeling. But all technology interacts with other technology, so what are the limits or scope of how you approach this? The best answer when you're getting started is to focus on those technologies where you can most directly address threats. As your skills grow, looking along your supply chain (and possibly the supply chains you are part of) may be a good way to expand your horizons.

Development Requirements vs. Acquisition Requirements

When you're developing technology from scratch, the set of security requirements you might choose to address is much larger than when you're acquiring technology from someone else. This issue is exacerbated by technological ecosystems. For example, the Burroughs 5500 computers of the 1960s had a memory architecture that was resistant by design to stack-smashing sorts of attacks (Hoffman, 2008; Shostack, 2008). However, it is challenging to procure a system with such features today.

In reality, few systems are really developed "from scratch." The security requirements of every project are constrained by its inputs. It is helpful to everyone along the chain to document what security requirements you do or do not support. For example, if you are developing on Windows, defending against the administrator account is not supported (Culp, 2013). Similarly, before Windows 8, you cannot defend against apps running as the same user. Windows 8 adds some capabilities in this area (Hazen, 2012).

Compliance-Driven Requirements

An ever-expanding set of security requirements is driven by compliance programs. Those compliance regimes may be imposed on you or your customers, and they make an excellent source of security requirements. More rarely, they're even a source of excellent security requirements. (It's challenging to write broad requirements that are specific enough to engineer from.) This section covers three such requirement sets: the Cloud Security Alliance (CSA) control matrix and domains, the United States NIST Publication 200, and PCI-DSS (the Payment Card Industry Data Security Standard). To the extent that you're building technology for a single organization, you may have security requirements directly imposed. If you're building technology to sell, or give away, then your customers may have requirements like these. If you expect to encounter a set of compliance requirements from your customers, it will probably be helpful to create or use a single meta-framework that covers all the issues in the frameworks you need to comply with, rather than attempt working with each one. There are commercially available "unified compliance frameworks," and depending on the number of compliance requirements you face, it may be worth buying one for speed, coverage, or expertise. The CSA framework can be a useful starting point if you need something free. The requirements that follow are presented as places from which to derive more detailed requirements. They should not be used to replace an appropriately detailed understanding of your requirements for compliance purposes.

Cloud Security Alliance

The CSA is a non-profit organization dedicated to cloud security. They have produced two documents that are helpful for security requirements: the controls domains and the controls matrix.

The first document maps controls into a set of domains, including governance and enterprise risk management, legal issues, compliance and audit, information management and data security, traditional security, business continuity and disaster recovery, data center operations, incident response, application security, encryption and key management, identity and access management, virtualization, and security as a service. This is a fine list of areas to consider, and the CSA has a lot more documentation for you to dig into. (They also consider architecture, and portability and interoperability, but those seem somewhat less relevant for security.)

The CSA also has a Cloud Control Matrix of 98 control areas, with mappings that show their applicability to architectural areas (physical, network, compute, storage, application, and data), to corporate governance, to cloud service delivery models (SaaS/PaaS/IaaS), and to service providers versus tenants. Each control area is also mapped to COBIT, HIPAA/HITECH, ISO/IEC 27001–2005, NIST SP800–53, FedRAMP, PCI DSS, BITS Shared Assessments SIG v6 & AUP v5, GAAP, Jericho Forum, and the NERC CIP.

The requirements documented in the Cloud Controls Matrix are designed to be used as a basis for cloud operational security. Some of the requirements are most relevant to cloud services, but it's a fine resource to start with, with the advantages of being both freely available and already mapped to a large set of other sets of controls.

NIST Publication 200

Requirements in this publication are a mixed set, ranging from planning and risk assessment to physical environment protection and technical requirements, such as authorization and system integrity. Federal agencies are required to "develop and promulgate formal, documented policies and procedures . . . and ensure their effective implementation" (NIST, 2006). US Government agencies must also meet the controls laid out in NIST Special Publication 800–53. Items marked with a star align to one or more STRIDE threats, so you might cross-check the section "The STRIDE Requirements" later in this chapter.

For each item in this list, consider if there's a need to address the issue in your product requirements:

- Access control, including authorization*
- Awareness and training
- Audit and accountability including traceability of actions back to accounts*
- Certification, accreditation, and security assessments, including assessments of whether information systems are suitably protected
- Configuration management, which imposes configuration and management requirements
- Contingency planning
- Identification and authentication*
- Incident response
- Maintenance
- Motherhood and apple pie (just kidding)
- Media protection
- Physical and environment protection
- Planning, including plans for the organizational information systems and controls

- Personnel security, including criteria for who's hired, managing termination, and penalties for compliance failures
- Risk assessment of threats (including risks to mission, functions, image, or reputation) to the organization or individuals
- Systems and service acquisition, including allocating resources and deploying system development life cycles that address security
- System and communication protection*
- System and communication integrity*

PCI-DSS

The Payment Card Industry Data Security Standard (PCI-DSS) is a set of standards for those processing payment card data (PCI, 2010). These standards are generally incorporated into contracts associated with credit card processing. Note the wide variance in specificity—from "have a security policy" to "do not use default passwords"—in the following requirements:

1. Install and maintain a firewall configuration to protect cardholder data.
2. Do not use vendor-supplied defaults for system passwords and other security parameters.
3. Protect stored cardholder data.
4. Encrypt transmission of cardholder data across open, public networks.
5. Use and regularly update anti-virus software.
6. Develop and maintain secure systems and applications.
7. Restrict access to cardholder data by business need-to-know.
8. Assign a unique ID to each person with computer access.
9. Restrict physical access to cardholder data.
10. Track and monitor all access to network resources and cardholder data.
11. Regularly test security systems and processes.
12. Maintain a policy that addresses information security.

Privacy Requirements

You'll find there are a few main motivations for privacy, including legal compliance and a desire to make only those promises that can be kept—to avoid customer anger. This section covers a selection of important privacy requirements frameworks. They are important because they underlie many laws or are influential with regulators (Fair Information Practices, Privacy by Design), can help you avoid privacy blow-ups (Seven Laws of Identity), are pragmatic, and are designed to be accessible to non-specialist software developers (Microsoft's Privacy Standards for Developers).

Fair Information Practices

Fair Information Practices (FIP) is a concept that goes back to a 1973 report for the United States Department of Health, Education, and Welfare, which put forth five core fair information Practices. Along the way, practices were promoted to principles, and if you're paying close attention, you'll notice FIP expanded to either, or sometimes even both (Gellman, 2013). The difference is minor, but I'll hew to the term used in the source discussed. The original enumeration was as follows:

1. Notice/Awareness
2. Choice/Consent
3. Access
4. Security
5. Enforcement/Redress

These form the basis for the 1980 OECD "Guidelines on the Protection of Privacy and Transborder Flows of Personal Data." The OECD put forth eight Principles. The European Union's Data Protection Directive and Canada's Personal Information Protection and Electronic Documents Act are also based on FIPs, and each has divided them into slightly different lists. These high-level principles may be a useful checklist when evaluating security and privacy issues at design time. Which list you should use will depend on a number of factors, including the location of the organization and its customer base. Be aware that many software engineers find these lists are too generic to be of much use when designing a system.

Privacy By Design

Privacy by Design is a set of principles created by the Ontario Privacy Commissioner with the goal of helping organizations embed privacy into product design. It outlines seven main principles, quoted below:

1. Proactive
2. By Default
3. Embedded
4. Positive Sum
5. Life-cycle Protection

6. Visibility/Transparency
7. Respect for Users

Privacy by Design has been criticized as "vague" and leaving "many open questions about their application when engineering systems" (Gürses, 2011).

The Seven Laws of Identity

Kim Cameron of Microsoft has put forward a set of seven principles he calls the *Laws of Identity* for digital identity systems (Cameron, 2005). They are not overall privacy requirements, but a great deal of privacy relates to how a system treats "identity," a concept further discussed in Chapter 14 "Accounts and Identity." They may be an interesting complement to contextual integrity (discussed in Chapter 6 "Privacy Tools"). These are extracted from a document that describes and contextualizes each law:

1. **User Control and Consent:** Technical identity systems must only reveal information identifying a user with the user's consent.
2. **Minimal Disclosure for a Constrained Use:** The solution that discloses the least amount of identifying information and best limits its use is the most stable long-term solution.
3. **Justifiable Parties:** Digital identity systems must be designed so the disclosure of identifying information is limited to parties having a necessary and justifiable place in a given identity relationship.
4. **Directed Identity:** A universal identity system must support both omni-directional identifiers for use by public entities and uni-directional identifiers for use by private entities, thus facilitating discovery while preventing unnecessary release of correlation handles.
5. **Pluralism of Operators and Technologies:** A universal identity system must channel and enable the inter-working of multiple identity technologies run by multiple identity providers.
6. **Human Integration:** The universal identity metasystem must define the human user to be a component of the distributed system integrated through unambiguous human-machine communication mechanisms offering protection against identity attacks.
7. **Consistent Experience Across Contexts:** The unifying identity metasystem must guarantee its users a simple, consistent experience while enabling separation of contexts through multiple operators and technologies.

These laws can be reasonably easily inverted into threats, such as "does the system get appropriate consent before revealing information?" or "does the system disclose identifying information not required for a transaction?" However, this runs the risk of losing the richness of the Laws of Identity, so it's left as an exercise for you.

Microsoft Privacy Standards for Development

The Microsoft Privacy Standards for Developers (MPSD) is a prescriptive document that, for a set of scenarios, gives advice about how to address them. However, the standards are not focused on the discovery of privacy issues. They focus instead on a set of scenarios (notice, choice, onward transfer, access, security, and data integrity) and requirements for those scenarios (Friedberg, 2008).

The difference between these privacy standards and the more principle-oriented approaches is a result of the customer-focus. The MPSD are explicitly based on the FIPs, but are designed to provide practical advice for developers. Making it easy for (a defined) someone to use the document increases the effectiveness of an approach, and the audience-focus of the MPSD could well be emulated by other documents to help improve privacy.

Which of these privacy requirements frameworks will best inform your technology depends on what you're building, and for whom. FIPs or Privacy by Design may spark valuable discussion of your designs or goals. If your system is focused on people, the "Seven Laws" can help. If you lack privacy expertise, the MPSD will help (but it is not intended to replace professional advice).

The STRIDE Requirements

You may recall that STRIDE is the opposite of properties that you want in a system, so properly this section ought to be called "The AINCAA Requirements," but that's just not very catchy. The relationship between STRIDE and the desired properties is shown in Table 12-1.

Table 12-1: STRIDE and AINCAA

THREAT	DESIRABLE PROPERTY
Spoofing	Authentication
Tampering	Integrity
Repudiation	Non-Repudiation
Information Disclosure	Confidentiality
Denial of Service	Availability
Elevation of Privilege	Authorization

The following subsections are organized according to the desirable property shown in Table 12-1.

Authentication

Authentication is the processes or activity which increases your confidence that something is genuine. For example, entering a password increases the system's confidence that the person behind the keyboard really is authorized to use the system.

Is Authentication Required for Various Activities?

Different systems require different levels of authentication. As discussed in the chapter introduction, many websites offer read content to anonymous people (that is, no authentication is required). Some, like Wikipedia, offer write access as well. Some requirements you can build on include:

1. Anonymous people can create/read/update/delete items.
2. All authenticated users can create/read/update/delete items.
3. An enumerated subset of users can create/read/update/delete items.

How Strong an Authentication Is Required?

As stated above, different systems require different levels of authentication, and different forms of control for the authentication system. Sample requirements include:

1. Single-factor authentication is sufficient for activity *X*.
2. Single-factor authentication plus a risk management check is sufficient for activity *X*.
3. Two-factor authentication is sufficient for activity *X*.
4. We will control the authentication database.
5. The IT/marketing/sales department will control the authentication database.
6. We will allow an outside organization (such as Facebook) to control our authentication database.
7. We will allow an outside organization (such as Facebook) to control part of our authentication database, such as "signed-in users" but not administrators.
8. Authentication should only be possible for people in IP range *X*.
9. Authentication should only be possible for people in physical location *X* (such as in the building or in the United States).

Note that systems to physically locate people are either weak, buggy (that is, high false positive, false negative rates) or exceptionally expensive (such as a dedicated air-gap network).

Account Life Cycle

The ways in which accounts are managed will vary based on your requirements. Sample requirements include:

1. Anyone can create an account.
2. Anyone with an e-mail address can create an account.
3. Anyone with a validated e-mail address can create an account.
4. Anyone with a credit card number can create an account.
5. Anyone with a valid, authorizable credit card can create an account.
6. Anyone with a credit card who can tell us how much we charged can create an account.
7. Anyone with a bank account who can tell us how much we charged can create an account.
8. Only an authorized administrator can create normal accounts.
9. Only two authorized administrators can create a new administrator account,
    a. and all other admins are notified,
    b. and an auditing team is notified. (This is perhaps a non-repudiation requirement, but you can also think of it as part of the account life cycle.)
10. Anyone can close their account at any time, and the data is deleted as soon as possible.
11. Anyone can close their account at any time, and the data is deleted after a cooling off period.
12. Anyone can close their account at any time, and the data is kept for business purposes.
13. Anyone can close their account at any time, and the data is kept for *N* time to satisfy regulatory requirements.
14. Administrator participation is required to close an account.
15. When administrator participation is required to close an account, the account must be globally inaccessible within *N* minutes.

Integrity

Sample integrity requirements include:

1. Data will be protected from arbitrary tampering.
2. This data will only be subject to modification by an enumerated set of authorized users.

3. These files/records will only be subject to modification by enumerated authorized users.
4. These files/records will only be subject to modification by enumerated authorized users, and edit actions will be logged.
5. These files/records will only be subject to modification by enumerated authorized users, and edit content will be logged.
6. These files/records will be unwritable when the system is in operation.
7. These files/records will be append-only when the system is in operation.
8. Modifications to these files/records will be cryptographically detectable.
9. Modifications to these files/records will be cryptographically detectable with commonly available tools.
10. Data sent over this inter-process channel will be protected from tampering by the operating system.
11. Data sent over this channel will be protected from tampering by a cryptographic integrity mechanism.
12. Messages will be protected from tampering by a cryptographic integrity mechanism.

You'll notice that there are integrity requirements on channels and messages. The channel is what the message travels down. Protection in the channel doesn't protect the data once it has left the channel.

For example, consider e-mail. Imagine a well-encrypted, tamper-resistant, replay-protected channel between two mail servers. The operators of those servers have confidence that the messages are well protected in that channel; but a person on one end or the other could alter a message, and forward it. If the messages themselves have tamper resistance, then that can be detected. Such tamper resistance could be imparted, for example, by a cryptographic signature scheme.

Non-Repudiation

Recall that non-repudiation can cover both business and technical requirements. Sample requirements include:

1. The system shall maintain logs.
2. The system shall protect its logs.
3. The system shall protect its logs from administrators.
4. The logs will survive compromise of a host; for example, by writing logs to a remote system.

5. The logs will allow account compromise to be differentiated from a behavior change.
6. The logs will resist counterparty fraud; for example, by using cryptographic signatures.
7. The logs will resist insider tampering; for example, with hash chains or write-once media.

Confidentiality

Sample confidentiality requirements include:

1. Data in file/database will be available only to these authorized users.
2. Data in file/database will be available only to these authorized users, even if computers/disks/tapes are stolen.
3. Data in file/database will be available only to these authorized users, even if computers are stolen while turned on.
4. The name/existence of this datastore will only be exposed to these authorized users.
5. The content of communication between Alice and Bob will only be exposed to these authorized users.
6. The topic of communication between Alice and Bob will only be exposed to these authorized users.
7. The existence of communication between Alice and Bob will only be exposed to these authorized users.

Availability

Sample availability requirements include:

1. The system shall be available 99 percent of the time.
2. The system shall be available 100 percent of the time.
3. The system shall be available 100 percent of the time, and we will pay our customers if it's not.
4. The system shall be available for *N* percent of the time, including planned maintenance.
5. Only authenticated users will be able to cause the system to spend 10× more CPU than they have spent.
6. The system will be able to resist a simple DoS such as synflooding by a 50,000-host botnet.

7. The system will be able to resist a simple DoS such as HTTPS connection initiation by a 50,000-host botnet.
8. The system will be able to resist a customized DoS by a 50,000-host botnet.

The selection of 50,000 is only somewhat arbitrary. It is large enough to be a substantial threat, while small enough that there are likely quite a few of them out there.

Authorization

Sample authorization requirements include:

1. The system shall have a central authorization engine.
2. The system shall have a central authorization engine with a configurable policy.
3. Authorization controls shall be stored with the item being controlled, such as with an ACL.
4. Authorization controls shall be stored in a central location.
5. The system shall limit who can read data at a higher security level.
6. The system shall limit who can write data to a higher integrity level.
7. The authorization engine should work with accounts or account groups.
8. The authorization engine should work with roles (properties of accounts).

There is a tension between storing authorization controls centrally versus with the objects being protected. The former is easier to manage but harder for normal people to understand (often to the point of being unsure where to go). The system controlling who can read from a higher integrity level is analogous to military data classification schemes. Someone with a secret clearance can't read a top-secret document. (This was first formalized as the Bell-LaPadula model [Bell, 1973]). Controlling who can write to a higher integrity level is also very useful, and is described by the Biba model (Biba, 1977). The Biba model is a description of how an operating system protects itself from programs running as a normal user.

Cloud and DevOps Authorization and Audit

Much of cloud operations eventually boils down to a set of authorization questions. Who is authorized to make which changes, and who made which changes. The lists might not line up, because policy and implementation don't always perfectly line up. As organizations move, intentionally or not, toward DevOps models, these questions become trickier. The requirements also change. Rather than a formal handoff from development to test, the code is promoted to pre-production, and then to production. Sample DevOps requirements include:

1. Any developer is authorized to push code to pre-production.
2. Any developer is authorized to push code to production.
3. Any production change requires only test pass complete.
4. These production changes only are possible with test pass completion.
5. Every production change requires human signoff.
6. Every change must be designed and tested to roll back.
7. Every production change can be tracked to a person.
8. Every production change can be tracked to a test run.

Non-Requirements

Just as enumerating requirements is important, so is being explicit about what the system won't do. Some attacks are too expensive to deal with (for example, you might accept that the KGB could subvert your employees). Others may require capabilities that the operating system, chip-maker, and so on, do not currently supply. Whatever the reason, the things that your system doesn't do should be explicit, so your management, operations, or customers are not surprised. The following sections consider three ways to express and communicate non-requirements: operational guides, warnings and prompts, and Microsoft's "10 Immutable Laws of Security."

Operational Non-Requirements

Sometimes there will be things that can't be secured in the code but must be addressed in operations. The simplest example is reading the logs to detect attacks. Other goals, such as defending against malware or a malicious admin, can be attractive distractions. They generally fall outside of what you should worry about. You should document these as either requirements or non-requirements and engineer appropriately.

Have an Operational Guide

Documenting these in an operational guide serves two purposes: transparency and requirements elicitation. Transparency is useful because it helps your customers set their expectations appropriately, and avoid unpleasant surprises. The second purpose, requirements elicitation, means that as you document what an operator needs to do, you may well decide that the requirements are unrealistic, and decide to either add features to make something more feasible, or remove features that can't be used securely.

Defend against Malware in the Right Way

Trying to defend a system against malware that is already on the system is a complex and probably futile effort for most products. The exceptions are operating systems creators and security software creators. If you're not in either group, and if the malware is running inside the same trust boundaries as your code, there's little you can do.

Most software systems should focus on preventing the elevation of privilege threats that allow malicious software to run. You should assume that the system is working on behalf of the people authorized to run code. (Obviously, this doesn't apply if you're creating an operating system or anti-virus product.)

Decide if Defending against Admin Is a Requirement

Most systems should not try to defend against the malicious admin. (The same principle as malware applies, but worse.) If the admin of a system is malicious, then they can do a wide variety of things. Some cryptographic systems may allow your data to transit these systems safely, but if you decrypt data on a system controlled by a malicious admin, they can capture your password or the plaintext of your documents. (Worse, they can get tricky. For example, telling you that a good cryptographic key didn't work, tricking you into entering other passwords you commonly use.)

If you're creating a high-assurance system of some form, you might have a requirement to always apply a two-person rule to defend against administrators. If that's the case, then you have a fine challenge ahead.

Warnings and Prompts

Some things that can't be secured in the code are sufficiently dangerous that there should be a warning before allowing the system to proceed. These things can be considered non-requirements, or they can be used to drive requirements that improve the architecture of the system. See Chapter 15 "Human Factors and Usability" for more information.

Microsoft's "10 Immutable Laws"

Microsoft's "10 Immutable Laws of Security" are an example of how to explain what your system doesn't do. The second paragraph of that document opens with "Don't hold your breath waiting for an update that will protect you from the issues we'll discuss below. It isn't possible for Microsoft or any software vendor to 'fix' them, because they result from the way computers work" (Culp, 2013). The first several "laws" are as follows:

> Law #1: If a bad guy can persuade you to run his program on your computer, it's not solely your computer anymore.
>
> Law #2: If a bad guy can alter the operating system on your computer, it's not your computer anymore.
>
> Law #3: If a bad guy has unrestricted physical access to your computer, it's not your computer anymore.
>
> Law #4: If you allow a bad guy to run active content in your website, it's not your website anymore.
>
> Law #5: Weak passwords trump strong security.
>
> Law #6: A computer is only as secure as the administrator is trustworthy.

You might note that laws 1, 2, and 4 sure do seem like slight variations on one another. That's to draw out the implications.

Summary

In this chapter, you've learned that good security requirements act as a complement to threat modeling, enabling you to make better decisions about threats you discover with the techniques in Part II of this book.

You've been given a set of base requirements that are designed to help you do the following:

- Understand the space of security requirements better.
- Quickly crystalize more precise requirements.

This chapter should serve as a practical, go-to resource when you're working through requirements at a business or technology level. The business level includes requirements driven by competitive pressure and industry, and requirements to handle vulnerabilities that your code might contain.

You've also seen how to use people/process/technology and prevent/detect/respond to inform your requirements process. Compliance frameworks, including those from the Cloud Security Alliance, the U.S. government, and the payment card industry can be used as a base for your requirements.

You've learned about a variety of sources for privacy requirements. Lastly, you've been reminded how the STRIDE threats violate properties, and how those properties can be developed into requirements.

CHAPTER 13

Web and Cloud Threats

In many ways, threat modeling for the web and cloud are very much like threat modeling for anything else, but these unique environments have some recurring threats, which are covered in this chapter.

This chapter is organized into web threats, cloud threats, cloud provider threats, and mobile threats. Web threats are broken into website threats, web browser, and plugin threats. Many of the cloud threats are expressed with respect to infrastructure as a service (IaaS) and platform as a service (PaaS). It closes with a section on mobile threats.

Web Threats

The web is composed of a simple and powerful set of protocols and languages. It has become a cliché to say that it has changed everything. It's easy to forget that the web is software like other software. Although you might assume that you need to threat model it in some new ways, the truth is that it's like most other software, so techniques such as STRIDE and attack trees work well for web technologies.

Website Threats

Public websites receive large amounts of scrutiny, and suffer from all that the world can throw at them. The classic STRIDE threats all apply, as do a slew of web-specific attacks that happen when you forget that there's a trust boundary between them and the apparently nice doggy that is wagging its tail and slobbering in remarkably cleverly formed SQL in your forms and JavaScript in your URLs in order to cause harm.

Usually, threats such as SQL injections and XSS are handled later in the software engineering process. You'll be developing using patterns, libraries, and frameworks that make each threat less likely, using appropriate testing tools to catch problems during testing, and watching the logs after deployment. So you're done, right? Unfortunately, no. You should be threat modeling to find the unique threats your site will be vulnerable to, such as your ad provider, your analytics code, and that authentication database you're using from some crazy start-up in San Francisco. A standard data flow diagram (DFD) showing where the data comes from for your server is essential, and a client-side DFD is also a pretty good idea, if only to ensure that you have a good test suite. A client-side DFD can also be a good way to create a list that helps you track when your dependencies issue security updates.

Web Browser and Plugin Threats

The web browser has become people's primary portal onto the Internet, and occasionally their last line of automated defense against attacks. Anyone considering building a web browser needs at least one expert with a deep knowledge of the history of browser security issues.

Browser companies could substantially help matters by being super-diligent about their security goals, and how those goals manifest between tabs, websites, and the OS hosting the browser. Clarity from browser creators on how to create a plugin that does not violate security would also be most welcome.

Web plugins or add-ons that extend browser security are becoming less and less common, in part because the two best-known and widely deployed plugins, Java and Flash, have both suffered serious and ongoing security problems. Another reason plug-ins are becoming less common is Apple's willingness to exclude Flash from the iPhone.

Any of the building blocks for finding threats can be applied to a web browser. For example, the STRIDE threats all apply to a web browser. There's spoofing of web pages for phishing or other goals, cross-tab tampering and tampering with files included from other servers. There's information disclosure about browser history vis CSS sniffing, and similar examples exist for each STRIDE threat. There are also very specific attack libraries available for web browsers and website designers.

If you're going to create a browser plugin, there are two unique elements to consider: the browser's security model and the browser's privacy model. You should also realize that auto-update is important and must be done securely.

Browser Security Model

You must deeply understand and respect the browser's security model, and not accidentally break it. This security model includes elements such as the same-origin policy, the boundaries between pages, and what can and can't open a new window, resize a window, and so on. You must also remember to treat the other sides of connections as malicious with respect to the browser. That is, from the browser's perspective, your component that sits on a web server could be under the control of an attacker, who can then send malicious content to your plugin and compromise additional systems. (Similarly, your plugin may be modified or run through a proxy that rewrites data to attack the server components.) However, there are times when breaking the browser security model is intentional and appropriate. For example, some security testing plugins do so.

Several experts have told me in all seriousness that browser security models are now so complex that I should not even write a section about this. I'm tempted to say that browser plugins, like crypto, is a domain for which you need expertise and penetration testing. It would be wonderful if browser manufacturers could fix this, and offer easier to understand plugin models so that plugins could be developed without putting the people who install them at risk. For a history of the three flaws in one popular plugin, see Mark Pilgrim's article "Avoid Common Pitfalls in Greasemonkey" (O'Reilly Network, 2005). (As an aside, Pilgrim's blog post is a good example of a "Note to API Callers," as discussed in Chapter 7, "Processing and Managing Threats.") For a book-length treatment of the full complexity of modern browsers, see Michal Zalewski's *The Tangled Web* (No Starch Press, 2011).

Browser Privacy Model

Similar to respecting the browser's security model, your plugin should respect the browser's privacy model. You should not allow tracking or surveillance in any way that the browser does not, and you should ensure that your controls are at least as accessible as those offered by the browser.

Auto-Update

It is very likely that you will have numerous security issues with your plugin, and you should therefore ensure that it's easy to report bugs to you, and that your updater works well with the browser's auto-update mechanism, and that you have a security update process that can deliver security updates without any tradeoffs such as new or changed user interfaces, new licenses, or similar impediments to upgrading.

Cloud Tenant Threats

You can use an attacker grouping approach to break out cloud threats. There are two main classes of new attackers (threats) when you move an IT system to the cloud: those from insiders at the cloud operator, and those from your fellow tenants of the cloud system. There are generally some new instances of availability threats, based on the increased complexity of connectivity. There are also two sets of legal threats: those that add complexity and/or effort or reduce the assurance of compliance, and the different legal standards around data given to third parties. Lastly, there's a hybrid of those legal threats, which are threats to forensic response. In this section, you'll see the term *cloud provider* used to refer to an organization that offers any combination of infrastructure, platform, or software as a service. Their customer is you, and like their other customers, you are a tenant of their service. Attackers might be tenants, or those who have broken in.

Insider Threats

When you move your data or operations to someone else's cloud, you add a trust boundary. That boundary has the employees and contractors of the cloud operator inside of it, with your data. As administrators, they have unavoidable technical access to the data you provide. They may intentionally attack you, fall victim to an attack themselves, accidentally misconfigure software, or fail to perform maintenance, such as wiping disks between re-allocations.

There are two ways to mitigate this threat: contractually and cryptographically. Contractual approaches dominate today because they're easier; and for most of the risks, it turns out that a contract is sufficient. However, contracts may not be subject to negotiation unless you're spending lots of money. Unfortunately, companies often use contracts to protect personal information, where much of the risk is external to the companies signing the contracts.

The cryptographic approach is to encrypt the data (and possibly obfuscate the code) before sending it. This is easier with a cloud storage system than with software as a service. Well-encrypted, integrity-protected, and authenticated data can be stored anywhere with a very low reduction in safety. (The encrypted state of the data will influence what processing can be done on the encrypted data. There is interesting cryptographic research on processing encrypted data, which as of this writing usually isn't part of the standard crypto libraries that you should use.) Of course, the keys need to be stored securely, or you're trading confidentiality and integrity for availability.

Co-Tenant Threats

These threats are to tenants of "infrastructure as a service" (IaaS) and to a lesser degree "platform as a service" (PaaS), whereby the provider/tenant trust boundary allows tenants to execute arbitrary code inside the data center. In IaaS, the code execution privileges are effectively unlimited, although they may formally be limited to what a non-administrative account can do. In PaaS, the code that is supposed to execute is far more limited. Historically, few platforms were constructed with a threat model that the most important attacker is already on the system. It is far more common, and probably even appropriate, for platform designers to worry about the trust boundary between the system and those who cannot execute any code. Unless the platform software has been carefully constructed to resist elevation of privilege attacks and to prioritize finding and fixing those, there are likely vulnerabilities that allow an attacker to violate the rules. That leads to second-order threats to the cloud tenants.

There is also a set of threats from other tenants, ranging from the trivial to the movie plot. At the trivial end, you may be behind the same single firewall as your competitor, or someone without an IT department. You might also be on the same domain as they are, such as cloudapp.net or s3.amazonaws.com. Some defenses, such as firewalls, need to be managed as part of the cloud deployment. Your systems may also come under attack as stepping-stones to other tenants of the cloud provider. Beyond that, another tenant might try to bust out of their virtual machine and take over a host, giving them access to your machine as well (if you're sharing machines). An attacker might also be able to access the network or storage (either local cache or storage specific to the cloud). Another tenant might be taken over to run a DoS attack against you, or an attacker might sign up to do so.

Threats to Compliance

There are three typical issues here. First, for many compliance regimes—but most notably PCI and HIPAA—the entire stack, including physical security, needs to be compliant. Therefore, the only way to have a PCI assessed app is for your cloud provider to be assessed PCI compliant. Second, there can be issues with auditing and logging. Not all cloud operators will provide logs of access to their APIs or web consoles. This can lead to technical issues, such as it may be impossible to see who added or changed accounts. That technical issue can lead to a compliance issue. The final issue is when you get into the PaaS and SaaS market, you often lose the ability to leverage cryptography at the filesystem or database level, as well as any concept of end-to-end encryption.

Legal Threats

The primary new legal threat when you move data to the cloud relates to laws that (at least in the U.S.) substantially reduce your ability to know about or challenge legal requests for your information, such as subpoenas or warrants. Data you store on your own systems is often more legally protected than data you store on someone else's systems. The legal demands served on your cloud provider may also contain provisions forbidding them from telling you about those demands, or you may be informed after the data has already been provided.

Of course, there's also the need to negotiate agreements related to privacy, security, and reliability. Contractual provisions for both privacy and security need to cover your business needs and your compliance needs. Privacy is covered by a hodge-podge of U.S. regulations. In the European Union, and those places with a safe harbor agreement for data from European countries, there's a set of requirements, most importantly for the organization holding the data to name a data custodian. That custodian has certain responsibilities, and you'll need to address those if you're moving data collected under EU or other similar privacy regimes.

It is, of course, important to consider these issues with your attorney; this section is intended only to outline some of the points you should discuss with them. Your attorney may have additional concerns.

Threats to Forensic Response

After an intrusion, your VM may be shut down by the cloud provider. You may have instantiated a system large enough that performing complete snapshot or a memory dump is time consuming; but most important, you may not have a defensible chain of custody.

Miscellaneous Threats

Some cloud providers offer easy to use virtual machine images, uploaded by kind strangers for your convenience, and out of the goodness of their hearts.

Sometimes, the people who uploaded them really did so out of the goodness of their hearts. Other times, the images are not so safe, and trusting them for anything serious is probably foolish.

Cloud Provider Threats

There is also a set of threats to the cloud provider that cloud providers must consider, and cloud customers should consider. These are all threats from or caused by the folks to whom you give access to your systems. These are split into threats caused by malicious behavior by the tenant that targets the provider, such as attempts by the tenant to hack the provider; and threats caused by tenant behavior, such as blacklisting.

Threats Directly from Tenants

The largest threat is that a tenant will find a way to break out of whatever sandbox you put them in, and be able to take actions you don't want them taking. Those actions might be on the order of running code on the raw hardware and tampering with either your billing or your other customers, or it might be connecting to networks that should be firewalled off. In particular, US-CERT has warned about threats to the IPMI (Intelligent Platform Management Interface) (US-CERT, 2013). These threats are sometimes managed by putting IPMI on an isolated network. If a tenant breaks out, they may be able to access such a management network. The sandbox escape threats are more likely when clients are held back by fewer security boundaries. Thus, a client in a Software as a Service (SaaS) environment has more barriers than one trying to escape from an Infrastructure as a Service offering.

There's also a fraud (repudiation) threat, which is that a new tenant might sign up with someone else's personal data and/or credit card, preparatory to committing fraud, running a botnet, or DDoSing a game server. These threats can be partially addressed by charging the card immediately for the first portion of service, or charging a sign-up fee, although that may be inhibitory to new business. If there are throttles for e-mail sent or similar things, it may be useful to tie them to length of tenancy.

Unfortunately, many of the ways to address these threats are at odds with the low-friction, get-started-quickly value proposition that cloud providers want to offer. There may be interesting ways to address these trade-offs that have yet to be invented, but for now appropriate monitoring for anomalies is important.

Such monitoring has to build on the unique elements of the business, so custom code will be needed.

Threats Caused by Tenant Behavior

There's a set of threats that tenants can cause, including spamming and piracy. These problems are magnified in those cases where accounts are free to anyone, and essentially anonymous. These threats are less clear-cut than issues such as spoofing, tampering, or information disclosure. If your requirements are clear, there's no question about whether the threat violates them. In contrast, perhaps the e-mails are all going to an authorized list? Perhaps the person who uploaded that song is the artist, or is authorized to do so? Or perhaps the use of an image is permissible under the law? This lack of clarity makes these threats harder to manage than the classical security violations.

The United States has a somewhat clear set of rules regarding *notice and take down*. These give cloud providers a legal defense against copyright claims until they receive a formalized notice of infringement, after which they must take certain actions, generally taking down the content. Following those processes is prudent, as jumping to judgment and action on a notice may threaten the protections you otherwise have.

These threats lead to an indirect threat to the provider and other tenants, which is backlash from the attacks. That backlash can include visits or calls from law enforcement, reports from other parties that require investigation or response, and blacklisting. Once a tenant has sent spam, been part of a botnet, and so on, there's a risk that the IP, subnet, or ASN may be blacklisted. The behaviors that lead to blacklisting may be violations of the terms of service. Responding to the behavior and getting IP addresses de-listed is likely a manual and time-consuming task.

Mobile Threats

Threats to mobile devices are generally similar to threats to other computers. For example, someone who can run code on the device may read your files, use your authentication data, etc. There are a few additional threats for mobile devices, including increased likelihood of device loss, difficulty managing the devices, and business models conflicting with security updates.

The threat of device loss is clearly higher for mobile devices than for servers. The two main ways to address device loss are device wipe and data wipe. Device wipe can cause conflict, as many devices are owned by your employees or contractors, so in wiping their device, you may be deleting data that is not yours to delete. Data wipe can be accomplished by sending encrypted data to the device, and only sending the key needed to access the data when the data is accessed.

Many mobile devices are locked to specific software providers, and constrain which software can be loaded onto the device. This may threaten the ability of a compliance team to load them up with compliance-ware. When a mobile device is locked, then you define the person holding the device as a threat. The device and its physical shell become a trust boundary that you must carefully consider, as all communication is subject to tampering, denial of service, and information disclosure.

Lastly, many wireless carriers threaten the ability of the software makers to deliver patches to devices in the field, claiming that arbitrary patching threatens them with bricked devices and support costs. This means that fielded mobile devices can be vulnerable to security problems that are fixed in newer versions of software.

Summary

The web is comprised of software which can be threat modeled like any other software. There are a variety of recurring threat classes that are best managed by using safer languages and test frameworks that focus on those classes. These threats are things like XSS and SQL injection. There are also recurring patterns within the web and cloud that you should consider when threat modeling.

The browser and its plugins have threat models that should be documented by the browser maker. Those threat models should cover both security and privacy, and you need to understand them to program the browser.

Cloud tenants come under threat from insiders at the cloud provider and from co-tenants. Limits on code execution make attacking your co-tenants harder, so as you move up the stack from IaaS to PaaS to SaaS, co-tenant attacks become less likely. There are also a variety of threats to compliance and legal threats that cloud tenants must account for. In addition, forensic response may be threatened if you are a cloud tenant.

Cloud providers have to worry about threats of their tenants attacking them, and the side effects that can occur when their tenants attack others. In particular, if tenants can access management networks that are normally isolated, the impact on security can be exceptionally large.

Mobile computers, including laptops, tablets, and phones are much like other computers, except the frequency of device loss is far higher. Some mobile devices are locked in ways that restrict the loading of software, making it hard to add compliance-ware, and possibly changing the threat model to include the person who uses the device. Such locking may also threaten patching, leaving devices vulnerable to known issues, and effectively removing the "need to find a vulnerability" barrier to attack.

CHAPTER

14

Accounts and Identity

If you don't get account management right, you open the door to a slew of spoofing threats. Your ability to rely on the person behind a keyboard being the person you've authorized falls away. This chapter discusses models of how computers identify and account for their users, and the interaction of those accounts with a variety of security and privacy concerns. Much of the chapter focuses on threat modeling, but some of it delves into thinking about elements of security and the building blocks that are used. The repertoire in this chapter is specialized, but frequently needed, which makes it worth working through these issues in detail.

As the world becomes more digital, we interact not with a person in front of us but with their digital avatars and their data shadows. These avatars and shadows are models of the person. Remember: All models are wrong, and some models are useful. When the model is a model of a person, he or she may take offense at how they have been represented. The offense may be fair or misplaced, but effective threat modeling when people are involved requires an understanding of the ways in which models are wrong, and the particular ways in which wrong models can impede your security, your business, as well as the well-being, dignity, and happiness of your current or prospective customers, citizens, or visitors.

Despite the term *identity* being in vogue, I do not use it as a synonym for account. The English word identity has a great many meanings. At its core is the idea of oneness, a consistency of nature—that this person is the same one you spoke with yesterday. Identity refers to self, personhood, character, and the presentation of self in life. To speak of "identity issuance" reveals either a lack of grounding in sociology and psychology, or a worrisome authoritarian streak, in which the identity of a human is defined and controlled by an external authority.

It is often tempting to model accounts as permanently good or bad, as a description of the person behind it. This is risky. Accounts can change from good to bad when an attacker compromises one, or when a bad creator decides to abuse them, which may be immediate or after a long period of "reputation establishment."

This chapter starts with the life cycle of accounts, including how they are created, maintained, and removed. From there, you'll learn about authentication, including login, login failures, and threats against authenticators, especially the most common authentication technology, passwords, as well as the various threats to passwords. That's followed by account recovery techniques, threat models for those, and a discussion of the trade-offs associated with them. The chapter closes with a discussion of naming and name-like systems of identifiers such as social security numbers.

Account Life Cycles

Over the lifetime of most systems, accounts will be created, maintained, and removed. Creation may take many forms, including the authorization of a federated account. Maintenance can include updating passwords or other information used for security. People are often not aware of or motivated to perform such maintenance, which has resulted in the creation of technical tools such as password expiry, which tries to either prod them or force their hand. People's awareness varies and is usually lower with lower-value accounts (when was the last time you looked at your e-mail from Friendster, or logged into your home wireless router?) Lastly, accounts will eventually need to be removed for a variety of reasons, and doing so exposes threats such as identifier re-use.

Account Creation

The life cycle of an account starts when the account is opened. Ideally, that happens with proper authorization, which means very different things in different contexts. You can roughly model this based on how deep the relationship is between the person and an organization.

For Close Relationship Accounts

Some accounts require and validate a good deal of information about a person as the account is created. These accounts are typically of very high value to the person, and incur high risk to the organization. Examples include a bank account or a work account with access to corporate e-mail and documents. Because of the sensitive nature of these accounts, the account creation process is typically more cumbersome, possibly including verification steps and approvals. Such accounts are likely to be strictly limited in terms of how many a person may have at one time.

When people understand that the security requirements for these accounts may exceed those of other types of accounts, they might use better (or at least different) passwords, and the threat of lying about key data is somewhat reduced.

For Free Accounts

There are many online accounts that require little to nothing when signing up: an e-mail address, perhaps. For these types of accounts, people will often provide personal information that is funny, aspirational, or completely inaccurate. They do this to present an identity or persona, or for political or privacy reasons. (I discovered recently that several of my online accounts say I am in Egypt, a country I haven't visited in 20 years. I likely set it during the Arab Spring, and had no reason to change it since then.) If you rely on this information, these tendencies to enter funny or aspirational information are a threat to you, while your attempts to "validate" or constrain it can seem like a threat to your customers.

Free accounts are more likely to be used by more than one person—for example, a family or team calendar. When someone leaves the team, the account management implications are less than when someone is no longer authorized to access a bank account. In the worst case scenario, the free account can be replaced trivially, although the contents might not be. Free accounts are often used for a variety of mischief, including but not limited to spam, or file-sharing for music, books, or movies. Each of these threatens to annoy you, your customers, or the Internet at large in various ways and to various degrees.

At the Factory

Systems that ship with a single default account created at the factory should require a password change at setup; otherwise, the password will be available to anyone via a search engine. You might also be able to ship with a unique password printed onto a device or a sticker.

Federated Account Creation

Accounts are often created based on an account elsewhere, such as a Facebook or Twitter login, or a corporate (active directory) account. Federation systems such as OAUTH or Active Directory Federation Services (ADFS) allow this to happen somewhat seamlessly. While federation reduces the burden on individuals who want to create new accounts, it exposes risk in that a breached federated system may be a stepping-stone to your system (depending on where and how authentication tokens are stored). It may pose privacy threats by requiring the linkage of accounts. It may also increase the impact of threats by making the federated account a more valuable target. Lastly, users are often forgetful about where they've federated, and leave federation in place even after they no longer use it.

Creating Accounts That Don't Correspond to a Person

We often want to think "one account for one person." Security experts advise against shared accounts for good reasons of (ahem) accountability. There are many reasons why that advice is violated. Some accounts are set up for more than one person—for example, a married couple may have a joint bank account. Often times, they will share a single login/password combination, even if you've made it easy to set up several (computer) accounts to connect to a single bank account. Similarly, many people might share one work account. It is important to think about what happens when one or more participants in such a shared account are no longer authorized to use it. For the married couple with a joint bank account, what's the right system? That both spouses have a (system) account that is authorized to access the (bank) account? Similarly, a traditional landline phone is an account for a family. If you call 867–5309, you might get someone in Jenny's family.

Andrew Adams and Shirley Williams have been exploring these issues and have a short, readable paper "What's Yours Is Mine, and What's Mine Is My Own" (Adams, 2012). Taking a cue from the world of law, they suggest considering several types of joint accounts: several, shared, subordinate, and nominee. *Several accounts* are those that reflect the intersection of individuals where each has complete authority over the account. *Shared accounts* are those for which all members of a group can see information, but some subset of users can control what others can change. For example, members of an LLC could all see the financials, but only the treasurer can issue payments. *Subordinate accounts* might be created by a parent or guardian, and allow one or more supervisory accounts to see some, but perhaps not all, of the child's activity. (For example, parents might be able to see correspondent e-mail addresses, but not contents.) Finally, *nominee accounts* might allow access to the account after some circumstance, such as death. (Nominee accounts in this sense relate closely to Schechter, Egelman, and Reeder's trustees, covered later in the section "Active Social Authentication.") In any or all of these sorts of systems, there might be one login account that is used by everyone who has access to the joint account, or one login per person—it depends primarily on your development decisions and the usability of a joint account system.

It's also important to avoid believing that there is a one-to-one correspondence between the existence of an account and a human being who controls it. This is easily forgotten, although identity masking is common enough that it has many names, such as *sockpuppets, astroturfing, Sybyls,* and *tentacles.* Each of these is a way to refer to a set of fake people under the control of a group or person hoping to use social proof for the validity of their position. (Social proof is the idea that if you see a crowd doing something, you're more likely to believe it's OK.) Credit for this point belongs to Frank Stajano and Paul Wilson, as described in their paper "Understanding scam victims: seven principles for systems security" (Stajano, 2011).

Account Maintenance

Over time, it turns out that nearly everything about the person who uses an account can change, and many of those changes should be reflected with the account. For example, almost everyone will change data such as their phone number or address; but other things about them can change as well—name, gender, birthday, biometrics, social security number. (Birthdays can change because of inaccurate entry, inaccurate storage, or even discovery of a discrepancy between documents and belief.) Even biometrics can change. People can lose the body part being measured, such as a finger or an eye. Less dramatically, cuts to fingers can alter a fingerprint pattern, and older people have harder to read fingerprints.

If you store such data, you need mechanisms for changing it. It's important to align the change of these records with the security implications of a change. If you use the phone or physical mail to authenticate, ensure that you do everything appropriate to authenticate a phone number change. For a customer change of address, many wise banks send letters to both the new address and the old address, and turn their risk algorithms way up for a month or so after such a change. When users are not aware that data such as phone number will be used as an authentication channel, they are far less likely to keep it up to date. Even when they are aware that such data may be used for that purpose, they are unlikely to remember to update every system with which their phone number is associated.

Notifying the Real Person

Many services will let their customers know about unusual security events. For example, Microsoft will send text messages or e-mail to notify that additional e-mail addresses have been added to an account, and LiveJournal will send an e-mail if a login happens from a browser without a cookie. Such notifications are helpful, insofar as your customers are probably motivated to protect their accounts; and risky, as your customers may not understand the messages. They may become more concerned than is appropriate, driving customer support costs, dissatisfaction, or brand impact. Additionally, there's a risk that attackers will fake your security messages for phishing-like attacks. The right call is a matter of good threat modeling, including good models of scenarios.

You can mitigate the risks by using scamicry-resistant advice (see Chapter 15 "Human Factors and Usability"), ensuring that you have low false positives, and using time as your ally. Time is an ally because you can delay authorizing important changes such as payments or backup authentication options until you have more information. That might be someone logging in from a frequently seen IP address or computer, demonstrating access to e-mail, or otherwise adding more information to your decisions. For more on delays, see "Avoiding Urgency" in Chapter 15. See also the "Account Recovery" section later in this chapter.

Account Termination

Customers may stop paying, leave, or pass away. Workers may quit or be fired. Therefore, it is important to have ways to terminate accounts fully and properly. Changing their passwords may not be enough. They might have e-mail forwarding or scheduled processes that run; or they may be able to use account recovery tools to get back in. This is actually the space in which many "identity management systems" play: helping enterprises manage the relationship between a person and the dozens to hundreds of accounts on disparate systems that they might possess. (Now get off my lawn before I hit you with my typewriter.)

When you terminate an account, you need to answer at least two important questions. First, what do you do with the objects that the account owns, including files, e-mail messages, websites, database procedures, crypto keys, and so on? Second, is the account name reserved or recycled? If you recycle account names, then confusion can result. If you don't, you risk exhausting the namespace.

Account Life-Cycle Checklist

This checklist is designed to be read aloud at a meeting. You're in a bad state if for any of these questions:

- You can't answer yes.
- You can't articulate and accept the implications of a no.
- You don't know.

1. Do we have a list of how accounts will be created?
2. Do all accounts represent a single person?

3. Can we update each element of an account?
4. Does each update notify the person behind the account?
5. Do we have a way to terminate accounts?
6. Do we know what happens to all the data associated with an account when it's terminated?

Authentication

Authentication is the process of checking that someone is who they claim to be. Contrast that with authorization, which is checking what they're allowed to do. For example, the person in front of you might really be Al Cohol, but that doesn't entitle them to a free drink.

Figure 14-1 shows a simple model of the authentication process. First, a person enrolls in some way, which varies from the simple (entering a username and password on a website) to the complex (going through an extensive background check and signing paperwork to trigger a create account process). Later, someone shows up and attempts to authenticate as the person who enrolled.

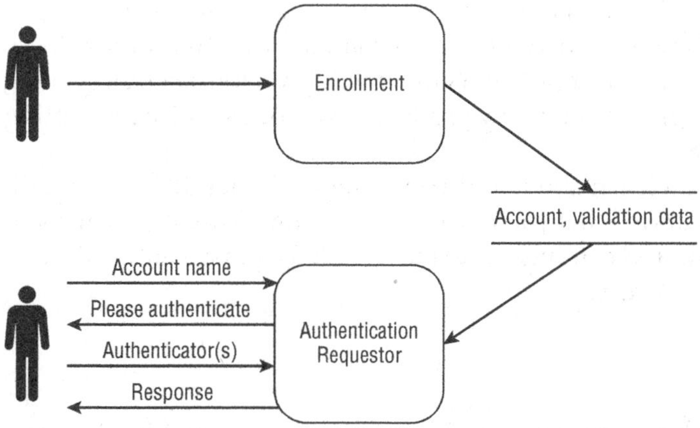

Figure 14-1: A simple model of authentication

Many of the threats covered in this chapter can be discovered by applying techniques such as STRIDE or attack trees to Figure 14-1. However, because the threats have been discovered, and the mitigations have been worked through, this chapter summarizes much of what's known so that you don't have to re-invent it.

The traditional three ways to authenticate people have required either "something you know, something you have, something you are," or some combination of those. Passwords are an example of something you know. Something you have might include proximity cards or cryptographic devices such as RSA tokens. Something you are is measured with tools such as fingerprint or retina scanners.

These methods of authenticating people are often termed *authentication factors*, and multi-factor authentication refers to the use of several factors at one time. It is important that factors be independent and different. If a system consists of something you have, an ATM card, and something you know, a PIN, and you write your PIN on the card, the security of the system is substantially reduced. Similarly, if the something you have is a phone infected with malware because it's synced to a desktop computer, then the ability of the phone to add security as a second factor is greatly reduced. Using more than one of the same sort of factor is sadly frequently confused with multi-factor authentication.

These three factors have been sarcastically reframed as "something you've forgotten, something you've lost, and something you were." (This is often attributed to Simson Garfinkel, although he does not take credit for it [Garfinkel, 2012]). This reframing stings because each is a real problem. Two additional factors are also sometimes considered: who you know, also called *social authentication*, and discussed later in the section "Account Recovery," and how you get the message, sometimes called *multi-channel authentication*. Multi-channel is heavily threatened by the integration of communication technologies, and good modeling of the channels often reveals how they overlap. For example, if you think that a phone is a good additional channel, walking through how phones are used might uncover possible vulnerability vectors such as syncing (and associated infection risk) and how products like Google Voice are putting text messages in e-mail.

In this section, you'll learn about login and especially handling login failures, followed by threats to what you have, are, and know. Threats to what you know spans passwords and continues into the knowledge-based authentication approach to account recovery.

Login

We're all familiar with the login process: Someone presents an identifier and authenticator, and asks to be authenticated in some way. As shown in Figure 14-2, there are many spoofing threats in this simple process, including that the client or server may make false claims of identity, and the local computer may be presenting a false UI. (It's that last threat which pressing Ctrl+Alt+Delete [CAD] addresses: CAD is a secure attention sequence, one that the operating system will always respond to, rather than passing to an application.)

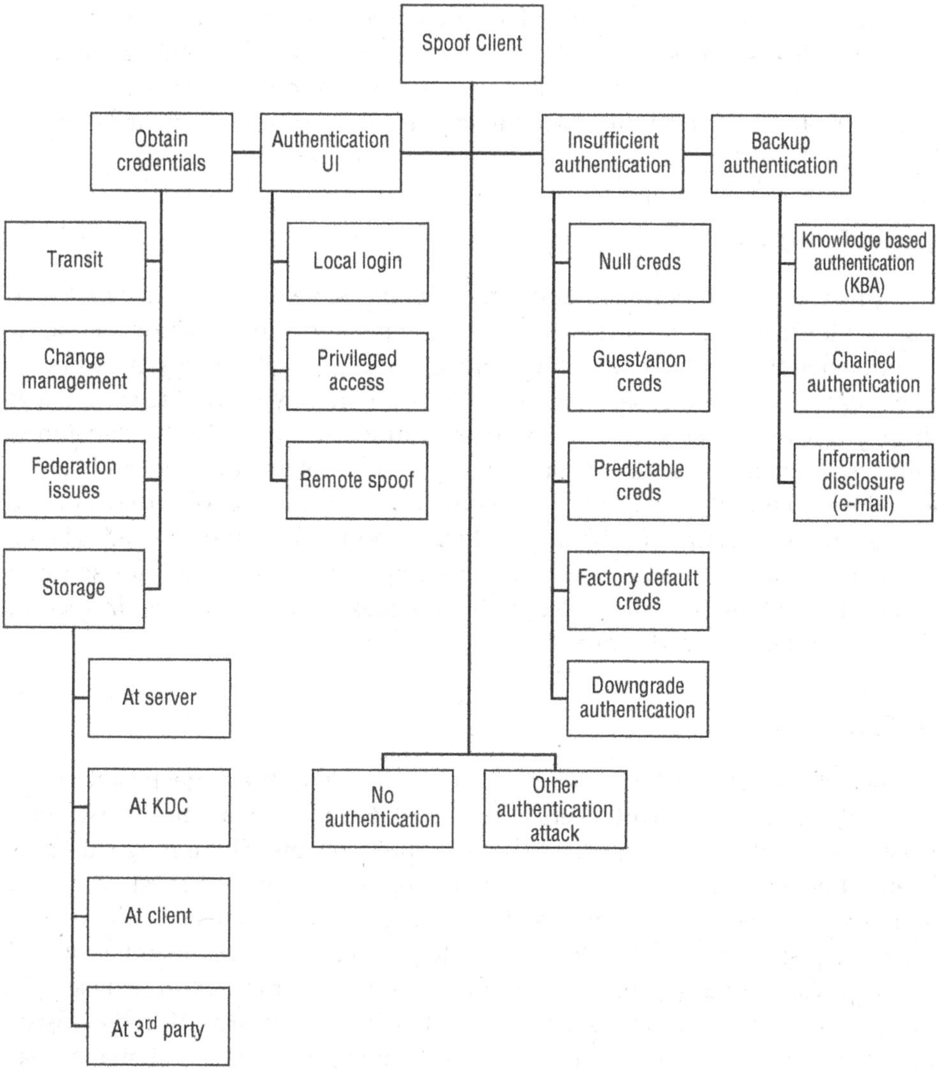

Figure 14-2: Spoofing an external entity threat tree

Let's first consider spoofing threats at the server, whether you describe the threat as threats of the server being spoofed or of the server spoofing; it's six of one, half a dozen of the other. The key is that the client is, for whatever reason, confused about the identity of the server it's talking to. As discussed previously, the key to mitigating these threats is mutual authentication, and in particular cryptographic authentication. If you're implementing a new login system, performing a literature review of the many previous systems and their failure modes is a very worthwhile endeavor. Spoofing of the client occurs in several forms, and an attack tree is a useful way to keep track of them.

The spoofing of an external entity threat tree is discussed in detail in Appendix B, "Threat Trees."

Login Failures

A login system is designed to keep the wrong people out. In a very real way, it's an interface that's intended to stymie people and present error messages, except when the right person jumps through a set of carefully designed hoops. Therefore, you have to design for failures by both those you want to see fail and those you want to see succeed. These are a first tension. Keep that tension in mind as you make choices. Do you tell the person what went wrong, and do you lock the account in some way? The second tension is that people are frustrated with security measures, and angry if their accounts are compromised. They'll be angry if their low-value accounts are compromised and used for spam or whatnot, and they'll be more deeply hurt if their bank account is drained or there are other real-world impacts.

No Such Account

"Incorrect username or password" is a common error message, based on the reasonable thinking that attackers who cannot discern if an account exists must waste energy attacking it, possibly also tripping alarms. There may well have been a time when this was commonly true, and there may yet be systems where account existence is hard to check. Today, with account recovery systems, it is harder to justify the usability loss associated with the "username or password" message. Additionally, with many systems using an e-mail address as a login mechanism, even if your system diligently hides all information disclosure threats around the existence of an account, someone else may well give it away (Roberts, 2012). It is time to accept that account existence is something an attacker can easily learn, and gain the usability benefits of telling real people that they've misspelled their account identifier.

Insufficient Authentication

As the many inadequacies of passwords become increasingly apparent, services are choosing to look at more data available at login time to make an authentication decision. With a classical web browser, this will frequently include checking the IP address, a geolocation based on that IP, browser version information, cookies, and so on. If you are going to create such a system, note that there's a threat. The specific version is cookie managers. You should plan for 20 percent–50 percent of your real customers to regularly delete their cookies (Nguyen, 2011; Young, 2011). Tell people if cookie deletion will affect the need for account recovery.

This can be generalized to a mismatch between expectations and your system. If other events will trigger account recovery, you should strongly consider setting people's expectations. Be very clear about what information you expect would be difficult for an attacker to determine about your algorithms. That's not to say you should reveal the information. Joseph Bonneau makes the claim that obscurity is an essential part of doing authentication well (Bonneau, 2012a). His arguments are solid, but they resolve the tension between limiting attacker information and usability in a way that leads to frustration for the real account owners. Of course, the frustration of your having a bank account drained is also very real. For more on obscurity, see the section "Secret Systems: Kerckhoffs and His Principles" in Chapter 16 "Threats to Cryptosystems."

Account Lockout

When a login attempt fails, you can choose to lock the account for some length of time—ranging from a few seconds to forever. The forever end of the spectrum requires some form of reset management, an exercise left to the reader. If you select shorter lengths of time, you can use fixed or increasing delays (also called *backoff*). You can apply delays to accounts or endpoints, such as an IP address or an address range, or both.

If the number of failures is represented as f, something like $(f-3) \times 10$ or $(f-5)^2$ seconds offers a reasonable mix of increasing security with each failure while not annoying people with unreasonable delays. (Of course, $(f-5)^2$ is sort of pathological if you don't handle the small integers well.) The system designer can either expose the backoff or hide it. Hiding it (by telling the person that their attempt to log in failed) may result in people incorrectly believing that they've lost their password, and thus driving the need for backup authentication that works faster.

Requirements for scenarios of keyboard login attempts versus network login attempts may be different. It might be reasonable to allow more logins via a physical keyboard. Of course, a physical keyboard is sometimes a slippery concept, easily subject to spoofing over USB or Bluetooth.

Threats to "What You Have"

Using the authentication categories of what you have, what you are, and what you know, "what you have" includes things such as identity cards or cryptographic hardware tokens. The main threats to these are theft, loss, and destruction.

The threat of theft is in many ways the most worrisome of the threats to "what you have." Some of these authenticators, such as proximity cards to unlock doors do not require anything else. (That is, you don't login to most doors with your handprint.) In most organizations, there is not a strong norm ensuring that the card is worn such that the face is easily visible, and an attacker who steals a card can simply put it in their wallet. Even with a "visible face" norm, matching photo to face tends to be challenging (see the next section for more discussion about this).

Other authenticator devices are often carried in bags, so someone who steals a laptop bag will obtain both the laptop and the authentication token. Some of these tokens only have a display, while others also have an input function, so using the token is a matter of what you have and what you know. The display-only tokens are cheaper, easier to use, and less secure. The appropriate trade-off is likely a matter of "chess playing." If you use the display-only tokens, is that still what an attacker would go after, or does it make it hard enough that the attacker will attack somewhere else? As of 2012 or so, a number of companies are making authenticators that are the same size and thickness as credit cards and which have both input buttons and e-ink displays. These are more likely to be carried in a wallet than the older "credit card–size" tokens, which were very thick compared to a credit card.

The threats of loss and destruction are relatively similar. In each case, the authorized person becomes unable to authenticate. In the case of destruction or damage, there's more certainty that the authentication token wasn't stolen.

Threats to "What You Are"

Measuring "what you are" is a tremendously attractive category of authentication. There's an intuitive desire to have ways to authenticate people as people, rather than authenticate something they can loan, lose, or forget. Unfortunately, it turns out that the desire and the technical reality are different. All biometric systems involve some sort of sensors, which take measurements of a physical feature. These sensors and their properties are an important part of the threat model. The data that is stored must be stored in a way which the sensor can reliably generate. The form into which sensor data is converted is called a *template*. All of this is shown in Figure 14-3, which looks remarkably similar to 14-1. Clever readers may notice that neither figure contains trust boundaries. Different systems place the trust boundaries in different places. For example, if you log in to your bank over the Internet using a fingerprint reader, there's a different trust boundary than if that reader is located in their branch office. Many of the threats against biometrics can be quickly derived from a model like the one shown in Figure 14-3.

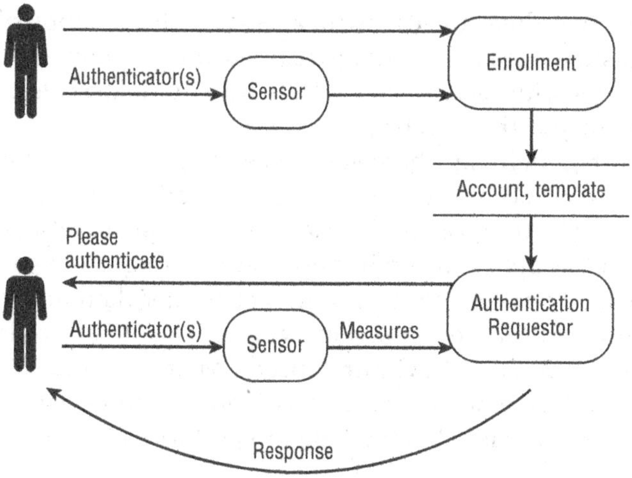

Figure 14-3: A model of biometric authentication

Some of those threats include the following:

- Attacking templates, either tampering with them to allow impersonation, or analyzing disclosed templates to create input that will fool the system
- Acquiring an image of the body part being measured, and using it to create input that will fool the system. This is spoofing against the sensor.
- Adjusting the body so that the measurement changes. This is often a denial-of-service attack against the system, possibly executed for innocent reasons.

Each of these is discussed in more depth over the next several paragraphs.

Attacking templates may be easier than is comfortable for advocates of biometrics, many of who have claimed that the stored template data could not be used to reconstruct the input that will pass the biometric. This has proven to be false for fingerprints (Nagar, 2012), faces (Adler, 2004), and irises (Ross, 2005), and will likely prove false for other templates. Resisting such attacks is probably in tension with managing the false positive and false negative rates associated with the system. Worse, the people who are being authenticated are usually not given a choice about the system. Therefore, even if reconstruction-resistant templates were designed, the distribution of incentives likely argues against their use.

Acquiring an image of the body part being measured can often come from an "in the wild" image. For facial biometrics, this may be as easy as searching (ahem) Facebook or LinkedIn. Fingerprints can come from a fingerprint left on a glass, a car door, or elsewhere. A search for "fingerprint" on Flickr shows thousands of images of people's fingerprints. One person's art leads to another's artful attack. Of course, there are less artful attacks, such as chopping off the body part to be measured. This has actually happened to the owner of a Mercedes-Benz with a fingerprint reader—a Mr. Kumaran in Malaysia (see "Malaysia car thieves steal finger." [Kent, 2005]).

Once you have a body part or an image thereof, you need to present it to the sensor in a convincing way. To reduce the incentive for taking body parts, there is sometimes "liveness" testing by the sensors. For example, fingerprint sensors might look for warmth or evidence of a pulse, while eye scanners might look for natural movements of the eye. Such testing turns out to be harder than many people expect, with facial recognition bypassed by waving a photo around; and, famously, fingerprints rendered with Gummy Bears (Matsumoto, 2002), recently repeated to some fanfare when a well known phone manufacturer experienced the same problem, possibly having failed to perform a literature review (Reiger, 2013).

Some systems measure activity, such as typing or walking, so the "image" captured needs to be more complex, and replaying it may similarly be harder, depending on where the sensor and data flows are relative to the trust boundaries. Attacks that are easy in a lab may be hard to perform in front of an alert, motivated, and attentive guard. However, in 2009, it was widely reported that Japan deported a South Korean woman who "placed special tapes on her fingers" to pass through Japan's fingerprint checks at immigration (Sydney Morning Herald, 2009).

For honest people, changing their fingerprints (or other biometrics) seems very difficult. However, there are a variety of factors and scenarios that make fingerprints harder to take or measure, including age; various professions such as surgeons, whose fingerprints are abraded by frequent scrubbing; hobbies such as woodworking, where heavy use of sandpaper can abrade the ridges; and cancer treatment drugs (Lyn, 2009).

There are also a few threats that are harder to see in the simple model. The first is "insult rates," the second is suitability and externalities. The biometrics industry has long had a problem with what they call the "insult rate." People are deeply offended when the machine doesn't "recognize" them, and if the people being measured are members of the general public, staff need to be trained to handle the problem gracefully. The second insult issue is that many people associate fingerprinting with being treated like a criminal. Is it suitable to treat your customers in a way that may be so perceived? Organizations should carefully consider the issue of offense, and well-meaning people should also consider the issue of desensitization caused by overuse of biometrics. This is an externality, where the act of an organization has a cost on others.

Many of the desirable properties of authenticators are not available in biometrics. Biometric sensors are less precise than a keyboard, which makes it harder to derive cryptographic keys. Another property that you'd like for your authentication secrets is that they are shared between one person and one organization, and you want to change those secrets now and then. But most people only have 10 fingers. (A few have more, and more have less.) Therefore, the threat of information disclosure by anyone who has a copy of your fingerprint has an impact on everyone who relies on your fingerprint to authenticate you. Of course, that applies to all biometrics, not just fingerprints. Overuse of biometrics makes these threats more serious for everyone who needs to rely on them.

One last comment on biometrics before moving on: Photographs are also a biometric, one that people can use very well, if the photograph is shown to motivated people in a high quality and reasonable size. People do an excellent job of recognizing family and friends. However, using photographs to match strangers to their ID photos turns out to be far more difficult, at least when the photograph is the size that appears on a credit card. (See Ross Anderson's *Security Engineering, Second Edition* [Wiley, 2008] for a multi-page discussion of the issue. To summarize, participants in an experiment rarely detected that a photo ID did not match the person using it. However, it appears that the use of such photos may act as a deterrent to casual crime.)

Threats to "What You Know"

Passwords are the worst authentication technology imaginable, except for all those others that have been tried from time to time. We all have too many of them, decent ones are hard to remember, and they're static and exposed to a potentially untrustworthy other party. They are also memorizable, require no special software, can be easily transmitted over the phone, and are more crisp than a biometric, which allows us to algorithmically derive keys from them. For a detailed analysis of these trade-offs, see Joseph Bonneau's "The quest to replace passwords" (Bonneau, 2012c). These tradeoffs mean that passwords are unlikely to go away, and most systems that have accounts are going to need to store passwords, or something like them, in some way.

In the aforementioned paper, Bonneau and colleagues lay out a framework for evaluating the usability, deployability, and security of authentication systems. Their security characteristics are outlined in the form of a security properties checklist, which will be useful to anyone considering the design of a new authentication scheme. They are listed here without discussion because anyone considering such a task should read their paper:

1. Resilient to physical observation
2. Resilient to targeted impersonation (such as attacks against knowledge-based backup authentication)
3. Resilient to throttled guessing (this is my online attacks category)
4. Resilient to unthrottled guessing (this is offline attacks)

5. Resilient to internal observation (such as keylogging malware)
6. Resilient to leaks from other verifiers
7. Resilient to phishing
8. Resilient to theft
9. No trusted third party
10. Requiring explicit consent
11. Unlinkable

Threats to Passwords

Threats to password security can be categorized in several different ways, and which is most useful depends on your scenario. I'll offer up a simple enumeration:

- Unintentional disclosure, including passwords on sticky notes, wikis, or SharePoint sites, and phishing attacks
- Online attacks against the login system
- Offline attacks against the stored passwords

Online attacks are attempts to guess the password through defenses such as rate limiting. Offline attacks bypass those defenses and test passwords as quickly as possible, often many orders of magnitude faster. Password leaks are a common problem these days, and they're a problem because they enable offline attacks, ranging from simple lookups to rainbow tables to more complex cracking. Good password storage approaches can help guard against offline attacks. Passwords stored on web servers is a common issue in larger operational environments. Phishing attacks come in a spectrum from untargetted to carefully crafted after hours of research on sites such as Facebook or LinkedIn. There's a model of online social engineering attacks is in Chapter 15.

Password Storage

This section walks you through information disclosure threats to stored passwords, building up layers of threats and cryptographic mitigations to bring you to an understanding of the modern approaches to password storage.

If you don't cryptographically protect your list of usernames and passwords, then all that's required to exploit it after information disclosure is to look up the account the attacker wishes to spoof, and then use the associated login. The naive defense against this is to store a one-way hash of the password. (A one-way hash is a cryptographic function that takes an arbitrary input and produces a fixed-length output.) The way to attack such a list is to take a list of words and for each word in the list, hash the word, and search for that hash in the list of hashed passwords. The list of words is called a dictionary, and the attack is called a dictionary attack. Each hashed dictionary word can be compared to each stored password. (If it matches, then you know what word you hashed, and that's the password.)

The defense against the speedup from comparing to each stored password is to add a *salt* to the password before hashing it. A salt is a random string intended to be different with different account passwords. Using a salt slows down an attacker from comparing each hash to all stored passwords to comparing each hash to that one password with the same salt (or those few passwords with the same salts). Salts should be random so that `Alice@example.com` has a different salt at different systems, and thus her stored, hashed password will be different even if she's using the same password at different systems. Salts are normally stored as plaintext with the hashed passwords.

Attackers might try to use modified versions of dictionary words. Software has been available for a long time that will take a list and permute each word in it, by changing o to 0, l (the letter, el) to 1, adding punctuation, and so on. Dictionaries are available for a wide variety of common languages, ranging from Afrikaans to Yiddish. There are also password-cracking lists of proper names, sports teams, and even Klingon. It's possible to store the hashed wordlist for a given hash, engaging in a "time-memory trade-off." These lists are called *rainbow tables*, and many are downloadable from the Internet. (Technically, rainbow tables store a special form of chains of hashes, which matter more if you are going to design your own storage mechanism; but given that smart people have spent time on this, you should use a standard mitigation approach.)

Unless you're implementing an operating system, it's almost certain that you'll want to store passwords that have been hashed and salted. The best pattern for this is roughly to take a password and salt, and shove them through a hash function thousands of times. The goal is to ensure that there's time after the detection of an accidental information disclosure for your customers to change their passwords. There are three common libraries for this: bcrypt, scrypt, and PBKDF2. All are likely to be better than anything you'd whip up yourself, and they are freely available in many languages.

- **bcrypt:** This is what I recommend. There is more freely available code, which is better documented and has more examples (Muffett, 2012). The bcrypt library also has an adaptive feature, which enables password storage to be strengthened over time without access to the cleartext (Provos, 1999). Do note that the name bcrypt is overloaded; at least one Linux package named bcrypt performs Blowfish file cryptography.
- **scrypt:** This may offer more security if you use it correctly. However, while documentation explains how to use the function for file encryption, it does not clearly address its use as a password storage tool (as opposed to a file encryption tool).

- **PBKDF2 (Password-Based Key Derivation Function 2):** This offers less defense, does not offer adaptivity, and there's only one reason to use it when bcrypt is available for your platform: because it's a NIST Standard (Percival, 2012; Openwall, 2013).

Even after you hash the passwords, you want to ensure that the hashes are hard to get. Even with salting, modern password cracking with dictionaries of common passwords is shockingly fast, on the order of eight billion MD5 passwords tested per second (Hashcat, 2013). At that speed, testing the million most common passwords with 100 variants of each takes less than a second.

If you are implementing an operating system, then the storage of passwords (or password equivalents) is a more complex issue. There are good usability reasons to keep authenticators in memory. This allows for the authenticator to be used without bothering the user. For example, Windows domain members can authenticate to a file share or Exchange without retyping their password, and unix users will often use ssh-agent, or the Mac OS keychain to help them authenticate. These patterns also lead to issues where an attacker can impersonate the account if they're inside the appropriate trust boundary.

There is no great solution short of keeping them out, which is, empirically, challenging. Relying on hardware such as smartcards or TPMs to ensure that the secrets don't leave the machine is helpful, as it provides a temporal bound, but an attacker who can execute code as the user can still authenticate as the user. The alternative of requiring action per authentication is highly inconvenient and would probably not solve the problem, because frequent authentication requests would desensitize people to requests for authentication data.

Using static strings for authentication means that the system to which a person is authenticating can spoof that person. There are a variety of clever cryptographic ways to avoid this, all of which have costs at deployment time, or other issues that make them harder to deploy than passwords (as noted earlier in "Authentication").

Password Expiration

In an attempt to respond to the threat of information disclosure involving passwords, many systems will expire them. By forcing regular changes, an attacker who comes into possession of a password has a limited window of time in which to use it. When systems force password changes, there are a few predictable ways in which people respond. Those include changing their password and then changing it back, transforming it to generate a new password (password1 becomes password2, or Decsecret becomes Jansecret), or picking a completely new password. (Hey, it could happen, and the person might not even write down the new password.)

This leads to an argument for controlling those human behaviors by storing password history, and sometimes also limiting the rate of password change.

Systems that store password history create an additional risk, which is that the stored passwords might be obtained, and an attacker who has access to a series of passwords can use either human or algorithmic pattern recognition to make very accurate guesses about what a person's next password is likely to be (Thorsheim, 2009; Zhang 2010). If you must store history, it is probably sensible to use an in-place adaptive algorithm such as bcrypt to store the historical passwords with a level of protection that would lead to unacceptable performance in interactive login.

I am not aware of any evidence that password expiration systems have any impact on the rate at which compromises happen. There is excellent evidence that normal people do not change their passwords unless forced, and as such there is a cost to password expiry that is hard to justify. The main reason to pay the cost of such a system is because a compliance program insists on it.

Authentication Checklist

This checklist is designed to be read aloud at a meeting. You're in a bad state if for any of these questions:

- You can't answer yes.
- You can't articulate and accept the implications of a no.
- You don't know.

1. Do we have an explicit list of what data is used in authentication?
2. Is it easy for us to add factors to that list?
3. Do we have easy to understand error messages?
4. If we're hiding authentication factors, what is our estimate of how long it would take for an attacker to find out about each?
5. Have we reviewed at least the information in the book for each authentication factor?
   a. Have we looked up the relevant references?
   b. Have we looked for additional threats based on those references?
6. Are we storing passwords using a cryptographically strong approach?

Account Recovery

We've all seen the "Forgot your password?" feature that so many sites offer. There are many varieties of this, including the following:

- E-mail authentication
- Social authentication

- Knowledge-based authentication
- Secret question/secret answer (or)
- Data from public records, such as your address on a given date

There are many varieties of these systems because, much like passwords, they are highly imperfect. This section provides an overview of the trade-offs involved. It begins with a discussion of time in account recovery, then explains account recovery via e-mail and social authentication, both of which are simple and relatively secure when compared to the more familiar knowledge-based ("secret question") systems covered at the end of this section.

All of these systems are abused by attackers. Famous examples include U.S. vice presidential candidate Sarah Palin's e-mail being taken over (the questions were birth date, zip code, and "Where did you meet your husband?" [Campanile, 2008]).

These systems should focus on recovering the account. The focus on "forgotten passwords" often leads system designers into the trap of giving people their previous password. This leads to the plaintext storage of passwords, which is usually not needed. Customers don't really care about their password or need it back. They care about the account (or what it enables) and need access to the account. Therefore, you should focus on restoring account access. The only substantial exception to this is encrypted data, for which it may be the case that an encryption key is derived from the password. You should investigate other ways to back up those encryption keys, such that you don't need to store passwords in plaintext.

When an account is recovered, it may be possible to throw away information that an attacker could exploit, such as payment information or mailing address. This information is usually easy to re-enter and has value to an attacker. (Addresses are useful for chained authentication attacks and stalking.) If you inform people why the data is gone, they are likely to be understanding. What data you choose to destroy as part of the account recovery process will depend on your business.

Time and Account Recovery

Time is an important and underrated ally in account recovery systems. The odds that users will need to use their account recovery option within five minutes (or even five days) of their last successful login are low. You might want the account recovery options for an account to be disabled until some specified amount of time has elapsed since the last successful login. (This point was made by my colleague and usable security expert Rob Reeder.) It is tempting to suggest offering fake account recovery options until then, but that might frustrate your real users.

The person driving an account recovery process might be the authorized account holder or an attacker. Your process should balance ease of use with challenge, and speed with an opportunity for the real account holder to intervene. For example, if you send password recovery e-mails, you should notify the person via every channel available to you. These notifications should contain instructions for the case that the receiver didn't initiate the account recovery, and possibly an explanation of why you're "spamming" them. These notifications and delays are more important when other risk factors are visible (for example, the account logs in from one IP address 90 percent of the time, but today logged in from the other side of the world).

Time also plays into account recovery in terms of what happens after the instant of getting into the account. Some system designers think they're done when a new password has been set. If the password was changed by an attacker, how does your customer recover his or her account? Perhaps after account recovery (but not normal password changes) the old password could work for some time period? However, then an attacker with the password is not locked out. There is no single obvious answer, and the right answer will differ for accounts associated with close relationships (work, banks, etc.) versus casual accounts.

Time is also a threat to account recovery systems. Over time, information that people have given you will decay. Their credit cards will become invalid, and their e-mail addresses, billing addresses, and phone numbers will likely change. If you rely on such information, consider allowing it to decay over time, being revalidated or removed from the system's recovery options.

E-mail for Account Recovery

If you have an e-mail address for your customer, you can send mail to it. That mail can contain a password or a token of some form. If you e-mail the customer a password, you should e-mail a new, randomly generated password. In fact, that should be all you can do, because you should take the preceding advice and not be able to e-mail them their old password. However, e-mailing them a password exposes the password to information disclosure threats on a variety of network connections and in storage at the other end. Some people will argue that it's better to not expose the password, but instead use a one-use token that allows the person to reset their password. The token should be a large random number, say 128–1,024 bits. You can send this either as a string they copy and paste into a browser form or as a URL. Hopefully it is obvious that the code which actually resets the password must confirm that the account actually requested a password reset, that the e-mail didn't bounce, and that the token is the one that was sent.

Either approach is vulnerable to information disclosure attacks. These attacks rely on either network sniffing or access to the backup e-mail address. You can partially mitigate these threats by crafting a message that does not contain all the information needed to recover the account. For example, if the system sends a URL with a recovery token, then it should not contain the account name. Thus, someone who intercepts or obtains the e-mail would need additional information if the account name is not the e-mail address. In systems where the e-mail address is the account name, that obviously doesn't work. You can add a layer of mitigation by checking cookies and possibly also by confirming that the browser they're using is sending the same headers as it was when someone requested a password reset. If you do that, there is a cookie deletion threat, which can be managed by telling people that they need to keep the page where they've requested a password reset.

Knowledge-Based Authentication

A variety of systems use various non-password information, which, it is hoped, only the real person behind the account knows. Of course, such information isn't really perfect for authentication. It must be known by the relying party so that it can be confirmed. Such information has the weakness that it may be known to other relying parties, or it may be discoverable by an attacker. The spectrum of such information runs from information that's widely available to the public through information that might be known only to the relying party. (Known only to the relying parties is a property that many hope is true of passwords.) This section considers three forms of knowledge-based authentication:

- Secret questions/secret answers
- Data from public records, such as your address on a given date
- Things only a few groups other than the organization and customer know, such as the dollar amount of a given transaction. "What is your password?" is one logical end of this knowledge-based authentication spectrum.

As mentioned earlier, ideally, the answers to these questions are known only to the real person behind the account, are exposed only to the proper account system, and people know they should keep it secret. Each of these systems can be threat modeled in the same ways.

Security

There are several classes of attack on the security of questions. The biggest ones are guessing and observation. The difficulty of each can be quantified, (possibly with respect to a specific category of attacker). Guessing difficulty is based on the number of possible answers. For example, "what color are your eyes?" has very few possible answers. Guessing difficulty is also based on probability. Brown eyes outnumber blue, which outnumber green. There are also attacks where the answer to the question can be found (observed) elsewhere. For example, information about addresses is generally public. This approach to measurement has been formalized by Bonneau, Just, and Matthews (Bonneau, 2010). They measured the guessing difficulty for people's names (parent names, grandparent names, teacher names, best friends) and place names (where you went to school, last vacation). They also comment on the relatively small number of occupations that our grandparents engaged in, and the small number of movies that are common favorites.

Observation difficulty refers to how hard it would be to find the answer from a given perspective. For example, mothers' maiden names are often accessible because of genealogy websites. Some questions are also subject to attack by memes such as "Your Porn Star Name" or "20 Facts About Me." The current first search result for "porn star name" suggests that you should form it from "your first pet's name and the street you grew up on." Relying on such information being secret is a bad choice. It is a bad choice because people don't expect that the information in question will need to be kept private. No one would find it entertaining to be asked for a password in order to generate a porn star name; they'd find it worrisome. Observation difficulty can only be measured in relation to some set of possible observers. Therefore, attacker-centered modeling makes sense for measuring observation difficulty.

Usability

Knowledge-based authentication systems also suffer many usability problems, including the following:

- **Applicability:** Does the item apply to the whole population? Questions about the color of your first car only apply to those who have owned cars; questions about the name of your first pet only apply to pet owners.
- **Memorability:** Will people remember their answer? Studies have shown that 20 percent or so will forget their answers within three months (Schechter, 2009a).
- **Repeatability:** Can someone correctly re-enter their answer ("Main St" vs. "Main Street"), and is the answer still the same as it was 10 years ago? (Is Avril Lavigne still your favorite singer?) Repeatability is also called stability in some analyses.
- **Facts versus preferences:** There is some evidence that preferences are more stable over time. However, entropy, and thus resistance to guessing attacks, is lower, and some preferences may be revealed to observation.

- **Privacy:** Some questions can seem intrusive, creepy, or too personal to users. Also, under the privacy laws of many countries, information can only be used for the purpose for which it was collected. Using such information for authentication may run afoul of such laws.
- **Internationalization:** The meaning of some questions does not carry across cultures. Facebook has reported that people in Indonesia don't name their pets, and so the usual answer to that question is "cat" (Anderson, 2013b).

Aligning security with the mental models of your customers is great if you can manage it, but it may be sufficient to avoid surprising your customer. To illustrate the difference, a website decided that cookies were part of the login process, and if your cookies were deleted, you would need not only your password, but also your secret question. Because my secret answer was something like "asddsfdaf," this presented a problem. The design surprised me, and prevented me from logging back in, which is the state my account is probably in to this day.

Additionally, systems can be open question or open answer. Open-question systems are of the form "please enter your question." It turns out that such systems result in questions with few answers (e.g., "What color are my eyes?"; "What bank is this?").

If You Must Use a Knowledge-Based Authentication System

Look for information in your system that can be used, such as "What was the dollar amount of your last transaction?" The information should be available to few parties;, thus, the last LinkedIn connection you added is poor. If your organization has features to enable social sharing, nothing that is shared should be usable to authenticate. It should also be hard for an attacker to influence; thus, "Who was the last person who e-mailed you?" is bad. Finally, it should be hard for an attacker who has broken in to extract all the information they would need to retake the account.

One way to reduce the chance that the attacker can extract all the information from the account is to augment the last dollar amount question with a financial account number question. If you use financial account numbers, be sure to require more than five digits. (Four digits is the U.S. limit to how many may be displayed; using five means an attacker only needs to guess, on average, five times to get in. Consider asking for six or eight.) When someone gets the answers right, consider sending a message to all the backup contact information you have, offering the real account owner a chance to challenge the authentication. That said, however, consider using social authentication, covered in the section of the same name, in place of knowledge-based authentication.

Chained Authentication Failures

As many organizations develop backup authentication schemes, avoiding chained and interlock authentication failures is an important issue. A *chained failure* is where an attacker who takes over an account at one site can see all the information they'll need to authenticate to another site. An interlocking failure is where that's bi-directional. For example, if you set your Gmail account recovery to Yahoo mail, and your Yahoo mail to recover with Gmail, then your recovery options are interlocked. Unfortunately, it's normally an issue that end users must manage for themselves.

NOTE This issue came to widespread attention after an August 2012 article in Wired, "How Apple and Amazon Security Flaws Led to My Epic Hacking" (Honan, 2012). It's worth recounting the details and then analyzing them. The names of the companies are taken from the Wired story. Note that these are large, mature companies with employees focused on security. The story is presented solely to help others learn. The steps that led to the "epic hacking" are as follows:

1. Attacker calls Amazon and partially authenticates with victim's name, e-mail address, and billing address. Attacker adds a credit card number to the account.
2. Attacker calls Amazon again, authenticating with victim's name, e-mail address, billing address, and the credit card number added in step 1. Attacker adds a new e-mail address to the account.
3. Attacker visits Amazon.com, and sends password reset e-mail to e-mail address from step 2.
4. Attacker logs in to Amazon with the new password. Attacker gathers last four digits of real credit card numbers.
5. Attacker calls Apple with e-mail address, billing address, and last four digits of the credit card. Apple issues a temporary credential for an iCloud account.
6. Attacker logs into iCloud and changes passwords.
7. Attacker visits Gmail and sends account reset e-mail to compromised Apple account.
8. Attacker logs into Gmail.

So what went wrong here?

- All the attacks used backup authentication methods.
- Several places used data that's mostly public to authenticate.
- Amazon allowed information that can be used to authenticate to be added with less authentication.
- The Wired writer took the advised approach and interlinked all of his accounts.

Returning to the issue of chained authentication failures, it is hard to prevent people from using their preferred e-mail provider. It is perhaps impossible for a company to determine where it stands in a daisy chain of authentications. It might be possible to detect authentication loops, manage the privacy concerns such a process could raise, and handle the loop in a clever way.

Social Authentication

As mentioned earlier, the traditional methods of authentication are what you have, what you know, and what you are. In a 2006 paper, John Brainard and colleagues suggested a fourth: who you know, presenting it as a way to handle primary authentication (Brainard, 2006).

Social authentication is authentication based on social contact of various forms. It is already in use at a great many businesses that send a replacement password to your manager if you're locked out. This leverages the expectation that managers ought to be able to get in touch with their employees and authenticate them. Social authentication may also help with making your system more viral. When someone is selected as a trustee, you might want to round-trip an e-mail message to them to ensure that the details are valid, and you may want to recheck that address from time to time. Such messages can have the added value of marketing your service, as you might need to explain what the service is. Try hard to not eliminate the security value by spamming.

Passive Social Authentication

In early 2012, Facebook deployed a backup authentication mechanism that asks users to identify a set of people connected to that user (Fisher, 2012; Rice, 2011). This is passive authentication in the sense that your Facebook contacts are not actively involved in the authentication process. Such systems are easier to deploy if you have a rich social graph of some type.

However, the data needed to bypass such a system is sometimes available to (and perhaps via) Facebook, LinkedIn, Google, and a growing number of other companies. Other problems include photos that don't include an identifiable face and photos that contain a name badge (for example, from a conference). Facebook also explored use of their social graph to make collaboration more difficult, selecting people who are less likely to be known to a single attacker, or friends of the attacker. Of course, because the attacker is unknown, they can only do this by looking for distinct subgraphs (Rice, 2011).

Active Social Authentication

Active social authentication uses a real-world relationship to recover access to an account. Such systems are most obvious when a manager gets a new password and provides it to an employee, but it's possible to build deeper systems that use a variety of account "trustees." One such system was developed experimentally by Stuart Schechter, Serge Egelman, and Rob Reeder (Schechter, 2009b). It is reviewed here in depth because it's superior in many ways to knowledge-based systems, and because many of the details show interesting design points.

They use a system of trustees who reauthorize access to an account. Their test used a system of four trustees selected by the account holder, and required concurrence of three trustees. When an account goes into recovery, each trustee is sent an e-mail with a subject line of "**FOR YOU ONLY**." The body of the message starts with "Do not forward any part of this e-mail to anyone," and continues with an explanation of what to do. The e-mail then goes on to encourage the recipient to visit a given URL. When the recipient does so, he or she is asked to explain why an account recovery code is being requested. The reasons are listed from riskiest to least risky so that someone who selects the first option(s) will see an additional level of warning before being allowed to get a recovery code. The reasons given are as follows:

- **Someone helping William Shakespeare** (or who claimed to be helping) **asked** for the code
- An e-mail, IM, SMS, or other text message that **appears to be from William Shakespeare** asked for the code
- **William Shakespeare left me a voicemail** asking for the code, and I will call him back to provide it
- **I am speaking to William Shakespeare by phone** right now and he has asked for the code
- **William Shakespeare is here with me** in person right now and he has asked me for the code
- None of the above reasons applies. I will provide my own:

After selecting one of these, and possibly seeing additional warnings about signs of fraud, the trustee is asked to pledge to the veracity of the answer and their understanding of the consequences of being duped. They are required to type their name and then press a button that says "I promise the above pledge is true." The trustee is then given a six-character code, and instructed to provide it either in person or in a phone call. The system will then e-mail all the other trustees, encouraging them to call or visit the account holder. This process has several useful properties, including increased security and alerting the account holder if they didn't initiate the account recovery.

There are a number of issues with the system as presented. One is time. This social approach takes longer to complete than knowledge-based approaches. Another is that in the initial reliability experiment, many participants did not succeed at recovering their account. Of 43 participants in the weeklong reliability experiment, 17 abandoned the experiment. Of the 26 who actively participated, 65 percent were able to recover their account. Two of the failures didn't remember their trustees or use the "look them up" feature, and another two were too busy to participate in the study. Looking at the 22 who actively participated, 77 percent of them succeeded at account recovery, which seems poor, but it's comparable to knowledge-based systems. It seems likely that more people would succeed if they really were trying to recover their account, and had nominated appropriate trustees.

Despite these concerns, social authentication is a promising area for account recovery, and I am optimistic that new systems will be developed and deployed, replacing knowledge-based account recovery for casual accounts.

Attacker-Driven Analysis of Account Recovery

Knowing who is attacking is a useful lens into how account recovery systems work, because there are sets of attackers who obviously have more access to data. Spouses or ex-spouses, family members, and others will often know (or be able to tease out information about) your first car, the street you grew up on, and so on. Attackers include, but are not limited to, the following:

- Spouses
- Friends
- Social network "friends" and contacts
- Attackers with current access to your account
- Attackers with access to an account on another system
- Attackers with access to a data broker's data

In "It's No Secret: Measuring the Security and Reliability of Authentication via 'Secret' Questions" (Schechter, 2009a), the authors categorize 25 percent of question/answer pairs in use at large service providers as vulnerable to guessing by family, friends, or coworkers. Spouses generally have unfettered access to records, financial instruments such as credit cards, and the like. Friends will often know about biographical information. Social network contacts can use attacks like the "Your Porn Star Name" game to get access to elements of personal history that social networks such as Facebook don't make public. The social networks themselves change what information they show as public, meaning your analysis of knowledge-based account recovery must be regularly revisited.

Another important set of attackers is online criminals, who have found ways to access information stored by data brokers. This information is often marketed as "out of wallet" authentication. That criminals have access to such data emphasizes the need to use data known only to you and your customers (Krebs, 2013).

Multi-Channel Authentication

Many systems claim to use additional channels for authentication. Some of them even do, but modeling what counts as a channel in a converged world is challenging. In particular, when a smartphone is synced to a computer, the act of syncing often involves giving one computer full authority to read or write to anything in the other. This means that smartphones are a risky source of additional channels. The computer is a threat to the smartphone, and vice versa. Physical mail is a fine example of an additional channel, with the obvious issue that it's quite slow.

Account Recovery Checklist

This checklist is designed to be read aloud at a meeting. You're in a bad state if for any of these questions:

- You can't answer yes.
- You can't articulate and accept the implications of a no.
- You don't know.

1. Do we have explicit reasons that we need an online account recovery feature?
2. Have we investigated active social authentication as an approach?
3. If you're using active social authentication, then have we tried to address the attacks by friends problem?
4. Have we tested the usability and efficacy of our approach for both the authorized customer and one or more sorts of attacker?

If you've decided to use a knowledge-based authentication system, you'll probably jump from #2 to the following list:

1. Will our system use only information that only we and our customer should know?
2. Will our system resist attacks like "Your Porn Star Name" game?
3. Will our system resist attack by spouses?
4. Will our system resist attackers who have broken in and scraped the account?
5. Will our system resist attackers who have access to information bought and sold by data brokers?

6. Have we considered the various usability aspects of knowledge-based authentication?
7. Do we use time and account-holder notification as allies?

Names, IDs, and SSNs

A great many technological systems seem to end up using human names and identifiers. The designers of these systems often make assumptions that are not true, or are perhaps even dangerous. A good model of names, identifiers, and related topics helps you threat model effectively, limiting what you expect to gain from using these identifiers. Many reliability and usability threats are associated with these topics. In this section, you'll learn about names, identity cards and documents, social security numbers and their misuse, and identity theft.

Names

"What's in a name?" asked Shakespeare, for a very good reason. A name is an identifier, and between diminutives, nicknames, and married names, many people use more than one name in the course of their life. Useful names are also relative. You and I mean something different by "mom"' or "my wife." I often mean different people when I say "Mike." (At work, my three-person team has a Mike, and my boss's boss is named Mike; and that's just at work.)

"Real Names"

It is tempting to set up a new system that requires people to use their "real names." It is widely believed that a real-name system is easier to validate, and that people will comment more usefully under their real names. Both of these claims are demonstrably false. South Korea rolled out and then scrapped a regulation requiring real names, having found that it did not prevent people "from posting abusive messages or spreading false rumors" (Chosunilbo, 2011). Internet comment management company Disqus has analyzed its data and discovered that 61 percent of its commenters were obviously using pseudonyms, and only 4 percent used what appeared to be a real name. They also found that both real name and pseudonym comments were marked as spam at approximately the same rates (9 percent and 11 percent respectively).

However, the cost of real name requirements can be high. Google's G+ system required real names on rollout. They did so with a set of "name police," who rejected real names and violated their own policies. These "nymwars" as they came to be known had a dramatic effect on the adoption of Google+, and I've argued elsewhere that it was singularly responsible for G+ not killing Facebook

(Shostack, 2012b). Germany has a law forbidding such policies (Essers, 2012). Both demands for real names and attempts to impose rules on those names continues to happen and cause outrage. For example, see "Please Enter a Valid Last Name" (Neilsen Hayden, 2012).

Patrick McKenzie published a list titled "Falsehoods Programmers Believe About Names." The list is worth reading in full, but here are the first nine items (McKenzie, 2010):

1. People have exactly one canonical full name.
2. People have exactly one full name which they go by.
3. People have, at this point in time, exactly one canonical full name.
4. People have, at this point in time, one full name which they go by.
5. People have exactly *N* names, for any value of *N*.
6. People's names fit within a certain defined amount of space.
7. People's names do not change.
8. Peoples names change, but only at a certain enumerated set of events.
9. Peoples names are written in ASCII, or some other single character set.

The list continues through another 30 false assumptions. Two items can be added to the list, based on reading the comments. First, you can exclude certain characters from people's names without offending them. Second, the name people give you is one they use outside your system. Many programmers seem offended at being asked to deal with this. A great many comments are of the form "people should just deal with it and offer a Romanized version of their name." Other commenters point out that lying about your name is in some instances a felony, and how changes in names or transliteration can lead to real problems. Many Americans were introduced to this by the TSA (airport security) when they checked that identity documents matched names on tickets. Discrepancies such as "Mike/Michael" lead to trouble. At best, a system that refuses people's preferred names threatens to appear arrogant and offensive to those who are mis-addressed.

So what should you do? Don't use human names as account names. Treat human names as a single field, and use what people enter. If you'd like to be informal, ask your customers for both a full name and how the system should address them.

Account Names

Unlike human names, it is possible to make account names unique by having some authority that approves names before they can be used. (I am aware of some countries that do this at birth, but none that require a renaming when someone moves there.) Names can be unique or currently unique. Someone had my `microsoft.com` e-mail before me. The last I heard, his kids were knocking it out of the little league park, and his wife still loved him (muscle memory on typing his e-mail address, or so she claimed). Therefore, uniqueness is helpful, but it leads to all the easily remembered e-mail addresses being taken.

If your account system relies on someone else maintaining uniqueness forever, while in fact they maintain uniqueness at a given time, you can run into trouble. For example, if that other Adam and I both sign up for LinkedIn with our @microsoft.com addresses, what should LinkedIn do? They can probably handle that by now, and you'll need to do so as well. (A draft of this section threatened to magnify this problem by including my e-mail address.)

"Meaningful ID"

Carl Ellison has coined the term *meaningful ID* and defined it as follows: "A meaningful ID for use by some human being is an identifier that calls to that human user's mind the correct identified entity" (Ellison, 2007). This is a good model for an important use case for names, which is to call to mind a specific person.

Ellison provides some requirements for meaningful IDs:

1. Calling a correct entity to the human's mind implies that the human being has a body of memories about the correct entity. If there are no such memories, then no ID can be a meaningful ID.
2. What works to call those memories to one observer's mind may not work for another observer. Therefore, a meaningful ID is in general a function of both the identified entity and the person looking at it.
3. The meaningful ID needs to attract attention or be presented without distracting clutter, so that it has the opportunity to be perceived.
4. When a security decision is to be made, the meaningful ID(s) must be derived in a secure manner, and competing IDs that an attacker could introduce at-will should not be displayed.

Ellison suggests that the best identifier to present to a person is probably a nickname selected by the person who must rely on it, or a picture taken by that relying party. Implicitly, a system must perform the translation, and be designed to mitigate spoofing threats around the nickname shown.

Zooko's Triangle

You may have noticed that the requirements for a meaningful ID are in tension with the requirements for account names. Meaningful IDs are selected by people, to be evocative for themselves, while account names are mediated by some authority. It turns out that there are many such tensions associated with names. One very useful model of these tensions is "Zooko's Triangle," named after its creator, Zooko Wilcox-O'Hearn, and shown in Figure 14-4. The triangle shows the properties of decentralized, secure, and human-meaningful (Zooko, 2006).

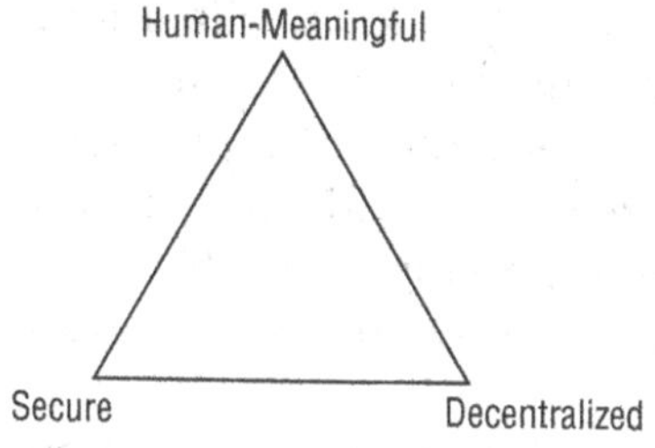

Figure 14-4: Zooko's Triangle

The idea is that every system design focuses on one or two of these properties, which requires a trade-off with the others. The choice can be implicit or explicit, and the Triangle is a useful model for making it explicit.

Identity Documents

Deferring the issue of identifying your users to a government agency is attractive. Having someone look at or make a copy of a government-issued identity document may constitute sufficient due diligence, especially if you are in a regulated industry. Looking at the documents and storing copies exposes you to very different threats. If you store them and lose control of the storage, you'll need to notify those people if you lose control of the documents (under a wide variety of state breach disclosure laws). This is an information disclosure threat against a data store, and the risk elimination mitigation is to not have that data store. It may be sufficient to ensure that you check the documents. If you are not required by law to expose yourself to such liabilities, then having copies of identity documents seems foolishly risky.

Another issue with identity documents is that many people lack them for a wide variety of reasons. Many American citizens lack identity documents. This issue gained attention in the run-up to the 2012 election, as many states passed voter ID laws. Setting aside the emotional political questions, these laws drew attention to the fact that roughly 11 percent of voting-age Americans do not have current and valid government-issued photo ID (Brenner, 2012). It is important to consider how you'll handle those customers without valid ID, or whose ID is not of the form you expect. For example, 20 million Americans don't have a driver's license (Swire, 2008). Your response to those without the ID you want might be to threaten to or actually refuse them service, but check with your sales and marketing departments before cutting off so many of your potential customers.

Many times, it seems attractive to address fraud issues by asking people to show copies of such documents. If the document is shown over the Internet, any fool with a printer can make a spoof that's good enough for their webcam. Similarly, any college student or illegal immigrant can acquire a document that's good enough to fool the majority of people paid to check the documents. As the value of such documents increases, so does the motivation to either forge them or corrupt the official issuance process. This is an economic threat to both your system and the integrity of the system as a whole. Regardless, knowing what an ID card says does not mean that the person with a given ID card is the same person who opened the account. This is a spoofing threat. (After all, given the breaches that happen, all the data on a given ID card may be available to a fraudster.)

In short, looking at ID cards may be a helpful step, but it would reflect poor threat modeling to assume that it will solve all your authentication problems.

Social Security Numbers and Other National Identity Numbers

This section reviews risks associated with the United States social security number (SSN). Over the last five to ten years, the use of SSNs has declined substantially as a result of new laws. As of this writing, it is illegal to deny someone goods or services because they will not give you their SSN in Alaska, Kansas, Maine, New Mexico, and Rhode Island (Hillebrand, 2008). A large number of state laws also restrict their use, too numerous to list here (Bovbjerg, 2005). The first problem is that many developers are unaware of these laws, and their lack of awareness may put their employers at risk. The second problem with SSNs is that some organizations use them as identifiers, while others use them for authenticators. (Recall that an identifier is a label for a person or other entity. An authenticator is how you prove that claim.) A few remarkable organizations manage to use them for both, but that's not a model you want to emulate.

SSNs Are Poor Identifiers

Social security numbers make poor identifiers even if all your customers are American citizens who happen to be willing to give you their SSN. Not every American has an SSN, and not everyone legally residing in the United States is a citizen. For example, many teachers participate in the Teacher Retirement System, which does not use SSNs. Many legal residents are not able to get an SSN. Second, SSNs lack a check digit, so it's easy to accidentally transpose or mistype digits. When you do, you have a roughly one-in-three chance of getting someone else's SSN. (Roughly 300–400 million SSNs have been issued, and the number space is nine digits.) Third, except for those who work at the Social Security Administration, the identifiers are outside your control.

SSNs Are Poor Database Keys

Even if you collect SSNs, you should ensure that your account identifier and database keys are ones that you control. Otherwise, you'll need to deal with a way to change your account identifier. As the Social Security Administration notes, "Applying for a new number is a big decision. It may impact your ability to interact with federal and state agencies, employers, and others. This is because your financial, medical, employment and other records will be under your former Social Security number . . ." (Social Security Administration, 2011). It is unclear whether the SSA is using SSNs as account identifiers, or if they are warning that many others do so. If they are using the SSA as an account identifier, that might be reasonable, but it would also seem reasonable that they have a way to manage an update. If they have chosen a mitigation strategy of risk transfer to citizens, then reasonable people might be skeptical that that's a decision a government should be making.

SSNs Are Poor Authenticators

SSNs are known to many parties. As stated earlier in the discussion of knowledge-based authentication, answers to authentication questions should be known to only a few parties. Unfortunately, between schools, banks, insurance companies, utility companies, employers, tax preparation, gyms, and other entities that have made SSNs a condition of participation, the SSNs of most Americans are available fairly widely, and are often leaked in data breaches.

Even if they were not, Alessandro Acquisti and Ralph Gross have shown that they can predict many SSNs based on date and location of birth. They could "identify in a single attempt the first five digits for 44 percent of deceased individuals who were born after 1988 and for 7 percent of those born between 1973 and 1988." They were also able to "identify all nine digits for 8.5 percent of those individuals born after 1988 in less than 1,000 attempts" (Power, 2009). In further work with Fred Stutzman, they were able to add facial recognition, using a dataset of faces on Facebook and an online dating site to find names and birth dates. They were able to guess a substantial number of SSNs or partial SSNs from three webcam pictures (Acquisti, 2011). As they point out, this technology will get better and better as facial recognition technology improves, and as labeled face data becomes more widely available.

Finally, social security numbers are routinely published by the Social Security Administration after people die, in the Social Security Death Master File (SSDMF) [Social Security Administration, 2012]. Some organizations check the SSDMF to prevent new account fraud. However, when someone dies, their account does not necessarily go away. For example, bank accounts might be maintained by an estate during probate. A phone might be kept active for several months to enable people to get in touch. If you are using SSNs or some portion of the SSN as an authenticator, it will have been made public, making your authenticator far less useful.

Why Not Publish the SSN List?

One innovative response to the issue of "are SSNs well known?" is to simply publish the list, thus clarifying the true state of the system (Lindstrom, 2006). This is attractive in a number of ways. However, the law states "Social security account numbers and related records that are obtained or maintained by authorized persons pursuant to any provision of law enacted on or after October 1, 1990, shall be confidential, and no authorized person shall disclose any such social security account number or related record" (42 USC 405(c)(2)(C)(viii)). Therefore, any source with an authoritative list is legally prohibited from publishing it. Rather than change the law to allow publication of the list, a sane new law should prohibit the use of SSNs as identifiers or authenticators, and restrict their use in both the public and private sectors. (Given the lack of a check digit, associating two records based on an SSN should probably be treated as negligent.)

Other National Identity Schemes

The preceding section is very U.S.-centric, and may therefore seem irrelevant to those in other countries, but it is not. The same sorts of issues crop up with any national identifier scheme, although the semi-private nature of the SSN seems to have exacerbated the conflation of its use as both identifier and authenticator.

Wherever you are considering using a government-issued identifier, (or other identifier provided by another organization) you should ask the following questions:

- Does everyone have one?
- Does it have a check digit?
- Will you ever serve tourists, students, refugees, or other foreigners?
- Can an individual get a new ID, and if so does it have the same field values?
- How will the system handle identity fraud in the future? (Even if the citizen can't change their number now, they may be able to in the future. You should store it as a field, not as your identifier or database key.)

If you want to use it as an authenticator, perhaps as part of an electronic ID scheme, ask how many people have access to the authentication data associated with the card.

Identity Theft

There is a common worry in the United States, referred to as identity theft. Elsewhere, I've written that the term *fraud by impersonation* is a more accurate description of the crime, and that it's a crime facilitated by inappropriate allocation of costs and benefits (Shostack, 2003). In particular, it's easy for organizations that trade in information to be paid even when the information turns out to be highly inaccurate. The cost to them is that they may need to update it. The threat to a data subject may be denial of credit, denial of a job or a volunteer opportunity, or even an inappropriate arrest. Other cost distributions would likely result in more socially desirable outcomes.

However, the term *identity theft* may be appropriate when you consider its emotional impact on a subset of victims where records with information about them have become inextricably linked to those of the perpetrator, and whose ability to engage in normal activities is inhibited by the emotional burden of further false accusations, and the fear of those accusations. Those people really have had their "good name" stolen (Identity Theft Resource Center, 2009). There may be a good case that their good name isn't stolen by the impersonator, but by those who intermix records and re-distribute the misinformation.

How does this play into threat modeling? Linkage is a threat to your data integrity and to your customer's satisfaction. System designers should take care when linking information from disparate sources. If your system has features or processes that allow people to access and correct information you store, you should ensure that those corrections are not accidentally overridden by the same data from a source whose data has been corrected. (That is, if Alice tells you that Bob is a deadbeat, and Bob shows you his cancelled checks paying his debt to Alice, you'll correct your record. Next month, Alice may well include Bob in her list of deadbeats again. Do you want Bob to be a happy customer? If so, you should be careful to not require that he correct your data repeatedly.) Tracking where your data is from can help with these issues. If you sell data about people, you can provide information about where you got the data to help your customers deliver better service. The most important distinction is between your direct observation and information you receive from elsewhere. You can either name the source, or, if the source is commercially sensitive, give them an alias.

Names, IDs, and SSNs Checklist

This checklist is designed to be read aloud at a meeting. You're in a bad state if for any of these questions:

- You can't answer yes.
- You can't articulate and accept the implications of a no.
- You don't know.

1. Do we know who controls our account namespace?
2. Do we have a way for our customers to assign a meaningful ID to things they need to securely identify?
3. Do we know what trade-offs we've made between global, meaningful, and secure?
4. Are we relying on identity documents? If so, are we storing copies of those documents, and who has signed off on that risk?
5. Are we using SSNs or similar identifiers at all?

Summary

In a good model of accounts, they exist at the intersection of the human and the machine, and threats are abundant at that boundary. Those threats include authentication threats and confusion about names and identifiers.

Accounts are a focal point for threats, which occur throughout the account life cycle, including account creation, maintenance, and termination. Risks of information disclosure to bad actors cause many systems to treat the people behind the accounts as attackers, rather than allies. Many of the authentication factors that are hidden are easily learned by a motivated attacker, while your real customers are left frustrated and in the dark. Good modeling that exposes how easy or hard it is to learn the obscured elements of authentication can help you make good choices, especially about notifying the person behind the account of what's happening.

Authentication is hard. Creating a workable authentication system that satisfies both an organization and its customers is hard. The framework of what you know, what you have, and what you are gives you a way to think about authentication, with "what channel are we using?" and "who you know" being interesting additions to the framework. However, each of these elements has threats against it, which have been worked through in great depth, and there are established patterns and limits for each.

If authentication is hard, backup authentication is even harder. A variety of knowledge-based authentication techniques can be used to recover access to an account. When you use one, you should focus on account recovery, not password recovery, because you should not store passwords in plaintext. There are many problems with knowledge-based authentication, including security and usability. It may be preferable to use a social authentication technique; although they are new and less familiar, they are likely more secure.

Unlike authentication, names are relatively easy, once you accept that they lack certain properties, and you understand the risks that they carry. Avoid the "real name" trap, and consider where on Zooko's Triangle your system should be: Are names memorable, globally unique, or secure? (Pick any two.) It is tempting to defer the problem to identity documents, which can help a carefully designed system but carry risks of their own. Designers often want to use social security numbers, which are poor identifiers, poor database keys, and poor authenticators. Despite those flaws, they are often used, bringing privacy and security threats along with them. One of those threats is identity theft, and there are patterns that can help you avoid contributing to the problem.

CHAPTER

15

Human Factors and Usability

Usable security matters because people are an important element in the security of any system. If you don't consider how people will use your system, the odds are against them using it well. The security usability community is learning to model people, the sorts of decisions you need them to make, and the sorts of scenarios in which they act. The toolbox for addressing these issues is small but growing, and the tools are not yet as prescriptive as you might like. As such, this chapter gives you (in particular the security expert) deeper background than some other chapters, and the best advice available.

Because humans are different from other elements of security, and because the models, threats, and means of addressing them are different, this chapter covers challenges of modeling human factors in terms of security, and the techniques available to address them.

The chapter starts with models of people, as they motivate everything in this chapter. It continues with models of software which are useful for human factors work. These two models interact with threat elicitation techniques which are covered next, and are similar to those you learned about in Part II of this book. Threats in this chapter include those in which an attacker tries to convince a person to take action, and threats in which the computer needs to defer to a person for a decision. After threat elicitation, you'll learn tools and techniques for addressing human factors issues, as well as some user interface principles for addressing those threats, and advice for designing configuration, authentication, and warnings. These are the human-factors equivalents of the defensive tactics and technologies covered Chapter 8 "Defensive Tactics and Technologies." From there, you'll learn about testing for human factors issues, mirroring what you learned in Chapter 10 "Validating That Threats are Addressed." The chapter closes with my perspective on usability and ceremonies.

Threat modeling for software or systems generally involves keeping two models in mind: a model of the software, and a model of the threats. Considering human factors adds a third model to the mix: a model of people. Ironically, that additional cognitive load can present a real usability challenge for those threat modeling human factors.

A FEW BRIEF NOTES ON TERMINOLOGY

- *Usability* refers to the subset of human factors work designed to help people accomplish their tasks. Usability work includes the creation of user interfaces. User interfaces, along with their discoverability, suitability for purpose, and the success or failure of the people using those interfaces, make up one or more user experiences.
- *Human factors* covers how technology needs to help people under attack, how to craft mental models, how to test the designs you're building.
- *Ceremony* refers to the idea of a protocol, extended to include its "human nodes." For now, consider a ceremony to be similar to a user experience, but from the perspective of a protocol analyst. Ceremonies are explained in depth later in the chapter.
- *People* are at the center of this chapter. You'll see them referred to as users in user testing, user interface, and similar terms of art, and sometimes as humans, to align with sources.

Models of People

This chapter opens with models of people because they are at the center of the work you will sometimes need to do when addressing security where people are in the loop. This is a new type of model which parallels models of software and threats.

We all know some people, know how they behave, what they want. Aren't these informal models enough? Unfortunately, the answer seems to be no. (Otherwise, security wouldn't have a usability problem.) There are two reasons to create more structured models. First, people who work in software usually construct informal models of people that appear good enough for day-to-day use (but are often full of contempt for normal folks). They aren't robust enough to lead us to good decisions. Second, and more important, our implicit models of people are rarely focused on how people make security decisions.

As a profession, we need better models showing how people arrive at a security task, their mental models of the security tasks they're being asked to do, or the security-related skills or knowledge we can expect various types of people to have. It might be possible to build all that into a single model, or we might have several models which are designed to work together. Additionally, we'd like a set of models that help those who are not experts in usable security.

Even if we had those models, attaining a consistent and repeatable automated analysis of the human beings within a ceremony is unlikely. (There's an argument that it is probably equivalent to developing artificial intelligence: If a computer could perfectly predict how a human being will respond to a set of stimuli, then it could exhibit the same responses. If it could exhibit the same responses, then it could pass the Turing test.) However, recall that all models are wrong, and some models are useful. You don't need a perfect model to help you predict design issues. All of the models in this chapter are on the less structured end of the spectrum and are most useful in a structured brainstorm or expert consideration of a ceremony.

Applying Behaviorist Models of People

Does the name Pavlov ring a bell? If so, one explanation is that your repeated exposure to a stimulus has conditioned a response. The stimulus is stories about Pavlov's famous dog experiments. The behaviorists believe that all observable behaviors are learned responses to stimuli. The behaviorist model has obvious and well-trod limitations, but it would not have had such a good run if it didn't at least have some explanatory or predictive power. Some of the ways in which behavioral models of people can apply to ceremonies are explored in this section.

Conditioning and Habituation

People learn from their environment. If their environment presents them with frequently repeated stimuli, they'll learn ways to respond to those stimuli. For example, if you put a username/password prompt in front of people, they're likely to fill it out. (That's a conditioned response, as pointed out by Chris Karlof and colleagues [Karlof, 2009].) It is hard for people to evoke deep, careful thought each time they encounter the stimulus, because such effort would usually be wasted. Closely related to this idea of a conditioned response is a habituation response such as automatically clicking a button in a dialog you have repeatedly seen (e.g., "Some files might be dangerous").

It's hard to argue that such behavior is even wrong. Aesop's tale about the boy who cried wolf ends with the boy not getting help when a real wolf appears.

People learn to ignore repeated, false warnings, for good reasons. If thinking carefully about the dialog mentioned in the example takes five seconds and a person sees it 30 times per day, that's three minutes per day, or 1,000 minutes per year spent thinking about that one dialog. Suppose someone were successfully attacked once per year by a malicious file that exploits a bug not yet patched on the computer, and their anti-virus wouldn't catch it. Will the cost of cleanup exceed 16 hours? If not, then the person is rationally ignoring the advice to spend those five seconds (Herley, 2009).

Conditioning and habituation can be addressed by reducing the frequency of the stimulus. For example, the SmartScreen feature in Windows and Internet Explorer checks whether a file is from a leading publisher or very frequently downloaded and simply asks the person what to do with the file, rather than issuing a warning. Conditioning can also be addressed by ensuring that the ceremony conditions people to take steps for their security (see "Conditioned-Safe Ceremonies" later in this chapter for more information).

Wicked Environments

Educators have a concept of "kind" learning environments. A kind learning environment includes appropriate challenges and immediate feedback. These environments can be contrasted with wicked environments, which make learning hard. Jay Jacobs has brought the concept of wicked environments to information security. Quoting his description:

> *[Feedback is] the prime discriminator between a kind and wicked environment and consequently the quality of our intuition. A kind environment will offer unambiguous, timely, and accurate feedback. For example, most sports are a kind environment. When a tennis ball is struck, the feedback on performance is immediate and unambiguous. If the ball hits the net, it was aimed too low, etc. When the golf ball hooks off into the woods, the performance feedback to the golfer is obvious and immediate. However, if we focus on the feedback within information security decisions, we see feedback that is not timely, extremely ambiguous, and often misperceived or inaccurate. Years may pass between an information security decision and any evidence that the decision was poor. When information security does fail, proper attribution to the decision(s) is unlikely, and the correct lessons may not be learned, if lessons are learned at all. Because of this untimely, ambiguous, and inaccurate feedback, decision makers do not have the opportunity to learn from the environment in which the risk-based decisions are being made. It is safe to say that these decisions are being made in a wicked environment.*
>
> —Jay Jacobs, "A Call to Arms" (ISSA Journal, 2011)

As a simple heuristic, you can ask, is this design wicked or kind? What can you do to provide better feedback or make the feedback more timely or actionable?

Cognitive Science Models of People

Cognitive science takes an empirical approach to behavior, and attempts to build models from observation of how people really behave. In this section, you'll learn about a variety of models of people that are in the cognitive science mold. They include the following:

- Carl Ellison's "ceremonies" model of people
- A model based on the work of behavioral economist Daniel Kahneman
- A model derived from the work of safety expert James Reason
- A framework explicitly for reasoning about humans in computer security by CMU professor Laurie Cranor
- A model derived from work on humans in security by UCL professor Angela Sasse

These models overlap in various ways. Each is, after all, a model of people. In addition, each of these can inform how you threat model the human aspects of a system you're building.

Ellison's Ceremonies Model

A ceremony is a protocol extended to include the people at each end. Security architect and consultant Carl Ellison points out that we, as a community, can learn from post-mortems of real ceremony errors, or perform tests on candidate ceremonies. He describes a model of "installing" programs on "human nodes" by means of a manual, training, or a contract that mandates certain user behavior. Models that require people to make decisions using the identity of the source require that the system effectively communicates about identity to the human node, using a meaningful ID—a concept covered in depth in Chapter 14, "Accounts and Identity."

Ellison defers the creation of a full model to experimental psychologists or cognitive scientists; and in that mode, the following sections summarize a few models that reflect some of the more insightful cognitive scientists whose work applies to security.

The Kahneman Model

This model is an attempt to extract some of the wisdom in *Thinking Fast and Slow* (Straus and Giroux, 2011). That excellent book is by Daniel Kahneman, the

Nobel Prize-winning founder of behavioral economics. It is chock-full of ways in which people behave that do not resemble a computer, and anyone preparing to threat model for human factors will probably find it repays a close reading. Following are some of the concepts presented in Kahneman's book and ideas about how they can be applied to threat modeling:

- **WYSIATI, or What You See Is All There Is:** This concept appears so frequently that Kahneman abbreviates it. The concept is important to threat modeling because it underscores the fact that the information currently presented to a person carries great weight in terms of any decisions they're being asked to make. For example, if a person is told they must contact their bank right now to address a problem, they are perhaps unlikely to remember that their bank never answers the phone after 4:00 P.M., never mind on a Saturday. Similarly, if a person doesn't see a security indicator (such a lock icon in a browser), they're unlikely to notice it's not there. If an attacker presents cleverly designed advice "for security," it might crowd out other advice the person has already received.
- **System 1 versus System 2:** System 1 refers to the fast part of your brain, which does things like detect danger, add 2+3, drive, or play chess (if you're a chess master). System 2 refers to the part of your brain that makes rational, considered decisions. System 1 influences our decision-making more than most people realize, or are willing to admit, perhaps including clicking away annoying dialogs. If clicking away dialogs is really system 1 activity, a system design that relies on system 2 when a dialog appears requires you to work hard to ensure that system 2 kicks in.
- **Anchoring:** Anchoring effects are absolutely fascinating. If you ask people to write down the last two digits of their SSN, people with low values for those digits will subsequently estimate unrelated numbers to be lower, whereas those with high values will estimate higher. Similarly, the sales technique of saying something like "this is a $500 camera, but just today it's $300" makes you think you're getting a great deal, even if your budget a moment ago was $200. Perhaps anchoring effects crowd out wisdom when people are presented with scams or are being conned into behaving in ways that they otherwise would not.
- **Satisficing:** Satisfice is a rotten word but it'll do, absent a better one to describe the reality that people attempt to make decisions that are good enough, because the cost of a great decision is too high, or because "decision-making energy" has been exhausted. For example, most people's savings

and investment choices are based on a subset of all possible investments, because evaluating options is time-consuming. In security, perhaps people allow system 1 to assess something, make a call regarding whether it's sufficient, and move on.

Reason's Many Models

Professor James Reason studies the ways in which accidents happen in large systems. His work has lead to the creation of a plethora of models of human error. It could be highly productive to take those models and create prescriptive advice for threat modeling.

For example, his model of "strong habit intrusions" describes how the rules, or habits, that help us get through the day can be triggered inappropriately by "environment[s] that contain elements similar or identical to those in highly familiar circumstances. (For example, 'As I approached the turnstile on my way out of the library, I pulled out my wallet as if to pay—although I knew no money was required.')" These strong habit intrusions might be usable as a threat elicitation heuristic.

Some of the other models he has presented include the following:

- A Generic Error-Modeling System, or GEMS (covering errors, lapses, and slips)
- An intention-centered model
- A model driven by the ways errors are detected
- An action model that includes omissions, intrusions, repetitions, wrong objects, mis-orderings, mis-timings, and blends
- A model based on the context of the errors

All but the first model are covered in depth in *The Human Contribution: Unsafe Acts, Accidents and Heroic Recoveries* (Ashgate Publishing, 2008).

The Cranor Model

In contrast to the creators of the previous models, CMU Professor Lorrie Faith Cranor focuses specifically on security and usability. She has created "A Framework for Reasoning About the Human in the Loop" (Cranor, 2008). Like Ellison's ceremonies paper, her paper is easy and worthwhile reading; this section simply summarizes her framework, which is shown in Figure 15-1.

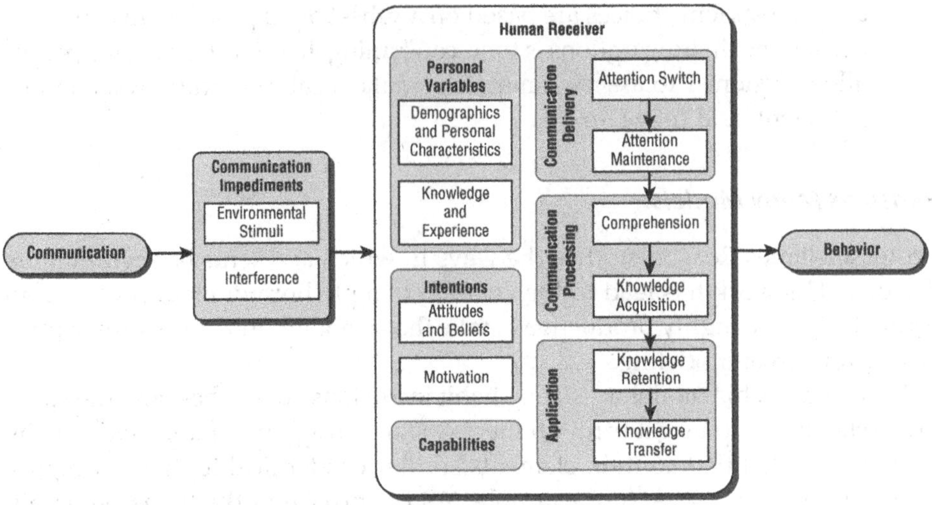

Figure 15-1: Cranor's human-in-the-loop framework

Much like Ellison, Cranor's model puts a person at the center of a model in which communication of various forms may influence behavior. However, "it is not intended as a precise model of human information processing, but rather it is a conceptual framework that can be used much like a checklist to systemically analyze the human role in secure systems." The components of her model are:

- **Communications:** The model considers five types of communication: warnings, notices, status indicators, training, and policy. These are roughly ordered by how active or intrusive the communications are, and they are generally self-explanatory. One noteworthy element of training that Cranor calls out is that effective training (by definition) must lead people to recognize a situation where their training should be applied. There is an interesting relationship to what Reason calls rule misapplication. Rule misapplication may be more common when training is not regularly re-enforced or when the situations in which the training should be triggered are infrequent.
- **Communications impediments:** These include any interference that prevents the communication from being received, and environmental stimuli that may distract the person from a communication that they have received, leading them to perform a different action. It is important to look for both behavior under attack and under non-attack, and ensure that communications reliably occur at the right time and only the right time.
- **The human receiver:** This has six different components, and the "relationships between the various components are intentionally vague." However, the left-hand column relates to the person, while the right-hand column roughly reflects the chain of events for handling the message.

- **Personal Variables:** Includes the person's background, education, demographics, knowledge, and experience, each of which may play into how a person reacts to a message
- **Intentions:** Includes attitudes, beliefs, and motivations
- **Capabilities:** Even a person who gets a message, wants to act on it, and knows how to act on it may not be able to. For example, he or she might not have a smartcard or a smartcard reader.
- **Communication Delivery:** This is related to the person's attention being switched to the communication and maintained there.
- **Communication Processing:** Determine whether the person understands the message and has the knowledge to act on it.
- **Application:** Does the person understand, from formal or informal training, how to respond to the situation, and can they transfer that knowledge to the specific facts at hand?

Cranor presents a model that describes how to use her framework, shown in Figure 15-2. It consists of task identification, task automation, failure identification in two ways (her framework and user studies), and mitigating those failures, again using user studies to ensure that the mitigations are functional. Cranor also usefully presents a set of questions to ask and factors to consider for each element of the model.

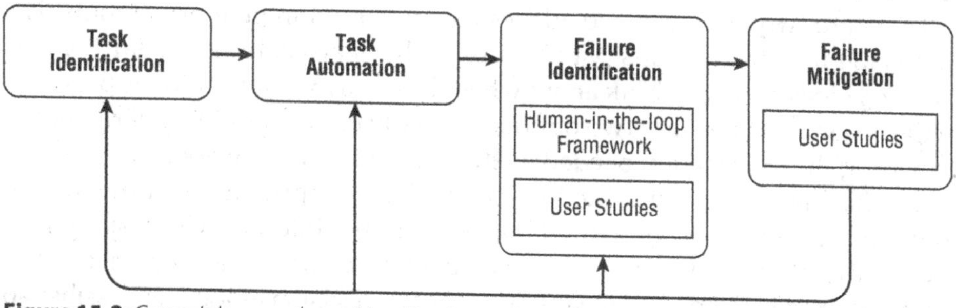

Figure 15-2: Cranor's human threat identification and mitigation process

Sasse's Model

UCL Professor Angela Sasse also has a model of failures situated in organizational systems, including management and policies, preconditions, productive activities, and defenses that surround the decision-makers (meaning any person, rather than only executives). It is fundamentally a compassionate model of people, based on the reality that most people generally want to be secure, and that their deviations from security are understandable if you take the time to "walk a mile in their shoes."

The most important threat modeling take-away from Sasse is her approach to those who make decisions that conflict with the suggestions of security experts. Oftentimes, security experts bemoan that "in a contest between being secure and dancing pigs, dancing pigs will win every time" or "stupid users will click anything you put in front of them." In contrast, she seeks to understand those decisions and the logic that underlies them. Such an understanding is essential to useful models of people.

Heuristic Models of People

The models of people described in this section are less associated with a single researcher, or otherwise don't quite fit into the way behaviorist or cognitive science models of people are presented, but they have been repeatedly and effectively used in studying how people's observed behavior differs from the expectations embedded in systems.

Goal Orientation

People want to get to the task at hand. If a security process stands between them and their goal, then they are likely to view that process as a hindrance. That means they may read a warning dialog as if it says "Do you want to get the job done?" and click OK. Because of this usability, practitioners will often state that, "security is a secondary task."

There are two main ways to address issues found in goal orientation. The first is to make the obvious path secure. If that's possible, it's by far the best course. The second is to think about when the security information is provided in the ceremony. There are two options: Go early or go late. Going early means providing the information needed as the person is thinking about what to do, rather than as they're committed to a path. For example, an operating system could display an application downloaded from the Internet with a spiky icon overlay, rather than (or in addition to) displaying a warning after someone has double-clicked it. Going late means delaying the decision as long as possible, so that the person has a chance to back out. This approach is used in the *gold bar pattern*, whereby the secure option is taken by default, and insecure options are made available in a gold bar along the top of the window. This is sufficient to review the document, but not to edit or print it. A nontargeted attack is unlikely to convince anyone to exit the sandbox and expose themselves to more risk. See "User Interface Tools and Techniques" later in this chapter for more information about the gold bar pattern.

Confirmation Bias

Confirmation bias is the tendency people have to look for information that will confirm a pre-existing mental model. For example, believers in astrology will remember the one time their horoscope just nailed what was about to happen, and discount the other 364 days when it was vague or just plain wrong. Similarly, if someone believes they urgently need to contact their bank, they may be less likely to notice slight oddities in the bank's login page.

Scientists and engineers have learned that looking for ways to disprove an idea is much more powerful that looking for evidence which confirms it. Unfortunately, looking for counter-evidence seems to be at odds with how people tend to work. Recalling the discussion of system 1 and system 2 in the section on Kahneman's work, there may be elements of system 1 versus system 2 at play here. System 1 may see a data point and collect it (feeding confirmation bias) or discard it as anomalous, preventing you from seeing the problem.

Addressing confirmation bias is tricky in general, and may be trickier in security circumstances. It might be possible to condition or train people to look for evidence of evil, and use that to undercut confirmation bias.

IS THIS SECTION FULL OF CONFIRMATION BIAS?

It is easy to find examples of these hueristics once you watch for them, which raises a worry that they are easy, rather than good explanations. Worse, in putting them here, I may be subject to confirmation bias. Perhaps in reality, some other factor is at work, and using one of these will be misleading. This risk is associated with many of the heuristics in this section, and a poor understanding of the cause may lead to selecting a poor solution. This should not be taken as an argument against using them, but a caution and a reminder of the importance of doing usability testing.

Compliance Budget

The term *compliance budget* appears in the work of Angela Sasse (introduced above), who has performed anthropological studies of British office workers. Her team noticed that after repeated exposure to the same security policies or tasks they were supposed to perform, the workers would respond differently (Beautement, 2009). During their interviews about security compliance, she noted that the workers were effectively allocating a "budget" to perform security tasks. They may or may not understand the tasks, but they would spend time and energy on them until their budget was exhausted, and then move on to other work tasks. When security requests were considered not as platonic tasks to be accomplished, but as real tasks situated against other tasks, worker behavior was fairly consistent.

Therefore, as you design systems, track how many security demands are being made in each of your scenarios. There is no "right" amount, but fewer is better.

Optimistic Assumptions

Many protocols impose optimistic assumptions about the capabilities of their human nodes. For example, people are sometimes expected to know where a browser's lock icon should be. (Top or bottom, left or right? In the main display area, obviously.) The lock cleverly disappears when it's not needed, which we optimistically assume doesn't make this question harder.

So how do you use this in threat modeling? As you go through the process, you should be keeping a list of assumptions you find yourself making (see Chapter 7, "Processing and Managing Threats"). For each optimistic assumption, look for a weaker assumption, or a way to buttress the assumption.

Models of Visual Perception

In work released as this book was being completed, Devdatta Akhawe and colleagues argue that limitations of human perception make UI security difficult to achieve. They present a number of attacks, including destabilizing perception of the pointer, attacking peripheral vision, attacking motor adaptations of the brain, mislocalization related to fast-moving objects, and abusing visual cues (Akhawe, 2013). Studying models of visual perception will probably be a fruitful area of research over the next few years.

Models of Software Scenarios

There are (at least) two ways to model a scenario, including a software-centered model and an attack-centered model. In this section, you'll learn about modeling both for threat modeling human factors. The software-centered models are somewhat easier, insofar as you know what sorts of circumstances will invoke them. The software models include scenario models of warnings, authentications, and configurations and models that use diagrams to represent the software. The attack-centered model is somewhat more broad. That is, if an attacker wants your software to do something, where can they force it?

Modeling the Software

You can model the goals and affordances of the software that a particular feature is intended to offer. (An affordance is whatever element of the user interface that communicates about the intended use.) One useful model of the interactions you'll offer includes warnings, authentications, and configuration (Reeder, 2008b). In that model, warnings are presented in the hope of deterring dangerous behavior, and include warnings dialogs, prods, and notifications. Authentications include the person authenticating to a computer either locally or via a network, and the remote system authenticating to the person. Configuration includes all those ways in which the person makes a security decision regarding the configuration of a computer or system.

These are not always distinct in practice. A single dialog will commonly both warn and ask for configuration or consent. Considering them separately helps you focus on the unique aspects of each, and ensure that you're providing the information that a person needs. In addition, the same advice applies to the warning regardless of the further content. So it applies to authentication, configuration, and consent. The types of information that you'll need to present so that the warning is clear doesn't change because of the additional context or decisions.

Warnings

A warning is a message from one party to another that some action carries risk. Generally, such messages are intended as a risk transference from one party to another, and they may have varying degrees of legal or moral effectiveness in actually transferring risk. Good warning design is covered later in this chapter in the section "Explicit Warnings."

Good warning design clearly identifies the potential problem, how likely it is, and what can be done to avoid it. Good warnings avoid "the boy who cried wolf" syndrome.

Authentication

People are astoundingly good at recognizing other people. It's probably an evolved trait. However, it turns out to be very difficult to authenticate people to machines or machines to people. Authentication is the process of proving that you are who you've said you are in a manner that's sufficient for a given context—authenticating that you're a student at State University is generally less important than authenticating that you're the missing heir to a massive fortune. Authentications are generally one party authenticating to another, such as a client authenticating itself to a server. They are sometimes bi-directional, and the authentication system in use in each direction may differ. For example, a web browser might connect to a bank and validate a digital certificate to start SSL. This is the server being authenticated via PKI to a client. The client will then authenticate via a password to the bank. There are also authentications that involve more parties.

The best advice on authentication (in both directions) is to treat it as a ceremony and pay close attention to where information comes from, how it could be spoofed, and how it will be validated in the real world.

Configuration

There are many ways to group configuration choices that can be made, including configurations made in advance, and configurations to allow or deny a specific activity. For each, it is helpful to consider the person's mental model, and the difficulty of testing their work. Useful techniques might include asking "how others might see the state of the system," whether "X can do Y," or having the person "describe the changes just made." Configuring a system for security is hard. The person performing the configuration needs to instruct the computer with a degree of precision that's required in few other areas of life, and constructing tests to ensure that it's been done right is often challenging for both technical and nontechnical people. Configuration tasks can be broken out into:

- **Configuration** such as altering a setting
- **Consenting** to some set of terms
- **Authorization** or permission settings
- **Verification** of settings or claims (such as the state of a firewall or identity of a website)
- **Auditing** or other investigation into the state of a system so people can view and act if appropriate

As you think about configuration, consider using a framework of who, what, why, when, where and how:

- **Who** can perform the configuration? Is it anyone? An administrator? Is there a parental role?
- **What** can they configure, and to what granularity? Is it on/off? Is it details intrinsic to the feature being configured (e.g., the firewall can block IP addresses or ports), or extrinsic, such as "this user cannot contact me"? The latter requires each channel of contact to know it must check the ACL.
- **Why** would someone want to configure the feature, and use those scenarios to determine what the user interface will be, and what mistakes they might make.
- **When** will someone be making configuration choices? Is it proactive or reactive? Is it just in time?

- **Where** will someone make the change? (And how will they find that interface?)
- **How** will users implement their intent? "How" is not only how they make a change, but how they can test it—for example, Windows "effective permissions" or the LinkedIn "Show me how others see this profile." Consider how users can see the configuration of the system as a whole.

Good design of a configuration system is hard. Decisions made early can make changes impossible or extremely expensive. For example, Reeder has shown that people have a hard time with elements of the Windows file permission model, and that changing to a "specificity preference" over the deny precedence appears to align better with people's expectations (Reeder, 2008a). However, changing that ordering would break the way one access control rules have been configured on possibly hundreds of millions of systems, and each rule would require manual analysis to understand why it's set the way it is, what the change would mean, and how to best repair it.

Diagramming for Modeling the Software

There are a variety of diagram types that can be useful for human factors analysis, including swim lanes, data flow diagrams, and state machines. Each is a model of the software, system, or protocol. In this section, you'll learn about how each can be modified for use in looking at the human in the loop.

Swim Lanes

You learned about swim lane diagrams for protocols in Chapter 2, "Strategies for Threat Modeling." These diagrams can be adapted for modeling people. In ceremony analysis, you add swim lanes representing each participant, as shown in Figure 15-3 (reproduced from Ellison's paper on ceremonies [Ellison, 2007]). There is an implicit trust boundary between each lane. In this diagram, S is the server, A1 and A2 are attackers, CC is the client, and CA is a certificate authority.

This diagram is worth studying, especially when you realize that A1 and A2 are machines controlled by attackers. Note that the attacker A is not shown; what this attacker knows is not relevant to the security of C, the person being tricked. Also note that messages from computers to humans ("S," short for server) and humans to computers ("click") are shown as protocol messages. It is very important to ensure the messages between computers and humans are clearly shown, and the contents of each is modeled. Such modeling will help you identify unreasonable assumptions, information not provided, and other communications issues.

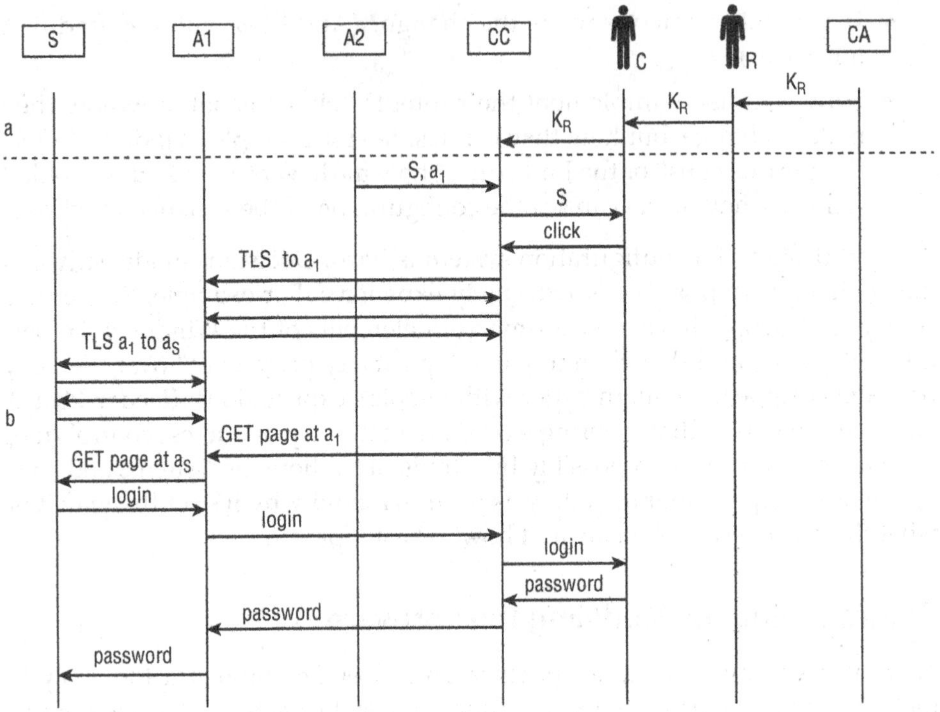

Figure 15-3: Ellison's diagram of the HTTPS ceremony

State Machines

State machines are often used to model the state of inanimate objects. The states of machines are simple compared to the states of humans. However, that doesn't mean that a state machine can't help you think about the state of people using your software. For example, consider Figure 15-4, which explores possible states of a person trying to visit a website and being blocked by a security warning. The state machine has two exit states: reading a web page and considering alternative options. They are indicated by darker lines around the states.

Quick consideration of this model reveals several issues:

- If a "bypass this warning" button is easily visible, it may be pressed by an annoyed person.
- If people feel overwhelmed by security decisions, they'll likely bypass the warning.
- The "stars must align" to get someone to the state of considering alternative plans.

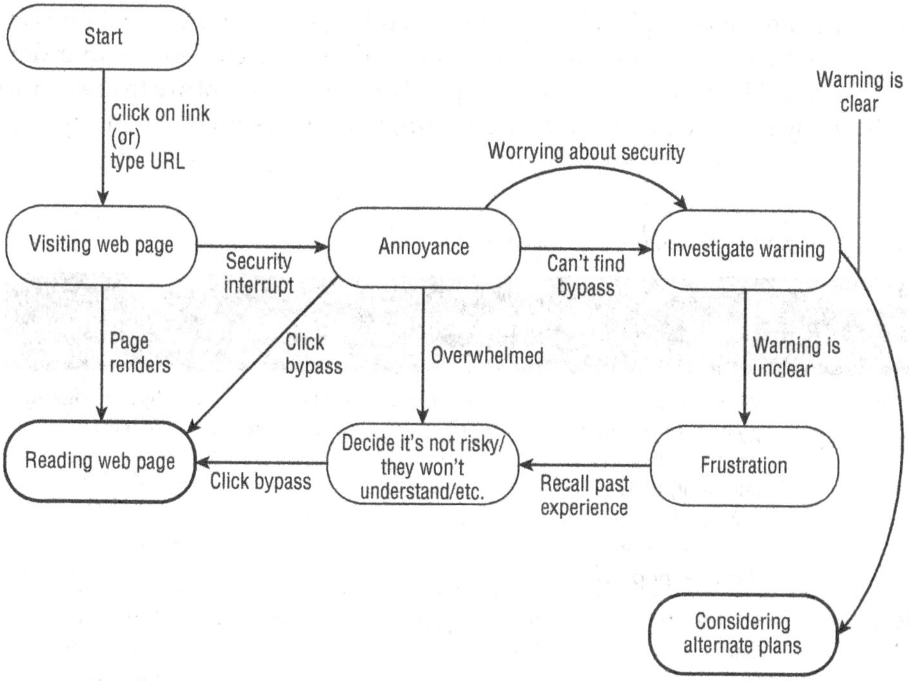

Figure 15-4: A human state machine

You can also use state machines in conjunction with ceremonies. In a ceremony, a node can be modeled as state (including secrets), a state machine with its inputs and outputs, service response times, including bandwidth and attention, and a probability of errors of various sorts. (Ellison provides a longer list with finer granularity for the same set of attributes [Ellison, 2007].)

Modeling Electronic Social Engineering Attacks

A project at Microsoft needed a comprehensive way to describe electronic social engineering attacks. In this context, electronic means roughly all those social engineering attacks that are not in person or over the phone.

We came up with the channels and attributes shown in Table 15-1, which we have found to be a useful descriptive model. It is intended to be used like a Chinese menu, whereby you choose one from column A, one from column B, and so on.

You'll probably find that the descriptors here are sufficient for describing most online social engineering attacks. Unfortunately, some evocative detail is lost (and some verbosity is gained) as you generalize from "a Nigerian prince spam" to "e-mail pretending someone to be someone you don't know, exploiting greed" or from "phishing" to "a website pretending to be an organization you have a relationship with and for which you need to enter credentials in order to do business." However, the resultant model descriptions capture the relevant details in a way that can inform either training or the design of technology to help people better handle such attacks.

Table 15-1: Attributes of Electronic Social Engineering Attacks

CHANNEL OF CONTACT	THING SPOOFED	PERSUASION TO INTERACT	HUMAN ACT EXPLOITED	TECHNICAL SPOOFING
E-mail	An operating system or product user interface element, such as a Mac OS warning, or a Chrome browser pop-up	Greed/promise of reward	Open document	System dialog or alert
Website	A product or service	Intimidation/ fear	Click link	Filename (extension hiding)
Social network	A person you know	Maintaining a social relationship	Attach device/ USB stick	File type (other than extension hiding)
IM	An organization you have a relationship with	Maintaining a business relationship	Install/run program	Icon
Physical*	An organization you don't have a relationship with	Curiosity	Enter credentials	Filename (multi-lingual)†
	A person you don't know	Lust/prurient interest	Establish a relationship‡	
	An authority			

* Physical is at odds with the online nature of most of these, but sometimes there's an interesting overlap, like a USB drive left in a parking lot.

† Multi-lingual spoofing involves use of languages written left to right and right to left in the same name. There is no way to do so which meets all cultural and clarity requirements.

‡ Establishing a relationship also overlaps; much, but not all electronic social engineering is focused on the installation of malware.

The Technical Spoofing column contains details that are sometimes clarifying. Those elements are more specific versions of the "user interface element" at the top of the Thing Spoofed column.

Threat Elicitation Techniques

Any of the threat discovery techniques covered in Part II of this book can probably be applied to a user experience. Spoofing seems particularly relevant. You can bring any of those to bear while brainstorming. The ceremony approach offers a more structured way to find threats. You can also consider the models of humans presented earlier while considering what a "human state machine" might do, or as ways to explain the results of the tests you perform.

Brainstorming

The models of people and scenarios provided so far can help anyone find threats by brainstorming. That's much more likely to be productive with participation from either security or usability experts. Different goals of these specialists may lead to clashes, however, as usability experts will likely tend toward making it easy to get back to the primary task, and security experts will tend to focus on the risk of doing so. Either structure or moderators may help you.

The Ceremony Approach to Threat Modeling

The ceremony approach to threat modeling, created by Carl Ellison, (and mentioned briefly earlier) is most like "traditional" threat modeling. It starts from the observation that any network protocol, sufficiently fully considered, involves both computers and humans on each end. He developed this observation into an approach to analyzing the security of ceremonies. "Ceremony Design and Analysis," the paper in which Ellison presents his model, is free, easy to understand, and worth reading when considering the human aspects of your threat model. It introduces ceremonies as follows:

> *[The ceremony is] an extension of the concept of network protocol, with human nodes alongside computer nodes and with communication links that include UI, human-to-human communication and transfers of physical objects that carry data. What is out-of-band to a protocol is in-band to a ceremony, and therefore subject to design and analysis using variants of the same mature techniques used for the design and analysis of protocols. Ceremonies include all protocols, as well as all applications with a user interface, all workflow and all provisioning scenarios. A secure ceremony is secure against both normal attacks and social engineering. However, some secure protocols imply ceremonies that cannot be made secure.*
>
> —Carl Ellison, "Ceremony Design and Analysis" (IACR Cryptology ePrint Archive 2007)

In a "normal" protocol, there are two or more nodes, each with a current state, a state machine (a set of states and rules for transitioning between them), and a set of messages it could send. Ellison extends this to humans, noting that humans can be modeled as having a state, messages they send and receive, and ways to transition into different states. He also notes that they are likely to make errors parsing messages. Ellison calls out three important points about ceremonies:

- "Nothing is out of band to a ceremony." If there's an assumption that something happens out of band, you must either model it or design for it being insecure.
- Connections (data flows) can be human to human, human to computer, computer to computer, physical actions, or even legal actions, such as Alice sells Bob a computer.
- Human nodes are not equivalent to computer nodes. Failure to take into account the way humans really act will break the security of your system.

Ceremony Analysis Heuristics

There are a set of threats that can be discovered simply and easily with some heuristics, and a set of threats that are more likely to be found with more structured work. Each heuristic has advice for addressing the threat. The first four are extracted from Ellison's "Ceremony Design and Analysis" (IACR Cryptology ePrint Archive 2007) to contextualize them as heuristics, while the final two are other heuristics that may help you.

Missing Information

The first issue to look for is missing information. Does each node have the information you expect it to act upon? For one trivial example, in the HTTPS scenario, the person is expected to know that the server name (S) does not match the URL (A1). However, the message from the computer contains only a server name, not a URL. Therefore, the analysis is particularly trivial: The designer has asked a person to make a decision but has not provided the information necessary to make it.

Ensure that you're explicit about decisions people will need to make, what information is needed to make them, and display it early enough that the person won't anchor on some other element, and close enough to where it is needed that other information will not be distracting.

Distracting Information

If you'd like to ensure that a person acts on information you present, keep in mind that each additional piece of information acts as a distractor, and may feed into confirmation bias. In discussing the human phase of verifying that a cryptographically signed e-mail was really signed, Ellison offers the screenshot shown in Figure 15-5, pointing out five elements that a human might look at, including the "From: address," the picture, the "Signed by" address, the text of the message, and other contextual information that the human might have available. The only element that the (cryptographic) protocol designer wants you to look at is the "Signed by" address, which is the fifth element displayed, after "From," "To," "CC," and "Subject"—all of which appears underneath various GUI elements, including the window title, taken from the e-mail subject. There is also a picture, and a small icon (reproduced from Ellison, 2007).

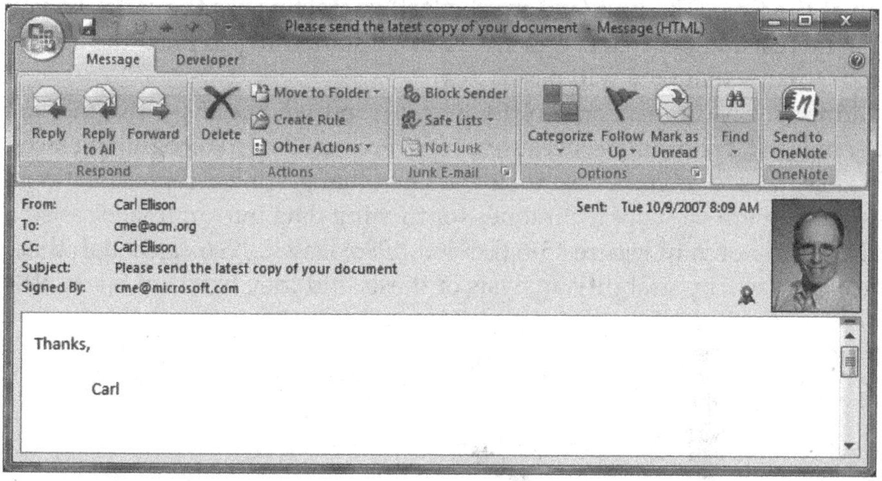

Figure 15-5: An e-mail interface

To address the possibility of distraction, information not key to the ceremony either should not be displayed or should be de-emphasized in some way or ways. In particular, you should take care to avoid showing information that is easily substituted or confused for the information that you want the person to use in the ceremony.

Underspecified Elements

Because a ceremony is all inclusive, it requires us to shine light where system architects might otherwise hand-wave. For example, how did a PKI root key on a system become authorized to suppress or send messages to the owner of that computer? (PKI root keys often suppress warning messages, and may activate messages, such as a green URL bar or a lock within the browser.) To address underspecified elements, specify them. It may be a practical requirement to accept risks associated with them, but a concrete statement of the risk might enable you to find a way to address it.

Fuzzy Comparison

People are pretty bad at comparing strings. For example, are the strings 82d6937ae236019bde346f55bcc84d587bc51af2 and 82d6937ae236019bde346f55bcc84d857bc51af2 the same string? Go on, check. It's important. I'm hopeful that when this book is laid out, the strings don't show up one above the next (and put in extra words to try to mitigate that threat from layout). So, did you check? I'm willing to bet that even most of you, reading the freaking gnarly specifics part of a book on threat modeling, didn't go through and compare them character by character. That may partly be because the answer doesn't really matter; but mostly it's because people satisfice—that is, we select answers that seem good enough at the time. The first (and maybe last) characters are the same, so you assume the rest are too. Often, attackers can do something to push the person to a fuzzy match that they will pass.

To address fuzzy comparison, look for ways to represent the bits so that they are easily compared. For example, because people are excellent at recognizing faces, can you use faces to represent data? How about other graphical representations? For example, there's a set of techniques for turning data into an image called a *visual hash*, as shown in Figure 15-6 (Levien, 1996; Dalek, 1996), although there is little or no security usability analysis of these, and they have not taken off.

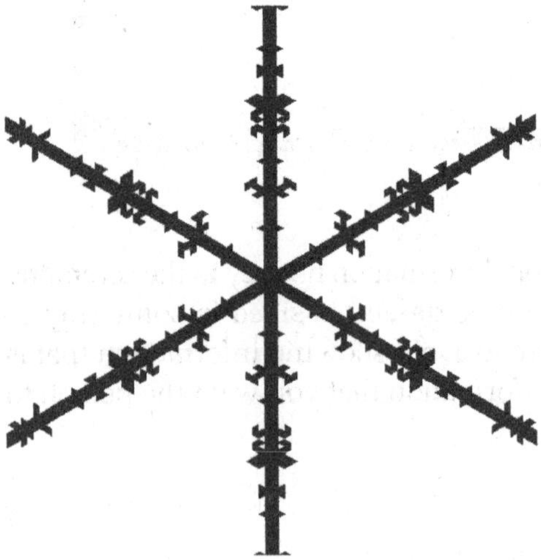

Figure 15-6: The snowflake visual hash

It may be possible to replace a long string of digits with a string of words, tapping into system 1 word recognition and improving comparability. Lastly, if none of those methods will work, try to create groups of four or five digits so that at least people find natural breakpoints when carrying out the comparative task.

Kahneman, Reason, Behaviorism

The entire section "Models of People," presented earlier, is suffused with perspectives that can be used as heuristics, or as a review list, asking yourself "how could this apply?"

The Stajano-Wilson Model

Frank Stajano and Paul Wilson have worked with the creators of the BBC's "Real Hustle" TV show to create a model of scams (Stajano, 2011). Their principles are quoted verbatim here, and could be adapted to use for threat elicitation:

1. **Distraction Principle:** While we are distracted by what grabs our interest, hustlers can do anything to us and we won't notice.
2. **Social Compliance Principle:** Society trains people to not question authority. Hustlers exploit this "suspension of suspiciousness" to make us do what they want.
3. **Herd Principle:** Even suspicious marks let their guard down when everyone around them appears to share the same risks. Safety in numbers? Not if they're all conspiring against us.
4. **Dishonesty Principle:** Our own inner larceny is what hooks us initially. Thereafter, anything illegal we do will be used against us by the fraudsters.
5. **Kindness Principle:** People are fundamentally nice and willing to help. Hustlers shamelessly take advantage of it.
6. **Need and Greed Principle:** Our needs and desires make us vulnerable. Once hustlers know what we want, they can easily manipulate us.
7. **Time Principle:** When under time pressure to make an important choice, we use a different decision strategy, and hustlers steer us toward one involving less reasoning.

The discussion of the herd principle points out how many variations of the sock puppet/Sybil/tentacle attacks exist, a point for which I'm grateful.

Integrating Usability into the Four-Stage Framework

This chapter advocates looking at usability and ceremony issues as a distinct set of activities from modeling technical threats. It may also be possible to bring usability into the four-stage framework by considering it in two places: mitigation and validation. If the general approach of thinking of mitigations as "change the design, use a standard mitigation; use a custom mitigation, accept the risk" is extended with "transfer risk by asking the person," then that makes a natural jumping off point to the techniques outlined in this chapter. Similarly, in validation, if a user interface asks the person to make a security or privacy decision, then assessing it with techniques from this chapter will help. This approach, illustrated in Figure 15-7, was developed by Brian Lounsberry, Eric Douglas, Rob Reeder, and myself.

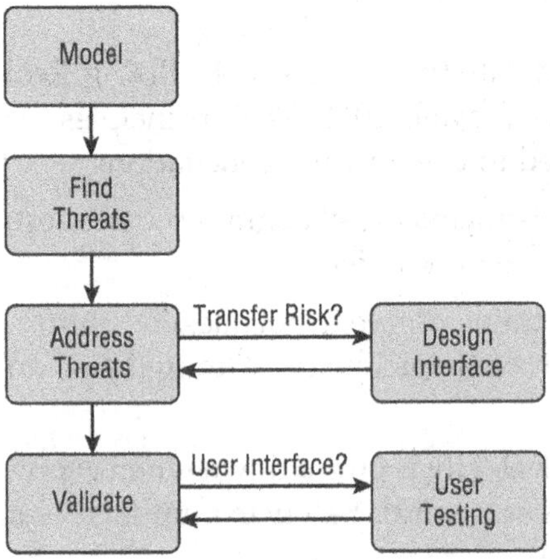

Figure 15-7: Integrating usability into a flow

Tools and Techniques for Addressing Human Factors

Having discussed how to find threats, it's now time to talk about how you can address them. This section begins with myths about people that we as a community need to set aside, it continues with design patterns for helping you find a good solution, and then describes a few design patterns for a kind learning environment.

In an ideal world, everyone would have time to carefully consider each security decision that confronts them, research the trade-offs, and make a call that reflects their risk acceptance given their goals and options. (Also in that ideal world, technology producers would be happy to invest the effort needed to help them.) In the real world, people typically balance their investment of effort against perceived risk, their perception of their own skill, time available, and a host of other factors. Worse, in the case of security, there sometimes is no "right" decision. If you get an e-mail from your boss asking you to print a presentation for an impromptu meeting with the CEO that's happening right now, you can't call to make sure it's really from the boss. You might want to accept the risk that someone has taken over your boss's e-mail. You want to make it easy for people to quickly reach the decision that they would make if they had all the time in the world. You want to make it possible for people to dig deeper, without requiring they do so.

Myths That Inhibit Human Factors Work

There are a number of myths that are threats to human factors work in security. They all center on contempt for normal people. People are not, as is often claimed, the weakest link, or beyond help. The weakest link is almost always a vulnerability in Internet-facing code. Society trusts normal adults to drink alcohol, to operate motor vehicles (ideally not at the same time), and to have children. Is using a computer safely so much harder? If so, whose fault is that? Following are some common myths about human behavior in terms of security:

- "Given a choice between security and dancing pigs, people will choose dancing pigs every time." So why make that a choice? More seriously, a better way to state this is, "Given a choice between ignoring a warning that they've clicked through a thousand times before without apparent ill effects and without being entertained, people will bypass a warning every time."
- "People don't care about security," or "People don't want to think about security." Either or both may well be true. However, people do care about consequences such as having to clean their system of a virus or dealing with fraudulent charges on their debit cards.
- "People just don't listen." People do listen. They don't act on security advice because it's often bizarre, time consuming, and sometimes followed by, "Of course, you'll still be at risk." You need to craft advice that works for the people who are listening to you.
- "My mom couldn't understand that." Your mom is very smart. After all, she raised you, and you're reading this book. QED. More seriously, you should design systems that your customers will understand.

Design Patterns for Good Decisions

The design patterns for mitigating threats that exploit people are similar to those for other categories of threats. This section describes the four high-level patterns: minimize what you ask of people, conditioned-safe ceremonies, avoid urgency, and ensure a path to safety.

Minimize What You Ask of People

If people are not good at being state machines running programs, it seems likely that the less that is asked of them, the fewer insecurities a ceremony will have. People must be involved when they have (or can reasonably be expected to have) information that other nodes need to make appropriate decisions. For example, Windows Vista introduced a dialog that asked people what sort of network they had just connected to. This elicited information (such as home, work, or coffee shop) that the computer can't reliably determine, and it was used to configure the firewall appropriately. A person must also be involved when making decisions about meaningful IDs. There are likely other data points or perspectives that a program must ask of a person.

There are two specific techniques to minimize what's asked of people: listing what they need to know, and building consistency:

- **Listing what people need to know:** Simply making a list of what people need to know to make a security decision is a powerful technique that Angela Sasse advocates. The technique has several advantages. First, it's among the simplest techniques in this book. It requires no special training or equipment. Second, the act of writing down a list tends to impose a reality check. When the list gets longer than one unit (whiteboard, page, etc.), even the most optimistic will start to question whether it's realistic. Finally, making a list enables you to use that list as a checklist, and asking how the customer will learn each item on the list is an easy (and perhaps obvious) next step.
- **Building consistency:** People are outstanding at finding patterns, sometimes even finding patterns where none exist. They use this ability to build models of the world, based on observations of consistency. To the extent that your software is either inconsistent with itself or with the expectations of the operating environment, you are asking more of people. Do not do so lightly. Consistency relates to the wicked versus kind environment problem raised by Jacobs. Ensuring that your security user experiences are consistent within a product is a very worthwhile step, as is ensuring that it's consistent with the interfaces presented by other products. This consistency makes your product a kind learning environment. Of course, this must be balanced with the value of innovation and experimentation. If everything is perfectly consistent, then we can't learn from differences. However, we can try to avoid random inconsistency.

Conditioned-Safe Ceremonies

Consistency will probably help the people who use your system, but a conditioned-safe approach may be even better. The concept of a conditioned-safe ceremony (CSC) is built on the observation that conditioning may play both ways. In other words, rather than train people to expect random shocks or interruptions from security, you could train or condition them to act securely. In their paper introducing the idea (Karlof, 2009), Chris Karlof and colleagues at University of California, Berkeley, proposed four rules governing the use of conditioned-safe ceremonies:

1. CSCs should only condition safe rules, those that can safely be applied even in circumstances controlled by an adversary.
2. CSCs should condition at least one immunizing rule—that is, a rule which will cause attacks to fail.
3. CSCs should not condition the formation of rules that require a user decision to apply the rule.
4. CSCs should not assume people will reliably perform actions which are voluntary, or that they have not been trained/conditioned to perform each time.

They also discuss the idea of *forcing functions*. In this context, a forcing function is "a type of behavior-shaping constraint designed to prevent human error," for example, a car that can be started only when the brake pedal is pressed. People regularly make the mistake of omitting steps in a process (it may be one of the most common types of mistakes), and they rarely notice when they've omitted a step. Forcing functions can help ensure that people complete important steps. The forcing function will only work when it is easier to execute than avoid, where avoidance may include avoiding use of the feature set that includes a forcing function. They use the example of Ctrl+Alt+Delete to bring up the Windows Login screen as a forcing function.

Avoiding Urgency

One of the most consistent elements of current online scams is urgency. Urgency is a great tool for the online attackers. They maintain control of the experience, sending the prospective victim to actions of their choice. For example, in a bank phishing scam, if the person sets the e-mail aside, they may later find a real e-mail from the organization, they may use a bookmark, or they may call the number on the back of their card. The fake website may be taken down, blacklisted, or otherwise become unavailable. Therefore, avoiding urgency helps your customers help themselves.

Avoiding urgency can involve something like saying, "We will take no action unless you visit our site and click OK. You can always reach our real security actions through a bookmark, or by using a search engine to get to our site."

If you've conditioned your customers to expect urgency from you, then urgency is less likely to act as a red flag. Make it harder for the attacker by avoiding urgency in your messages to customers.

Ensuring an Easy Path to Safety

When people are being scammed, is there a way to get back to a safe state? Is it easy to discover (or remember) and take that path to safety? For example, is there always an easy way to access messages you send from your home page? If there is, then potential phishing victims can take control of the experience. They can go to their bookmarked website and get the message. You might use a pattern like the gold bar (discussed in the section "Explicit Warnings," later in this chapter) or an interstitial page to notify people about important new messages, so they learn that they can find new messages from your site.

If that's always available, then attackers will need to convince people that that system is broken for whatever reason. Today, that's easy, because "go to your bookmark" is lumped in with a barrage of confusing and questionable security advice. (The path to safety pattern was identified by Rob Reeder.)

Design Patterns for a Kind Learning Environment

A kind learning environment contrasts with a wicked one. If you're an attacker, you want the world to be wicked. You want people to be confused and unsure of how to defend themselves, because it makes it easier to get what you want. The following sections provide advice for how to promote a kind environment.

Avoid "Scamicry"

Scamicry is an action by a legitimate organization that is hard for a typical person to distinguish from the action of an attacker—for example, a bank calling a customer and demanding authentication information without an easy way to call back and reach the right person. How can Alice decide whether it's her bank or a fraudster? Trust caller ID? That's trivial to spoof. Similarly, the bank can choose how to track clicks on its marketing campaigns. It can use the domain of the marketing company (`example.com/bank/?campaign=123;emailid=345`) or it can use a tracking URL within its own domain (`bank.com/marketing/?campaign=123;emailid=345`) Alice might want to look at the domain to make a decision (and many security people advise her to do so); but if the bank routinely sends e-mail messages with links to tracking domains, then Alice can't look at the URL and decide if it's really her bank. Scamicry makes the world a more wicked environment, disempowers people, and empowers attackers.

WHAT IS SCAMICRY?

My team coined the term *scamicry* after I received a voicemail claiming to be from a bank. The caller said they needed a callback that day to a number that wasn't listed on their website's Contact Us page. I had written a large check for something, and it triggered their fraud department. However, there was no clear reason for the "call in the next four hours" requirement in the voicemail. The bank could presumably have put their fraud team's number on their website, held the check for a day or so (although this may have been constrained by regulations on check processing). In discussing the experience, we realized that it was a common pattern, and that perhaps naming it would help to identify and then overcome it.

Sometimes it can be remarkably hard to avoid violating common advice, and that should cause us to question the wisdom of that advice. (See the next section for more on good security advice.)

If the steps of a ceremony involve one party violating common security advice, or encouraging another party to do so, then that's a sub-optimal ceremony design. You can think of scamicry as an organization making the usable security problem more wicked.

In their paper on scams, Frank Stajano and Paul Wilson include an insight closely related to scamicry:

> *System architects must coherently align incentives and liabilities with overall system goals. If users are expected to perform sanity checks rather than blindly follow orders, then social protocols must allow "challenging the authority"; if, on the contrary, users are expected to obey authority unquestioningly, those with authority must relieve them of liability if they obey a fraudster. The fight against phishing and all other forms of social engineering can never be won unless this principle is understood.*
>
> —Stajano and Wilson, "Understanding Scam Victims" (Communications of the ACM, 2011)

I would go further, and say that understanding is insufficient; intentional design and coordination between a variety of participants in the "phished ecosystem" is needed.

Properties of Good Security Advice

There's a tremendous amount of advice about how people should act online. In the discussion of behaviorist models of people, you learned about people rationally ignoring security advice. Part of the problem is that there's too much of it, creating a wicked environment. The reasonable question is how should you form good advice? Consider whether your advice meets the following five properties (Shostack, 2011b; Microsoft, 2011):

- **Realistic:** Guidance should enable typical people to accomplish their goals without inconveniencing them.
- **Durable:** Guidance should remain true and relevant, and not be easy for an attacker to use against your people.
- **Memorable:** Guidance should stick with people, and should be easy to recall when necessary.
- **Proven effective:** Guidance should be tested and shown to actually help prevent social engineering attacks.
- **Concise and consistent:** The amount of guidance you provide should be minimal, stated simply, and be consistent within all the contexts in which you provide it.

User Interface Tools and Techniques

Ideally, you should address threats in a way that doesn't require a person to do something. This has the advantage of being more reliable than even the most reliable person, and not conditioning people to click through warnings. Unfortunately, it's not always possible. The methods in this section are a strong parallel to those in Chapter 8. You'll learn about configuration, and how to design explicit warnings and patterns that attempt to force a person to pay attention. This section does not cover authentication, as threats to such systems are covered under spoofing in Chapter 3, "STRIDE," in the discussion of threats to usability in this chapter, and in Chapter 14.

Configuration

Configuration tasks are generally performed by people because a prompt encourages them to check or improve their security. That prompt could be a story in the news or told by a friend, a policy or reminder e-mail, or an attacker trying to reduce their security (probably as a step to a more interesting goal).

The goals of configuration are as follows:

- Enable the person to complete a security- or privacy-related goal.
- Enable the person to complete the goal efficiently.
- Help people understand the effects of the task they're undertaking.
- Minimize undesirable side-effects.
- Do not frustrate the person.

Some metrics you can consider or measure as you're building configuration interfaces include the following:

- **Discoverability:** What fraction of people can go from getting a prompt to finding the appropriate interface to accomplish their task? Obviously, it's important that a test not tell the person how to do this, nor start them on the configuration screen.
- **Accuracy:** What fraction of people can correctly complete the task they are given?
- **Time to completion:** How long does it take to either complete the task or give up? Time to abandonment is likely to be higher, as test subjects will try to please the experimenter or appear diligent or intelligent.
- **Side-effect introduction:** What fraction of people do something else by accident while accomplishing the main task?
- **Satisfaction:** What fraction of people rate the experience as satisfying, given a scale from "satisfying" to "frustrating"?

The preceding two lists are derived from (Reeder, 2008b).

Explicit Warnings

A useful warning consists of a message that there's danger, an assessment of the impact associated with the danger, and steps to avoid the danger. A good warning may also contain some sort of attention-capturing device, such as a picture of a person falling off a ladder. That's a very general definition of a useful warning. For more specific advice, consider the NEAT/SPRUCE combination or the Gold Bar pattern.

NEAT and SPRUCE

NEAT and SPRUCE are mnemonics for creating effective information security warnings. Wallet cards created by Rob Reeder read: "Ask yourself: Is your security or privacy UX (user experience)":

- Necessary? Can you change the architecture to eliminate or defer this user decision?
- Explained? Does your UX present all the information the user needs to make this decision? Have you followed SPRUCE (see below)
- Actionable? Have you determined a set of steps the user will realistically be able to take to make the decision correctly?
- Tested? Have you checked that your UX is effective for all scenarios, both benign and malicious? (Our cards refer to the UX being NEAT, which has been changed here to effective to encourage testing the warning.)

SPRUCE is a checklist for what makes an effective warning:

- Source: State who or what is asking the user to make a decision
- Process: Give the user actionable steps to follow to make a good decision
- Risk: Explain what bad result could happen if the user makes the wrong decision
- Unique knowledge user has: Tell the user what information they bring to the decision
- Choices: List available options and clearly recommend one
- Evidence: Highlight information the user should factor in or exclude in making the decision

The cards are available as a free PDF from Microsoft (SDL Team, 2012). So why a wallet card? In a word, usability. Rob Reeder reviewed everything he could find on creating effective warnings, and summarized it in a 24-page document. That document contained 68 elements of advice. In working with real programmers, however, he discovered that was way too long, and created our NEAT guidance: Warnings should be necessary, actionable, explained, and tested. The SPRUCE extension was joint work with myself and Ellen Cram Kowalczyk (Reeder, 2011a).

The "Gold Bar" Pattern

A gold bar pattern combines warning, configuration, and sometimes other safety features into a non-intrusive dialog bar appearing across the top or bottom of a program's main window. You've probably seen the pattern in Microsoft Office and in browsers, including IE and Firefox.

The interface appears non-modally while the program does as much as it safely can. For example, a Word document from the Internet will render, allowing you to read it. A bar appears across the top, informing you that this is a safer, limited version of Word. (Underneath, Word has opened the document in a sandboxed and limited version of the program that has less attack surface and functionality. If you watch carefully when clicking one of these, you'll notice that Word disappears and reappears. That's the viewer closing and the full version launching (Malhotra, 2009).)

This pattern has a number of important security advantages. First and foremost, it may eliminate the need for the person to make a decision at all. Second, it delays security decision-making to a point when more information is available. Third, it replaces dialogs that said things like "While files from the Internet can be useful, this file type can potentially harm your computer," or "Would you like to get your job done?"

The gold bar pattern has limits. The bars are intended to be subtle, which can result in them being overlooked. Their size limits the amount of text within the bar. They can also fail to align with the mental model of the person experiencing them. For example, someone might ask, "Why is e-mail from my boss treated as untrusted, and why do I need to leave the protected mode to print?" (Because your boss's computer might be infected, and because printing exposes substantial attack surface. However, those are neither obvious nor explained in the interface.) Lastly, because the bars are subtle, they fail to impose a strong interrupt and may therefore fail to invoke system 2, described earlier. System 1 is the faster, intuitive system, whereas system 2 processes complex problems. They were introduced earlier in the section "Cognitive Science Models of People."

Patterns That Grab Attention

There is a whole set of patterns that try to force people to slow down before doing something they'll regret. This section reviews some of the more interesting ones. It might help to conceptualize these as ways to invoke system 2. The goal of these mechanisms is to get people encountering them to avoid jumping to the answer using system 1 and instead bring in their system 2.

Hiding the Dangerous Choice

Internet Explorer's SmartScreen Filter doesn't put the dangerous run button directly in front of people. It has used a variety of strategies for this. For example, one post-download dialog, shown in Figure 15-8, has buttons labeled Delete, Actions, and View Downloads. When shown this warning, IE users choose to delete or not run malware 95 percent of the time. This interface design has been combined with other usable security wins, including showing the dialog (on average) only twice per year, which may make the hiding pattern less intrusive

(Haber, 2011). It is hard to disentangle the precise elements that make this so effective, but much of it has to do with the combination of elements, refined through extensive testing.

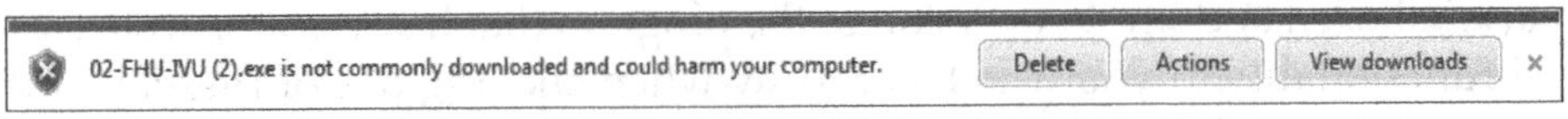

Figure 15-8: An IE SmartScreen Filter warning dialog

Modal Dialogs

Modal dialogs are those that capture focus and cannot be closed until a person resolves the choice in the dialog. Modal dialogs fell out of favor for a variety of accidental reasons. For example, a floating modal dialog box was not always the front-most window in an interface, or it could pop up on another monitor or virtual workspace. Modal dialogs interrupt task flow. *Lightboxing* is the practice of displaying a darkened interface with only the modal dialog "lit up." This addresses many of the accidental issues with modal dialogs, and it is commonly used by websites.

Spiky Buttons

Keith Lang has proposed the use of less friendly user interface elements, such as spiky buttons (Lang, 2009). A sample is shown in Figure 15-9. In a blog discussion about it, the question of how quickly people would habituate to it was raised. Others suggested more standard stop imagery would work better (37Signals, 2010). Spiky buttons may be more of a "don't jump there" message than a "pay attention" message, but without experimentation and a set of people with ongoing exposure to them, it's hard to say. To the best of my knowledge, it has not been used.

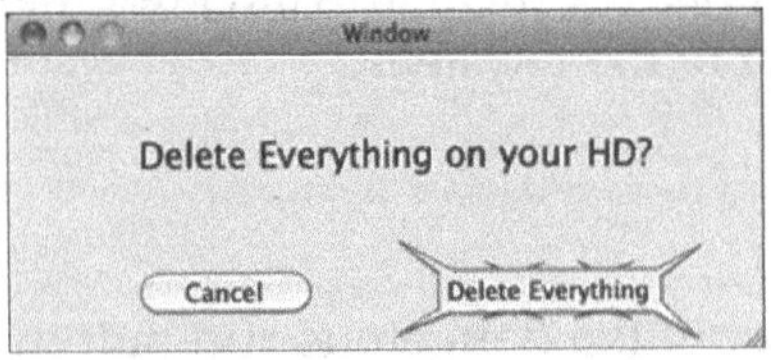

Figure 15-9: A spiky button

Delay to Click

When you attempt to install a Firefox add-in, Firefox imposes a delay of four seconds. As shown in Figure 15-10, the Install button is grayed out, and displays a countdown from (4). Somewhat surprisingly, this is actually not designed to get you to stop and read the dialog, although it may have that effect. It is intended to block an attack whereby a site shows a CAPTCHA-like interface with the word "only" displayed. The site attempts to install the software when you type the "n," triggering a security dialog; when you type the "y," it triggers the "yes" in the dialog, which now has focus (Ruderman, 2004). A related technique, a 500ms delay, is used for other dialogs, such as the geolocation prompt (Zalewski, 2010).

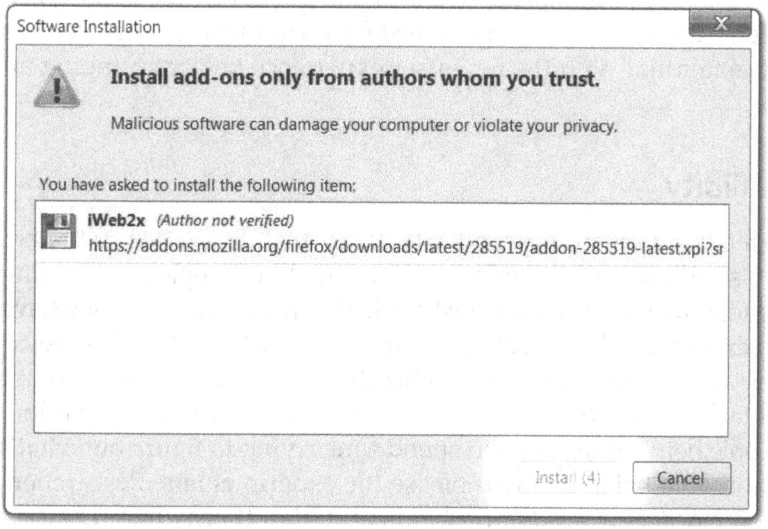

Figure 15-10: Firefox doesn't care if you read this.

Testing for Human Factors

Like every way you address threats, it is important that you test those mitigations for threats that involve people. If an attacker is trying to convince someone to take action, does your interface help the potential victim make a security choice, while letting them get their normal work done? Unfortunately, people are surprising, so testing with real people is a useful and important step.

There are a few issues that make the testing of any security-relevant user interface challenging. The best summary of those issues is in a document by usable security researcher Stuart Schechter (Schechter, 2013). That document is focused on writing about usable security experiments (rather than designing or performing them). However, it still contains very solid advice that will be applicable. You can also find excellent guidance on usability testing in books such as Rubin's "*Handbook of Usability Testing*" (Wiley, 2008), which unfortunately doesn't touch on the unique issues in testing security scenarios.

Benign and Malicious Scenarios

Normal usability testing asks a question such as "Can someone accomplish task X with reasonable effort?" Good ceremony testing requires testing "Can someone accomplish task X and raise the right exception behavior only when under attack?" That requires far more subtle test design. (That is, unless you expect that your attackers will start with "This file really is malicious! Please click on it anyway!") It also requires at least twice as many tests. Lastly, unless you have reason to believe that most people will only encounter the user experience being tested extremely rarely, a good test needs to include some element of getting people familiar with the new user experience before springing an attack on them.

Ecological Validity

Participants in modern user studies tend to be aware that they're being studied. The release forms and glass walls tend to give it away. Also, people participating in a user study tend to expect that the tasks asked of them are safe. They have good reason to expect that. The trouble is that if you think what's being asked of you is safe, or at least a designed experience, then you may not worry about things (such as tasks, indicators, or warnings) that would normally worry you. Alternately, people being studied often spend time trying to figure out what's being studied, or what behaviors will please the experimenters. Researchers refer to this as the *ecological validity* problem, and it's a thorny one. The best sources of current thinking are SOUPS (the Symposium On Usable Privacy and Security) and the security track of the ACM SIGCHI conference. (SIGCHI is the Special Interest Group on Computer-Human Interaction.)

General Advice

The following list is derived from a conversation with Lorrie Cranor, who accurately points out that a simple checklist will be sufficient to explain how to perform effective usability testing. Any errors in this are mine, not Dr. Cranor's:

- It is hard to predict how people are going to behave without doing a user study, so user studies are important.
- Find someone, either a colleague or a consultant, who knows how to do user studies and work with that person.
- The user study expert you work with is unlikely to know much about threat modeling or to have done a usable security study before. You will need to help them understand what they need to know about security and threat modeling.

- As you work with the usability expert to design a user study, keep in mind that you need to find a way to study how people behave in situations where they are under an active attack. The tricky part is figuring out how to put your study participants in a situation that simulates these threats without actually putting anyone at risk. (See the preceding section on "Ecological Validity.")
- Security user studies frequently use deception in order to simulate a security threat. For example, a study on web browser phishing warnings was advertised as being about online shopping. Participants were instructed to make an online purchase and check their e-mail to get the receipt so they could be reimbursed. When they checked their e-mail, they had a message that appeared to be from the vendor where they made a purchase, encouraging them to log in to a website that was actually a phishing website. When they tried to log in to that website, it triggered a warning in their web browser and experimenters could observe how participants responded to such warnings. Use of deception in a study design will raise ethical issues.
- Some security user studies use role-playing or hypothetical scenarios. For example, a study on text passwords asked participants to imagine that their e-mail account password had been compromised and they were required to create a new password. (Ur, 2012) A study on the usability of PGP asked participants to play the role of a campaign volunteer in a political election and send and receive e-mails, being careful to use PGP to ensure that campaign strategy information didn't fall into the wrong hands (Whitten, 1999).

Perspective on Usability and Ceremonies

As of 2011, roughly half of the malware running on Windows computers was being installed using techniques that tricked a person into doing something they didn't intend (Microsoft, 2011). Phishing attacks continue to plague the Internet, although it's hard to measure how much impact they have. The time when we can design systems without considering the people using them is long past. We need to learn how to do better at modeling both people and systems, and integrating the models, but we have ways that can be made to work. They are less prescriptive than I would like to see, and that should inform your decisions about who engages with them, and how you plan for them.

You'll need people with more breadth than is required for many other security tasks. People with backgrounds in sociology, anthropology, or psychology will have perspectives that are different from those with a computer science or engineering background. Usability specialists will also be useful in threat modeling sessions that focus on people, and in discussions of design changes to address usability. In addition, keep in mind that performing ceremony analysis or using other techniques in this chapter will take longer than other threat modeling techniques, and you'll also need more time for ancillary tasks like training and making sure everyone agrees on the goals and scope of an analysis. There is a risk of getting bogged down in elements which feed into your ceremony, rather than analyzing what's unique to you.

Ceremonies provide a fascinating framework for bringing humans into threat modeling. They show us ways to integrate people into existing analysis techniques, and support the assertion that ignoring people is no longer acceptable. At the same time, they do have limitations, many acknowledged in Ellison's paper. I'd like to address two:

- Effective ceremony analysis requires more maturity and experience than other forms of threat modeling, as it involves an understanding of both technology and people. I am hopeful that this will not dissuade anyone from trying it, and that we will learn a great deal about how to do it well over the next few years.
- The other aspect is the idea that "nothing is out of band to a ceremony." This is challenging for a prescriptive and bounded threat modeling exercise. It summons and celebrates the specter of projects designed to run forever, so when can you effectively say that a ceremony analysis has run its course? One part of the answer is that you know where all data needed for, or used in, the ceremony crosses a trust boundary. You may not need to know where it ultimately came from, but only how much trust you're placing in the provider. Similarly, in looking for threats, it may be sufficient for your business purposes to run through the section "Ceremony Analysis Heuristics," or you might prefer to run usability tests. Similarly, you may get to a point where the next useful mitigation requires 25 percent of the project's budget, and decide that a particular risk is thus acceptable and document it.

A last quote from Reason sums up issues relating to human factors and usability better than I can.

The managers of complex and hazardous technologies face a very tough question: how do they control human behavior so as to minimize the likelihood of unsafe violations without stifling the intelligent wariness necessary to recognize inappropriate procedures and avoid mis-appliances? The answer must surely lie in how they choose to deploy the variety of systemic controls that are available for shaping the behavior of its human elements.

James Reason, *The Human Contribution* (Ashgate Publishing, 2008)

It's a fine issue to consider in designing and analyzing technologies of any complexity, and all technology today operates in the hazardous world of the Internet.

Summary

If you don't try to help the people who will use your system to use it securely, they will probably fail. Modeling for systems that involve people is harder than other threat modeling. You must add models of people to both your model of the software and your model of the threats. Working with three models is harder than working with two, and models of people are less crisp than models of technology.

Models of people from behaviorists and cognitive scientists are useful for understanding how people will behave in a variety of circumstances. The behaviorist models include conditioned responses and kind versus wicked learning environments. Kahneman teaches us that what you see is all there is; that system 1 and 2 interact in surprising but predictable ways; and that anchoring and satisficing are common and important biases we all have. Others, like Reason, Cranor, and Sasse, also offer important lessons. Reason has many models of errors; Cranor provides a systematic approach to thinking about security with a human in the loop; and Sasse reminds us that security is but one of many things people want.

There are also heuristics you can use when working to help people, ranging from goal orientation to confirmation bias or a compliance budget. You also saw that there's a tendency for system designers to make optimistic assumptions about people. Models of the software can be extended to take into account human factors issues. You can model scenarios as warnings, authentications, or configuration; and you can extend a variety of diagrams to include or represent people. Lastly, you can model the techniques of electronic social engineering.

All the techniques for finding threats work when you include models of people. Brainstorming about them is, like other brainstorming, a tool that works better when you have security and usability experts in the room. You can also use ceremony analysis and a variety of ceremony-specific heuristics for finding threats, including missing information, distracting information, underspecified elements, fuzzy comparison, and a set of principles taken from cognitive scientists.

There are a plethora of building blocks for addressing threats. Many of these are design patterns, such as minimizing what you ask of people, conditioned safe ceremonies, avoiding urgency, and ensuring an easy path to success. There are also patterns for kind learning environments, such as avoiding scamicry and creating good security advice. You can also use more specific techniques, such as Gold Bars, NEAT and/or SPRUCE, and a set of patterns for grabbing people's attention.

Lastly, like all solutions to threats, you need to test for human factors. Such testing is challenging and worthwhile. You need to test in both benign and malicious scenarios, ensure that your tests don't cause people to behave differently (that is, ensure they have ecological validity), and work with people who have experience with testing for human factors.

CHAPTER

16

Threats to Cryptosystems

Cryptography is the art of communicating securely in the presence of adversaries. Cryptography, or crypto, as nearly everyone calls it (to save two syllables), figures into a good number of defenses. You can use it as part of how you address spoofing, tampering, repudiation, and information disclosure. It's important for people working in and around security to understand cryptographic tools; and perhaps more important, to understand the common mistakes made while using them, because failing to understand these mistakes can lead to overconfidence, and mistakes made by overconfident people are a major source of real-world problems.

Cryptographers have been enumerating threats for a very long time. They have done more than most other branches of security to quantify the security of their systems, and have over a long time evolved their thinking about threat models (in the sense of what attacks they worry about). And frankly, crypto can be a lot of fun. If you want to dabble in cryptography, the right place to get started is by breaking cryptosystems. (In a lab, not breaking into other people's systems in possible violation of ethics or law. Thanks! I knew you'd understand.) There are many targets, and the worst you'll do is *not* break anything. In contrast, if you try to get started by building cryptosystems without developing knowledge of how to break them, you'll inevitably have false confidence in what you've built. It's easy to build a cryptosystem whose flaws you can't see.

This chapter is mostly a reference chapter. It does not replace a good text on cryptography, but encourages you to use the largest building blocks available, rather than rolling your own. If you need to roll your own, you need to first read all of *Cryptography Engineering* by Niels Ferguson, Bruce Schneier, and Yoshi Kohno (Wiley, 2012). I don't want to scare anyone away from crypto, nor do I want you to be overconfident.

In this chapter, you'll first learn about cryptographic primitives. Primitives are the smallest units of cryptography that anyone will ever use. (They're often called building blocks, but this book uses "building block" to refer to the building blocks in the 4-stage model.) After the cryptographic primitives, you'll learn about the classic crypto attackers and attacks against cryptosystems. Those are followed by advice on building with crypto, and a set of things worth remembering. The chapter closes with a discussion of an over-reliance on secrecy to protect a system in the context of Kerckhoffs, the person who crystalized that discussion.

Cryptographic Primitives

There are only a few basic cryptographic primitives: symmetric and asymmetric encryption, hash functions, and pseudo-random number generators (PRNGs). Understanding them will help you avoid mistakes in their use. This section also covers a set of techniques that are useful for preserving privacy—that is, preventing certain types of information disclosure attacks. Lastly, you'll look at a few important modern constructions that you should be familiar with.

Basic Primitives

The primitives just mentioned are at the very heart of cryptography. If you don't understand them, they're easy to confuse, and confusing them will leave you or your customers insecure. This section uses some standard conventions and terminology: Alice and Bob are typically the people who want to communicate. They do this by sending messages, which are also called *plaintext*. The cryptosystems they've agreed to use often have *ciphers* and sometimes *keys*. A cipher has various functions, such as *encrypt* and *decrypt*. The following sections begin with the category of system you're most likely familiar with, symmetric cryptosystems. The others are shown in table 16-1.

Table 16-1: Cryptographic Primitives

PRIMITIVE	GOAL	INPUT	OUTPUT
Symmetric cryptography	Confidentiality	Plaintext (any length)	Ciphertext (same length)
Asymmetric	Authentication	Plaintext (any length)	Fixed length signature

PRIMITIVE	GOAL	INPUT	OUTPUT
Asymmetric	Key agreement	Counterparty information	A session key
Hash	Fingerprint	Plaintext (any length)	Fixed length message dependent fingerprint
PRNG	Randomness	Various	Hard to predict bits

Symmetric Cryptography

Symmetric encryption systems—also known as private key or secret key systems, or even just ciphers—use a key known to both (or all) sides of a conversation, thus the name symmetric. The Caesar cipher is an example of a (very simple) symmetric system. Letters are shifted three letters to the right, with A being represented by D, B by E, and so on. Someone must either know the key, guess the key or break the system to read the message. Ideally, you use a system that is harder to break.

Assume that Alice and Bob have shared a key. The original, unencrypted message Alice wants to send to Bob is the plaintext. She and Bob have previously agreed on a symmetric cipher to use, along with a key. The plaintext and key are inputs to the cipher's encryption function, which outputs a ciphertext. She sends this ciphertext to Bob, not worrying about who might see it, because if the cryptosystem is strong, that ciphertext is unintelligible to everyone without the key. Those with the key feed the key and the ciphertext to the decryption function, which outputs the plaintext. The symmetry of the system results from the same key being used on both ends. Symmetric systems protect against information disclosure attacks when the key is secure. Unfortunately, establishing the key in a secure way is tremendously tricky. Years ago, governments would send keys in briefcases handcuffed to couriers, which is expensive and slow.

There are two types of symmetric algorithms, *block ciphers* and *stream ciphers.* A block cipher takes a block of input (often 128 bits) and encrypts it with a key, producing an output block of the same size as the input. Many constructions that use a block cipher also use an *initialization vector (IV)*. This is a random number that is input to the cipher along with the key and the first block to ensure that identical plaintexts are not encrypted the same way.

A stream cipher takes a key and produces a key stream. That key stream can be XORed with a plaintext bit stream to produce ciphertext. The same key stream is produced at the receiver, which can then use XOR to get the plaintext. If you ever reuse a key stream, your ciphertexts can be XORed, and the output of that is the XOR of the plaintexts. That's highly undesirable. The most common stream cipher, RC4, has a host of issues. Be sure to review the advice in

Cryptography Engineering before you use RC4. (Let me save you time—RC4 is not mentioned in *Cryptography Engineering*, because it's so hard to use securely, but as you review the advice there, you'll find something that will work safely. Just don't use RC4.)

The simple rule for symmetric encryption is to use AES in CBC or CTR mode. AES is the U.S. "Advanced Encryption Standard," and the modes refer to the precise ways bits are managed. (CBC is "cipher block chaining," while CTR is "counter" mode.) The pros and cons of each are subtle, and debate rages on. However, using one or the other will almost always be the right choice. To be explicit, this means you should avoid ECB mode. ECB stands for "electronic code book," although you can think of it as "extreme cryptographic blunder" because it's an extreme cryptographic blunder to use the mode.

Asymmetric Cryptography

In an asymmetric encryption system, each party has a set of mathematically related keys, and through the use of really cool math, manages a variety of useful results, including encryption, key agreement, and digital signatures. Asymmetric encryption systems are also called public key systems, because one of the keys is made public.

NOTE **Asymmetric cryptography is also known as *public key encryption*.**

This section presents a simplified version of the math that doesn't use much more than high school algebra and then discusses how asymmetric systems can be used.

Alice and Bob each pick a number. Alice picks a, Bob picks b. They then agree on a number g. Maybe their number is the closing of the Dow Jones index on the previous day. It can be public; it just needs to be hard for an adversary to influence.

Alice calculates $A = g^a$ and Bob calculates $B = g^b$. Alice then sends A, and Bob sends B. Then Alice calculates a secret key, $s = B^a$, and Bob calculates $s = A^b$. Now, because multiplication is commutative, $A^b = B^a$ (or, really, $g^{ab} = g^{ba}$). If you assume that it's hard to calculate a from g and ga, then it's hard for anyone who doesn't know a or b to figure out what s is. Alice and Bob have now agreed on a secret without ever sending that secret back and forth. It's not that hard to figure the *n*th root of g^a, and from there you can approximate, but this is a simplified description. Therefore, to get more security, we'll add one more element, which is that Alice and Bob do all of this math *modulo p*. Math modulo p is like clock arithmetic. 12 hours after 7, it's 7. So 7 modulo 12 is 7, and 19 modulo 12 is also 7. We can replace 12 with any other number, which is called p. When a, b, g, and p are large, and satisfy certain mathematical properties, then figuring out a or b from g^a and g^b is hard. Because it's hard, Alice and Bob could use s as a key in a symmetric encryption system. They want to do this because symmetric encryption is fast, and asymmetric encryption is slow.

This is way cool, and it's worth taking a few moments to work through some of the math yourself to see it work. However, if you use the preceding system as presented, you will be successfully attacked. The example is designed to help you get a feel for what's possible and why. It is not intended to replace a full college-level course in mathematical cryptography, which is needed before you can make interesting mistakes in this space.

Once you've worked through the math, you can use asymmetric systems for three things beyond online key agreement: encryption, offline key exchange, and signatures. The cryptosystem's encrypt function allows anyone to encrypt a message using a public key so that only the person with the private key can read it. If the message is the key to another, then that key can be used to encrypt or decrypt messages. (The usual reason for this is that symmetric systems are much, much faster than asymmetric systems.) Most important, asymmetric signature systems can be used to sign a message, and anyone with the public key can verify the signature. A quirk of the math in RSA, one of the first public key cryptosystems, leads many people to overgeneralize with the claim that signatures are the inverse of encryption.

The pitfalls related to effective key exchange, signatures, and encryption are substantial and often subtle. Using systems such as Diffie-Hellman, RSA, or DSA as originally presented is foolish.

Hashes

The third important building block are hashes, also called one-way functions, or message digests. A hash takes an input of some arbitrary length and produces a fixed-length digest or hash of the input. Ideally, any change to the input completely transforms the output. This means that other building blocks can assume they'll always see a fixed-length input. For example, a signature algorithm can assume that it will always see input of the same length, and defer the problem of arbitrary length input to the hash function.

Hashes are also used to store passwords, usually with a *salt*. A salt is an additional input to a hash function, designed to ensure that identical inputs create different outputs. Therefore, if Alice and Bob are both using the password Secret1, then the simple approach to storing a hash of each of their passwords would reveal that Alice and Bob have the same password (but not what it is). With salting, the threat from sorting is mitigated. There's other threats, and more information on the storage of passwords in Chapter 14, "Accounts and Identity."

Hashes can also be used to create *fingerprints*. A fingerprint in this context is a hash of something longer, designed to be used by people to authenticate that each person has the same copy of the longer thing (such as a file or message).

This approach is useful because hashes are faster to calculate than digital signatures. For example, if you want to sign a copy of a web browser, you could calculate the signature on all the millions of bytes of the browser, or you could calculate the signature on the 16 to 64 bytes (128 to 512 bits) of a hash. It's also possible for people to validate a fingerprint. Some people will print public key fingerprints on a business card to allow you to validate the authenticity of that public key. Printing the entire key would be less usable.

Lastly, hashes can be used to calculate message authentication codes (MACs). A message authentication code uses a key known to each side of a protocol, and the key and message are hashed together to produce a MAC. The key is kept private on each endpoint, while the message and MAC are sent.

The most famous of these hashes, MD5, has now been effectively and publicly broken. Do not expect MD5 to give you any security, although sometimes you'll need to use it because of a counterparty. Instead, use the latest in the SHA series from NIST.

Randomness

The final important cryptographic primitive is random numbers, sometimes provided by dice. But of course dice are too slow to provide enough random numbers for cryptographic use, so they are usually provided by pseudo-random number generators (PRNGs). For a simple example, if Alice chooses her public key based on a bad random number source (say, microseconds since boot), then an attacker can decide how long he thinks most systems will stay up, and start searching at the median value. If Alice uses a good random number, then the search is much harder. The essence here is that you have some entropy (information unknown to the attacker), and you want to make the best possible use of that entropy.

If you have access to a good hardware source of randomness, which produces lots of entropy, use it. Otherwise, you'll need to use a PRNG to give you more pseudo-random bits. Unfortunately, PRNGs are incredibly difficult to build well, and many things that appear random in computer systems turn out to be somewhat predictable. That's why John von Neumann has said "Anyone who considers arithmetical methods of producing random digits is, of course, in a state of sin" (von Neumann, 1951). Fortunately, most operating systems now include decent-quality PRNGs. Make sure you're using one everywhere you need randomness.

Note that randomness is easier for human-operated endpoints, which can take randomness from keyboard interrupts, mouse movements, and other inputs that are hard for an attacker to observe. If you have machines in a data center, you may need to augment randomness. There are hardware devices to do this, sometimes included in a CPU.

NOTE **As this book went to press, a great deal of controversy erupted over possible backdoors in random number generators. The advice remains that you should rely**

on the operating system. The risk associated with altering PRNGs is larger than the risk that your library's RNG is malicious. You want to avoid the sorts of mistakes the Debian maintainers introduced into OpenSSL (Debian, 2008). If you are implementing an operating system, then use the hardware RNG with the mixing approach now used by FreeBSD (Goodin, 2013).

Privacy Primitives

There is a small number of primitives that are useful for addressing information disclosure:

- **Steganography:** This is the art of hiding messages—for example, encoding your message in the least-significant bits of an image file, such as a photograph. Effective steganography is useful for hiding messages from attackers to conceal the existence of communication. It is also used to encode anti-piracy information in audio and video ("watermarking"). If you need to implement steganography, the best work tends to appear at the Information Hiding Conference.
- **Mixes and Mix networks:** These are tools for taking a set of messages, mixing them together, and then sending them out in a way that unlinks the messages from the sender. They generally require latency to work.
- **Onion routing:** This is a technique for sending messages over a network that unlinks messages from senders, like mix networks. Each message is wrapped in multiple layers of encryption which are wrapped or unwrapped one at a time (like an onion). Tor is the best-known onion router implementation today.
- **Blinding:** These techniques allow a system to sign a message without seeing it. Blinding is covered in Chapter 8, "Defensive Tactics and Technologies," in the section on mitigating privacy threats.

Modern Cryptographic Primitives

These primitives are more specific than the basic primitives introduced above. When your problem can be addressed with one of these, that's far better than cobbling something together.

Perfect Forward Secrecy

Perfect forward secrecy (PFS) is a property that ensures that if one of the (long-term) keys involved in a protocol is later compromised, then the messages which were sent under a forward secrecy scheme cannot be decrypted.

Authenticated Key Exchange

Authenticated key exchange (AKE) is so hard to do right that cryptographers are now developing primitives to address it. AKE is focused on channels (confidential, authenticated, integrity-protected) created over an adversary-controlled connection. There is a related problem, authenticated and confidential channel establishment (ACCE), which is similarly complex. If you find yourself in these spaces, defer to experts and their work. See "On the Security of TLS Renegotiation"(Giesen, 2013) for the state of the art as this book is being written.

Random Oracles

An oracle is a construct that answers questions put to it. In cryptography, the answers an oracle gives are consistent. The random oracle is one that responds to any query with a response chosen randomly from all possible responses. For any given query, it will always return the same response. A random oracle acts much the way we want hash functions to act, but it is mathematically simple. Oracles are almost always available to the attacker.

If you see a proof of something with a random oracle, be aware that today's hash functions are not random oracles.

Proven Cryptosystems

When reading about a cryptosystem, you will occasionally see that it is accompanied by a mathematical proof, and you may be tempted to consider any proven cryptosystem superior to those without proofs. It is helpful to be aware of three things. First, the proofs may or may not cover the same things that you're worried about (unless you have a personal burning hatred of second preimages). Second, the proofs are sometimes exceptionally complex mathematical constructs, which can be hard even for mathematicians to follow. If the system has been altered to make a proof possible, then there's a trade-off. It may be the right one, and you should evaluate that against your needs. Lastly, most proofs rest on a set of implicit assumptions that cryptographers expect their audience will understand (Koblitz, 2007).

Certificates and PKI

If Alice publishes a public key, such as A, then anyone who knows that the private part of key A is maintained by Alice can encrypt a message such that only Alice can read it. You can think of this like a set of public mailboxes with names on them. One is labeled Alice, another is labeled Bob. Anyone can walk up to the appropriate mailbox and drop in a letter for Alice or Bob. Only Alice can decrypt messages dropped in the Alice box, and only Bob can decrypt messages in the Bob box, because each has the appropriate private key. Anyone can create a mailbox with their name on it, and anyone can (virtually) walk up and drop a message in that mailbox. Of course, nothing prevents me from creating a mailbox with your name on it, which means I have a key needed to read messages intended for you. If I can trick some senders into sending me messages for you, then I can read those messages. If I'm clever, once I read them, I can forward them on so you'll never know they were read by someone else.

In theory, if all these public keys are collected into a directory, then anyone can use the directory to look up the key for a person. Among the many troubles with this in practice are the many people named Alice, or figuring out if Bob is Bob, Bobby, Robert, or something else in the directory. Some party may attempt to vouch for who's who, creating certificates of various forms, by signing a public key and some associated identifying information. These parties are often called certificate authorities or certificate issuers. The snarky may ask who made them authorities.

Each certificate has either two or three parts, depending on how you count. Using the most common way of counting, a certificate has two parts: the public and the private. The public part includes a public key and a signature on it. The other counting method identifies a public part, a private part, and a certificate file. When sending certificates, it is important to only send the public part or the certificate file. The private part should never be shared. You want to share the public part and the certificate, and it's fine to do so, or to reveal the fingerprint of either. Ideally, the private key is generated on the machine on which it will be used, and never leaves that machine.

Classic Threat Actors

In discussing protocols, cryptographers use names for the participants. This helps people keep track of the human meaning of the variables. The first letter of the name is used as the mathematical variable:

- *Alice and Bob* are the classic actors in cryptographic protocols. They were introduced in the first paper on RSA, and have been with us ever since, communicating in the presence of adversaries. Sometimes there are additional participants, with names added in alphabetic order, such as Carol, Chuck, or Dave. The additional participants will usually not include "E" names, because those are reserved for Eve, the oldest attacker. Generally, references to "Alice and Bob" mean "the parties trying to communicate securely."
- *Eve* is an eavesdropper. She is able to tap into the network between Alice and Bob, but is either unwilling or unable to modify their communications. Another way to state this is that Eve only takes advantage of information disclosure threats to violate confidentiality. If you're a movie fan, you'll

know that Eve may have three faces, but she almost always goes by "Eve." Other actor names show more variation.

- *Mallory* can also tap into the network but is willing and able to create, destroy, or modify communication content. Usually, Mallory is able to eavesdrop as well, and if he can't, the reason why should be clearly and convincingly articulated. Mallory is occasionally called some other M name. Mallory takes advantage of network spoofing, tampering, information disclosure, and denial-of-service threats. Sometimes a message created by Mallory can implement a repudiation threat, but that's a second-order effect of successful spoofing or tampering.
- *Alice or Bob as traitor* can happen because sometimes Alice or Bob are not only communicating in the presence of adversaries. Sometimes after a betrayal, blackmail, or other threat, Bob has actively turned against Alice (or vice versa). These attacks commonly subvert a shared secret or, by carefully constructing messages, convince Alice to solve equations that either leak information about her private keys or trick her or her software into having those keys perform operations not intended by Alice. These threats map less well to STRIDE, but they are usually information disclosure or elevation of privilege (insofar as Bob is getting answers not intended by Alice). Even when Alice and Bob are trustworthy, insufficient authentication can lead to the same impacts.
- Trent is a "trusted third party" who, by mutual agreement, can perform operations that everyone will believe. (See the "Perspective" sidebar immediately after this list for more on trust.)
- Victor is also a trusted third party, but one who only performs verification operations.

NOTE **The word "trust" is used in a somewhat unusual way by cryptographers: Trusted parties can betray the people who trust them. The term is used to describe what the trusted party *can* do, rather than what you *expect* them to do. Therefore, "a trusted, but not trustworthy person was caught selling secrets." This use of "trust" leads to a great deal of confusion. Terms like "relied-upon" are more clear, but sometimes awkward to use. When you see systems that assert trust in Trent or Victor, ask yourself, do you want to rely on that party to behave in a trustworthy way, and what's the downside if they betray you? Are there alternatives that allow you to address that threat?**

Attacks Against Cryptosystems

Successful cryptographic attacks usually either lead to information disclosure or allow tampering that the cryptography is intended to prevent. The following list of cryptographic attacks, focuses both on attacks that help you understand what can go wrong with your systems and on attacks that are reasonably understandable to those who are not specializing in cryptography.

NOTE **Linear and differential cryptanalysis are intentionally excluded from this list. They are mathematical attacks on the design of cryptosystems, and if you're engineering software, then the recommended algorithms have been vetted against those attacks, so you can't accidentally make yourself vulnerable. The excluded attacks are complex to describe and easy to describe incorrectly. More importantly, if you are applying the overall advice to use well-understood primitives, they are unlikely to be relevant.**

- **Known ciphertext:** Known ciphertext attacks are those for which nothing but the ciphertext is available to Eve (or the ciphertext and addressing information). For example, a radio intercept of a ciphertext might include some indicator of the recipient. Ideally, the best attack against such messages is a brute-force one, whereby Eve (who we assume has knowledge of the cryptosystem) must try each possible key to determine whether the message can be decrypted.
- **Chosen ciphertext:** A chosen ciphertext is an attack in which Mallory can insert a chosen ciphertext. For example, if your payroll database has (block-)encrypted salary values, you might not know the CEO's salary, but it might be fun to insert the ciphertext of his salary in the database cell that applies to you. There's also a set of attacks in which inserting chosen ciphertext gets you less information than the full plaintext, but such information disclosure can often be leveraged into a larger attack.
- **Chosen plaintext:** Choosing your opponent's plaintext is a great attack and often seems fanciful. However, during World War II, allied cryptanalysts were trying to figure out Japanese code names for islands. They instructed the base at Midway Island to radio (in the clear) that they were running out of water. Shortly after that, they intercepted a message that stated "AF is short on water," thus indicating that AF was Midway. (Presumably, the intercept was in Japanese. [Kahn, 1996].) It is usually surprisingly easy to get your plaintext into modern protocols, because everything is being done by programs that have no ability to notice that their input is bizarre.
- **Adaptive chosen:** These are variants of the chosen ciphertext or plaintext attacks in which the adversary can inject something, observe your response, and then inject something else.
- **Man-in-the-middle (MITM):** These are executed by Mallory, sitting on the network and altering traffic as it goes by, preventing Bob from seeing Alice's real messages. It is almost always a mistake to assume that Mallory can't do this because of any non-cryptographic reason. Even if you are building for a very specific and controlled environment, over the lifetime of your implementation the environment is likely to change in

unpredictable ways. MITM attacks include (but are not limited to) relay, replay, reflection, and downgrade attacks.

- **Relay, or chess master, attacks:** How do you beat a chess master if you're a rank amateur? It's easy! Play chess by mail against two masters at once. If you're trying to convince one chess master to vouch for your skills, this is an interesting attack. Of course, not everyone cares how good you are at chess, but the attack generalizes.

  The modern approach is to be a MITM between Alice and Bob. If Alice is a web browser, and Bob is a web server, then Mallory can present a web server to Alice, Alice will dutifully enter her password, and Mallory will submit it via HTTPS to Bob.
- **Replay:** A replay attack is one in which Mallory captures messages and resends them. For example, let's say Mallory knows that spymaster Alice uses time to address messages to her field agents. (That is, Bob listens at 7:30, Charlie listens at 8:00.) After Alice sends the encrypted, authenticated message "You've been discovered! Flee!" at 7:30, Mallory gleefully rebroadcasts it every half-hour for weeks, with police waiting by the ticket counters at the train station.
- **Reflection:** In these attacks, Mallory plays back Alice's content to Alice. They're a little more subtle than replay, reflection, or other MITM attacks. For example, let's say there's an authentication protocol that relies on a secret key, k, and the authentication consists of encrypting a random nonce with k. Then Alice would send a hello, Bob sends n, and Alice sends n back encrypted with key k. When Bob receives n encrypted with k, he moves to an authenticated state. If Mallory wants to impersonate Alice, then he watches Bob send n, and then asks Bob to authenticate himself, with the same nonce, n. Bob conveniently sends Mallory the encrypted nonce, which Mallory then sends, pretending to be Alice.
- **Downgrade attacks:** These are attacks against protocols, executed by a MITM. Downgrade attacks can occur when an insecure version of a protocol is updated but the client or server is unsure what version the other side speaks. Mallory stands in the middle, impersonating each to the other, and forces them to use the less secure version. There are three classes of defense against downgrades: The first hashes all previous messages into the later messages; the second relies on one side or the other (or both) having a memory of what version its counterparties use, and that memory is used to detect and either alert or refuse the change; while the third and most secure defense involves not speaking the old version.
- **Birthday attacks:** These are named after the surprising fact that if you have just 23 people in a room, there's a 50 percent chance that two of them

will have the same birthday, and a 99 percent chance with 57 people. You can find many good explanations of this online, so let's discuss the attack. An attacker generates a set of documents, looking for any two that will hash to the same value. Hashes, like birthdays, have a fixed set of possible values. When an attacker has two documents that have the same hash, she can substitute one for the other. For example, one document might say "attack at dawn," the other might say "retreat at 7:15." If they hash to the same thing, software is unlikely to catch the substitution.

- **Traffic analysis:** These attacks involve looking at a set of messages and learning things from the patterns without ever actually understanding the message. For example, if Bob and Charlie routinely retransmit Alice's messages, perhaps Alice is more senior to them in the organization. Similarly, if Alice always responds quicker to Charlie's messages than to Bob's, then perhaps Alice reports to Charlie. Thus, information is disclosed to Eve even if she can't obtain any message content. Message size can also play an important role in traffic analysis. For example, if your "buy" button is the only 3,968 byte image on your site, an attacker watching HTTPS traffic can identify the request for that image.
- **Length extension attacks:** If Mallet knows the hash of "foo," it is trivial for him to calculate the hash of "foobar." That's true even if "foo" is a complex data structure containing secrets known only to Alice and Bob. This attack affected a lot of people using hashes for authentication in URLs, to which attackers could add extra parameters (Duong, 2009).
- **Timing attacks:** Subtle differences in the time it takes to perform cryptographic operations can reveal information such as the length of a message, where in your code an operation fails, or the hamming weight of a private key. (Hamming weight is the sum of the 1 bits in a string.) These differences can be detected over network connections. The simplest mitigation is to always specify a fixed length of time before returning.
- **Side channel attacks:** These are focused on extracting information from the physical state of the computer. For example, the power draw of a computer changes as it executes instructions and the CPU makes a small amount of sound. In various quantum cryptographic systems, mirrors are used, and the positions and movements of the mirrors reveal information. "Acoustic Cryptanalysis: On Nosy People and Noisy Machines" (Shamir, 2013) contains a clear introduction to acoustic cryptanalysis.
- **Rubber hose cryptanalysis:** Sometimes the easiest way to beat a cryptosystem is to beat the person using it until they give you the key. The degree of violence varies by locale and attacker. Some may literally use a rubber hose, others may just lock Alice up until she gives in.

Building with Crypto

This section discusses a few points of cryptographic engineering, including making choices about cryptosystems to use, planning for upgrades, authenticating at the outermost layer, and some techniques for managing keys.

Making Choices

Because cryptography is hard, it's easy to decide that the right design includes flexibility and negotiation. If you're designing a protocol, and you're not sure if you should use CBC or CTR mode, why not negotiate it at the start? The reason is because such negotiation explodes your attack surface, your analysis work, your future compatibility work, and your test plan. It provides all sorts of places for a MITM or other attacker to wedge themselves in. Therefore, make a decision about what you're building, and keep it simple. (This point derives from Thomas Ptacek's blog article "Applied Cryptography Engineering" [Ptacek, 2013]). If you have multiple authentication options, then the attacker gets to choose the weakest one to attack. Once they can attack authentication, they can perform all sorts of other attacks.

Preparing for Upgrades

To the extent that you're building your own protocols, you should assume that there will be failures. A useful defensive pattern is to incorporate a hash of all previous messages you've sent into the next message. However, a MITM who is terminating the connections and relaying the data can still bypass this. If you do not have a plan and test suite for upgrades, you almost certainly will end up being unable to securely upgrade.

Key Management

Key management is about ensuring that each party has the right cryptographic keys, and that there's some mapping between each cryptographic key and an account or roles within a system.

The cryptographic methods for key management can be split into symmetric systems—that is, those that rely on a shared key—and asymmetric systems.

Shared key systems usually mean Kerberos. If you need to use a shared key system, Kerberos has much to recommend it. Such systems suffer from spoofing problems, whereby each entity which knows a key can use it in ways that implicate the other parties associated with that key.

Asymmetric systems reduce the problem of distributing keys in a confidential and authentic way by removing the confidentiality requirement; therefore, asymmetric systems are generally preferable. You still need to authenticate keys, and there are a number of ways to do so:

- Perhaps the simplest is variously called *TOFU* (*trust on first use*) or *persistence*. The idea, introduced to a broad audience by SSH, was to get a key on first connect and to then persist that key, warning the user if it changed. There are two malicious scenarios in which it would change, and one benign one. The malicious scenarios are the start or end of a man-in-the-middle attack (either way, the key changes). In the benign scenario, the systems administrator changes the key. Key rotation is generally desirable, as it limits exposure to undetected compromise, however, it can be operationally difficult to do in a secure and smooth way.
- A system called *Convergence* builds on the idea of memory by sharing the key that various participants see. Discord between perspectives is generally indicative of an attack (Marlinspike, 2011). A wrinkle is the common security goal of "one key, one service, one machine." For example, a 100-machine "web farm" at a bank might have 100 different keys, one per machine, and the Convergence system will issue a lot of alarms.
- PGP introduced a system called *web of trust*. The idea is that each participant maintains their own set of keys, and any participant can sign a key. Such a signature indicates that they vouch for the key mapping to an identifier (in PGP's case, e-mail addresses and names). Web of trust doesn't scale particularly well, in part because of usability, and in part because the meaning of a signature varies from person to person.
- Another option is having a limited set of parties vouch for the keys, by issuing certificates. There's an entire industry of organizations that will sign cryptographic keys for a fee under the banner of "public key infrastructures" or PKI. There are also mechanisms such as DNSSEC. DNSSEC is built on a root key, operated by Verisign on behalf of ICANN, which is responsible for delegating (signing) various zones, such as .com. There are a variety of systems, most prevalently DANE, for inserting other keys into the DNSSEC root of trust. Criticisms of DNSSEC include that Verisign also operates a wiretapping infrastructure business, the Verisign NetDiscovery Lawful Interception Service, (Verisign, 2007) and that the company is based primarily in the United States, where it may be subject to a variety of interference.
- PKI can be seen as a limited web of trust, with only a few entities able to vouch for a key. *Certificate Pinning* takes that limitation a step further, with software deciding that only a small set of certificate issuers will be allowed to issue certificates that will be relied upon. For example, Google's Chrome web browser limits who can issue a certificate for Gmail.

Authenticating before Decrypting

Moxie Marlinspike, who created the Perspectives system, asserts that all cryptographic systems should ensure that they authenticate a message before doing anything else (Marlinspike, 2011). He outlines a number of attacks that were made possible by violating what he calls his "Cryptographic Doom Principle." Of course, you need to remember to check the message authentication code in constant time. (The authenticate before decrypting approach is also called "encrypt-then-MAC.")

Things to Remember About Crypto

This advice is more general than the advice for builders, but it's a set of things which you should remember as you're using crypto.

Use a Cryptosystem Designed by Professionals

The design and analysis of new cryptosystems is a specialized field of mathematics, and the tools that cryptanalysts have developed over the last 40 years go through amateur systems like a chainsaw goes through puppies. Really. It's that ugly. If you don't know what an adaptive chosen plaintext attack is or why you'd need to worry about it, let me simplify this: Use the highest level protocol or system designed by professionals which meets your security requirements.

There is only one exception to this advice: If you work for a national cryptographic agency, you may have in-house algorithms. Please send me a copy. I'll review them and let you know if they're acceptable. Other than that, just don't do it.

Use Cryptographic Code Built and Tested by Professionals

This might look like a restatement of the previous point. It's not. Rather, you should use the crypto libraries built into your operating system, or otherwise use an implementation that's solid and well tested. A lot of subtle mistakes can creep in if you implement your own. In short, it is faster, cheaper, and more reliable to use crypto than to re-implement it.

NOTE Several of the issues discussed in this chapter are the subject of fierce debate in the cryptographic engineering or research communities. Which block cipher mode to use or how to gather and manage randomness are not simple questions. If you're interested in those debates, you can find them. Or you can leave them to those professionals.

Cryptography Is Not Magic Security Dust

Cryptography offers a powerful toolset for solving problems. However, you have to apply the tools appropriately to solve a well-defined problem at hand. For example, if you're coding an SSL connection (using a standard SSL library, of course), have you thought through the failure modes and what you want to have happen in each, and implemented that error-handling code?

Assume It Will All Become Public

This is a restatement of Kerckhoffs's Principle, "The system must not require that it is a secret, and it must be able to fall into enemy hands." The upshot of this is that your system will almost always include two parts: a system, which is widely known and deployed, and a key, which is regularly and easily changed—see, for example, the password management systems in Chapter 14 Those password management systems are the best we know how to do, in large part because security experts have discussed them at length. The only secrets are the passwords themselves; and those are (relatively) easily changed. See the "Secret Systems: Kerckhoffs and His Principles" section later in this chapter for more details on Kerckhoffs's Principle.

There are many ways in which programmers violate this principle, but one is so common it's worth calling out: embedding a symmetric key in your code. That key is available to everyone with a debugger. Don't do it.

You Still Need to Manage Keys

Key management is hard. All the preceding discussion aside, there are times when you want to manage keys either with local code or manually to ensure that what's happening is what you think is happening. For example, OpenSSL can't check whether the domain name matches the certificate presented, because that's a separate layer. Similarly, the `CertGetCertificateChain()` call will by default chain to any of the 100 or so roots in the Windows Root Certificate Store.

Whatever keys you are managing, you'll need to ensure that you can create them (with sufficient entropy available), store them securely, and revoke or expire them appropriately.

Secret Systems: Kerckhoffs and His Principles

Auguste Kerckhoffs proposed a set of principles for cryptosystems in 1883. There are two that are generally referred to as "Kerckhoffs's Principle." They follow his first principle, which is that a system must be undecipherable. The two that are often invoked today are as follows:

1. [The cryptographic system] must not be required to be secret, and it must be able to fall into the hands of the enemy without inconvenience.
2. Its key must be communicable and retainable without the help of written notes, and changeable or modifiable at the will of the correspondents.

From these, we get a variety of restatements, many of which lose the subtlety of the original (and in at least one case, the translation adds an interesting subtlety) [Kerckhoffs, 1883; Petitcolas 2013]. The core concept is that the system must not be secret, which implies that we need something that users can modify. This can be read as an early statement that security by obscurity doesn't work. While that's true, at some level, security requires that some things (such as keys) remain secret. It may be helpful to consider the difference between obscurity, in the sense of difficult to find, and secret, in the sense of intentionally hidden.

Kerckhoffs's principles survive because they carry with them a lot of subtle wisdom. For example, the first part of Kerckhoffs's third principle relates to useful properties of passwords.

There is nothing inherently wrong with a system being secret, as long as everyone relying on the security of the system has sufficient confidence that it has undergone sufficient security scrutiny. If your customers or prospects are arguing about the security of your secret sauce, then by definition they do not have sufficient confidence in the scrutiny and threat modeling it has undergone.

There is another aspect of secrecy, which is that it works differently in the physical and computer worlds. In the physical world, attackers who wants to steal the Colonel's secret recipe have to physically enter the kitchen and watch as the secret herbs and spices are blended. Doing so puts them at risk. They are at risk of exposure, being challenged, or even arrested for trespassing. Even probing the security measures around the kitchen involves a degree of risk. Contrast that with trying to break the security of a popular program. It's popular, so anyone can get a copy. You can set up a computer, and probe away to your heart's content. You can debug your exploit code in the comfort of your own home, with zero risk.

This difference is usually implicit, and leads to very different thinking about the value of secrecy around security measures in various communities. Protecting the location of a security camera makes a lot less sense if you've released a brick-for-brick model of your headquarters (Swire, 2004). Similarly, it may be that when you operate a service, you can get more value from obscurity than when you ship a product. That's because you may be able to observe probing. However, you only get that value from obscurity if you actually have ways to detect such probes, analyze what you detect, and respond when appropriate.

Summary

Cryptography is an important set of tools and techniques for addressing threats. There are a wide variety of very sharp tools in the cryptographer's toolbox. The most important are symmetric and asymmetric cryptosystems, hashes, and randomness. You should understand each of these well enough to avoid misusing them. There are more specific primitives for privacy, and a wide set of more specific tools such as forward secrecy and certificates. Cryptographers like to name the parties to their protocols. The names have a pattern and you'll sometimes see that pattern outside of cryptographic documents.

There are a wide variety of threats to cryptosystems; it is likely the area where threats and mitigations have been studied the longest. This chapter has presented a small attack library; more complete ones fill entire books.

If you find yourself building with cryptography, you'll want to make choices, not offer up an infinite list of options (and test cases). Such a list of options will make it harder to plan for upgrades, which is a tremendously important thing to get right from the start. Many of your problems will involve key management. Key management ranges from persistence to a trusted third party vouching for a key. Recall that "trusted" in security is an inverse of its use in polite society: The trusted party is the one who can betray you, and minimizing trust (who can betray you) is a good engineering goal.

You should always use a cryptosystem designed, implemented, and tested by professionals. Your operating system probably comes with a library of these. You should assume that your cryptosystem will become public, and not let that worry you.

What you should worry about is that cryptography is hard. Your goal should be to do it well enough that rather than attacking your crypto, the attackers bypass it. That brings you back into the chess games and "how deep to go" questions which you learned about in Chapter 7 "Processing and Managing Threats."

Part

V

Taking It to the Next Level

Up to this point, you've been learning what's known about threat modeling. From this point on, it's all focused on the future: the future of threat modeling in your organization, and the future of threat modeling approaches.

This part of the book contains the following three chapters:

- **Chapter 17: Bringing Threat Modeling to Your Organization** includes how to introduce threat modeling, who does what, how to integrate it into a development process, how to integrate it into roles and responsibilities, and how to overcome objections to threat modeling.
- **Chapter 18: Experimental Approaches** includes a set of emerging approaches to operations threat modeling, the "Broad Street" taxonomy, adversarial machine learning, threat modeling a business, and then gets cheeky with threats to threat modeling approaches and a few thoughts on effective experimentation.
- **Chapter 19: Architecting for Success** provides some final advice on going forward—all the mental models, touchpoints, and process design advice to help you develop new and better approaches to threat modeling, along with a few last words on artistry in your threat modeling.

CHAPTER
17

Bringing Threat Modeling to Your Organization

This chapter starts from the assumption that your organization does not threat model. If that assumption is wrong, the chapter may still help you bring more advanced threat modeling to your organization, or better organize the threat modeling you perform to generate greater impact. What you've learned through this point in the book can be applied by an individual without organizational support. This chapter is for those who want to influence the practices of the organization they're working for. (Consultants will also find it helpful.)

There are many ways to introduce a new practice to your organization. One is to stand up in front of everyone and say, "I just read this awesome book, and we should totally do this!" Another is to say, "I just tried this, and look how many bugs I found!" Yet another would be to intrigue people with a copy of *Elevation of Privilege*, saying "Check out this cool card game!" Each of these represents a strategy, and different strategies will work or not in different situations. There are many good books on how to work within an organization. Sam Lightstone's *Making It Big in Software* is one of the more comprehensive for software professionals (Pearson, 2010). Obviously, one chapter can't provide all the information that a full book will, but in this chapter you'll learn a few key strategies and how to apply each of them to individual contributors. The chapter also includes a section on convincing management because management will almost always want evidence that threat modeling is worthwhile, and that evidence will almost certainly involve the experiences of individual contributors.

Up to now, you've been learning about the tasks and processes of threat modeling, with the focus on threat modeling itself. In this chapter, you'll learn about how threat modeling interfaces with how an organization works. The chapter opens with a discussion about how to introduce threat modeling to an organization including how to convince individual contributors and how to convince management. From there, it covers who does what, including prerequisites, deliverables, roles and responsibilities, and group interaction issues such as decision models and effective meetings. Next, the chapter discusses integrating threat modeling into a software development process, including agile threat modeling, how testing and threat modeling relate, and how to measure threat modeling, along with HR issues such as training, ladders, and interviewing. The chapter closes with a discussion of how to overcome objections. Of course, overcoming objections is part of convincing people, but the details you learn about who does what and how to integrate into a process will inform how you overcome objections. For example, you can't overcome an objection that "we're an agile shop" until you know how threat modeling connects to agile development.

How To Introduce Threat Modeling

This section covers how to "sell" an idea in general, then how to sell it to individual contributors and then management. That's the path you'll need to follow, both in the book and in the workplace. Figure out how to make a convincing case, then make that case to the people who will be doing the work, and the people who will be managing them.

After reading the preceding chapters and exploring the techniques, you're obviously excited to ask your organization to start threat modeling. Your excitement may not lead to their excitement. Even with *Elevation of Privilege*, threat modeling may not be enough fun for a game night with your family. Threat modeling is a serious tool to reach a goal. The more clearly you can state your goal, the better you'll be able to achieve it. The more clearly you can state how your goal differs from your current state, the easier it will be to draw a straight line between the two. For example, if your organization does no threat modeling and has no one with experience doing so, perhaps a useful goal would be a threat modeling exercise that results in fixing a security bug in the next release. You might also consider that as a milestone along the way to a greater goal, such as not losing sales because of security concerns.

In order to introduce threat modeling into an organization, you need to convince two types of people that it's worthwhile: the individual contributors who will participate and the managers who reward them. Without both of those sets of people on board, threat modeling will not be adopted. And so you're going to need to "sell" them. Technical people are often averse to sales, but competent enterprise sales people have many tricks and even a few skills which may help you get your ideas implemented. The salespeople you want to borrow from aren't the type who sell used cars. They're the type who spend weeks or months to understand an organization and get their product paid for and implemented. Salespeople have ways of understanding the world and bending it to their will. They understand the value of knowing who can sign a check, and who can effectively say "no." They know that as you "work an organization" to get someone to sign that check, it's valuable to identify how each person you work with gets both an "organizational win" and a "personal win." For example, if you're buying a new database system, the organizational win might be more flexibility in designing new queries, and the personal win might be gaining a new skill or technology for your resume. Salespeople also learn that it's useful to have a "champion" who can help you understand the organization and the various decision makers you'll need to convince along the way. Within larger organizations, having such a champion you can bounce such ideas off of and strategize with can be a good complement to your technical arguments.

Applying those sales lessons to threat modeling, you can ask the following: Who signs off? It's probably someone like a VP of R&D who could require that no code goes out the door without a threat model. Why will your VP sign off? Fewer bugs? More secure products? Competitive edge? Fewer schedule changes due to fixing security bugs late? What will their personal win be? That's hard to predict. It might be something like helping their engineers add new skills, or less energy spent on making hard security decisions about those bugs.

Convincing Individual Contributors

If you're the only person in the room who wants the team to do something, few managers will sign off. You must convince individual contributors that threat modeling is a worthwhile use of their time. You should start with fun, which means *Elevation of Privilege*. If you don't have one of the professionally produced Microsoft or Wiley decks, spend a bit of energy to print a copy or two in color. Making an activity fun keeps people engaged, and it may help you overcome past poor experiences. Besides, fun is fun. Bringing pizza and beer rarely hurts.

But fun is not enough. At some point you'll need to give everyone a business reason to keep showing up. Maybe modeling the software with good diagrams helps people stay aligned with what's being built. Maybe good security bugs are being found and fixed. Maybe a competitor is falling behind because they're spending all their time cleaning up after a security failure. Identifying the value your team will receive is key to convincing management. Additionally, your effort may not be enough. Having a respected engineer as a champion can be a tremendous help.

NOTE **A test lead in Windows wrote "I can't overstate how much having Larry's support for [this tool] helped us gain credibility in the development community. You should find a Larry equivalent . . . and make sure he is sold on evangelizing the new process/tool."**

There are many objections you might face, which are covered in depth in the "Overcoming Objections to Threat Modeling" section at the end of this chapter. One objection is so common and important that it's threaded throughout the chapter, and worth discussing now: YAGNI. (For those who haven't encountered it, YAGNI is the agile development mantra of "You Ain't Gonna Need It.") YAGNI is a mantra because it's a great way to push back on red tape in the development or operations process. The really tricky challenge in bringing in any new process is that your organization has not gone out of business despite not having that new process—so how do you convince anyone to invest in it?

Convincing Management

Management, at its core, is about bringing people together to accomplish a task (Magretta, 2002). You need management to accomplish tasks that are bigger than one person can do alone. That management can be implicit and shared when two people are collaborating, it can be a general ordering troops into a dangerous situation, and it can be all sorts of things in between. Tim Ferris has written: "The word decision, closely related to incision, derives from the meaning "a cutting off." Making effective decisions—and learning effectively—requires massive elimination and the removal of options" (Ferriss, 2012).

This matters to you because management is management in part because of their ability to say no to good ideas. That sounds harsh, and it is; but you and your coworkers probably have dozens of good ideas every month. A manager who says yes to all of them will never bring a project to fruition. Therefore, an important part of management's job is to eliminate work that isn't highly likely to add enough business value. By default, you don't need whatever the flavor of the month is, and this month, what you don't need may appear to be threat modeling.

Therefore, to convince management, you need a plan with some "proof points." (I really hate that jargon, but I'm betting your management loves it, so I'm going to hold my nose and use it.) One of the very first proof points will probably be buy-in from a co-worker.

Your plan needs to explain what to do, the resources required, and what value you expect it to bring. The way to present your play will vary by organization. The more your proposal aligns with management's expectations, the less time they'll spend figuring out what you mean, and that means more time spent on the content itself. Do you want to train everyone, or just a particular group? Do you want to stop development for a month to comprehensively threat model everything? You'll need more proof points for that. Do you want to require a formal, documented threat model for each sprint? What resources will be required? Do you need a consultant or training company to come in? How much time do you want from how many people? What impact is this investment going to have? How does that compare to other efforts, either in security or some other "property," or even compared to feature work? What evidence do you have that that impact will materialize?

If you are at a smaller organization, this will be less formal than at a large organization. At a large organization, you may find yourself presenting to layers of management and even senior executives. If you are used to presenting to engineers, presenting to executives can be very different. Nancy Duarte has an excellent and concise summary of how to do that in a *Harvard Business Review* article titled "How to Present to Senior Executives" (Duarte, 2012). Whoever you're presenting to, if you are not used to presenting at all, consider it a growth opportunity, not a threat.

Who Does What?

If you want an organization to start doing something, you'll need to figure out exactly who does what and when. This section covers a set of project management issues, such as prerequisites, deliverables, roles and responsibilities, and group interaction topics such as decision models and effective meetings.

Threat Modeling and Project Management

Project management is a big enough discipline to fill books and offer competing certifications. If your organization has project managers, talk to them about fitting threat modeling into their approach. If not, some baseline questions you'll need to answer include the following:

- **Participants:** Who's involved?
- **Tasks:** What do they do?
- **Training:** How do we help them do it?
- **Prep work:** What needs to be done before a kick-off?
- **Help:** What do they do when confused?
- **Conflict management:** Who makes a call when different participants disagree and can't reach a consensus?
- **Deliverables:** What do the people produce?

- **Milestones:** When are deliverables due?
- **Interaction:** How does communication occur (in-person meetings, e-mail, IRC, wikis, etc.)?

As you roll out threat modeling, you'll also need to define tactical process elements for deliverables such as the following:

- What documents need to be created?
- What tooling should be used, and where do you get it?
- Who creates those documents, and who signs off on them?
- When are those documents required, and what work can be held up until they're done?
- How are those documents named?
- Where can someone go to find them?

Most of both lists are self explanatory. The answer to "who" are roles. For example, developers create software diagrams, and development managers sign off on them. Naming is a question of what conventions have been established. For example, is it TM-Featurename-owner.html? Featurename-threat-model .docx? Feature.tms? Feature/threatmodel.xml?

Once you've answered these questions, you'll need to inform those who will be threat modeling. That might be done with a training course, an e-mail informing people of a new process, or it might be a wiki that defines your development or operational process. The approach should line up with how other processes roll out.

Prerequisites

In thinking about threat modeling, it's helpful to define what you need to kick off the threat modeling activity and what the deliverables will be. For example, creating a preliminary model of the software such as a data flow diagram (DFD) and gathering the project stakeholders in a room might be your prerequisites, along with getting *Elevation of Privilege* (and enough copies of this book for everyone!). How you divide the tasks is up to you. Having explicit prerequisites and deliverables can help you integrate threat modeling into other software engineering. It's important to have the right amount of process for your organization, and to respect the YAGNI mantra. Even if your organization isn't one where that's regularly invoked, it's a good idea to focus on the highest value work.

Deliverables

If you're part of an organization that thinks in terms of projects and deliverables, you can consider threat modeling as a project with its own deliverables, or you can integrate smaller activities into other parts of development.

If you treat threat modeling as a project in and of itself, there are a number of deliverables you could look for. The most important include diagrams, security requirements and non-requirements, and bugs. These should be treated like any other artifact created as part of the project, with ownership, version control, and so on. These documents should be focused on the security value you gain from creating them. Some approaches suggest that documents be created especially for the security experts involved in threat modeling, or that the documents must have large sections of introductory text copied in from elsewhere, such as requirements or design documentation. That doesn't add a lot of value. You might be surprised that a list of threats is not a deliverable. That's because lists of threats are not consumed anywhere else in development. Unlike architectural diagrams, requirements, and bugs, they are not easily added. (Bugs are a good intermediate deliverable, and are the way to bring threat lists beyond the threat modeling tasks.)

You'll need to define what the deliverables are called, where they're stored, what gates or quality checks are in place, and where they feed into. These deliverables are delivered to, and must be of a quality that's acceptable to, the project owner. Even if they are created or used by security experts, they should be designed for use by the folks to whom they are delivered. Depending on how structured an approach to threat modeling you have, there may be other, intermediate documents created as part of the process.

So when should you produce these deliverables? If you consider threat modeling as part of other work, you could look at maintaining or updating your software model as something that happens at the start of a sprint. Finding threats could happen as part of that model, as part of test planning, or at another time that makes sense for your project. Addressing threats can become a step in bug triage.

As the participants become more experienced and an organization's threat-modeling muscles develop, the approach will likely become less rigid, and more fluid, and stepping between activities more natural. Such a process might look like what is illustrated in Figure 17-1.

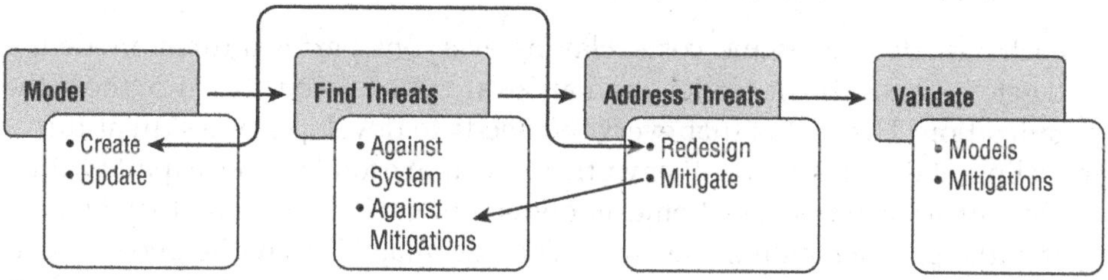

Figure 17-1: A four-stage approach with feedback

It's also possible to develop an organization's capabilities around the interplay of requirements, threats, and mitigations, as discussed in Chapter 12, "Requirements

Cookbook." As described there and shown in Figure 12-1, reproduced here as Figure 17-2, real threats violate requirements and can be mitigated in some way.

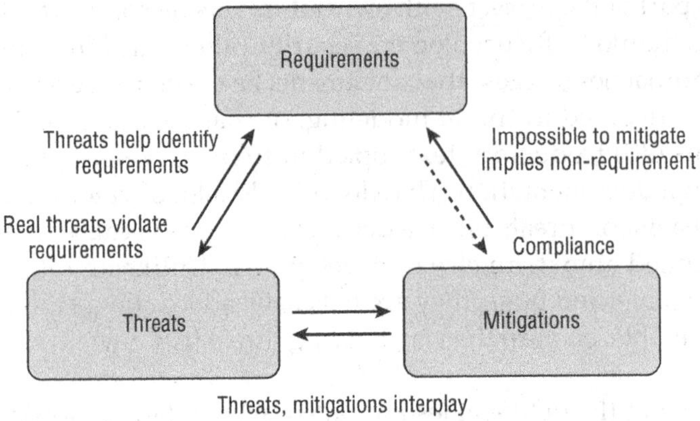

Figure 17-2: The interplay of threats, requirements, and mitigations

Direct interaction is much more common between threats and requirements and threats and mitigations. The interaction between threats and requirements may lead to you trying to implement both a threat modeling process and a requirements process at the same time. Doing so would be a challenging task, and should not be taken on lightly.

Individual Roles and Responsibilities

When an organization wants work done, it assigns that work to people. This section covers how you can do so.

There are roughly three models that can be employed:

- Everyone threat models.
- Experts within the business are consulted.
- Consultants (internal or external) are used.

Each has advantages and costs. Having everyone perform threat modeling will get you basic threat models, and an awareness of security throughout the organization. The cost is that everyone needs to develop some skill at threat modeling, at the expense of other work. Using the second model, experts within the organization report to whomever owns product delivery, and they work as part of the product team on security. The advantage is that one person owns delivery of the threat model and how that's integrated into the product. The disadvantage is that person needs to be present at all the right meetings, and that won't always happen. Even with the best intentions, people may not realize they're going to make security decisions, or the security person may be triple-booked when everyone else is available. The final model uses consultants, either from within the company or external. Either way, consultants offer the advantage of specialization in threat modeling, but the disadvantage of lacking product context. External consultants can be extra valuable because management values what it pays for, and external consultants can sometimes deliver bad news with less worry about politics. However, external consultants may be more restricted than internal ones in terms of what they may be exposed to. Furthermore, external consultants often deliver a report that is filed away, without further action taken. You can mitigate that risk by having one of their deliverables be a list of bugs, which either they or someone in your organization can file.

An additional consideration is how people get help when needed. In smaller organizations, this can be organic; in larger ones, having a defined way to get help can be very helpful.

The next question is what sort of skill sets or roles should be assigned threat modeling tasks? The answer, of course, is that there's more than one way to do it, and the right way is the one that works for your organization. Even within one organization, there might be multiple right ways to do it, and multiple right ways to split up the work.

For example, one business unit within Microsoft has made threat modeling a part of the program management job. In another it is driven by the software developers. Yet another has split it up so that development owns creating the diagrams, and test owns ensuring that there's an appropriate test plan, including finding threats against the system with STRIDE per element. What works for your organization cannot be a matter of one person succeeding at the tasks. Don't get me wrong—that's a necessary start. If no enthusiast has succeeded at the tasks and produced bugs that were worth fixing, you can't expect anyone else to waste their time. That may seem harsh, but if you, as the enthusiast reading this book, can't demonstrate value, how can others be expected to?

Group Interaction

Three important elements of group interaction are who's in the group, how they make decisions, and how to hold effective meetings.

Group Composition

As you move from an individual threat modeling to a group effort, a natural question is what sorts of people form the group? Generally, you'll want to include the following (example job titles are shown in parentheses):

- People who are building the system (developers, architects, systems administrators, devops)
- People who will be testing the system (QA, test)

- People who understand the business goals of the system (product managers, business representatives, program managers)
- People who are tracking and managing progress (project managers, project coordinators, program managers)

Decision Models

In any group activity, there is a risk of conflict, and organizations take a variety of approaches to managing those conflicts and reaching decisions. It is important to align threat modeling decision making with whatever your organization does to make decisions, and consider where decisions may need to be made. The issues most likely to be contentious are requirements and bugs. For requirements, the issue is "what's a requirement?" For bugs, issues can include what constitutes a bug, what severity bugs have, and what bugs can be deferred or not fixed. Tools like bug bars can help (as covered in Chapter 9, "Trade-Offs When Addressing Threats"), but you will still need a way to resolve disputes.

There are a variety of decision matrices that break out decision responsibility in various ways. One of the most common is RACI: Responsible, Approver, Consulted, Informed. Responsible indicates those people who are assigned tasks and possibly deliverables. The approver makes decisions when conflict can't be handled otherwise. Those who are consulted may expect that someone will ask for their opinions, but they do not have authority to make the decisions. The last group is kept informed about progress. Various implementations will define who is expected to escalate or object in various ways, with those in the informed or consulted categories less expected to escalate. Table 17-1 shows part of a sample RACI matrix for security activities including threat modeling (Meier, 2003). The line listed as design principles is similar to my use of "requirements."

Table 17-1: A Sample RACI Matrix for Threat Modeling and Related Tasks

TASKS	ARCHITECT	SYSTEM ADMINISTRATOR	DEVELOPER	TESTER	SECURITY PROFESSIONAL
Threat Modeling	A		I	I	R
Security Design Principles	A	I	I		C
Security Architecture	A	C			R
Architecture Design and Review	R				A

Another large (product) team at Microsoft broke out threat modeling by discipline and activity within threat modeling, using a model of "own (O), participate (P), and validate (V)," as shown in Table 17-2.

Table 17-2: Threat Modeling Tasks by Role

SESSION	ARCHITECT	PROGRAM MANAGER	SOFTWARE TEST	PENETRATION TEST	DEVELOPER	SECURITY CONSULTANT
Requirements	O	O	V	P	V	
Model (software)	P	P	O	V	O	
Threat Enumeration	P	P	V	O	V	
Mitigations	P	P	O	V	O	
Validate	O	O	P	P	P	V

Effective TM Meetings

A great deal has been written about how to run an effective meeting, because running an effective meeting is hard. Common issues include missing or unclear agendas, confusion over meeting goals, and wasting time. This leads to a lot of people working hard to avoid meetings, and I'm quite sympathetic to that goal. Threat modeling often includes people with different perspectives discussing complex and contentious topics. This may make it a good candidate for holding one or more meetings, or even setting up a regular meeting for a long threat modeling project. It's also helpful to define the meetings as either decision meetings, working meetings or review meetings. Each may be required, and clarity about the goals of a meeting makes it more likely that it will be effective.

The agenda for a threat modeling meeting can be complex because numerous tasks might need to be handled, including the following:

- Project kickoff
- Diagramming or modeling the software
- Threat discovery
- Bug triage

These different tasks may lead to different meeting structure or goals:

- Creating a model of the software with a diagram can be a collaborative, action-oriented meeting with a clear deliverable. If the right people are in the room, they can likely judge whether the model of the software is complete.
- Threat discovery can be a collaborative brainstorming meeting, and while the deliverables are clear, completeness is less obvious.
- Bug triage may be performed in a decision meeting with an identified decision process or decision maker.

These different goals are often overlapped into a single "threat modeling" meeting. If you need to overlap, consider using three whiteboards or easels: one for diagrams, one for threats, and one for the bugs. Label each clearly and explain that each is different and has different rules. Physically moving from one whiteboard to the next can help establish the rule set for that portion of a meeting. However, it is challenging to go from collaborative to authoritative and back within a single meeting. Generally, that means it will be challenging to triage bugs in a diagram or threat-focused meeting. Similarly, threat modeling meetings with a goal of creating a document are probably not a good use of everyone's time. Finally, holding a meeting without a designated note taker will be a lot less effective.

A good threat modeling meeting focuses on tasks that require each person in the room to be present. It is likely that the meeting will require people from each discipline in your organization (such as programmers and testers). A threat model review with the wrong folks is not just a waste of time, it risks leaving you and your organization with a false sense of confidence. Make sure that you have the right architects, drivers, or whatever else is organizationally appropriate. These people can be quite busy, so it helps to ensure that they get value from the meetings, which in turn helps to ensure that the entire team shares a mental model of the system, which makes development and operations flow more smoothly.

One last comment about meetings. Words matter greatly. Threat modeling can be contentious under the best of circumstances. Meetings are far more likely to be effective if discoveries and discussions are about *the* code or *the* feature, rather than *Alice's* code or *Bob's* feature. They'll also be more effective if those presenting the system focus on what's being built, rather than the whys. (I recall one meeting in which every third sentence seemed to be about why the system was impenetrable. What turned out to be impenetrable was the description, not the system.) Similarly, you want to avoid words that inflame anyone. For example, if people believe that discussing attacks implies advocating criminal activity, then it's probably best to use another word such as threat or vulnerability; or if a team is concerned that the term "breach" implies mandatory reporting, it might be better to discuss incidents. As a last fallback, you can say "issue" or "thing." If your threat modeling meetings become contentious, it may help to start with a brief statement from the meeting leader about the scope, goals, and process for the meeting, or even to have neutral moderators join in. The skill sets required of the moderators will depend on what turns out to be contentious.

Diversity in Threat Modeling Teams

Regardless of what you're threat modeling, it's useful to bring a diverse set of skills and perspectives to bear on analyzing a system. If you're building software, that includes those who write and test code, while if it's an operational project, it might be systems managers and architects. Unless it's a small project, it will probably also include project management.

You'll need to figure out to what extent customers or customer advocates should be involved. Often, these perspectives will inform your decisions about what's important, what's an acceptable threat, or where you need to focus your attention.

For example, in discussing their voting system threat model, Alec Yanisac and colleagues mention the enormous value they observed from bringing together technologists, election officials, and accessibility experts with voting systems vendors. They attributed a great deal of their success to having the various parties in the same place to discuss trade-offs and feasibility (Yanisac, 2012).

Bringing in a wide set of skills, perspectives, and backgrounds can slow down discussion as people go through the team formation process of "storming, forming, norming and performing." The more diversity in the group, the longer such a process will take. However, the more diverse group will also be able to find a broader set of threats.

Threat Modeling within a Development Life Cycle

Any organization that is already developing software has some sort of process or system that helps it move the software from whiteboard to customers. Smart organizations have formalized that process in some way, and try to repeat the good parts from cycle to cycle. Sometimes that includes security activities, but not always.

NOTE **A full discussion about how to bring security into your development life cycle is beyond the scope of this book. One could make the case that threat modeling should always be the first security activity an organization undertakes, but that sort of one-size-fits-all thinking is one of the ideas that I hope this book puts to rest. Other activities, such as fuzzing, may have a lower cost of entry and produce bugs faster.**

On the other hand, an hour of whiteboard threat modeling can point that fuzzer in the right direction. More important, it's helpful to think of security as something that permeates through development and deployment. One good resource for thinking about this is the Security Development Lifecycle Optimization Model (`http://www.microsoft.com/security/sdl/learn/assess.aspx`).

Development Process Issues

In this section, you'll learn about bringing threat modeling into either waterfall or agile development, how to integrate threat modeling into operational planning, and how to measure threat modeling.

Waterfalls and Gates

If you're using something like a waterfall process, then threat modeling plays in at several stages, including requirements, design, and testing. (You doubtless slice your development process a little differently than the next team, but you should have roughly similar phases.) During requirements and design, you create models of the software, and you find threats. Of course, you let those activities influence each other. During testing, you ensure that the software you built matches the model of the software you intended to build, and you ensure that you're properly resolving your bugs.

If your process includes gates (sometimes also called functional milestones), such as "we can't exit the design phase until . . . ," then those gates can be helpful places to integrate threat modeling tasks. Following are a few examples:

- We can't exit design without a completed model of the software for threat identification, such as a DFD.
- We can't start coding until threat enumeration is complete.
- Test plans can't be marked complete until threat enumeration is complete.
- Each mitigation is complete when there's a feature spec (or spec section) to cover the mitigation.

Threat Modeling in Agile

The process of diagramming, identifying, and addressing threats doesn't need to be a waterfall. It's been presented like that to help you understand it, but you can jump back and forth between the tasks as appropriate for your team or organization. There's nothing inherent to threat modeling that is at odds with being agile. (There is an awful lot of writing on threat modeling that is process heavy. That's not the same as threat modeling being inherently process heavy.) Feel free to apply YAGNI to whatever extent it makes sense for you.

Now, you might get super-duper agile and say, "Threat models? We ain't gonna need them." That may be true. You've probably gotten away without threat models to date, and you're worried that threat modeling as described doesn't feel agile. (If that's the case, thanks for reading this far.) One agile practice that seems to relate very closely to threat modeling is test-driven design. In test-driven design, you carefully consider your tests before you start writing code, using the tests to drive conversations about what the code will really do. Threat modeling is a way to think through your security threats, and derive a set of test cases.

If you believe that threat modeling can be useful, you'll need a model of the software and a model of the threats. That can be a whiteboard model, using STRIDE or *Elevation of Privilege* to drive discussion of the threats.

Even if you're not an agile maven, YAGNI can be a useful perspective. When you're adding something to the diagram, are you going to need that there? When you identify a threat, can you address it? Someone taking out the hard drive and editing bits is hard to address. You won't need that threat.

If you're in the YAGNI camp, you might be saying, "That last security problem was really a painful way to spend a week," or you might be looking at these arguments and asking, "Do we have important security threats?" If you are in an "already experiencing pain" scenario, then you probably don't need any more selling. Pick and choose from the techniques in this book to find a set of trade-offs that work in your agile environment. If you're in the skeptical camp, you've looked at a lot of arguments for an appropriately sized investment in threat modeling. That is, invest in a small agile experiment: Try it yourself on a real system, and see if the result justifies doing more.

Operations Planning

Much like planning development, there's more than one way to plan for new deployments of networks, software, or systems. (For simplicity, please read systems as inclusive of any technology you might be planning to deploy.) Integrating threat modeling into deployment processes involves the maintenance of models of the system. These models are, admittedly, rarely prioritized, but without knowing what a system looks like, understanding the scope or impact of a change due to a new deployment is more challenging.

Finding threats against a system is a matter of understanding the changes that occur as systems are operated or modified, and ensuring that you look for threats where changes are happening. Often, but not always, the new threats are associated with changes to connectivity (including firewalls).

The (acceptance or deployment) testing of a change should include any planned mitigations, checking to see whether the mitigations were deployed, and checking that they both allow what's planned, and prevent what they are expected to deny. Checking the deny rules can be a tricky step. It's easy to find one case and see if it's denied, but checking the full set of what should be denied can be challenging.

Testing and Threat Modeling

Don't underestimate the value of skilled testers to threat modeling. The testing mindset that asks the question "How can this break?" overlaps with threat modeling. Each threat is an answer to that question. Each layer of threat mitigation and response is a bug variant. Looking for the weakest link is similar to test planning. Unit tests can look like vulnerability proof-of-concept code. Therefore, your testers (under whatever name they work) are natural allies. Furthermore, threat modeling can solve a number of problems for testers, including the following:

- Testing is undervalued.
- Limited career advancement
- Exclusion from meetings

Testing is sometimes undervalued, and testers often feel their work is not valued. Helping them find important bugs can increase the importance of testing, and help security practitioners get those bugs fixed.

Related to the problem of being undervalued, testers often feel like their career path is more limited than that of developers. Working with testers to enable them to perform effective security tests can help open new career paths.

Lastly, developers and architects often feel that architectural choices are detached from testing or testability, and do not bother to include testers in those discussions. When threat modeling drives security test planning, seeing the software models early becomes an important part of test activity, and this may drive greater inclusion.

This can be a virtuous circle, in which quality assurance and threat modeling are mutually reinforcing.

Measuring Threat Modeling

In any organization, it is helpful to be able to measure the quality of a product. Measuring threat modeling is a complex topic, in the same way that measuring software development is tricky. The first blush approaches, such as measuring the number of diagrams or lines of code, don't really measure the right things. The appropriate measurements will depend on the threat modeling techniques you're using and the security or quality goals of the business. You can measure how much or how broadly a larger business is applying threat modeling, and you can measure the threat model documents themselves. When you measure the models themselves, two approaches can be used: *pass or fail*, and *additive scoring*.

Either approach can start from a checklist. For example, in the Microsoft SDL Threat Modeling Tool, there's a four-element checklist per threat. (Does the threat have text? Does the mitigation have text? Is the threat marked "complete"? Is there a bug?) At the end, each threat has either a score of 0–4 or a pass (at 4). You could apply similar logic to a data flow diagram. Is there at least one process and one external entity? Is there a trust boundary? Is it labeled? You can assess the model as a whole. In *The Security Development Lifecycle*, Howard and Lipner present the scoring system shown as Table 17-3 (Microsoft Press, 2006).

Table 17-3: Measuring Threat Models

RATING	COMMENTS
0 – No threat model	No TM in place, unacceptable
1 – Not acceptable	Out of date indicated by design changes or document age
2 – OK	DFD with "assets" (processes, data stores, data flows), users, trust boundaries At least one threat per asset Mitigations for threats above a certain risk level Current
3 – Good	Meets the OK bar, plus: Anon, authenticated local and remote users shown S,T,I,E threats all accepted or mitigated
4 – Excellent	Meets the good bar, plus: All STRIDE threats identified, mitigated, plus external security notes and dependencies identified Mitigations for all threats "External security notes" include plan for customer-facing documentation

A more nuanced approach would score the various building blocks separately. Diagram scoring might involve a quality ranking by participants, tracking the rate of change (or requested changes), and the presence of the appropriate external entities. Threat scoring could entail a measure of threats identified (as in Table 17-3), or perhaps coverage of first- and second-order threats.

You might also use a combination of pass/fail and additive. For example, if you were using a bar and each threat needs a 5 on some 7-point scale, you could then sum the threats, requiring a 50, or 10 points per DFD element, or you could start from whatever level the "good" threat models you look at seem to be hitting. You might also require an improvement over a prior project, perhaps 10 percent or 15 percent higher scores. Such an approach encourages people to do better without requiring an unreasonable investment in improvement for a given release.

MEASURING THE WRONG THING

People focus their energy on the things that are measured by those who reward them. People also expect that if you're measuring something, there's a pass bar that indicates what is good enough. Both of these behaviors are risks for threat modeling for the same reason that few organizations measure lines of code or bugs as a measure of software productivity: Measurements can drive the wrong behavior. (There's a classic Dilbert on wrong behaviors, with the punch line, "I'm gonna write me a new minivan this afternoon!" [Adams, 1995])

Therefore, measuring threat modeling might be counterproductive. It may be that measuring is a useful way to help people develop threat modeling muscles. You might be able to use people's instinct to "game" the scoring system by awarding points for reporting (good) bugs in the threat modeling approach .

One other possible issue with a measurement scale is that it's likely to stop too early. The Howard-Lipner scoring system described earlier stops at "excellent," reducing the incentive to strive beyond that point. What if it had an "awesome" level, which was awarded at the discretion of the scorer?

When to Complete Threat Modeling Activities

The tasks discussed in this section relate closely to the section "Iteration" in Chapter 7, "Digging Deeper into Mitigations." The difference is that as threat modeling moves from an individual activity (as discussed in Chapter 7 to an activity situated within an organization (as discussed in this chapter), the organization may want some degree of consistency.

Two organizational factors affect when to complete threat modeling:

- Is it a separate activity?
- How deep do you go?

Threat modeling can be a separate activity or integrated into other work. It is very helpful to threat model early in the development cycle, when requirements and designs are being worked out. This is threat modeling in the sense of requirements analysis, finding threats, and designing mitigations. As you get close to release or delivery, it is also helpful to validate that the models match what you've built, that the mitigations weren't thoughtlessly pushed to the next version or a backlog, and that the test bugs have been addressed.

The question of how deep you go is an important one. Many security practitioners like to say "you're never done threat modeling." Steve Jobs liked to say "great artists ship." (That makes you wonder, was he familiar with the career of Leonardo da Vinci? On the other hand, Leonardo's work languished in obscurity for hundreds of years.) It is almost always a good idea to start with breadth first, and then iterate through threat modeling your mitigations. How long you should continue is an understudied area. In a security-perfect world, you could continue as long as you're productively finding threats, and then stop. One good way to justify needing more time to threat model mitigations is if you can find attacks against them with a few minutes of consideration or by reviewing similar mitigations. Unfortunately, that requires experience, and that experience is expensive.

Postmortems and Feedback Loops

There are two salient times to analyze your threat modeling activity: immediately after reaching a milestone and after finding an issue in code that was threat modeled and shipped. The easiest is right after some milestone, while the potentially more valuable is when threats are found by outsiders. After a milestone, memories are fresh, the work is recent, and the involved participants are available. You can ask questions such as the following:

- Was that effective?
- What can we do better?
- What tasks should we ensure that we continue to perform?

All of the standard sorts of questions that you ask in a development or operations after-incident analysis can be applied to threat modeling.

The second sort of analysis is after an issue is found. You'll want to consider whether it's the sort of thing that your threat modeling should have prevented; and if you believe it is, try to understand why it was not prevented. For example, you might have not thought of that threat, which might mean spending more time finding threats, or adding structure to the process. You might misunderstand the design or deployment scenarios, in which case more effort on appropriate modeling might be helpful. Or you might have found the threat and decided it wasn't worth addressing or documenting.

Organizational Issues

These issues relate less to process and more to the organizational structures that surround threat modeling. These issues include who leads (such as programmers or testers or systems architects), training, modifying ladders, and how to interview for threat modeling.

Who Leads?

The question of who is responsible for ensuring that threat modeling happens varies according to organization, and depends heavily on the people involved and their skills and aptitudes. It also depends on to what degree the organization is led by individuals driving tasks versus having a process or collaborative approach.

Breaking threat modeling into subtasks, such as software modeling, threat enumeration, mitigation planning, and validation, can offer more flexibility to assign the tasks to different people. The following guidelines may be helpful:

- Developers leading threat modeling activity can be effective when developers are the strongest technical contributors or when they have more decision-making power than people in other roles. Developers are often well positioned to create and provide a model of the software they plan to build, but having them lead the threat modeling activity carries the risk of "creator blindness"—that is, not seeing threats in features they built, or not seeing the importance of those threats.
- Testers driving the process can be effective if your testers are technical; and as discussed earlier in the section "Testing and Threat Modeling," it can be a powerful way to align security and test goals. Testers can be great at threat enumeration.
- Program managers or project managers can lead. A threat model diagram or threat list is just another spec that they create as part of making a great product. Program/project managers can ensure that all subtasks are executed appropriately.
- Security practitioners can own the process, as long as they understand the development or deployment processes well enough to integrate effectively. Depending on the type of practitioner, they can be intensely helpful in threat enumeration, mitigation planning, and validation.
- Architects (either IT architects or business architects) can also own threat modeling, ensuring that it's a step that they execute as they develop a new design. Much like developers, architects are well positioned to provide a model of the system being built, but can be at risk of creator blindness.

Regardless of who owns, leads, or drives, threat modeling tasks tend to span disciplines and require collaboration, with all the trickiness that can entail.

Training

From the dawn of time, threat modeling has been passed down from master to apprentice. Oh, who am I kidding? People have learned to threat model from their buddies. It's typically experiential learning, without a lot of the structure that this book is bringing to the field. That kind of informal apprenticeship has (you'll be shocked to learn) pros and cons. The advantage is having someone who can answer questions. The disadvantage is that without any structure, when the mentor leaves sometimes the "apprentices" flail around. Thus, the trick for security practitioners is to truly mentor, rather than dominate. That might involve leading questions, or debriefs before or after tasks.

When an organization begins its foray into threat modeling, participants need to be trained and told how they'll be evaluated. Threat modeling includes a large set of tasks, and it's important to be clear about what those tasks entail and how they should be accomplished. This takes very different forms in different organizations, including approaches like written process documentation, brown bag lunches, formal classroom training, computer-based training, and my favorite, *Elevation of Privilege*. Of course, *Elevation of Privilege* doesn't cover process elements such as what documents need to be created, so that can be integrated into the skill-teaching portion of a training.

Modifying Ladders

Job "ladders" are a common way to structure and differentiate levels of seniority within an organization. For example, someone hired right out of school would start as a junior developer, be promoted to developer, then senior developer. So let me get this out of the way. Ladders are a big company thing. They're bureaucracy personified, and reflect what happens when humans are treated as resources, not individuals. If your company is a small start-up, ladders are antithetical to the artisanal approach that it personifies; but if you want to introduce threat modeling to a company that uses them, they're a darned useful tool for setting expectations.

When you have an idea of what threat modeling approach and details work for your organization, and when you have a set of people repeatedly performing threat modeling tasks and demonstrating impact, talk to your management about what they see. Are all the people doing the same tasks in the same way? Are they delivering to the same quality and with similar impact, or are there distinctions? If there are distinctions, do they show up among individuals at different levels on the current ladders? If so, great; those distinctions are candidates for addition to the core or optional skills that define a ladder.

If, for example, your organization has five levels on the software engineering ladders, with a 1 being just out of college, and a 5 being the top, determine whether some level of subcompetency in threat modeling, such as diagram creation or using STRIDE per element, can be added to the ladder, at level 2 or 3, and then everyone who wants to be promoted must demonstrate those skills. At the higher end, perhaps refactoring or operational deployment changes have been rolled out to address systemic threats. Those would be candidate skills to expect to see at level 4 or 5.

Interviewing for Threat Modeling

When threat modeling becomes a skill set you hire or promote for, it can help to have some interview techniques. This section simply presents some questions and techniques to get you started. The same questions apply effectively to software and operations folks, but the answers will be quite different.

General knowledge

1. Tell me about threat modeling.
2. What are the pros and cons of using DFDs in threat modeling?
3. Describe STRIDE per element threat modeling.
4. How could you mitigate a threat such as X?
5. How would you approach mitigating a threat such as X?

Questions 4 and 5 are subtly different; the former asks for a list, whereas the latter asks the interviewee to demonstrate judgment and be able to discuss trade-offs. Depending on the circumstance, it might be interesting to see if the candidate asks questions to ensure he or she understands the context and constraints around the issue.

Skills testing

1. Have the candidate ask you architectural questions and draw a DFD.
2. Give the candidate a DFD, and ask them to find threats against the system.
3. Give the candidate one or more threats and ask them to describe (or code) a way to address it.

Behavior-based questioning

Behavior-based interviewing is an interview technique in which questions are asked about a specific past situation. The belief is that by moving away from generic questions, such as "How would you approach mitigating a threat such as X?" to "Tell me about a time you mitigated a threat such as X," the interviewee is moved from platitudes to real situations, and the interviewer can ask probing questions to understand what the candidate really did. Of course, the questions suggested here are simply starting points, and much of the value will result from the follow-up questions:

1. Tell me about your last threat modeling experience.
2. Tell me about a threat modeling bug that you had to fight for.
3. Tell me about a situation in which you discovered that a big chunk of a threat model diagram was missing.
4. Tell me about the last time you threat modeled an interview situation.

Threat Modeling As a Discipline

The last question related to who does what is: "Can we as a community make threat modeling into a discipline?" By a discipline, I mean, can enthusiasts expect threat modeling to be a career description, in the way that software engineer or quality assurance engineering is a career?

Today, it would be an unusual VP of engineering who didn't have a strategy for achieving a predictable level of quality in any releases, and a person or team assigned to ensure that it happens. It's no accident that the past few decades have seen the development of software quality assurance as a discipline. The people who cared greatly about software quality spent time and energy discussing what they do, why they do it, and how to sell and reward it within an organization.

Whatever name it goes by, and whatever nuances or approaches an organization applies, quality assurance has become a recognized organizational discipline. As such, it has career paths. There are skill sets that are commonly associated with titles or ladder levels. There are local variations, and an important division between those who write code to test code and a shrinking set that is paid to test software manually. However, there are recognized types of impact and leadership, along with a set of skills related to strategy, planning, budgeting, mentoring, and developing those around you—all of which are expected as one becomes more senior. Those expectations (and the associated rewards) are a result of testers forming a community, learning to demonstrate value to their organization and sharing those lessons with their peers, and a host of related activities. Furthermore, the discipline exists across a wide variety of organizations. You can move relatively smoothly from being a "software development engineer in test" at one company to a "software engineer in test" at another.

Should threat modelers aspire to the same? Is threat modeling a career path? Is it the sort of skill set that an organization will reward in and of itself, or is threat modeling more analogous to being able to program in Python? That is, is it a skill set within the professional toolbox of many software developers, but one that you don't expect every developer to know? It may be something your organization already does, and if a candidate knows Perl, not Python, then you'll expect that he or she can pick up Python. Or threat modeling may be more similar to version control in your organization. You expect a candidate at one level above entry grade to be able to talk about version control, branches, and integration, but that may not be sufficient to hire the person. Conversely, perhaps only a basic skill level is required, and hiring managers don't expect most people to develop much beyond that.

Perhaps threat modeling is more similar to performance expertise. There are tools to help, such as profilers, and it's easy to get started with one. There are also people with a deep knowledge of how to use them, who can have detailed conversations about what the tools mean. Expertise in making systems fast can be a real differentiator for some engineers in development or operations.

Nothing in this section should be taken as an argument that threat modeling can't develop to the extent that quality has. Quality as a discipline has been developing for decades, and it's entirely possible that over time, the security, development, or operations communities will see ways to make threat modeling a discipline in and of itself. In the meantime, we need to develop its value proposition within today's disciplines and career ladders.

Customizing a Process For Your Organization

As discussed in Chapter 6 "Privacy Tools," the Internet Engineering Task Force (IETF) has an approach to threat modeling that is focused on their needs as a standards organization. You can treat it as an interesting case study of how the situation and demands of an organization influence process design. The approach is covered in "Guidelines for Writing RFC Text on Security Considerations" (Rescorla, 2003). The guidelines cover how to find threats, how to address them, and how to communicate them to a variety of audiences. What threats the IETF will consider was the subject of intense discussion at their November, 2013 meeting (Brewer, 2013). That discussion continues as this book goes to press, but the approach used over the last decade will remain a valuable case study.

The document by Rescorla focuses on three security properties: confidentiality, data integrity, and peer authentication. There is also a brief discussion of availability. Their approach is explicitly focused on an attacker with "nearly complete control of the communications channel." The document describes how to address threats, providing a repertoire of ways that network engineers can provide first and second order mitigations and the tradeoffs associated with those mitigations. The threat enumeration and designing of mitigations are precursors to the creation of a security consideration section. The security considerations section is required for all new RFCs, and so acts as a gate to ensure that threat enumeration and mitigation design have taken place. These sections are a form of external security note, focused on the needs of implementers, and they also disclose the residual threats, a form of non-requirement. These forms are discussed further in Chapter 7 and Chapter 12.

You'll note that their threats are a subset of STRIDE, without repudiation or elevation of privilege. This makes sense for the IETF, defining the behavior of the network protocols, rather than the endpoints. The IETF's situation is somewhat unusual in that respect. Few other organizations define network protocols. But many organizations ship products in a family, and the products in that family will often face similar threats, allowing for a learning process and some reuse of work. The IETF is also a large organization that can amortize that work over many products.

However, the IETF, like your organization, can make decisions about what threats matter most to them, to assemble lessons about mitigation techniques, and to develop an approach to communicating with those who use their products. You can learn from what the IETF does.

Overcoming Objections to Threat Modeling

Earlier, you learned that your plan needs to explain what to do, what resources are required, and what value you expect it to bring. Objections can be raised against each of these, so it's important to talk about handling them. As you develop a plan, many of the objections that will be raised are valid. (Even invalid objections probably have a somewhat valid basis, even if it's only that someone doesn't like change or they like to argue.) Some of these objections will be feedback-like, and expressed as ways to improve your plan. To the extent that they don't remove value, incorporating as many of these as possible helps people realize that you're listening to them, which in turn helps them "buy in" and support your plan. Obviously, if a suggestion is counterproductive, you want to address it. For example, someone might say, "Don't we need to start threat modeling from our assets?" and you could respond, "Well, that's a common approach, but I haven't seen it add anything to threat models and it often seems to be a rathole. And since Alice has already expressed concern about the cost of these tasks, maybe we should try it without assets first."

As you listen to objections, it may be helpful to model them as threats to one or more elements of the plan (resource, value, or planning), and start from the overall response, getting more specific as needed. Note that (all models are wrong) these meld together pretty quickly, and (some models are useful) it might be useful to ask clarifying questions. For example, if someone is objecting to the number of people involved, is that a concern about the resourcing involved, or about the quality of the evidence relative to the proposal?

Resource Objections

Objections in this group relate to the input side of the equation. At some point, even the largest organizations have no more money to spend on security, and management will start making trade-offs; but before you get there, you may well reach objections to the size of the investment. Examples include too many people or too much work per person.

Too Many People

How many people are you proposing get involved in threat modeling? It may be that your proposal really does take time from too many people. This may be a resource objection, or it may be a way of presenting a value objection (it's too many people for the expected value), or it may be a proof objection—that is, your evidence is insufficient for the organization to make the investment.

Too Much Work per Person

There are only 24 hours in a day, and only 8 or 10 of them are working hours. If you're proposing that your most senior people should spend an hour per day threat modeling, that requires pushing aside that much other work. Especially if they're senior people, that work is probably important and requires their time. A typical software process might incorporate not only the feature being worked on, but properties such as security, privacy, usability, reliability, programmability, accessibility, internationalization, and so on. Each of these is an important property, and at the end of the day, it can overwhelm the actual feature work (Shostack, 2011b). You'll need to craft your proposal to constrain how much time is asked of each person. You may want to suggest what should be removed from people's workload, but doing so may anger someone who has worked to ensure that those tasks happen.

Too Much Busywork/YAGNI

A lot of activities associated with older approaches to threat modeling are like busywork, or they invite the objection that "you ain't gonna need it". Examples include entering a description of the project into a threat modeling tool (hey, it's in the spec) or listing all your assumptions (what do you do with that?). If you get this objection, you'll want to show how each of your activities and artifacts is used and valued by people later in the chain.

Value Objections

Objections in this group relate to the output side of the equation. Someone might well believe that security investments are a good idea, but this particular proposal doesn't reach the bar.

"I've Tried Threat Modeling. . ."

Many people have tried various threat modeling approaches, and many of those approaches provided incredibly low value for the work invested. It is tremendously important to respect this objection, and to understand exactly what the objector has done. You might even have to listen to them vent for a while. Once you understand what they did and where it broke down, you'll need to distinguish your proposal by showing how it is different.

There are both practical and personal objections based on past experience. The practical objections stem from complex, inefficient, or ineffective approaches that have been advocated elsewhere. Those objections inform the approaches in this book. However, there are also personal objections, from where those ineffective approaches were pushed in ways that repelled people. There are a number of mistakes you should avoid, including:

- Not training people in what you want them to do
- Give people contradictory or confusing advice.
- Threat model when it's too late to fix anything.
- Condescend to people when they make mistakes.
- Focus on process, rather than results.

"We Don't Fix Those Bugs"

If your approach to threat modeling is producing many bugs that are resolved with something like `WONTFIX`, then that's a problem. It might be that the approach finds bugs that don't matter, or it might be that the organization sets the bar high for determining which bugs matter. In either event, some adjustment is called for. If it's the approach, can you categorize the bugs that are being punted? Is it entities outside some boundary? Stop analyzing there. Is it a class of unfixable bugs? Document it once, and stop filing bugs for it. If it's one of the STRIDE types, perhaps lowering the priority until the organization is more willing to accept those bugs will help you address other security bugs. If it's the organizational response, is a single individual making the call? If so, perhaps talking to that person to understand their prioritization rationale would help.

"No One Would Ever Do That"

This objection (and its close relative, "Why would anyone do that?") is less an objection to threat modeling per se than to specific bugs being fixed. Generally, the best way to address these concerns is to look through the catalog of attackers in Appendix C "Attacker Lists" and find one who plausibly might "do that," and/or find an instance of a similar attack being executed, possibly against another product. If you respond by saying "If I can find you an example, will you agree to fix it?" then you distinguish between where the objector really thinks no one would ever do that, and where the real objection is that the fix seems hard or changes a cherished feature.

Objections to the Plan

If you have a reasonable amount of investment to produce a reasonable return, you may still not get approval. Recall that management is management because they'll say no to good ideas. Therefore, your threat modeling proposal not only has to be good enough to overcome that bar, it has to overcome that bar in the particular circumstances when the proposal is made. Several of those circumstances relate to the state of the organization, and include factors such as timing and recent change, among other things. They also include things particular to your plan, such as other security activity or the quality of evidence you provide for your plan.

Timing

Management may already be investing in a couple of pilot projects, or one may have just blown up in their face. It may be the day after the budget was locked. A global recession may have just hit. These are hard objections to overcome. The best bet may be to ask when would be the right time to come back.

Change

Changing the behavior of individuals is hard, and changing the behaviors of an organization is even harder. Change requires adjustment of people, processes, and habits. Each adjustment, however much it will eventually help, requires time and energy that are taken away from productive work. Each person involved in a change wants to know how it will impact them; and if the impact is not positive, they may oppose or impede it. As such, people often fear change, and managers fear kicking off changes. If your organization has just been through a big change or a difficult change, appetite for more may be lacking.

Other Security Activity

The challenge may be that you have a decent investment proposal and decent return but the return on another security investment is higher. The ways to overcome this are either an adjustment to the investment or finding a way to improve the return. A key part of that strategy is emphasizing that finding bugs early is cheaper than finding them late. For some bugs that's because you avoid dependencies on the bug, but for many it's because the cheapest bugs to fix are the ones that you head off before you implement them. Similarly, if you can show that threat modeling could have prevented a class of bugs that continue to cause problems, then that may be sufficient justification.

Quality of Evidence

A final challenge to your plan may be that the quality of your proof points is insufficient in some way. If so, ask clarifying questions as discussed earlier, but it may simply be that you need more local experience with threat modeling before it can be formally sanctioned, or you need to gather additional data through a pilot project or something similar.

Summary

Getting an organization to adopt a new practice is always challenging. On the one hand, the issues you face will have a great deal in common with the issues faced by others who have introduced threat modeling. On the other hand, how you face them and overcome them will have aspects unique to your organization. Everyone will need to "sell" their case to individual contributors and to management.

Along the way to convincing people, you'll have to answer a variety of questions related to project management and roles and responsibilities, and ensure that those answers fit your organization's approach to building systems. Generally, that will include understanding the prerequisites to various tasks, and what deliverables those tasks will produce. As you execute the required tasks, you'll run into interaction issues, so you need to understand how decisions will be made. The decision models are likely different for different threat modeling tasks. Some of those tasks will require meetings, and making meetings effective can be tricky, especially if you overload agendas, meeting goals, and decision models. Such overload is common to threat modeling.

Organizations vary in terms of delivering technology, and they deliver technology of different types. Some organizations use waterfalls with gates and checkpoints; others are more agile. All organizations need to roll out systems, and some also deliver software. Each development and deployment approach will have different places to integrate threat modeling tasks. Most organizations also have organized testing, and testing can be a great complement to threat modeling. How an organization approaches technology also has implications for how it hires, rewards, and promotes people, including factors such as training, career ladders, and interviewing.

When attempting to bring threat modeling to an organization, you'll encounter a variety of objections that you'll need to address. Those objections can be roughly modeled as resource objections, value objections, and objections to the plan; and each can be understood and approached in the various ways described in this chapter.

CHAPTER
18
Experimental Approaches

Today's approaches to threat modeling are good enough that a wide variety of people with diverse backgrounds and knowledge can use them to find threats against systems they are developing, designing, or deploying. However, there's no reason to believe that current approaches are the pinnacle of threat modeling. The same smart people who are finding new ways to reconceptualize programming and operations will find new ways to approach threat modeling.

This chapter presents some promising approaches with one or more identifiable issues to overcome. Those issues can include a lack of success with the method when used by those other than its inventors or a lack of prescriptiveness. Those approaches include looking in the seams; operational threat modeling approaches, including the FlipIT game and kill chains; the Broad Street taxonomy; and adversarial machine learning. This chapter also discusses threats to threat modeling approaches, risks to be aware of as you create your own techniques or approaches, and closes with a section on how to experiment.

Some of these approaches are like Lego building blocks, and can easily be attached to modeling software with DFDs and STRIDE, while others take a different approach to a problem, and are harder to snap together. The approaches that can be plugged into other systems include a discussion about how you can do that.

Looking in the Seams

You can find threats by bringing teams together to discuss the design of their software, and using the resultant arguments as a basis for investigation. The premise is that if two teams have different perspectives on how their software works, then it's likely the software has seams that an attacker could take advantage of. This technique has been around for quite a long time, and is routinely borne out in conversations with experts (McGraw, 2011). Why then is it listed under experimental? Because there is limited advice available about what to do to actually make it work.

One team at Microsoft has produced a methodology it calls *intersystem review* (Marshall, 2013). This methodology was designed to build on DFDs and STRIDE, and it works well with them. The questions (listed below) can probably be applied to other approaches. What follows is a version of the intersystem review process, edited to make it more generally applicable. Thanks to Andrew Marshall of Microsoft for agreeing to share the work which forms the basis for this section.

The participants in an intersystem review are development, test, and program management contacts for both (or all) sides of the system, along with security experts. Before meeting in person, someone responsible for security should ensure that the threat models for each team are documented, and pay close attention to the external dependency lists. Unless otherwise noted/decided, that responsible person should ensure that each step in the process, described as follows, is completed.

The terms *product* and *product group* are intended to be interchangeable with "service," and the approach here may even be applied between companies, agencies, or other entities. The first two steps are assigned to the product group, as they are most likely to understand their own systems.

1. For each system, the product group should document data obtained from other products:
   a. For what purpose or purposes is data validated?
   b. What purposes/use cases/scenarios are known not to be supported?
   c. Is there an assumption that specific validation or tests will be performed by the receiver? (If so, is that in the developer documentation and any sample code?)
   d. Does inbound data have any particular storage, security, or validation concerns associated with it?
   e. What edge cases are developers and testers concerned about?

2. For each system, the product group should document data sent to other products:
   a. What promises does the product make about content, format, integrity or trustworthiness of the data?
   b. What purposes is the data suitable for?
   c. What validation is the recipient expected to perform? Where are those requirements documented?
   d. What expectations are there for privacy or data protection by the receiver?
   e. What edge cases are developers and testers concerned about?
3. Create a system model including each system and the trust boundaries. The model can be imperfect, and imperfection may provoke discussion.
4. Have the cross-system group meet in person. The agenda should include:
   a. If the participants are new to intersystem-review, explain the goals of the process and meeting.
   b. A walk-through of the diagrams and scenarios each component supports
   c. Document design, coding, and testing assumptions made by each team on data received by dependencies. Outside the meeting, these assumptions can be checked.
   d. Deep-dive into edge cases, especially around error handling and recovery.
   e. Review prior security bugs specific to services or interfaces exposed at the trust boundaries.

Depending on the relationship between the systems involved, it may be helpful to pre-define a decision model with respect to bugs identified during the meeting. Such a decision model is especially important if participants may suggest or demand bugs be filed or addressed in code other than their own, and if that otherwise wouldn't be the case. For example, participants might not have that ability if the seams are between two organizations. Also helpful is an assigned note taker or recording of the meeting.

Operational Threat Models

The models described in this section, FlipIT and kill chains, are designed to be of value to people operating systems. They span a gamut, from the deeply theoretical approach of FlipIT to the deeply practical kill chains.

FlipIT

FlipIT is a game created by Ari Juels, Ron Rivest, and colleagues. (Ari is Chief Scientist for RSA, Inc., and Ron is one of the creators of the RSA cryptosystem.) FlipIT is played by two players, each of whom would like to control an IT system for as long as possible. Each can, at any time, and at some cost, check to see if they control the system, and if they do not, take control. Whoever controls the system at a given time is earning points, but the score is hidden until the end of the game (otherwise, it would leak information about who's in control). The object of the game is to have more points than your opponent at the end. Perhaps obviously, FlipIT is more a game in the sense of the Prisoner's Dilemma than a game like Monopoly. To help you get a sense for the game, there is a simple online demonstration (Bowers, 2012), and it has a certain charm and ability to pull you into playing.

FlipIT is a model of an IT system and an intruder. Each would like to control the system at a minimal cost. Its authors have used FlipIT as a model to demonstrate how password changes can be made more secure at a lower cost. I'm optimistic that FlipIT can be effectively used to model a system's security in additional interesting ways. FlipIT is listed as experimental because to date only its authors have used it to find new insights.

FlipIT is a very different sort of model compared to other forms of operational threat modeling, and if it's possible to integrate it with other approaches, how to do so is not yet clear.

Kill Chains

The concept of "kill chains" comes from analysis at the US Air Force. There have been several attempts to apply *kill chain* approaches to operational threat modeling. The essential idea of a kill chain is that most attacks involve more than simply taking over a computer or gathering usernames and passwords via phishing. There is a chain of events that includes such steps, but as technology exploitation becomes commercialized and weaponized, understanding the chain of activity gives defenders more opportunities to interfere with it. These kill chain models seem to benefit from customization to align with the mental models of defenders who are using them.

The models in a kill chain approach model both the actions of the attackers and the reactions of the defenders. The idea was introduced in a paper "Intelligence-Driven Computer Network Defense Informed by Analysis of Adversary Campaigns and Intrusion Kill Chains," by Eric Hutchins and colleagues at Lockheed Martin (Hutchins, 2011). You'll see these referred to as

"LM kill chains" in this section. There is also work from Microsoft on "threat genomics" which is closely related and discussed below.

Kill chains are fairly different from other threat elicitation approaches. They are like Erector Sets while STRIDE is like Legos. There might be an opportunity to use the defensive technologies as a bridge to other defensive techniques or tools, but it could be awkward.

LM Kill Chains

The LM kill chain paper presents the idea of using kill chains to drive defensive activity. The authors' approach models attacker activity in terms of indicators. These indicators are either atomic, computed, or behavioral. An atomic indicator is one that cannot be further broken down while retaining meaning. A computed indicator is also derived from data in the incident (rather than an interpretation), and can take forms such as a regular expression. A behavioral indicator is created by combining atomic and computed indicators, and might be a sentence designed for a person to read and consider.

The LM kill chain model outlines seven phases that attackers go through:

- **Reconnaissance:** Research, identification and selection of targets
- **Weaponization:** Combining an exploit and remote access tool into a package for delivery
- **Delivery:** Delivering the package to the target. LM reports that e-mail, websites, and USB media were most commonly observed.
- **Exploitation:** Some action to trigger intruder code, often via a vulnerability in an OS or application (See also the section "The Broad Street Taxonomy," later in this chapter.)
- **Installation:** Installing the remote access tool into the targeted system
- **Command and Control (C2):** Establishing and using a communications channel with the attacker
- **Actions on Objectives:** The actual work that motivates all of the above

The model also posits that there are defensive actions that a defender can take, and includes a table (redrawn as Table 18-1) with an information operations doctrine of detect, deny, disrupt, degrade, deceive, and destroy. The defensive doctrine is derived from the U.S. military. The acronyms used are: IDS (Intrusion Detection System), NIDS (Network IDS), HIDS (Host IDS), NIPS (Network Intrusion Prevention System), and DEP (Data Execution Protection).

Table 18-1: LM Courses of Action Matrix

PHASE	DETECT	DENY	DISRUPT	DEGRADE	DECEIVE	DESTROY
Recon	Web analytics	Firewall ACL				
Weaponize	NIDS	NIPS				
Deliver	Vigilant User	Proxy Filter	In-Line AV	Queuing		
Exploit	HIDS	Patch	DEP			
Install	HIDS	"chroot" Jail	AV			
C2	NIDS	Firewall ACL	NIPS	Tarpit	DNS Redirect	
Actions on Objectives	Audit Log			Quality of Service	Honeypot	

Source: Hutchins, et al. 2011.

The paper usefully shows how indicators can provide a way to look earlier and later in the chain to find other aspects of an intrusion, and how common indicators may show that multiple intrusions were made by the same attacker. Taking data from other phases to find places to look for indicators of attack is an important way to model and focus defender activity.

Threat Genomics

Another approach that shows promise is Espenschied and Gunn's threat genomics (Espenschied, 2012). This work models the detectable changes that attackers introduce into an operational system. In contrast to the LM model, the threat genomics model focuses on detectable changes, rather than operational steps, that an attacker would progress through. The approach aims to build a model of an attack from those changes, and then apply the models to improve detection and predictive capabilities. Threat genomics models are a set of what the authors call *threat sequences*. A sequence is a set of state transitions over time. The states are as follows:

- Reconnaissance
- Commencement
- Entry
- Foothold
- Lateral movement
- Acquired control

- Acquired target
- Implement/execute
- Conceal and maintain
- Withdraw

Note that the states are not sequential, and not all are required. For example, an attack that installs a remote access tool may involve entry and foothold as the same action. Steps such as reconnaissance or lateral movement may not be required at all. (This is in contrast to the LM model.) The sequences are based on observable indicators, such as log entries. Note that this model "sits above" many of the "security indicators" systems, such as OpenIOC, STIX, and so on. The sequences are intended to move analysts away from interpreting individual indicators or correlations to interpreting correlations between sequences.

After an attack, if investigators piece together enough elements of the sequence, then the sequence and/or its details may provide information about an attacker's tools, techniques, and procedures. If these are graphed, then different graphs may help to distinguish between attackers. A sample sequence from Espenschied and Gunn's paper is shown in Figure 18-1.

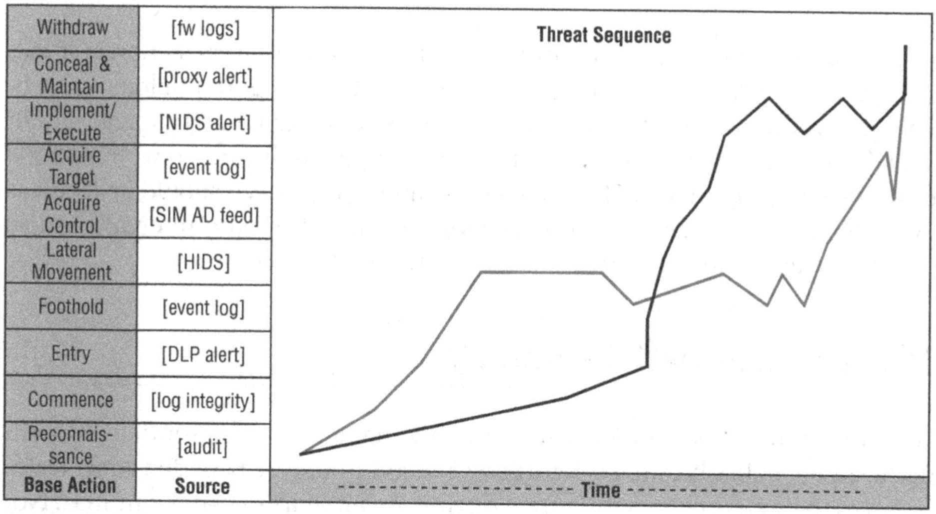

Figure 18-1: Threat genomics example

The sequences model enables an investigator to understand where indicators should be present. For example, before a target can be acquired, the attacker has to enter and establish a foothold.

This model is also a helpful way to consider what data sources would detect which state transitions. For example, domain controller change reports may help discover control acquisition, but they will not directly help you find the initial point of entry. Figure 18-2, taken from the paper, shows a sample mapping of data sources to transitions.

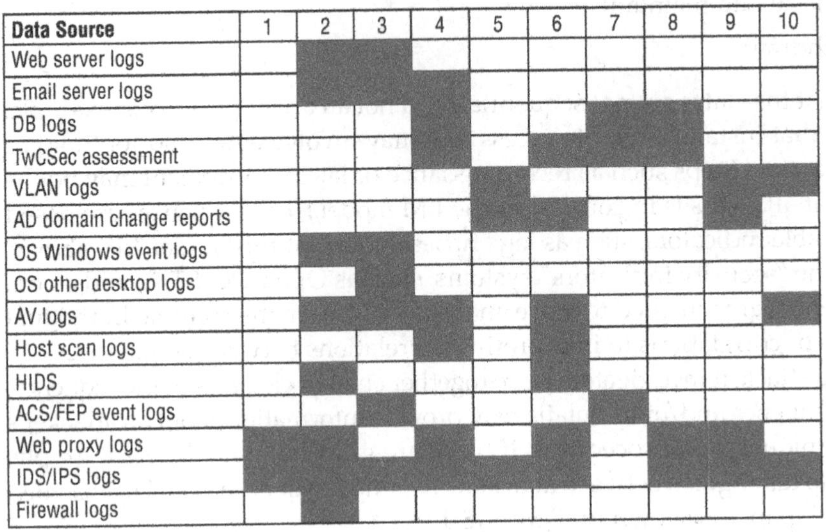
Data Source
1
2
3
4
5
6
7
8
9
10
Web server logs
Email server logs
DB logs
TwCSec assessment
VLAN logs
AD domain change reports
OS Windows event logs
OS other desktop logs
AV logs
Host scan logs
HIDS
ACS/FEP event logs
Web proxy logs
IDS/IPS logs
Firewall logs

Figure 18-2: Mapping data sources to transitions

If a column is missing, you should consider whether that transition is something you want to detect. The list of possible rows is long. If a defensive technology row doesn't match any column, it's worth asking what it's for, although the failure to find a match may result from it simply not lining up well with the threat genomics approach. The defensive technologies shown should be taken as examples, not a complete list. Threat genomics is listed as experimental because to date (as far as I know) only its authors have made use of it.

The "Broad Street" Taxonomy

I developed the "Broad Street Taxonomy" and named it after a seminal event in the history of public health: Dr. John Snow's identification of a London street water pump as the source of contamination during an outbreak of cholera in 1854. Not only did he demonstrate a link, but he removed the handle of the water pump, and in doing so probably altered the course of the epidemic. For more on the history of that event, see *The Ghost Map* by Steven Johnson (Penguin, 2006). It is both a taxonomy, that is a system for categorizing things, and a model, in that it abstracts away details to help focus attention on certain aspects of those events. I chose the name Broad Street to focus attention on the desire to understand how computers come to harm, and it enables activities to address those causes. The use of an aspirational, rather than a functional name, was also driven by the fact that the taxonomy categorizes a set of things that are somewhat tricky to describe. Part of the reason they are tricky to describe is that the taxonomy groups them together for the first time. By analogy, before Linnaeus built a tree of life, vertebrae referred only to backbones, not the set of creatures with backbones. By categorizing living organisms, he created a new way of seeing them. (My aspirations are somewhat less . . . broad.)

So what does Broad Street model? The taxonomy is designed to clarify how computers are actually compromised ("broken into") for malware installations, and it has shown promise for use in incident root cause analysis. It focuses only on issues that have been repeatedly documented in the field. The taxonomy helps understand compromises in a way that can effectively drive product design and improvement. The value of the model is its focus on the means of compromise for an important set of compromises. However, Broad Street is neither a model of compromise nor a model of how malware gets onto systems. It's not a model of compromise because it doesn't touch on compromises that start with stolen credentials. Nor is it a complete model of how malware gets onto systems, as it excludes malware that is installed by other malware.

NOTE **The model has had a deep impact at Microsoft, resulting in an update to AutoPlay being shipped via Windows Update, but its use has been limited elsewhere (so far).**

Before getting into the taxonomy itself, note that Broad Street does not align well with software development threat modeling; its model of the world is too coarse to be of use to most developers, who consider particular features. Thus, continuing with the toy analogies, Broad Street is like Lincoln Logs.

When represented as a taxonomy, Broad Street includes a set of questions that are designed to enable defenders to categorize an attack in a consistent way. The questions are ordered, and presented as a flowchart, as shown in Figure 18-3. The questions are designed to be applied to a single instance of compromise, or, in the case of malware that uses several different approaches to compromise a system, serially across each technique, resulting in each technique having a label. The questions are explained after the flowchart. The simplified presentation in a flowchart is easy to use, but many nodes have nuances that are hard to capture in the short labels. The exit condition for categorizing an attack is that an attack must have a label. Note that in Figure 18-3, there are boxes labeled "I'm unsure" and "hard to categorize." These are intended for those using the taxonomy to record those problems. (Figure 18-3 shows version 2.7 of the taxonomy.)

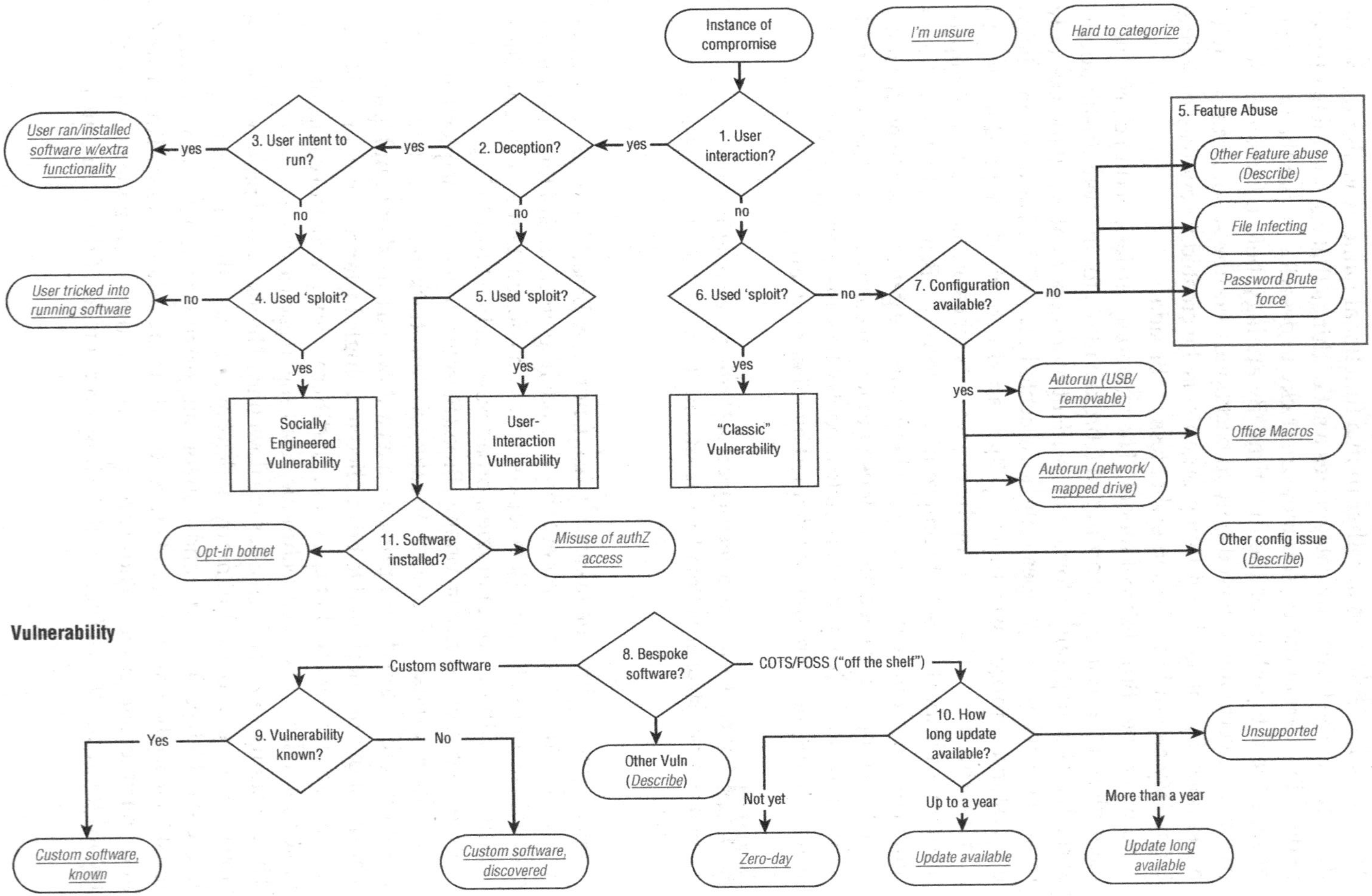

Figure 18-3: The Broad Street Taxonomy

1. **User interaction?** The first question the taxonomy poses is whether a person has to perform some action that results in a compromise. Asked another way, if no one is logged into the computer, can the attack work? If the answer is yes, the flow proceeds to question 2; if no, the flow proceeds to question 6.
2. **Deception?** The second question is one of deception. Deception often entails convincing someone that they will get some benefit from the action, or suffer some penalty if they don't do it, using any of a variety of social engineering techniques. (Table 15-1 provides ways to describe such techniques.) Examples of deception might include a website telling people that they need to install a codec to watch a video, or an e-mail message that claims to be from the tax authorities. There are a variety of actions that a "normal person" will believe are safe, such as browsing well-known websites or visiting a local file share. (Earlier variants of the taxonomy addressed this by asking, "Does the user click through a warning of some form?" and while that is still a good criterion, it is hard to argue that removing warnings from software should lead to changing the way something is categorized.) If propagation requires deceiving the victim, the flow proceeds to question 3. If it doesn't, question 3 is skipped and the flow proceeds to question 5.
3. **User intent to run (software)?** If interaction is required, is the person aware that the action they are taking will involve running or installing software? If the answer is yes, the incident can be categorized by the endpoint: *User ran/installed software (with unexpected functionality)*. The person runs the software, which does unexpected and malicious actions in addition to, or instead of, the software's desired function. A significant overlap exists between this and the traditional definitions of Trojan Horse software. The analogy with the Trojan Horse from Greek mythology refers to the way a lot of malware gains access to victims' computers by masquerading as something innocuous: malicious programs represented as installers for legitimate security programs, for example, or disguised as documents for common desktop applications. This label can cause two types of confusion. First, it could lead to multiple endpoints with the same label. Second, many security vendors define "trojan" [sic] as a program that is unable to spread of its own accord.
4. **Used 'sploit?/Deserves a CVE?** These questions have the same intent. Different presentations of the taxonomy use different presentations of this question, selected to be more usable for a particular audience. This question has the same meaning for nodes (4, 5, and 6) of the process flow, and determines whether or not a vulnerability is involved. Because the term "vulnerability" can be open to interpretation, the question asks whether the method used to install the software is of the sort often documented

in the Common Vulnerabilities and Exposures list (CVE), a standardized repository of vulnerability information maintained at `cve.mitre.org`. ("Deserves" is used to cover situations in which the method meets the CVE criteria but has not yet been assigned a CVE number, as with a previously undisclosed vulnerability. However, the CVE does not cover less frequently deployed systems, so "deserving of a CVE" may be read as "a thing which would get a CVE if it were in a popular product.") This question can also be read as "Was an exploit used?" (where exploit refers to a small piece of software designed to exploit a vulnerability in software, and often written as "sploit"). If question 4 is answered no, then the incident is categorized: *User tricked into running software*. This result indicates a false badging, such as a malicious executable named document.pdf.exe with an icon similar or identical to the one used for PDF files in Adobe Reader. The victim launches the executable, believing it to be an ordinary PDF file, and it installs malware or takes other malicious actions. If question 4 is answered yes, then you can categorize the means of compromise as *socially engineered vulnerability*, and possibly further categorize it through the vulnerability subprocess (nodes 8, 9 and 10).

5. **Deserves a CVE?** If question 5 is answered yes, then you can categorize it as a *user-interaction vulnerability*, and possibly further categorize it through the vulnerability subprocess. The taxonomy does not use the popular "drive-by-download" label because that term is used in several ways. One is analogous to these issues; the others are what are labeled: *User runs/installs software with extra functionality* and *User tricked into running software*. If it does not deserve a CVE, then you can refer to the endpoint as an *Opt-in botnet*, a phrase coined by Gunter Ollman (Ollman, 2010). In some cases, people choose to install software that is designed to perform malicious actions. For example, this category includes Low Orbit Ion Cannon (LOIC), an open-source network attack tool designed to perform DoS attacks.
6. **Deserves a CVE?** If question 6 is answered yes, then you should categorize it as a *classic vulnerability*, and possibly further categorize it through the vulnerability subprocess.
7. **Configuration Available?** Can the attack vector be eliminated through configuration changes, or does it involve intrinsic product features that cannot be disabled through configuration? Configuration options would include things like turning the firewall off and using a registry change to disable the AutoRun feature. If the answer is yes—in other words, if the

attack vector can be eliminated through configuration changes—the flow terminates in one of four endpoints:

a. **AutoRun (USB/removable)**: The attack took advantage of the AutoRun feature in Windows to propagate on USB storage devices and other removable volumes.

b. **AutoRun (network/mapped drive)**: The threat takes advantage of the AutoRun feature to propagate via network volumes mapped to drive letters.

c. **Office Macros**: The threat propagates to new computers when victims open Microsoft Office documents with malicious macros.

d. **Other configuration issue**: This catch-all is designed to accumulate issues over time until we can better categorize them.

If the answer is no—in other words, if the attack vector uses product features that cannot be turned off via a configuration option—then the vector is called *feature abuse*, which includes three subcategories:

a. **File infecting viruses**: The threat spreads by modifying files, often with .exe or .scr extensions, by rewriting or overwriting some code segments. To spread between computers, the virus writes to network drives or removable drives.

b. **Password brute force**: The threat spreads by attempting brute-force password attacks—for example, via ssh or rlogin or against available SMB volumes to obtain write or execute permissions.

c. **Other feature abuse**: This is another catch-all, designed to accumulate issues over time until we can better categorize them.

8. **Bespoke Software Project?** This question is designed to distinguish locally developed software from widely available software. Vulnerabilities are not unique to commercial (or open-source) software, and other exploit analyses have found that vulnerabilities in custom software, such as website code, account for a significant percentage of exploitation (Verizon, 2013).
9. **Vulnerability known?** This question serves to distinguish between issues discovered by the owner/operator/creator of the software and those found by an attacker. For vulnerabilities discovered by an organization, there is some period of time between discovery and patching while the vulnerability is reproduced, and code is fixed and tested. One endpoint here, *Custom software, known (to owner)*, is for that set. The other

endpoint, *Custom software, discovered (by attacker)*, is for those vulnerabilities first found by an attacker.

10. **How long update available?** (The abbreviated text fits in a box, and means "how long has the update been available to install?"):
    a. **Zero-day**: Refers to a vulnerability for which no patch was available from the software creator at the time of exploitation.
    b. **Update available**: Refers to a vulnerability for which a patch was available from the software creator for up to a year at the time of exploitation.
    c. **Update long available**: Refers to a vulnerability for which a patch was available from the software creator for over a year at the time of exploitation.
    d. **Unsupported**: Refers to a vulnerability in the software that the creator no longer supports, including when the creator is out of business.

The Broad Street Taxonomy is a way to categorize and model an important set of things which are not otherwise brought together. Modeling those things in a new way has helped to improve the security of systems, and that modeling and categorization is worth exploring in additional areas.

Adversarial Machine Learning

Because machine learning approaches help solve a wide variety of problems, they have been applied to security, some in authentication, others in spam or other attack detection spaces. Attackers know this is happening, and have started to attack machine learning systems. As a result, academics and defenders are starting to examine a security subfield called *adversarial machine learning*. In a paper of that name, the authors propose a categorization with three properties (Huang, 2011). The properties are influence, security goals, and attacker goals. The influence property includes attacks against the training data, and exploratory attacks against the operational system. The second property describes what security goal is violated, including integrity of the detector's ability to detect intrusions; and availability, meaning the system becomes so noisy that real positives cannot be detected. The security goals also include privacy, meaning attacks that compromise information about the people using the system, and it appears to be a subset of information disclosure attacks. The third category is a spectrum of attacker goals, from targeted to indiscriminate.

The paper lays out the taxonomy including descriptions of further attacks in detail, walks through a number of case studies, and discusses defenses. (False negatives are included in their bulleted explanation of availability, but not in the text. Their taxonomy may be more clear if you treat induction of false negatives as an integrity attack, and caused false positives as an availability attack.) This is a field that is likely to explode over the next few years, as more people believe that big data and machine learning will solve their security problems.

Adversarial machine learning can be contextualized as a second-order threat that is relevant when machine learning is used as a mitigation technique. Currently, there is no clean model demonstrating how machine learning can help mitigate threats, which inhibits saying exactly where adversarial machine learning will help or hurt.

Threat Modeling a Business

How to threat model something bigger than a piece of software or a system being deployed is a fair question, and one that security and operations people would like to be able to address in consistent, predictable ways that offer a high return on investment.

There appears to be tension between scope and the value that organizations receive for their threat modeling investments. That is, threat modeling more specific technologies is easier than threat modeling something as large and complex as a business. Perhaps at some level, all organizations are similar? At another level, each one has unique assets and threats against those assets. The most mature system for modeling a business is OCTAVE-Allegro from CERT-CC.

OCTAVE is the Operationally Critical Threat, Asset, and Vulnerability Evaluation approach to risk assessment and planning. There are three, interlinked methods: the original; an OCTAVE-S method for smaller organizations; and OCTAVE-Allegro, which is positioned as a streamlined approach. All are designed for operational risk management, rather than development time, and all focus on operational risks.

The methodology is freely available from the CERT.org website, and it is clearly organized into a set of phases and activities, with defined roles and responsibilities. The free materials include worksheets, examples and a book. Training classes are also offered. It is one of the more fully developed methodologies available, and those looking to create a new approach should examine OCTAVE and understand why each element is present.

OCTAVE Allegro consists of eight steps organized into four phases:

1. Develop risk measurement criteria and organizational drivers.
2. Create a profile of each critical information asset.
3. Identify threats to each information asset.
4. Identify and analyze risks to information assets and begin to develop mitigation approaches.

Risks are to be brainstormed (or approached with a provided threat tree) in six areas, each of which has an associated worksheet:

- Reputation and customer confidence
- Financial
- Productivity
- Safety and health
- Fines/legal penalties
- User-defined

The documentation notes that "working through each branch of the threat trees to identify threat scenarios can be a tedious exercise." This is an ongoing challenge for all such methodologies, and one that offers a real opportunity for helping a large set of organizations if someone finds a good balance here. OCTAVE and its family do not interconnect in obvious ways with other methods. Perhaps this family of systems is like Revel model airplanes. If the kit is what you need, it's what you need, but it may be a little tedious to put it together?

Threats to Threat Modeling Approaches

Henry Spencer said, "those who don't understand Unix are condemned to reinvent it, poorly." The same applies to threat modeling. If you don't understand what has come before, then how can you know if you're doing something new? If you know you're doing something new but you're changing training, tasks, or techniques at random, how can you expect the outcome to be better? If you don't understand the issues in what came before, how do you know if you're tweaking the right things?

There are a number of common ways to fail at threat modeling. The first is not trying, which is self-evident. Some additional important ones are discussed in this section. They are broken into dangerous deliverables and dangerous approaches.

Dangerous Deliverables

These are two outputs which tend to lead to failure. The first is to create an enumeration of all assumptions (made worse by starting with that list), the second is threat model reports.

Enumerate All Assumptions

The advice to "enumerate all assumptions" is common within threat modeling systems, yet it is full of fail. It's full of fail for a number of reasons, including that enumerating all assumptions is impossible; and even if it were possible, it would be an unbounded and unscoped activity. It's also highly stymieing. Let's start with why enumerating all assumptions is not possible.

Using a simple example, I could write, "I assume readers of this book speak English." That sentence contains a number of assumptions, such as that this book will be read, and that it will be read in English. Both assumptions are, in part, false. I could assume that reading, in the sense I'm using it, incorporates an audio-book (hey, an author can hope, or at least look forward to text-to-speech improving). It also incorporates the assumption that the book won't be translated. Underlying the word "English" is the strange belief that there exists a definable thing that we both call the English language, and that each of the terms I use will be read by the reader in the manner in which I intend it. You could reasonably argue that those assumptions are silly and irrelevant to our purposes. You could do so even if you were steeped in arguments over what a language is, because our goal here is to discuss threat modeling; and to the extent that we're within the same communities of practice and considering threat modeling as a technical discipline, you'd be right. However, threat modeling is not a single community of practice. Experts in different things are expert in different things, and the assumptions they make that matter to one another are not obvious in advance. That's why they are assumptions, rather than stated. Therefore, asking people to start a threat modeling process by enumerating assumptions is going to stymie them.

Even though enumerating all assumptions is impossible, tracking assumptions as you go can be a valuable activity. There are a few key differences that make this work. First, it's not first—that is, it doesn't act as an inhibitor to getting started. Second, it relies on documenting what you discover through the natural flow of work. Third, assumptions are often responsible for issues falling between cracks, so investigating and validating assumptions often pays off. (See the discussion of *intersystem review* in the "Looking in the Seams" section earlier in this chapter for advice on teasing out assumptions from large systems.)

Threat Model Reports

Threat modeling projects have a long and unfortunate history of producing a report as a final deliverable. That's because very early threat modeling was done by consultants, and consultants deliver reports. Their customers turn those into bugs, or perhaps more commonly, shelfware. Reports are not, in and of themselves, bad. A good threat analysis can be a useful input to requirements, can help software engineers think about problems, and can be a useful input into a test plan. Good notes to API callers or non-requirements can help things not fall through the seams. A good analysis might turn the threats into stories so they stay close to mind as software is being written or reviewed. This is an area where attacker-centric modeling may help. A good story contains conflict, and conflict has sides. In this case, you are one side, and an attacker is the other side.

Dangerous Approaches

Sometimes, looking at what you should not do can be more instructive than looking at what you should do. This section describes some approaches to threat modeling that share a common characteristic: They are all ways to fail.

- **Cargo culting:** The term *cargo cult science* comes to us from Richard Feynman:

> *In the South Seas there is a cargo cult of people. During the war they saw airplanes with lots of good materials, and they want the same thing to happen now. So they've arranged to make things like runways, to put fires along the sides of the runways, to make a wooden hut for a man to sit in, with two wooden pieces on his head to headphones and bars of bamboo sticking out like antennas—he's the controller—and they wait for the airplanes to land. They're doing everything right. The form is perfect. It looks exactly the way it looked before. But it doesn't work. No airplanes land. So I call these things cargo cult science, because they follow all the apparent precepts and forms of scientific investigation, but they're missing something essential, because the planes don't land.*
>
> from *Surely You're Joking, Mr. Feynman!* (Feynman, 2010)

  The complexities of threat modeling will sometimes combine with demands by leadership to result in cargo-cult threat modeling. That is, people go through the motions and try to threat model, but they lack an understanding of the steps, completing them by rote. If you don't understand why a step is present, you should eliminate it, and see if you get value from what remains.

- **The kitchen sink:** Closely related to cargo culting is the "kitchen sink" approach to the threat modeling process. These systems are sometimes developed by adherents of several approaches who need to work together. No one wants to leave out their favorite bit, and either no one wants to make a decision or no one is empowered to make it stick. The trouble with the kitchen sink approach is that effort is wasted, and momentum toward fixing problems can be lost.
- **Think like an attacker:** The advice to think like an attacker is common, and it's easy to repeat it without thinking. The problem is that telling most people to think like an attacker is like telling them to think like a professional chef. Even my friends who enjoy cooking have little idea how a chef approaches what dishes to put on a menu, or how to manage a kitchen so that 100 people are fed in an hour. Therefore, if you're going to ask people to think like an attacker, you need to give them supports,

such as lists of attacker goals or techniques. Effort to become familiar with those lists absorbs "space in the brain" that must be shared with the system being built and possible attacks (Shostack, 2008b). "Think like an attacker" may be useful as an exhortation to get people into the mood of threat modeling (Kelsey, 2008).

- **You're never done threat modeling:** Security experts love to say that you're never done threat modeling, and there are few better ways to ensure that you're never going to get it included in a project plan. If you can't schedule the work, if you can't describe a deliverable that fits into a delivery checklist, then threat modeling is unlikely to be an essential aspect of delivery.
- ***This* is the way to threat model:** Another idea that hurts threat modeling is the belief that there's one right way to do it. One outgrowth of this is what might be called the "stew" model of threat modeling: just throw in whatever appeals, and it'll probably work out. Similarly, too much advice on threat modeling currently available is not clearly situated or related to other advice, and as such there is often an implicit stew approach. If you select ingredients from random recipes on the Internet, you're unlikely to make a tasty stew; and if you select ingredients from random approaches to threat modeling, do you expect anything better? Good advice on threat modeling includes the context in which an approach, methodology, or task is intended to be used. It also talks about prerequisites and skills. It is made concrete with a list of deliverables, but more important, how those deliverables are expected to be used.
- **The way I threat model is...:** Every approach that has been criticized in this book has not only advocates, but advocates who have successfully applied the approach. They are likely outraged that their approach is being questioned, and with good reason. After all, it worked for them. However, that's no guarantee that it will work for others. One key goal of this book is to provide structured approaches to threat modeling that can be effectively integrated into a development or operations methodology in a cost-effective way. A useful approach to threat modeling will scale beyond its inventor.
- **Security has to be about protecting assets:** This is so obvious a truism that it's nearly unchallengeable. If you're not investing to protect an asset, why are you investing? What is the asset worth? If you're investing more than the value of the asset, why do it? All of these are great questions, and well worth asking. It's hard to argue with the importance of either. If you have no assets to protect, don't invest in threat modeling. At the same time, these questions aren't always easy to answer. Modeling around assets is

easier with operational systems than with "boxed" software (although the software-centric approach does tend to work well for operational systems). The importance of the question, however, isn't always aligned with when it should be asked, or even with the project at hand. "What gives meaning to your life?" is an important question, but if every software project started with that question, a lot of them wouldn't get very far.

How to Experiment

After reading about all the ways that threat modeling can go astray, it can be tempting to decide that it's just too hard. Perhaps that's true. It is very hard to create an approach that helps those who are not expert threat modelers, and it's very hard to create an approach that helps experts—but it is not impossible. If you have an understanding of what you want to make better, and an understanding of what has failed, many people will make something better, something that works for their organization in new ways. To do that, you'll want to define a problem, find aspects of that problem that you can measure, measure those things, introduce a change, measure again, and study your results.

Define a Problem

The first step is to know what you're trying to improve. What is it about the many systems in this book and elsewhere that is insufficient for your needs? Why are they not working? Define your goal. You may end up solving a different problem than you expect, and that may be OK; but if you don't know where you're going, you're unlikely to know if you've arrived.

Developing a good experiment around threat modeling is challenging. Perhaps more tractable is interviewing developers or surveying them after a task. Knowing what you're trying to improve can help you decide on the right questions to ask. Are you trying to get threat modeling going? In that case, perhaps ask participants if they think it was worthwhile and how many bugs they filed. Are you comparing two systems to find more threats? Are you trying to make the process run faster? See how long they spent, and how many bugs they filed. Knowing what you're trying to achieve is a key part of measuring what you're getting.

Find Aspects to Measure and Measure Them

It's easy to make changes and hope that they have the appropriate results. It can be harder to experiment, but the best way to understand what you've done is to structure an experiment. Those experiments can be narrow, such as creating better training around STRIDE, or broader, such as replacing the four-stage model. At the core of an experiment should be some sort of testable hypothesis: If we do *X*, we'll get better results than we do with *Y*.

Designing a good experiment involves setting up several closely related tests, with as few variances between them as possible. Therefore, you might want to keep the system used in the test the same. You might want to use the same people, but if they're threat modeling the same system twice, then data from one test might taint the other. Putting people through multiple training sessions might show a different result from putting them through one (in fact, you'd hope it would). Therefore, you might bring different people in, but how do you ensure they have similar skills and backgrounds? How do you ensure that what you're testing is the approach, rather than the training? Perhaps one training has a better-looking presenter, or show more enthusiasm when covering one approach versus another. You should also review the advice on running user tests in Chapter 15 "Human Factors and Usability."

Study Your Results

If you've done something better, how much better is it? What's the benefit? Does it lead you to think that the line of inquiry is complete, or is there more opportunity to fix the issues that are causing you to experiment? What will it cost to roll it out across the relevant population? Can the new practices coexist with the old, or will they be confusing? These factors, along with the size and dispersion of an organization, influence the speed and frequency of new rollouts.

When you've built something new and useful, you should give it a name. Just as you wouldn't call your new programming language "programming language," you shouldn't name what you created "threat modeling." Give it a unique name.

Summary

There are many promising approaches to threat modeling, and a lot of ways in which experimentation will improve our approaches. Knowing what has been done and what has failed are helpful input to such experiments.

The first promising approach is to look in the seams between systems, and this chapter gives you a structured approach to doing so. You also looked at a few other approaches to operational threat modeling that show promise, including the FlipIT game and two kill chain models. There is also a Broad Street Taxonomy, which is designed to help understand bad outcomes in the real world. Lastly, there is an emergent academic field studying adversarial machine learning, which will be an important part of understanding when machine learning systems can help you mitigate threats.

This chapter also examined a long list of threats to threat modeling approaches, including dangerous deliverables (lists of assumptions and threat model reports) and dangerous approaches. The dangerous approaches include cargo culting and throwing in everything but the kitchen sink. They also include exhorting people to "think like an attacker"; telling them (or yourself) "you're never done threat modeling"; saying "the way to threat model is"; or "the way I threat model is"; and the ever-popular distraction, "security has to be about assets."

Knowing all of this sets you up to innovate and experiment. You should do so for a problem that you can clearly articulate and for which you can measure the results of an experiment (as challenging as that can be).

CHAPTER
19

Architecting for Success

There is no perfect or true way to threat model; but that is not to say that there are no poor approaches documented, approaches that have never worked for anyone but their author, and it is not to say that you can't compare approaches and decide that some are better or worse. One readily observable indicator is whether the authors describe organizational factors in depth, such as the degree of expertise needed, or inputs and outputs. Another indicator is whether the system has proponents (other than its creators) who make use of it in their own work.

This chapter closes the book by looking at the ways in which the threat modeling practitioner's approach, framing, scope, and related issues can help you design new processes or roll processes out successfully. In other words, it moves from focusing on how threat modeling can go wrong to how to make it work effectively.

This chapter begins with a discussion of flow and the importance of knowing the participants, and then covers boundary objects and how "the best is the enemy of the good." It closes with a discussion of how "the threat model" is evolving and artistry in threat modeling.

Understanding Flow

Flow is the state of full immersion and participation in an activity. It reflects a state of undistracted concentration on a task at hand, and is associated with effective performance by experts in many fields. In his book *Finding Flow,* Mihaly Csíkszentmihályi (Basic Books, 1997) describes how "the person is fully immersed in what he or she is doing, characterized by a feeling of energized focus, full involvement, and success." Many structured approaches to threat modeling actively inhibit flow in both beginners and experts, and few allow it to emerge. The documented and common elements of flow include the following:

1. The activity is intrinsically rewarding
2. People become absorbed in the activity*
3. A loss of the feeling of self-consciousness*
4. Distorted sense of time
5. A sense of personal control over the situation or activity*
6. Clear goals*
7. Concentrating and focusing
8. Direct and immediate feedback*
9. Balance between ability level and challenge*

Items with an asterisk (*) are those for which I have personally witnessed regular or systematic failures of threat modeling systems to achieve this property.

Flow is the most important test of an approach, methodology, or task for threat modeling. Knowing who will find flow in an approach is a key to architecting for success. If your audience can't find flow, their ability to find threats will be dramatically inhibited. Without flow, threat modeling is a chore, and it is less likely to be a part of an engineering process.

This is not to argue that flow is always a criteria for assessing security processes, especially those beyond threat modeling, but it offers a model for addressing a class of issue. As an example, many approaches to threat modeling have no clearly stated and achievable goal. For example, a goal might be to "find all possible security problems." This is an exceptionally broad goal and one whose achievement is subject to extended argument. Similarly, many processes require diagrams but offer no criteria for what constitutes "sufficient" diagramming. These sorts of problems can be predicted or addressed using flow as a model of people.

One element of flow is the balance of ability level and challenge, which is sometimes represented as a flow channel (see Figure 19-1). The idea is that a person starts an unfamiliar task in state A1. From there, if the challenge is too low relative to their skills, they move to boredom (A2). If the challenge is too high relative to their skills, they move to anxiety (A3). When challenge and skills are balanced, they can learn new skills, take on greater challenges, and experience flow (A4).

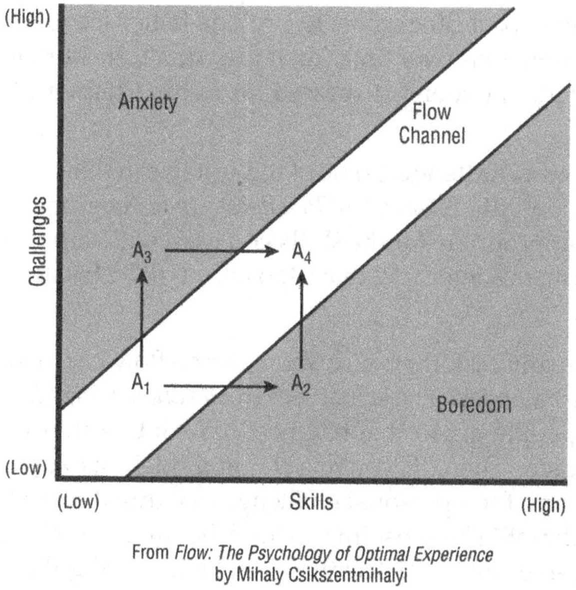

Figure 19-1: The flow channel

If you are developing a system and find that your participants are either bored or anxious, look for ways to better help them achieve a flow state.

Flow and Threat Modeling

For far too many people, the attempt to threat model leaves them anxious or scared. The balance is skewed toward challenge, and people don't see a way to develop their skills. They're overwhelmed by the details and the requirements. Advocates of threat modeling can unintentionally push people toward anxiousness by overwhelming them with details and possibilities. When someone has no basis for comparison or decision making, they're easily overwhelmed with "you might do it like this or that," or with decision fatigue. (The reason it's so hard to choose between 80 varieties of toothpaste is because most people don't have any idea what makes one toothpaste better than another, and the differences may not matter a lot.)

Following are three key aspects of aligning threat modeling with finding flow:

- **Clear goals:** Many threat modeling processes are focused on a report, or don't have clear internal steps. To the extent that it's possible, each system in this book has clear goals, exit criteria, and self-checks.
- **Direct and immediate feedback:** There are a variety of levels at which feedback is important. Is this a good threat? Have we examined this system "sufficiently"? Microsoft's SDL TM Tool provides instant feedback

on diagrams, and you can expect other tools to provide better feedback on other elements of threat models over time (or, if they don't, encourage their creators to consider it). The tool is disucssed further in Chapter 11, "Threat Modeling Tools."

- **Balance between ability and challenge:** Some of the systems in this book are for experts. Others (especially *Elevation of Privilege*) are for beginners. Selecting a system that's appropriate for the skills you have will help you develop new ones. Jumping to something that's too hard will be frustrating, and too easy to quit.

The ideal state for anyone, in any task they care about, is the flow channel, where ability and challenge are balanced. The structures in *Elevation of Privilege* are useful because they help people get to that balance in a nonthreatening way—but the challenges don't stop there. If you're a threat modeling expert, you can often find flow by looking for a personal challenge in a threat modeling session. The most elegant threat? The most impactful? The threat that will crystalize a requirement or non-requirement? The threat that will highlight the technical debt impact of a design? Perhaps it's not the best threat, but the most threats, or the most ways in which a certain STRIDE type can appear. Maybe it's a beginner who needs effective coaching?

This idea of finding something to improve relates to a body of work on *deliberate practice*. Deliberate practice is a term of art meaning an assigned practice task with a defined focus area (Ericsson, 1993). A good music teacher might assign two new students vastly different pieces to play, with one focusing on rhythm, the other focusing on dexterity. Each piece would be selected against a weakness that the teacher can see. (A popular author contorted this into "10,000 hours of work will make you an expert.") There's good evidence that expertise develops faster with deliberate practice, and threat modeling will improve when we start to develop example systems that help people work through common failings.

In the SDL TM Tool, people model software at the start of threat modeling. They do so in whiteboard-like diagrams to minimize cognitive load (see the section "Beware of Cognitive Load" later this chapter.) They happen at the beginning to enable a positive feedback experience ("You've successfully created a diagram!"). Contrast this with other approaches that begin with something like "Create a list of all the assets in the system." Making a list of assets is not something most developers do, so starting a threat modeling exercise from a diagram can be seen as more likely to lead to a flow experience, and less likely to inhibit one.

The most trenchant critique of the SDL Threat Modeling Tool (which I created) is that it can be tedious. The STRIDE-per-element approach used in the tool can be seen as problematic in that similar issues tend to crop up repeatedly in a threat model. Therefore, as people use the tool, they find themselves repeatedly entering the same threat, copying and pasting, or entering a reference. It's not a great use of people's precious time. I take some small pride in having created a tool that helps people who previously couldn't perform these tasks reach the point where they can execute the key elements of the tasks and even get bored with them.

But my pride is not what's important. What's important is a tool that challenges people more appropriately, enabling them to do better at threat modeling. Someone once said that a video game is a program with a user interface that's so compelling that you keep using it for fun. A compelling video game offers tools for you to master, trickier environments for you to explore, and bigger monsters to fight so that the challenge presented keeps increasing. Threat modeling tools could do the same.

Stymieing People

One of the opposites of flow is when people feel stymied by what's in front of them. Sometimes that's because the problem at hand is hard. Often, it's because the person doesn't know where to start, because the problem is too big, or they don't know what success looks like. When no one knows what success looks like, one way to overcome that is to look for ways to break the problem into smaller chunks, or look for other ways to get started. (The trope that "you need to crawl before you can walk" often comes up in these circumstances.)

A variant of this is the claim that threat modeling doesn't find anything interesting (see, for example, Osterman, 2007). Sometimes, threat modeling can involve walking through a lot of possibilities but finding few interesting threats. This doesn't feel good; but if you have skilled practitioners performing the threat modeling and still not finding anything, you can rest easier. You have assurance that the designers probably did a good job of threat modeling, either explicitly or implicitly.

Beware of Cognitive Load

Cognitive load is the amount of information you're asking someone to keep in their working memory at one time. When there's too much, people are forced to fall back to cheat sheets, work much more slowly, or go back to their e-mail. Cognitive load can be another inhibitor of flow.

Whiteboard diagrams are familiar to almost everyone in software. Data flow diagrams and swim lane diagrams are almost as familiar. Their cognitive load is small. UML and other diagrams are both more complex and less familiar, so for many, the load is greater. Therefore, you should generally prefer data flow and swim lane diagrams, so that the energy can be spent on the unique security tasks in threat modeling. If everyone on a team is deeply familiar with UML, then it may be a better choice, as UML is more expressive than DFDs. See the section "Boundary Objects," later in this chapter.

Formal systems can offer an interesting example of cognitive loading. When people encounter a new notational system for the first time, or the first time in a long time, they have to think about what something like ∩ means (hint, it's set union or intersection), or how to pronounce φ ("phi"). The energy spent on such subtasks distracts from the nominal goal. Of course, there are good reasons to use such notations, including precision. There is no universal "good decision" regarding something like notation. There are simply decisions that provide various participants with different value in different situations. One such value would be that the expected participants can discover and address threats. You should focus on that.

Avoid Creator Blindness

Another important aspect to understanding people in a threat modeling session is what I call *creator blindness*. This is the set of cognitive factors that make it difficult to proofread your own work, or judge an artistic work in progress. When the technology you're creating is a program of any complexity, making it work properly, meeting all the stated and unstated requirements, will expand to take up all available room. The cognitive load involved in thinking about the technology and how to attack it is enough to overwhelm nearly anyone. This is part of why Eric Raymond claims that "All bugs are shallow with enough eyes" (Raymond, 2001). Other people will see your bugs faster than you will. Security professionals will see security bugs faster than others, but trying to threat model your own creation is a tough challenge. If you need to analyze your own technology, use the structures in Part II of this book to help draw you into looking at it in a new light.

The problem of being unable to assess your own system also shows up in the design of threat modeling approaches. The person who designs a new threat modeling approach is emotionally involved with the pride of creation, which hinders their ability to assess their own work. The use of structured experiments, as described at the end of the previous chapter, can help with this variant of creator blindness, as can the tools in this chapter.

Assets and Attackers

This book has been critical of asset-centered modeling, and it has been critical to attacker-centric modeling. Not to beat a dead horse, this section examines them again in light of factors such as flow and boundary objects. Asset-centric approaches require developers to focus on something other than the software they're building. That takes them into an unfamiliar space. The jargon "everything in the diagram is an asset" leads to extra cognitive load from using a different word (asset) than is natural (such as computer).

Attacker-centric approaches also stymie flow. The initial requirement to create a set of attackers means putting energy into a subdeliverable, although Appendix C, "Attacker Lists" can reduce or replace that work. Flow is also stymied by the demand to "think like an attacker" or even "this attacker." As discussed in the previous chapter, asking someone to "think like an attacker" can be a tall order (like "think like a professional chef"), and many people will be stymied and have no idea where to start.

Knowing the Participants

The better you understand the people who will be doing threat modeling, the better you can select or design a system that will work for them, and teach them how to perform. Are you designing a system for experts or newcomers? Those new to threat modeling will appreciate structure, while experts will find that it chafes. Are you teaching people who work on a particular technology? If your audience is the Microsoft Windows product group, you might find that a set of unix examples fails to resonate or communicate the details that matter to you.

You can divide participants into two major groups: those who want to develop deep expertise in threat modeling and those who don't. Both are reasonable desires. Many people are far more skilled in database design than I am; but I know enough to know what I don't know, and enough that I can sit in a design meeting and not feel like a waste of a chair. I used to refer to people who are not expert in threat modeling as "non-experts" until I realized how deeply situated in my worldview that is, and how dismissive it can sound. It's important to respect people's desires regarding the skills they want to develop (although it is reasonable to respectfully try to influence those choices and desires). I sometimes fall into the term non-expert, but I prefer to use "expert in other things."

Those who don't want to become threat modeling experts can still be asked to develop a basic degree of familiarity. As discussed in Chapter 17, "Bringing Threat Modeling to Your Organization," much like version control, you can reasonably expect a skilled software engineer to have some familiarity with concepts such as checking code into a branch, and managing branches. Similarly, you can look forward to a world in which every reasonably skilled software engineer will have some familiarity with threat modeling and why it's worthwhile, and in which a shop that doesn't threat model is viewed with as much disdain as one that does version control by copying source onto a random USB drive once a week and throwing them in a drawer.

Threat modeling experts will have to engage differently in such a world, and it will be a better world for many people. A typical engagement will have much deeper questions, and that puts a different burden on the threat modeling experts. Less frequently will a threat modeling expert be able to enter a room and have something useful to say after a simple glance at a diagram. The "obvious" threats will be found and addressed more frequently by experts in other things.

Security experts will get value from experts in other things when those folks are not leaning on the security experts all the time. They can review instead of create, which frees up time to focus on the trickier, more challenging, deeper threats. At the same time, it can be scary to have experts in other things learn some of the magic tricks that you perform. It threatens the way security professionals self-identify and how they present themselves. Some security professionals will be scared of the change, and not want to move it ahead. Those who do drive change to their organization will find themselves increasingly valued by management and future employers.

These comments on participants are quite general. Understanding your own participants and especially the technical leaders will be a key part of making a process that works. Not understanding the participants is a sure route to failure. Understanding your participants and explicitly documenting the salient attributes of your environment are important components of a successful threat modeling process, both within your organization and when others try to learn from it.

Boundary Objects

The concept of a *boundary object* has been quite useful to me in designing threat modeling approaches that work for a wide set of participants. It is perhaps most easily understood through an example: A set of experts were working on a museum exhibit about birds. Some experts focused on the learning objectives and how the exhibit as a whole would come together. Other experts focused on the individual displays. The bird watchers wanted to focus on comparing the birds, such as markings on the chest, the different beaks. The evolutionary biologists wanted to show the birds in their niches, and how they could have evolved into them. The exhibit wasn't coming together. Each group had its own jargon, its own perspective, its own way of thinking about what made a given bird interesting or not interesting. Long story short, what helped was when the participants had the bird under discussion in the room with them, and could point to salient features. The bird acted as a boundary object, something they could all focus on in their discussions (Star, 1989). Ironically and unfortunately, there is no easy introduction to this field. That is, it lacks a boundary object.

In crafting a threat modeling approach that will include a variety of participants, boundary objects can help. The Microsoft SDL TM Tool includes two by-design boundary objects: diagrams and bugs. At the beginning of this chapter, you learned how creating those diagrams at the start of the process reduces friction to a flow state, and how the choice of diagram type interacts with cognitive load. There's another important aspect to the diagram, which is that it acts as a boundary object. Both software developers and security geeks can point at the diagram and use it as a focal point for conversation. Their individual jargon, perspectives, and ways of thinking meet when someone goes to the whiteboard, jabs at a line, and says, for example, "Right here, what data goes from foo to bar?" That data flow is the boundary object.

The second boundary object in the tool is the bug. The bug acts as an object that both developers and threat modeling experts can point to when discussing an issue. This is why the SDL TM Tool includes buttons that file bugs with a single click, and threats are portrayed as less complete if a bug hasn't been filed. Using boundary objects at the beginning and end of a process is a good design pattern for any system passed between people with different skill sets. There may be other boundary objects, and looking for them as you work with different communities is a great practice in architecting for success.

The Best Is the Enemy of the Good

There are a number of scenarios in which aspirations of security perfection lead to either not shipping or shipping without security. Aspiring to the best security is admirable, as is delivering good security. Finding the right balance between the good and the best is tricky in many areas of life. Getting the wrong balance can have all sorts of downsides.

There are some threat-modeling-specific risks to be aware of. One is that effort focused on defending against a more powerful adversary might distract from effort to defend against attacks by other adversaries. For example, effort to make it harder to exploit vulnerabilities by corrupting memory and exploit vulnerabilities is deeply technically challenging. It may be that work to prevent the more common social engineering attacks is set aside to focus on the interesting technical challenge. Paul Syverson has shown that in comparing privacy technologies of low- and high-latency mixes, some simple attacks work better on the higher security, high-latency mixes. In each of these cases, the trade-offs are not simple ones (Syverson, 2011).

Another risk is that your security may be different with respect to different adversaries with different capabilities. It's not always the case that adversaries are a strict superset of one another. For example, two attackers might have different risk tolerance. A technically weaker attacker—say, a criminal running malware—might be more willing to take risks than a technically more powerful attacker such as an intelligence agency. There is also a risk that a threat is anchored in defenders' minds. That is, they become overly-focused on a threat to the exclusion of others. For example, privacy threats from smart meters are complex to defend against, and easily understood. There is a set of threats to privacy that are easier to execute and easier to defend against, but the more subtle surveillance threats get more attention (Danezis, 2011). A real-world example of this can be found in the Predator drone system. The story is well summarized in a *Wired* article:

> *The original Predator, just 27 feet long, was little more than a scaled-up model plane with an 85-horsepower engine. It had a payload of just half a ton for all its fuel, cameras and radios. And encryption systems can be heavy. (Big crypto boxes are a major reason the Army's futuristic universal radio ended up being too bulky for combat, for example.) With the early Predator models, the Air Force made the conscious decision to leave off the crypto. The flying branch was well aware of the risk. "Depending on the theater of operation and hostile electronic combat systems present, the threat to the UAVs could range from negligible with only a potential of signal intercept for detection purpose, to an active jamming effort made against an operating, unencrypted UAV" the Air Force reported in 1996. "The link characteristics of the baseline Predator system could be vulnerable to corruption of down links data or hostile data insertions."*
>
> "Most U.S. Drones Openly Broadcast Secret Video Feeds" (Shachtman, 2012)

The threats are easily found via STRIDE or other threat modeling, and include signal intercept (information disclosure of location), active jamming (DoS), corruption of downlinks (tampering, information disclosure), and hostile data insertions (EoP). The standard approach to mitigating network threats is the use of cryptography. Thus, the mitigations are also well understood, with the possible exception of location tracking, for which military aircraft typically use spread spectrum or narrow-beam communications.

However, the mitigation description in the article is slightly inaccurate. It is more clearly stated as "NSA-approved encryption systems can be heavy." The NSA wants a variety of shielding and self-destruct mechanisms to address threats of electromagnetic emissions and disclosure of cryptosystems or keys. These are reasonable threats to mitigate in the NSA's book, but as a result of requiring these as a "package deal," the version 1 system used no crypto. Application compatibility concerns have kept crypto out ever since. This is a great example of allowing the best to be the enemy of the good. It might have been possible to deploy with publicly available cryptographic systems without additional layers of protection in the first releases, and then add more protections later. (There are possible concerns about key management, which are likely solvable with public key cryptography. Again, if you allow the best to be the enemy of the good, you end up with control channels in the clear.)

Closing Perspectives

As this book draws to a close, there are two topics that remain. The first is the claim that the threat model has changed, and what you can do with such a claim.

The second is the matter of artistry in threat modeling. It will likely surprise no one that I am fond of threat modeling, and see room for artistry.

"The Threat Model Has Changed"

If I had a dollar for every time I'd heard that "the threat model has changed" in the last few months, I certainly wouldn't tell readers of this book where I was keeping them. It's worth breaking this claim down a little, and understanding what it means.

So first, what's "the threat model?" This phrase often means some set of threats that everyone needs to worry about. And over the last 50 years, that's been revolutionized at least twice. One revolution was the rise of personal computers, when anyone could obtain a computer that was under their control and use it as a base of operations. The second was the rise of interconnected networks. Most important was the Internet, but the rise of networks in general made it possible for remote attackers to come after you. There's a good case that the extension of the Internet and inexpensive computers to the poorest parts of the world represents a third such revolution, in which our assumptions about the economics of attacks have been shattered.

There are other, smaller, but still important changes recently. These include the rise of criminal markets, the normalization of the Internet as a battlefield, and the rise of online activism. There has been a rise of online marketplaces where specialists in techniques such as exploit development, phishing, or draining bank accounts can buy and sell their skills. This rise in the efficiency of attackers and their ability to collaborate is clearly important, although how much the change in attacker economics will change the threat model is still playing out. Another important change is the apparent willingness of governments to invest in the continuation of politics by "cyber" means. Some label this war, others espionage. I think it is probably something new, and the ways in which organizations can find themselves under sustained, persistent attack by paid attackers is a change to the threat model. The third change is the rise of online activists. Although the term "hacktivism" was coined in 1996, the eagerness of people around the world to take up attack tools and apply them seems new and different.

There is another sense in which the phrase "the threat model has changed" is used. It also means the threats which matter enough to influence requirements has changed. This is how many people are using it in the wake of Edward Snowden's revelations about Internet spying. We have long known (in general terms) that the Internet is either heavily monitored or highly susceptible to such monitoring, and that knowledge was insufficient to motivate action. Many of those asserting that the threat model has changed are really asserting that the valid requirements have changed.

Not all of the revelations are things we knew. For example, efforts by US agencies to introduce weakened cryptosystems into American standards represent new threats. (This is simplified for the sake of an example.) Nonetheless, many of the revelations are changing the requirements end of the threat model, rather than revealing new threats.

Lastly, there is a tension between two perspectives. The first is that "all this has happened before, and all this will happen again." In many ways, the attacks change slowly, and new threats are often slight variations on the old threats. The other perspective is that attacks always get better. Both are right. What is perhaps most important is when someone tells you that the threat model has changed, you understand the ways in which it has changed, and what that may require or enable you to better secure.

On Artistry

"If you have to ask what jazz is, you'll never know."

Louis Armstrong

Many security experts learned to threat model the way blues or jazz musicians would learn to play: apprenticed to a master. This has many advantages, and a huge downside. The downside first: It's hard to decide if the heroin addiction is part of what you need to learn. More to the point, it's hard to know if the masters are doing it the way they do it because that's the best way, or because that's how they learned it.

An early reviewer commented that this book turns threat modeling into a mechanical exercise, and takes the art out of it. For the early parts of this book, that is correct, intentional, and essential. Truly excellent threat modeling is not something that everyone can achieve. Anyone can pick up a camera and take a picture. It's easy to produce a .jpg file that captures the light in a scene. With an understanding of technique, deliberate practice, and critiques someone can regularly produce a decent picture. With all that and talent, they can produce great pictures. This book introduces the practitioner to the techniques and provides guidance and structure; but all the books in the world don't obviate the need to practice and learn. Systems to be threat modeled abound. Find a teacher or even a partner student and take them on. Competency requires a mastery of the "tools" that can only result from using them. It requires critiques and asking how you can do better. It requires someone telling you where your work is lacking. With decent tools and feedback, anyone can become competent.

It's perfectly reasonable to want to aim higher than that, and many of the people who read the closing chapters of a book on threat modeling are likely aiming higher—and to them I want to say that the mechanical aspects are necessary but not sufficient.

To produce art requires practice and experience. It may be that you're the Salvador Dali of threat modeling. That's awesome. As anyone who's ever really studied a Dali painting knows, Dali had incredible technique to back up his talent. He didn't just say, "Hey, this would be a fun image." He made the clock melt on canvas. Anyone can put a urinal in a room and call it art. Developing a deep understanding of what makes a threat model good and what helps an organization deliver good threat models is part of greatness, and technique provides a needed foundation for your artistry.

Another interesting question is should an organization aim for process or artistry? In a fascinating Harvard Business Review article ("When Should a Process Be Art?"), Joseph Hall and M. Eric Johnson take aim at this question. They say when a process has variable inputs and customers value distinctive outputs, an artistic process might be a good answer. In their model, an artistic process is one where highly skilled professionals exercise judgment. They give the example of Steinway pianos, each made with wood whose variation impacts the instrument. Threat modeling certainly has varied inputs of requirements and software, and the output that's most helpful can be different. So it may well be a good candidate for an artistic process if your organization can support one. The essence is to figure out where artistry is appropriate, to create processes to support and judge the artistic work, and to periodically re-evaluate the balance between art and science. See (Hall, 2009) for more.

Summary

There is a set of prescriptive tools that you can use to design better processes. The first is attention to flow, that state of full engagement that can lead to outstanding results. There is a set of conditions for flow, and each can be considered by a system designer. Doing so requires that you understand who will be executing the tasks using the approach you're designing. People with different backgrounds will have different skills, and thus respond differently to the same challenge. They will also see objects differently. Artifacts such as diagrams and bugs can work as boundary objects, enabling people with different skills and from different disciplines to meet on common ground.

With these tools, and with all the good aspirations in the world, it can be tempting to aim for perfect security. Perfect security is a worthwhile goal, but so is shipping. Unfortunately, sometimes the two goals are at odds, and a team will need to make trade-offs. It's important to not allow the "best," or your highest aspirations for a system, to become the enemies of shipping with good security.

Finding a balance between all these factors is where threat modeling moves from practical and prescriptive toward artistry. This book has focused on the practical and prescriptive, because those have been lacking. The tasks involved in threat modeling have often been too hard. There is a great deal of artistry to be found in finding the best threats, the most clever redesigns, or the most elegant mitigations.

Now Threat Model

So now we arrive at the end of this book, and the start of something better. This book has presented the state of threat modeling as 2013 draws to a close. I hope it has come together in a form that you can use either to begin threat modeling or to improve your threat modeling. Parts II and III should provide enough prescriptive advice and detailed, actionable information that you feel comfortable assembling the "Lego blocks" into something that works for your organization. Part IV on specifics should get you through those gnarly spots. This closing chapter should help you understand what makes a threat modeling approach succeed or fail. I encourage you to now put the knowledge you've gained to good use. Go threat model, and make things more secure.

APPENDIX

A

Helpful Tools

This appendix provides you with a set of lists containing common answers to "What's your threat model?" and "What are your assets?"

Common Answers to "What's Your Threat Model?"

The question "What's your threat model?" can help you quickly express who or what you're worried about. Some typical answers include the following:

- Someone with user-level access to the machine
- Someone with admin-level access to the machine
- Someone with physical access to a machine or site

Network Attackers

Attackers that are in a good position to attack via the network include the following:

- Eve or Mallory
  - Using available software
  - Creating new software
- Your ISP

- Your cloud provider, or someone who has compromised them
- The coffee shop or hotel network
- The Mukhbarat or the NSA
- A compromised switch or router
- The node at the other end of a connection
- A trusted node that's been compromised

Physical Attackers

This section considers those physically attacking a technical system, not those attacking people. Examples include the following:

- Possession of a machine for unlimited time
  - A thief who has stolen the machine
  - Police or border agents who seize the machine
- Time-limited but physically unconstrained access
  - For five minutes
  - For an hour
  - The janitor*
  - Hotel maids*
- Physically constrained access to a machine
  - Can insert a USB key ("Can I just plug my phone in to recharge?")
  - Physical, in-line keyloggers
  - Access via Bluetooth or other radio protocols
- Ninjas
- Pirates (the kind with guns)

*Either of whom can be a techie in a uniform

There is an equivalent set of threats to the integrity and confidentiality of a network:

- Access to the network for an (effectively) unlimited time (easiest with wireless networks, including WiFi, microwave or satellite links)
- Time-limited access that allows plugging in of a "leave behind" box, such as those made by the company Pwnie Express
- Physically and temporally constrained access, such as a guest plugging into a conference room network

Attacks against People

There's a variety of ways in which people are attacked. Cryptographers are fond of talking about "rubber hose" cryptanalysis (also known as beating someone until they talk). It can be fascinating to consider what happens if each person (or class of person, such as sysadmins) in a system goes bad, but these attacks can be tremendously expensive to prevent.

For example, there is a model outlining how secret agents convince people to become spies using the following four methods (Shane, 2008):

- Money
- Ideology
- Coercion
- Ego

In this micro-model, coercion includes persuasions like rubber hose cryptanalysis, the Zapata cartel kidnapping a family member, and so on. Similarly, ego includes using sex as bait. Always remember to focus on the threats that you can mitigate.

Supply Chain Attackers

There is a set of people who can attack you through the supply chain that delivers technology to your environment. These attackers are commonly worried about, but they are hard to protect yourself against. They can attack hardware, software, and firmware, along with documentation. What's more in the era of using search engines to solve all technical problems, an attacker can augment their attacks with well-crafted untrustworthy advice on random websites in the hopes of influencing people to act in certain ways. Supply chain attackers include the following:

- System designers
  - For your system
  - For components on which you depend
- System builders
  - The factory in China building your widgets
  - A supplier to that factory who delivers parts
  - A supplier to that factory who delivers machines
- The delivery chain

Privacy Attackers

These are attackers who might violate people's privacy. They include the following:

- Marketers
  - Systems designers who rely on advertising models
  - Component libraries who sell to marketers
- Data brokers
- Stalkers
- Identity thieves
- The NSA or other national intelligence agencies
- Police
  - Constrained by laws in the way democracies expect
  - Not/less constrained by law
- Those linking databases

Non-Sentient "Attackers"

Non-sentient attackers such as the following generally don't attack the confidentiality or integrity of your systems, but they can absolutely impact its availability:

- Natural disasters (as appropriate for your region)
- Public health disasters

The Internet Threat Model

As discussed in Chapter 17, "Bringing Threat Modeling to Your Organization," the IETF has adapted a standard threat model for the design of new Internet protocols. The document is a fascinating example of how security experts can design a custom threat modeling approach for an organization. Note that revelations by Edward Snowden in late 2013 may change this model.

> *The Internet environment has a fairly well understood threat model. In general, we assume that the end-systems engaging in a protocol exchange have not themselves been compromised. Protecting against an attack when one of the end-systems has been compromised is extraordinarily difficult. It is, however, possible to design protocols which minimize the extent of the damage done under these circumstances.*

> *By contrast, we assume that the attacker has nearly complete control of the communications channel over which the end-systems communicate. This means that the attacker can read any PDU (Protocol Data Unit) on the network and undetectably remove, change, or inject forged packets onto the wire. This includes being able to generate packets that appear to be from a trusted machine. Thus, even if the end-system with which you wish to communicate is itself secure, the Internet environment provides no assurance that packets which claim to be from that system in fact are.*
>
> Rescorla and Korver, *Security Considerations Guidelines* (RFC 3552)

The IETF also considers two classes of limited threat models: passive attackers who will read from but not write to the network, and active attackers who can write, and possibly read.

Assets

Please only use this section after you have considered the risks and difficulties of asset-centric modeling, as discussed in Chapters 2 "Strategies for Threat Modeling" and 19 "Architecting for Success."

Computers as Assets

You can label various types of computers as assets, including the following:

- Computers used by individuals
  - This computer
  - A laptop
  - A mobile phone
  - iPad/Kindle/Nook
  - etc.
- Servers
  - Web server
  - E-mail server
  - Database server
  - etc.
- Security systems
  - Firewall
  - VPN concentrator
  - Log server

- Functional groups
    - Development systems
    - Financial systems
    - Manufacturing systems

People as Assets

You can think of people as assets who could come under attack. (Of course, it is more correct to consider them as resources.) Some groups of people you might consider include the following:

- Executives
    - Executive assistants
- Sysadmins
- Sales people
- Janitorial staff
- Food-processing staff
- Contractors of various stripes
- Any employee
- Citizens
- Immigrants
- Minorities
- People living with disabilities

Processes as Assets

You can consider your processes as assets. Examples include the following:

- Issuing a check/money transfer (including refunds)
- Shipping product (or product keys)
- Software or product development
    - Deployment
- Manufacturing
    - Integrity of product
    - Safety of workers
- Hiring

Intangible Assets

The reasoning behind including intangible assets is that because they're listed on the balance sheet, they should be listed in the threat model. However, there's a chasm between these assets and threats that you can mitigate. Regardless, here are some examples:

- Reputation or goodwill
- Intellectual property
- Stock price
- Executive attention
- Operational staff attention
- Employee morale

Stepping-Stone Assets

These are assets in the most limited sense, but they are sometimes used:

- Authentication data
    - Username/password
    - Physical access tokens
    - Mobile phones pretending to be access tokens
- Network access
- Access to a particular computer

APPENDIX

B

Threat Trees

These threat trees are worked-through analyses, intended to act as both models and resources. Each tree is presented twice, first as a graphical tree and then as a textual one. The versions contain the same data, but different people will find one or the other more usable. The labels in the trees are, by necessity, shorthand for a longer attack description. The labels are intended to be evocative for those experienced with these trees. Toward this goal, some nodes have a label and a quoted tag, such as "phishing." Not all nodes are easily tagged with a word or an acronym. The trees in this appendix are OR trees, where success in any node leads to success in the goal node. The rare exceptions are noted in the text and diagrams.

This appendix has three sections: The main body is a set of 15 STRIDE threat trees. That is followed by three trees for running code on a server, a client, or a mobile device, as those are common attacker targets. The last tree is "exploiting a social program," illustrating how systems such as e-mail and instant messenger programs can be exploited. The appendix ends with a section on tricky filenames, and their use in certain classes of attacks which trick people.

STRIDE Threat Trees

These trees are organized according to STRIDE-per-element. Each has as its root node the realization of a threat action. These STRIDE trees are built on the ones presented in *The Security Development Lifecycle* (2006). The trees are focused on first-order threats. Once you have elevated privileges to root, you can do an awful lot of tampering with files on that system (or other mischief), but such actions are not shown in the trees, as including them leads to a maze of twisty little trees, all alike.

Each tree in this section is followed by a table or tables that explains the node and discusses mitigation approaches, both for those developing a system and those deploying it ("operations") who need stronger security. The term "few" in the mitigations column should be understood as meaning there is no obvious or simple approach. Each of the ways you might address a threat has trade-offs. In the interests of space and focused threat modeling, those trade-offs are not discussed in this appendix. In a very real sense, when you start considering those trade-offs, threat modeling has done its job. It has helped you find the threat. What you do with it, how you triage and address the bugs from those threats, is a matter of good engineering.

The trees presented in this section are shown in Table B-0. In this appendix, the labels differs from normal Wiley style, in ways that are intended to be easy (or easier) to use given the specific information in this appendix.

- Tables are numbered to align with the figures to make it easier for you to go back and forth between them. Thus, figure B-1 is referenced by Tables B-1a, B-1b, B-1c, B-1d and B-1e, while figure B-2 is referenced by a single table B-2.
- Many tables are broken into smaller logical units. The breakdown is driven by a desire to have tables of reasonable length.
- Where there are multiple tables per tree, they are referred to as subtrees. Each subtree is labeled with a combination of category ("spoofing") and subnode ("by obtaining credentials").
- Numbering of tables starts at zero, because you're a programmer and prefer it that way. (Or perhaps because we wanted to start figures at B-1, making this table hard to number.)

Table B-0 does not have a figure associated with it.

Table B-0: STRIDE-per-Element

		DFD APPLICABILITY			
THREAT TYPE	MITIGATION	EXTERNAL ENTITY	PROCESS	DATA FLOW	DATA STORE
S – Spoofing	Authentication	B-1*	B-2	B-3*	
T – Tampering	Integrity		B-4	B-5	B-6
R – Repudiation	Non-repudiation	B-7	B-7		B-8*
I – Information Disclosure	Confidentiality		B-9	B-10	B-11
D – Denial of Service	Availability		B-12	B-13	B-14
E – Elevation of Privilege	Authorization		B-15		

*(B-1) Spoofing an external entity is shown as spoofing a client in the following tables.

*(B-3) Spoofing of a data flow is at odds with how STRIDE-per-element has been taught.

*(B-8) Repudiation threats matter when the data stored is logs.

NOTE **The spoofing of a data flow is at odds with how STRIDE-per-element has generally been taught or presented, but it is in alignment with how some people naturally think of spoofing. It's less-tested content; and as you gain experience, you're likely to find that the threats it produces overlap heavily with spoofing of a client or tampering with a data flow.**

Each tree ends with "other," a node without further discussion in the explanatory text because given its unanticipated nature, what to add is unclear. Each tree is technically complete, as "other" includes everything. Less glibly, each tree attempts to focus on the more likely threats. Therefore, for example, although backup tape data stores are subject to both tampering and information disclosure, the disclosure threats are far easier to realize, so the backup threats are not mentioned in the tree for tampering with a data store. Generally, only security experts, those aspiring toward such expertise, or those with very high value targets should spend a lot of time looking for those "others." It is tempting, for example, when writing about tampering with a process, to declare that those threats "matter less." However, which threats matter is (ahem) a matter of requirements.

As a community, we know relatively little about what threats manifest in the real world (Shostack, 2009). If we knew more about which threats are likely, we could create trees optimized by likelihood or optimized for completeness, although completeness will always need some balance with pedantry and usability. Such balance might be provided by tree construction or how the tree is presented. For example, a software system that contains the trees could present various subsets.

Spoofing an External Entity (Client/ Person/Account)

Figure B-1 shows an attack tree for spoofing by/of an external entity. Spoofing threats are generally covered in Chapter 3, "STRIDE," and Chapter 8, "Defensive Tactics and Technologies," as well as Chapter 14, "Accounts and Identity."

- Goal: Spoof client
- Obtain existing credentials
  - Transit
  - Federation issues
  - Change management
  - Storage
    - At server
    - At client
    - At KDC
    - At 3rd party
- Backup authentication
  - Knowledge-based authentication (KBA)
  - Information disclosure (e-mail)
  - Chained authentication
- Authentication UI
  - Local login Trojan ("CAD")
  - Privileged access Trojan (./sudo)
  - Remote spoof ("phishing")
- Insufficient authentication
  - Null credentials

- Guest/anonymous credentials
- Predictable credentials
- Factory default credentials
- Downgrade authentication
- No authentication
- Other authentication attack

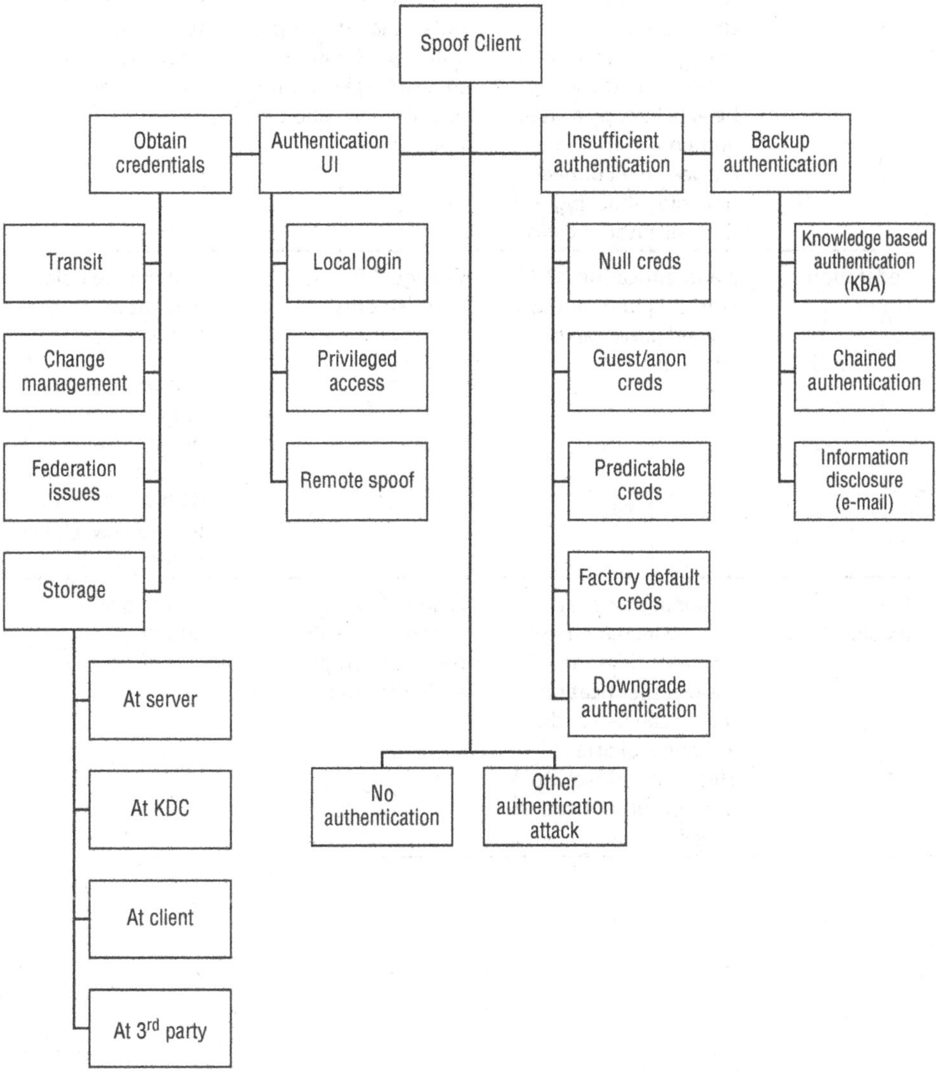

Figure B-1: Spoofing an external entity (client)

Also consider whether tampering threats against the authorization process should be in scope for your system.

Table B-1a: Spoofing by Obtaining Existing Credentials Subtree

TREE NODE	EXPLANATION	DEVELOPER MITIGATION	OPERATIONAL MITIGATION
Transit	If the channel over which authenticators are sent is not encrypted and authenticated, an attacker may be able to copy a static authenticator or tamper with the connection, piggybacking on the real authentication	Use standard authentication protocols, rather than develop your own. Confirm that strong encryption and authentication options are used.	Tools such as SSL, IPsec, and SSH tunneling can be added to protect a weak transit.
Federation issues	If authentication is federated, failures at the trusted party can be impactful.	Change the requirements.	Logging, to help you know what's happening Tunneling, to improve network defense (but a federation system with weak cryptography will have other issues)
Change management	If your authentication change management is weaker than the main authentication, then it can be used as a channel of attack. This relates closely to backup authentication issues.	Ensure that change management is strongly authenticated.	Logging and auditing

Table B-1b: Spoofing by Obtaining Existing Credentials: Attacking Storage Subtree

TREE NODE	EXPLANATION	DEVELOPER MITIGATION	OPERATIONAL MITIGATION
At server	The server stores the authenticator in a way that's vulnerable to information disclosure or tampering. Information disclosure is worse with static approaches such as passwords than with asymmetric authentication.	Ensure that the authenticators are well locked down. Seek asymmetric approaches. If using passwords, see Chapter 14 for storage advice.	Consider adjusting permissions on various files (and the impact of doing so).
At client	The client stores authenticators in a way that an attacker can steal.	The balance between usability and credential prompting can be hard. Ensure that the credentials are not readable by other accounts on the machine. If you're designing a high-security system, consider hardware techniques to augment security (TPM, smartcards, hardware security modules).	Treat authentication as a probabilistic decision, and use factors such as IP or machine fingerprints to augment authentication decisions.
At KDC (key distribution center)	If a KDC is part of a symmetric-key authentication scheme, it may need to store plaintext authenticators.	To minimize the attack surface, design the KDC to perform as few functions as possible. Write your security operations manual early.	Protect the heck out of the machine with firewalls, IDS, and other techniques as appropriate.
At third party	People reuse passwords, and other parties may leak passwords your customers use.	Avoid static passwords altogether. If your usernames are not e-mail addresses, exploiting leaks is much harder. For example, if the Acme company leaks that "foobar1" authenticates Alice@example.com, attackers can simply try Alice@example.com as a username; but if the username which leaks is Alice, the odds are that another person has that username at your site.	Code to detect brute-force attempts, or an upswing in successful logins from a new location or IP.

Table B-1c: Spoofing Backup Authentication Subtree

TREE NODE	EXPLANATION	DEVELOPER MITIGATION	OPERATIONAL MITIGATION
Knowledge-based authentication (KBA)	KBA schemes have many problems, including memorability and secrecy. See Chapter 14."	Use social authentication or other schemes rather than KBA.	Use a password management tool, and treat each KBA field as a password.
Information disclosure	Attacker can read backup authentication messages containing secrets that can be used to authenticate. This most frequently appears with e-mail, but not always.	Use social authentication. If you can't, don't store passwords in a form you can send, but rather create a random password and require the person change it, or send a one-use URL.	If the product you're using has this problem, it's probably non-trivial to graft something else onto it.
Chained authentication	Attackers who take over e-mail can abuse e-mail information disclosure as well as disclosures after taking over accounts. See "How Apple and Amazon Security Flaws Led to My Epic Hacking,"(Honan, 2012) for more information.	Use social authentication, and consider treating authentication in a probabilistic fashion. If you can't, avoid relying on authenticators that other organizations can disclose. (No claim that's easy.)*	These issues are hard to fix in development, and even harder in operations.

*It is tempting to suggest that you should not display data that other sites might use for authentication. That advice is a "tar pit," leading to more questions than answers. For example, some organizations use the last four digits of a SSN for authentication. If you don't display those last four digits, should you display or reveal other digits to someone who can authenticate as your customer? If you do, you may help an attacker construct the full number. It is also tempting to say don't worry about organizations that have made poor decisions, but backup authentication is a real challenge, and characterizing those decisions as poor is easy in a vacuum.

Table B-1d: Spoof Authentication UI Subtree

TREE NODE	EXPLANATION	DEVELOPER MITIGATION	OPERATIONAL MITIGATION
Local login Trojan ("CAD")	An attacker presents a login user interface to someone	Use of secure attention sequences to reach the OS	Always press Ctrl+Alt+Delete (CAD) to help keep your login information secure.
Privileged access Trojan (./sudo)	An attacker alters the `PATH` variable so their code will load first.	Hard to defend against if the environment allows for customization	Don't use someone else's terminal session for privileged work.
Remote spoofing ("phishing")	A website* presents itself as a different site, including a login page.	Reputation services such as IE SmartScreen or Google's Safe Browsing	Reputation services that search for abuses of your trademarks or brand

* Currently, phishing is typically performed by websites, but other forms of remote spoofing are feasible. For example, an app store might contain an app falsely claiming to be from (spoofing) Acme Bank.

Table B-1e: Spoofing Where There's Insufficient Authentication Subtree

TREE NODE	EXPLANATION	DEVELOPER MITIGATION	OPERATIONAL MITIGATION
Null credentials	The system allows access with no credentials. This may be OK, for example, on a website.	Add authentication.	Disable that account.
Guest/anonymous credentials	The system has a guest login. Again, that may be OK.	Remove the guest account.	Disable that account.

Continues

Table B-1e *(continued)*

TREE NODE	EXPLANATION	DEVELOPER MITIGATION	OPERATIONAL MITIGATION
Predictable credentials	The system uses predictable user-names or a poor random generator for passwords.	If assigning passwords, use strong randomness. If usernames are unlikely to be easily discovered, arbitrary usernames may help.	Reset passwords, assign new usernames.
Factory default credentials	The system ships with the same credentials, or credentials that can be guessed, like those based on Ethernet ID.	Force a password change on first login, or print unique; passwords on each device/documentation.	Change the password.
Downgrade authentication	An attacker can choose which of several authentication schemes to use.	Remove older/weaker authentication schemes, turn them off by default, or track which each client has used.	Turn off weaker schemes.

There is no table for either no authentication (which is hopefully obvious; change that if the requirements warrant such a change) or other authentication attack.

Spoofing a Process

Figure B-2 shows an attack tree for spoofing a process. Spoofing threats are generally covered in Chapter 3, and Chapter 8. If an attacker has to be root, modify the kernel, or similarly, use high privilege levels to engage in spoofing a process on the local machine; then, generally, such attacks are hard or impossible to mitigate, and as such, requirements to address them are probably bad requirements.

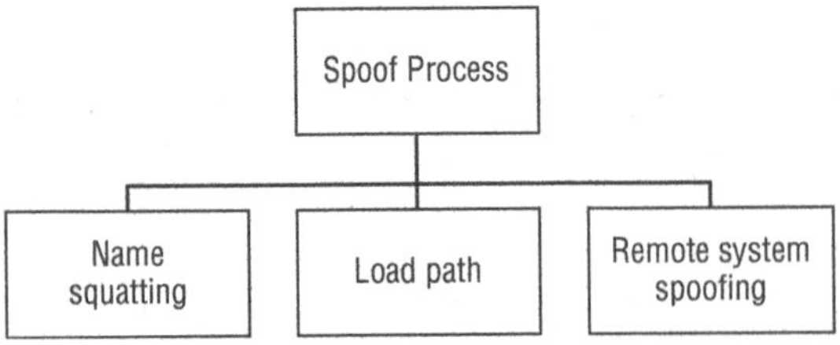

Figure B-2: Spoofing a process

Goal: Spoof process

- Name squatting
- Load path
- Remote system spoofing

Table B-2: Spoofing a Process

TREE NODE	EXPLANATION	DEVELOPER MITIGATION	OPERATIONAL MITIGATION
Name squatting	The attacker connects to a communication endpoint, such as a file, named pipe, socket, or RPC registry and pretends to be another entity.	Use the OS for naming, permissions of synchronization points.	Possibly permissions
Load path	The attacker deposits a library, extension, or other element in a way that the process will trust at next load.	Name the files you want with full paths (thus, refer to %windir%\winsock.dll, not winsock.dll or ~/.login, not .login).	Check permissions on files.
Remote system spoofing	Confuse a process about what a remote process is by tampering with (or "spoofing") the data flows.	See tampering, spoofing data flow trees (B5 and B3).	See tampering, spoofing data flow trees.

Spoofing of a Data Flow

Figure B-3 shows an attack tree for spoofing a process. Spoofing threats are generally covered in Chapter 3, and Chapter 8; and many of the mitigations are cryptographic, as covered in Chapter 16, "Threats to Cryptosystems." Spoofing a data flow is an amalgamation of tampering with a data flow and spoofing a client, which may be a more natural way for some threat modelers to consider attacks against network data flows. It is not traditionally considered in STRIDE-per-element, but it is included here as an experimental approach.

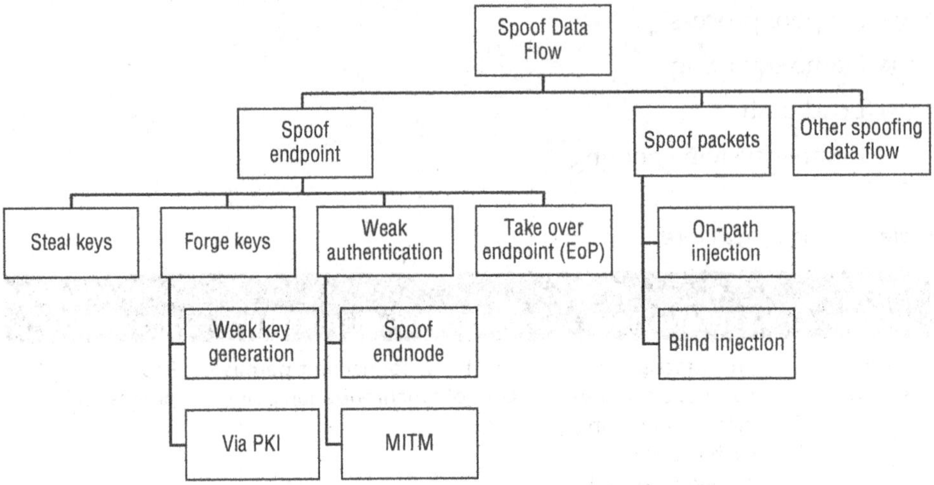

Figure B-3: Spoofing of a data flow

Goal: Spoof a data flow

- Spoof endpoint
  - Steal keys
  - Forge keys
    - Weak key generation
    - Via PKI
  - Weak authentication
    - Spoof endnode
    - MITM
  - Take over endpoint
- Spoof packets
  - Blind injection
  - On-path injection
- Other spoofing data flow

Table B-3a: Steal/forge Keys Subtree

TREE NODE	EXPLANATION	DEVELOPER MITIGATION	OPERATIONAL MITIGATION
Steal keys	Information disclosure where the data is crypto keys. Generally, see the information disclosure trees (B11, and also B9 and B10).	OS tools for secure key storage	Hardware security modules

Table B-3b: Forge Keys Subtree

TREE NODE	EXPLANATION	DEVELOPER MITIGATION	OPERATIONAL MITIGATION
Weak key generation	If a system is generating keys in a weak way, an attacker can forge them.*	Avoid generating keys at startup, especially for data center machines or those without hardware RNGs.	Regenerate keys
Via PKI	There are many ways to attack PKI, including misrepresentation, legal demands, commercial deals, or simply breaking in.†	Key persistence, perspectives/Convergence-like systems	Few

* Some examples of weak key generation include (Debian, 2008) and (Heninger, 2012).

† Examples of misrepresentation include Verisign issuing certificates for Microsoft (Fontana, 2001). A legal demand might be like the one issued to Lavabit (Masnick, 2013). Commercial deals include ones like Verisign's operation of a "lawful intercept" service (Verisign, 2007).

Table B-3c: Weak Authentication Subtree

TREE NODE	EXPLANATION	DEVELOPER MITIGATION	OPERATIONAL MITIGATION
Spoof endnode	Any non-cryptographically secured method of referring to a host, including MAC address, IP, DNS name, etc.	Use cryptography properly in the authentication scheme.	Tunneling
MITM	Man-in-the-middle attacks	Strong authentication with proper crypto	Tunneling

Table B-3d: Spoof Packets Subtree

TREE NODE	EXPLANATION	DEVELOPER MITIGATION	OPERATIONAL MITIGATION
On-path injection	A network attacker can see the normal packet flow and insert their own packets.	Cryptographic channel authentication and/or message authentication	Tunneling
Blind injection	An attacker cannot see packets and learn things such as sequence numbers, or see responses, but injects packets anyway.	Cryptographic channel authentication and/or message authentication	Tunneling

The "take over endpoint" node should be self-explanatory.

Tampering with a Process

Figure B-4 shows an attack tree for tampering with a process. Tampering threats are generally covered in Chapter 3, and Chapter 8, and are touched on in Chapter 16.

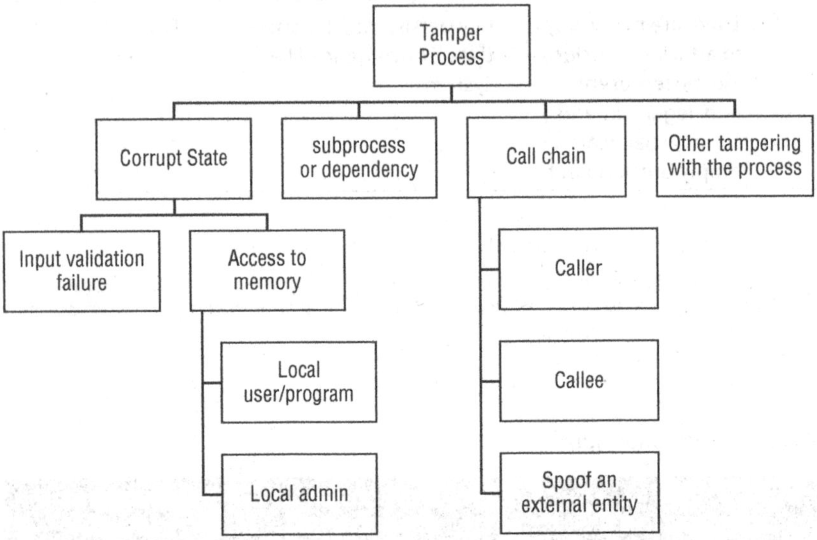

Figure B-4: Tampering with a process

Goal: Tamper with a process

- Corrupt state
  - Input validation failure
  - Access to memory
    - Local user/program
    - Local admin
- Call chain
  - Caller
  - Callee
  - Spoof an external entity
- Subprocess or dependency
- Other tampering with the process

Also consider whether these threats apply to subprocesses, or what happens if callers or callees are spoofed.

Table B-4a: Corrupt State Subtree

TREE NODE	EXPLANATION	DEVELOPER MITIGATION	OPERATIONAL MITIGATION
Input validation failure	If inputs are not appropriately validated, memory corruption can result in EoP or DoS.	Carefully validate all input for the appropriate purpose.	None for the threat, sandboxing can contain impact
Access to memory (local user/ program)	A user with authorized write access to memory can tamper with the process. It's important to realize that on many operating systems, this is the case for all programs the user runs. (Can you freely attach a debugger? If so, a program you're running can do the same.)	Create new account; Review shared memory permissions.	few
Access to memory (local admin)	A local admin with a debugger can be a threat (e.g., you're trying to use DRM).	Memory protection and anti-debugging schemes, generally used by DRM and other malware	separate machines

Table B-4b: Call Chain Subtree

TREE NODE	EXPLANATION	DEVELOPER MITIGATION	OPERATIONAL MITIGATION
Caller	Untrusted code may call your code, passing it malicious parameters.	Input validation	Permissions can be used to ensure that lower-trust code can't execute untrustworthy applications.
Callee	Your callees can tamper with memory (e.g., via extension points).	Design more constrained APIs.	Ensure that only trusted/ trustworthy callees are called, or trustworthy plugins are installed.
Subprocess or dependency	This is the same as the previous two, expressed differently in the hopes of being evocative.		

Tampering with a Data Flow

Figure B-5 shows an attack tree for tampering with a data flow. Tampering threats are generally covered in Chapter 3, and Chapter 8, cryptography will often play a part in addressing them, and is covered in Chapter 16.

Generally, if you don't prevent spoofing of a data flow, you have tampering and information disclosure problems.

Data flow threats can apply to channels or messages, or both. The difference is easiest to see with examples: E-mail messages travel over an SMTP channel, whereas HTML (and other format) messages travel over HTTP. The question of which you need (either, neither, or both) is a requirements question.

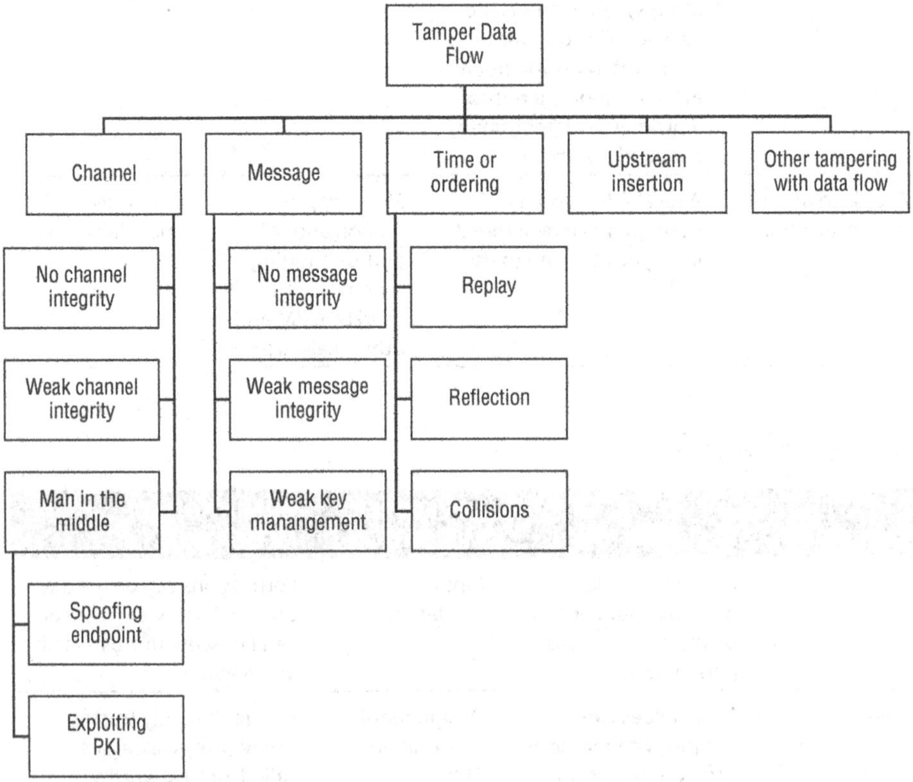

Figure B-5: Tampering with a data flow

Goal: Tamper with a data flow

- Message
  - No message integrity
  - Weak message integrity

- Weak key management
- Channel
  - No channel integrity
  - Weak channel integrity
  - Weak key management
  - Man in the middle
    - Spoof endnode (or endpoint)
    - Exploiting PKI
- Time or ordering
  - Replay
  - Reflection
  - Collisions
- Upstream insertion
- Other tampering with data flow

Table B-5a: Tampering with a Message Subtree

TREE NODE	EXPLANATION	DEVELOPER MITIGATION	OPERATIONAL MITIGATION
No message integrity	Nothing protects message integrity from tampering.	Add integrity controls.	Very dependent on the data flow. Tunneling may help address parts of the threat, but really provides channel integrity.
Weak message integrity	Weak algorithm, such as MD5	Use a better algorithm.	As above
Weak key management	Weak key management can lead to problems for the messages.	Use better key management.	As above

Table B-5b: Tampering with Channel Integrity Subtree

TREE NODE	EXPLANATION	DEVELOPER MITIGATION	OPERATIONAL MITIGATION
No channel integrity	Nothing protects channel integrity.	Add integrity controls.	Tunneling over an integrity-protected transport can help.
Weak channel integrity	Weak algorithm, such as MD5	Use a better algorithm.	As above

Continues

Table B-5b (*continued*)

TREE NODE	EXPLANATION	DEVELOPER MITIGATION	OPERATIONAL MITIGATION
Weak key management	Key management can be bad for either channels or messages or both.	Use better key management.	As above
Man in the middle	Man in the middle attacks that allow data tampering	Strong authentication	Tunneling
Spoofing endpoint	See tree B3.		
Exploit PKI	Attack the PKI system	Key pinning	Convergence, Persistence

Table B-5c: Tampering with Time or Ordering Subtree

TREE NODE	EXPLANATION	DEVELOPER MITIGATION	OPERATIONAL MITIGATION
Replay	Attacker resends messages that the system really sent .	Message identifiers, and tracking what's been seen	Tunneling may help.
Reflection	Attacker takes a message and sends it back to the sender.	Careful protocol design	Tunneling may help.
Collisions	Attacker sends (possibly invalid) messages with sequence numbers, causing real messages to be ignored.	Manage identifiers after validation.	Few

Table B-5d: Tampering via Upstream Insertion Subtree

TREE NODE	EXPLANATION	DEVELOPER MITIGATION	OPERATIONAL MITIGATION
Upstream insertion	Rather than tamper with the data flow directly, convince an endnode to insert the data you want.	Input validation on places where messages could be inserted; output validation on places where you send them.	Possibly firewalling

Tampering with a Data Store

Figure B-6 shows an attack tree for tampering with a data store. Tampering threats are generally covered in Chapter 3, and Chapter 8.

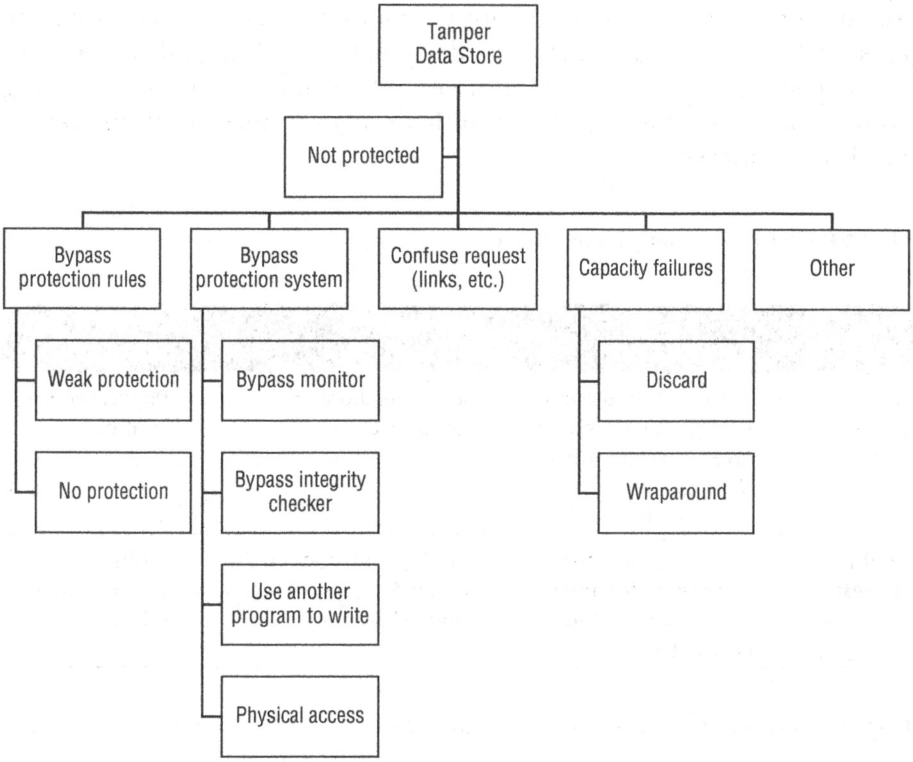

Figure B-6: Tampering with a data store

Goal: Tamper with a data store

- Not protected
- Confuse request
- Bypass protection rules
  - Weak rules
  - No protection
- Bypass protection system
  - Bypass monitor
  - Bypass integrity checker
  - Use another program to write
  - Physical access
- Capacity failures
  - Discard
  - Wraparound
- Other

You might consider tampering with the monitor or elevation of privilege against it; however, often at that point the attacker is admin, and all bets are . . . more complex. Capacity failures are an interesting balance of tampering and denial of service, but they can certainly result in tampering effects that are valuable to an attacker.

Table B-6a: Tamper with a Data Store Subtree

TREE NODE	EXPLANATION	DEVELOPER MITIGATION	OPERATIONAL MITIGATION
Not protected	There's no protection for data; for example, it's on a filesystem with no permissions, or a globally writable wiki.	Add protections as appropriate.	Physical access control
Confuse request	Can a data element have multiple names, for example through links or inclusion?	Check permissions on the resolved object (after name canonicalization).	Probably none with reasonable effort

Table B-6b: Tamper by Bypassing Protection Rules Subtree

TREE NODE	EXPLANATION	DEVELOPER MITIGATION	OPERATIONAL MITIGATION
Weak protection	The rules (ACLs, permissions, policies) allow people with questionable justification to alter the data.	Ensure your code creates data with appropriate permissions.	Change the permissions.
No protection	The rules allow anyone to write to the data store.	As above	As above

Table B-6c: Tamper by Bypassing a Protection System Subtree

TREE NODE	EXPLANATION	DEVELOPER MITIGATION	OPERATIONAL MITIGATION
Bypass monitor	Exploit the lack of a "reference monitor" through which all access requests pass, or take advantage of bugs.	Good design, extensive testing	Use a better system.
Bypass integrity checker	Attack either the integrity checker code or its database (often out of scope).	None	Read-only database, boot from separate OS
Use another program to write	If you can't put data into a store, can another program do so on your behalf? Can you put it somewhere else?	Ensure you understand the data you're writing on behalf of other processes.	Remove/block the proxy program.
Physical access	Reboot the system into another OS.	Encrypted filesystem or integrity checks with a crypto key stored elsewhere	Encrypted filesystem, physical protection

Table B-6d: Tampering via Capacity Failures Subtree

TREE NODE	EXPLANATION	DEVELOPER MITIGATION	OPERATIONAL MITIGATION
Discard	Refers to new data not being recorded	Shutdown or switch to wraparound.	More storage
Wraparound	Refers to the oldest data being deleted to make room	Shutdown or switch to discard.	More storage

The developer mitigations in Table B-6d are slightly less tongue-in-cheek than it may appear. After all, when you are out of storage, you're out of storage; and at that point you must choose either to allow the storage issue to stop the system or to make room in some fashion. Not shown in the table are compression and moving data to another store somewhere, both of which can be legitimate approaches.

Repudiation against a Process (or by an External Entity)

Figure B-7 shows an attack tree for repudiation against a process, or by an external entity. Repudiation threats are generally covered in Chapter 3, and Chapter 8, as well as in Chapter 14.

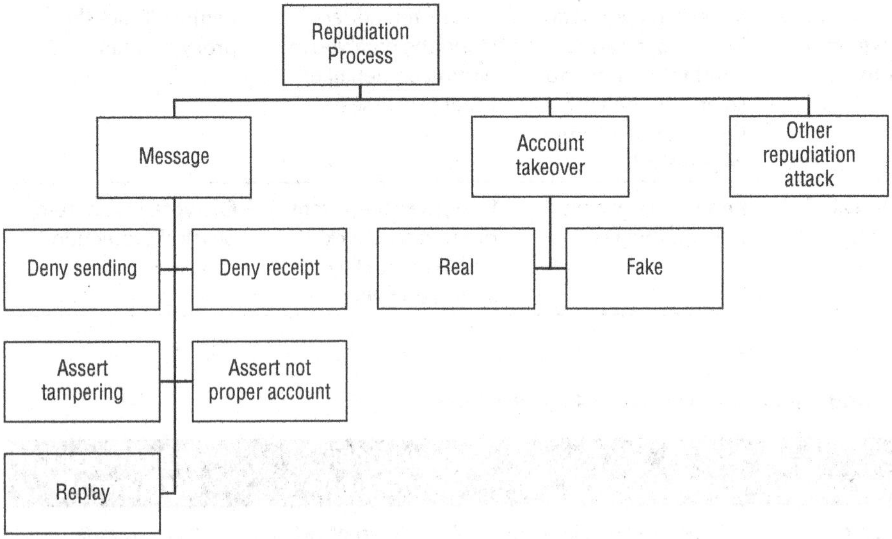

Figure B-7: Repudiation against a process

Goal: Repudiation

- Account takeover
  - Real
  - Fake
- Message
  - Deny sending
  - Deny receipt
  - Assert tampering
  - Assert not proper account

- Replay
- Other

Table B-7a: Repudiate by Account Takeover Subtree

TREE NODE	EXPLANATION	DEVELOPER MITIGATION	OPERATIONAL MITIGATION
Real	The account was actually compromised.	Stronger authentication	Additional authentication tools
Fake	Someone asserts that the account was taken over.	Strong logging	Strong logging, penalties*

* If you impose penalties, you will inevitably impose them on innocent customers. Be judicious.

Table B-7b: Message Repudiation Subtree

TREE NODE	EXPLANATION	DEVELOPER MITIGATION	OPERATIONAL MITIGATION
Deny sending	Claim that a message wasn't sent.	Digital signatures	Logging
Deny receipt	Claim that a message wasn't received.	Web bugs, logs	Logging, possibly firewalls to block web bugs
Assert tampering	Claim that a message has been altered.	Digital signatures	Log message hashes in a reliable way.
Assert not proper account	E-mail from barack.obama37@example.com is probably not from the president of the United States.	Meaningful IDs, nicknames (See Chapter 15, "Human Factors and Usability.")	Process?
Replay	If your messages are of the form "sell 1,000 shares now," then an attacker might be able to claim your sale of an extra 1,000 shares was in error.	Design protocols that are more precise.	Logging

Repudiation, Data Store

Figure B-8 shows an attack tree for repudiation in which logs are involved. Repudiation threats are generally covered in Chapter 3, and Chapter 8.

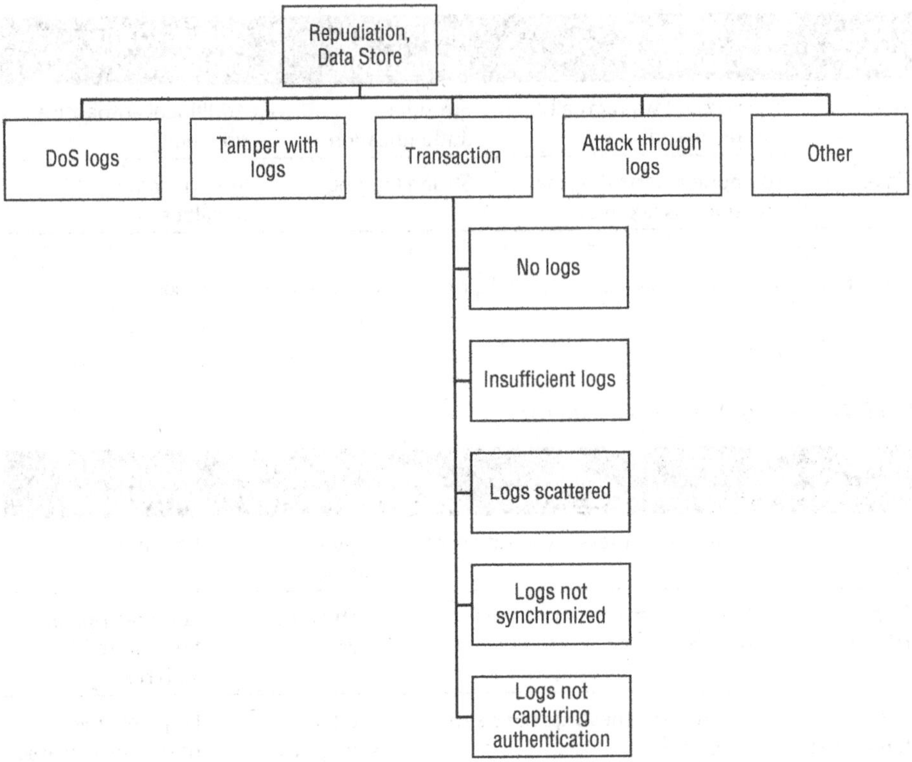

Figure B-8: Repudiation, Data Store

Goal: Repudiation (data store focus)

- Transaction
  - No logs
  - Insufficient logs
  - Logs scattered
  - Logs not synchronized
  - Logs not capturing authentication

- Tamper with logs
- DoS logs
- Attack through logs
- Other

Table B-8a: Transaction Repudiation Subtree

TREE NODE	EXPLANATION	DEVELOPER MITIGATION	OPERATIONAL MITIGATION
No logs	There are no logs.	Log	Log (It's better than bad, it's good!)
Insufficient logs	The logs don't tell you what you need.	Scenario analysis	Perhaps a logging proxy
Logs scattered	Your logs are all over the place, responding to a repudiation claim is too expensive.	Scenario analysis	Log consolidation
Logs not synchronized	Your systems have different times, meaning correlating your logs is hard.	Few	Set all systems to work in UTC and use a local time server.
Logs not capturing authentication	Your logs don't capture the inputs to authentication decisions, such as Geo-IP or fingerprinting.*	Log more	Few

* Also, manage privacy issues here, and information disclosure risks with logs exposing authentication information.

Table B-8b: Redupidation Attacks through Logs Subtree

TREE NODE	EXPLANATION	DEVELOPER MITIGATION	OPERATIONAL MITIGATION
Attack through logs	Logs are often seen as "trusted" but usually contain information of varying trustworthiness.	Be careful about what assumptions you make, and ensure you document what your logs contain.	Few

See also denial of service (Figure and Tables B14) and tampering with data stores (Figure and Tables B-6).

Information Disclosure from a Process

Figure B-9 shows an attack tree for information disclosure from a process. Information disclosure threats are generally covered in Chapter 3, and Chapter 8.

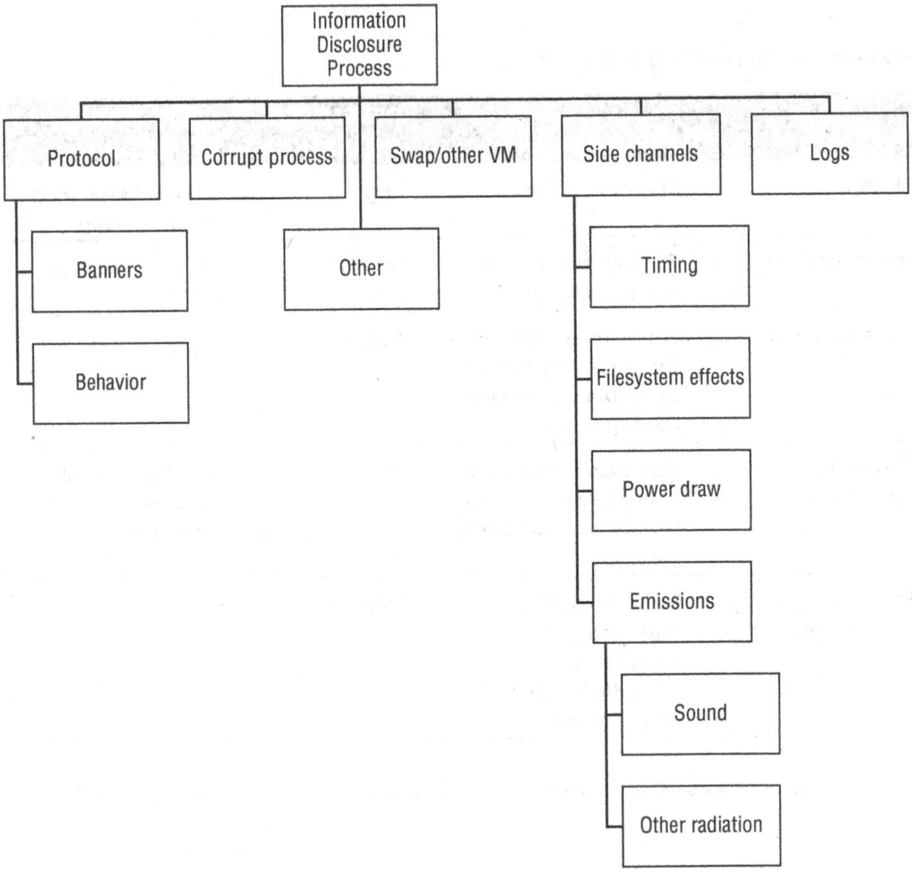

Figure B-9: Information disclosure from a process

Goal: Information disclosure from a process

- Side channels
  - Timing
  - Power draw
  - Filesystem effects
  - Emissions
    - Sound
    - Other radiation

- Protocol
  - Banners
  - Behavior
- Logs
- Corrupt process
- Other
- Swap/Virtual memory

As a class, side channels are like metadata; they're unintentional side-effects of computation, and they are often surprisingly revealing.

Table B-9a: Information Disclosure via Side Channels Subtree

TREE NODE	EXPLANATION	DEVELOPER MITIGATION	OPERATIONAL MITIGATION
Timing	How long the code takes to complete can reveal information about its secrets, especially cryptographic secrets.	Design for cryptography to take constant time. Yes, that's annoying.	None
Power draw	Power draw can be surprisingly revealing about operations.	Cryptographic blinding can help.	If you have power supplies that monitor draw, ensure the logs they produce are protected.
Filesystem effects	Code will often write revealing information to disk.	Create a private directory and put your interesting tidbits in there.	Separate VMs.
Emissions			
Sound	Startlingly, processors make sound that can be used to learn about cryptographic keys (Shamir, 2013).	Architect to keep untrustworthy parties off (and far from) machines with important keys.	Remove microphones.
Other radiation	Other forms of radiation, including van Eck (sometimes called "TEMPEST") and light can reveal information.	There are fonts that are designed to make van Eck attacks challenging; they may violate rules regarding accessibility.	Shielding

Table B-9b: Information Disclosure via Protocol Subtree

TREE NODE	EXPLANATION	DEVELOPER MITIGATION	OPERATIONAL MITIGATION
Banners	If your process announces what it is (for example, "HELO sendmail 5.5.1"), that may be valuable to an attacker.	Consider the risk trade-offs for banners; what value do you get by revealing a version?	Sometimes, banners can be altered; the value of doing so may or may not be worth the effort.
Behavior	Oftentimes, new versions of a program behave differently in ways that an attacker can observe.	It can be hard to avoid subtle behavior changes when you update code for security purposes.	Ensure that your security does not depend on keeping the versions you're running secret.

Table B-9c: Additional Information Disclosure Threats Subtree

TREE NODE	EXPLANATION	DEVELOPER MITIGATION	OPERATIONAL MITIGATION
Logs	Logs often contain important process data. Ensure that you log the right data to the right logs. (For example, log login failures to a log that only admin can read; don't log passwords at all.)	If you control the logs (e.g., a database system with its own logs), design your logs with information disclosure in mind. If you're using system logs, don't attempt to change permissions on them.	Ensure that you keep log permissions properly set.
Swap/Virtual memory	Important secrets like cryptographic keys should not be swapped out.	Use the appropriate system calls to protect them.	No extra activity
Corrupt process	If you can tamper with or elevate privileges against a process, you can use that to disclose information.	Use a security development life cycle to prevent these.	None

Information Disclosure from a Data Flow

Figure B-10 shows an attack tree for information disclosure from a data flow. Information disclosure threats are generally covered in Chapter 3, Chapter 8 and Chapter 16.

Generally, if you don't prevent spoofing of a data flow, you have tampering and information disclosure problems.

Data flow threats can apply to channels or messages, or both. The difference is easiest to see with examples: E-mail messages travel over an SMTP channel, whereas HTML (and other format) messages travel over HTTP. The question of which you need (either, neither, or both) is a requirements question.

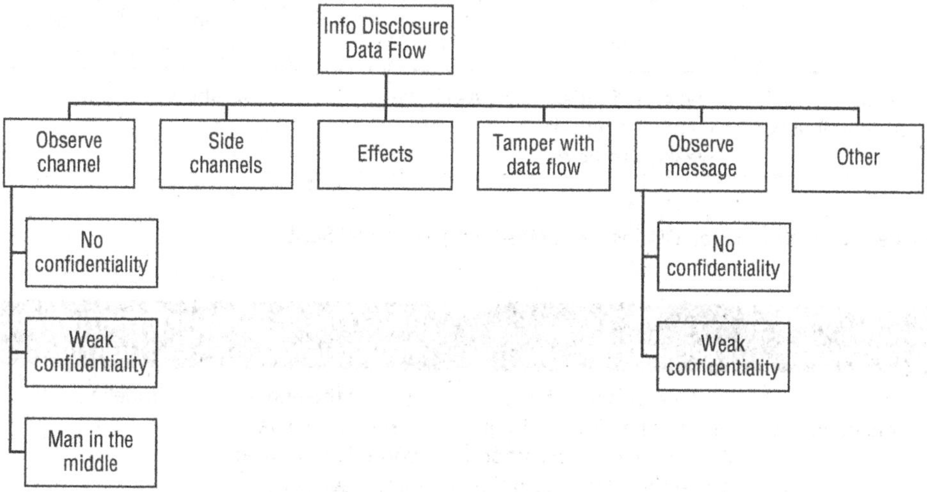

Figure B-10: Information disclosure from a data flow

Goal: Information disclosure from a data flow

- Observe message
  - No confidentiality
  - Weak confidentiality
- Observe channel
  - No confidentiality
  - Weak confidentiality
  - Man in the middle (See Tables B3 spoofing data flows.)
- Side channels
- Effects
- Other and spoofing

See also tampering with data flows (Figure and Tables B3 and B5, many of which can lead to information disclosure.

Table B-10a: Information Disclosure by Observing a Message Subtree

TREE NODE	EXPLANATION	DEVELOPER MITIGATION	OPERATIONAL MITIGATION
No confidentiality	Nothing protects the contents of a message.	Cryptographic (or permissions for on-system flows)	There may be message protection add-ons available, such as PGP, or tunneling for channel protection may help.
Weak confidentiality	The confidentiality of messages is weakly protected.	As above	As above

Table B-10b: Information Disclosure by Observing a Channel Subtree

TREE NODE	EXPLANATION	DEVELOPER MITIGATION	OPERATIONAL MITIGATION
No confidentiality	Nothing protects the contents of the channel. Even if you have good message protection, data about the messages (who talks to whom) can be revealing.	Encrypt the entire channel. If you're worried about who talks to whom, see B-10c.	Tunneling
Weak confidentiality	The contents of the channel are weakly protected.	Improve the encryption.	Tunneling
MITM	See B3, spoofing data flows.		

Table B-10c: Other Information Disclosure Threats Subtree

TREE NODE	EXPLANATION	DEVELOPER MITIGATION	OPERATIONAL MITIGATION
Side channels	Data about who talks to whom can be interesting. See the discussion of traffic analysis in Chapter 3.	See Chapter 3.	Private network connections may help.
Effects	However well you protect the data flows, sometimes you take action, and those actions can be revealing.	None	Operational discipline

Information Disclosure from a Data Store

Figure B-11 shows an attack tree for information disclosure from a data store. Information disclosure threats are generally covered in Chapter 3, Chapter 8, and Chapter 16.

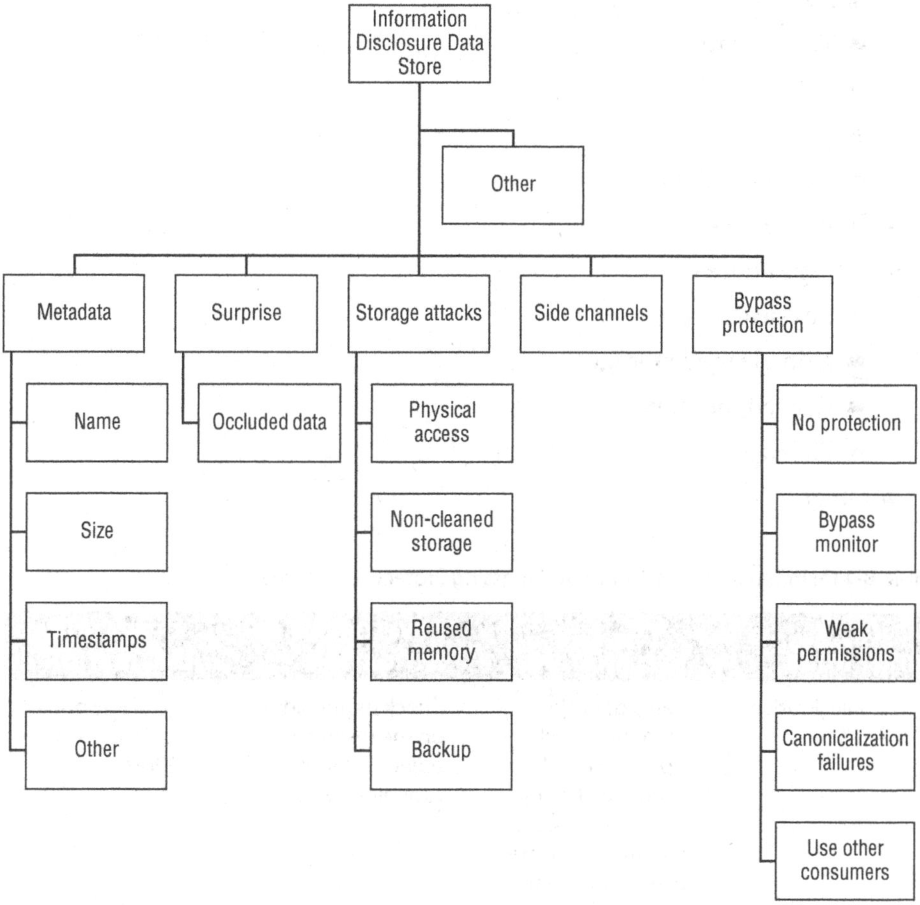

Figure B-11: Information disclosure from a data store

Goal: Read from a data store

- Bypass protection
  - Canonicalization failures
  - No protection
  - Bypass monitor

- Weak permissions
- Use other consumers
- Metadata
  - Name
  - Size
  - Timestamps
  - Other
- Surprise
  - Occluded data
- Side channels
- Storage attacks
  - Physical access
  - Non-cleaned storage
  - Reused memory
  - Backup
- Other

Table B-11a: Information Disclosure by Bypassing Protection Subtree

TREE NODE	EXPLANATION	DEVELOPER MITIGATION	OPERATIONAL MITIGATION
Canonicalization failures	Can a data element have multiple names—for example, through links or inclusion? If so, different names may be processed differently.	Check permissions on the resolved object (after name canonicalization).	Probably none with reasonable effort
No protection	The system offers no protection, perhaps by design.	Use another system, or add protection.	Physical protection
Bypass monitor	Exploit the lack of a "reference monitor" through which all access requests pass, or take advantage of bugs.	Redesign is probably easier than the sorts of extensive testing that might find all the bugs.	Use a better system.

TREE NODE	EXPLANATION	DEVELOPER MITIGATION	OPERATIONAL MITIGATION
Weak permissions	The permissions are too permissive.	Stronger permissions	Stronger permissions
Use other consumers	Find another program that can read the data and use it to read for you.	Don't open arbitrary files and pass on their contents.	Remove or block that program with permissions.

Table B-11b: Information Disclosure through Metadata and Side Channels Subtree

TREE NODE	EXPLANATION	DEVELOPER MITIGATION	OPERATIONAL MITIGATION
Name	A filename can reveal information, such as "Plans to layoff Alice.docx".	Private directories, and allowing people to define where data is stored	Permissions
Size	The size of a file can reveal information.	Ensure that your files are of standard size. (This is rarely needed but it might be for your data types.)	Permissions
Timestamps	When a file is created can reveal interesting information.	Private directories, and allowing people to define where data is stored	Operational security to conceal timestamps
Side channels	Aspects of behavior such as a disk filling up or being slow can reveal information.	Possibly quotas, pre-allocating space to conceal actual usage	Reducing side channels is a large investment.
Other	If you're concerned about the preceding issues, there's a wide variety of ways to be clever.	Steganography, encryption	Isolation

Table B-11c: Information Disclosure from Surprise Subtree

TREE NODE	EXPLANATION	DEVELOPER MITIGATION	OPERATIONAL MITIGATION
Occluded data	Data for purposes such as change tracking, etc., can be revealing.	Tools to help view, inspect, or remove such data	Procedures and training for publication

Table B-11d: Information Disclosure via Storage Attacks Subtree

TREE NODE	EXPLANATION	DEVELOPER MITIGATION	OPERATIONAL MITIGATION
Physical access	Physical access is awesome if you believe your operating system will protect you.	Encryption	Physical security
Non-cleaned storage	When you release storage, does the OS clean it?	Manually overwrite sensitive data, usually repeatedly. Note that this works poorly with flash-based storage.	Destroy disks, rather than resell them. You can overwrite spinning media, but flash storage wear leveling makes information disclosure threats hard to manage.
Reused memory	When you release storage, does the OS clean it?	As above	None
Backup	What happens to those offsite tapes?*	Cryptography	Cryptography

* Threats to backup can also allow tampering. However, completing a tampering attack with a backup tape is far more complex than information disclosure through such tapes.

Denial of Service against a Process

Figure B-12 shows an attack tree for denial of service against a process. Denial-of-service threats are generally covered in Chapter 3, and Chapter 8.

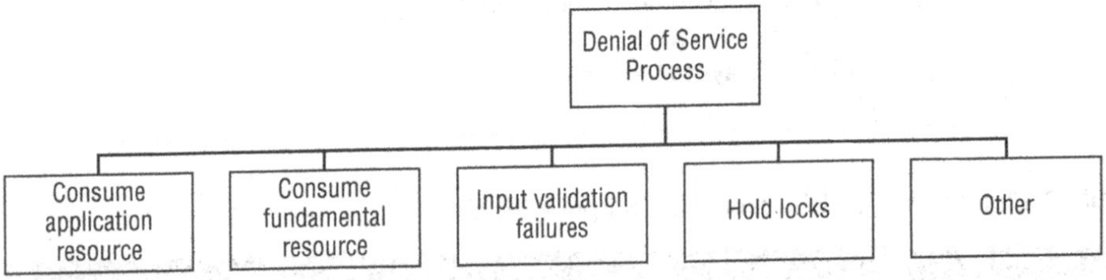

Figure B-12: Denial of service against a process

Goal: Denial of service against a process

- Consume application resource
- Consume fundamental resource
- Input validation failures
- Hold locks
- Other

Table B-12: Denial of Service against a Process

TREE NODE	EXPLANATION	DEVELOPER MITIGATION	OPERATIONAL MITIGATION
Consume application resource	Application resources include connections, or buffers or structures that manage business logic.	Dynamically allocated resources	VMs or load balancing
Consume fundamental resource	Fundamental resources include disk, memory, or bandwidth.	Use OS quotas.	VMs or load balancing
Input validation failures	An input failure that crashes the application	Careful input validation	Process restarting. (Be careful that you don't allow DoS to turn into EoP by giving attackers as many chances as they need.)
Hold locks	To the extent that an application can hold locks, it can deny service to other locks.	Give up your locks quickly.	One VM per application

Denial of Service against a Data Flow

Figure B-13 shows an attack tree for denial of service against a data flow. Denial-of-service threats are generally covered in Chapters 3, and Chapter 8.

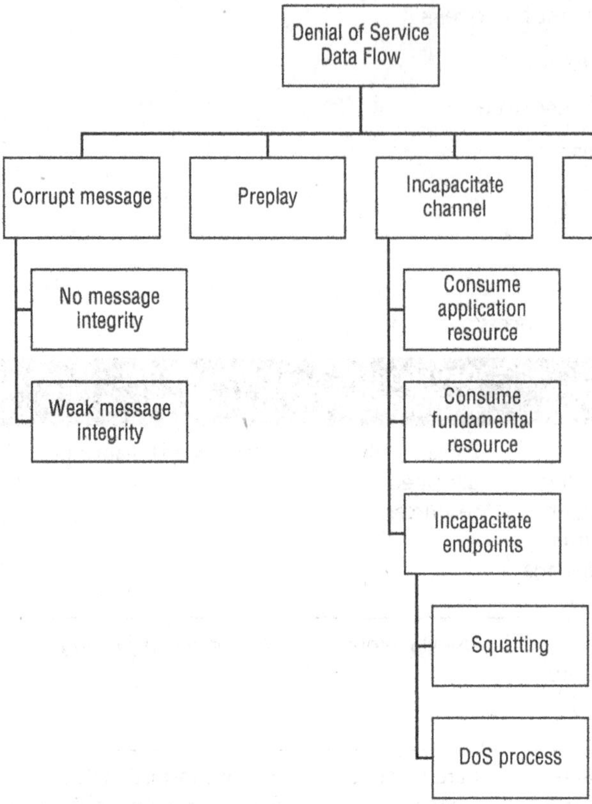

Figure B-13: Denial of service against a data flow

Goal: Denial of service against a data flow

- Preplay
- Corrupt messages
  - No integrity
  - Weak integrity
- Incapacitate channel
  - Consume fundamental resource
  - Consume application resource
  - Incapacitate endpoints
    - Squatting
    - DoS against process
- Other

Table B-13a: Denial of Service via Preplay Subtree

TREE NODE	EXPLANATION	DEVELOPER MITIGATION	OPERATIONAL MITIGATION
Preplay	An attacker initiates a connection or action before you, absorbing cycles.	Proof of work doesn't work, but consider dropping connections that seem slow.	Mmm, capacity

Table B-13b: Denial of Service via Corrupt Messages Subtree

TREE NODE	EXPLANATION	DEVELOPER MITIGATION	OPERATIONAL MITIGATION
No integrity	If the channel has no integrity, an attacker along or close to the path can corrupt messages.	Add integrity checks.	Add capacity or, if feasible, tunneling.
Weak integrity	Similar to no integrity, but with an unkeyed checksum, or a non-cryptographic checksum	Use a cryptographically strong checksum with keying.	Add capacity or, if feasible, tunneling.

Table B-13c: Denial of Service By Incapacitating a Channel Subtree

TREE NODE	EXPLANATION	DEVELOPER MITIGATION	OPERATIONAL MITIGATION
Consume fundamental resource	Typically, bandwidth is the fundamental resource, but it can also be CPU.	Use TCP, not UDP, so you can at least require that endpoints be able to respond.	Bandwidth—sweet, sweet bandwidth
Consume application resource	Anything that your application can provide can be consumed. For example, if you have a state-based firewall with static tables of state data, that table can be filled.	Avoid fixed allocations.	VMs and load balancers

Continues

Table B-13c (*continued*)

TREE NODE	EXPLANATION	DEVELOPER MITIGATION	OPERATIONAL MITIGATION
Incapacitate endpoints	Do something to kill the endpoint.	Ensure your end-points can't be incapacitated.	fail-over
Squatting	Show up before the real application to claim a port, a named pipe, etc.	None	Permissions
DoS against process	Cause the process to spin in some way, making the channel unusable.	As above	VMs and load balancers

Denial of Service against a Data Store

Figure B-14 shows an attack tree for denial of service against a data store. Denial-of-service threats are generally covered in Chapter 3, and Chapter 8.

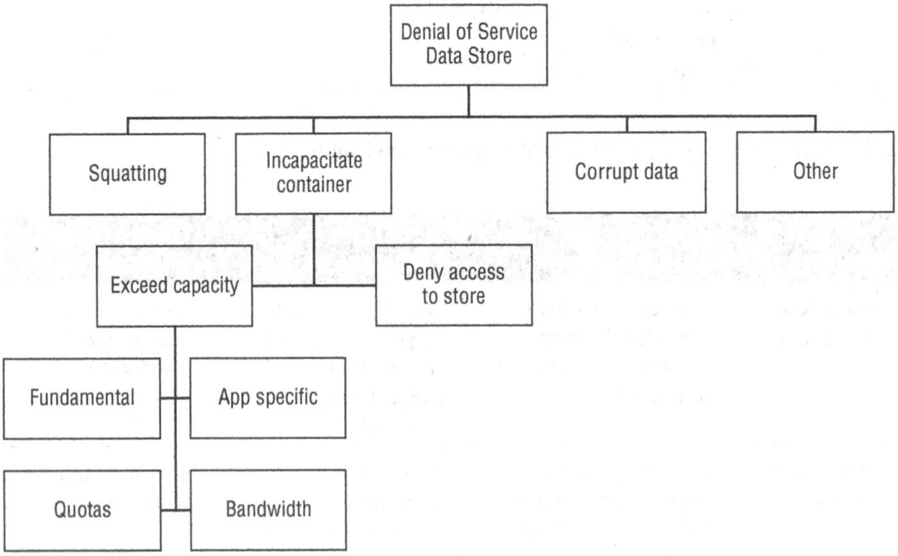

Figure B-14: Denial of service against a data store

Goal: Denial of service against a data store

- Squatting

- Corrupt data (See tamper with data store, Figure B-6.)
- Incapacitate container
  - Deny access to store
  - Exceed capacity
    - Fundamental
    - App specific
    - Quotas
    - Bandwidth
- Other

Exceed capacity or bandwidth means I/O operations per second, and if sustained, that can have knock-on effects as I/O is queued.

Table B-14a: Deny Service by Squatting Subtree

TREE NODE	EXPLANATION	DEVELOPER MITIGATION	OPERATIONAL MITIGATION
Squatting	Show up before the real application to claim a port, a named pipe, etc.	Assign permissions to the object in question.	Assign permissions to the object in question.

Table B-14b: Deny Service by Incapacitating a Container Subtree

TREE NODE	EXPLANATION	DEVELOPER MITIGATION	OPERATIONAL MITIGATION
Deny access to store	An attacker might deny access to a store by adding an ACL or taking and holding a lock.	Put the store somewhere that attackers are limited in their ability to add ACLs or locks. Test to see if you can access the store; fail gracefully.	Move the store somewhere an attacker can't change permissions, possibly using a link to redirect.
Exceed capacity	Fill the data store in some way, either fundamental, or app specific, or by hitting quotas or bandwidth constraints.		

Continues

Table B-14b *(continued)*

TREE NODE	EXPLANATION	DEVELOPER MITIGATION	OPERATIONAL MITIGATION
Fundamental	Absorb a fundamental resource such as disk space.	Fail gracefully.	More storage
App specific	If the application has resource limits, fill them up; for an example, see US-CERT, 2002.	Avoid fixed allocations.	None
Quotas	A quota can work like a fundamental resource restriction, while holding the DoS to a single application or account, rather than a system.	Design choices about appropriate trade-offs	Deployment choices about appropriate trade-offs
Bandwidth	Even if the data store can hold more data, network bandwidth or buffers on either end of a connection can fill up.	Dynamic buffers may help postpone the issues.	More bandwidth, or (especially in cloud/ data centers) move the processes closer to the system that is writing.

Elevation of Privilege against a Process

Figure B-15 shows an attack tree for elevation of privilege against a process. Elevation of privilege threats are generally covered in Chapter 3, and Chapter 8.

Goal: Elevation of privilege against a process

- Dynamic corruption
  - Input validation failure
  - Access to memory

- Static corruption (See tamper with data store, Figure B-6.)
- Insufficient authorization
  - Cross domain issues
  - Call chain issues
  - Design issues
    - Usability

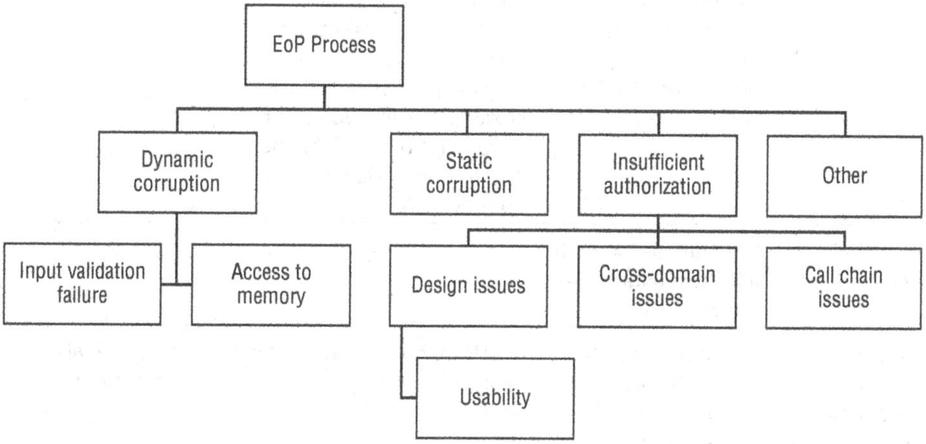

Figure B-15: Elevation of privilege against a process

Table B-15a: Elevate Privilege by Dynamic Corruption Subtree

TREE NODE	EXPLANATION	DEVELOPER MITIGATION	OPERATIONAL MITIGATION
Input validation failures	Input can alter control flow (e.g., via stack smashing or heap overflow).	Careful design, input validation for purpose, fuzzing	Sandboxing can partially mitigate the effects.
Access to memory	Sometimes code will attempt to defend against administrators or other local accounts.	See "Tampering with a Process".	Use the OS.

Table B-15b: Exploit Insufficient Authorization to Elevate Privileges Subtree

TREE NODE	EXPLANATION	DEVELOPER MITIGATION	OPERATIONAL MITIGATION
Cross-domain issues	Applications that use a "same origin" policy or a "no cross domain" policy can be impacted by failures in that security model. These models are frequently used in web applications.	Ensure that security checks are centralized into a reference monitor that makes names canonical and then runs checks. Be careful with common domains and DNS issues that can result from load balancing or cloud services. (For example, is Amazon S3 or Akamai, along with all their customers, inside your trust boundary?)*	Your own domain(s) will probably help.
Call-chain issues	See "Tampering with a Process (Figure B4) above.		
Design issues (usability)	If your authorization system is hard to use, people are less likely to use it well.	Perform human-factors tests early in the design.	Tools to analyze permissions

* Amazon and Akamai are mentioned to be evocative, not to disparage their services.

Other Threat Trees

These trees are intended to be templates for common modes of attack. There are several tensions associated with creating such trees. First is a question of depth. A deeper, more specific tree is more helpful to those who are experts in areas other than security. Unfortunately, through specificity, it loses power to shape mental models, and it loses power to evoke related threats. Second, there is a tension between the appearance of completeness and the specificity to an operating system. For example, exploit domain trust is Windows specific, and it can be derived from either "abuse feature" or "exploit admin (authentication)" or both, depending on your perspective. As such, consider these trees and the audience who will be using them when deciding if you should use them as is or draw more layers.

Unlike the STRIDE trees shown earlier, these trees are not presented with a catalog of ways to address the threats. Such a catalog would be too varied, based on details of the operating systems in question.

Running Code

The goal of running code can also be seen as elevation of privilege with respect to a system. That is, the attacker moves from being unable to run code (on that system) to the new privilege of being able to run code (on that system). These trees also relate to the goal of exploiting a social program, which is presented next. The key difference is that the trees in this section focus on "run code," and that is not always an attacker's goal. These trees do not contain an "other" node, but the categories are designed to be broad.

On a Server

In this context, a server is simply a computer that does not have a person using it, but rather is running one or more processes that respond to network requests. The goal is "run code" rather than "break into," as breaking in is almost always a step along a chain, rather than a goal in itself, and the next step toward that goal is almost always to run some program on that machine. This tree, as shown in Figure B-16, does not distinguish between privilege levels at which an attacker might run code.

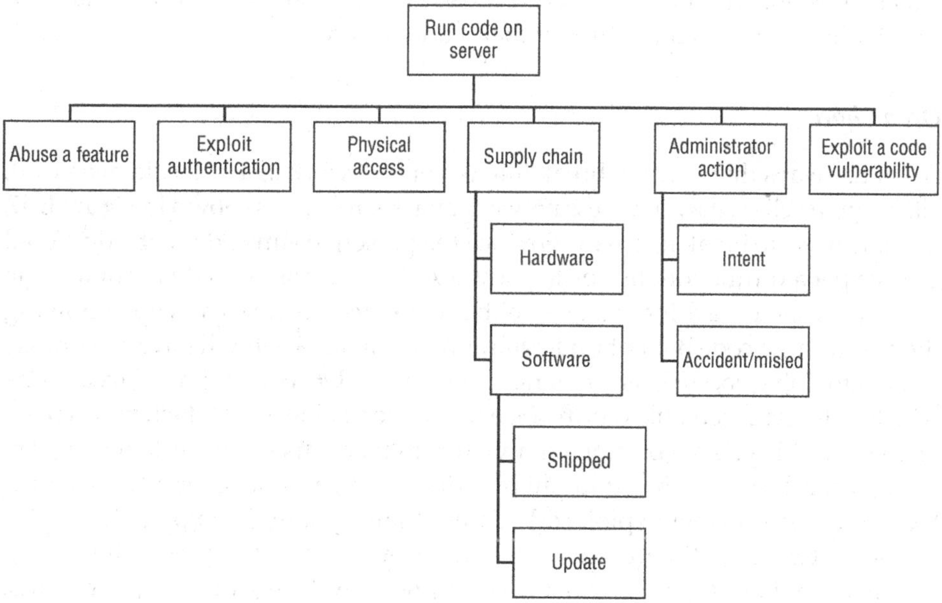

Figure B-16: Run code on a server

Goal: Run code on a server

- Exploit a code vulnerability
  - Injection vulnerabilities

      - Script injection
      - Code injection (including SQL and others)
    - Other code vulnerabilities
- Abuse a feature
- Exploit authentication
- Physical access
- Supply chain
    - Tamper with hardware
    - Tamper with software
      - As shipped
      - Tamper with an update
- Administrator action
    - Intentional
    - Accident/mislead

Tampering with software updates may be targetable or may require a broad attack. Injection vulnerabilities are a broad class of issue where code/data confusion allows an attacker to insert their code or scripts.

On a Client

All of the ways that work to break into a "server" work against a client as well, although the client may have less network attack surface. As shown in Figure B-17, the new ways to break in are to convince the person to run code with additional or unexpected functionality or to convince them to pass unsafe input to code already on their machine. You can either convince them to run code knowing they're running code but not understanding what impact it will have, or confuse them into doing so, such as by using a file with a PDF icon and displayed name which hides its executable nature. (See the section below on "Attack with Tricky Filenames.") If you're convincing a victim to pass unsafe input to a program on their machine, that input might be a document, an image, or a URL (which likely will load further exploit code, rather than contain the exploit directly).

These attacks on the person can come from a variety of places, including e-mail, instant message, file-sharing applications, websites, or even phone calls.

Goal: Run code on a client

- As server
- Convince a person to run code
    - Extra functionality

    - From a website
    - Tricked into running
- Convince person to open an exploiting document (possibly via a document, image, or URL)
- Watering hole attacks
    - Website
    - Filesharing
    - Other
- "What's this?"

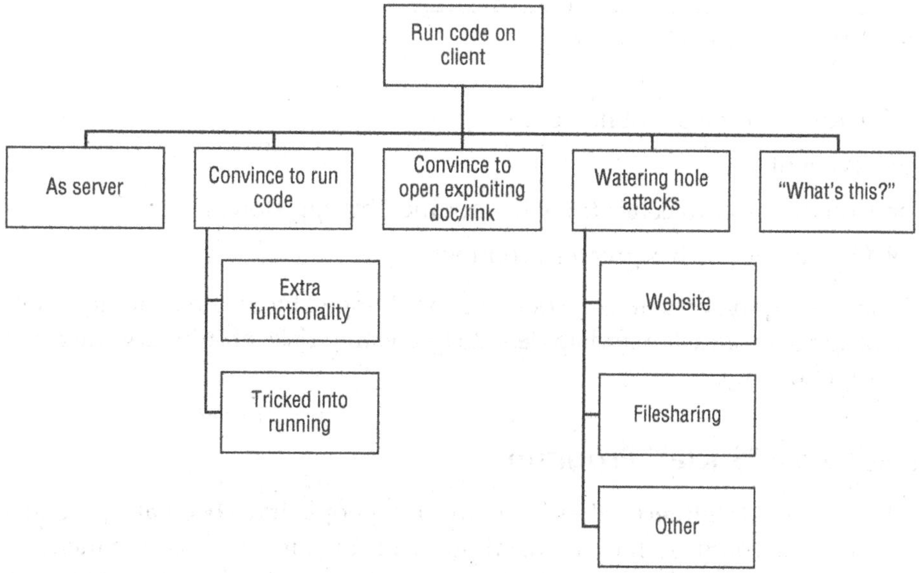

Figure B-17: Run code on a client

Those paying attention might notice that this is informed by the Broad Street Taxonomy, as covered in Chapter 18, "Experimental Approaches." Watering hole attacks are similar to "convince person to open an exploiting document," but they target a possibly broad class of people. That may range from targeting those interested in an obscure government website to those visiting a programming site. (Attack code in either place may involve some discretion based on target IP, domain, or other factors.) Watering hole attacks can also impact those downloading content from file-sharing services and the like. The last category ("What's this?") refers to attacking a person via a file on a file share, USB key, or other device, so curious users click an executable because they're curious what it does.

On a Mobile Device

The term *mobile device* includes all laptops, tablets, or phones. Attacks against mobile devices include all client attacks, and physical access has added prominence because it is easier to lose one of these than a refrigerator-size server. The additional attacks are shown in Figure B-18.

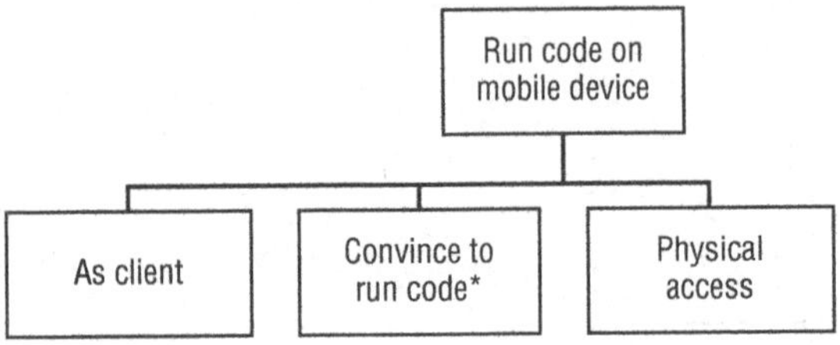

Figure B-18: Run code on a mobile device

Goal: Run code on a mobile device

- As client
- Convince to run code* (may be modified by app stores)
- Physical access has greater prominence

*Convincing someone to run code may be changed by the presence (or mandate) of app stores. Such mandates lead to interesting risks of jailbreaks carrying extra functionality.

Attack via a "Social" Program

For longer than the Internet has been around, people have been attacked at a distance. Most countries have a postal police of some form whose job includes preventing scammers from taking advantage of people. The Internet's amazing and cheap channels for connecting people have brought many of these online, and added a set of new ways people can be taken advantage of, such as exploiting vulnerabilities to take over their computers.

The threat tree shown in Figure B-19 can be used in two ways. First, it can be used as an operational threat model for considering attack patterns against e-mail clients, IM clients, or any client that a person uses in whole or in part to connect with other people. Second, it can be used as a design-time model to ensure that you have defenses against attacks represented by each part of the tree.

Goal: Attack via a "social" program

- Run code
  - Unattended exploit
  - Exploit vulnerability via document

    - Reason to act + belief in safety
    - Belief in safety
- Human action
  - Visit a website
    - Phishing
    - Exploit vulnerability*
    - Ad revenue
    - Other
- Drive other action

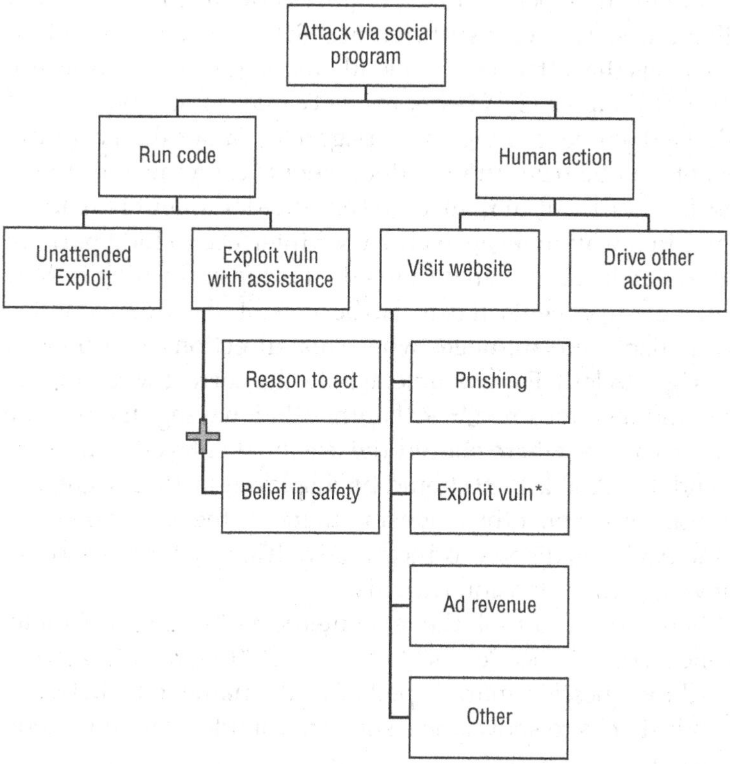

Figure B-19: Using a social program to attack

*The "Exploit vulnerability" reason to get a person to visit a website means that the attacker does something to convince a person to visit a website where there's exploit code waiting. It is duplicative of the "exploit vuln with assistance." It is sufficiently common that it's worth including in both places. (There is an alternative for attackers, which is to insert their exploit into an advertisement shown on the web.)

This tree intentionally treats attacks by administrators or the logged-in account as out of scope. The "logged-in account" here refers to acts taken either by that person or by code running with the privileges of that account. Once code is inside that trust boundary, it can most effectively (or perhaps only) be managed by code running at a higher privilege level. Almost by definition that is out of scope for such a social program. You might have an administrative module that runs at higher privilege and, for example, acts as a reference monitor for certain actions, but code running as the logged-in account could still change the user interface or generate actions.

Attack with Tricky Filenames

A simple model of convincing a person to act requires both a reason for them to act and a belief that the act is safe, or sufficiently safe to override any caution they may feel. The reasons that attackers frequently use to get people to act are modeled in Table 15-1 of Chapter 15. A belief in safety may come from a belief that they are opening a document (image, web page, etc.) rather than running a program. That belief may be true, and the document is carrying a technical exploit against a vulnerability. It may also be that the document is really a program, and named in a way that causes the user interface to hide parts of the name. Hiding parts of the name can be a result of extension hiding in Mac OS, Windows, or other environments. It can also be a result of various complex issues around mixing displayed languages whose text directions are different (read left to right or right to left). For example, what's the correct way to write Abdul's Resume? Should it be resume دبع? If, rather than having that resume in a file named .doc, it's a .exe, where should the .exe be displayed relative to دبع? On the one hand, the Arabic دبع should be displayed farthest right, but that will confuse those who expect the extension there. If the extension is on the far right, then the Arabic is displayed incorrectly. It's easy for a person to get confused about what a file extension really is.

Entertainingly, Microsoft Word took the text entered as "Abdul (in Arabic) Resume" and re-rendered it as "R" "e" "s" "u" "m" "e" "L/lam" etc. Abdul, and then re-arranged the question mark typed after the name to be between those words. (Which just goes to show...the issues are complex, and there's no obviously right answer.)

APPENDIX

C

Attacker Lists

As discussed in Chapter 2, "Strategies for Threat Modeling," focusing on attackers is an attractive way to make threats real. This appendix provides you with an understanding of attackers at a variety of levels of details. The first section is four lists of attackers with limited detail about each. That is followed by a discussion of "personas," and then a fully worked out system of threat personas.

Many projects have floundered because creating these models is challenging. This appendix is presented with the hope that it will help you, and the (cynical) expectation that it will help you by helping you "fail faster." That is, by providing these lists, you can experiment with a variety of attacker models, rather than needing to create your own to try them out. By failing faster, you can learn lessons and move along, rather than getting mired in an approach.

There is one other attacker worth considering, and that is the expert witness. If you expect your product (or evidence from it) to be used in court, consider how each element of the product, process, or system might come under attack by a motivated skeptic. For an example of this, see "Offender Tagging" by Ross Anderson (Anderson, 2013).

Attacker Lists

This section lays out four sets of attackers which have been developed to various degrees.

Barnard's List

One set of attackers was developed by Robert Barnard in *Intrusion Detection Systems* (Barnard, 1988) and is covered in Ross Anderson's *Security Engineering, 2nd Edition* (Wiley, 2008, pp. 367-68). It consists of four attackers. Derek, a 19-year-old addict, is looking to steal to pay for his drugs. Charlie is a cat burglar who has been convicted seven times. Bruno is a "gentleman criminal" who steals art or other high-value items. Abdurrahman heads a cell of militants with military weapons training and technical support from a small government.

Verizon's Lists

Another set of attackers appears in the Verizon Data Breach Intelligence Report, and is derived from observation of their data. It consists of three types of actors who appear regularly: organized crime, state affiliated, and activists. Each is characterized by the industry of victims they attack, the region in which they operate, common actions, and the sorts of assets they go after. (Verizon, 2013).

NOTE **Verizon uses the word "asset" to refer to either a machine type, such as "mail server," or the data that the attackers want, or both. This is yet another example of how the term can reduce clarity, rather than add it, as discussed in Chapter 2.**

This attacker set is best suited for operational threat modeling. A slight variant of this is used by the security company Securosis, which adds "competitor," and replaces "activists" with "unsophisticated" (Securosis, 2013).

Verizon's RISK team also has what they call the "A4 Threat Model." A4 refers to Actors, Actions, Assets, and Attributes. (Verizon, 2013). Based on conversations with the creators, that model may be better for categorizing incidents than predicting them.

OWASP

The Open Web Application Security Project (OWASP) has a set of attackers in (OWASP, 2012). The OWASP enumeration of threat agents is quoted verbatim below:

- **Non-Target Specific:** Non-Target Specific Threat Agents are computer viruses, worms, trojans, and logic bombs.

- **Employees:** Staff, contractors, operational/maintenance personnel, or security guards who are annoyed with the company
- **Organized Crime and Criminals:** Criminals target information that is of value to them, such as bank accounts, credit cards, or intellectual property that can be converted into money. Criminals will often make use of insiders to help them.
- **Corporations:** Corporations who are engaged in offensive information warfare or competitive intelligence. Partners and competitors come under this category.
- **Human, Unintentional:** Accidents, carelessness
- **Human, Intentional:** Insider, outsider
- **Natural:** Flood, fire, lightning, meteor, earthquakes

Intel TARA

Intel has a system called Threat Agent Risk Assessment (TARA) that includes a Threat Agent Library and a Methods and Objectives Library. The system is described in a white paper from Intel, but the complete libraries are considered confidential (Rosenquist, 2009). The Intel TAL consists of 22 threat agents, and a 16-agent derivative is included in the U.S. Department of Homeland Security's "IT Sector Baseline Risk Assessment." A list of "Threat Agent Profiles" is included in Figure 4 of the TARA paper, and it includes the following agents:

- Competitor
- Data miner
- Radical activist
- Cyber vandal
- Sensationalist
- Civil activist
- Terrorist
- Anarchist
- Irrational individual
- Government cyber warrior
- Organized criminal
- Corrupt government official
- Legal adversary
- Internal spy
- Government spy

- Thief
- Vendor
- Reckless employee
- Untrained employee
- Information partner
- Disgruntled employee

Personas and Archetypes

It's possible to start from a simple list of attacker archetypes, such as those shown in the previous section. When doing so, it's easy to find yourself arguing about the resources or capabilities of such an archetype, and needing to flesh them out. For example, what if your terrorist is state-sponsored, and has access to government labs? These questions make the attacker-centric approach start to resemble *"personas,"* which are often used to help think about human interface issues. You can use lessons from that community to inform your approach.

Although he didn't invent the word, usability pioneer Alan Cooper developed the concept of personas in his 1998 book, *"The Inmates are Running the Asylum"* (SAMS, 1999). In more recent work, *"About Face 3: The Essentials of Interaction Design"* (Wiley, 2012), Cooper and his colleagues integrate personas into a more in-depth process, and stress that personas are based on research. Cooper defines a seven step process for creating personas.

1. Identify behavioral variables.
2. Map interview subjects to behavioral variables.
3. Identify significant behavior patterns.
4. Synthesize characteristics and relevant goals.
5. Check for completeness and redundancy.
6. Expand descriptions of attributes and behaviors.
7. Designate persona types.

They defined this process because experience with less structured approaches didn't lead to effective product design. They stress that persona development must be an intensive data- and research-driven process. If you're willing to go through that sort of process for an attacker set, then you may find more success with attacker-driven threat modeling. For step 2, you may be able to find multiple attackers of each type and induce them to go through your interviews. Then, with such a persona set in hand, you may able to create useful scenarios and requirements.

A key aspect of Cooper's approach to scenarios and requirements is that people are using a product to accomplish goals, and the reason for the personas is to ensure that features are created in support of those goals. Unless you include a "give me administrator access" button, attackers are unlikely to use the features you create in the way you intend to accomplish their goals.

With that explanation of personas, let's proceed to a fully-worked set of attacker personas.

Aucsmith's Attacker Personas

The remainder of this appendix is a reformatted and very gently edited version of a document, "Threat Personas," (Aucsmith, 2003) created between 1999 and 2003 by Dave Aucsmith, Brendan Dixon, and Robin Martin-Emerson at Microsoft, and it appears here with the kind permission of Microsoft. Note that some of the list elements were left empty in the original, and those have been left empty here.

It is included because it is a well-worked-through and empirical approach to persona-driven threat modeling. It can help you by accelerating experiments with such approaches. However, you should also see the cautions in Chapter 2, before attempting to use these personas.

Background and Definitions

All computer systems have both users and, in some sense, anti-users: those trying, for one reason or another, to break into, control, or misuse a computer system and the data it manages. Anti-users, like computer users, fall into a few patterns that describe "threat personas" engaged in "threat scenarios."

Classification of anti-users, based on an analysis of FBI cyber-attack data, clusters best when using two key axes: Motivation and Skill. There are four different motivations driving anti-users:

- **Curiosity:** "Because it was there" compels some anti-users. They want to experiment and try things out, perhaps indulging in a little vandalism along the way. They're not motivated by fame or gain (yet), but wile away the hours for their own enjoyment. A common physical analogy is kids who vandalize local parks for no apparent reason.
- **Personal fame:** Some anti-users want fame; they like to see their name "in lights" or to be known among their friends and comrades. Financial gain is not a goal. These anti-users purposely leave marks for others to see, to build their own reputation. A physical analogy might be those who block streets to protest the WTO.

- **Personal gain:** A growing number of anti-users use their skills for personal gain. These range from spammers (who co-opt innocent systems for use as spam mailers) to those that commit financial fraud (such as by stealing credit card numbers). What sets these apart is the desire for personal financial gain. Bank robbers, in the physical world, have the same motivation.
- **National interests:** Political interests drive a select number of anti-users. To them, "hacking" is just another tool for accomplishing a political end. There are *legitimate* anti-users, such as those protecting a country's national interests, and *illegitimate* anti-users seeking to undermine that same interest. A legitimate anti-user, for example, might crack into a terrorist's computer to learn of an impending attack; an illegitimate anti-user, by contrast, may attack an airline reservation system to learn flight passenger details. The nation they serve, by standard definitions, might or might not exist (such as Al-Qaeda). Physical analogies abound and span the globe. They include the NSA (National Security Agency) in the US, the GCHQ in Britain, and other known (or unknown) organizations.

Anti-users also have varying levels of skill:

- **The script kiddie:** Because programs, once written, may be used by anyone, not all anti-users are themselves programmers. Some merely use the tools and applications others develop. These script-kiddies do not have any real system knowledge—they only understand how to follow instructions and use the different available tools.
- **The undergraduate:** A little knowledge can go a long way. A number of anti-users have bits of experience coupled with some undergraduate experience. They employ these much like the script kiddies: They mostly use tools and applications other write. They might try some minor modifications, such as tailoring the attack or slightly altering the data used, but they lack the skills to do anything more than twist and adjust a few dials and settings.
- **The expert:** Advanced anti-users supply the tools and applications. They write the worms and viruses. They write the worm generators and virus generators. They write the applications that snoop networks for weaknesses. They're quite comfortable working in the kernel of their favorite operating system or reading protocol traces. Advanced anti-users are the experts of the underground.

- **The specialist:** Virtually any skill has a value to someone, and "hacking" skills are worth a great deal to some. A few anti-users, through very specialized training (such as Ph.D. work) and access to critical resources (such as significant monetary funds and source listings), develop extremely specialized abilities. These specialists do not often leave traces of their work. They work carefully and methodically. Snooping and breaking computer systems is their job, not just their pastime.

When applied to the FBI data, these motivation and skill categories yield eight, distinct threat personas grouped by five different "behaviors"—a two-way interaction between motivation and skill—as depicted in the following figure. The following sections cover each persona in detail.

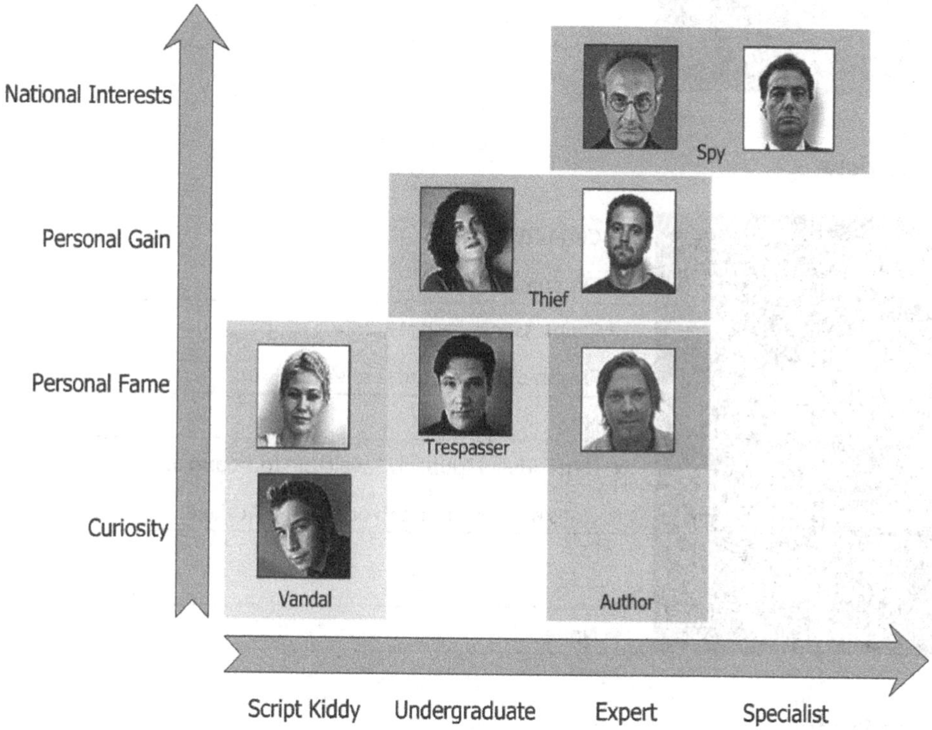

Personas

David "NeOphyate" Bradley – Vandal

Overview

MOTIVATION	❖ Curiosity ❖ Experimentation
SKILL AND EDUCATION	❖ Quintessential script kiddie ❖ Freshman in computer science
SPAN OF INFLUENCE	❖ None
COLLABORATION	❖ Depends on "publicly" available tools and applications ❖ Does not contribute to others; is a "lurker"
TOOLS AND TECHNOLOGIES	
IT EXPERIENCE	❖ None

Core Profile

Chief Motivation

- Curiosity

Background, Experience, and Education

- Most common type of attacker; frequently participates in DDoS attacks
- Has played with computers for years; is the computer "expert" for his family and friends
- Frequently plays computer games
- Very little programming experience, restricted to scripting websites
- Has "no clue" regarding details of the attacks he launches, but he is persistent and has the time. He'll try anything without regard for the consequences (e.g., run attacks meant for Windows against Linux systems).
- Never attacks early in the morning (because he's sleeping); attacks most always occur late in the evening or on weekends
- Currently a freshman in computer science

Employer

- None, is a full-time student

Previous Accomplishments

- Launched a three-day TCP/IP "SYN flood" DoS attack against a non-profit organization; also tried using an ICMP "ping-of-death" attack (which failed)
- Recently knocked all friends off of an IRC (Internet Relay Chat) session using a DoS (Denial of Service) script
- Unsuccessfully attempted to gain administrator (aka "root") access to the Department of Computer Science lab computers
- Took part in two of the large DDoS attacks launched against well-known sites (e.g., Yahoo!)
- More or less attended class during the last week

Span of Influence

- None, depends highly on others

Scope of Attacks

- Popular websites
- His school's network

- Friends' computers
- Computers on his cable modem network segment (e.g., his neighbors)

JoLynn "NightLily" Dobney – Trespasser

Overview

MOTIVATION	❖ Personal fame; bragging rights ❖ Experimentation
SKILL AND EDUCATION	❖ Basic programming and network knowledge ❖ Self-taught ❖ Heavily reads news groups
SPAN OF INFLUENCE	❖ None
COLLABORATION	❖ Depends on "publicly" available tools and applications ❖ Does not contribute to others; is a "lurker"
TOOLS AND TECHNOLOGIES	
IT EXPERIENCE	❖ Limited; typical low-level system jockey

Core Profile

Chief Motivation

- Personal fame

Background, Experience, and Education

- Has played with computers for years; is the computer "expert" for her family and friends
- Frequently plays computer games
- Has a little more knowledge and experience than script kiddies, but not much more—likes to experiment, though, and try new things
- Some programming experience; can write some system scripts and configure standard components (e.g., network router)
- Mostly self-taught; possible computer tech degree

Employer

- Computer technician in a medium-size manufacturing plant

Previous Accomplishments

- Periodically shuts down local library website through IRC-based DDoS (distributed denial-of-service) attacks
- Nightly runs scripts to find open computers on cable modem network segment
- Planted a Sub7 Trojan horse program (a "backdoor" allowing continued access to the computer) on open computers
- Attacked her local community library, with persistent DoS attacks, to contest a $0.25 late-return fine
- Unintentionally destroyed data used by a medium-size website when the Trojan horse she implanted caused the web server to fault

Span of Influence

- None, depends highly on others

Scope of Attacks

-

Sean "Keech" Purcell – Defacer

Overview

MOTIVATION	❖ Seeks to change public opinion; vent personal anger ❖ Conscience; morally-motivated political goals ❖ Personal fame
SKILL AND EDUCATION	❖ Enrolled in an MS in computer science program ❖ Attends Black Hat ("hacker" convention)
SPAN OF INFLUENCE	
TOOLS AND TECHNOLOGIES	
IT EXPERIENCE	

Core Profile

Chief Motivation

- Political purposes

Background, Experience, and Education

- Moderate programming and network experience, mostly in applications
- Completed an undergraduate in computer science
- Enrolled in an MS in computer science program
- Relatively sophisticated and reasonably skilled (He doesn't write the original exploit but he can cobble together new combinations and modify how the exploit works.)
- Active member of the "Animal Liberation Front" (ALF) that recently released 10,000 minks from "captivity" on a local mink farm
- Differs from a terrorist only by a matter of degree; he has the same essential motivation and uses similar (though less sophisticated) methods

Employer

- Currently a full-time student

Previous Accomplishments

- Recently changed the FRAMESET URLs of a wood products company's home page; he left the company's name intact but replaced the content with a political diatribe against their tree harvesting techniques
- Changed the home page of a wood products company, by exploiting an IIS vulnerability, to point to the home page of an environmental advocacy group
- Successfully launched a DDoS attack against the same wood products company

Span of Influence

-

Scope of Attacks

-

Bryan "CrossFyre" Walton – Author

Overview

MOTIVATION	❖ Personal fame among his small circle of "authors"
SKILL AND EDUCATION	❖ Holds an MS in computer science
SPAN OF INFLUENCE	
COLLABORATION	❖ Contributes "public" tools for others to use
TOOLS AND TECHNOLOGIES	
IT EXPERIENCE	

Core Profile

Chief Motivation

- Personal fame among fellow "authors"

Background, Experience, and Education

- Has played with computers for years; is the computer "expert" for his family and friends

- Extensive programming and network experience, both in applications and systems
- Holds an MS in computer science
- Reads and contributes to news groups; seen as one of the "experts"
- Is hard to track down and little concrete information is known about him; what is known has been learned by rumor and innuendo.
- He writes the exploit, perhaps just the kernel of the attack; he lets others (using toolkits) build and launch the actual worm or virus.
- Often learns about holes by examining the patches and fixes we ship (e.g., he compares the code before and after applying the patch)

Employer

- A medium-size network management company

Previous Accomplishments

- Wrote and launched *Slammer* (a very sophisticated worm); it was unusual that he elected to write and launch the worm himself.
- Wrote the core of the MSBlaster worm; others packaged his exploit and launched the worm.
- Wrote a few less successful exploits against IIS and Apache
- Wrote a series of time-limited worms to test propagation techniques
- Recently contributed a new worm tool that makes it easy to launch the same worm against different operating systems

Span of Influence

- Highly influential

Scope of Attacks

-

Lorrin Smith-Bates – Insider

Overview

MOTIVATION	❖ Personal gain ❖ Intense dislike for her employer
SKILL AND EDUCATION	❖ Holds a BS in computer science ❖ Three years of experience as a database administrator
SPAN OF INFLUENCE	❖ Very limited ❖ Does not actively participate in the underground community
COLLABORATION	❖ None
TOOLS AND TECHNOLOGIES	
IT EXPERIENCE	❖ Three years of experience as a database administrator ❖ Held two summer internships while completing her undergraduate degree (one as a phone-support technician, another as a network jockey)

Core Profile

Chief Motivation

- Personal gain

Background, Experience, and Education

- Regularly uses computers but is not avid user (e.g., not a frequent gamer)
- Some programming experience; mostly application level, some systems level
- Has held internships as a phone-support technician and as a network jockey
- Has been employed for the last three years as a database administrator for the accounting database; highly trusted by the organization, usually has access to bookkeeping functions and/or systems

Employer

- Medium-size retail firm

Previous Accomplishments

- Recently modified the access permissions on the purchasing database. Set herself up as a vendor and billed the company for consumables; was caught when the discrepancy was detected during an in-depth audit
- In her previous job, with a large NY bank, she initiated a false interbank transfer (SWIFT) into an accomplice's London account.

Span of Influence

- Very limited
- Does not actively participate in the underground community

Scope of Attacks

- Limited to her current employer

Douglas Hite – Thief

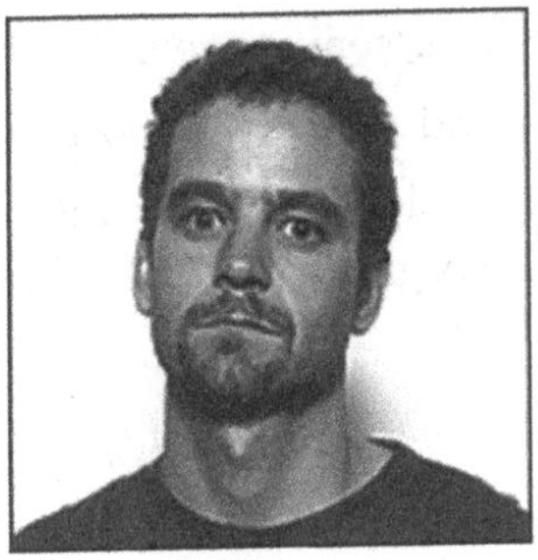

Overview

MOTIVATION	❖ Personal gain ❖ The thrill of succeeding
SKILL AND EDUCATION	❖ Holds a BS in computer science ❖ Has eight (or more) years of system-level programming experience
SPAN OF INFLUENCE	
COLLABORATION	
TOOLS AND TECHNOLOGIES	
IT EXPERIENCE	❖ Systems-level programmer for several years

Core Profile

Chief Motivation

- Personal gain

Background, Experience, and Education

- Has played with computers for years; is the computer "expert" for his family and friends

- Frequently plays computer games
- A great deal of programming experience, in both applications and especially systems
- Holds a BS in computer science
- Has eight (or more) years of system-level programming experience writing drivers for remote-control devices
- He is, effectively, a member of organized crime moving into the computer world; the fastest growing segment of computer crime (e.g., the Russian Mafia is getting very good at this).

Employer

- Crime-based organization
- May hold a day job?

Previous Accomplishments

- Obtained credit-card numbers from CDNow via a 24-byte SQL injection attack. He then offered goods on eBay, which, when purchased, he bought using one of the stolen numbers (pocketing the auction price and leaving the victim with "hot" goods).
- Attacked a medium-size doctor's office just before payday, redirecting all direct-deposit information to his own account(s). Then, after payday, he redirected the direct-deposit information back to the correct entries, covering his tracks.
- Modified DNS entries for a ticket agency's computers. This redirected a FORM POST to purchase tickets to a false clearinghouse. He collected the real tickets and cashed them in for face value at different airports.

Span of Influence

-

Scope of Attacks

-

Mr. Smith – Terrorist

Overview

MOTIVATION	❖ National interests ❖ Highly motivated by ideology
SKILL AND EDUCATION	❖ Holds an MS in computer science ❖ Seven (or more) years experience in systems-level programming
SPAN OF INFLUENCE	❖ Limited to his ideological organization ❖ Quiet and does seek to influence "outsiders"
COLLABORATION	❖ Member of an ideological organization ❖ Works with assigned "team" members
TOOLS AND TECHNOLOGIES	
IT EXPERIENCE	❖ Several years of experience as a systems-level programmer

Core Profile

Chief Motivation

- National interests (motivated by ideology)

Background, Experience, and Education

- Holds an MS in computer science
- Seven (or more) years experience in systems-level programming
- Trained in weapons and explosives
- Deeply committed to the ideological principles of his organization

Employer

-

Previous Accomplishments

- Hacked into a Kuwaiti airline reservation system and found flights carrying members of the Kuwaiti royal family. He relayed this information to a compatriot who then blew up the plane in flight.
- Stole information on aerosol physics to assist with manufacturing chemical weapons
- Located a truck shipment of organophosphates (used to make nerve gas) in England. He then assisted with hijacking the truck.

Span of Influence

- Limited to his ideological organization
- Quiet and does seek to influence "outsiders"

Scope of Attacks

- Worldwide

Mr. Jones – Spy

Overview

MOTIVATION	❖ National interests
SKILL AND EDUCATION	❖ Holds a Ph.D. in computer science ❖ Continuous and ongoing education and training
SPAN OF INFLUENCE	
COLLABORATION	
TOOLS AND TECHNOLOGIES	
IT EXPERIENCE	

Core Profile

Chief Motivation

- National interests

Background, Experience, and Education

- Holds a Ph.D. in computer science (His thesis was "Fault Injection into Cryptographic Protocols.")
- Actively engaged in continuous education and training
- Has access to most source code (legally or illegally obtained)

Employer

- Government agency

Previous Accomplishments

- By bridging through a dual-homed (two network cards) laptop, he simultaneously connected to both the Internet and a VPN. He then "echoed" every packet sent or received, using modified network drivers, to a secure collection point.
- Modified the random number generator in an OEM software image by reducing the complexity of the LFSR and then encrypting the output with a public key.

Span of Influence

-

Scope of Attacks

- Worldwide

APPENDIX

D

Elevation of Privilege: The Cards

This appendix discusses the threats in the *Elevation of Privilege* card game. It goes beyond the material included in the game, with the goal of making the game more helpful. Each bulleted item in the lists that follow includes the card, the threat, a brief discussion, and possibly a reference or comments about how to address it.

The aces are all of the form "You've invented a new type of attack." The intent of "new" is "not clearly covered in a card," rather than "never before seen." How to interpret "clearly covered" is up to the group that's playing. You might be liberal, and encourage use of the aces, especially by those who are not security experts. You might be harsh, and set a high bar for security experts. It depends on the tone of your gameplay. However you decide to interpret it, be sure to write down the threat and address it. There is no per-threat-type discussion of Aces.

For more on the motivation, design, and development of *Elevation of Privilege,* see my paper "Elevation of Privilege: Drawing Developers into Threat Modeling" (Shostack, 2012).

Spoofing

Many of the concepts here are discussed at length in Chapter 14 "Accounts and Identity."

2 of Spoofing. *An attacker could squat on the random port or socket that the server normally uses.* Squatting is a term of art for a program that occupies the resource before your program starts. If you use a random port (registered with some portmapper), how can a client ensure that they're connecting to the right place? If you use a named object or a file in /tmp, the same sort of issues will apply. You can address this by using ACLs to ensure that the named object is restricted to your code, and that it is not transient (that is, it exists regardless of whether your code is running). You can also use an object in a private directory, rather than /tmp. If you use a port, you'll need to authenticate after connection, as other programs can start listening on that port. Unix systems have reserved ports on which only root can listen, but using that requires that your code runs as root or SUID root; or, if you break your code into a privileged listener and a larger unprivileged processor, the root component has to synchronize over some mechanism that then may be vulnerable to squatting.

3 of Spoofing. *An attacker could try one credential after another and there's nothing to slow them down (online or offline).* This refers to brute-force attacks. Online as a term of art here means all attacks for which some code you've written has a chance to intercede; offline means the attacker has a copy of the datastore on which your authentication code relies, and the attacker can use whatever attack tools they'd like. Resisting online attacks involves backoff and possibly lockout, while resisting offline attacks involves salts and iterated hashes (as discussed in Chapter 14.

4 of Spoofing. *An attacker can anonymously connect because we expect authentication to be done at a higher level.* This may be a reasonable assumption, but have you validated it?

5 of Spoofing. *An attacker can confuse a client because there are too many ways to identify a server.* This can refer to the human or software clients. If your systems have several names (for example, a WINS name, a DNS name, and a branding name), what ensures that the client always sees the same thing?

6 of Spoofing. *An attacker can spoof a server because identifiers aren't stored on the client and checked for consistency upon reconnection (that is, there's no key persistence).* This refers to "trust on first use," (TOFU) as performed by SSH and other protocols.

7 of Spoofing. *An attacker can connect to a server or peer over a link that isn't authenticated (and encrypted).* This can result in the server, peer, or client being spoofed.

8 of Spoofing. *An attacker could steal credentials stored on the server and reuse them (for example, a key is stored in a world-readable file).* Or the key could be stored so that only a few principals can read it, but it's still vulnerable to theft. You may want to use hardware that is designed to hold high-value keys, rather than store them on the file system.

9 of Spoofing. *An attacker who obtains a password can reuse it (use stronger authenticators).* This may have a complex interplay with your requirements, but it's always worth asking whether passwords can be removed from the system. (There's a discussion of those trade-offs in Chapter 14.)

10 of Spoofing. *An attacker can choose to use weaker or no authentication.* Many systems have negotiated authentication, sometimes including no authentication. Consider the options that you want or need to make available.

Jack of Spoofing. *An attacker could steal credentials stored on the client and reuse them.* There's a wide variety of ways that credentials are stored on clients, and you cannot directly prevent any of them. These mechanisms include primarily cookies and passwords. Consider additional authentication mechanisms such as IP addresses or device fingerprinting, and be careful to not break the person's mental model. Also remember that many people delete cookies.

Queen of Spoofing. *An attacker could go after the way credentials are updated or recovered (account recovery doesn't require disclosing the old password).* Backup authentication is hard, so don't miss the discussion of threats in Chapter 14.

King of Spoofing. *Your system ships with a default admin password and doesn't force a change.* If your systems all have the same default admin password, it will end up on the web and available to unskilled attackers. If you use an algorithm to determine it, such as the media access control (MAC) address, or some hash of the address, that too will likely become known.

Tampering

Many of the issues brought up by tampering threats are addressed with crypto, covered in depth in Chapter 16 "Threats to Cryptosystems."

2 of Tampering. There is no 2 of Tampering card, as we were unable to find a tampering threat we thought would be common enough to warrant a card. Suggestions to the author are welcome, care of the publisher, or via various social media. (Naming platforms is attractive, and at odds with my aspiration towards having written a classic text.)

3 of Tampering. *An attacker can take advantage of your custom key exchange or integrity control that you built instead of using standard crypto.* Creating your own cryptosystem can be fun, but putting it into production is foolhardy.

4 of Tampering. *Your code makes access control decisions all over the place, rather than with a security kernel.* A security kernel (sometimes called a reference monitor) is a single place where all access control decisions can be made. The advantage of creating one is consistency, and the forcing function of considering what the API should be, which means you need to consider the appropriate parameters in each authentication.

5 of Tampering. *An attacker can replay data without detection because your code doesn't provide time stamps or sequence numbers.* Generally, time stamps are harder to use well, because they require synchronized clocks. Also, time stamps may have a larger attack surface than sequence numbers used only for your purposes. (Additionally, someone might attack your clock for unrelated reasons, so again, time stamps are riskier.)

6 of Tampering. *An attacker can write to a datastore on which your code relies.* If you like it, then you should have put an ACL on it.

7 of Tampering. *An attacker can bypass permissions because you don't make names canonical before checking access permissions.* If your code checks permissions on ./rules, and attackers can make ./rules a link, then they can add whatever permissions they would like. Expand that to a full and canonical path.

8 of Tampering. *An attacker can manipulate data because there's no integrity protection for data on the network.* Generally, the ways to fix this will be SSL, SSH, or IPsec.

9 of Tampering. *An attacker can provide or control state information.* If your system relies on something that an attacker can change, such as a URL parameter of authenticated=true or username=admin, then a redesign is probably in order.

10 of Tampering. *An attacker can alter information in a datastore because it has weak ACLs or includes a group that is equivalent to everyone ("all Live ID holders").* These two examples (of weak ACLs and everyone groups) are not exactly the same things, but we wanted to get them both in. The fix to either involves changing the permissions.

Jack of Tampering. *An attacker can write to some resource because permissions are granted to the world or there are no ACLs.* This is a slightly more broad version of number 10.

Queen of Tampering. *An attacker can change parameters over a trust boundary and after validation (for example, important parameters in a hidden field in HTML, or passing a pointer to critical memory).* Generally, you address these with pass-by-value, rather than pass-by-reference. You validate and use the values you're passed.

King of Tampering. *An attacker can load code inside your process via an extension point.* Extension points are great. It's very hard to create systems that load someone else's code in a library without exposing yourself to security (and reliability) risks.

Repudiation

Many of these threats are threats to logging, as logging is an essential part of non-repudiation. Repudiation threats are often an interesting foil for requirements, but they are covered less well by *Elevation of Privilege.*

2 of Repudiation. *An attacker can pass data through the log to attack a log reader, and there's no documentation regarding what sorts of validation are done.* Attackers can be distinguished by what data elements they can insert. Any web user can insert a URL into your HTTP logs by requesting it. The time stamp field is under the control of (a possibly subverted) web server. Your logs should distinguish who can write what.

3 of Repudiation. *A low privilege attacker can read interesting security information in the logs.* You should ensure that interesting security information is stored in logs that are protected.

4 of Repudiation. *An attacker can alter digital signatures because the digital signature system you're implementing is weak, or uses MACs where it should use a signature.* This attack is less about logs, more about the use of crypto to either authenticate or provide non-repudiation. If you're using MACs (message authentication codes), those are generally based on symmetric crypto, and as such provide only integrity, not non-repudiation with respect to the other end of a connection.

5 of Repudiation. *An attacker can alter log messages on a network because they lack strong integrity controls.* Over a network, where the threat includes those from untrusted entities with network access, a MAC can provide integrity to support non-repudiation. This threat assumes both ends are trustworthy, unlike the 4 of Repudiation.

6 of Repudiation. *An attacker can create a log entry without a time stamp (or no log entry is time stamped).* If you trust the other end of a connection to provide time stamps, what happens when they don't?

7 of Repudiation. *An attacker can make the logs wrap around and lose data.* A challenge with logs is what to do when you have a lot of them. You can either lose data or availability (by shutting down when you can't log). You should make a decision based on which is appropriate for your system.

8 of Repudiation. *An attacker can make a log lose or confuse security information.* For example, if you have a system that compresses logs ("previous message repeated a gajillion times") does that work only on identical messages?

9 of Repudiation. *An attacker can use a shared key to authenticate as different principals, confusing the information in the logs.* This relates to the 4 of Repudiation, and showcases the value of asymmetric cryptography versus shared keys.

10 of Repudiation. *An attacker can get arbitrary data into logs from unauthenticated (or weakly authenticated) outsiders without validation.* If you have a centralized logging point, what does it record about where data comes from, and how does it authenticate those systems?

Jack of Repudiation. *An attacker can edit logs, and there's no way to tell (perhaps because there's no heartbeat option for the logging system).* You can heartbeat so that there's some indication logs were working, and there are more robust systems that use cryptography (often in the form of hash chains or trees).

Queen of Repudiation. *An attacker can say, "I didn't do that," and you would have no way to prove them wrong.* This is a business requirement threat, and your logs must capture the sorts of things that your customers might deny having done.

King of Repudiation. *The system has no logs.* (It's tempting to say that this one is self-explanatory, but *Elevation of Privilege* is designed to draw developers into threat modeling.) Logs can be helpful not only in debugging and operations, but also in attack detection or reconstruction, and in helping to settle disputes. Your logs should be designed to address each of those scenarios.

Information Disclosure

Many information disclosure threats are best addressed with cryptography.

2 of Information Disclosure. *An attacker can brute-force file encryption because no defense is in place* (example defense: password stretching). Password stretching refers to taking a password and iterating over it thousands of times to make a better cryptographic key, which is then used to encrypt the document (rather than using the password directly).

3 of Information Disclosure. *An attacker can see error messages with security-sensitive content.* For example, your web error page says "Cannot connect to database with password foobar1." The right pattern is a unique error code and perhaps pointing to the relevant logs. This can also relate to the 3 of Repudiation (a low-privilege attacker can read interesting security information in the logs).

4 of Information Disclosure. *An attacker can read content because messages (for example, an e-mail or HTTP cookie) aren't encrypted even if the channel is encrypted.* The distinction between channel and message encryption is important. The channel is something like an SMTP connection, and even if that's encrypted, data is in the clear at endpoints.

5 of Information Disclosure. *An attacker might be able to read a document or data because it's encrypted with a nonstandard algorithm.* Use standard cryptographic algorithms.

6 of Information Disclosure. *An attacker can read data because it's hidden or occluded (for undo or change tracking) and the user might forget that it's there.* Change tracking is a lovely feature, and modern Microsoft products tend to have a "prepare for sharing" sort of function. If your data formats have similar issues, you'll want similar functionality.

7 of Information Disclosure. *An attacker can act as a "man in the middle" because you don't authenticate endpoints of a network connection.* Failures to authenticate lead to failures of confidentiality. You'll generally need both.

8 of Information Disclosure. *An attacker can access information through a search indexer, logger, or other such mechanism.* This can refer to a local search indexer, such as the Mac OS Spotlight; or a web indexer, such as Google.

9 of Information Disclosure. *An attacker can read sensitive information in a file with bad ACLs.* Bad ACLs! No biscuit! This really should have read "weak," rather than "bad," and the fix is more restrictive ACLs or permissions.

10 of Information Disclosure. *An attacker can read information in files with no ACLs.* Therefore, add some.

Jack of Information Disclosure. *An attacker can discover the fixed key being used to encrypt.* You likely don't use the same physical key to unlock every door you're authorized to open, so why use the same cryptographic key?

Queen of Information Disclosure. *An attacker can read the entire channel because the channel (for example, HTTP or SMTP) isn't encrypted.* As more and more data passes over untrustworthy networks, the need for encryption will continue to increase.

King of Information Disclosure. *An attacker can read network information because there's no cryptography used.*

Denial of Service

Threats 3–10 are constructed from three properties, shown in parentheses after the text description:

- **Is the threat to a client or a server?** Threats to servers likely affect more people.
- **Is the attacker authenticated or anonymous?** Threats in which an attacker needs credentials have a smaller pool of attackers (or require a preliminary step of acquiring credentials), and it may be possible to retaliate in some way, acting as a deterrent.
- **Does the impact go away when the attacker does (temporary versus persistent)?** Persistent issues that require manual intervention or destroy data are worse than threats that will clear up when the attacker leaves.

There is no discussion of these threats per card, but the cards are listed for reference or use in checking aces.

2 of Denial of Service. *An attacker can make your authentication system unusable or unavailable.* This refers to authentication systems that use either backoff or account lockout to prevent brute-force attacks. Fixing the issues raised by the 3 of Tampering can lead you here.

3 of Denial of Service. *An attacker can make a client unavailable or unusable but the problem goes away when the attacker stops (client, authenticated, temporary).*

4 of Denial of Service. *An attacker can make a server unavailable or unusable but the problem goes away when the attacker stops (server, authenticated, temporary).*

5 of Denial of Service. *An attacker can make a client unavailable or unusable without ever authenticating, but the problem goes away when the attacker stops (client, anonymous, temporary).*

6 of Denial of Service. *An attacker can make a server unavailable or unusable without ever authenticating, but the problem goes away when the attacker stops (server, anonymous, temporary).*

7 of Denial of Service. *An attacker can make a client unavailable or unusable and the problem persists after the attacker goes away (client, authenticated, persistent).*

8 of Denial of Service. *An attacker can make a server unavailable or unusable and the problem persists after the attacker goes away (server, authenticated, persistent).*

9 of Denial of Service. *An attacker can make a client unavailable or unusable without ever authenticating, and the problem persists after the attacker goes away (client, anonymous, persistent).*

10 of Denial of Service. *An attacker can make a server unavailable or unusable without ever authenticating, and the problem persists after the attacker goes away (server, anonymous, persistent).*

Jack of Denial of Service. *An attacker can cause the logging subsystem to stop working.* An attacker who can cause your logging to stop can execute attacks that are then harder to understand and possibly harder to remediate.

Queen of Denial of Service. *An attacker can amplify a denial-of-service attack through this component with amplification on the order of 10:1.* Amplification refers to the defender's resource consumption versus the attacker's. An attacker who just sends you a lot of data is consuming bandwidth at a ratio of 1:1. An attacker who sends a DNS request for a public key is sending dozens of bytes and receiving hundreds, so there's an amplification of 10:1 or so.

King of Denial of Service. *An attacker can amplify a denial-of-service attack through this component with amplification on the order of 100:1.* As per the Queen, but tenfold worse.

Elevation of Privilege (EoP)

2–4 of Elevation of Privilege. There are no cards for the 2, 3, or 4 of Elevation of Privilege, as we were unable to find EoP threats we thought would be common enough to warrant cards. Suggestions are welcome.

5 of Elevation of Privilege. *An attacker can force data through different validation paths which give different results.* If you have different code performing similar validation, then it's hard for your other functions to know what will be checked. This is a great opportunity to refactor.

6 of Elevation of Privilege. *An attacker could take advantage of .NET permissions you ask for but don't use.* The .NET Framework is an example; since the game was created, frameworks with permissions have become quite trendy, appearing in many mobile and even desktop operating systems. Asking for permissions you don't need reduces the security value of these frameworks.

7 of Elevation of Privilege. *An attacker can provide a pointer across a trust boundary, rather than data that can be validated.* This is the pass-by-reference/ pass-by-value issue yet again. If you're going to make trust decisions, you need to ensure that the resources on which you're acting are outside the control of a potential attacker. This issue often appears when pointers are used to make kernel/userland or interprocess communication faster.

8 of Elevation of Privilege. *An attacker can enter data that is checked while still under the attacker's control and used later on the other side of a trust boundary.* This is a more open variant of the 7, using any data, rather than a pointer.

9 of Elevation of Privilege. *There's no reasonable way for callers to figure out what validation of tainted data you perform before passing it to them.* This can be solved by API design, so that fields are marked as "trustworthy" or not, or by documentation, which people are unlikely to read.

10 of Elevation of Privilege. *There's no reasonable way for a caller to figure out what security assumptions you make.* Perhaps this card should read "what security requirements you impose on them," but it's late for that. This card is a variant of the 9, intended to frame the issue because it's so frequent that extra chances to find it are good.

Jack of Elevation of Privilege. *An attacker can reflect input back to a user, such as cross-site scripting.* This card combines the 9 and 10, throwing in a trust boundary and some jargon. Here, an attacker finds a way to make data that comes from them appear to come from you, taking advantage of trust in you. Performing input and output validation can help here.

Queen of Elevation of Privilege. *You include user-generated content within your page, possibly including the content of random URLs.* This should be read more broadly than simply web pages (although there's a lot of fun to be had there). If what you think came from Alice came from Bob, what are the security implications of sending that back to Alice?

King of Elevation of Privilege. *An attacker can inject a command that the system will run at a higher privilege level.* Command injection attacks include use of control characters, such as the apostrophe or semicolon. When these are inserted in the right way to dynamic code, they can lead to an attacker being able to run code of their own choosing. You need to transform your input into a canonical form. Loop until the input doesn't transform anymore, then check it.

APPENDIX

E

Case Studies

This appendix lays out four example threat models. The first three are presented as fully worked-through examples; the fourth is a classroom exercise presented without answers in order to encourage you to delve in. Each example is a threat model of a hypothetical system, to help you identify the threats without getting bogged down in a debate over what the real threat model or requirements are for the particular product.

The models in this appendix are as follows:

- The Acme database
- Acme's operational network
- Sending login codes over a phone network
- The iNTegrity classroom exercise

Each model is structured differently because there's more than one way to do it. For example, the Acme database is modeled element by element, which is good if your primary audience is component owners who want to focus their reading on their components; while the Acme network is organized by threat, to enable systems administrators to manage those threats across the business. The login codes model shows how to focus on a particular requirement and consider the threats against it.

The Acme Database

The Acme database is a software product designed to be run on-premises by organizations of all sizes. The currently shipping version is 3.1, and this is the team's first threat model. They have chosen to model what they have and then determine how each new feature interacts with this model as part of the same process in which they do performance and reliability analysis. This modeling is inspired by a series of recent design flaws that affected company revenue. The output of this modeling would be a clear list of bugs and action items. Because the important take-away from this appendix is not the bugs or action items, but the approach that finds them in your software or system, the bug list is not provided as a list.

Security Requirements

Acme has formalized security requirements for the first time. Those requirements are as follows:

- The product is no less secure than the typical competitor (Acme's software is currently very insecure, and as such, stronger goals are deferred to a later release).
- The product can be certified for sales to the U.S. government.
- The product will ship with a security operations manual. A security configuration analysis tool is planned but will ship after the next revision.
- Non-requirement: protect against the DBA.
- As the product will hold arbitrary data, the team will not be actively looking for privacy issues but nor will they be willfully blind.
- Additional requirements will be applied to specific components.

Software Model

After a series of design meetings over the course of a week, run by Paul (project management lead) and attended by Debbie (architecture), Mike (documentation), and Tina (test), the team agrees on the model shown in Figure E-1. These meetings took longer than expected, because details emerged whose relevance to the threat model was not initially clear, leading to a discussion of questions such as "Does this add a trust boundary," and "Does this accept connections across a trust boundary?"

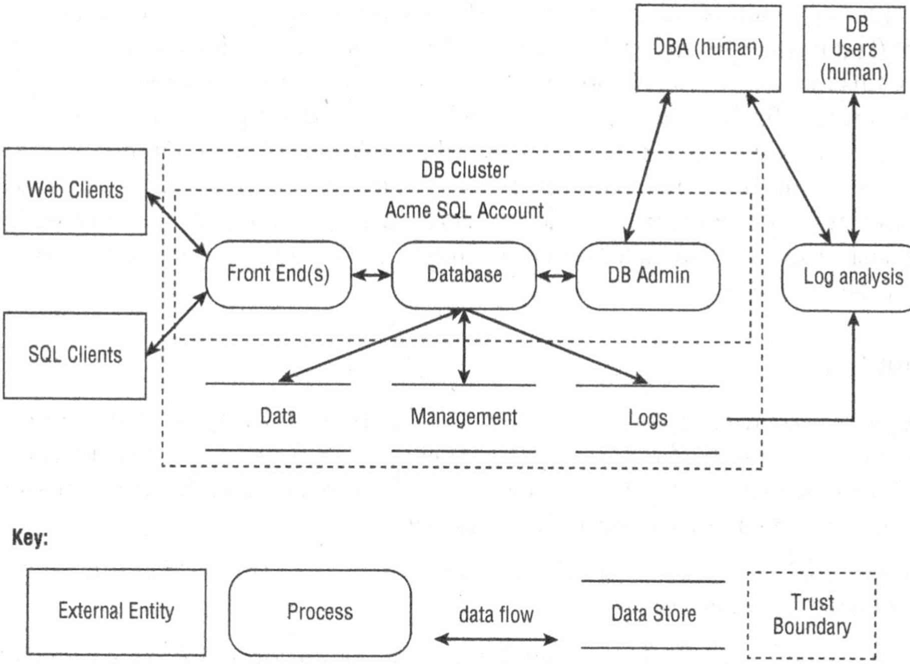

Figure E-1: The Acme database

Threats and Mitigations

The threats identified to the system are organized by module, to facilitate module owner review. They were identified three ways:

- Walking through the threat trees in Appendix B, "Threat Trees"
- Walking through the requirements listed in Chapter 12, "Requirements Cookbook"
- Applying STRIDE-per-element to the diagram shown in Figure E-1

Acme would rank the threats with a bug bar, although because neither the bar nor the result of such ranking is critical to this example, they are not shown. Some threats are listed by STRIDE, others are addressed in less structured text where a single mitigation addresses several threats. The threats are shown in italic to make them easier to skim.

Finding these threats took roughly two weeks, with a one-hour threat identification meeting early in the day during which the team examined a component and its data flows. The examination consisted of walking through the threat trees in Appendix B and the requirements checklist in Chapter 12, and then considering whether other aspects of STRIDE might apply to that one component (and its data flows). Part of each meeting was reserved for follow-up from previous meetings. Part of the rest of the day was used for follow-up to check assumptions, file bugs as appropriate, and ensure that component owners were aware of what was found. Those two weeks could have been compressed into a "do little but threat model" week, but the team chose a longer time period to avoid blocking other work that depended on them, and to give the new skills and tasks time to "percolate"—that is, time for reflection, and consideration of what the team was learning.

Front Ends

The *front ends* are the interface between the database and various clients, ranging from websites to complex programs that make SQL queries. The front ends are intended to handle authentication, load balancing, and related functions so that the core database can be as fast as possible.

Additional requirements for the front end are taken from the "Requirements Cookbook," Chapter 12:

- Only authenticated users will have create/read/update/delete permissions according to policies set by database designers and administrators. (This combines authorization and confidentiality requirements.)
- Single-factor authentication will be sufficient for front-end users.
- Accounts will be created by processes designed by customers deploying the Acme DB software.
- Data will be subject to modification only by enumerated authorized users, and actions will be logged according to customer configuration. (Such configuration will need to be added to the security operations guide.)

The threats identified are as follows:

- **Spoofing:** The authentication from both web and SQL clients is weaker than the team would like. However, the requirement to support web browsers and third-party SQL clients imposes limits on what can be required. Product management has been asked to determine what current customers have in place, and a discussion will be added to the product security operations guide.
- **Tampering:** A number of modules included for authentication were poorly vetted for security properties. It seems at least one has an auto-update feature whose security properties and implications require analysis.
- **Repudiation:** Logging at the front end is nearly non-existent, but what logs exist are stored on the front end, and will need to be sent to the back end.

- **Information Disclosure:** There are both debugging interfaces and error messages, which reveal information about the database connection parameters.
- **Denial of Service:** Reliability engineering has already removed most of the application-specific static limits, but how to configure a few will be added to the operations guide.
- **Elevation of Privilege:** A separate security engineering pass will perform a variety of testing on input validation. Additionally, the front-end team will document the limited validation it performs on data, and review that against assumptions that the core database makes about protection.

Connections to Front Ends

The web front end always runs over SSL, addressing *tampering* and *information disclosure* issues. The SQL client and client libraries will be upgraded so that connecting without SSL requires setting special options (one on the server to allow such connections, one on the client to allow fallback). The Acme client and libraries will always attempt to connect with SSL first, unless a second option, "DontEvenBotherWithSecurity," is set.

Denial-of-service threats are again generally well addressed by the reliability and performance engineering that has already been done. The security team sends a congratulatory box of donuts to the reliability team.

Core Database

Requirements:

- All database permissions rules will be centralized into a single authorization engine to enforce confidentiality, integrity, and authorization policies.

Threats:

- **Spoofing:** The core database is designed to run on a dedicated system, and as such is unlikely to come under spoofing attacks. The one exception, which will be analyzed further, is that the front end has the ability to impersonate and perform actions as any user account.
- **Tampering:** Input validation raises questions of SQL injection, and those lead to questions about what assumptions are being made about the front ends. An intersystem review is planned according to the approach described in Chapter 18 "Experimental Approaches."
- **Repudiation:** Reviews found that the database logs nearly everything originating from the front end, except several key session establishment APIs fail to log how the session was authenticated.

- **Information Disclosure:** SQL injection attacks against the database can lead to information disclosure in all sorts of ways. The team plans to investigate ways to architecturally restrict SQL injection attacks.
- **Denial of Service:** Various complex cross-table requests may have a performance impact. A tester is assigned to investigate clever ways to perform small, expensive queries.
- **Elevation of Privilege:** A review finds two routines that by design allow any caller to run arbitrary code on the system. The team plans to add ACLs to those routines and possibly turn them off by default.

Data (Main Data Store)

Preventing *tampering, information disclosure,* and *denial of service* all rely on the presence of a limited set of connections, with those connections controlled by operating system permissions. If the data store is remote and runs on network attached storage, the storage controller can bypass all the controls on the data. Additionally, the network connections would be vulnerable. The team will document this, and perhaps add additional cryptographic features in a future release that address such threats with untrusted data stores. That decision will hinge on how important the business requirement is, the effort involved in implementation, and possible performance impact.

Management (Data Store)

The same problems that could affect the data store are magnified if the management data store is on remote storage. The team plans to move management data to the same device as the database, and document the security effect of moving it elsewhere.

Connections to the Core Database

The team has been assuming that these connections are within a security boundary, with the previously unstated assumptions that the front ends, database, and DB admin portals would be on a trusted network. Given the work to address all the threats that this assumption allowed, and to ensure performance, that assumption is updated to an isolated network for those with a packet filter. That assumption is added to the operations guide. A bug to encrypt and authenticate between components is filed for a future version.

DB Admin Module

The requirements are as follows:

- **Authentication Strength:** Required authentication strength is debated, and a bug is opened to ensure that the agreed upon requirement is crisp.
- **Account creation:** Creating new DBA accounts will require two administrators, and all administrators will be notified. (This will be a new feature.)
- **Sensitive Data:** There can be requirements to protect information from DBAs—for example, a column of social security numbers. This will be supported in two ways: first, with the option to create a deny ACL for an object, and second, with the option to encrypt data with a key that's passed in. (There's a third option, which is for the caller to encrypt the data, but that's always been implicitly present.) All three are to be documented, along with a discussion of the importance of key management, and the known plaintext attacks against simplistic encryption of a small set of a billion SSNs.
- **Spoofing:** The DBA can connect in two ways: via a web portal and via SSH. The web portal uses SSL, which incorporates by reference all several hundred SSL CAs in a browser, and as such the portal may be spoofable. That may or may not be acceptable risk, so it is now documented in the operations guide. The DBA currently connects with single-factor authentication, and it may be that support for stronger authentication makes sense.
- **Tampering:** The DBA can tamper, and in some sense that's their job.
- **Repudiation:** The admin can change logs. This is documented as a risk, and while logged, the risk is recursive.
- **Information Disclosure:** Previously, the DBA login page provided a great deal of "dashboard" and overview information pre-login as a convenience feature. That is now configurable, and the default state is under discussion. It may also be necessary to protect against DBAs, a requirement set that the team (and author) missed when applying STRIDE-per-element, and discovered when checking requirements.
- **Denial of Service:** The DBA module can turn off the database, re-allocate storage space, and prioritize or de-prioritize jobs. Ancillary denial-of-service attacks may also be possible, which are not logged.
- **Elevation of Privilege:** There is a single type of DBA. It may be sensible to add several layers, and clarifying customer requirements should precede such work.

Logs (Data Store)

Unlike the main data store, logs are, by design, read by log analysis tools that are outside the trust boundary.

- **Tampering:** The logs are presented as read-only to the analysis tools.
- **Repudiation:** The logs are key to analyzing an attempt at repudiation, but it turns out that not all logs are delivered to the central log store. Some are held in other locations, which is tracked in a set of bugs.
- **Information Disclosure:** Because the log analysis code is outside the trust boundary, the logs must not contain information that should not be disclosed, and a review of logging will be required, especially focused on personal information.
- **Denial of Service:** The log analysis code has the capability to make numerous requests. If logs are stored on the same system as the main database, then managing log requests could limit database performance by consuming resources needed for controller bandwidth, disk operations, and other tasks. This issue is added to the operations guide, with a suggestion to send logs to a separate system.

Log Analysis

The threats are as follows:

- **Spoofing:** All the typical spoofing threats are present (roughly everything covered in Appendix B's figure and table B-1 applies). As the number of database users is typically small, the team decides to add persistent tracking of login information to aid in authentication decisions.
- **Tampering:** The log analysis module has several plugins to connect to popular account management tools, each of which presents a tampering threat. As the logs are already read-only with respect to the log analysis tool, tampering threats are less important.
- **Repudiation:** The log analysis tools may help an attacker figure out how to engage in a repudiation that is hard to dispute.
- **Information Disclosure:** The log analysis tools, by design, expose a great deal of information, and a bug was filed based on the Information Disclosure item under "Logs (Data Store)" to control that information. (In a real threat model, you'd just refer to a bug number.)
- **Denial of Service:** Complex queries from log analysis can absorb a lot of processing time and I/O bandwidth.
- **Elevation of Privilege:** There are probably a number of elevation paths based on calls from the log analysis module to other parts of the system, designed in before trust boundaries were made explicit.

In summary, it seems that Acme's development team has learned a lot, and has a good deal of work in front of them. Because this work was kicked off after a series of embarrassing security incidents, management is cautiously optimistic. They have a set of issues to work on, and if more incidents happen, they can use those incidents to see if their threat modeling work found the threats, and prioritize that fix. They believe such surprises are far less likely than they were before they started threat modeling.

Acme's Operational Network

The Acme Corporation are makers of fine database software. It used to produce jet-propelled pogo sticks, tornado seeds, and other products before a leveraged buyout drove it to a more traditional corporate structure, including a more traditional operational network. After its project to threat model its software goes well, producing useful and actionable bugs, it decides to take a crack at modeling its internal network.

Security Requirements

These requirements were built on those from the Requirements Cookbook (see Chapter 12):

1. Operational vulnerability management will track all products deployed on the attack surface.
    a. Henceforth, all newly deployed software will be checked to ensure it has a vulnerability announcement policy.
    b. Paul, a project coordinator, has been assigned to track down vulnerability announcement policies per product in use, and to subscribe to all of them.
2. Operations will ensure that its firewalls align with the trust boundaries shown in diagrams.
3. The sales portion of the network will need to be PCI compliant.
4. Complete business requirements are somewhat hard to pin down, and of the form "Let's not have bad stuff happen." Those will be made more precise as questions of how to mitigate are analyzed, using the feedback process between threats, mitigations, and requirements shown in Figure 12-1 (in Chapter 12).

Acme has decided to focus on a STRIDE threat-oriented approach, as it worked reasonably well for their software threat modeling. They are aware that a balance between prevent, detect, and respond is probably also important, but wanted to build on their success with software modeling, and so will consider those requirements at a later date.

Operational Network

Acme's operational network was shown earlier in Chapter 2, "Strategies for Threat Modeling" and is reproduced here as Figure E-2. The remainder of this section is written in the form of a summary, as if it were from the team. The main thing missing is bug numbers, because adding fake bug numbers won't make the examples more readable.

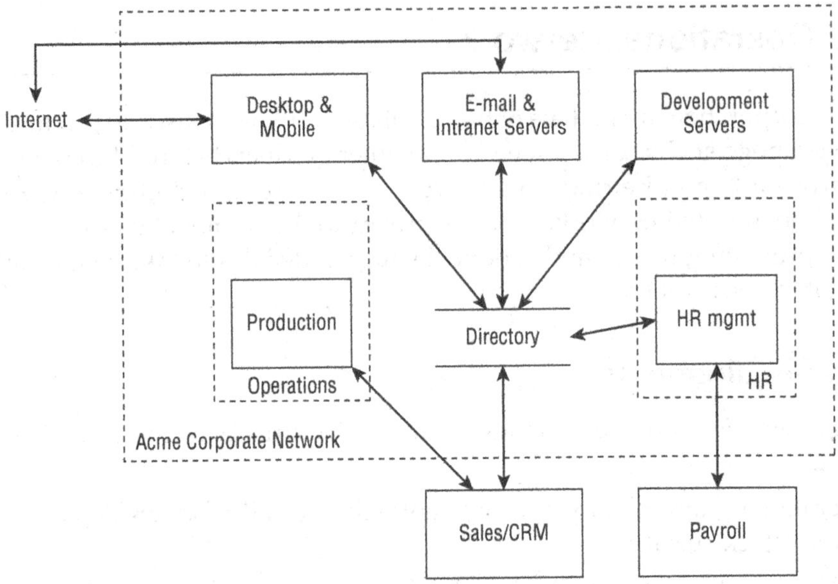

Figure E-2: Acme's operational business network

The team has decided that this diagram will suffice to get started even though there are several obvious bugs, including the fact that it does not show payment processing. That will be considered later, as making sure no one steals the plans for the rocket-powered pogo sticks or dehydrated boulders is considered a top priority.

The systems that make up the operational network are as follows:

- **Desktop and mobile:** are the end-user systems that everyone in the company uses.
- **E-mail and intranet:** are an Exchange server and a set of internal wikis and blog servers.
- **Development servers:** includes the local source-control repository, along with bug tracking, build, and test servers.
- **Production:** This is where products are made using a just-in-time approach. It includes an operations network that is full of machine tools and other equipment that is finicky and hard to keep operational, never mind secure.

- **Directory:** This is an Active Directory server, which is used for account management across most of the systems at Acme.
- **HR Management:** This is a personnel database, time-card system for hourly employees, and related services.
- **Website/Sales/CRM:** This is the website through which orders are placed. The website runs at an IaaS cloud provider. It has a direct connection to the production shop. The website is locally built and managed with a variety of dependencies.
- **Payroll:** This is an outsourced payroll company.

Threats to the Network

The team made an initial decision to look at operations threat by threat, rather than system by system, as looking at the systems makes it a little harder to rank threats (and would result in a threat model that looks like the prior example). In the interests of presenting a somewhat compact example, additional requirements are only called out occasionally.

Spoofing

The team decided to look at spoofing threats by the victim—that is, what happens if someone spoofs the connection to each system or set of systems within the diagram.

The requirements for Acme's network are as follows:

- No anonymous access to corporate systems.
  - There may be a requirement for whistleblower anonymity. The question is sent to legal.
- Single-factor authentication is sufficient for all systems.
- All systems should default to authorization against the directory system.
- Account creation is performed by a single administrator.

The requirements for the website are as follows:

- Facebook logins will be accepted.
- Anyone with a validated e-mail account can create an account.

Spoofing threats to specific areas of the operational network include:

- **Desktop and mobile:** Several developers have installed their own remote access software, believing that "no one would ever find it" is sufficient security. Rather than have a debate on the subject, the team realized there's no good alternative, and adds this as justification for the VPN project to move faster.

- **E-mail and intranet services:** These services are exposed to the Internet. Password protection on the intranet servers is spotty, as some of them were deployed with the assumption that they're "behind the firewall," while others were deployed with a shared username/password, and yet others really do need exposure to the Internet for mobile workers. That last need will be addressed with a VPN, which is not yet deployed.
- **Development servers:** These servers being spoofed seems to turn largely into an integrity (tampering) threat against either source or development documents.
- **Production:** Most obviously, someone could drive the creation of extra products, have those products either stack up in the warehouse or, worse, be delivered to fake customers. More subtly, a rascally attacker might be able to deliver fake product plans, resulting in product malfunctions, unhappy customers, and bad press for the company and its products.
- **Directory:** The biggest issue would be spoofing of HR management. If someone can pretend to be HR, they end up with a lot of power.
- **HR Management:** The digital data flows are almost exclusively outbound. Inbound processes still involve a lot of face-to-face discussion and paper forms.
- **Sales/CRM:** These systems have a direct connection to production, where orders are sent. It turns out that the server in production will take entries authenticated only by IP address, and anyone with that address can enter orders.
- **Payroll:** Spoofing threats to the payroll system loom large in everyone's mind, especially because HR e-mails payroll data every week. Unfortunately, the payroll company has no options to use anything stronger than a username and password. After a raucous debate, the team decides to file a bug (also noting the information disclosure and tampering threats associated with e-mail), and then moves to other threats.
- **Other spoofing:** A single directory server acts as a single point of failure for spoofing security. While this worries some team members, the "solution" of adding a second directory system doesn't help because even after a lot of work to keep them in sync, most spoofing attacks will have two potential targets.

Tampering

Currently, a great deal of reliance is placed on firewalls to prevent tampering attacks. Few of the internal data flows are integrity protected. Many of the following threats can be implemented either against the endpoint or against network data flows:

- **Desktop and mobile:** There is little control over what software runs on desktops across the company. Developers run high-privilege accounts on both their e-mail and development machines. There's no integrity checking or whitelisting software in use.
- **E-mail and intranet:** The e-mail servers are reasonably well protected, while the intranet servers are a mixed bag. One wiki runs off a common account, known to most of the developers.
- **Development servers:** The source control server is fairly locked down, with constrained access that seems to have been implemented to log all changes. The test servers are known to be a mess, with anyone able to make changes; and tracking what has changed when and where is manual.
- **Production:** The department has a wide variety of equipment, some of which even talks to each other without humans involved. Tampering threats abound, from tampering with raw materials to tampering with computer-controlled devices in order to produce either subtly or very wrong output, to tampering with delivery instructions.
- **Directory:** This is fairly locked down, with a limited number of administrator accounts, all of whom can tamper by design. However, anyone who breaks in or misbehaves here can likely obtain full credentials to do so elsewhere in the network.
- **HR management:** These systems are not as locked down as anyone would like. An employee who made changes there could likely do so undetected by technology. The change would have to be noticed by a person. Changes, such as not paying a salary, would be caught by employees, while paying too much would (we hope) be caught by accounting. Changes to job titles, dates of hire (which affect pension, vacation, and other benefits) would likely go undetected.
- **Sales/CRM:** There are a number of issues. Perhaps most important, someone who can alter data on that site can alter prices, either subtly or aggressively. Someone can also alter customer records, making a new customer

appear long-standing or vice-versa, and changing how they are treated by customer service or anti-fraud.

- **Payroll:** The tampering attacks here range from the obviously bad, such as adding employees or changing salaries, to the more subtle, such as changing tax withholding or deductions at the same time ("We're sorry, Mr. Smith, but we have not received insurance premiums from you. . .").

Repudiation

The team decided to focus most repudiation attention on sales order repudiation, and has planned a review of logs on the sales server. There are certainly other repudiation issues they could examine, including repudiation of check-ins to the development servers, repudiations of HR changes, or repudiation of changes to production. However, for a first pass at threat modeling, other threats are given priority.

Information Disclosure

Acme is very protective of trade secrets regarding product creation, and worried about the contents of the customer support database, as a few customers seem to regularly encounter product reliability issues. Customer support believes that many of these customers are merely hasty, not taking time to read the instructions. Threats apply to:

- **Desktop and mobile systems:** Unfortunately, these must have access to most data. Data encryption software may be an important addition here, to protect against information disclosure if the machines are stolen. This mitigation applies across most of the systems in the company, and is not repeated per section.
- **E-mail servers:** E-mail contains a tremendous amount of confidential information. The team considers a pilot project for e-mail encryption.
- **Intranet servers:** These servers are a different beast. It's challenging to add encryption for application data such that only certain readers have the keys (in contrast to full disk encryption). It might be possible to use a more well-considered set of permissions. Additionally, it's possible to add SSL to most of these servers.
- **Development servers:** It is similarly challenging to use encryption for application data.
- **Production servers:** These are locked down primarily for reliability reasons, which has nice side effects for security.

- **HR management:** These include information on salaries, performance reviews, sufficient personal data to commit identity theft, as well as a host of information on prospective candidates.
- **Sales/CRM:** These systems contain information about upcoming sales, coupon codes, customer names and addresses, and—probably accidentally—credit card numbers. The data flow from sales to production needs to have encryption added.

Denial of Service

Somewhat similar to repudiation, denial-of-service threats are treated as a lower priority than spoofing, tampering, or information disclosure. The team notes that production is dependent on a non-scalable set of machines and skilled machine operators, and so a leap in sales would be a denial of vacation.

Elevation of Privilege

Outsiders can attempt to elevate to insider privileges via desktop (attacking via e-mail, IM, and web browsing), and attacking sales/CRM or payroll, each of which is exposed to the Internet. To address the desktop elevation attacks, the team looks to vulnerability management and sandboxing. The web applications that deliver sales and CRM are exposed to a variety of attacks, including SQL and command injection, cross-site scripting (XSS), cross-site request forgery (CRSF), and other web attacks. Testing for those attacks will be managed by the QA team, which will need additional security training. The team resolves to ask external vendors some questions about patching and secure development at the payroll company. Acme has decided to defer insider threats for now, as there's a lot to be done in the near term.

In summary, Acme has used STRIDE threat modeling and a model of their operational network to identify many threats. Again, they have moved from a vague sense of unease to a well justified set of concerns, which they can work through. From here, they'd need to decide on a prioritization scheme for those concerns, or consider additional security requirements, depending on their unique needs.

Phones and One-Time Token Authenticators

Chapter 9, "Trade-Offs When Addressing Threats," describes a threat model (shown in Figure E-3) that illustrates how threat models can be used to drive the evolution of an architecture. This model is also a useful example of a focused threat model. It ignores a great deal of important mechanisms, and shows how the trust boundaries and requirements can quickly identify threats. It should not be taken as commentary on any particular commercial system, some of which may mitigate threats shown here. Also, many of these systems support text to speech that can read the code to a person using an old-fashioned telephone; the alternatives suggested in the following material do not have that capability.

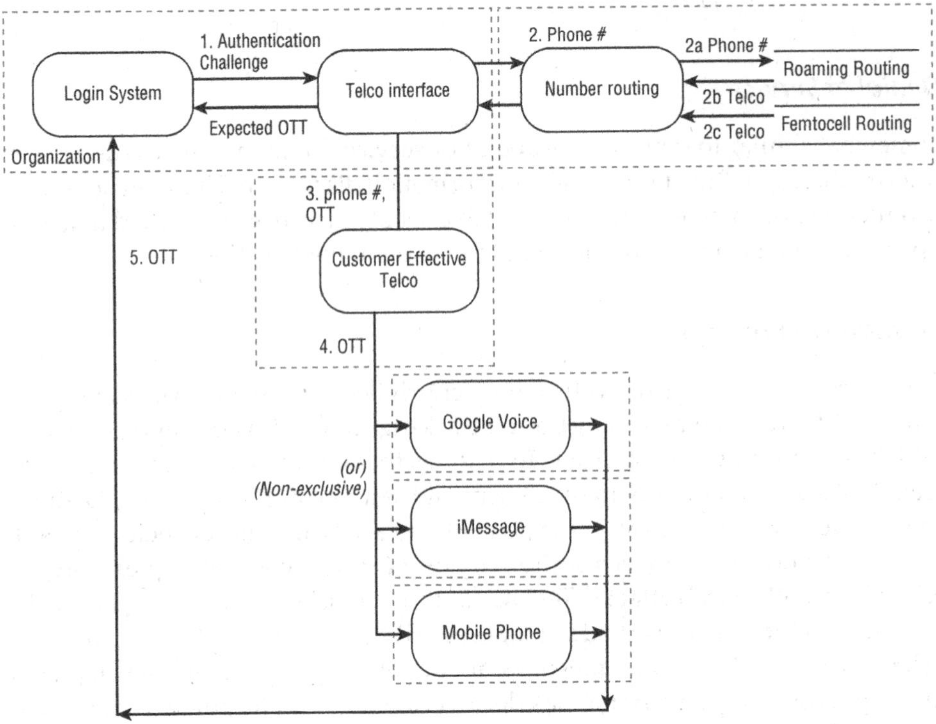

Figure E-3: A one-time token authentication system

The Scenario

A wide variety of systems are designed to send auxiliary passwords—*one-time tokens* (*OTT*)—over the phone network to someone's phone. During an enrollment phase, the user is asked to provide a phone number, which is then associated with the account. The scenario shown in Figure E-3 starts when someone attempts to log in (to an account with which a phone is associated) at the "Login system." A model of how that works is as follows:

1. The login attempt triggers a message to some telephone company ("telco") interface, and that message is a phone number and a message to be sent to the phone number.

2. The telco interface does some form of lookup to find out how to route the message. That's modeled as a "number routing" process in a separate trust domain. There are a number of ways in which mobile phones associate with other phone carriers, including roaming and *femtocells*. Similarly, but not shown, with U.S. phone number portability, simple routing by area code and exchange no longer works, even for landlines. The number routing system returns a pointer to a "Customer effective telco."
3. The telco interface then sends the phone number and OTT to the customer's effective telco.
4. The OTT is then sent to one or more systems that may be delivering the message. That might simply be the phone in question, but it could also be an interface such as Google Voice or Apple iMessage. (All products are listed for illustrative purposes only.)
5. The person enters the OTT at the login page, and it is compared to the expected value.

The security requirement is that the OTT is not disclosed to an attacker. There are three requirements which might apply. First, the OTT should get through intact—that is, free of tampering. Second, the system should remain operational. Both those requirements apply to almost any variant of this system, and as such they do not enhance the value you get from a comparative threat model. The third requirement which may be relevant is privacy; people may not want to give you their mobile phone number and risk it being abused for sales calls or other purposes. This is a threat to your ability to use OTT to improve authentication. The privacy issue would weigh in favor of applications on mobile devices.

The Threats

This model focuses on threats to the confidentiality of the OTT. Some of those are direct threats, others are impacts of first-order threats such as spoofing and tampering:

1. The login system and telco interface communicate inside a trust boundary, and you can ignore threats there for this model.
2. The phone number being sent to a routing service outside the trust boundary presents a number of threats. If the reply is not accurate, step 3 will expose the OTT. The reply can be inaccurate for a variety of reasons, including but not limited to the following:
   - Lies (inaccurate or misleading data regardless of whether that's accidental, intentional by the database, or intentional by someone who's hacked the database) from the roaming database
   - Lies from the femtocell database

- Attacks against the routing service (EoP, tampering, spoofing)
- Attacks against the return data flow (tampering, spoofing)

3. The "customer effective telco" can see the OTT.
4. Systems designed to improve text message processing can see the OTT.

Possible Redesigns

Information disclosure threats can be addressed by adding cryptographic functions. Simplified versions of ways to do that include the following:

- Send a nonce, encrypted to a key held on a smartphone, then send the decrypted nonce to the authentication server (message 1 = $e_{phone}(nonce_n)$, message 2 = $nonce_n$). Then the server checks whether the $nonce_n$ is the one that it encrypted for the phone, approving the transaction if it is.
- Send a nonce to the smartphone, and then send a signed version of the nonce to the server [message 1 = $nonce_{phone}$, message 2 = $sign_{key(phone)}(nonce_{phone})$]. The server validates that the signature on the $nonce_{phone}$ is from the expected phone's key, and is a good signature on the expected nonce. If both those checks pass, then the server approves the transaction.
- Send a nonce to the smartphone. The smartphone hashes the nonce with a secret value it holds, and sends back the hash.

For each of these, it's important to manage the keys appropriately, and it's probably useful to include time stamps, message addressing, and other elements to make the system fully secure. Including those in this discussion makes it hard to see how cryptographic building blocks could be applied.

The key in all design changes is understanding the differences introduced by the changes, and how those changes interact with the software requirements as a whole.

Redesigns that focus on using the phone as a processor preclude the use of an old-fashioned telephone, or even a mobile phone (of the kind where the end user can't easily install software). Because such phones still exist, it may be that the threats just enumerated are considered acceptable risk, or even an improvement over traditional passwords.

Sample for You to Model

You can use the models presented above as training models with answer keys. (That is, use the software model in Figure E-1 and the operational model in Figure E-2 and find threats against them yourself. You can treat the example threats as an answer key; but if you do, please don't feel limited to or constrained by them. There are other example threats.) In contrast this section presents a model without an answer key. It's a lightly edited version of a class exercise that was created by Michael Howard and used at Microsoft for years. It's included with their kind permission. I've personally taught many classes using this model, and it is sufficiently detailed for newcomers to threat modeling to find many threats.

Background

This tool, named iNTegrity, is a simple file-integrity checking tool that reads resources, such as files in the filesystem, determining whether any files or registry keys have been changed since the last check. This is performed by looking at the following:

- File or key names
- File size or registry data
- Last updated time and date
- Data checksum (MD5 and/or SHA1 hash)

Architecturally, the tool is split into two parts: a host component and an administrative console. As shown in Figure E-4, one client can communicate with multiple servers, rather than running the tool locally on each computer.

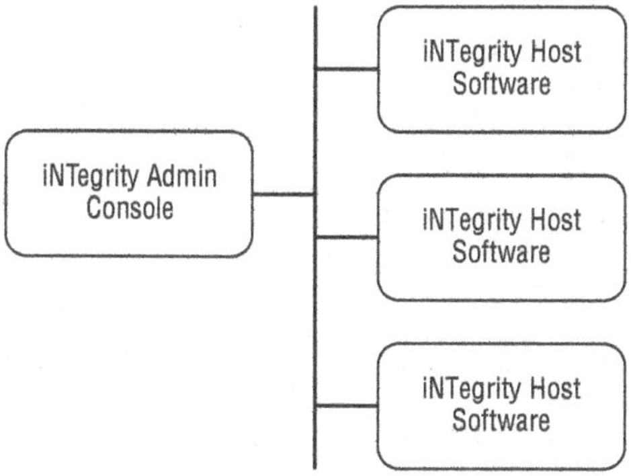

Figure E-4: The networked host/admin console nature of the iNTegrity tool

In another operational environment, it might be known that a machine has been compromised and can no longer be trusted, and the server and client software can be run off, say, a bootable CD or USB drive. In this case, the integrity-checking code is running under a trusted, read-only Windows environment, and the host and admin components both read data from the compromised machine, but not using the potentially compromised OS. The host process does not run as a Windows service in this mode, but as a standalone console application.

The Host Component

This small host component is written in C++ and runs as a service on a Windows server. Its role is to take requests from the admin console and respond to those requests. Valid requests include getting information about host component version, and recursive and non-recursive file properties. Note that the host software performs no analysis; it sends raw integrity data (filenames, sizes, hashes, ACLs, and so on) to the admin console, which performs the core analysis.

The Admin Console

The admin console code stores and analyzes resource (file, registry) version information that comes from one or more host processes. A user can instruct the admin console to connect to a host running the iNTegrity host software, get resource information, and then compare that data with a local, trusted data store of past resource information to see if anything has changed.

The iNTegrity Data Flow Diagrams

The iNTegrity data flow diagrams are shown in Figures E-5 and E-6.

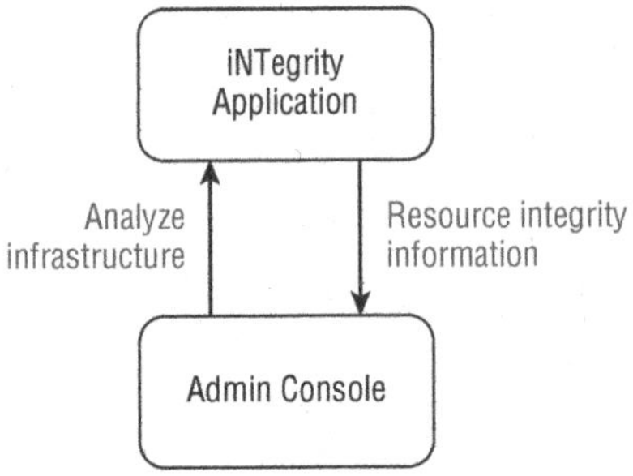

Figure E-5: Context diagram

NOTE **The iNTegrity example comes from a time when the standard advice was to create a *context diagram*, which can be helpful when an external threat modeling consultant is being used, acting as a forcing function to consider the scope and boundaries of the threat model.**

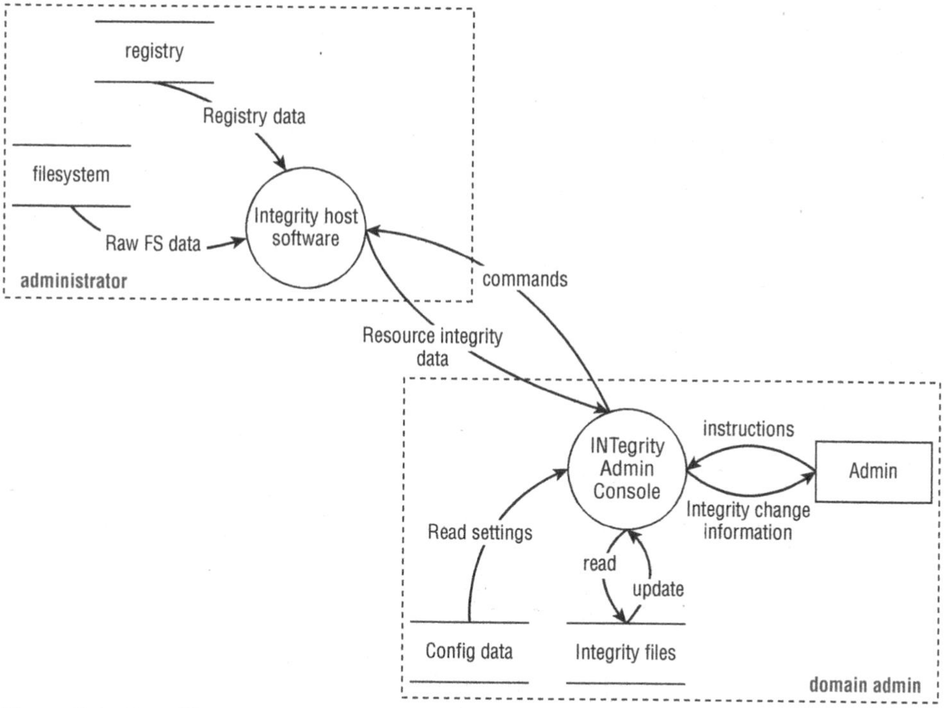

Figure E-6: Main DFD

Exercises

The following exercises were designed to walk students through the activities they'll need to perform to find threats. They can be used by readers of this example without modification:

1. Identify all the DFD elements. (People often miss the data flows.)
2. Identify all threat types to each element.
3. Identify three or more threats: one for a data flow, one for a data store, and one for a process.
4. Identify first-order mitigations for each threat.

Extra credit: The level 1 diagram is not perfect. What would you change, add, or remove?

Glossary

This glossary is intended to provide practical definitions of terms to help you understand how they are used in threat modeling and in this book. I have aimed for clarity, consistency, and brevity.

I have tried to be clear in context, but I avoid attempts to declare one meaning or another "correct" or superior to others.

ACL (access control list) — This allows or denies access to files. ACL is often used interchangeably with permissions, despite the fact that Windows or other ACLs have some technically important differences from unix permissions—in particular, the flexibility of the semantics of a list of rules, rather than a fixed set of permission bytes.

administrator — The most privileged account on a system, and the name of the most privileged account on a Windows system. The text is contextually clear when an issue is specific to a design element or feature of Windows. Often used in the text interchangeably with "root," the most privileged account on unix systems.

AINCAA — The properties violated by the STRIDE threats. Those properties are as follows: Authentication, Integrity, Non-repudiation, Confidentiality, Availability, and Authorization.

AJAX (Asynchronous JavaScript and XML) — Generally, AJAX refers to a style of programming websites and the relevant design of the back end which results in a more fluid and interactive experience than pushing the Submit button.

Alice and Bob — Protagonists in cryptographic protocols since time immemorial, or perhaps since Rivest, Shamir, and Adleman used them when introducing the RSA cryptosystem.

API (application programming interface) — A way for programmers to control a piece of technology.

archetype — A kind of model of a personality or behavior pattern.

ASLR (Address Space Layout Randomization) — Randomizing the address space of a process makes writing effective stack-smashing attacks more difficult. While ASLR is a specific technique, it is usually used in this book as an exemplar of a set of defensive techniques with the goal of preventing memory corruption or control-flow attacks.

ASN (Autonomous System Number) — Used in Internet routing, the ASN refers to a complete set of Internet addresses that should be routed to the same place.

asset — An object of value, possibly intangible, in the sense that goodwill is an asset carried on a company's books. In threat modeling, it has two particular meanings. One, it is a thing that either an attacker will pursue or someone wants to protect or is a stepping stone to either. Two, it can mean a computer or other piece of technology, where asset is a synonym for a more common word.

attack surface — Places where a trust boundary can be traversed, whether by design or by accident.

authentication — The process of increasing another's confidence in an identification. "Alice Smith authenticated herself by showing her company badge."

AuthN, AuthZ — These abbreviations for authentication and authorization, respectively, are often used because they are both shorter to write and can be easily skimmed.

authorization — The process of checking whether an identified entity is allowed to take some action. The entity can be a person or a technological system of some form. "Alice is not authorized to view the contents of the layoffs directory."

availability — The property of being available for intended service. Denial-of-service attacks are intended to reduce, impair, or eliminate availability.

Bell-LaPadula — A classic model of confidentiality, based on military classification schemes. In Bell-LaPadula's model, systems with higher privilege can read from lower privilege systems, but not write to them.

(Think of a system running as "secret"; it can read unclassified systems but not write to them, as that could reveal secret information.)

belt-and-suspenders — An approach in which you have multiple controls in place—for example, using both a belt and suspenders to hold your pants up.

best practice — A term used either aspirationally or as a means of stifling debate. The aspirational use is of the form "we should use best practices for securing this system." The debate-stifling form is "you need to enforce password changes, it's on our best practices list." It is a best practice to apply "five whys" when told something is a best practice. "Five whys" is a practice attributed to Toyota for understanding root causes. At its core, ask why, and then ask why of the answer five times to find a root cause.

Biba — Another classic security model, this one based on integrity. Systems at a lower integrity level cannot write to a higher integrity level.

Bob — *See* Alice and Bob.

CAPTCHA (Completely Automated Public Turing test to tell Computers and Humans Apart) — Those irritating and often unreadable words and/or numbers presented online before you can submit something are designed to be easy for humans and hard for computers, but they end up being easy for computers and hard for everyone except those people who are paid a dollar or two to sit and solve them all day. On the bright side, at least those poor folks have a job.

ceremony — A term for a protocol that has been defined to include the people involved in the protocol. This is a useful way to analyze usability and human factors issues, and is covered at length in Chapter 15.

ciphertext — The encrypted version of a message. If *e* means encrypt, *k* is a key, and *p* is plaintext, a ciphertext message is ek(p).

ciphertext, known — *See* known ciphertext.

confidentiality — The security property describing information restricted to a set of authorized people, and only disclosed to them.

control-flow attack — An attack on a program which alters the control flow. Stack-smashing attacks are an example of control flow attacks, where attacker-supplied data overwrites the program's stack.

CSA (Cloud Security Alliance) — Quoting its website, "The Cloud Security Alliance (CSA) is a not-for-profit organization with a mission to promote the use of best practices for providing security assurance within Cloud Computing, and to provide education on the uses of Cloud Computing to help secure all other forms of computing."

CSC (Conditioned-safe ceremony) — A ceremony that involves a step designed to result in people engaging in that step by rote. *See also* ceremony.

CSRF (Cross-site request forgery) — A type of web attack whereby an attacker convinces your browser to request one or more web pages, using your cookies, without your participation.

DBA (Database administrator) — The privileged person or set of people who have administrative rights to a database.

DDoS (distributed denial of service) — A denial-of-service attack carried out by more than one machine.

DFD (data flow diagram) — Diagrams which show the data flow of a system. Sometimes called threat model diagrams, because they're so useful in threat modeling.

DoS (denial of service) — The class of attack that violates availability.

DREAD (Damage, Reproducibility, Exploitability, Affected Users, Discoverability) — Developed and then retired by Microsoft. Discussed in Chapter 9.

DRM (digital rights management) — Schemes that treat the purchaser of a digital object as a threat, and attempt to prevent them from usefully accessing a file except using certain programs. Also called digital restrictions management.

EAL (Evaluation Assurance Level) — An EAL is an element of the *Common Criteria* for security evaluation promulgated by major Western governments and Japan.

EoP (elevation of privilege) — Both a category of threat and (capitalized) the name of the threat modeling game. As a threat, EoP refers to a way in which people can exceed their authorization (or privileges). This includes gaining the capability to run code on a computer (aka breaking in), or moving from a restricted account to a more privileged one.

escalation of privilege — A synonym for elevation of privilege.

exploit — In its traditional sense, exploit refers to taking advantage of or unfairly benefitting from the work of another. In the technical sense, it can mean taking advantage of a program flaw such that an attacker gains some benefit. For example, "The document contains an exploit" means that a flaw in the program has been identified, and the document has been carefully constructed to take advantage of that flaw.

femtocell — A small computer with integrated radios and networking, designed to augment cellular phone service. A femtocell is a natural place to execute man-in-the-middle attacks.

formal — Either a structured approach (often with pre- and post-conditions) or a mathematical structuring. It is used in both ways in this book.

FQDN (fully qualified domain name) — A domain name ending in a recognized top-level domain (such as .com) or, more precisely, ending with "."—the root of domain trust. (Thus, `microsoft.com.` is an FQDN.)

friendly fraud — Term used by payments processors to refer to when a family member, roommate, or other person uses a credit card, and the owner of the card denies knowing anything about the charges.

GEMS (Generic Error Modeling System) — James Reason's model describing how people make mistakes.

global passive adversary — An entity which can eavesdrop around the world. Used either to specify a precise capability with which to judge the security of a design, or to avoid political discussion that can result from naming a particular country's spies. Revelations of NSA practices in the summer of 2013 should lead to skepticism over the euphemistic variant.

GOMS (Goals, Operators, Methods, and Selection) — Rules to an early model of how people process information.

heap overflow — An exploitable condition whereby attackers can write data to the dynamically allocated heap in a way that allows them to influence or replace normal operation of a program.

IaaS (Infrastructure as a Service) — A cloud offering in which clients buy power, network, and CPU cycles, and run their own systems on top of them, often in the form of complete virtual machines. *See also* PaaS, SaaS.

IC (individual contributor) — Someone whose work does not involve managing others.

IETF (Internet Engineering Task Force) — The folks who define how computers on the Internet talk to each other.

IETF threat modeling — Personal shorthand for my interpretation of RFC 3552 as an approach to threat modeling. To the best of my knowledge, the IETF does not endorse a methodology for, or a structured approach to, threat modeling.

information disclosure — A threat that violates confidentiality.

IOI (item of interest) — In privacy threat modeling, an IOI is an aspect of the system of interest to attackers. For an excellent source for privacy terminology, see "A Terminology for Talking About Privacy by Data Minimization" (Pfitzman, 2010).

integrity — The property that an object is whole, undivided, and of the form that its creators intended and its reliant parties expect. The property violated by tampering.

known ciphertext — An attack that works when the encrypted version of a message is available to the adversary.

meaningful ID — An identifier that is meaningful to the human using it, which brings to mind exactly one entity. See both Chapter 14, and Chapter 15.

MITM (man-in-the-middle) — An attack in which someone can intercede between the participants in a protocol, spoofing Alice to Bob (so that Bob believes that someone else is Alice) and Bob to Alice (such that Alice believes that same someone else is Bob). Often, cryptographers call this MITM "Mallory." Thus, Bob believes that Mallory is Alice, and Alice believes that Mallory is Bob. Hijinks, as they say, tend to ensue.

model — As a noun, a simplified or abstracted description of a thing, system, or process; as a verb, the act of devising, creating, or using such an abstracted or simplified description.

Mukhabarat — The Arabic term for an intelligence or state security agency. Sometimes invoked as an alternative to talking about the U.S. National Security Agency or other passive adversaries, although events of the Arab Spring exposed a willingness to engage in active attacks.

NIST — The United States National Institutes of Standards and Technology.

non-repudiation — The security property that people cannot falsely repudiate (deny) their actions.

NSA (National Security Agency [United States]) — Often invoked because of its powerful capabilities to listen to a wide swath of traffic, or its skills in making or breaking cryptographic algorithms. Generally, NSA is used as an example of a global passive adversary.

OECD — Organization for Economic Cooperation and Development.

PaaS (Platform as a Service) — A cloud computing offering whereby the client buys a system, such as a web stack on a given OS, and runs their own applications on top of it. For example, Google App Engine is a Platform as a Service.

permissions — *See* ACL.

persistence — keeping track of cryptographic keys you receive to detect changes. Also called "TOFU."

PKI (public key infrastructure) — An approach to key authentication in which a trusted third party authenticates keys. Subject to a variety of threats.

PM — Program manager or program management. At Microsoft, program managers are engineers with responsibility for all non-code, non-test deliverables, often including vision, specs, timelines, and delivery of the product. This role carries a great deal of implicit meaning and expectation, and the best description I know of can be found in "The Zen of Program Management" (Microsoft, 2007).

race conditions — A class of security incidents in which there's a delay and a possibility of changing things between the checking of a condition (such as the target of a symbolic link) and the use of that check's results. Also called TOCTOU (time of check, time of use).

reference monitor — The software that enforces security policies, such as access to objects. Acting as a reference monitor for operating system objects is one function an OS kernel provides.

repudiation — The act of denying responsibility for an action.

RFC (Request for Comments) — The standards documents issued by the IETF (Internet Engineering Task Force).

root — The most privileged account on a unix system. The text is contextually clear when an issue is specific to a design element or feature of unix. Often used in the text interchangeably with "administrator".

SaaS (Software as a Service) — A cloud offering in which the client buys a business package of some type, such as CRM, and the CRM is operated by a company, such as `Salesforce.com`. Contrast with PaaS and IaaS.

Scamicry — Behavior which is hard to distinguish from behavior by scammers. For example, the use of obscure domains to accept e-mail click through is used by attackers (leading to advice to check URLs) and by legitimate organizations (leading to that advice being less valuable, and to people being confused.) Scamicry prevents people's natural pattern recognition from working well around information security.

SDL (Security Development Lifecycle) — The set of activities undertaken by an organization to prevent the introduction of security issues in software development.

SIPRNet (Secret Internet Protocol Router Network) — The air-gapped IP network operated by the United States defense department.

social proof — A phenomenon where people believe that what others are doing is acceptable (or safe) behavior. Sometimes exploited by attackers whose collaborators act the way they want you to act.

sockpuppet — The account used in a sockpuppet attack.

sockpuppet attack — Describes an attack whereby someone creates a set of accounts to create the impression that their position has more support than it otherwise might appear to have. Also called in various communities *Sybils* or *tentacles*. The offline versions include social proof and, in politics, astroturfing.

spoofing — The category of threats that violate authentication by pretending to be someone or something else.

SQL injection — A category of attack whereby a SQL command is "injected" into a query by an attacker.

SSDL (secure software development lifecycle) — A synonym for SDL.

SSN (social security number) — *See* Chapter 14 for discussion.

stack smashing — A subset of buffer overflow in which the attacker overwrites the program stack, leading to a change in control flow.

steganography — The art of secret writing. Invisible inks are an example of a steganographic technique, as is altering the least significant bits of an image to carry a message.

stepping-stone asset — Something an attacker wants to take over in order to gain access to some further target. *See* things attackers want asset, things you protect asset.

STRIDE — Spoofing, Tampering, Repudiation, Information Disclosure, Denial of Service, and Elevation of Privilege. A mnemonic for finding threats. Often incorrectly (and sometimes frustratingly) called a classification system or taxonomy.

Sybil, Sybil attack — *See* sockpuppet, sockpuppet attack.

System 1, System 2 — Psychological terms describing two approaches to thinking and decision making—a fast automatic system, and a slower, more deliberative system. System 1 responses are fast and require little conscious thought; in contrast, System 2 is slower and more deliberate. See Chapter 15, or *Thinking, Fast and Slow* (Kahneman, 2011) for more information.

tampering — Attacks that violate the integrity of a system, file, or data flow.

tentacles — *See* sockpuppet attack.

things attackers want asset — An asset with the property that an attacker wants to copy, delete, tamper with, or otherwise attack for gain. Contrast with stepping-stone asset.

things you protect asset — An asset with the property that you protect because it's important to you, rather than because you expect an attacker to go after it.

threat discovery — A synonym for threat enumeration.

threat elicitation — A synonym for threat enumeration.

threat modeling — The use of abstractions to aid in thinking about risk. See the Introduction for explicit discussion of the various ways in which the term is used.

Time of check/Time of use issue — Sometimes abbreviated TOCTOU; *see* race condition.

TM (threat modeling) — Not to be confused with trademark or ™, a legal process for the protection of brands to reduce confusion.

TMA (Threat model analysis) — Either an activity to look for threats, or the written output of such a process. Used in the early days of threat modeling at Microsoft, but it sometimes crops up elsewhere.

TOFU (trust on first use) — Keeping track of cryptographic keys you've seen to avoid asking people repeated questions about trusting those keys. Also called persistence.

transitive asset — A phrase used in Swiderski and Snyder's *Threat Modeling* (Microsoft Press, 2004) to refer to what I call a stepping-stone asset.

trust boundary — The place where more than one principal interacts—thus, where threats are most clearly visible. Threats are not restricted to trust boundaries but almost always involve actions across trust boundaries.

trust levels — A description of the security context in which an entity works. Things at the same level are isomorphic—there is no advantage to going from one to another. If some code has different privileges (permissions, etc.), then that code is at different trust levels.

trusted — A way of describing an entity that can violate your security rules, and is trusted not to do so.

trusted third party — A party who, by mutual agreement, can screw other participants. Seriously, that's what trusted means. You expect them to perform reliably, and if they don't, you're out of luck.

TOCTOU (time of check/time of use) — *See* race condition.

tunneling — An approach to networking whereby one protocol is encapsulated in another to gain some advantage. Common examples include SSH and SSL.

TTL (time to live) — A value set in a network protocol with the intent of decrementing the value at each network hop. Not all tunneling systems will reduce TTL as they move packets.

UX (user experience) — A superset of the user interface elements, including how the person experiences them, and expectations about the skills, experiences, and training the person may have.

vendor — The person or people who create software. Used because it's less verbose than "the people who make your software," but I mean no disrespect to the creators of open-source or free/libre software.

WYSIATI (What You See Is All There Is) — A term coined by Daniel Kahneman (Farrar, Straus and Giroux, 2011) to refer to a set of ways in which human perception and recollection diverge from what we might hope.

WYTM — What's your threat model? A question asked to clarify understanding of risks. The answer is generally a few words, such as "global passive adversary" or "someone who can run code as a different account on the machine."

YAGNI (You Ain't Gonna Need It) — This saying comes from the extreme programming (XP) movement, and emphasizes building only the product you're shipping, and as little else as you can get away with shipping. Security requirements and threat models are often viewed as things you ain't gonna need, which is often incorrect.

Bibliography

37 Signals. "Aggressive, spiky button vs. rounded corner button," Signal vs. Noise, April 5, 2010, https://37signals.com/svn/posts/2255-aggressive-spiky-button-vs-rounded-corner-button.

Abi-Antoun, Marwan, and Jonathan Aldrich. "Static Extraction and Conformance Analysis of Hierarchical Runtime Architectural Structure Using Annotations." In ACM SIGPLAN Notices, vol. 44, no. 10, pp. 321–40 (ACM, 2009).

Abi-Antoun, Marwan, and Jeffrey M. Barnes. "Analyzing Security Architectures," Proceedings of the IEEE/ACM International Conference on Automated Software Engineering, pp. 3–12 (ACM, 2010).

Acquisti, Alessandro, Ralph Gross, and Fred Stutzman. "Faces of Facebook: Or, How the Largest Real ID Database in the World Came to Be." BlackHat USA, August, 2011. Draft available online at http://www.heinz.cmu.edu/~acquisti/face-recognition-study-FAQ/acquisti-faces-BLACKHAT-draft.pdf.

Adams, A. A., and S. A. Williams, "What's Yours Is Mine and What's Mine's My Own," unpublished draft, May 8, 2012, http://opendepot.org/id/eprint/1096.

Adams, Scott, Dilbert cartoon, published November 13, 1995, http://thedilbertstore.com/comic_strips/1995/11/13.

Adida, Ben, et al. "CALEA II: Risks of Wiretap Modifications to Endpoints," Center for Democracy and Technology, May 17 2013, https://www.cdt.org/files/pdfs/CALEAII-techreport.pdf.

Adler, Andy. "Images Can Be Regenerated from Quantized Biometric Match Score Data," Electrical and Computer Engineering, Canadian Conference on, vol. 1, pp. 469–72 (IEEE, 2004).

Akhawe, Devdatta, Warren He, Zhiwei Li, Reza Moazzezi, and Dawn Song. "Clickjacking Revisited: A Perceptual View of UI Security," BlackHat USA, August, 2013, http://www.cs.berkeley.edu/~devdatta/clickjacking.pdf.

Alexander, Christopher, Sara Ishikawa, and Murray Silverstein. *A Pattern Language* (New York: Oxford University Press, 1977).

Anderson, Ross. *Security Engineering: A Guide to Building Dependable Distributed Systems* (Indianapolis: Wiley, 2008).

———. "Offender Tagging," Light Blue Touchpaper blog, last modified September 2, 2013, http://www.lightbluetouchpaper.org/2013/09/02/offender-tagging/.

———. "Security and Human Behavior 2013," Light Blue Touchpaper blog, last modified June 6, 2013, http://www.lightbluetouchpaper.org/2013/06/03/security-and-human-behaviour-2013/.

ANSI Z535. "Brief Description of all Six Standards and Safety Color Chart," accessed October 15, 2013, http://www.nema.org/Standards/z535/Pages/ANSI-Z535-Brief-Description-of-all-Six-Standards-and-Safety-Color-Chart.aspx.

Asadollahi, Yahya, Vahid Rafe, Samaneh Asadollahi, and Somayeh Asadollahi. "A Formal Framework to Model and Validate Event-Based Software Architecture," *Procedia Computer Science 3* (2011): 961–66 and http://asmeta.sourceforge.net/.

Asadollahi, Yahya, Vahid Rafe, Samaneh Asadollahi, and Somayeh Asadollahi. "A Formal Framework to Model and Validate Event-Based Software Architecture," *Procedia Computer Science 3* (2011): 961–66 and http://asmeta.sourceforge.net/.

Aucsmith, David, Brendon Dixon and Robin Martin-Emerson, "Threat Personas", Microsoft internal document, version 0.9, 2003.

Barnard, R.L. *Intrusion Detection Systems* (Buttersworth, 1988) as cited in Anderson (2008), supra.

Beautement, Adam, M. Angela Sasse, and Mike Wonham. "The compliance budget: managing security behaviour in organisations," In *Proceedings of the 2008 workshop on New security paradigms*, pp. 47-58. ACM, 2009.

Beckert, Bernhard, and Gerd Beuster. "A Method for Formalizing, Analyzing, and Verifying Secure User Interfaces." In *Formal Methods and Software Engineering*, pp. 55–73 (Berlin: Springer, 2006).

Bell, D. Elliott, and Leonard J. LaPadula. "Secure Computer Systems: Mathematical Foundations," MTR-2547 (Bedford: The MITRE Corporation, 1973).

Bella, Giampaolo, and Lizzie Coles-Kemp. "Seeing the Full Picture: The Case for Extending Security Ceremony Analysis," *Proceedings of the 9th Australian Information Security Management Conference*, Edith Cowan University, Perth Western Australia, 5–7 December, 2011.

Biba, K. J. "Integrity Considerations for Secure Computer Systems." MTR-3153. (Bedford: The MITRE Corporation, 1977).

Biham, Eli, Alex Biryukov, and Adi Shamir. "Cryptanalysis of Skipjack reduced to 31 rounds using impossible differentials." In *Advances in Cryptology --Eurocrypt'99*, pp. 12-23 (Berlin Heidelberg: Springer, 1999).

Bonneau, Joseph. "Authentication Is Machine Learning," Light Blue Touchpaper blog, December 14, 2012 (see in particular comment 2 by Bonneau), `http://www.lightbluetouchpaper.org/2012/12/14/authentication-is-machine-learning/`.

———. "Authenticating Humans to Computers: What I Expect for the Next Ten Years," streamed live on November 29, 2012, `https://www.youtube.com/watch?v=_bnj5Qa_9iU&feature=plcp`.

Bonneau, Joseph, Cormac Herley, Paul C. Van Oorschot, and Frank Stajano. "The Quest to Replace Passwords: A Framework for Comparative Evaluation of Web Authentication Schemes." In Security and Privacy (SP), 2012 IEEE Symposium on, pp. 553-67 (IEEE, 2012).

Bonneau, Joseph, Mike Just, and Greg Matthews. "What's in a Name?" In *Financial Cryptography and Data Security*, pp. 98–113 (Berlin, Heidelberg: Springer, 2010).

Bovbjerg, Barbara D. "Federal and State Laws Restrict Use of SSNs, Yet Gaps Remain," U.S. GAO, GAO-05-1016T, September 15, 2005, `http://www.gao.gov/new.items/d051016t.pdf`.

Bowers, Kevin D., Marten van Dijk, Robert Griffin, Ari Juels, Alina Oprea, Ronald L. Rivest, and Nikos Triandopoulos. "Defending Against the Unknown Enemy: Applying FLIPIT to System Security." In *Decision and Game Theory for Security*, pp. 248–63 (Berlin: Springer, 2012), `http://www.emc.com/emc-plus/rsa-labs/presentations/flipit-gamesec.pdf`.

Bowker, Geoffrey C., and Susan Leigh Star. *Sorting things out: Classification and its consequences*, (Cambridge: The MIT Press, 2000).

Boyd, Colin, and Anish Mathuria. *Protocols for Authentication and Key Establishment* (Berlin: Springer, 2003).

Brainard, John, Ari Juels, Ronald L. Rivest, Michael Szydlo, and Moti Yung. "Fourth-Factor Authentication: Somebody You Know," In 2006 ACM Conference on Computer and Communications Security, pp. 168–78.

Brenner Center for Justice. "Voter ID," last updated October 15, 2012, http://www.brennancenter.org/content/section/category/voter_id.

Brewer & Darrenougue. "Minutes of the IETF 88 Plenary," November 6, 2013, http://www.ietf.org/proceedings/88/minutes/minutes-88-iab-techplenary.

Buley, Taylor. "Netflix settles privacy lawsuit, cancels prize sequel," Forbes Firewall blog, March 12, 2010, http://www.forbes.com/sites/firewall/2010/03/12/netflix-settles-privacy-suit-cancels-netflix-prize-two-sequel/.

Cameron, Kim. "The Laws of Identity," last revised May, 2005, http://www.identityblog.com/?p=352.

Campanile, Carl. "Dem Pol's Son Was 'Hacker'," *New York Post*, September 19, 2008.

Celis, David. "Stop Validating E-mail Addresses with Complicated Regular Expressions," September 12, 2006, http://davidcel.is/blog/2012/09/06/stop-validating-email-addresses-with-regex/.

Chandler, Raymond. *Trouble Is My Business: A Novel*. Random House Digital, Inc., 2002, http://books.google.com/books?id=TrGxX4kZNLIC

Chen, Raymond. "It rather involved being on the other side of this airtight hatchway. . ." The Old New Thing blog, May 8, 2006, http://blogs.msdn.com/b/oldnewthing/archive/2006/05/08/592350.aspx.

Chosunilbo. "Real-Name Online Registration to Be Scrapped," The Chosunilbo, last revised December 30, 2011, http://english.chosun.com/site/data/html_dir/2011/12/30/2011123001526.html.

Clarke, Roger. "An Evaluation of Privacy Impact Assessment Guidance Documents," *International Data Privacy Law* 1, no. 2 (2011): 111–20, http://idpl.oxfordjournals.org/content/early/2011/02/15/idpl.ipr002.full.pdf, http://idpl.oxfordjournals.org/content/1/2/111.abstract.

———. "Privacy Impact Assessment," May 26, 2003, http://www.rogerclarke.com/DV/PIA.html.

———. "Privacy Impact Assessment: Its Origins and Development," April 2009, http://www.rogerclarke.com/DV/PIAHist-08.html.

———. "Cloud Controls Matrix," Version 3, September 26, 2013, https://cloudsecurityalliance.org/research/ccm/.

Cloud Security Alliance (CSA). "Security Guidance," Version 3, November 14, 2011, https://cloudsecurityalliance.org/research/security-guidance/peer-review/.

Convery, S., D. Cook, and M. Franz. "An Attack Tree for the Border Gateway Protocol (Draft 1), Routing Protocol Security, expired March 17, 2004, http://web.eecs.umich.edu/~zmao/eecs589/papers/draft-convery-bgpattack-01.txt.

Cooper, Alan, and Paul Saffo. *The Inmates Are Running the Asylum* (Indianapolis: SAMS, 1999).

Cooper, A., H. Tschofenig, B. Aboda, J. Peterson, J. Morris, M. Hansen, R. Smith. "Privacy Considerations for Internet Protocols," RFC 6973, July 2013, `http://www.rfc-editor.org/rfc/rfc6973.txt`.

Cooper, Alan, Robert Reimann, and David Cronin. *About Face 3: The Essentials of Interaction Design* (Indianapolis: John Wiley & Sons, 2012).

Cranor, Lorrie Faith. "A Framework for Reasoning About the Human in the Loop," *UPSEC 8* (2008): 1–15.

Csikszentmihalyi, Mihaly. *Finding flow: The psychology of engagement with everyday life.* (New York: Basic Books, 1997).

———. *Flow: The psychology of optimal experience. (New York: Harpercollins, 1990).*

Culp, Scott, and Angela Gunn. "Ten Immutable Laws of Security (Version 2.0)," accessed October 16, 2013, `http://technet.microsoft.com/en-us/library/hh278941.aspx`.

CyberSource. "2012 Online Fraud Report," CyberSource, Fourteenth Annual Industry Report, accessed October 16, 2013, `http://forms.cybersource.com/forms/NAFRDQ12012whitepaperFraudReport2012CYBSwww2012`.

Dalek, Calum T, "Fingerprinting," *Wired*, vol. 4, no. 9, page 47, September 1996, `http://www.wired.com/wired/archive/4.09/eword.html`.

———. "Covert Communications Despite Traffic Data Retention." In *Security Protocols XVI*, pp. 198–214 (Berlin: Springer, 2011).

Danezis, George. Personal communication, 2011.

Debian Project. "Debian Security Advisory DSA-1571-1 openssl — Predictable Random Number Generator," published May 13, 2008, `http://www.debian.org/security/2008/dsa-1571.`, `https://wiki.debian.org/SSLkeys#Technical_Summary`

Deng, Mina. "Privacy preserving content protection," Ph.D diss., Ph. D. thesis, Katholieke Universiteit Leuven-Faculty of Engineering, 2010.

Disquss. "Pseudonyms Drive Community," Disquss corporate blog, accessed October 16, 2013, `http://disqus.com/research/pseudonyms/`.

Duarte, Nancy. "How to Present to Senior Executives," *Harvard Business Review*, October 4, 2012, `http://blogs.hbr.org/cs/2012/10/how_to_present_to_senior_execu.html`.

Duong, Thai, and Juliano Rizzo. "Flickr's API Signature Forgery Vulnerability," September 2009, `http://netifera.com/research/flickr_api_signature_forgery.pdf`.

EAC Advisory Board. "Elections Operations Assessment: Threat Trees and Matrices and Threat Instance Risk Analyzer," Elections Assistance Commission, December 23, 2009, submitted by University of South Alabama, `http://www.eac.gov/assets/1/Page/Election%20Operations%20Assessment%20`

Threat%20Trees%20and%20Matrices%20and%20Threat%20Instance%20Risk%20Analyzer%20%28TIRA%29.pdf.

Ellison, Carl M. "Ceremony Design and Analysis," IACR Cryptology ePrint Archive (2007): 399. https://eprint.iacr.org/2007/399.pdf.

Ericsson, K. Anders, Ralf T. Krampe, and Clemens Tesch-Römer. "The role of deliberate practice in the acquisition of expert performance." Psychological review 100, no. 3 (1993): 363.

Espenschied, Jonathan, and Angela Gunn. "Threat Genomics," MetriCon 7, August 7, 2012, http://www.securitymetrics.org/blog/2012/08/19/metricon-7/?page=Metricon7.0.

Essers, Loek. "German Privacy Regulator Orders Facebook to End Its Real Name Policy," *ITworld*, December 17, 2012, http://www.itworld.com/print/328387.

Ferguson, Niels, Bruce Schneier, and Tadayoshi Kohno. *Cryptography Engineering* (Indianapolis: Wiley, 2012).

Ferriss, Timothy. *The 4-Hour Chef: The Simple Path to Cooking Like a Pro, Learning Anything, and Living the Good Life*, as cited in "Cheat Sheets for Everything." *Boing Boing*, November 21, 2012, http://boingboing.net/2012/11/21/timothy-ferriss-cheat-sheets.html.

Feynman, Richard P. *"Surely You're Joking, Mr. Feynman!": Adventures of a Curious Character* (New York: W.W. Norton & Company, 2010).

FIPS. "Data Encryption Standard," Federal Information Processing Standards Publication 46-2, supersedes FPS PUB 46-1, January 22, 1988, http://www.itl.nist.gov/fipspubs/fip46-2.htm.

Fisher, Dennis. "Inside Facebook's Social Authentication System," ThreatPost blog, March 8, 2012, http://threatpost.com/inside-facebooks-social-authentication-system-030812/76300.

Fontana, John. "VeriSign Issues Fraudulent Microsoft Code-Signing Certificates," Network World Fusion, March 22, 2001, http://www.networkworld.com/news/2001/0322vsign.html.

Friedberg, Jeffrey, et al. "Privacy Guidelines for Developing Software Products and Services," version 3.1, September, 2008.

Garfinkel, Simson, personal communication, November 2012.

Gawande, Atul. *The Checklist Manifesto* (Penguin Books: 2010).

Gellman, Robert. "Fair Information Practices: A basic History," version 2.02 of November 11, 2013, http://bobgellman.com/rg-docs/rg-FIPShistory.pdf.

Green, Robert Lane. *You Are What You Speak* (New York: Random House, 2011).

Giesen, Florian, Florian Kohlar, and Douglas Stebila. "On the Security of TLS Renegotiation," 2013, http://eprint.iacr.org/2012/630.pdf.

Goldberg, Ian Avrum. "A Pseudonymous Communications Infrastructure for the Internet." Ph.D diss., University of California, 2000.

Goldberg, Ian A., Matthew D. Van Gundy, Berkant Ustaoglu, and Hao Chen. "Multi-Party Off-the-Record Messaging," 2008, `http://www.cypherpunks.ca/~iang/pubs/mpotr.pdf`.

Goodin, Dan "'We cannot trust' Intel and Via's chip-based crypto, FreeBSD developers say" December 10, 2013 `http://arstechnica.com/security/2013/12/we-cannot-trust-intel-and-vias-chip-bas\ ed-crypto-freebsd-developers-say/`

Gordon, Lawrence A., and Martin P. Loeb. "The Economics of Information Security Investment," ACM Transactions on Information and System Security (TISSEC) 5, no. 4 (2002): 438–57.

———. *Managing Cybersecurity Resources: A Cost-Benefit Analysis* (New York: McGraw-Hill, 2006).

Gürses, Seda, Carmela Troncoso, and Claudia Diaz. "Engineering Privacy By Design," COSIC 2011, last accessed October 16, 2013, `http://www.cosic.esat.kuleuven.be/publications/article-1542.pdf`.

Haber, Jeb. "SmartScreen® Application Reputation in IE9," *IEBlog*, May 17, 2011, `http://blogs.msdn.com/b/ie/archive/2011/05/17/smartscreen-174-application-reputation-in-ie9.aspx`.

Hall, Joseph M., and M. Eric Johnson. "When Should a Process Be Art," Harvard Business Review, March 2009.

Hashcat, Hashcat advanced password recovery product page, `http://hashcat.net/oclhashcat/`, visited December 7, 2013.

Hazen, John. "Delivering Reliable and Trustworthy Metro Style Apps," Building Windows 8, May 17, 2012, `http://blogs.msdn.com/b/b8/archive/2012/05/17/delivering-reliable-and-trustworthy-metro-style-apps.aspx`.

Heckman, Rocky. "Application Threat Modeling v2," TechRepublic /U.S., March 7, 2006, `http://www.techrepublic.com/article/application-threat-modeling-v2/6310491`.

Heitgerd, Janet L., et al. "Community Health Status Indicators: Adding a Geospatial Component," accessed October 15, 2013, *Preventing Chronic Disease* 2008;5(3). `http://www.cdc.gov/pcd/issues/2008/jul/07_0077.htm`.

Heninger, Nadia, Zakir Durumeric, Eric Wustrow, and J. Alex Halderman. "Mining Your Ps and Qs: Detection of Widespread Weak Keys in Network Devices," In *Proceedings of the 21st USENIX Security Symposium*, August 2012.

Herley, Cormac. "So Long, and No Thanks for the Externalities: The Rational Rejection of Security Advice By Users," In *Proceedings of the 2009 Workshop on New Security Paradigms Workshop*, pp. 133–44 (ACM, 2009).

Hill, Sad. "Caution Sign Has Sharp Edges Do Not Touch," Sad Hill News, November 9, 2010, `http://sadhillnews.com/2010/11/09/us-bans-toner-travel-and-font-usage-unknown-missile-launches/caution-sign-has-sharp-edges-do-not-touch-sad-hill-news`.

Hillebrand, Gail. "Social Security Number Protection Legislation for States," Consumers Union, June 2008, http://www.consumersunion.org/pub/core_financial_services/004801.html.

Hoffman L. Personal communication. See also the Burroughs tribute page, available at http://www.ianjoyner.name/Burroughs.html.

Honan, Mat. "How Apple and Amazon Security Flaws Led to My Epic Hacking," *Wired*, August 6, 2012, http://www.wired.com/gadgetlab/2012/08/apple-amazon-mat-honan-hacking/.

Howard, Michael. "Secure Coding Secrets," Microsoft Security Development Lifecycle blog, November 18, 2008, http://blogs.msdn.com/b/sdl/archive/2008/11/18/secure-coding-secrets.aspx.

Howard, Michael, and David LeBlanc. *Writing Secure Code* (Redmond: Microsoft Press, 2002) and also 2nd edition, 2009.

Howard, Michael, and Steve Lipner, *The Security Development Lifecycle*, (Redmond: Microsoft Press, 2006)

Huang, Ling, Anthony D. Joseph, Blaine Nelson, Benjamin I.P. Rubinstein, and J. D. Tygar. "Adversarial Machine Learning," In *Proceedings of the 4th ACM Workshop on Security and Artificial Intelligence*, pp. 43–58. ACM, 2011, http://blaine-nelson.com/research/pubs/Huang-Joseph-AISec-2011.

Hutchins, Eric M., Michael J. Cloppert, and Rohan M. Amin. "Intelligence-Driven Computer Network Defense Informed By Analysis of Adversary Campaigns and Intrusion Kill Chains," *Leading Issues in Information Warfare and Security Research 1* (2011): 80; http://www.lockheedmartin.com/content/dam/lockheed/data/corporate/documents/LM-White-Paper-Intel-Driven-Defense.pdf.

Identity Theft Resource Center. "Identity Theft: The Aftermath 2008," May 28, 2009, http://www.idtriskmgtgroup.com/documents/Aftermath_2008_Highlight.pdf.

Ingoldsby, Terrance R. "Attack Tree-Based Threat Risk Analysis," Amenaza Technologies Ltd. Copyright 2009, 2010; http://www.amenaza.com/downloads/docs/AttackTreeThreatRiskAnalysis.pdf and http://www.screencast.com/users/Amenaza/folders/Default/media/a18cb16a-f88f-4161-b1a4-124e5f06376d.

Jacobs, Jay. "A Call to Arms: It Is Time to Learn Like Experts," *ISSA Journal*, November 2011, http://beechplane.files.wordpress.com/2011/11/a-call-to-arms_issa1111.pdf.

Jakobsson, Markus, Erik Stolterman, Susanne Wetzel, and Liu Yang. "Love and Authentication," *Proceedings of the SIGCHI Conference on Human Factors in Computing Systems*, pp. 197–200 (ACM, 2008).

Johnson, Steven. *The Ghost Map: The Story of London's Most Terrifying Epidemic and How It Changed Science, Cities, and the Modern World* (New York: Penguin, 2006).

Jones, J. "An introduction to factor analysis of information risk (fair)," Norwich Journal of Information Assurance 2, no. 1 (2006): 67, riskmanagementinsight.com/media/documents/FAIR_Introduction.pdf.

Just, Mike. "Designing and Evaluating Challenge-Question Systems," *Security and Privacy*, IEEE 2, no. 5 (2004): 32–39.

Kahn, David. *The Codebreakers* (New York: Scribner, 1996).

Kahneman, Daniel. *Thinking, Fast and Slow* (New York: Farrar, Straus and Giroux, 2011).

Kahney, Leander, "Twist a pen, open a lock," Wired.com, Sep 17 2004, http://www.wired.com/culture/lifestyle/news/2004/09/64987.

Karlof, Chris, J. Doug Tygar, and David Wagner. "Conditioned-Safe Ceremonies and a User Study of an Application to Web Authentication," SOUPS, 2009.

Kelsey, John. Comment on "Think Like an Attacker?" Emergent Chaos blog, September 19, 2008, http://emergentchaos.com/archives/2008/09/think-like-an-attacker.html.

Kent, Jonathan. "Malaysia Car Thieves Steal Finger," BBC News online, March 31 2005, http://news.bbc.co.uk/2/hi/asia-pacific/4396831.stm.

Kerckhoffs, Auguste. "La cryptographie militaire," Journal des sciences militaires, vol. IX, pp. 5–38, Jan. 1883, pp. 161–191, Feb. 1883.

Kim, Gene, Kurt Milne, and Dan Phelps. "Prioritizing IT Controls for Effective Measurable Security," IT Process Institute (2006).

Kim, Gene H., and Eugene H. Spafford. "The Design and Implementation of Tripwire: A File System Integrity Checker," In *Proceedings of the Second ACM Conference on Computer and Communications Security*, pp. 18–29. ACM, 1994, http://dl.acm.org/citation.cfm?id=191183.

Klien, Gary, *Sources of Power* (Cambridge: MIT Press, 1999).

Koblitz, Neal, and Alfred J. Menezes. "Another look at 'provable security'," Journal of Cryptology 20, no. 1 (2007): 3–37. And generally, http://anotherlook.ca.

Kocher, Paul, "Surviving Moore's Law: Security, AI, and Last Mover Advantage," Usenix Security 2006, https://www.usenix.org/conference/15th-usenix-security-symposium/surviving-moores-law-security-ai-and-last-mover-advantage.

Kohnfelder, Loren, and Praerit Garg, The threats to our products, Microsoft Interface, April 1, 1999. Available at http://blogs.msdn.com/sdl/attachment/9887486.ashx.

Komanduri, Saranga, Richard Shay, Patrick Gage Kelley, Michelle L. Mazurek, Lujo Bauer, Nicolas Christin, Lorrie Faith Cranor, and Serge Egelman. "Of Passwords and People: Measuring the Effect of Password-Composition Policies," *In Proceedings of the SIGCHI Conference on Human Factors in*

Computing Systems, pp. 2595–2604. ACM, 2011, http://www.pdl.cmu.edu/PDL-FTP/Storage/mazurek-chi11_abs.shtml.

Krebs, Brian, "Data Broker Giants Hacked by ID Theft Service," September 25, 2013, http://krebsonsecurity.com/2013/09/data-broker-giants-hacked-by-id-theft-service/.

Lang, Keith. "The Science of Aesthetics," UXAustralia 2009, http://vimeo.com/6527897, and comments https://twitter.com/songcarver/status/283070446990151681.

Laser Software. http://laser.cs.umass.edu/release/.

Laurie, Ben, and Richard Clayton. "Proof-of-Work Proves Not to Work, version 0.2," Workshop on Economics and Information Security, 2004.

LeBlanc, David, "Practical Windows Sandboxing" blog series, July 27, 2007, http://blogs.msdn.com/b/david_leblanc/archive/2007/07/27/practical-windows-sandboxing-part-1.aspx.

Levien, Raph. "Snowflakes As Visual Hashes," post to "Best of Security" mailing list, May 17, 1996, http://marc.info/?l=best-of-security&m=96843702220490&w=2.

Lightstone, Sam. *Making It Big in Software: Get the Job. Work the Org. Become Great* (Boston: Pearson, 2010).

Lindstrom, Peter. "A Modest Proposal to Eliminate the SSN Façade," Spire Security Viewpoint blog, April 11, 2006, http://spiresecurity.typepad.com/spire_security_viewpoint/2006/04/a_modest_propos.html.

Lipner, Steve. Personal communication, 2008.

Lyn, Tan Ee. "Cancer Patient Held at Airport for Missing Fingerprint," Reuters, May 27, 2009, http://www.reuters.com/article/2009/05/27/us-fingerprints-idUSTRE54Q42P20090527?feedType=RSS&feedName=oddlyEnoughNews&rpc=22&sp=true.

Magretta, Joan. *What Management Is* (New York: Simon and Schuster, 2002).

Malhotra, Vikas. "Protected View in Office 2010," Microsoft Office 2010 Engineering blog, August 13, 2009, http://blogs.technet.com/b/office2010/archive/2009/08/13/protected-view-in-office-2010.aspx.

Marlinspike, Moxie. "The Cryptographic Doom Principle," Thought Crime blog, December 13, 2011, http://www.thoughtcrime.org/blog/the-cryptographic-doom-principle/.

———. "The Convergence System: SSL and The Future of Authenticity," a talk given at BlackHat, July 2011, http://www.blackhat.com/html/bh-us-11/bh-us-11-briefings.html#Marlinspike.

Marshall, Andrew. "Intersystem Review: Tearing at the Seams Between Dependent Threat Models," Microsoft internal document, January 2013.

Martina, Jean Everson, and Marcelo Carlomagno Carlos. "Why Should We Analyze Security Ceremonies?," First CryptoForma Workshop, May 2010, http://www.marcelocarlomagno.com/downloads/pdf/martina2010.pdf.

Masnick, Mike. "Lavabit Details Unsealed: Refused to Hand Over Private SSL Key Despite Court Order and Daily Fines," *TechDirt*, October 2, 2013, http://www.techdirt.com/articles/20131002/14500424732/lavabit-details-unsealed-refused-to-hand-over-private-ssl-key-despite-court-order-daily-fines.shtml.

Margosis, Aaron, "Problems of Privilege, Find and Fix LUA Bugs," Technet Magazine, August 2006, http://technet.microsoft.com/en-us/magazine/cc160944.aspx.

Matsumoto, Tsutomu, Hiroyuki Matsumoto, Koji Yamada, and Satoshi Hoshino. "Impact of Artificial 'Gummy' Fingers on Fingerprint Systems," Proceedings of SPIE Vol. #4677, Optical Security and Counterfeit Deterrence Techniques IV, Thursday-Friday 24-25 January 2002, http://cryptome.org/gummy.htm.

McCullagh, Declan, "AOL's disturbing glimpse into users' lives", August 7, 2006 CNet, http://news.cnet.com/2100-1030_3-6103098.html.

McGraw, Gary, and John Steven. "An Interview with John Steven," Silver Bullet Security Podcast, Show 068, November 30, 2011, http://www.cigital.com/silver-bullet/show-068/.

McKenzie, Partick, "Falsehoods Programmers Believe About Names," June 17, 2010 http://www.kalzumeus.com/2010/06/17/falsehoods-programmers-believe-about-names/

McMillan, Robert. "CSO says Cisco security is growing up," Infoworld, August 6, 2008, http://www.infoworld.com/d/security-central/cso-says-cisco-security-growing-705.

———. "Google Attack Part of Widespread Spying Effort," *Computerworld*, January 13, 2010, http://www.computerworld.com/s/article/9144221/Google_attack_part_of_widespread_spying_effort.

McRee, Russ, "IT Infrastructure Threat Modeling Guide" June 22, 2009 http://blogs.technet.com/b/secguide/archive/2009/06/22/it-infrastructure-threat-modeling-guide.aspx

McWhorter, John. *The Power of Babel: A Natural History of Language* (New York: HarperCollins, 2003).

Meier, J. D. *Improving Web Application Security: Threats and Countermeasures* (Redmond: Microsoft Press, 2003) or http://msdn.microsoft.com/en-us/library/ms994812.aspx.

Microsoft. "Assess Your Security," Microsoft Security Development Lifecycle (SDL) Optimization Model, last accessed October 16, 2013, http://www.microsoft.com/security/sdl/learn/assess.aspx.

Microsoft. SIR, vol. 11, Microsoft Security Intelligence Report, 2011, Last accessed October 16, 2013, http://www.microsoft.com/security/sir/default.aspx.

———. "The Zen of Program Management," Microsoft JobsBlog, February 14, 2007, http://microsoftjobsblog.com/zen-of-pm.

Microsoft SDL Team. "Appendix N: SDL Security Bug Bar (Sample)," 2012, http://msdn.microsoft.com/en-us/library/windows/desktop/cc307404.aspx.

Miller, George A. "The magical number seven, plus or minus two: some limits on our capacity for processing information," Psychological review 63, no. 2 (1956): 81.

Miller, Robert B., Stephen Heiman, and Tad Tuleja. *The New Strategic Selling: The Unique Sales System Proven Successful by the World's Best Companies* (New York: Business Plus, 2005).

MITRE. "Attack Patterns: Knowing Your Enemies in Order to Defeat Them," BlackHat, Washington, D.C., 2007, http://capec.mitre.org/documents/Attack_Patterns-Knowing_Your_Enemies_in_Order_to_Defeat_Them-Paper.pdf.

———. "CAPEC-89: Pharming," last updated June 21, 2013, http://capec.mitre.org/data/definitions/89.html.

———. "CAPEC-1000, Mechanism of Attack," last updated June 21, 2013, http://capec.mitre.org/data/definitions/1000.html.

Moore, Andrew P., Robert J. Ellison, and Richard C. Linger. "Attack Modeling for Information Security and Survivability," No. CMU-SEI-2001-TN-001. Carnegie-Mellon University, Pittsburgh, PA, Software Engineering Institute, 2001, http://www.sei.cmu.edu/library/abstracts/reports/01tn001.cfm.

Muffett, Alec. "Regulators, Password Hashing & Crypto Considered As a Branding Exercise: #bcrypt #security /cc @schneierblog @glynwintle," dropsafe blog, June 15, 2012, http://dropsafe.crypticide.com/article/9439/comment-page-1#comment-47595.

Murray, Mike. *Forget the Parachute, Let Me Fly The Plane* (Seattle: Amazon Digital Services, 2011) http://www.amazon.com/Forget-Parachute-Let-Fly-Plane-ebook/dp/B004ULVMKC.

Nagar, Abhishek. "Biometric Template Security," Ph.D diss., Michigan State University, 2012.

Narayanan, Arvind, and Vitaly Shmatikov. "Robust de-anonymization of large sparse datasets," In Security and Privacy, 2008. SP 2008. IEEE Symposium on, pp. 111-125. IEEE, 2008.

Nather, Wendy. "All about 'cheeseburger risk'," 415 Security Blog, January 15, 2013, http://informationsecurity.451research.com/?p=4851.

National Bureau of Standards. "Guidelines for Automatic Data Processing Physical Security and Risk Management," FIPS Pub 31, 1974, pp. 12–14.

Neighly, Madeline, and Maruice Emsellem. "Wanted: Accurate FBI Background Checks for Employment," National Employment Law Project, July 2013, http://www.nelp.org/page/-/SCLP/2013/Report-Wanted-Accurate-FBI-Background-Checks-Employment.pdf.

Neilsen Hayden, Patrick. "Please Enter a Valid Last Name," Making Light blog, December 11, 2012, http://nielsenhayden.com/makinglight/archives/014624.html.

Netflix. "Lessons Netflix Learned from the AWS Outage," Netflix, April 29, 2011, http://techblog.netflix.com/2011/04/lessons-netflix-learned-from-aws-outage.html.

Nguyen, Duc. "Your Face Is Not your password," BlackHat DC 2009, http://www.blackhat.com/presentations/bh-dc-09/Nguyen/BlackHat-DC-09-Nguyen-Face-not-your-password.pdf.

Nguyen, Joe. "Cookie Deletion: Why It Should Matter to Advertisers and Publishers," ClickZ.com, March 2, 2011, http://www.clickz.com/clickz/column/2281571/cookie-deletion-why-it-should-matter-to-advertisers-and-publishers.

Nissenbaum, Helen. *Privacy in context: Technology, policy, and the integrity of social life* (Palo Alto: Stanford University Press, 2009).

NIST. "Minimum Security Requirements for Federal Information and Information Security," FIPS Pub 200, March 2006, http://csrc.nist.gov/publications/fips/fips200/FIPS-200-final-march.pdf.

OECD. "OECD Guidelines on the Protection of Privacy and Transborder Flows of Personal Data, updated 2013, http://www.oecd.org/document/18/0,3746,en_2649_34223_1815186_1_1_1_1,00.html.

Office of the Victorian Privacy Commissioner. "A Guide to Completing Parts 3 to 5 of Your Privacy Impact Assessment Report," Office of the Victorian Privacy Commissioner, Australia, 2009, https://www.privacy.vic.gov.au/privacy/web2.nsf/files/privacy-impact-assessments-report-accompanying-guide/$file/guideline_05_09_no2.pdf.

———. "Privacy Impact Assessment: A Guide for the Victorian Public Sector," Office of the Victorian Privacy Commissioner, Australia, April 2009, https://www.privacy.vic.gov.au/privacy/web2.nsf/files/privacy-impact-assessments-guide/$file/guideline_05_09_no1.pdf.

Ollman, Gunter. "The Opt-In Botnet Generation: Social Networks, Hacktivism, and Centrally-Controlled Protesting," Damballa, Inc. white paper, retrieved 2010.

Openwall. "ASIC/FPGA Attacks on Modern Hashes," pg. 45, last accessed October 16, 2013, http://www.openwall.com/presentations/Passwords12-The-Future-Of-Hashing/mgp00045.html.

———. "GPU Attacks on Modern Hashes," pg. 46, last accessed October 16, 2013, http://www.openwall.com/presentations/Passwords12-The-Future-Of-Hashing/mgp00046.html.

Osterman, Larry. "Threat Modeling Again, Presenting the PlaySound Threat Model," Larry Osterman's Weblog, September 17, 2007, http://blogs.msdn.com/b/larryosterman/archive/2007/09/17/threat-modeling-again-presenting-the-playsound-threat-model.aspx.

OWASP. "2013 Top 10 List," OWASP.org, last modified June 23, 2013, https://www.owasp.org/index.php/Top_10_2013-Top_10.

———. "Attack Template," OWASP.org, last modified May 6, 2008, https://www.owasp.org/index.php/Attack_template.

———. "Cache Poisoning," last revised April 23, 2009, https://www.owasp.org/index.php/Cache_Poisoning.

———. "Category: Attack," OWASP.org, last modified on August 10, 2012, https://www.owasp.org/index.php/Category:Attack.

———. "XSS Filter Evasion Cheat Sheet", last revised September 17, 2013 https://www.owasp.org/index.php/XSS_Filter_Evasion_Cheat_Sheet

PCI Security Standards. "PCI DSS Quick Reference Guide: Understanding the Payment Card Industry Data Security Standard Version 2.0," 2010, https://www.pcisecuritystandards.org/documents/PCI%20SSC%20Quick%20Reference%20Guide.pdf.

Percival, Colin. "SCrypt: A Key Derivation Function," December 4, 2012, http://www.daemonology.net/papers/scrypt-2012-slides.pdf.

Perlow, Jon. "New in Labs: Stop Sending Mail You Later Regret," Official Gmail Blog, October 6, 2008, http://gmailblog.blogspot.com/2008/10/new-in-labs-stop-sending-mail-you-later.html.

Peterson, Gunnar, personal communication 2009.

Petitcolas, Fabien A. (translator) "La Cryptographie Militaire: Journal des Sciences Militaires," Janvier 1883, last updated May 29, 2013, http://www.petitcolas.net/fabien/kerckhoffs/crypto_militaire_1.pdf and http://www.petitcolas.net/fabien/kerckhoffs/.

Pfitzmann, Andreas, and Marit Hansen. "A Terminology for Talking About Privacy by Data Minimization: Anonymity, Unlinkability, Undetectability, Unobservability, Pseudonymity, and Identity Management." Version

0.34, Aug 10 (2010), https://kantarainitiative.org/confluence/download/attachments/45059055/terminology+for+talking+about+privacy.pdf.

Pilgrim, Mark. "Avoid Common Pitfalls in Greasemonkey. How the History of Greasemonkey Security Affects You Now," O'Reilly Network, November 11, 2005, http://www.oreillynet.com/lpt/a/6257.

Power, Richard. "There Is an Elephant in the Room; and Everyone's Social Security Numbers Are Written on Its Hide," CyBlog, July 6, 2009, http://www.cyblog.cylab.cmu.edu/2009/07/there-is-elephant-in-room-everyones.html.

Provos, Niels, and David Mazieres. "A Future-Adaptable Password Scheme," In *USENIX Annual Technical Conference, FREENIX Track*, pp. 81-91. 1999.

Ptacek, Thomas. "Applied Cryptography Engineering," Sockpuppet.org blog, July 22, 2013, http://sockpuppet.org/blog/2013/07/22/applied-practical-cryptography/.

Ptacek, Thomas H., and Timothy N. Newsham. "Insertion, evasion, and denial of service: Eluding network intrusion detection," Secure Networks Inc., Calgary, Alberta Canada, 1998.

Rabkin, Ariel. "Personal Knowledge Questions for Fallback Authentication: Security Questions in the Era of Facebook," In *Proceedings of the Fourth Symposium on Usable Privacy and Security*, pp. 13–23. ACM, SOUPS, July 23–25, 2008, Pittsburgh, PA.

Radke, Kenneth, Colin Boyd, Juan Gonzalez Nieto, and Margot Brereton. "Ceremony Analysis: Strengths and Weaknesses," In *Future Challenges in Security and Privacy for Academia and Industry*, pp. 104–15 (Berlin: Springer, 2011).

Rains, Tim. "Software Vulnerability Management at Microsoft," post to Microsoft Security Blog, June 30, 2013, http://blogs.technet.com/b/security/archive/2013/07/01/software-vulnerability-management-at-microsoft.aspx and linked white paper of the same name, July 2010.

Raymond, Eric S. *The Cathedral and the Bazaar: Musings on Linux and Open Source by an Accidental Revolutionary* (Sebastopol: O'Reilly, 2001).

Reason, James T. *The Human Contribution: Unsafe Acts, Accidents and Heroic Recoveries* (Burlington: Ashgate Publishing, 2008).

Reeder, R. W. "Expandable Grids: A User Interface Visualization Technique and a Policy Semantics to Support Fast, Accurate Security and Privacy Policy Authoring." Ph.D thesis, Carnegie-Mellon University Computer Science Department. CMU tech report number CMU-CS-08-143 (July 2008).

Reeder, Rob, E. Kowalczyk, and Adam Shostack. "Helping engineers design NEAT security warnings," In *Proceedings of the Symposium On Usable Privacy and Security (SOUPS), Pittsburgh, PA*. 2011.

Reeder, Robert W. "Measuring Trust User Experiences," Microsoft internal document, March 10, 2008.

Reeder, Robert W., Lujo Bauer, Lorrie F. Cranor, Michael K. Reiter, and Kami Vaniea. "More Than Skin Deep: Measuring Effects of the Underlying Model on Access-Control System Usability," In *Proceedings of the SIGCHI Conference on Human Factors in Computing Systems*, pp. 2065–74. ACM, 2011, `http://www.ece.cmu.edu/~lbauer/papers/2011/chi2011-semantics.pdf`.

Reiger, Frank, "Chaos Computer Club breaks Apple TouchID," Blog post 21 September, 2013, `http://www.ccc.de/en/updates/2013/ccc-breaks-apple-touchid`.

Reiner, Rob. *The Princess Bride*. Buttercup Films, Ltd. 1987. (DVD)

Remes, Wim. "wow. . . Hotwire removes stored CC information from account upon password reset. That's actually awesome," Twitter, July 20, 2013, `https://twitter.com/wimremes/status/358709749585416193`.

Rescorla, Eric, and Brian Korver. "Guidelines for Writing RFC Text on Security Considerations," BCP 72, RFC 3552, July 2003, `http://www.ietf.org/rfc/rfc3552.txt`.

Revuru, Anil. "Threat Analysis and Modeling (TAM) v3.0—Learn about the New Features," `http://blogs.msdn.com/b/threatmodeling/archive/2009/07/20/threat-analysis-and-modeling-tam-v3-0-learn-about-the-new-features.aspx`.

Rice, Alex. "A Continued Commitment to Security," January 26, 2011, `https://blog.facebook.com/blog.php?blog_id=company&blogger=503683099` and `https://www.facebook.com/notes/486790652130`.

———. "Social Authentication," Microsoft Blue Hat, December 14, 2012, `https://channel9.msdn.com/Events/Blue-Hat-Security-Briefings/BlueHat-Security-Briefings-Fall-2012-Sessions/BH1202`, and personal communication.

Ristiȅ, Ivan, SSL Threat Model, September 9, 2009 `http://blog.ivanristic.com/2009/09/ssl-threat-model.html`

Roberts, Paul F. "Leaky Web Sites Provide Trail of Clues About Corporate Executives," *IT World*, August 13, 2012, `http://www.itworld.com/it-managementstrategy/289519/leaky-web-sites-provide-trail-clues-about-corporate-executives`.

Rosenquist, Matt, "Prioritizing Information Security Risks With Threat Agent Risk Assessment," Intel Corporation White Paper, December 2009.

Ross, Arun A., Jidnya Shah, and Anil K. Jain. "Toward Reconstructing Fingerprints from Minutiae Points," In *SPIE Proceedings Vol. 5779*, pp. 68–80. International Society for Optics and Photonics, 2005.

Rubin, Jeffrey, and Dana Chisnell. *Handbook of Usability Testing: How to Plan, Design, and Conduct Effective Tests, 2nd Edition* (Indianapolis: Wiley, 2008).

Ruderman, Jesse. "Race Conditions in Security Dialogs," SquareFree .com, July 1, 2004, `http://www.squarefree.com/2004/07/01/race-conditions-in-security-dialogs/`.

Ruiz, Guifré, Elisa Heymann, Eduardo César, and Barton P. Miller. "Automating Threat Modeling Through the Software Development Life-Cycle," *XXIII Jornadas de Paralelismo* (JP2012), Elche, Spain, September 2012. `http://www.jornadassarteco.org/js2012/papers/paper_92.pdf`.

———. "Detecting Cognitive Causes of Confidentiality Leaks," *Electronic Notes in Theoretical Computer Science 183* (2007): 21–38.

Rukšenas, Rimvydas, Paul Curzon, and Ann Blandford. "Modelling and Analysing Cognitive Causes of Security Breaches," *Innovations in Systems and Software Engineering 4*, no. 2 (2008): 143–60, `http://www.eecs.qmul.ac.uk/~pc/publications/2008/rrpcabISSE2008preprint.pdf`.

Ryan, Peter. *Modeling and Analysis of Security Protocols* (Boston: Addison Wesley, 2000).

Saitta, Paul, Brenda Larcom, and Michael Eddington. "Trike v. 1 methodology document [draft]," July 13, 2005, `http://dymaxion.org/trike/Trike_v1_Methodology_Documentdraft.pdf`.

Salter, Chris, O. Sami Saydjari, Bruce Schneier, and Jim Wallner. "Toward a Secure System Engineering Methodology," In *Proceedings of the 1998 workshop on New Security Paradigms*, pp. 2–10 (ACM, 1998), `http://www.schneier.com/paper-secure-methodology.html`.

Sassaman, Len, Meredith L. Patterson, Sergey Bratus, and Michael E. Locasto. "Security Applications of Formal Language Theory," IEEE Systems Journal 7(3): 489-500 (2013).

Sasse, Angela. Personal communication, 2012.

SC Magazine. "Amenaza Technologies Ltd. SecurITree" review, February 1, 2007, `http://www.scmagazine.com/amenaza-technologies-ltd-securitree/review/1105/`.

Schechter, Stuart. "Common Pitfalls in Writing About Security and Privacy Human Subjects Experiments, and How to Avoid Them," Microsoft Research,

January 15, 2013, MSR-TR-2013-5, http://research.microsoft.com/apps/pubs/default.aspx?id=179980.

Schechter, Stuart, A. J. Bernheim Brush, and Serge Egleman. "It's No Secret: Measuring the Security and Reliability of Authentication via 'Secret' Questions," Microsoft Research, May 17, 2009, http://research.microsoft.com/apps/pubs/default.aspx?id=79594.

Schechter, Stuart, Serge Egelman, and Robert W. Reeder. "It's Not What You Know, But Who You Know: A Social Approach to Last-Resort Authentication," In *Proceedings of the SIGCHI Conference on Human Factors in Computing Systems*, pp. 1983–92 (ACM, 2009), http://research.microsoft.com/apps/pubs/default.aspx?id=79349.

Schmid, Joachim. "AsmGofer," last updated 2009, http://www.tydo.de/doktorarbeit.html.

Schnieier, Bruce. "Announcing: Movie Plot Threat Contest," Blog post, April 1, 2006, https://www.schneier.com/blog/archives/2006/04/announcing_movi.html.

———. "Attack Trees," *Dr. Dobb's Journal*, December 1999, Schneier blog, http://www.schneier.com/paper-attacktrees-ddj-ft.html.

SDL Team. "Necessary, Explained, Actionable, and Tested (NEAT) Cards" SDL blog, October 9, 2012, http://blogs.msdn.com/b/sdl/archive/2012/10/09/necessary-explained-actionable-and-tested-neat-cards.aspx.

SeaMonster. "Security Modeling Software," SourceForge, last updated May 7, 2013, http://sourceforge.net/projects/seamonster/.

Securosis, Mike Rothman. "The CISO's Guide to Advanced Attackers: Sizing Up the Adversary [New Series]," Securosis blog, April 16, 2013, https://securosis.com/blog/the-cisos-guide-to-advanced-attackers-sizing-up-the-adversary.

Shachtman, Noah. "Insiders Doubt 2008 Pentagon Hack Was Foreign Spy Attack," Wired online, August 25, 2010, http://www.wired.com/dangerroom/2010/08/insiders-doubt-2008-pentagon-hack-was-foreign-spy-attack/.

Shachtman, Noah, and David Axe. "Most U.S. Drones Openly Broadcast Secret Video Feeds," Wired online, October 29, 2012, http://www.wired.com/dangerroom/2012/10/hack-proof-drone/.

Shamir, Adi, and Eran Tromer. "Acoustic Cryptanalysis: On Nosy People and Noisy Machines," last accessed on October 16, 2013, http://tau.ac.il/~tromer/acoustic/.

Shane, Scott. "A Spy's Motivation: For Love of Another Country," *The New York Times*, April 20, 2008, http://www.nytimes.com/2008/04/20/weekinreview/20shane.html.

Shostack, Adam. "Adding Usable Security to the SDL," 2011, Microsoft Developer Network, http://blogs.msdn.com/b/sdl/archive/2011/05/04/adding-usable-security-to-the-sdl.aspx and http://blogs.msdn.com/b/sdl/archive/2012/10/09/necessary-explained-actionable-and-tested-neat-cards.aspx.

———. "Buffer Overflows and History: A Request" (including comments), Emergent Chaos, October 20, 2008, http://emergentchaos.com/archives/2008/10/buffer-overflows-and-history-a-request.html.

———. "Elevation of Privilege," Microsoft Security Development Lifecycle, February 7, 2013, http://www.microsoft.com/security/sdl/adopt/eop.aspx and http://www.homeport.org/~adam/Elevation-of-Privilege-BlackHat2010ShostackFinal.pptx.

———. "Elevation of Privilege: Drawing Developers into Threat Modeling," white paper, December, 2012, http://blogs.msdn.com/b/sdl/archive/2012/12/18/elevation-of-privilege-drawing-developers-into-threat-modeling.aspx.

———. "Engineers Are People, Too." Keynote at Software and Usable Security Aligned for Good Engineering (SAUSAGE) Workshop, reported in "DRAFT Report on the NIST Workshop - I3P" August 2011, http://www.thei3p.org/docs/publications/436.pdf (pg. 24); slides available at http://www.homeport.org/~adam/Engineers-are-people-too-SAUSAGE.pptx.

———. "Google+ Failed Because of Real Names," Emergent Chaos, January 25, 2012, http://emergentchaos.com/archives/2012/01/google-failed-because-of-real-names.html.

———. "Helping Engineers Design NEAT Security Warnings," Microsoft Security Development Lifecycle, May 4, 2011, http://blogs.msdn.com/b sdl/archive/2011/05/04/adding-usable-security-to-the-sdl.aspx and http://www.microsoft.com/en-us/download/details.aspx?id=34958.

———. "Think Like an Attacker?" Emergent Chaos, September 17, 2008, http://emergentchaos.com/archives/2008/09/think-like-an-attacker.html.

———. "The Discipline of 'Think Like an Attacker'," Emergent Chaos, September 22, 2008, http://emergentchaos.com/archives/2008/09/the-discipline-of-think-like-an-attacker.html.

Shostack, Adam, and Danny Dhillon. "Threat Modeling: Lessons Learned and Practical Ways to Improve Your Software," RSA, March 4, 2010.

Shostack, Adam, and Andrew Stewart. *The new school of information security.* (Boston: Addison Wesley, 2009).

Shostack, Adam, and Paul Syverson. "What Price Privacy?" (2003), http://citeseerx.ist.psu.edu/viewdoc/download?rep=rep1&type=pdf&doi=10.1.1.144.8657.

Simidchieva, Borislava. "Yolo County Election Process Model and Fault Tree Analysis," Laser Library, June 9, 2010, https://collab.cs.umass.edu/wiki/pages/T2i15688y/Yolo_County_Election_Process_Model_and_Fault_Tree_Analysis.html.

Simidchieva, B. I., Engle, S. J., Clifford, M., Jones, A. C., Allen, B., Peisert, S., Bishop, M., et al. (2010). "Modeling and Analyzing Faults to Improve Election Process Robustness," 2010 Electronic Voting Technology Workshop/Workshop on Trustworthy Elections, Washington, D.C. Retrieved from http://www.usenix.org/events/evtwote10/tech/full_papers/Simidchieva.pdf.

Social Security Administration. "Hearing on Identity Theft and Tax Fraud," May 8, 2012, http://oig.ssa.gov/newsroom/congressional-testimony/hearing-identity-theft-and-tax-fraud.

———. "New Numbers for Domestic Violence Victims," SSA Publication 05-10093, ICN 468615, August 2011, http://www.ssa.gov/pubs/10093.html.

Solove, Daniel J. *Understanding Privacy*, (Cambridge: Harvard University Press, 2008).

Sportsman, Nathan. "Threat Modeling," Praetorian presentation, 2011, http://www.praetorian.com/downloads/presentations/Praetorian_Threat_Modeling_Presentation.pdf.

Stack Overflow. "Using a regular expression to validate an email address," Stack Overflow, last accessed June 21, 2013, http://stackoverflow.com/questions/201323/using-a-regular-expression-to-validate-an-email-address.

Stajano, Frank, and Paul Wilson. "Understanding Scam Victims: Seven Principles for Systems Security," Communications of the ACM, March 2011, vol. 54, no. 3.

Star, Susan Leigh, and James R. Griesemer. "Institutional Ecology, Translations and Boundary Objects: Amateurs and Professionals in Berkeley's Museum of Vertebrate Zoology, 1907–39." *Social Studies of Science 19*, no. 3 (1989): 387–420.

Stevens, James F., Richard A. Caralli, and Bradford J. Willke. "Information Asset Profiling," Technical Note CMU/SEI-2005-TN-021. Carnegie-Mellon University, Pittsburgh, PA Software Engineering, 2005.

Sweeney, Latanya. "k-anonymity: A model for protecting privacy," International Journal of Uncertainty, Fuzziness and Knowledge-Based Systems 10, no. 05 (2002): 557-570.

Swiderski, Frank. "Threat Modeling Tool Revealed," Channel 9, July 9, 2004, last accessed October 17, 2013, http://channel9.msdn.com/Blogs/TheChannel9Team/Frank-Swiderski-Threat-Modeling-Tool-revealed.

Swiderski, Frank, and Window Snyder. *Threat Modeling* (Redmond: Microsoft Press, 2004).

Swire, Peter. "A model for When Disclosure Helps Security: What Is Different About Computer and Network Security?" *Journal on Telecommunications and High Technology Law 2* (2004).

Swire, Peter, and Casandra Q. Butts. "Addressing the Challenges of Identification and Authentication in American Society," Center for American Progress, June 2, 2008, http://www.americanprogress.org/issues/civil-liberties/report/2008/06/02/4520/the-id-divide/.

Sydney Morning Herald. "Woman Fools Japan's Airport Security Fingerprint System," *The Sydney Morning Herald*, January 2, 2009, http://www.smh.com.au/travel/woman-fools-japans-airport-security-fingerprint-system-20090102-78rv.html.

Syverson, Paul. "Sleeping Dogs Lie in a Bed of Onions But Wake When Mixed," Fourth Hot Topics in Privacy Enhancing Technologies (HotPETs 2011), http://petsymposium.org/2011/program.php.

TASM Toolset. "Specification, Simulation, and Formal Verification of Real-Time Systems," ACM Digital Library, 2007, http://dl.acm.org/citation.cfm?id=1770371.

Thorsheim, Per. "Why History May Be Bad for You," Security Nirvana, November 26, 2009, http://securitynirvana.blogspot.com/2009/11/why-history-may-be-bad-for-you.html.

ThreatModeler. "Getting Started with ThreatModeler," "Quick Start Guide," and "Data Sheet," MyAppSecurity, 2013, http://myappsecurity.com/threatmodeler/threatmodeler-resources/.

Torr, Peter. "Guerrilla Threat Modelling (or 'Threat Modeling' if you're American)," Microsoft Developer Network, February 22, 2005, http://blogs.msdn.com/b/ptorr/archive/2005/02/22/guerillathreatmodelling.aspx.

Towle, Holly K. "Personal Data as Toxic Waste: A Data Protection Conundrum." Privacy and Data Security Law Journal, June, 2009

Trike. "Trike Tools," Octotrike, last accessed October 17, 2013, http://octotrike.org/tools.shtml.

Ur, B. P.G. Kelley, S. Komanduri, J. Lee, M. Maass, M. Mazurek, T. Passaro, R. Shay, T. Vidas, L. Bauer, N. Christin, and L.F. Cranor. "How does your password measure up? The effect of strength meters on password creation." USENIX Security 2012.

US-CERT. "Risks of Using the Intelligent Platform Management Interface," US-CERT Alert TA13-207A, July 26, 2013, http://www.us-cert.gov/ncas/alerts/TA13-207A.

———. "State-Based Firewalls Fail to Effectively Manage Session Table Resource Exhaustion," CERT Vulnerability Note VU#539363, October 15, 2002, last revised January 6, 2003, http://www.kb.cert.org/vuls/id/539363.

Van Dijk, Marten, Ari Juels, Alina Oprea, and Ronald L. Rivest. "FlipIt: The Game of 'Stealthy Takeover'," *Journal of Cryptology* (2012): 1–59.

Van Duyne, Douglas K., James A. Landay, and Jason I. Hong. *The Design of Sites: Patterns for Creating Winning Web Sites* (Boston: Pearson, 2007).

VeriSign. "VeriSign® NetDiscovery Lawful Intercept Compliance Solutions," White paper 00017651, November 28, 2007, http://www.verisign.com/static/001927.pdf.

Verizon. "2013 Data Breach Investigations Report," Verizon, 2013, http://www.verizonenterprise.com/DBIR/2013/.

Visual Paradigm. "Data Flow Diagram," VisualParadigm.com, December 4, 2006, http://www.visual-paradigm.com/highlight/highlightdfd.jsp.

Von Neumann, John. "Various techniques used in connection with random digits," Applied Math Series 12, no. 36-38 (1951): 1.

Ware, Willis H. "Records, Computers and the Rights of Citizens," No. P-5077. Rand, 1973. http://epic.org/privacy/hew1973report/.

Wells, Joseph, *Corporate Fraud Handbook*. 3rd Edition (Indianapolis: Wiley, 2011).

White, Dominic. "Corporate Threat Modeler," SensePost, update 2010, http://www.sensepost.com/labs/tools/management/ctm/.

———. "Threat Modeling Workshop," SensePost, update 2010, http://www.sensepost.com/cms/resources/labs/tools/management/ctm/ThreatModelingWorkshop-ITWebSummit2010.zip.

Whitehouse, Ollie. "Real World Application Threat Modeling By Example," 44Con 2013.

Whitten, Alma, and J. Doug Tygar. "Why Johnny Can't Encrypt: A Usability Evaluation of PGP 5.0," In *Proceedings of the 8th USENIX Security Symposium*, 1999.

Wikipedia. "Battle of Midway: Allied Code-Breaking," Wikipedia.com, last modified October 7, 2013, http://en.wikipedia.org/wiki/Battle_of_Midway#Allied_code-breaking.

———. "Birthday Problem," Wikipedia.com, last modified October 1, 2013, http://en.wikipedia.org/wiki/Birthday_problem.

———. "Data Encryption Standard," Wikipedia.com, last modified October 5, 2013, http://en.wikipedia.org/wiki/Data_Encryption_Standard.

———. "Evaluation Assurance Level," Wikipedia.com, October 11, 2013, http://en.wikipedia.org/wiki/Evaluation_Assurance_Level.

———. "GOMS (Goals, Operators, Methods, and Selection rules)," Wikipedia.com, last updated August 7, 2013, http://en.wikipedia.org/wiki/GOMS.

———. "Kerkhoffs Principle," Wikipedia.com, last update October 12, 2013, http://en.wikipedia.org/wiki/Kerckhoffs%27s_principle.

———. "Responsibility Assignment Matrix (RAM)," Wikipedia.com, last modified October 15, 2013, http://en.wikipedia.org/wiki/Responsibility_assignment_matrix.

———. "Syn Flood," Wikipedia.com, last modified September 16, 2013, http://en.wikipedia.org/wiki/SYN_flood.

Williams, Laurie, Michael Gegick, and Andrew Meneely. "Protection Poker: Structuring Software Security Risk Assessment and Knowledge Transfer," In *Engineering Secure Software and Systems*, pp. 122–34. (Berlin: Springer, 2009).

"Windows 8 Integration," Mozilla Wiki, last modified on July 29, 2012, https://wiki.mozilla.org/Windows_8_Integration.

Yanisac, Alex, Harold Purdue, and Jeff Landry. Personal communication, 2012.

Young, Rupert. "How Often Do Users Reset or Delete Their Cookies?"; comment on thread, http://www.quora.com/How-often-do-users-reset-or-delete-their-cookies, Jan 26, 2011.

Yu, Persis S., and Shanon M. Dietrich. "Broken Records: How errors by criminal background checking companies harm workers and businesses," April 2012, available at http://www.nclc.org/issues/broken-records.html.

Zalewski, Michal. "Add a Security Delay to the Main Action of Popup Notifications (Bug #583175)," Bug report and discussion, July 29, 2010, https://bugzilla.mozilla.org/show_bug.cgi?id=583175.

———. *The Tangled Web: A Guide to Securing Modern Web Applications* (San Francisco: No Starch Press, 2011).

Zhang, Yinqian, Fabian Monrose, and Michael K. Reiter. "The Security of Modern Password Expiration: An Algorithmic Framework and Empirical Analysis," *Proceedings of the Seventeenth ACM Conference on Computer and communications security*, pp. 176–86 (ACM, 2010).

Zooko. "Names: Decentralized, Secure, Human-Meaningful: Choose Two," Zooko.com, last updated January 30, 2006, http://web.archive.org/web/20120125033658/http://zooko.com/distnames.html.

Index

B

S

U